ORGANIZATIONAL
BEHAVIOR

McGRAW-HILL SERIES IN MANAGEMENT
Keith Davis and Fred Luthans, Consulting Editors

THIRD EDITION

ORGANIZATIONAL BEHAVIOR

FRED LUTHANS

Professor of Management
University of Nebraska

McGRAW-HILL BOOK COMPANY

New York   St. Louis   San Francisco   Auckland   Bogotá   Hamburg   Johannesburg
London   Madrid   Mexico   Montreal   New Delhi   Panama   Paris   São Paulo
Singapore   Sydney   Tokyo   Toronto

This book was set in Melior by Black Dot, Inc. (ECU).
The editors were Kathi A. Benson, John F. Carleo, and Peggy Rehberger;
the designer was Anne Canevari Green;
the production supervisor was Leroy A. Young.
The drawings were done by Fine Line Illustrations, Inc.
R. R. Donnelley & Sons Company was printer and binder.

ORGANIZATIONAL BEHAVIOR

34567890DODO898765432

Library of Congress Cataloging in Publication Data

Luthans, Fred.
    Organizational behavior.

    (McGraw-Hill Series in management.)
    Includes indexes.
    1. Organizational behavior. I. Title.
HD58.7.L88 1981 658.4 80-14707
ISBN 0-07-039144-0

ACKNOWLEDGMENTS FOR EXPERIENTIAL EXERCISES

Exercises for Part 1: "Synthesis of Student and Instructor Needs" was suggested by Professor Philip Van Auken and is used with his permission; "Work-Related Organizational Behavior: Implications for the Course" is adapted from "Getting Acquainted Triads" in J. William Pfeiffer and John E. Jones (eds.), *A Handbook of Structured Experiences*, vol. I, University Associates, San Diego, Calif., 1969, and "Defining Organizational Behavior" in James B. Lau, *Behavior in Organizations*, Irwin, Homewood, Ill., 1975.

Exericses for Part 2: The questions in "The Eye of the Beholder" were suggested by Richard E. Dutton in "Expectations and the Perception of Others," *The Behavior Laboratory*, Goodyear, Pacific Palisades, Calif. 1975, p. 7. The exercise "Self-Perception and Development of the Self-Concept" was suggested by Philip Van Auken and is used with his permission.

Exercises for Part 3: "Motivation Questionnaire" is reprinted from "Motivation: A Feedback Exercise," in John E. Jones and J. William Pfeiffer (eds.), *The Annual Handbook for Group Facilitators*, University Associates, San Diego, Calif., 1973, pp. 43–45, and is used with permission; "Job Design Survey" is adapted from J. R. Hackman and G. R. Oldham, "Development of the Job Diagnostic Survey," *Journal of Applied Psychology*, vol. 60, 1975, pp. 159–170; "Role-Playing and O.B. Mod." is adapted from Fred Luthans and Mark J. Martinko, *The Power of Positive Reinforcement*, McGraw-Hill, New York, 1978, pp. 35–38.

Exercises for Part 4: "Groups and Conflict Resolution" is from Alan Filley, *Interpersonal Conflict Resolution*, Scott, Foresman, Glenview, Ill., 1975, pp. 139–142, as adapted from William H. Haney, *Communication and Organizational Behavior*, Irwin, Homewood, Ill., 1967, pp. 319–320; "Power and Politics" is reprinted with permission from Andrew J. DuBrin, *Human Relations*, Reston, Va., 1978, pp. 122–123; "Leadership Questionnaire," is reprinted with permission from J. William Pfeiffer and John E. Jones (eds.), *A Handbook of Structured Experiences for Human Relations Training*, vol. 1, University Associate, San Diego, Calif., 1974. The questionnaire was adapted from Sergiovanni, Metzeus, and Burden's revision of the Leadership Behavior Description Questionnaire, *American Educational Research Journal*, vol. 6, 1969, pp. 62–79.

Exercises for Part 5: "Organizations" is reprinted with permission from Fremont E. Kast and James E. Rosenzweig, "Our Organizational Society," *Experiential Exercises and Cases in Management*, McGraw-Hill, New York, 1976, pp. 13–15; "Paper Plane Corporation" was contributed by Professor Louis Pothreu and is used with his permission.

Exercises for Part 6: "Selection and Appraisal: The Case of Naylor Product Corporation" is reprinted with permission from Andrew D. Szilagyi and Marc Wallace, "The Performance Dilemma," *Organizational Behavior and Performance*, Goodyear, Santa Monica, Calif., 1980, pp. 477–478; "Organization Development at J. P. Hunt" is reprinted with permission from Andrew D. Szilagyi and Marc Wallace, "Survey Feedback," *Organizational Behavior and Performance*, Goodyear, Santa Monica, Calif., 1980, pp. 605–606.

ABOUT THE AUTHOR

FRED LUTHANS holds the National Bank of Commerce Chair of Management at the University of Nebraska at Lincoln. He received his Ph.D. from the University of Iowa and taught at the U.S. Military Academy at West Point while serving in the Armed Forces. A prolific writer, he has published fifteen books and over fifty articles in applied and academic journals. His book *Organizational Behavior Modification*, coauthored with Robert Kreitner, won the ASPA (American Society of Personnel Administration) award for the outstanding contribution to human resource management. His articles are widely reprinted and have brought him the ASHPA (American Society of Hospital Personnel Administration) award. The consulting co-editor for the McGraw-Hill Management Series, Professor Luthans also serves on a number of editorial boards. He has served on the editorial board of the *Academy of Management Review* since its beginning. He has been very active in the Academy over the years and currently is the President of the Midwest Division. Professor Luthans has a very extensive research program at the University of Nebraska and teaches courses in organizational behavior and management at both the graduate and undergraduate levels. In addition, he is an active consultant to both private and public sector organizations and conducts workshops on behavioral management both in this country and abroad.

FOR
KAY, KRISTIN, BRETT, KYLE, AND PAIGE

CONTENTS

PART 2   **A MICRO PERSPECTIVE OF ORGANIZATIONAL BEHAVIOR:
               COGNITIVE PROCESSES AND PERSONALITY**

PREFACE

The field of organizational behavior is rapidly progressing. I am amazed how much more we know about human behavior in organizations today than we did when I wrote the first edition of this text. Yet, despite this progress in our knowledge, human problems continue to be the major challenge facing managers today and in the foreseeable future.

As with the previous editions, this latest version provides a strong conceptual framework for the study, understanding, and application of organizational behavior. The book has been thoroughly revised and updated to reflect emerging perspectives in the organizational behavior field as a whole, changes in the specific topics covered, and the great number of research studies published in the last four years. In addition, although the book retains its coverage of time-proven material, it is also much more student- and applications-oriented. The changes in this edition are more specifically summarized in the following sections.

Conceptual framework   The book contains twenty-two chapters in six major parts. Part 1 provides an overview and foundation for the reader. After an introductory chapter which defines the field and gives some historical background on the practice of management, the next two chapters provide a behavioral science/research methodology foundation and a specific conceptual framework for the study and application of organizational behavior. Part 2 examines organizational behavior from a micro perspective, with chapters on perception and personality. Part 3 presents the very heart of the micro approach to organizational behavior. Chapters on theoretical aspects of both motivation and learning are followed by chapters on practical application. The psychological processes of motivation and learning covered in these five chapters are more closely associated with organizational behavior than is any other concept. The applications evolving out of the study of motivation and learning directly lead to more effective management of people and result in improved organizational performance. Part 4 explores the dynamics of organizational behavior. Separate chapters are devoted to the specific topics of groups, communication, conflict and stress, power and politics, and leadership. These topics begin to move the study of organizational behavior away from a strictly micro orientation. Part 5 on organization theory and the management processes completes the transition by presenting a more macro perspective on organizational behavior. The four chapters on management processes and organization theory take a broader-based approach to the study of organizational behavior. Finally, Part 6 deals with direct applications of organizational behavior to human resource management, organizational development, and personal development. There are chapters on selection and appraisal, organizational development, and self-management and career development. Although applications of concepts are discussed throughout the book, these last three chapters are directly concerned with actual skills and techniques that will lead to "bottom line" results for the conceptual and human dimensions of the practice of human resource management. Some comments about the future of management conclude the book.

The parts of the book are generally arranged so that the units of analysis and study progress from very micro-oriented individual concepts (perception, personality, motivation, and learning) to groups and their dynamics (communication, conflict, stress, power, and leadership) and finally to the macro end of the spectrum with the study of organization structure and management processes. These sections are fairly self-contained so that selected chapters could be dropped or studied in a different sequence without damaging the flow or content of the book. The same is true of the foundation part near the front and the direct applications part near the back of the book.

New topical coverage In addition to the reorganization of the book, there are three new chapters:

Chapter 8 Goal Setting and Job Design
Chapter 14 Power and Politics
Chapter 22 Self-Management, Career Development, and the Future

There are also numerous new sections within the other chapters. Some new topics covered include:

Threats to the internal validity of research studies
The use of multiple measures
A social learning framework for organizational behavior
Attributions in perception
Split-brain psychology
The socialization process
Social theories of personality
Alderfer's ERG motivation theory
Attribution models of motivation
Cognitive learning theories
Modeling learning processes and applications
New applications of O.B. Mod. in industrial, retail and public organizations
Groupthink problems
Mintzberg's managerial roles
Communications feedback
Strategies for managing organizational conflict
Leader/match training
A social learning approach to leadership

A general contingency framework for management
An information processing view of organizations
The Perrow contingency model of organizations
The Galbraith contingency model of organizations
Duncan's decision tree analysis of organizations
Content, predictive, and construct validities
Judgmental techniques for performance appraisal
New organization development techniques for the future

Pedagogical changes To make this edition more applications- and student-oriented, several new pedagogical features have been added. First, each chapter opens with a vignette drawn from the real world. These *vignettes* help the student relate the more theoretical content of each chapter to real events, real people, and real organizations. Second, in keeping with the recent trend toward *experiential learning* in the teaching of organizational behavior, at the end of each major part there is a new section containing a case study followed by two or three experiential exercises. Also, a new shorter case has been added to the existing cases at the end of each chapter. Finally, there is a *supplementary book* (Fred Luthans and Kenneth Thompson, *Contemporary Readings in Organizational Behavior*, 3d ed., McGraw-Hill, 1981) that correlates outside readings to give added depth and a different perspective to the major topics covered in the text.

Intended audience Despite the reorganization, changes, and additions described above, the purpose and the intended audience of the book remain the same. Similar to the earlier editions, this new edition is aimed at those who wish to take a totally modern, research-based approach to organizational behavior and human resource management. It does not assume the reader's prior knowledge of either management or the behavioral sciences. Thus, the book can be used effectively in the first or only course in four-year or two-year colleges. It is primarily aimed at the behavioral follow-up course to the more traditional introductory management course or the organizational behavior course in the MBA program. Moreover, the book should be helpful to practicing managers who want to understand and more effectively manage their most important asset—human resources.

Acknowledgments Every author owes a great deal to others, and I am no exception. I would like to acknowledge the interaction I have had with my colleagues John Cullen, Daniel Ganster, and Bronston T. Mayes in the organizational behavior area at the University of Nebraska. In particular, I would like to acknowledge the total support and standards of excellence provided by my departmental chairman, Sang M. Lee. Dean Gary Schwendiman has also been very supportive. In getting started in my academic career I never want to forget the help, encouragement, and scholarly values I received from Professors Henry H. Albers and Max S. Wortman. In addition, Professor Richard M. Hodgetts has been an especially valuable colleague. Over the years, I have been very lucky to be around excellent doctoral students. I would like to thank them all for teaching me as much as I have taught them. In particular, I would like to mention Professors Tim R. V. Davis of Cleveland State University, Robert Kreitner of Arizona State University, Terry Maris of the University of Kentucky, Mark Martinko of Florida State University, Kenneth Thompson of Notre Dame University, and Diane Lockwood and Douglas Baker of the University of Nebraska as having an especially important impact on my recent thinking about organizational behavior. I am also very grateful to those professors who used the previous editions of the book and gave me valuable feedback for making this revision. In particular, I would like to thank Professors Kermit Cudd of the University of Tennessee at Chattanooga, Keith Davis of Arizona State University, Phil Fisher of the University of South Dakota, Larry Frye of St. Petersburg Junior College, Eugene Koprowski of the University of Colorado, and David Van Fleet of Texas A & M University, who read and gave their comments on the manuscript. Finally, as always, I am deeply appreciative of my wife and children, who gave me the time and encouragement to complete this book.

Fred Luthans

AN INTRODUCTION TO ORGANIZATIONAL BEHAVIOR

INTRODUCTION
AND BACKGROUND

PRODUCTIVITY*

The productivity of American employees is at a very low ebb. In the period from 1948 to 1966 productivity had an average annual percentage increase of 2.8 percent. Between 1966 and 1973 this had slipped to 1.6 percent, and between 1973 and 1978 it plummeted to a dismal 0.8 percent annual increase. This is by far the lowest increase among industrial powers, and the projections for the 1980s are not very encouraging. The causes of this declining productivity can be traced to a number of problems such as inflation and the rising costs of government intervention. However, it is also true that today's employees are simply not producing up to their capacity. This employee productivity problem has spawned a number of organized efforts to examine ways to improve the performance of the American worker. Groups such as the National Center for Productivity and the Quality of Working Life, the American Productivity Center, the Work in America Institute, and the American Quality of Work Center have all directed their efforts toward improving working conditions and motivating today's employees. To date, these efforts have generated a lot of concern and have focused attention on the improvement of the quality of work life for employees. The reasoning is that a better working climate will lead to a more productive employee. While there has been some success with these programs, a much better understanding of the basic quality of work life elements of organizational behavior is needed for the future.

*Adapted from "How to Promote Productivity," *Business Week,* July 24, 1978, pp. 146–151; and John W. Kendrick, "Background and Overview of Productivity Improvement Programs," in *Proceedings of Managing Productivity Enhancement,* Utah State University, Logan, 1979, p. 18.

Management is generally considered to comprise three major dimensions—technical, conceptual, and human. The technical dimension consists of the manager's expertise in computers or accounting or engineering or marketing. There seems little question that today's managers are technically competent. They know the technical requirements of their jobs inside and out. This is a major reason why this country remains the most powerful in the world. Our managers have the technical know-how to get the job done. But few today would question that our once dominant position in the world seems to be slipping. There are many complex reasons for our problems, but certainly the declining productivity of our organizations is a major factor.

To improve our effectiveness in producing goods and services, we need better management. If we are already doing a good job on the technical aspects, then it follows that more needs to be done on the conceptual and human dimensions of modern management. This is where the field of organizational behavior comes into the picture. Organizational behavior is directly concerned with the conceptual and human side of management.

AN ORGANIZATIONAL BEHAVIOR APPROACH

Traditionally, managers either ignored the conceptual and human dimensions of their job or they made some overly simplistic assumptions. Although there were certainly exceptions, managers generally thought, and many still do, that their employees were basically lazy, that they were only interested in money, and that if you could make them happy they would be productive. When such assumptions were accepted, the human problems facing management were relatively clear-cut and easy to solve. All management had to do was devise monetary incentive plans, ensure security, and provide good working conditions; morale would be high and maximum productivity would result. It was as simple as one, two, three. Human relations experts, industrial psychologists, and industrial engineers supported this approach, and personnel managers implemented it.

Unfortunately, this traditional approach has not worked out in practice. Although no real harm has been done and some good actually resulted in the early stages of organizational development, it is now evident that such a simplistic approach falls far short of providing a meaningful solution to the complex human problems facing today's management. The assumptions have been questioned and for the most part have been invalidated by research and experience.

The major fault of the traditional approach is that the assumptions overlook far too many aspects of the problem. Human behavior at work is much more complicated and diverse than is suggested by the economic, security, working-conditions approach. The new organizational behavior approach assumes that employees are extremely complex and that there is a need for theoretical understanding backed by rigorous empirical research before applications can be made for managing people effectively. The transition has now been completed. The traditional human relations approach no longer has a dominant role in the behavioral approach to management. Few people would question that the organizational behavior approach, with its accompanying assumptions, dominates the behavioral approach to management now and will do so in the foreseeable future.

Now that organizational behavior has become the widely accepted approach, it is beginning to develop and mature as an academic discipline. As with any other relatively new academic endeavor, however, there have been some rough spots and sidetracks in its development. Besides the healthy academic controversies over theoretical approach or research findings, perhaps the biggest problem that organizational behavior has had to face is an identity crisis. Exactly what is meant by *organizational behavior*? Is it an attempt to replace all of management with behavioral science concepts and techniques? How, if at all, does it differ from good old applied or industrial psychology? Fortunately, these questions have now largely been answered to the satisfaction of most management academicians, behavioral scientists, and management practitioners.

In a recent comprehensive analysis of the field of organizational behavior, the former head of the organizational behavior division and current president of the Academy of Management, Larry L. Cummings, distinguished between organizational behavior and other closely related disciplines, as shown in Table 1-1. He also emphasized that organizational behavior is a way of thinking—a way of conceiving problems and articulat-

Table 1-1

DISTINCTIONS AMONG ORGANIZATIONAL BEHAVIOR, ORGANIZATIONAL PSYCHOLOGY, ORGANIZATION THEORY, AND PERSONNEL AND HUMAN RESOURCES

Organizational Behavior— Organizational Psychology (OP)	Both fields focus upon explaining human behavior within organizations. Their difference centers on the fact that OP restricts its explanatory constructs to those at the psychological level. OB draws constructs from multiple disciplines. As the domain of OP continues to expand, the difference between OB and OP is diminishing, perhaps to the point of identity between the fields.
Organizational Behavior— Organization Theory (OT)	The distinction is based on two differences: unit of analysis and focus of dependent variables. OB is defined as the study of individual and group behavior within organizations and the application of such knowledge. OT is the study of structure, processes, and outcomes of the organization per se. The distinction is neither that OB is atheoretical and concerned only with behavior nor that OT is unique or exclusive in its attention to theory. Alternatively, the distinction can be conceived as between micro and macro perspectives on OB. This removes the awkward differentiation of behavior and theory.
Organizational Behavior— Personnel and Human Resources (P&HR)	This distinction usually depicts OB as the more basic of the two and P&HR as more applied in emphasis. OB is seen as more concept-oriented, while P&HR is viewed as emphasizing techniques or technologies. The dependent variables, behavior and affective reactions within organizations, are frequently presented as similar. P&HR can be seen as standing at the interface between the organization and the individual, focusing on developing and implementing the system for attracting, maintaining, and motivating the individual within the organization.

Source: L. L. Cummings, "Toward Organizational Behavior," *Academy of Management Review,* January 1978, p. 92.

ing research and action solutions. He suggests several characteristics of organizational behavior that reflect this point of view.[1] Briefly summarized, they are the following:

1. Problems and questions are typically formulated within an independent variable(s)–dependent variable(s) framework. The models attempt to search for cause and effect.
2. The field is oriented toward change as a desirable outcome for organizations and persons within organizations.
3. The field has a distinctly humanistic tone, reflected in the concern for self-development, personal growth, and self-actualization. However, there is another side that emphasizes operant learning models and behavior modification, which reflects a concern with environmental determinism rather than with self-actualization.
4. The field is becoming increasingly performance-oriented. Most studies include a performance-oriented dependent variable.
5. The field is greatly influenced by norms of skepticism, caution, replication, and public exposure of knowledge based on facts. In other words, it follows the scientific method.

In summary then, organizational behavior is directly concerned with the understanding, prediction, and control of human behavior in organizations. It represents the *behavioral* approach to management, not the whole of management. Other recognized approaches to management include process, quantitative, systems, and contingency. In other words, organizational behavior does not intend to replace the whole of management theory. The charge that old wine, applied/industrial psychology, has merely been poured into a new bottle, organizational behavior, has also proved to be groundless. Although it is certainly true that the behavioral sciences make a significant contribution to both the theoretical and research foundation of organizational behavior, it is equally true that applied/industrial psychology should not be equated with organizational behavior. For example, organizational structure and management processes (decision making and control) play an integral, direct role in organizational behavior but have at most an indirect role in applied/industrial psychology. The same is true of many important dynamics and applications of organizational behavior. Although there will probably never be total agreement on the exact meaning and domain of organizational behavior—which is not necessarily bad, because it makes the field more exciting—there is little doubt that organizational behavior has come into its own as a field of study, research, and application.

This book on organizational behavior attempts to give the specific necessary background and skills to make the managers of today and tomorrow as effective with the conceptual and human dimensions of management as they have been in the past with its technical dimensions.

The remainder of this chapter gives the necessary historical background on management. The field of management in general and the behavioral

---

[1] L. L. Cummings, "Toward Organizational Behavior," *The Academy of Management Review,* January 1978, pp. 93–94.

approach in particular do have a rich heritage. Practitioners and students of management sometimes ignore this important history or feel that it is totally removed in time from today's problems and irrelevant to them. "Old-timers," who know and have actually experienced firsthand some of this development of the field of management, often chide their younger counterparts for "reinventing the wheel." There is certainly some truth to this accusation. The purpose of the following discussion is to trace some of the important phases and provide a foundation for the practice of management. The next chapter will take a similar approach by providing a foundation for the behavioral sciences. Such a management/behavioral science foundation is necessary to more meaningfully interpret and apply what follows in the remaining parts of the book.

THE EARLY PRACTICE OF MANAGEMENT

Managers have been in existence for as long as individuals have put others in a position subordinate to them for the purpose of accomplishing predetermined goals. Some of the earliest recovered documents written by Sumerian temple priests about 5000 B.C. offer tangible evidence of managerial practices.[2] Throughout history, managers have played a vital role in their respective societies. Much of the success of the Egyptian and Roman civilizations can be credited to their astounding managerial accomplishments. Nevertheless, practicing managers were not initially recognized in academic circles. For example, in the writings of Adam Smith, the founding father of economics, only land, labor, and capital were viewed as specific agents of production. It was not until the beginning of the nineteenth century that economists such as J. B. Say added the entrepreneurial concept as an ingredient of production. The "undertaker of industry" was defined by Say as one who unites all means of production—the labor of the one, the capital or the land of the others—". . . and who finds in the value of the products which result from them, the reestablishment of the entire capital he employes, and the value of wages, the interest and the rent which he pays, as well as the profits belonging to himself."[3]

Say's requirements for the entrepreneurial role sound like a job description for modern executives. He felt that the necessary qualities were

. . . judgement, perseverance, and a knowledge of the world as well as of business. He is called upon to estimate, with tolerable accuracy, the importance of the specific product, the probable amount of the demand, and the means of its production: at one time he must employ a great number of hands; at another, buy or order the raw

---

[2]For a discussion of management practices in ancient civilizations, see Claude S. George, Jr., *The History of Management Thought*, 2d ed., Prentice-Hall, Englewood Cliffs, N.J., 1972, pp. 1–27; and Daniel A. Wren, *The Evolution of Management Thought*, Ronald, New York, 1972, pp. 14–22.

[3]Jean Baptiste Say, *Catechism of Political Economy*, trans. John Richter, Sherwood, Neely and Jones, London, 1816, pp. 28–29.

material, collect labourers, find consumers, and give at all times a rigid attention to order and economy; in a word, he must possess the art of superintendence and administration.[4]

Thus, the classical entrepreneurs were risk-bearing proprietors who coordinated labor and capital and practiced the art of management. At first they were termed "merchant princes" or "pretty capitalists," but later, with the advent of the industrial revolution, the term "captains of industry" became a more appropriate description. The successful captains were a rare combination of power and genius and were primarily responsible for launching modern industrialism.

The "captain" of General Motors

William C. Durant, the founder of General Motors, is an outstanding example of this initial phase of the practice of management in the twentieth century. In 1908 he laid the building blocks for the company that was to become the largest manufacturing concern in the world. Durant had the necessary managerial skills to build the giant corporation's foundation. The approach was essentially a one-man operation where Durant made all major decisions, and he preferred subordinates who were yes-men. All pertinent information and records were carried in his head. His day-to-day activities and decision making were based on hunch, experience, and intuition.

Other famous captains of industry were Henry Ford, Cornelius Vanderbilt, Andrew Carnegie, and John D. Rockefeller. All these men were brilliant but sometimes ruthless. They possessed the managerial qualities necessary for the initial stages of industrialization. However, when the industrial revolution began to mature and become stabilized, this approach was no longer appropriate. Although Durant's style was highly effective in the early days of General Motors, after a while "chinks began to appear in the armor."[5] By 1920, General Motors was in serious financial trouble. Within a few weeks' time Durant himself had lost nearly $100 million. In his analysis, Ernest Dale makes it clear that there were many contributing causes to the General Motors crisis. For example, insufficient use of accounting and inventory control was a big problem.[6] However, two major difficulties stood out from all the rest: Durant refused to utilize staff advice; and he failed to come up with an organizational plan that could hold together the tremendous corporate structure he had created.

Some of Durant's behaviorally oriented shortcomings are exemplified by his handling of two brilliant subordinates, Walter Chrysler and Alfred P. Sloan. Chrysler, who at the time headed the Buick Division of General Motors, remembered how he pleaded with Durant to

. . . please, now say what your policies are for General Motors. I'll work on them;

---

[4]Jean Baptiste Say, *A Treatise on Political Economy*, New American ed., Lippincott, Philadelphia, 1867, pp. 330–331. First printed in Paris in 1803.

[5]Ernest Dale, *The Great Organizers*, McGraw-Hill, New York, 1960, pp. 73–74.

[6]Ibid., p. 74.

whatever they are, I'll work to make them effective. Leave the operations alone; the building, the buying, the selling and the men—leave them alone, but say what your policies are.[7]

Chrysler also told of an almost unbelievable encounter he had with Durant.

Once I had gone to New York in obedience to a call from him [Durant]; he wished to see me about some matter. For several days in succession I waited at his office, but he was so busy he could not take the time to talk with me. . . . During a lull I gained his attention for a minute. "Hadn't I better return to Flint and work? I can come back here later." "No, no. Stay right here." I waited four days before I went back to Flint; and to this day I do not know why Billy [Durant] had required my presence in New York.[8]

Because of this kind of shabby treatment, Chrysler eventually quit General Motors and founded what was to become one of that company's biggest competitors.

A similar blunder was Durant's treatment of Alfred P. Sloan. In May 1920, when General Motors was in the beginning of its decline, Sloan submitted to Durant an ingenious plan of organization. The plan reflected many insights into the company's problems and contained some logical solutions. Durant apparently ignored the plan completely. Sloan was so distraught over the outright rejection without discussion or consultation that he was about to resign from the company when the du Pont family assumed control of the corporation. In December 1920, Pierre S. du Pont resubmitted Sloan's organizational plan to the board of directors, and this time it was accepted. Sloan was made president of the company and was allowed to implement his plan. Using his new methods of management, he practically single-handedly rescued General Motors from the sure-death management methods used by Durant. Captains of industry, such as Durant, played a necessary initial role, but it was organizational specialists such as Sloan who then perpetuated and strengthened what the captains had founded.

Organizational specialists

Two pioneering practicing managers, the French engineer and executive head Henri Fayol and General Motors' Alfred P. Sloan, best represent the "Great Organizers." Fayol's career embodied many different phases. He made his initial mark as a practicing mining engineer. Then, as a research geologist, he developed a unique theory on the formation of coal-bearing strata. This experience gave him a keen appreciation of the technical side of enterprise. However, the major portion of his career was spent practicing, and then writing about, the managerial functions and process.

In 1888, Fayol became managing director of Comambault, the well-known French combine. When he assumed the top position, no dividend had been paid for three years and bankruptcy was approaching. Fayol's

---

[7]Walter P. Chrysler, with Boyden Sparkes, *Life of an American Workman*, Dodd, Mead, New York, 1950, p. 148. Originally published in 1937.

[8]Ibid., pp. 156–157.

ingenious managerial and organizational methods soon paid off. The decline was shortly reversed, and by the time of World War I, the combine was able to make a significant contribution to the French cause. Fayol retired in 1918, but through writing and speaking engagements he succeeded in popularizing his theories and techniques of management. He maintained that the successful practicing manager should be able to handle people and should have considerable energy and courage, continuity of tenure, and a great deal of specialized and general experience.[9] He particularly stressed the methods of specialization and organization as necessities for success. In discussing specialization he stated:

The object of division of work is to produce more and better work with the same effort. The worker always on the same part, the manager concerned always with the same matters, acquire an ability, sureness, and accuracy which increase their output.[10]

Devoting most of his attention to the process of organizing, he observed:

To organize a business is to provide it with everything useful to its functioning: raw materials, tools, capital, personnel. All this may be divided into two main sections, the material organization and the human organization.[11]

Alfred P. Sloan is the other outstanding historical example of a Great Organizer. His basic organizational plan was for General Motors to maintain centralized control over highly decentralized operations. Although the du Ponts undoubtedly influenced Sloan, he is widely recognized to have made a tremendous managerial contribution.[12] His plan is largely responsible for the success story of General Motors. Dale states:

Sloan's organization study—the report on which the G.M. reorganization was based—is a remarkable document. Almost entirely original, it would be a creditable, if not a superior, organization plan for any large corporation today. It is a landmark in the history of administrative thought.[13]

In the first year after the du Ponts installed Sloan as president, the company almost doubled its manufacturing capacity. The reorganization went hand in hand with increased productivity and higher profits.

Scientific managers

The Great Organizers were primarily concerned with overall managerial organization in order for their companies to survive and prosper. The

[9]Henri Fayol, *General and Industrial Management*, trans. Constance Storrs, Pitman, London, 1949, p. 50.

[10]Ibid., p. 20.

[11]Ibid., p. 53.

[12]Dale, op. cit., p. 84.

[13]Ibid., p. 86.

scientific management movement around the turn of the century took a narrower, operations perspective. Yet the two approaches were certainly not contradictory. The managers in both cases applied the scientific method to their problems, and they thought that effective management at all levels was the key to organizational success. The two approaches differed chiefly in that the scientific managers worked from the bottom of the hierarchy upward, whereas the organizationalists worked from the apex downward. In other words, both had essentially the same goals, but they tried to reach them from different directions.

Frederick W. Taylor is the recognized father of scientific management. Although recent analysis questions the validity of some of the accomplishments attributed to Taylor,[14] there is little doubt that his name has become synonymous with this style of management. He had actual shop and engineering experience and therefore was intimately involved with tools, products, and various machining and manufacturing operations. His well-known metal-cutting experiments demonstrate the scientific management approach. Over a period of twenty-six years, Taylor tested every conceivable variation in speed, feed, depth of cut, and kind of cutting tool. The outcome of this experimentation was high-speed steel, considered one of the most significant contributions to the development of large-scale production.

Besides through his metal-cutting experiments, Taylor dramatically contributed to increased productivity through his scientific management philosophy and principles. In Taylor's words, this approach can be summarized as (1) science, not rule of thumb; (2) harmony, not discord; (3) co-operation, not individualism; (4) maximum output, in place of restricted output; and (5) the development of each person to his or her greatest efficiency and prosperity.[15] These concepts represented a total system of management as well as day-to-day operating procedures.[16]

Two of the most famous applications of Taylor's principles were to the pig-iron handling and shoveling operations at Bethlehem Steel Company. In the first situation, a gang of seventy-five workers loaded pigs of iron, each weighing 92 pounds, into boxcars. By applying scientific management, the company achieved about a threefold increase in productivity. A similar rise in productivity was attained when the principles were applied to the men who shoveled iron ore and rice coal.[17] At first, these achievements were not widely recognized, but it was not long before scientific management became practically synonymous with management itself. The upsurge in popularity was primarily a result of a 1910 railway rate hearing before the Interstate Commerce Commission. Testimony by Harrington Emerson, a consultant on efficiency engineering, indicated that the railroads could save "a million

---

[14]Charles D. Wrege and Amedes G. Perroni, "Taylor's Pig-Tale: A Historical Analysis of Frederick W. Taylor's Pig Iron Experiments," *Academy of Management Journal*, March 1974, pp. 6–27.

[15]Frederick W. Taylor, *The Principles of Scientific Management*, Harper, New York, 1911, p. 140.

[16]George, op. cit., p. 93.

[17]A detailed account of the Bethlehem experiments may be found in Taylor, op. cit., pp. 41–48 and 57–76.

dollars a day" through the use of scientific management. The newspapers headlined this testimony, and scientific management became renowned throughout American industry and also popular in Europe and Japan.

Taylor was by no means the only noteworthy scientific manager. Others in the movement, such as Frank Gilbreth and Henry L. Gantt, made especially significant contributions. Furthermore, the scientific managers were not the first or only group that recognized the importance of the operating function. A hundred years earlier, Adam Smith had carefully pointed out the advantages of division of labor, and in 1832, Charles Babbage, a British mathematician with some astounding managerial insights, discussed transference of skill in his book *Economy of Machinery and Manufacture*. Although Henry Ford could also be thought of as a captain of industry, the achievement of 10,000 Model T's a day would rival any scientific management accomplishment.

The emergence of functional specialists

The captains of industry were primarily financial specialists. They created most of today's large corporations from a series of combinations, mergers, and financial manipulations. This financial phase was then replaced by an organizational orientation. The Great Organizers established structures which permitted their corporations to survive and meet the challenges of increased production. The scientific managers fed the insatiable consumer appetite for goods and services. These experts achieved phenomenal production results. In fact, like the captains of industry, they did their job almost too well. Inventories began to pile up as a result of the tremendous increases in productivity. The managerial problem shifted from one of not being able to produce enough to one of trying to dispose of the deluge of manufactured goods. At this point marketing specialists entered the picture. The marketing functions, consisting of the promotion, distribution, and sale of goods and services, became an integral part of practicing management. Thus, the functions of finance, production, and marketing each in turn received emphasis in the practice of management. Each of these functional specialties is still very much in evidence today and makes extremely important contributions to modern organizations.

The personnel manager, the other traditionally recognized functional specialist, has not yet been mentioned. This does not imply that the functional specialists ignored the importance of the personnel function. Sloan, in reflecting on his years with General Motors, was careful to point out that as far back as the 1920s the company provided many employee benefits, such as excellent employee facilities, group life insurance, and a savings and investment plan.[18] Furthermore, the now famous General Motors bonus plan provided the necessary managerial incentives to make his decentralized organizational plan effective. In his book, Fayol emphasized the importance that incentive payments, especially profit sharing, played in

---

[18]Alfred P. Sloan, Jr., *My Years with General Motors*, John McDonald and Catharine Stevens (eds.), Doubleday, Garden City, N.Y., 1964. p. 391.

effective management. He also gave selection and training a great deal of attention.[19] The pioneering scientific managers developed sophisticated differential piece-rate incentive plans and recognized the impact that the group had on the individual.[20] Henry Ford, of course, was almost as famous for paying his workers $5 a day as he was for mass-producing the Model T. These examples offer ample evidence that the personnel function was very much in existence before the 1930s. However, the major change in the practice of management that included the personnel function, with its accompanying concern for the human element, did not occur until the sociopsychological upheavals in the late 1920s and early 1930s. At that time, in addition to creating personnel departments, practicing general managers also began to shift from a relatively strict production orientation to a growing awareness and concern for the human aspects of management.

THE HUMAN RELATIONS MOVEMENT

The practice of management which places heavy emphasis on employee cooperation and morale might be classified as human relations. Raymond Miles states that the human relations approach was simply to "treat people as human beings (instead of machines in the productive process), acknowledge their needs to belong and to feel important by listening to and heeding their complaints where possible and by involving them in certain decisions concerning working conditions and other matters, then morale would surely improve and workers would cooperate with management in achieving good production."[21] There are, of course, varied and complex reasons for this human relations position. Historically, three of the most important contributing factors would be the Great Depression, the labor movement, and the results of the now famous Hawthorne studies.

The Great Depression

The economy was operating in high gear just before the thundering financial crash occurred in 1929. The production and organizational specialists had achieved amazing results. What went wrong? With maximized production, would not the "invisible hand" of laissez faire economics take care of the rest? Obviously it did not. Most economic analyses include one or more of the following as major causes of a depression: (1) piling up of business inventories and accumulation of large stocks of new durables in consumers' hands; (2) consumer resistance to rising prices and increasing business costs; (3) an end of the upward acceleration effect and a resulting decline in investment spending; (4) accumulation of vast amounts of new productive

---

[19]Fayol, op. cit., pp. 26–32 and 78–81.

[20]For some of Taylor's insights into the impact of the group on human behavior, see his *Principles*, op. cit., p. 50.

[21]Raymond E. Miles, *Theories of Management*, McGraw-Hill, New York, 1975, p. 40.

capacity and new technological developments; (5) a growing scarcity of promising large-scale investment outlets and exhaustion of excess bank reserves; and (6) a weakening of confidence and expectations.[22]

Before the Great Depression, production specialists had contributed to some of these causes. After the crash, management began to realize that production could no longer be the only major responsibility of management. Marketing, finance, and personnel were also required in order for a business to survive and profit. The Depression's aftermath of unemployment, discontent, and insecurity brought to the surface human problems that managers were now forced to recognize and cope with. Personnel departments were either created or given more emphasis, and most managers now began to develop a new, awakened view of the human aspects of work. Human relations took on added significance as an indirect, and in some cases a direct, result of the Depression.

The labor movement

Another important contributing factor to the human relations movement was the organized labor movement. Although labor unions (for example, the Philadelphia Shoemakers) were in existence in America as early as 1792, it was not until the passage of the Wagner Act in 1935 that organized labor made a substantial impact on management. Why did the movement develop? Perhaps the best explanation is simply that practicing managers did not properly recognize the human contribution to the goals of the organization. A "fair wage," decent hours, and adequate working conditions were often sacrificed for more production. Some of the more enlightened pioneers in management, such as Taylor, Ford, and Sloan, openly expressed their sincere desire to give labor its fair share. However, except for these few exceptions and some scattered paternalistic managers, management often exploited labor.

In 1935, when unions became legally entrenched, managers began to wake up and take notice. The general reaction was either to fight the union movement or to realize that it was here to stay and might possibly have something to contribute. Although open conflicts were not uncommon in this era, most managers assumed the latter position and formed personnel departments either to deal with the unions or to keep them out. In either case, primary emphasis was placed on employee relations and secondary attention was given to wages, hours, and conditions of employment. The personnel department's activities carried over into all other management functions.

Unfortunately, the human relations role too often came about for the wrong reasons. In too many cases, it was forced on managers by labor's threatening them with the consequences of noncompliance with union demands. Ideally, it would have been better had human relations developed because of the intrinsic motivation of practicing managers to better understand and provide for the welfare of their employees.

---

[22]George L. Bach, *Economics*, 8th ed., Prentice-Hall, Englewood Cliffs, N.J., 1974, p. 173.

THE HAWTHORNE STUDIES

Although the Depression and the labor movement were at least important indirect causes of the practice of human relations, the Hawthorne studies dominate the academic historical development. Understanding all aspects of these well-known studies is vital to an appreciation of the historical development of organizational behavior.

Before the Hawthorne studies officially started, Elton Mayo headed a research team which was investigating the causes of very high turnover in the mule-spinning department of a Philadelphia textile mill in 1923 and 1924. After interviewing and consulting the workers, the team set up a series of rest pauses which resulted in greatly reduced turnover and more positive worker attitudes and morale.

About the same time that Mayo and his group were conducting the Philadelphia study, a typical scientific management study, sponsored by the National Research Council, was being made at Hawthorne. This latter study was attempting to determine experimentally the effects that varying degrees of illumination had on worker productivity.

Illumination experiments

The light experiments were conducted on female workers, who were divided into two groups. One group was placed in a test room where the intensity of illumination was varied, and the other group worked in a control room with supposedly constant conditions. The results were baffling to the researchers. Productivity increased in both rooms. Furthermore, in the test room no correlation developed. The production of the women continually increased whether the footcandles of light were raised, retained at the original level, or even brought down to moonlight intensity so that the workers could barely see. Obviously, some variables in the experiment were not being held constant or under control. Something besides the level of illumination was causing the change in productivity. This something, of course, was the complex human variable.

It is fortunate that the illumination experiments did not end up in the wastebasket. Those responsible for the Hawthorne studies had enough foresight and spirit to accept the challenge of looking beneath the surface of the apparent failure of the illumination experiment. In a way, the results of the illumination experiments were a serendipitous discovery. In reference to research, *serendipity* means accidental discovery.[23] The classic case is the breakthrough for penicillin which occurred when Sir Alexander Fleming accidentally discovered green mold on the side of a test tube. The reason why the green mold was not washed down the drain or why the results of the illumination experiment were not thrown in the trashcan can be credited to

---

[23]The term can be traced to Horace Walpole's story *The Three Princes of Serendip*. The princes in the story searched the world but did not find what they were seeking. Instead, they stumbled on many interesting and exciting events that they had not planned to encounter. An expanded discussion of serendipity appears in Arthur J. Bachrach, *Psychological Research*, 2d ed., Random House, New York, 1964, chap. 1.

the researchers' not being blinded by the unusual or seemingly worthless results of their experimentation. The serendipitous illumination experiment provided the impetus for the relay room phase of the Hawthorne studies.

Relay room experiments

In 1927, the relay room experiments got under way. These experiments represent the actual beginning of the Hawthorne studies attributed to Elton Mayo. In reality, he was only one member of a large research team composed of Harvard colleagues and company representatives.[24] This team of researchers utilized their earlier experience with rest pauses at the Philadelphia textile company. Thirteen variables tested the effects that place of work, place and length of rest pause, length of working day, length of workweek, method of payment, and a free midmorning lunch had on productivity.[25]

Taking a cue from the earlier illumination experiment at the plant, the researchers attempted to set up the test room so that there would be more control over the independent variables. Two female assemblers were selected for the experiment. They were permitted to choose four others to join them in the test room, which was segregated from the rest of the plant. During the experiment, the women were often consulted and sometimes allowed to express themselves about the changes that took place in the experiment. This had also been done in the previous studies in Philadelphia. In the relay test room, the female assemblers were insulated from the traditional restrictions of management. In total, they were treated and recognized as individuals with something to contribute.

The results in the relay room were practically identical with those in the illumination experiment. Each test period yielded higher productivity than the previous one had done. Even when the women were subjected to the original conditions of the experiment, productivity increased. The conclusion was that the independent variables (rest pauses and so forth) were not by themselves causing the change in the dependent variable (output). As in the illumination experiment, something was *still* not being controlled.

The relay room experiment was followed by a second relay room experiment and the mica splitting test room study. The results of these two studies were judged to be inconclusive.[26] Next, 20,000 interviews were

---

[24]In the preface to *Management and the Worker*, Mayo stated, "I cannot name all who have thus participated . . . An attempt to name everyone would read, a colleague suggests, like a telephone book." He specifically cited Fritz J. Roethlisberger and William J. Dickson, the authors of *Management and the Worker*, the most detailed account of the studies, as having been intimately involved. Roethlisberger was a Harvard colleague and Dickson represented the Western Electric Company. He also stated that Dean Wallace B. Donham and Dr. Lawrence J. Henderson of Harvard's Committee on Industrial Physiology were very active participants. An equally active group of company participants consisted of C. G. Stoll and W. F. Hosford of the New York office and C. L. Rice of the Hawthorne Works in support of G. A. Pennock, G. S. Rutherford, and M. L. Putnam.

[25]Unless otherwise noted, references made to the procedures and results of the Hawthorne studies are drawn from Fritz J. Roethlisberger and William J. Dickson, *Management and the Worker*, Harvard, Cambridge, 1939.

[26]Ibid., p. 160.

conducted between 1928 and 1930. These interviews generated a great amount of information. Table 1-2 depicts the actual topics that were discussed. Out of these data a great deal of insight into employee attitudes and group dynamics evolved. Specifically, the insights into the impact that informal work groups have on restriction of output led to the last major research effort in the Hawthorne studies.

Bank wiring room study

The final phase of the research program was the bank wiring study, which started in November 1931 and lasted until May 1932. Its primary purpose was to make an observational analysis of the informal work group. The

Table 1-2

TOPICS DISCUSSED IN THE MASS INTERVIEWING PROGRAM AT HAWTHORNE

Absence

Advancement

Aisles

Bogey

Club activities*
  General
  Entertainment
  Club store
  Educational
  Sports

Dirt

Fatigue

Floor

Furniture and fixtures
  Time clocks
  Drinking water and
    fountains
  Chairs
  Trucks
  Pans
  Elevators
  Fans
  Benches
  Miscellaneous

Hospital

Hours
  Standard
  Night
  Overtime
  Rest periods

Interest

Interviewing program

Light

Lockers

Material
  Quality
  Quantity
  Finished product
  Miscellaneous

Monotony

Noise

Payment
  Wages
  Group piecework
  Straight piecework
  Rate revision
  Piecework rate
  Piecework in general
  Payroll routine
  Miscellaneous

Placement
  Company placement
  Job placement
  Transfers
  Personnel organization

Restaurant

Safety and health

Sanitation
  Spitting
  General

Smoke and fumes

Social contacts

Steady work

Supervision

Temperature

Thrift
  Stock purchase plan
  Building and loan
  Life insurance
  Ready money plan
  General

Tools and machines
  Tools
  Machines

Transportation

Vacation

Ventilation

Washrooms

Welfare
  General
  Benefit plans
  Employment
  Service (continuous)
  Publications
  Pensions
  Loans to employees
  Christmas welfare
  Legal service

Working space

General
  Miscellaneous
  Education

*Hawthorne Club.

Source: F. J. Roethlisberger and William J. Dickson, *Management and the Worker,* Harvard, Cambridge, 1939, p. 221.

group chosen for observation consisted of fourteen male operators: nine wirers, three solderers, and two inspectors.

The methods used in this study were in some ways similar to the preceding relay room experiments. As in the relay experiments, the bank wirers were placed in a separate test room. The researchers were reluctant to segregate the bank wiring group because they recognized this would alter the realistic factory environment they were attempting to simulate. However, for practical reasons, the research team decided to use a separate room.[27] Unlike the relay room experiments, the bank wiring study involved no experimental changes once the study had started. Instead, an observer and an interviewer gathered objective data for study. The observer gained the confidence of the group and was recognized as a regular member. The interviewer, on the other hand, remained an outsider. The interviewer's major function was to obtain information about the workers' attitudes, thoughts, and feelings. With the exceptions of the separate room, the observer, and the interviewer, all the conditions were designed to duplicate those in the bank wiring department itself. Of particular interest was the fact that the department's regular supervisors were used in the bank wiring room. Just as in the department out on the factory floor, their main function was to maintain order and control.

Results of the bank wiring room study   The results in the bank wiring room were essentially opposite to those in the relay room. In the bank wiring room there were not the continual increases in productivity that occurred in the relay room. Rather, output was actually restricted by the bank wirers. By scientific management analysis, e.g., time and motion study, the industrial engineers had arrived at a standard of 7312 terminal connections per day. This represented two and one-half equipments. The workers had a different brand of rationality. They decided that two equipments was a "proper" day's work. Thus, two and one-half equipments represented the management norm for production but two equipments was the informal group norm and the actual output.

The researchers determined that the informal group norm of two equipments represented restriction of output rather than a lack of ability to produce at the company standard of two and one-half equipments. The following evidence supports this contention:

1. The observer noted that all the men stopped before quitting time.
2. Most of the men admitted to the interviewer they could easily turn out more work.
3. Tests of dexterity and intelligence indicated no relationship between capacity to perform and actual performance.

The logic for restriction of output revolved around factors such as the following:

1. *Fear of unemployment.* The lump-sum theory of work was supported by reasoning such as, "Don't work yourself out of a job."
2. *Fear of raising the standard.* Most workers were convinced that once they had reached the standard rate of production, management would raise the standard, reasoning that it must be too easy to attain.

---

[27]Ibid., pp. 387–388.

3. *Protection of the slower workers.* The workers were friendly off the job as well as on the job. They appreciated the fact that all workers, including the slower ones, had family responsibilities that required them to remain employed. Therefore, the faster workers protected the slower ones by not outproducing them by too much. The group did not want to make the slower workers look bad in the eyes of management.

4. *Satisfaction on the part of management.* Management seemed to accept the lower production rate. No one was being fired or even reprimanded for restricted output.

From a group dynamics standpoint, of particular interest were the social pressures used to gain compliance to the group norms. The incentive system dictated that the more an individual produced, the more money the individual would earn. Also, the best producers would be laid off last, and thus they could be more secure by producing more. Yet, in the face of this management rationale, almost all the workers restricted output. Social ostracism, ridicule, and name-calling were the major sanctions utilized by the group to enforce this restriction. In some instances, actual physical pressure in the form of a game called "binging" was applied. In the game, a worker would be hit as hard as possible, with the privilege of returning one "bing" or hit. Forcing rate busters to play the game became an effective sanction. These group pressures had a tremendous impact on all the workers. Social ostracism was more effective in gaining compliance to the informal group norm than money and security were in attaining the scientifically derived management norm.

Implications of the Hawthorne studies

The Hawthorne studies are unquestionably the single most important historical foundation for the behavioral approach to management. They have been cussed and discussed, revisited, discounted, and lauded throughout the succeeding years.[28] Despite some obvious methodological limitations, there are some interesting insights from the Hawthorne studies that contribute to the better understanding of human behavior in organizations. For instance, one interesting aspect of the Hawthorne studies is the contrasting results found in the relay room and the bank wiring room. In the relay room, production continually increased throughout the test period and the relay assemblers were very positive. The opposite was true in the bank wiring room; blatant restriction of output was practiced by disgruntled workers. Why the difference in these two phases of the studies?

One clue to the answer to this question may be traced to the results of a questionnaire administered to the women in the relay room. The original intent of the questions was to determine the health and habits of the women.

[28]For example, see Henry A. Landsberger, *Hawthorne Revisited*, Cornell, Ithaca, N.Y., 1958; Alex Carey, "The Hawthorne Studies: A Radical Criticism," *American Sociological Review*, June 1967, pp. 403–416; H. M. Parsons, "What Happened at Hawthorne," *Science*, Mar. 8, 1974, pp. 992–932; "Hawthorne Revisited: The Legend and the Legacy," *Organizational Dynamics*, Winter 1975, pp. 66–80; and Richard Franke and James Kaul, "The Hawthorne Experiments: First Statistical Interpretations," *American Sociological Review*, October 1978, pp. 623–643.

Their answers were generally inconclusive except that *all* the operators indicated they felt "better" in the test room.[29] A follow-up questionnaire then asked about specific items in the test room situation. In discussions of the Hawthorne studies, the follow-up questionnaire results, in their entirety, usually are not mentioned. Most discussions cite the women's unanimous preference for working in the test room instead of the regular department. Often overlooked, however, are the women's explanations for their choice. In order of preference, the women gave the following reasons:

1. Small group
2. Type of supervision
3. Earnings
4. Novelty of the situation
5. Interest in the experiment
6. Attention received in the test room[30]

It is important to note that novelty, interest, and attention were relegated to the fourth, fifth, and sixth positions. These last three areas usually are associated with the famous Hawthorne effect. Many social scientists imply that the increases in the relay room productivity can be attributed solely to the fact that the participants in the study were given special attention and that they were enjoying a novel, interesting experience. This is labeled the *Hawthorne effect* and is, of course, a real problem with all human experimental subjects. But to charge that all the results of the relay room experiment were the result of such an effect on the subjects seems to ignore the important impact of the small group, the type of supervision, and earnings.

In *Management and the Worker*, Roethlisberger and Dickson recognized the importance that the highly cohesive small group had for the women.

No longer were the girls isolated individuals, working together only in the sense of an actual physical proximity. They had become participating members of a working group with all the psychological and social implications peculiar to such a group. . . . They had become bound together by common sentiments and feelings of loyalty.[31]

The effect of earnings also was analyzed in the second relay room and mica splitting room experiments. Although earnings were shown to have a definite impact, no firm conclusions were drawn. Probably the most important insights can be gained from a more thorough analysis of the role that supervision played in the work groups studied at Hawthorne.

Supervision in the relay and bank wiring rooms

The relay and bank wiring rooms had some common variables. Both rooms contained small, highly cohesive groups that worked on an incentive basis

---

[29]Roethlisberger and Dickson, op. cit., p. 66.

[30]C. E. Turner, "Test Room Studies in Employee Effectiveness," *American Journal of Public Health*, June 1933, p. 584.

[31]Roethlisberger and Dickson, op. cit., p. 86.

and were segregated from the rest of the plant. The major difference was the supervisory climate. In the relay room there were no regular supervisors per se. Yet the relay women stated that after the small group it was the type of supervision that made them feel so good and produce at a high rate. They consistently mentioned "freedom" and "the nice way we are treated" as explanations for their attitudes and behavior. In other words, the women were perceiving the friendly, attentive, genuinely concerned researchers as their supervisors. The relay test room observers were directed to build a friendly rapport with the female operators. They made a point of constantly interacting with the women. Roethlisberger and Dickson noted, "Sometimes the topics he [the observer] brought up pertained to their work, sometimes to personal matters, and occasionally they took the form of a general inquiry as to the attitude of the operators toward the test."[32]

In the bank wiring room, an entirely different supervisory climate existed. Regular department supervisors were used to maintain order and control in the test room. It was observed that this supervisory arrangement produced an inhibiting atmosphere.[33] The observer played a different role from that performed in the relay room. In the bank wiring room, he was directed to be a disinterested spectator. His general conduct precluded the workers' perceiving him as a supervisor. For instance, he was not allowed to issue orders or answer any questions that implied the assumption of authority. Thus, in the bank wiring room the observer came to be viewed as a member of the group rather than as a supervisor.

The importance of supervisory climate

Elton Mayo's original analysis emphasized the importance of supervision in assessing the output record in the relay room. He noted that while the women in the relay room were ". . . getting closer supervision than ever before, the change is in the quality of supervision. This—change in quality of supervision—is by no means the whole change, but it is an important part of it."[34] Mayo and others, such as C. E. Turner, a consultant to the Hawthorne studies, played down the importance of the Hawthorne effect as an explanation for the results. Turner stated: "We at first thought that the novelty of test room conditions might be partly responsible for increased output but the continuing increase in production over a 4-year period suggests that it was not of great importance."[35]

Despite these initial observations, most contemporary discussions of the Hawthorne studies emphasize the novelty aspects and exclude the important implications concerning supervision. Much of the problem lies in the fact that the Hawthorne studies suffer from guilt by association stemming from

---

[32]Ibid., p. 37.

[33]Ibid., p. 458.

[34]Elton Mayo, *The Human Problems of an Industrial Civilization*. Viking, New York, p. 75. Original 1933 copyright held by the President and Fellows of Harvard College.

[35]Turner, op. cit., p. 584.

the general indictment against the Mayo ideological school of thought.[36] If novelty were, in fact, the only explanation for the results of the relay room, one could question why the bank wirers, who were also placed in a separate room, did not react the same way. Were the research methods so much improved that the bank wiring room perfectly simulated the factory floor and that no novelty was present? If the novelty argument is used in the relay room, should it not also apply to the bank wiring room?

To reiterate, the major difference between the two rooms was not necessarily that one situation was novel and the other was not. Rather, the important point seems to be the differing climates of supervision that existed in the two rooms. To be sure, one cannot and should not dismiss other disparities, such as male versus female, mere observation and interviewing versus quasi-experimental techniques, or even the degree of novelty that existed in the two rooms. Another difficulty in the interpretation of most discussions is the semantic problem of whether the novelty and special attention given the women are considered to be the Hawthorne effect, a unique, attentive type of supervision, or both. Regardless of these complications and definite methodological limitations, the analysis of the Hawthorne studies seems to point out the impact that climate of supervision has on human behavior in organizations.

SUMMARY

This introductory chapter first spelled out exactly what is meant by organizational behavior, and outlined the contents and aims of the book. The remainder was devoted to providing a brief historical foundation for the practice of management. Figure 1-1 gives a visual presentation of how management has changed over the decades, leading up to the organizational behavior approach to human resource management. The early practice of management evolved through several phases. About a hundred years ago the captains of industry, exemplified by General Motors founder William C. Durant, dominated. Their ruthless, one-person style then gave way to organizational specialists and scientific managers. These latter managers nurtured what the captains had founded. The financial and production function specialists were soon joined by marketing and personnel specialists. The personnel function is directly relevant to the behavioral approach to management, but all managers of people, regardless of functional specialty, are relevant to the study of organizational behavior. The human relations movement evolved from causes such as the Depression and the organized labor movement, but the Hawthorne studies dominate at least the

---

[36]This school of thought is presented in Mayo's books *The Human Problems of an Industrial Civilization*, 2d ed., 1946, *The Social Problems of an Industrial Civilization*, 1945, and *The Political Problems of an Industrial Civilization*, 1947, all published by Harvard University Graduate School of Business Administration, Division of Research, Boston; and in T. North Whitehead's *Leadership in a Free Society*, 1936, and Roethlisberger's book *Management and Morale*, 1955, both published by Harvard University Press, Cambridge, Mass.

academic historical development. These celebrated studies, which took place over a time span of several years, were the first attempt to systematically analyze human behavior in an organizational setting. Most modern behavioral scientists are very critical of the research design and discount the results. Admittedly, the design, as in any pioneering effort, was crude by modern standards. However, this should not completely negate the insights concerning the role that behavioral science analysis can play in the better understanding, prediction, and control of human behavior in the work place. The Hawthorne studies set an important precedent for establishing the value that the behavioral sciences can have for the behavioral approach to management. The next chapter is specifically devoted to this behavioral science foundation.

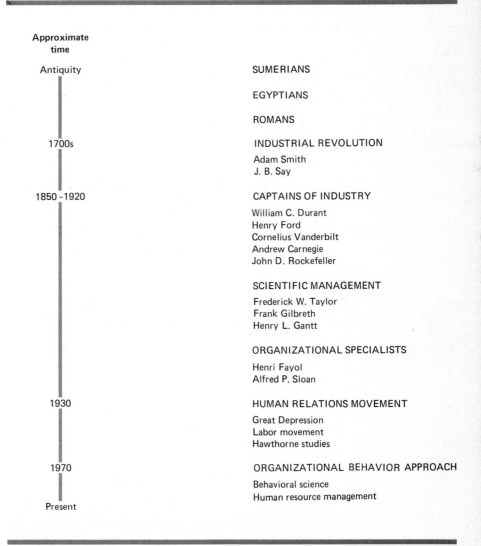

**Figure 1-1
A historical overview of the practice of management.**

QUESTIONS FOR DISCUSSION AND REVIEW

1. How does organizational behavior relate/differ from organizational psychology? From organization theory? From personnel and human resource management?
2. How did the "captains of industry" differ from the "organizational specialists" in their practice of management? Cite specific examples.
3. Identify and briefly summarize the major historical contributions to the human relations movement.
4. In the Hawthorne studies, how do you explain that in the relay room experiment there were continual increases in productivity but in the bank wiring study there was deliberate restriction of output?
5. Why do you feel the Hawthorne studies make such an important historical contribution to the study of organizational behavior?

CASE:
HOW IS THIS STUFF GOING TO HELP ME?

Jane Arnold wanted to be a manager. She enjoyed her accounting, finance, and marketing courses. Each of these had provided her with some clear-cut answers. Now her professor in this behavioral management course tells her that there are really very few clear-cut answers when it comes to managing people. Then he starts off with some history on management practice and says that behavioral science concepts play a big role in the course. She is very perplexed. She came to school to get answers on how to be an effective manager, but this course sure doesn't seem to be heading in that direction.

1. How would you relieve Jane's anxiety? How is a course on organizational behavior going to make her a better manager?
2. Why start off with a brief history of the practice of management?
3. How does a course in organizational behavior differ from courses in fields such as accounting, finance, or marketing?

CASE:
TOO NICE TO PEOPLE

John had just graduated from the College of Business Administration at State University and joined his family's small business, which employs twenty-five semiskilled workers. The first week on the job his dad called him in and said, "John, I've had a chance to observe your working with the men and women for the past two days and, although I hate to, I feel I must say something. You are just too nice to people. I know they taught you that human relations stuff at the university, but it just doesn't work here. I remember when the Hawthorne studies were first reported and everybody at the university got all excited about them, but believe me, there is more to managing people than just being nice to them."

1. How would you react to your father's comments if you were John?
2. Do you think John's father understood and interpreted the Hawthorne studies correctly?
3. What phases of management do you think John's father has gone through in this family business?

RESEARCH METHODS AND THE BEHAVIORAL SCIENCES

EBASCO, INC. RESEARCHES ITS PROBLEMS*

Ebasco Services, Inc. builds power plants. It is part of a network of companies that were subsidiaries of General Electric Company. Founded in 1905, Ebasco is currently part of Enserch Corporation, a diversified energy company which acquired Ebasco in August 1976. The management of Ebasco was concerned that the firm was not being as effective as it could be, but they had no real handle on either its promise or its problems. A few years ago, under the direction of Andrew O. Manzini, the director of manpower planning and development, the firm attempted to find out more about itself through extensive surveys and interviews with each of the employees and the 300 managers. The purpose of this effort was to make an accurate research assessment of the company's strengths and weaknesses. The end result was a 645-page research report of facts, figures, and conclusions. Management currently believe that they now have a much better understanding of the problems facing the company and that the data can be used to help them come up with solutions and help chart the future. Not only was there a great increase in management's overall awareness of the company, but specific internal problems relating to communications and misperceptions were revealed. Consequently, the company is embarking on a program that will improve its internal and external directions. The total cost invested in this effort so far is $74,000, but management believes the benefits are incalculable.

*Adapted from "When Bosses Look Back to See Ahead," *Business Week,* Jan. 15, 1979, pp. 60–61.

The last chapter gave a rationale and historical foundation for the study of organizational behavior. This chapter gives a behavioral science foundation. A working knowledge of the behavioral sciences and their research methods is a necessary prerequisite for the study of organizational behavior. A behavioral science foundation is what separates the organizational behavior approach from the older, more simplistic human relations approach. The disciplines of anthropology, sociology, and psychology and their accompanying rigorous research methods make an important contribution to a better understanding of human behavior in modern organizations.

BACKGROUND OF THE BEHAVIORAL SCIENCES

Compared to the physical or biological sciences, behavioral science is a relatively new academic discipline. The development of behavioral science can perhaps best be summarized by paraphrasing Galileo, that it is "a very new science of a very ancient subject."[1] No science can realistically pin its origin down to a specific date. As long as humans have inhabited the earth, their behavior has been a matter of concern and of attempts at understanding. Compared to the other sciences, however, the *scientific* study of human behavior is relatively new.

The use of the interdisciplinary term *behavioral science* is of very recent vintage. The term can be traced to the World War II era, but it was in the 1950s that the Ford Foundation popularized it. The foundation's multimillion-dollar program, Individual Behavior and Human Relations, became widely known as the behavioral sciences program. Probably the best definition of *behavioral science* is "the scientific study of human behavior." This definition differentiates behavioral science from the other biological and physical sciences, the humanities, and even certain disciplines within the social sciences. Table 2-1 clarifies the exact relationship of behavioral science to other academic disciplines. The table shows that behavioral science with its three primary disciplines is a subclassification in the social sciences. The social sciences, in turn, are a major subpart of the overall arts and sciences. The chief difference between the behavioral sciences and the other social sciences, such as history, economics, and political science, is the methodology used to accumulate knowledge. A behavioral science depends on rigorous scientific methodology in the collection of empirical data on human behavior. The other social sciences commonly use aggregate or indirect documentary practices in building their body of knowledge.

It is by means of the scientific methodology stemming from the behavioral sciences that organizational behavior researchers are able to accumulate meaningful knowledge to directly help managers better understand, predict, and control employees' behavior. This does not mean that there are no other ways of gaining insight into organizational behavior. For example, personal experience that is relayed through conversations, speech-

[1] Robert K. Merton, "The Mosaic of the Behavior Sciences," in Bernard Berelson (ed.), *The Behavioral Sciences Today*, Basic Books, New York, 1963, p. 249.

Table 2-1

RELATIONSHIPS AMONG ACADEMIC DISCIPLINES

ARTS AND SCIENCES
  Humanities
  Physical sciences
  Biological sciences
  and
  SOCIAL SCIENCES
    Economics
    History
    Political science
    and
    BEHAVIORAL SCIENCES
      Anthropology
      Sociology
      Psychology

es, or the popular press and movies is common. Although such insights are valuable to an extent, the scientific method which strives to minimize personal biases and establish cause-and-effect relationships between relevant variables is the best way.

RESEARCH METHODOLOGY

Discovering the truth of why humans behave the way they do is a very delicate and complex process. In fact, the problems are so great that many scholars, chiefly from the physical and applied sciences, argue that there can be no precise science of behavior. They maintain that humans cannot be treated like chemical or physical elements; they cannot be effectively controlled or manipulated. For example, the critics state that, under easily controllable conditions, two parts of hydrogen combined with one part of oxygen will always result in water, and that no analogous situation exists in human behavior. Human variables such as motives, learning, perception, values, and even "hangovers" on the part of both subject and investigator infect the controls that are attempted. For these reasons, behavioral scientists are often on the defensive and must be very careful to comply with accepted methods of science.

Behavioral scientists strive to attain the following hallmarks of any science:

1. The procedures are public.
2. The definitions are precise.
3. The data-collecting is objective.
4. The findings are replicable.
5. The approach is systematic and cumulative.
6. The purposes are explanation, understanding, and prediction.[2]

[2]Bernard Berelson and Gary A. Steiner, *Human Behavior*, Harcourt, Brace & World, New York, 1964, pp. 16–17.

Figure 2-1 summarizes the relationship among practical behavioral problems and unanswered questions, research methodology, and the existing body of knowledge. When a question arises or a problem evolves, the first place to turn for an answer is the existing body of knowledge. It is possible that the question can be immediately answered or the problem solved without going any further. Unfortunately, this usually is not true in the case of organizational behavior. One reason is that the amount of knowledge directly applicable to organizational behavior is relatively very small. The small body of knowledge is due primarily to the newness of the field. It must be remembered that behavioral science is relatively young, but organizational behavior is even younger—it is really a product of the 1970s. The Hawthorne studies go back over fifty years, but a behavioral-science-based approach to the study and application of human behavior in organizations is very recent. The sobering fact is that many questions and problems in organizational behavior cannot be directly answered or solved by existing knowledge. This situation is definitely changing, as more research expands the body of knowledge. The chapters in this book reflect the current status of this knowledge.

DESIGNS USED TO ANSWER QUESTIONS

The research design is at the very heart of scientific methodology. The three designs most often used in organizational behavior research today are the experiment, the case, and the survey. All three designs have played important roles in the development of meaningful knowledge. The experimental design is largely borrowed from psychology, where it is used

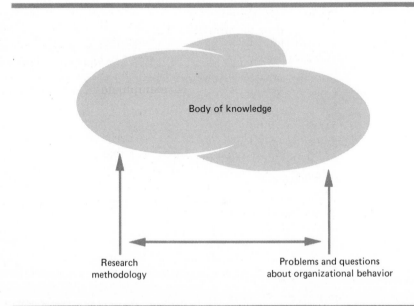

Body of knowledge

Research
methodology

Problems and questions
about organizational behavior

**Figure 2-1
Simple relation-
ships among prob-
lems, methodolo-
gy, and knowl-
edge.**

extensively, and the case and survey designs have traditionally played a bigger role in sociology. All three designs can be used effectively for researching organizational behavior.

Experimental design

A primary aim of any research design is to establish a cause-and-effect relationship. The experimental method offers the best possibility of accomplishing this goal. All other factors being equal, most researchers prefer this method of testing hypotheses. Simply defined, an experiment involves the manipulation of independent variables to measure their effect on, or the change in, dependent variables, while everything else is held constant or controlled. Usually, an experimental group and a control group are formed. The experimental group receives the input of the independent variable and the control group does not. Any measured change in the dependent variable in the experimental group can be attributed to the independent variable, assuming no change has occurred in the control group. The controls employed are the key to the successful use of the experimental design. If all intervening variables are held constant or equal, the experimenter can conclude with a high degree of confidence that the independent variable caused the change in the dependent variable.

Laboratory experiments   There are three general types of experimental designs—laboratory, natural, and field. The laboratory experiment permits high degrees of control but has a major disadvantage in its limited generalizability. Under laboratory conditions, it is relatively easy, for example in a learning experiment using white rats, to find the schedule of reinforcement that leads to the greatest resistance to extinction; or, among college sophomores, to determine the effects of cooperation versus competition on task efficiency and satisfaction. But, meaningful generalizations from this kind of experimentation are not always possible. In more complex and realistic settings, e.g., real employees in a real organizational setting, there is a constant interactive effect between the person and the situation, and it is very difficult to isolate and manipulate independent variables and almost impossible to control all relevant intervening variables. But it should also be remembered that a laboratory does not have to be a sterile situation in a campus psychology department. All you need for a laboratory is a setting (it could be in an organization), some subjects, and a task.[3] Some organizational behavior researchers argue that with these minimal requirements satisfied, the laboratory method can be used to study a virtually unlimited range of behavioral phenomena, including many that characterize the organizational environment.[4]

---

[3]Karl E. Weick, "Laboratory Experimentation with Organizations," in James G. March (ed.), *Handbook of Organizations*, Rand McNally, Chicago, 1965.

[4]W. Clay Hamner and Dennis W. Organ, *Organizational Behavior*, Business Publications, Dallas, 1978, p. 28.

Natural experiments Some of the artificiality and generalizability problems inherent in the laboratory experimental method can be eliminated or lessened by natural and field experiments. In a natural experiment, the independent variable is manipulated or changed by the normal course of events and not by the experimenter. Thus, the researcher does not have a *reactive effect* on the independent variable manipulation. This reactivity problem was first brought out in the Hawthorne studies, where it was pointed out that the mere fact that subjects are being experimented on, regardless of the experimental manipulations, will affect the results obtained. The subjects may try to do well or badly or try to figure out what is going on in the experiment, and this reactivity will impact on the dependent variables. The problem is minimized in natural experiments and the generalizability is enhanced, but the opportunities for utilizing the technique are very limited.

Field experiments Perhaps the most useful and adaptable experimental technique for understanding human behavior in organizations is the field experiment. "It differs from the natural experiment primarily in the fact that now changes are introduced in the group with the explicit purpose of testing some hypothesis or evaluating the effectiveness of some innovation in methods of group management."[5] This type of experiment is more applicable than the other two to most questions and problems in organizational behavior, but there are still some limitations.

Validity of experiments The value of a research study is dependent on its validity, i.e., whether the study really demonstrates what it is supposed to demonstrate. In particular, a study must have both *internal* and *external validity* in order to make a meaningful contribution to the body of knowledge. A study has *internal validity* if there are no plausible explanations to the reported results other than those reported. Table 2-2 summarizes the widely accepted classes of the factors that can confound experimental results and threaten internal validity. Laboratory studies usually control these threats to internal validity better than do field studies. But the reverse is true for *external validity*, which is concerned with the generalizability of the results obtained. In order for a study to have external validity, the results must be applicable to a wide range of people and situations. The field experiment tends to have better external validity because the experiment takes place in a real setting, but because there are less controls than in a laboratory setting, internal validity may be threatened.

In general, the best strategy is to use both laboratory and field designs to answer the same question. The weaknesses of the two designs can offset one another. Normally, the research would start with a laboratory study to isolate and manipulate the variable(s) in question. This would be followed by an attempt to verify the findings in a field setting. This progression from the laboratory to the field would lead to the soundest conclusions. But, as will be

---

[5]Dorwin Cartwright and Alvin Zander, *Group Dynamics*, 3d ed., Harper & Row, New York, 1968, p. 33.

Table 2-2

THREATS TO INTERNAL VALIDITY

Threat	Nature of the problem
History	Uncontrolled intervening events that occur between the time when the pre- and post-experiment measurements are taken.
Maturation	Changes in the subject(s) with the mere passing of time, irrespective of the experimental treatment.
Testing	The effect of previous testing on a subject's present performance.
Instrumentation	Changes in measures of subject performance because of changes in the instruments or observers over time.
Regression	Changes in performance due to subjects going from extreme scores to a more typical score.
Interactions	Confounding effects resulting from interactions of one or more of the above. For example, there may be a selection-maturation interaction that the experimenter may mistake for the effect of the manipulated variable.

Source: Adapted from D. T. Campbell and J. C. Stanley, *Experimental and Quasiexperimental Designs for Research,* Rand McNally, Chicago, 1963.

pointed out later, free observation in the naturalistic setting should even precede laboratory investigations of organizational behavior problems or questions.

Case method

The case design makes a complete examination and analysis of one or a few behavioral entities (worker, supervisor, executive work group, department, organization) over an extended period. The purpose is to discover and analyze *every* aspect of the particular case under investigation. The case researcher typically uses naturalistic observation, existing records, and questionnaires and interviews to gather data. As applied to organizational behavior research, the case design should not be confused with the case-study approach used by social workers and psychotherapists. The case method as used in organizational behavior research is much more rigorous and comprehensive.

The actual conduct of case research is most critical to its success. There are three areas generally recognized as being crucial for successful case research:

1. *The attitude of the investigator.* In order for the case technique to be successful, investigators must be alertly receptive and must be seeking rather than testing. They should be continuously reformulating and redirecting as they uncover new information.
2. *The intensity of study.* An effective case analysis should obtain all information unique to the particular unit being studied and also those features that are common to other cases.
3. *The integrative ability of the investigator.* The case approach must rely on the talent of the researcher to successfully pull together many diverse findings into a

unified interpretation. The final interpretation should not, however, merely reflect the investigator's predisposition.[6]

If careful attention is given to key points such as those just outlined, the case can be a very effective research design. The depth of analysis attained through the technique is its major advantage. The glaring disadvantage is that it is not usually practical or logical to generalize the results of one case analysis to other cases or to the whole. This limitation drastically reduces the external validity of the case method for building a meaningful body of knowledge. The case method does not normally provide enough evidence to prove cause and effect. On the other hand, this method does usually uncover some very meaningful insights, research questions, and hypotheses for further testing by an experimental design.

Survey technique

The third major design available to research on human behavior is the survey. This easy-to-use technique depends upon the collection of empirical data via questionnaires and interviews. It is extremely useful in solving some questions and problems of organizational behavior. "In general, whenever the investigator is interested in assessing or estimating the present state of affairs with regard to some variable that changes over time for a large group of subjects, a sample survey is the only practical way to get an answer."[7]

The survey overcomes the major disadvantage of the case design: if properly designed, the survey's results can be generalized. Whereas the case is restricted to a single, or to very few, units of analysis, the survey has very broad coverage. Another advantage is that the survey collects original data. Its major drawback is the lack of depth of information obtainable from the two major data collection tools, the questionnaire and the interview. Because of this limitation, some scholars within—and many outside—the behavioral sciences have totally discredited the survey as a legitimate research design. Some of this criticism, especially that relating to some of the early surveying done in the behavioral sciences, is certainly justified. Even today, some surveys concentrate only on empiricism (gathering data for data's sake) and neglect the necessary planning and design aspects. In addition, overdependence on questionnaire-generated data may be highly misleading. An indirect measurement technique, questionnaires reflect perceptions of behavior rather than the actual behavior in the real setting. Davis and Luthans contend that "The prospects of discovering, for example, whether leaders really do structure subordinates' paths to goals (e.g., the path-goal approach) or whether such procedures can actually be effective is more likely to be answered through real-time, in-situation observational studies,

---

[6]Claire Selltiz et al., *Research Methods in Social Relations*, rev. ed., Holt, New York, 1959, pp. 60–61.

[7]Berelson and Steiner, op. cit., p. 26.

than through questionnaire investigations which are many times removed from the actual behavior."[8]

There is little doubt that the field of organizational behavior has depended too much on questionnaire instruments to obtain data for all three designs—experiment, case, and survey. A multiple measures approach that gives a degree of convergence among the various data collection techniques is needed for the future.[9] Table 2-3 summarizes the various available data collection techniques and their strengths and weaknesses. The key is that

[8]Tim R. V. Davis and Fred Luthans, "Leadership Reexamined: A Behavioral Approach," *Academy of Management Review*, April 1979, p. 244.

[9]Eugene J. Webb, Donald T. Campbell, Richard D. Schwartz, and Lee Sechrest, *Unobtrusive Measures: Nonreactive Research in the Social Sciences*, Rand McNally, Chicago, 1966; and Diane L. Lockwood and Fred Luthans, "Multiple Measures to Assess the Impact of Organization Development Interventions," *The 1980 Annual Handbook for Group Facilitators*, University Associates, San Diego, Calif. pp. 233–245.

Table 2-3

MEASUREMENT TECHNIQUES AVAILABLE FOR ORGANIZATIONAL BEHAVIOR RESEARCH

Method	Variations	Types of measures/data
Questionnaire	Thematic apperception test (TAT) Pair comparison Q-sort Rank order Sociometric tests Thurstone's equal appearing intervals Guttman scalogram Likert's summated ratings Semantic differential Multidimensional scaling	Attitude, motivation, personality and perception measures Factual data (e.g., sex, age, job position, location) Past behavior data (e.g., "Did you complete a performance evaluation in the past week?") Prospective behavior (i.e., responses to hypothetical situations) Sociometric choice data Employee or supervisory performance ratings
Interview	Unstructured or semistructured Structured	Testimonial (usually written comments by interviewers or verbatim transcription of responses) Descriptive (e.g., "critical incident" recall of past events) Close procedure (i.e., sentence completion) Forced-choice measures
Observational	Naturalistic observation	Content-and-process descriptions from journals, diaries, or client logs Content analysis of verbal communication Unobtrusive measures (e.g., recordings of nonverbal communication, time, accretion, and erosion measures)

Table 2-3

Method	Variations	Types of measures/data
	Participant observation	Structural/hierarchial descriptions Technological measures Logistics measures (i.e., work flow) Task characteristics Response frequency data (e.g., Bale's interaction analysis) Communication network data
Archival	Organizational history documents	Corporate bylaws, stock issuance and transfer, minutes from board of directors meetings, policies of all types
	Productivity records	Quantity, quality, ratio, or percentage data (e.g., productivity, quality, maintenance, scrap, sales, and inventory control rates)
	Finance records	Monetary data (e.g., profit/loss, return on investment, labor cost, support system cost, forecasting error, taxes, reserves, bank notices)
	Personnel records	Job descriptions, promotion-demotion, transfers, recruitment, exit or debriefing data, attendance, absenteeism, turnover rates, grievances
	Time records	In/out time, overtime, turnaround time, shipping or delivery time, claim processing time
Self-Generated	Action plan charts	Data relevant to goal attainment and performance evaluation
	Behavioral contingency charts	Behavioral frequencies, baseline and post-intervention data
	Behaviorally anchored rating scales (BARS)	Performance-related behaviors, appraisal data

Source: Adapted from Diane L. Lockwood and Fred Luthans, "Multiple Measures to Assess the Impact of Organization Development Interventions," *The 1980 Annual Handbook for Group Facilitators,* University Associates, San Diego, Calif., pp. 241–244.

organizational behavior researchers need to use all of these measurement techniques. In particular, more attention should be given to observational techniques that allow measurement of the interactive nature of behaviors, persons, and situations. In their rush for respectability, organizational behavior researchers may be guilty of bypassing the most widely recognized first stage of any scientific development—observation of naturally occurring events. Obviously, it is much easier to ask than to observe, and this path of least resistance is the one that has been largely followed in accumulating knowledge about organizational behavior.

THE NEED FOR NEW RESEARCH DESIGNS

Besides the need for multiple measures in general and observational techniques in particular, there is also a need for new designs as alternatives to the traditional control group experimental design, cases, and surveys. Single case experimental designs are a potentially useful but greatly neglected alternative. These designs hold up very well when scrutinized in terms of internal and external validity criteria and lead to cause-and-effect conclusions.[10] They are already widely used in behavioral psychology, education, and mental health research[11] and have been demonstrated to be applicable to organizational behavior research as well.[12]

The single-case experimental design can take two forms—the *reversal* (or A-B-A-B) and the *multiple baseline*. The reversal is performed in the following manner:

1. First a baseline measure is obtained on the individual or group behavior in question. (A)
2. Then an intervention is made and the behavior is measured until the change stabilizes. (B)
3. Then the intervention is withdrawn and baseline conditions are reestablished. (A)
4. Once the behavior under baseline conditions stabilizes, the intervention is made again. (B)

Figure 2-2 shows an actual case where this reversal design was employed. The beauty of this design is that the subject(s) serve as their own control. The problem of intersubject variability inherent in a control group design is eliminated. The drawback of this potentially powerful design, however, is that it assumes that the behaviors are capable of being reversed when returning to baseline conditions. Other things taking place in the environment may take over to sustain the dependent variable and thus undermine this assumption. In addition, a very practical problem in using a reversal design is how to persuade results-minded management to return to baseline conditions if an intervention is working in the desired direction. Few managers are willing to sacrifice results in order to help prove a cause-and-effect relationship.

To get around some of the limitations of reversals, especially the practical problem of reversing desired results, a multiple-baseline design can be employed. In this design, baseline data are gathered for behaviors, individuals, or situations. The design is implemented as follows:

1. Baseline data are obtained on two or more behaviors (or individuals or situations).

---

[10] A. E. Kazin, "Methodological and Assessment Considerations in Evaluating Reinforcement Programs in Applied Settings," *Journal of Applied Behavioral Analysis*, Fall 1973, pp. 517–531.

[11] M. Hersen and D. H. Barlow, *Single-Case Experimental Designs: Strategies for Studying Behavior Change*, Pergamon, New York, 1976.

[12] Fred Luthans and Kenneth M. Bond, "The Use of Reversal Designs in Organizational Behavior Research," *Academy of Management Proceedings*, 1977, pp. 86–90; Judi Komaki, "Alternative Evaluation Strategies in Work Settings: Reversal and Multiple Baseline Designs," *Journal of Organizational Behavior Management*, Summer 1977, pp. 53–77; Peter W. Van Ness and Fred Luthans, "Multiple-Baseline Designs: An Alternative Strategy for Organizational Behavior Research," *Proceedings of the Midwest Academy of Management*, 1979, pp. 336–350; and Fred Luthans and Terry L. Maris, "Evaluating Personnel Programs Through the Reversal Technique," *Personnel Journal*, October 1979, pp. 692–697.

Attendance Rate by Category of Employment

Category of employment	PHASE A (Baseline)	PHASE B (Program)		PHASE A¹ (Withdrawal of program, baseline conditions)		PHASE B¹ (Reintroduction of program)
	1976			1977		
	Jan.-Dec.	April	May	June	July	August
40 hrs/wk	87.96	92.43	93.98	86.03	83.39	86.23
37.5 hrs/wk	95.15	94.11	91.30	87.50	75.90	88.28
32 hrs/wk	100.78	115.25	106.35	109.06	80.84	104.40
30 hrs/wk	.92.65	91.39	95.99	90.44	101.03	104.94
Attendance rate*	91.06%	95.27%	96.09%	90.87%	87.01%	94.63%

*Represents a weighted average per number of employees in each category.

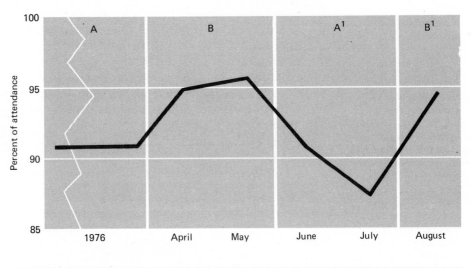

Figure 2-2
Example of a reversal design used to analyze the impact that a behavioral management program (O.B. Mod.) had on employee attendance at a bank. (*Source:* Fred Luthans and Terry L. Maris, "Evaluating Personnel Programs Through the Reversal Technique," *Personnel Journal,* October 1979, p. 694.)

2. An intervention is then made on one of the behaviors but baseline conditions are maintained on the other(s).
3. Once the behavior has stabilized after the intervention, the next behavior is given the intervention.
4. This continues until all the behaviors are brought under the intervention.

Figure 2-3 shows a graph of an actual case where a multiple-baseline design was used. This staggered intervention design has advantages similar to the reversal design and eliminates the practical problem of reversing the behavior but makes the assumption of noninterdependence. In some cases, changing one behavior (or individual or situation) may cause the other to change. So far, applications of these designs have been limited to assessing the impact of behavioral change intervention programs (e.g., reinforcement, feedback, or goal setting), but they could also be effectively used to assess the impact of any training or organization development intervention as well. In other words, these single-case designs are not restricted to behavior change studies. Despite some of the real or potential problems, both the reversal and multiple-baseline designs, especially when used in conjunction with more conventional control group designs, can make an important contribution to researching organizational behavior in the future.

ANTHROPOLOGY

In addition to a working knowledge of research methodology, an understanding of the basic behavioral science disciplines of anthropology, sociology, and, especially psychology is also vital to the study of organizational behavior. Clearly, a more detailed understanding of research methods and the behavioral science disciplines is needed than can be provided in this chapter; what is presented here is the necessary broad foundation which can provide points of departure for the more specific topics that are covered in the rest of the book.

Figure 2-3 Example of a multiple baseline design used to analyze the impact that a behavioral management program (O.B. Mod.) had on the productivity of two employees (Mr. BR and Mr. TL) in a manufacturing firm. (*Source:* Peter W. VanNess and Fred Luthans, "Multiple-Baseline Designs: An Alternative Strategy for Organizational Behavior Research," *Proceedings of the Midwest Academy of Management,* 1979, p. 346.)

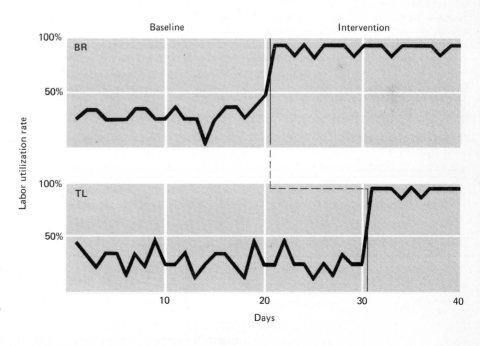

The first behavioral science discipline that will be examined is *anthropology*. This is literally defined as *the science of man*. The term combines the Greek stem *anthropo* ("man") and the noun ending *logy* ("science"). The use of the word *anthropology* can be traced back to the ancient Greek civilization. For example, Aristotle used the word to refer to a man who "talks about himself."[13] In this Greek sense, anthropology is as old as any academic discipline. As a modern discipline incorporating a scientific viewpoint and methodology, however, it is relatively new. The body of anthropological knowledge that has been accumulated by scientific methodology is currently relatively small but is rapidly expanding.

Anthropology is a discipline with a very wide scope. One noted anthropologist candidly observed that her colleagues ". . . have embraced enthusiastically and immodestly the literal meaning of the word anthropology—the science of man. Not satisfied with the science of man, they honor many in their profession who are avowed humanists."[14] Figure 2-4 summarizes the breakdown of anthropology into its various subfields. Cultural anthropology is particularly relevant to the study of organizational behavior.

Figure 2-4 Subfields of anthropology. (*Source:* Adapted from Felix M. Keesing, *Cultural Anthropology,* Holt, New York, 1966, p. 4.)

---

[13]Alfred C. Haddon, *History of Anthropology*, Watts, London, 1910, p. 6.

[14]Cora DuBois, "Anthropology—Its Present Interests," in Berelson (ed.), *The Behavioral Sciences Today*, op. cit., p. 26.

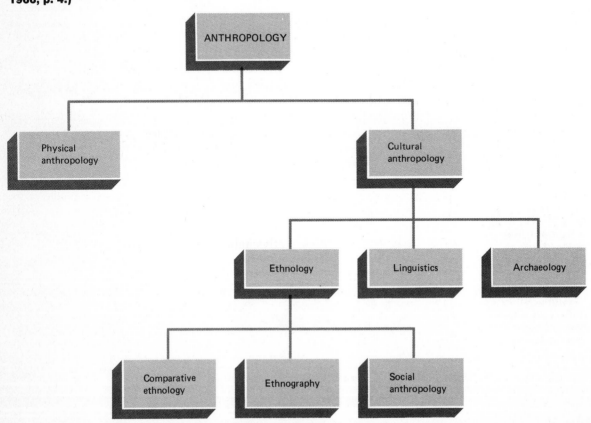

Cultural anthropology

Cultural anthropology deals with people's learned behavior as influenced by their culture. In more definitive terms, "cultural anthropology studies the origins and history of man's cultures, their evolution and development, and the structure and functioning of human cultures in every place and time."[15] Obviously, the overriding concept is culture.

Definition of culture   There are numerous definitions of culture. After a survey of more than a hundred of them, it was concluded that the following was the most comprehensive definition:

Culture consists of patterns, explicit and implicit, of and for behavior acquired and transmitted by symbols, constituting the distinctive achievement of human groups, including their embodiments in artifacts.[16]

To cite the major characteristics of the concept, culture

1. Is historical
2. Includes ideas, patterns, and values
3. Is selective
4. Is learned
5. Is based upon symbols
6. Is an abstraction from behavior
7. Is a product of behavior[17]

Theories of culture   Cultural anthropologists have developed several theories to explain the impact of culture on human behavior. The three most prominent theories may be summarized by the descriptive "isms," *evolutionism*, *historicalism*, and *functionalism*. These three theories have become schools of thought in anthropology. The oldest is evolutionism.

Evolutionism identifies three general stages of cultural development. The first stage is savagery, which is followed by barbarism, which is followed eventually by civilization. The evolutionists point out that at any given time the world contains geographic areas that are in each stage of cultural development. Today, the evolutionism theory is generally discounted by anthropologists. The argument is that the evolutionists' assumptions are too simplistic and that there is too much contradictory evidence to justify the adoption of this theory.

Historicalist theories directly challenge the assumptions of evolutionism and environmental determinism. The aim of the historical approach to cultural anthropology is to accumulate and analyze all the traits, customs, and characteristics of a given culture. The collection of data is accomplished

---

[15]Ralph L. Beals and Harry Hijer, *An Introduction to Anthropology*, 2d ed., Macmillan, New York, 1959, p. 9.

[16]Alfred L. Kroeber and Clyde Kluckhohn, "Culture: A Critical Review of Concepts and Definitions," in *Papers of the Peabody Museum*, vol. 47, no. 1, Harvard University, Cambridge, 1952, p. 181.

[17]Ibid., p. 157.

by objective observation and field research, which generate a wealth of empirical facts about a culture. The problem then becomes one of applying and generalizing the results.

Functionalist theories of culture take a systems viewpoint. As will be discussed in later chapters, the systems approach is playing an increasingly important role in all academic disciplines, and it is probably the approach most widely accepted by today's anthropologists. The functionalists concentrate on the various elements or functions that make up a cultural system. They recognize and emphasize that the cultural elements are interrelated and that they become integrated into a holistic system. Functionalism seems to provide the best framework for understanding the nature and significance of culture.

Significance of culture   The important role that culture plays in human behavior may be one of the most underrated concepts in the behavioral sciences. The culture dictates what people learn and how they behave. One management theorist points out the nature and significance of culture by making an analogy with the sea: "We are immersed in a sea. It is warm, comfortable, supportive, and protecting. Most of us float below the surface; some bob about, catching glimpses of land from time to time; a few emerge from the water entirely. The sea is our culture."[18]

Every organization has a type of culture, which may help explain much of employee behavior. For example, for years the IBM corporation had cultural values that dictated that all employees dealing with the public/customers should wear a white shirt and conservative suit and tie. There are also behavioral implications associated with whether the employee comes from a blue-collar, white-collar, or executive-suite culture. The culture not only tells an employee what is proper attire to wear, it can also dictate what is right and good or wrong and evil. For example, bribes and payoffs may be expected as a proper way to do business in certain foreign cultures but wrong and unethical/illegal in American culture. As the recent bribery and payoff scandals indicated, executives in many multinational corporations were caught in between these conflicting cultural demands.

SOCIOLOGY

Although anthropology can and does at least indirectly contribute to a better understanding of organizational behavior, the behavioral science discipline of sociology is more directly relevant. *Sociology* is traditionally defined as the *science of society*. To the uninformed, its purposes and goals are often unclear. Many equate sociology with social work and the solving of social problems. Some even relate sociology to the political philosophy of socialism. In reality, sociology is at the same time more narrow and broader than the areas with which it is often confused. Perhaps sociology can most accurately be described as an academic discipline that utilizes the scientific method in accumulating knowledge about social behavior. The other areas

---

[18]Ross A. Webber, *Culture and Management*, Irwin, Homewood, Ill., 1969, p. 10.

do not have this specific purpose and goal. The overall focus of sociology is on social behavior in societies, institutions, organizations, and groups.

Similar to the other behavioral sciences, sociology is a relatively young academic field, and the word itself did not come into existence until 1842. Auguste Comte (1798–1857) used the term *sociology* to identify a new science of society based upon systematic methodology rather than philosophical speculation. He used the concepts of statics and dynamics to delineate the field. Through the application of the static concept, Comte wanted to demonstrate how the various parts of society interact and interrelate. In his book *The Positive Philosophy* he wrote, "the statical study of sociology consists in the investigation of the laws of action and reaction of the different parts of the social system." In contrast, his concept of social dynamics focused on whole societies. Attention was devoted to the development and change of total societies through time. Both social statics and dynamics have greatly influenced the development of modern sociology.

After Comte, other pioneers in the field also made significant contributions. Emile Durkheim, who, like Comte, was French, Herbert Spencer of England, and Max Weber of Germany are the most widely known early sociologists, and they represent the national centers that substantially affected the development of the field. Herbert Spencer (1820–1903) is credited with writing the first book dealing directly with sociology. His three-volume *Principles of Sociology* was published in 1877. Spencer essentially refined what Comte had said approximately thirty-five years earlier, but it was Durkheim and Weber who really extended the discipline.

Emile Durkheim (1858–1917) was a prolific writer on a diversity of sociological topics. His best-known works include *Suicide, On the Division of Labor, Rules of Sociological Method,* and *The Elementary Forms of Religious Life.* One idea in particular illustrates Durkheim's far-reaching thinking. He developed the concept of *anomie* to explain certain sociological phenomena. Anomie can best be defined as a state of isolation or normlessness in which social rules or norms no longer have an effect on individual behavior. In modern times, the breakdown of traditional institutions like the family, and the societal disorganization and individual alienation created by industrialization and urbanization reflect Durkheim's anomie. Much of the dissatisfaction of today's work force expressed by such terms as "blue-collar blues" and "white-collar woes" are attributed to anomie.

Max Weber (1864–1920) is most often associated with the organization concept of bureaucracy. Using Comte's social dynamics as a starting point, he analyzed development and change in Western society. He noted that the common denominator for social change in the Western world was the cultural value of rationalization. The best example for Weber was the bureaucratic form of organization, which is completely rational. He was the first to utilize this phenomenon as a unit of analysis for society. The characteristics and ramifications of bureaucracy are thoroughly discussed in Chapters 18 and 19, on organization theory.

Closely related to the rationalization theme was Weber's institutional analysis of religion. He felt that religion played an important part in the development and change of Western civilization. His purposes "were to examine the effect of religious ideas on economic activities, to analyze the relation between social stratification and religious ideas, and to ascertain and explain the distinguishing characteristics of Western civilization."[19] His analysis, presented in *The Protestant Ethic and the Spirit of Capitalism*, accomplishes these purposes. This book is a classic study of the fundamental comparative relationships between religion and economic and social life in Western culture.

Modern perspectives of sociology

The above discussion demonstrates that sociology has a rich heritage. The early sociologists concentrated on immediate, practical social problems and strove for societal betterment. Contemporary sociology is characterized by rigorous methodology with an empirical emphasis and conceptual consciousness. The major thrust common to all areas of sociology is toward the goal of understanding interdependent social behavior. The primary units of analysis studied by modern sociologists, going from largest to smallest, are the society, institution, organization, group, and norms and roles. Most relevant to the study of organizational behavior are the latter three—organization, group, and norms/roles. In fact, whole chapters and parts of other chapters of this book are devoted to these units of analysis. The macro perspective of organizational behavior (Part 5 of the book) and many of the contemporary organizational development techniques covered in Chapter 21 are sociologically based.

PSYCHOLOGY

Whereas sociology plays a big part in the macro perspective, psychology is the most significant foundation for the micro approach to organizational behavior. As the introductory comments indicated, the micro perspective dominates contemporary organizational behavior, so it follows that a thorough grounding in psychology is necessary.

Modern *psychology* is almost universally defined as the *science of behavior*. It generally includes animal as well as human behavior. The inclusion of animal behavior has been criticized. In many types of psychological experimentation, animals such as rats or monkeys are utilized because of the high degree of control that can be exercised over them. As the earlier discussion on research methodology indicated, the difficulty comes from trying to generalize the results and conclusions drawn from animal experimentation to human behavior. Despite the differing opinions regarding the place of animal research, all psychologists are united in their belief that *individual human behavior* should be the principal focus of psychology. The understanding, prediction, and control of human behavior are the goals of modern psychology.

---

[19]Reinhard Bendix, *Max Weber: An Intellectual Portrait*, Doubleday, Garden City, N.Y., 1960, p. 266.

Common misconceptions

Psychology is a much misunderstood academic discipline. The problem stems from the fact that everyone from the illiterate to the Ph.D. is intimately involved with, and a student of, human behavior. Everyone has preconceived notions about human nature that are based on individual experience. These beliefs are staunchly defended. As a result, there are many misconceptions and sometimes ill feelings toward the academic discipline that tries to tell the individual about human behavior.

With regard to human behavior, it is not unusual to find common sense and science in opposition. The major differences between the two may be summarized as follows:

1. Common sense is vague compared to scientific knowledge.
2. Flagrant inconsistencies often appear in commonsense knowledge, whereas the demand for logical consistency is a hallmark of science.
3. Science systematically seeks to explain the events with which it deals; common sense ignores the need for explanation.
4. The scientific method deliberately exposes claims to the critical evaluation of experimental analysis; the informal methods of common sense fail to test conclusions in any systematic fashion.[20]

These differences are seen in the psychological and the lay approaches to human behavior. The psychologist possesses the scientific viewpoint and utilizes the scientific method in gathering facts about human behavior. The layperson relies on common sense and not science.

In the past and even to some extent today, psychologists are viewed by the general public with a great deal of misunderstanding and, in some cases, suspicion. Psychologists have tried to clear up some of the more common misconceptions by pointing out the following:

1. Psychologists cannot "read your mind" simply by looking at you.
2. Psychologists have no peculiar interest in psychoanalyzing you.
3. Psychologists are not fortune-tellers.
4. Neither a psychologist nor anyone else can tell anything about a person from the bumps on the skull (phrenology).
5. Neither psychologists nor anyone else can tell anything about you by the numbers of letters in your name (numerology) or by the lines in your hand (palmistry).
6. By and large, psychologists are not interested in mystical phenomena such as telepathy or clairvoyance.[21]

In other words, psychology does not deal with mysticism or superstition.

Too often, people seem interested only in the sensational aspects of psychology and are prone to accept "facts" without considering their source. One psychologist comments that "self-styled psychological experts who offer advice to anyone, anywhere, at any time after seeing two psychiatric

---

[20]Howard H. Kendler, *Basic Psychology*, 3d ed., W. A. Benjamin, Menlo Park, Calif., 1974, pp. 12–13.

[21]Gregory A. Kimble and Norman Garmezy, *General Psychology*, 2d ed., Ronald, New York, 1963, p. 3.

movies and reading one book by Freud are all too common."[22] Gaining an understanding of human behavior is a very complex and demanding undertaking. Although there are few simple answers, psychologists always attempt to approach their study from the viewpoint of science.

The founding and development of psychology

A common summary statement concerning the development of psychology is that it has a long past but a short history. Similar to the other behavioral sciences, psychology is a relatively new area of study. Also similar to other academic disciplines, a specific date for its founding cannot realistically be assigned. The generally agreed-upon starting point for the study of psychology as an independent science, and for the behavioral sciences in general, was Wundt's laboratory in 1879. There had been many indirect contributions previously, but "before Wundt there had been plenty of psychology but no psychologists."[23]

There are two ways to explore the trends and development of psychology. One method is to examine the changing concerns of those in the field. Early psychologists were mainly interested in the mind. As recently as fifty to sixty years ago, psychology was commonly defined as the *science of the mind*. As stated previously, the modern definition is the *science of behavior*. The contrasting definitions illustrate the change in emphasis during the past half-century. Early psychologists dwelled on mental processes of consciousness and experience. They concentrated on things like memory and measurement of sensation. Modern psychologists deal more objectively with behavior. The measurement and understanding of overt behavior dominate present-day psychological theory and practice. As is often pointed out, however, the shift of interest from the mind to behavior is only one of degree; "psychology has not yet lost its mind."[24]

The other way of tracing the development of an academic field is to note the changes in methods used in accumulating knowledge. Behavioral science in general and psychology in particular have moved from philosophical speculation to rigorous empiricism. Modern psychologists utilize primarily the laboratory experiment to analyze behavior. Most of them do not consider that psychology even existed before Wundt's laboratory was established. In the United States, the first psychological laboratory was founded at Johns Hopkins University in 1883. Today, every major university in the country has an extensive laboratory to study behavior.

Schools of thought

As an academic field develops, there is a natural tendency to logically relate and structure diverse theories into specific schools of thought. In a growing

---

[22]Kendler, op. cit., 2d ed., 1968, p. xi.

[23]Ibid., p. 33.

[24]Clifford Morgan and Richard King, *Introduction to Psychology*, 3d ed., McGraw-Hill, New York, 1966, p. 22.

discipline that has not fully matured or stabilized, adherents to a particular theory often become defensive of their position, and a sense of competition frequently results. The formative years of psychology were characterized by schools of thought which were highly competitive. The most widely known are structuralism, functionalism, behaviorism, gestalt psychology, and psychoanalysis.

Structuralism   Founded by Wundt, structuralism represents the earliest theoretical school. The theory revolved around conscious experience and attempted to build a science of the mind. Wundt and his followers proceeded by breaking down the mind into various structural units, hence the label *structuralism.*

The structuralists concentrated on mental states such as sensation, memory, imagery, and feelings. Drawing on their heritage in physiology and the physical sciences, they were determined to measure processes. Introspection was the primary tool developed for this purpose. Essentially, it is a self-observation technique where subjects are asked to describe in minute detail their reaction to sensory stimuli such as color, smell, and sound. Unfortunately, this technique did not produce any profound results or implications, and it soon became apparent that the structuralist approach was too narrow. The mind is much more complex than just a group of structural units made up of conscious sensation and experience.

Functionalism   Around the turn of the century, structuralism gave way to functionalism as the dominant school of thought. Functionalism developed in America, where philosophers William James (1842–1910) and John Dewey (1859–1952) were very critical of the structuralists. They felt the key to understanding the mind was an understanding of how it *functions*, not of how it is structured. Thus, emphasis was placed on people's adjustment and adaptation to their environment. Compared with the structuralists, the functionalists were all-encompassing and more pragmatic. Although they did borrow the introspection tool for analyzing mental states, they went one step further by observing and recording total behavior patterns. Besides their sensory experience, people's learning, forgetting, motivation, and general adaptability to a new situation were studied. "So functionalism had two chief characteristics; the study of the total behavior and experience of an individual, and an interest in the adaptive functions served by the things an individual does."[25]

Behaviorism   Behaviorism was a natural outgrowth of functionalism. The theoretical trend had been away from the mind and toward behavior. The structuralists had been concerned only with the mind, but the functionalists emphasized both mind and behavior. Now the behaviorists felt that only observable, objective behavior was of significance to psychology.

Behaviorism was influenced by the work of the Russian physiologist Ivan

---

[25]Ibid., p. 24.

Pavlov (1849–1936). However, the generally recognized founder of classical behaviorism (sometimes called the stimulus-response, or S-R, school of thought) was the American John B. Watson (1878–1958). In the early 1900s he questioned whether the use of the introspective technique was within the realm of science. He maintained that only observable, objective behavior qualified for scientific investigation. Therefore, psychology should be concerned only with S-R connections, or the observation, measurement, and analysis of stimuli and the resulting responses.

The results of Pavlovian experimentation convinced most early behaviorists that identifiable S-R conditioned reflexes were the basic elements of all behavior. In this regard, they were ironically similar to the structuralists whom they so vehemently rejected. Behaviorism promoted the learned aspects of behavior. The behaviorists did not attach any importance to unlearned or instinctual behavior. In fact, Watson and his followers believed that humans were solely products of learning, and they boasted that they could condition a person to become almost anything.

The behaviorist school of thought has greatly influenced modern psychology. By dealing only with observable, overt events, behaviorism forced psychology to become more research- and science-oriented. Even the currently used definition of psychology—the science of behavior—is attributable to behaviorism. A great many modern psychologists would probably consider themselves behaviorists. They agree on the importance of learned behavior and discount instincts as having any value in understanding human behavior; but, of course, modern behaviorism has gone way beyond the mechanistic S-R approach of Pavlov and Watson.

Starting with the work of B. F. Skinner, who made the significant distinction between respondent conditioning (S-R) and operant conditioning (behavior as a function of its consequences), behaviorism entered a new era. Very recently, some of Skinner's notions have been sufficiently tempered so that most psychologists would agree that behaviorism is once again entering a new era. Albert Bandura's social learning theory probably best represents the thinking of the new generation of behaviorists.[26] This latest approach still stresses that behavior is the appropriate unit of analysis and that it is still largely grounded in the environment, but it differs from Skinnerian behaviorism in recognizing and assigning an important role to cognitive mediating processes in understanding human social behavior. The next chapter will go into this in more detail, and Chapters 9, 10, and 22 examine in greater depth how behaviorism is applied to the study of organizational behavior.

Gestalt psychology   While functionalism and behaviorism were becoming popular in America, the *gestalt* school was replacing structuralism in Germany. Its founding is usually attributed to Max Wertheimer and dated around 1912. Whereas the structuralists were noted for their attempt to isolate sensory units of the brain and the behaviorists for their emphasis on

---

[26]Albert Bandura, *Social Learning Theory*, Prentice-Hall, Englewood Cliffs, N.J., 1977.

specific conditioned behaviors, gestaltists felt that the whole, not the parts, was the important subject matter of psychology.

Gestalt is difficult to define because the word was brought directly into English from German. Loosely, the term means "pattern," "configuration," "form," or "organization." A simplified explanation of the gestalt school of thought is that its adherents believe the whole to be greater than the sum of its parts. A simple illustration of how gestaltism works is the classic Müller-Lyer illustration in Figure 2-5. The lines X and Y are of exactly equal length. However, they are perceived to be unequal because of their relationship to the whole. In other words, the whole is perceived differently from the sum of the ways the parts would be perceived.

Just as German physical scientists had influenced structuralism, they also influenced gestaltism. The gestaltists made an analogy between the "field" of behavior and a magnetic field in physics. Such analysis has resulted in the label *field theorists* for those who adhered to this approach. For example, the pioneering social psychologist Kurt Lewin, who used the analogy of magnetic fields in explaining group dynamics, is often called a field theorist.

Like the structuralists, gestaltists used introspection—but with a different emphasis. They were more concerned with the free response of a subject than with the elaboration or interpretation of a trained observer. This different use of introspection dealt with phenomena of experience and perception and is commonly known as *phenomenology*. Along with the behaviorists, the gestaltists have had a great impact on modern psychology. Their thinking was the forerunner of general systems theory, which is currently playing an important role in all fields of study. Modern cognitive theorists also have roots in gestaltism and phenomenology.

Psychoanalysis   A discussion of the historical development of psychological thought would not be complete without mentioning the works of Sigmund Freud (1856–1939). His ideas about unconscious motivation and the development and structure of personality, and his treatment technique, which he called *psychoanalysis*, have all had a vast influence on the development of modern psychology. Freud and his colleagues, such as Alfred Adler and Carl Jung, both of whom later broke away to formulate their own theories, were active in Europe about the same time that functionalism was popular in America.

By itself, psychoanalysis is really not a separate school of psychological

**Figure 2-5
The Müller-Lyer il-
lusion.**

thought. More accurately, it is a treatment technique and form of therapy for persons suffering from psychological problems. The method utilizes free association to encourage the patient to cope consciously with underlying or repressed problems or trauma. Psychoanalysis is still a widely used technique for the therapeutic treatment of mental patients and even of healthy persons.

Freud was a practitioner—a medical physician and a psychiatrist. He was not an experimental researcher. However, in treating the mentally ill, he keenly observed that their problems were often subject to cause-and-effect relationships that the patients themselves were not consciously aware of. From this observation, Freud concluded that unconscious mental processes (usually sexually linked) motivated much of human behavior. Because Freud's conclusions were based on clinical observation and not on experimental methods, many behavioral scientists have been critical of psychoanalytic theories. Regardless of this criticism, Freudian concepts are widely recognized, and they are used as the starting point for discussions of motivation and the development and structure of personality in Chapters 5 and 6.

Modern approaches to psychology

All the historical schools of thought contribute some theoretical understanding and research techniques to the modern approach to psychology. In varying degrees, all are still in evidence today. In contrast to the pioneers in the field, modern psychologists do not necessarily identify themselves with any one school of thought. Nevertheless, in their basic theoretical orientations and research methods they certainly lean toward one or another of the schools. In particular, the behaviorist and gestalt schools have had a tremendous impact on the orientation of modern psychologists. On the whole, however, contemporary psychologists take an eclectic theoretical approach and utilize the laboratory-experiment method of research.

Contemporary psychological theory may be divided into several areas of concentration. There is no universal agreement on the divisions because they greatly depend on how finely one draws the lines between the various areas. Three broad classifications would include the biological-physiological aspects; the psychological processes; and the whole-person personality concept.

Biological-physiological aspects   One major approach taken by modern psychology is to give attention to the biological-physiological aspects of behavior. The behaviorist school generally played down the importance of biological-physiological analysis. But starting about twenty-five years ago there was an awakened interest in the role that this type of analysis could play in understanding behavior.

The biological contributions to behavior center on heredity. The impact of heredity is an old but still unsettled issue. The behaviorists almost completely discounted heredity, but most of today's psychologists recognize that it plays at least some role in determining behavior. One of the most controversial issues in psychology concerns the influence of heredity versus environment on intelligence, which is still being debated. In reality, heredity can never be completely separated from environment or vice versa. From the moment of conception on, the environment interacts with the genetic endowment of the human being.

The most direct physiological impact on behavior comes from the endocrine glands and the central nervous system. There are other physiologically related concepts in psychology, such as the "general adaptation syndrome," which is related to the analysis of stress, and the "reticular formation," which is related to sleep, waking, and energetic action. The endocrine glands secrete hormones directly into the bloodstream and have a definite effect on emotion and other psychological states. But the focus of psychologists' greatest interest has been the central nervous system, which consists of the brain and nervous system. The brain was the original concern of psychologists, and it has been determined that certain parts of it, particularly the hypothalamus, directly influence psychological states. But many other parts and functions of the brain remain a mystery. Part of the problem stems from the fact that physiologists have not helped much in providing an understanding of the brain's inner workings. Nevertheless, the brain's role in behavior is certainly not a dead issue in psychology. An example of this is the current interest in the preliminary results that are emerging from the study of the separate halves of the brain (right brain, left brain) and of electrical stimulation of the brain (ESB). (Some of the major findings and implications of the split brain and ESB are discussed in Chapter 5.) This research, plus the work being done in related areas, points to the almost unlimited potential of biological-physiological analysis as an aid to understanding human behavior.

Psychological processes   The most common topical breakdown of the discipline of psychology is into basic cognitive processes. Perception, motivation, and learning are the three most generally accepted classifications. These processes operate and interact to produce the psychologically whole person, and they represent the major units of analysis for modern psychology. They are given primary attention in psychological theory and research. In this book, Chapter 4 is devoted to perception, Chapters 6, 7, and 8 concentrate on motivation, and Chapters 9 and 10 discuss learning. An understanding of these basic micro processes is vital to the study of organizational behavior.

Personality   The third major conceptual area in psychology is the study of personality. The separation of psychology into the processes of perception, learning, and motivation, mentioned above, is largely artificial and unrealistic. An individual operates and behaves as a whole, not as a collection of separate parts. The study of personality is concerned with the whole person. A major area in psychology, it is principally concerned with the personality's development and structure. Chapter 5 focuses specifically on personality development and theories of personality structure. An understanding of personality, as well as of the psychological processes, is extremely relevant to the study of organizational behavior.

SOCIAL PSYCHOLOGY

Social psychology is generally not mentioned as a separate discipline in the behavioral sciences. There are two major reasons for this exclusion. First, social psychology is frequently classified as a subfield in both psychology and sociology. This often confuses students and committees concerned with the duplication of courses in universities. The typical university curriculum offers two separate courses called social psychology, one in the psychology department and one in the sociology department. The difference between the two is a matter of emphasis and professional orientation. The second reason that social psychology has not been treated separately is that it can almost be equated with behavioral science itself. Similar to behavioral science, social psychology is academically interdisciplinary. It consists of an eclectic mixture of psychology and sociology. The exclusion of social psychology as a behavioral science, however, in no way deemphasizes its importance. Social psychology, if considered a separate discipline, is more closely aligned with organizational behavior as a whole than any other single discipline.

There are many slight variations in definitions of social psychology. One comprehensive definition is that it is the study of individual behavior in relation to the social environment. The most important part of the social environment is other persons, individually and collectively. More simply, social psychology is the *study of individual behavior within a group*. This definition points out the close ties that social psychology has to psychology (individual emphasis) and sociology (group emphasis). It was only fitting that the first two books on social psychology, simultaneously published in 1908, were written by a psychologist, William McDougall, and a sociologist, Edward Ross.[27]

The logical breakdown for analysis and study in social psychology is the individual, the group, and the interaction between the individual and the group. The last-named provides the key difference between the study of social psychology and the study of psychology and sociology. An example is the approach taken in the study of groups. Social psychology is more concerned with why an individual joins a group (affiliation) and wants to remain a member of the group (cohesion). The social psychologist focuses primarily on group structure and function only to the extent that they affect individual behavior. Besides the study of groups, topics of general interest to the social psychologist include:

---

[27]William McDougall, *Introduction to Social Psychology*, Methney, London, 1908; and Edward A. Ross, *Social Psychology: An Outline and Source Book*, Macmillan, New York, 1908.

1. *Attitudes*, their formation and change
2. *Communication research*, the effect that networks have on individual and group efficiency and satisfaction
3. *Problem solving*, the analysis of cooperation versus competition
4. *Social influences*, the impact of conformity and other social factors on individual behavior
5. *Leadership*, especially the identification and function of leaders and their effectiveness

More specialized theories (such as cognitive dissonance) and analysis (such as approach-avoidance conflict) are also a vital part of social psychology.

As these topics indicate, social psychology is very closely related to organizational behavior. This is evidenced by the overall orientation and table of contents of this book. Part 4 in particular borrows heavily from the theories and research findings of social psychology. Moreover, a mutually beneficial relationship seems to exist between the disciplines of social psychology and organizational behavior. One of the major purposes of this book is to help develop and refine this relationship.

SUMMARY

Research methodology and the behavioral sciences provide a necessary foundation for the study of organizational behavior. Defined as the scientific study of human behavior, behavioral science is moving in the direction of becoming a truly interdisciplinary field of study. Behavioral science greatly depends on scientific methodology to accumulate knowledge. Experimental, case, and survey designs are widely used. New designs such as reversals and multiple baselines can make a contribution to future research in organizational behavior. The academic disciplines of anthropology, sociology, and psychology make up behavioral science. Anthropology, literally defined as "the science of man," concentrates primarily on the role that culture plays in human behavior. Sociology is directly concerned with social behavior—in societies, institutions, organizations, groups, and roles. Psychology makes the greatest contribution of any of the separate behavioral science disciplines to the study of organizational behavior. It gives primary attention to individual micro behavior from the perspective of the biological-physiological aspects, psychological processes, and personality. In particular, a knowledge of the psychological processes of perception, motivation, and learning is vital to the micro analysis and understanding of organizational behavior. Social psychology is closest to overall behavioral science and organizational behavior.

QUESTIONS FOR DISCUSSION AND REVIEW

1. How does behavioral science differ from social science?
2. What are the strengths and weaknesses of the three major research designs?

3. Explain how reversals and multiple-baseline designs work. How do these differ from traditional experimental designs?
4. Why is the study of culture important to organizational behavior?
5. What are the major units of analysis studied by modern sociologists? Which one do you think is most relevant to organizational behavior? Why?
6. Why do you think psychology is such a commonly misunderstood academic discipline?
7. Briefly summarize the various schools of thought in psychology.
8. How does social psychology relate to sociology? To psychology?

CASE:

MR. CHEMIST TACKLES THE PERSONNEL DEPARTMENT

Jerry Bradley brought a unique background with him into his new job in the personnel department of Huge Company. Jerry had majored in chemistry at college and had worked in the company's research and development laboratory on new-product development for the past five years. Jerry had a knack for getting along with people around the lab, so when the job in personnel opened up, his boss suggested that he try for it. Jerry had never thought of going into personnel work but decided it would be a new challenge, and he did like working with people. After getting the standard orientation for new employees, Jerry was appalled at the way in which the personnel department attacked their problems. As far as he could tell, no attempt was made to use accepted scientific methodology in solving personnel problems. For example, they had no idea whether supervisors should tell their subordinates the results of the performance evaluation. When Jerry asked his boss about this situation, the boss tersely replied, "Well, Mr. Chemist, how would you go about solving our problems?"

1. If you were Jerry, how would you answer the boss?
2. Briefly, how could an experiment be set up to answer the question of whether supervisors should communicate the results of the performance evaluation to their subordinates? What would be the independent, dependent, and control variables in such an experiment?
3. What contribution can knowledge of the behavioral sciences make to solving problems in a personnel department? In a research and development laboratory? Will Jerry be handicapped in his new job by having no knowledge of the behavioral sciences?

CASE:

DILEMMA FOR PROGRAM EVALUATION

Jane Dewy had just been assigned to the training department of a large federal agency. She was assigned to program evaluation and worked directly with the training and development program for first-line supervisors. She was charged with constructing a method of measuring the effectiveness of some of the agency's training programs. The usual evaluation procedure was to administer a reaction questionnaire, which was given to the supervisors at the end of the training program. The trainees had consistently rated the program very highly. Jane was skeptical though. She thought that anyone who received a week off of their regular job to go to a training program at a vacation resort might think the program was great. She wanted to find another means of evaluating the program, a means that would truly measure its results and effectiveness. She was thinking of sending a questionnaire to the subordinates whom the trainees supervised, but she felt uncomfortable just sending out such questionnaires. She knew how trite and meaningless those sorts of questionnaires could be. She remembered how she and most of her fellow trainees in training programs she had attended over the years treated surveys—as a joke and a waste of time. Yet she had to do something to evaluate the effectiveness of the training program. She reasoned that sending out another questionnaire was better than nothing.

1. Is sending out another questionnaire Jane's only alternative?
2. How could she design an experiment to evaluate the program. What would be the independent variable? What would be the dependent variable(s)?
3. Besides program evaluation, what are some other direct applications of research methodology by practicing managers?

A CONCEPTUAL MODEL FOR ORGANIZATIONAL BEHAVIOR

PROBLEMS ON THE HUMAN SIDE OF ENTERPRISE*

In a recently published special report on work it was made clear that there are many problems on the human side of enterprise. While management approaches and theories have given important guidance over the past hundred years, there are still no real answers to the growing human problems facing today's management. New solutions need to be found to both old and emerging problems. But, there is growing evidence that these solutions are not coming about. For example, almost two-thirds of the semiskilled or unskilled workers responding to the survey indicated that it was likely that they would change jobs, and in managerial and executive positions almost one-third indicated that they would probably change their occupations in the coming year. Such results seem to indicate that people are indeed dissatisfied with their jobs and their careers. Increased effort needs to be directed toward improving the understanding, prediction, and control of humans at work.

---

*Adapted from *Psychology Today,* May 1978, pp. 46–84.

What separates humans from animals, or other objects in the universe? What are people really like? Are employees naturally lazy or productive? Why do managers and workers behave the way they do? What is their real nature? These questions have been debated over the years. Philosophers, theologians, politicians, behavioral scientists, managers, and the person on the street have been and still are preoccupied with these questions. Most often, scholars and lay persons have ready answers to these questions and staunchly defend their positions. To date, however, the true nature of human behavior in general and organizational behavior in particular is still largely undefined and open for discussion and research.

One psychologist describes an intriguing situation that may be analogous to the current status of understanding human behavior.

Suppose the ill-fated occurrence of an atomic holocaust had come to pass on earth, and after the debris had cleared the only two remaining objects to be seen were an ultraprimitive man and a watch, still going, which he had picked up in the desert. Since the man might be presumed to be in a state of almost complete ignorance, all realization of the purpose of the watch had now been obliterated from the earth. . . . That this structure would present the primitive man with a puzzle if he were to try accurately to describe it, to say nothing of explaining its origin, seems evident. We, too, are like watches—lost in the desert of time. And similarly, we are at a loss to understand either our origin or our essential nature.[1]

Is the picture really as bleak as that described above? Is nothing known about human behavior? Whether scholar or layperson, everyone has had abundant experience in living and dealing with, reading about, and observing fellow human beings. A normal outgrowth of this lifetime of experience is that everyone has a definite opinion about human behavior. Unfortunately, when common-sense approaches to human behavior are put to the test of science, they are often proved wrong. Yet it is through the applications of science that human behavior can best be understood. This, of course, is the approach of behavioral science that was outlined in the last chapter.

The behavioral scientist analyzes human behavior on the basis of scientific methodology. The major goal of behavioral scientists is to understand behavior. Philosophers, theologians, and managers are interested primarily in evaluating behavior. The emphasis on understanding versus evaluation is the major difference between the behavioral sciences and the other approaches used in analyzing human behavior. The study of organizational behavior, of course, follows the lead of the behavioral sciences. The field of organizational behavior is interested in *understanding* human behavior in organizations, but since it is more of an applied field than the behavioral sciences as a whole, organizational behavior is also vitally concerned with *predicting* and *controlling* human behavior for improved organizational performance.

---

[1]Floyd H. Allport, "A Theory of Enestruence (Event-Structure Theory): Report of Progress," *American Psychologist*, January 1967, p. 1.

This chapter provides a conceptual framework and a specific model for attaining the goals of understanding, predicting, and controlling organizational behavior. A conceptual *framework* is perhaps best defined as a device that provides categories or labels which help us to collect and organize data; a *model* goes one step further by providing a representation of the real world and how it functions.[2] A model specifies the variables and how they relate to one another. Both frameworks and models fall short of an overall theory, but both make inputs into a theory. A theory is more comprehensive and represents the body of knowledge that is structured by the frameworks and models. The following discussion presents various approaches to human behavior. The term *framework* is used rather than *theory* because most of these approaches fall short of being comprehensive theories of human behavior; taken together, however, they provide background information important in developing a specific conceptual model for organizational behavior.

FREUDIAN PSYCHOANALYTIC FRAMEWORK

The Freudian approach relies on a psychoanalytic or conflict view of human behavior. At least in Western culture, the conception of people being in constant inner conflict is one of the oldest explanations. The conflict model portrayed primitive humans' constant inner struggle between good and evil. Good (angels) and evil (devils) were believed to be competing for the domination of the body and soul. Common sayings such as "he is possessed by the devil" or "she is a little angel," reflect this view. Under this model, individuals are merely innocent bystanders and the situation completely overwhelms them. This primitive view of conflict still exists in many parts of the world, even within subcultures of highly developed countries. Obviously, the primitive good-evil conflict model cannot be substantiated by scientific methodology. It is based on magic and the supernatural, which are outside the realm of science.

A more meaningful, comprehensive, and systematically based conflict view stems from the theories of Sigmund Freud. These ideas can be summarized into what can be called the *psychoanalytic framework*. Although Freud is most closely associated with the framework, others such as Carl Jung, Alfred Adler, Karen Horney, and Eric Fromm, who all broke away from Freud, made additional contributions and extended the approach.

Clinical techniques were used primarily to develop the psychoanalytic approach. Through the clinical techniques of free association and psychotherapy, Freud noted that his patients' behavior could not always be consciously explained. This clinical finding led him to conclude that the major motivating force in humans is unconscious in nature. The personality

---

[2]David A. Nadler, J. Richard Hackman, and Edward E. Lawler, III, *Managing Organizational Behavior*, Little, Brown, Boston, 1979, p. 8.

structure can be explained within the unconscious framework, Freud believed, by three interrelated, but often conflicting, psychoanalytic concepts: the *id*, the *ego*, and the *superego*.

The id concept

The id is the core of the unconscious. It is the unleashed, raw, primitive, instinctual drive of the Freudian approach. The id, constantly struggling for gratification and pleasure, is manifested mainly through the libido (sexual urges) or aggression. The libido strives for sexual relations and pleasure, but also for warmth, food, and comfort. Aggressive impulses of the id are destructive and include the urges to fight, dominate, and generally destroy. In a conflict sense, the id incorporates life instincts that compete with its death instincts. As individuals develop and mature, they learn to control the id. But even then it remains a driving force throughout life and an important source of thinking and behaving.

The ego concept

Whereas the id represents the unconscious, the ego is the conscious. It represents logic in the Freudian approach and is associated with the reality principle. The ego keeps the id in check through the realities of the external environment. The ego is constituted so that it can interpret reality for the id through intellect and reason. Instrumental behavior, such as dating or working, is developed by the ego to satisfy the needs of the id. However, many conflict situations arise between the id and the ego because the id demands immediate pleasure while the ego dictates denial or postponement to a more appropriate time and place. In order to resolve the conflicts, the ego gets support from the superego.

The superego concept

The superego is the third element of the Freudian framework. It can best be depicted as the conscience. The superego provides the norms that enable the ego to determine what is right or wrong. The superego conscience should not be confused with the conscious aspects of the ego. In fact, according to Freud, the superego is mostly unconscious.

The person is not aware of the workings of the superego. The conscience is developed by absorption of the cultural values and morals of a society. Accordingly, the parents have the most influence on the development of the superego. After resolving the Oedipus complex (love of parent), the child will unconsciously identify with the parents' values and morals.

The superego aids the person by assisting the ego to combat the impulses of the id. However, in some situations the superego can also be in conflict with the ego. An example is the situation where the reality-seeking ego violates the conscience. The conflict between ego and conscience provokes the wrath and vengeance of the largely unconscious superego. The inevitable struggles between the id, ego, and superego cause this to be considered a conflict framework for human behavior.

The Freudian approach in perspective

Freud's model is characterized by the conflicting personality constructs (id, ego, and superego) and unconscious motivation. Psychological adjustment occurs only when the ego properly develops to resolve the conflicts stemming from the id and superego. The ego concept implies that humans are rational, but the id, the superego, and unconscious motivation give the impression that humans are very irrational. Under the Freudian approach, behavior is based on emotion. If the ego cannot control the id, the person is an aggressive, pleasure-seeking menace to society. If the id is too severely checked by the ego, the person is equally maladjusted. The person may have an abnormal sex life and be extremely passive. Moreover, if the superego is very strong, the result may be acute anxiety and guilt.

Freud has had a great impact in many areas of twentieth-century thought. For example, he has had a great influence on treatment techniques for the mentally ill, and he did make some contribution to the understanding of human behavior in general and, at least indirectly, to organizational behavior. Some areas where the psychoanalytic approach has made an impact on organizational behavior include the following:[3]

1. *Creative Behavior.* For example, certain stages of the creative process are unconscious in nature.
2. *Dissatisfaction.* Employee behaviors such as daydreaming, forgetting, apathy, rationalization, and even absenteeism, tardiness, sabotage, and alcoholism/drug abuse can be analyzed in psychoanalytic terms.
3. *Organization Development Techniques.* Organization development techniques such as transactional analysis (e.g., attempts to improve interpersonal communication skills and eliminate "game playing") and group/team development rely to some degree on psychoanalytic thought.
4. *Leadership and Power.* The attention given to authority and dominance in psychoanalytic approaches is reflected in the study of leadership and power in organizational behavior.

The above shows that Freud's ideas have proved to be very far-reaching and long lasting. Yet overall, he is criticized as much today as he is praised. Most of the criticism centers on the overemphasis given to sexual motivation.

From a behavioral science viewpoint, however, the most valid criticism of the Freudian approach is that it is not based on empirically verifiable facts. The psychoanalytic elements are largely hypothetical constructs and are not measurable, observable items susceptible to scientific analysis and verification. The id, ego, and superego are primarily a "black box" explanation (a term used in management that means something is there but it cannot be understood) of human beings. This is why most modern behavioral

---

[3]H. Joseph Reitz, *Behavior in Organizations*, Irwin, Homewood, Ill., 1977, pp. 67–68.

scientists reject the psychoanalytic approach as the total explanation of human personality and behavior. Nevertheless, important insights, especially into personality structure and the idea of unconscious motivation, are significant contributions to understanding human behavior in general, and the points above have definite implications for understanding certain aspects of organizational behavior. They will be expanded upon in subsequent sections of the book.

EXISTENTIALISTIC FRAMEWORK

Existentialism, broadly understood as the search for meaning, is based on the analysis of existence and being. The existentialistic approach is not really a behavioral science approach. Its roots lie more in the realm of philosophy and the humanities and are not scientifically based.

Existentialism is European in origin and can be traced to the writings of the philosophers Kierkegaard, Nietzsche, and Schopenhauer. Among the philosophers with an existentialist orientation are Martin Heidegger, Martin Buber, and Jean-Paul Sartre. The best-known American spokesman, in recent years, has been Rollo May. May and Sartre, in particular, have been critical of the usual scientific approaches that are employed to gain an understanding of humans. They are afraid that a scientific behavioral analysis may destroy or lose sight of the person's true nature or "being." They are more interested in exploring the insides of the human mind and spirit, people's potential, rather than their actual behavior. Thus, most recently, their type of approach has often been called the "human potential" approach.

Existentialism is conceptually similar to Durkheim's sociological concept of anomie, which was discussed in Chapter 2. Similar to Durkheim, existentialists see a breakdown of traditional norms and the ties that individuals have traditionally had with society. For example, Rollo May views people as suffering from unconstructive anxiety. He defines "unconstructive" or "neurotic" anxiety as the "shrinking of consciousness, the blocking off of awareness; and when it is prolonged it leads to a feeling of depersonalization and apathy" which is "the state, to a greater or lesser degree, of those who have lost, or never achieved, the experience of their own identity in the world."[4] This feeling of "depersonalization and apathy" is what Durkheim referred to as *anomie*.

In modern times the individual is faced with a very large, urbanized environment. The existentialists believe that the depersonalizing effects of this environment force individuals to determine their own destiny. People shape their own identity and make their "existence" meaningful and worthwhile to themselves. This process is accomplished through the individual's experience of being. Coleman views this being as "a matter of commitment to increased self-awareness and self-direction, to true communication with others, to concern with values and evaluation, and to

---

[4]Rollo May, *Psychology and the Human Dilemma*, Van Nostrand, Princeton, N.J., 1967, p. 41.

acceptance of the responsibility for making choices and directing his own destiny."[5]

The emphasis attached to self-awareness and action in the existential or human potential scheme is different from that in the psychoanalytic approach. Existential people seek self-awareness, direction, and control. Their existence in a depersonalized environment is a given. What they make of this existence is entirely up to them, i.e., they try to attain their potential. The existentialist approach maintains that people have free will to chart their existence and being and reach their true potential as loving, living human beings.

The impact of the existentialistic model

The existentialistic approach becomes very relevant in a society suffering from environmental and moral decay. In a world that is overpopulated, undernourished, polluted, ravaged by war and crime, with racial injustice and poverty rampant amidst affluence and material excess, it is extremely difficult for an individual to carve out a meaningful existence. The problem is compounded if the old, tradition-bound values of the past linger on as norms for the present, even though they are irrelevant and incapable of practical application under current conditions or in the foreseeable future.

Certainly some aspects of the modern American scene seem directly relevant to an existentialistic approach. Similarly, on a micro level, human behavior in organizations seems appropriate for existentialistic study and analysis. Determining a meaningful occupational existence may be a severe challenge for an individual faced with the characteristics of the modern formal organization. One recent analysis of an existentialistic approach to organizational behavior concludes that the focus should be on goals and values. "The central belief is that existence precedes essence, and human systems exist and create their own image through actions."[6] Such a philosophical approach is not scientifically based and will not be conceptually integrated into this book. Yet, with modern values of self-gratification and self-fulfillment, existentialism does provide some very useful insights. It can be effectively used to set a tone and to supplement more scientifically based discussions of organizational behavior.

COGNITIVE FRAMEWORK

The psychoanalytic and existentialistic approaches are on the periphery of the study of human behavior. Two more scientifically based frameworks can be better used to explain human behavior in general and organizational behavior in particular. Although other names are sometimes applied and

---

[5]See James C. Coleman, *Psychology and Effective Behavior*, Scott, Foresman, Glenview, Ill., 1969, p. 33.

[6]Kurt Kourosh Motamedi, "Toward Explicating Philosophical Orientations in Organizational Behavior (OB)," *Academy of Management Review*, April 1978, p. 358.

there are many other distinct models contained within each framework, these two are best labeled the cognitive and the behavioristic.

The *cognitive* approach to human behavior has many sources of input. The gestalt and phenomenological schools of thought in psychology, which were discussed in Chapter 2, provide a historical base for the cognitive approach. In general, the cognitive framework came about as a reaction to the other approaches to human behavior. In particular, pioneering psychologists such as Edward Tolman became disenchanted with the psychoanalytic and early behavioristic approaches. They felt that Freudian thinking placed too much emphasis on negative, irrational, and sexually motivated behavior and that the early behavioristic framework was too simplistic, deterministic, and mechanistic. The alternative that was proposed gave humans much more ''credit'' than the other approaches. The cognitive approach emphasizes the positive and free-will aspects of human behavior and utilizes concepts such as expectancy, demand, and incentive. The term *cognition*, the basic unit of the cognitive framework, is the act of knowing an item of information. Cognitions precede behavior and constitute input into the person's thinking, perception, or problem solving.

The work of Tolman can be used to represent the cognitive approach. Although considered a behaviorist in the sense that he believed behavior was the appropriate unit of analysis, Tolman felt that behavior was purposive: it was directed toward a goal. In his laboratory experiments, he found that animals learned to expect that certain events will follow one another. For example, animals learned to behave as if they expected food when a certain cue appeared. Thus, to Tolman learning consisted of the *expectancy* that a particular event will lead to a particular consequence. This cognitive concept of expectancy implies that the organism is thinking about or is conscious of or aware of the goal. Table 3-1 briefly summarizes the role that expectancies and other cognitions play as mediating processes between the stimulus/situation and the behavior. Thus, Tolman and others in the cognitive approach (e.g., those mentioned in Table 3-1) felt that behavior is best explained by these cognitions.

Contemporary psychologists carefully point out that a cognitive concept such as expectancy does not reflect a guess about what is going on in the mind; it is a term that describes behavior.[7] In other words, the cognitive and behavioristic models are not as opposite as they appear on the surface and sometimes are made out to be—for example, Tolman considered himself a behaviorist. Yet, despite some conceptual similarities, there has been a controversy throughout the years in the behavioral sciences on the relative contributions of the cognitive versus the behavioristic framework. Although the sequence is reversed (only recently have behavioristic approaches been proposed in organizational behavior because of the dissatisfaction with the cognitive approach[8]), the controversy has carried over into the field of

---

[7]Robert C. Bolles, *Learning Theory*, Holt, New York, 1975, p. 84.

[8]For example, see Fred Luthans and Robert Ottemann, ''Motivation versus Learning Approaches to Organizational Behavior,'' *Business Horizons*, December 1973, pp. 55–62.

Table 3-1

A SUMMARY OF COGNITIVE APPROACHES

Cognitive classification	Cognitive structure	Description
Expectancy	S-Cognition-B	Thoughts and other cognitions intervene between incoming information and the final behavioral response. The main cognitive determinant of action is an "expectancy." Proponents include Atkinson, Lewin, Porter, Rotter, Tolman, and Vroom.
Extraexpectancy	S-Cognition-B	Thoughts and other cognitions intervene between incoming information and the final behavioral response. Many cognitive processes determine action, such as information seeking, causal attributions, etc. Proponents include Adams, Deci, Festinger, Heider, Kelley, and Lazarus.

Source: Adapted from Larry E. Pate, "Cognitive Versus Reinforcement Views of Intrinsic Motivation," *Academy of Management Review*, July 1978, p. 508.

organizational behavior. Before discussing the input that the cognitive approach can make to a conceptual model of organizational behavior, it is necessary to better understand the behavioristic approach.

BEHAVIORISTIC FRAMEWORK

Chapter 2 discussed the behavioristic school of thought in psychology. Its roots can be traced to the work of Pavlov and Watson. These pioneering behaviorists stressed the importance of dealing with observable behaviors instead of the elusive mind that had preoccupied the earlier structuralists and functionalists. They used classical conditioning experiments to formulate the stimulus-response (S-R) explanation of human behavior. Both Pavlov and Watson felt that behavior could be best understood in terms of S-R. A stimulus elicits a response. They concentrated mainly on the impact of the stimulus and felt that learning occurred when the S-R connection was made.

Modern behaviorism marks its beginning with the work of B. F. Skinner. Skinner is generally recognized as the most influential living psychologist. He felt that the early behaviorists helped to explain respondent behaviors (those behaviors elicited by stimuli) but not the more complex operant behaviors (those behaviors not elicited by stimuli, which simply occur; operant behaviors are emitted by the organism). In other words, the S-R approach helped explain physical reflexes; for example, when stuck by a pin (S), the person will flinch (R); or when tapped below the kneecap (S), the person will extend the lower leg (R). On the other hand, Skinner found through his operant conditioning experiments that the consequences of a response could better explain most behaviors than could eliciting stimuli. He emphasized the importance of the response-stimulus (R-S) relationship. The organism has to operate on the environment in order to receive the desirable consequence. The preceding stimulus does not cause the behavior in operant conditioning; it serves as a cue to emit the behavior. For Skinner, behavior is a function of its consequences.

Both classical and operant conditioning are given more detailed attention in Chapter 9. For now, however, it is important to understand that the behavioristic approach is *environmentally* based. It implies that cognitive processes such as thinking, expectancies, and perception do not play a role in behavior. However, as in the case of the cognitive approach, which includes behavioristic concepts, some psychologists feel that there is room for cognitive variables in the behavioristic approach. In particular, a social learning approach has emerged in recent years that incorporates both cognitive and behavioristic concepts and principles.

SOCIAL LEARNING FRAMEWORK

The cognitive approach has been accused of being mentalistic, and the behavioristic approach has been accused of being deterministic. Cognitive theorists argue that the S-R model, and to a lesser degree the R-S model, is much too mechanistic an explanation of human behavior. A strict S-R interpretation of behavior seems justifiably open to the criticism of being too mechanistic, but because of the scientific approach that has been meticulously employed by behaviorists, the operant model in particular has made a tremendous contribution to the study of human behavior. The same can be said of the cognitive approach. Much research has been done to verify its importance as an explanation of human behavior. Instead of polarization and unconstructive criticism between the two approaches, it now seems time to recognize that each can make an important contribution to the study of human behavior. The social learning approach tries to integrate the contributions of both approaches.

It must be emphasized that the social learning approach is a behavioral approach. It recognizes that behavior is the appropriate unit of analysis. Although there are a number of modern theorists associated with social learning,[9] the work of Albert Bandura is probably the most representative of this approach.[10] He takes the position that behavior can best be explained in

---

[9]Walter Mischel, "Toward a Cognitive Reconceptualization of Personality," *Psychological Review,* vol. 80, 1973, pp. 284–302; Michael J. Mahoney, *Cognition and Behavior Modification,* Ballinger, Cambridge, 1974; Donald Meichenbaum, *Cognitive Behavior Modification: An Integrative Approach,* Plenum, New York, 1977; Arthur W. Staats, *Social Behaviorism,* Dorsey, Homewood, Ill., 1975.

[10]Albert Bandura, "Social Learning Theory," in J. T. Spence, R. C. Carson, and J. W. Thibaut (eds.), *Behavioral Approaches to Therapy,* General Learning Press, Morristown, N.J., 1976; Albert Bandura, *Social Learning Theory,* Prentice-Hall, Englewood Cliffs, N.J. 1977; and Albert Bandura, "The Self System in Reciprocal Determinism," *American Psychologist,* vol. 33, 1978, pp. 344–358.

terms of a continuous reciprocal interaction between cognitive, behavioral, and environmental determinants. The person and the environmental situation do not function as independent units but, in conjunction with the behavior itself, reciprocally interact to determine behavior. Bandura explains that, "it is largely through their actions that people produce the environmental conditions that affect their behavior in a reciprocal fashion. The experiences generated by behavior also partly determine what a person becomes and can do, which, in turn, affects subsequent behavior."[11] He then transforms this approach into the model shown in Figure 3-1.

The specifics of social learning, such as vicarious or modeling processes, the role of cognitive mediating processes, and the importance of self-control procedures will be discussed in Chapters 9 and 22. But for now, it can be said that social learning with its very comprehensive, interactive nature serves as an excellent conceptual framework and point of departure for developing a meaningful model for organizational behavior.[12]

A SPECIFIC MODEL FOR ORGANIZATIONAL BEHAVIOR

Organizational behavior has the advantage of being a relatively young and growing field of study. It can legitimately borrow, in an eclectic manner, the best from the various established frameworks for human behavior. At one point in its early development, the field of organizational behavior seemed to be in a dilemma, searching for a theoretical orientation. Over the past couple of decades, most writers in organizational behavior have taken a humanistic, cognitive approach. For example, Douglas McGregor took a humanistic approach, and theorists such as Victor Vroom depended mainly on cognitive concepts in their writings on organizational behavior. In the last couple of years, the behavioristic model has begun to be utilized in theorizing and research on organizational behavior.[13] In many ways, what the field of

---

[11]Albert Bandura, *Social Learning Theory*, Prentice-Hall, Englewood Cliffs, N.J., 1977, p. 9.

[12]See Tim R. V. Davis and Fred Luthans, "A Social Learning Approach to Organizational Behavior," *Academy of Management Review*, April 1980, pp. 281–290.

[13]For a summary of the literature on the operant model in organizational behavior, see Fred Luthans and Robert Kreitner, *Organizational Behavior Modification*, Scott, Foresman, Glenview, Ill., 1975.

**Figure 3-1
Reciprocal determinism in social learning.(Source: Adapted from Albert Bandura, Social Learning Theory, Prentice-Hall, Englewood Cliffs, N.J., 1977).**

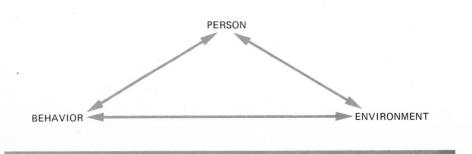

organizational behavior has been going through in recent years is a replay of the behavioristic-versus-cognitive controversy that has existed and, in many respects, still exists in psychology. Now, in organizational behavior, the time seems to have come to recognize the contributions of both approaches and to begin to synthesize and integrate both into a comprehensive model of organizational behavior. The social learning approach provides a good foundation for such an eclectic organizational behavior model.

The goals of an organizational behavior model

As stated earlier, the goal of presenting the frameworks so far discussed is to better understand, not evaluate, the complex phenomena collectively called *human behavior*. Understanding human behavior in organizations is also a vital goal for a model of organizational behavior. In addition, however, as was stated earlier, because organizational behavior is an applied field, two other desirable goals besides understanding are prediction and control. The field of organizational behavior serves as the basis for modern human resource management. Prediction and control of human resources are critical to the goals of modern management. Thus, the goals of a model of organizational behavior are to understand, predict, and control human behavior in organizations.

The cognitive approach seems essential to the understanding of organizational behavior. The behavioristic approach can also lead to understanding, but perhaps even more important is the contribution it can make to prediction and control. For example, on the basis of Edward Thorndike's classic law of effect, the behavioristic approach would say that organizational behavior followed by a positive or reinforcing consequence will be strengthened and will increase in subsequent frequency, and organizational behavior followed by an unpleasant or punishing consequence will be weakened and will decrease in subsequent frequency. In other words, organizational behavior can be predicted and controlled on the basis of managing the contingent environment. In any event, if the three goals of understanding, prediction, and control are to be met by a model of organizational behavior, both the cognitive and the behavioristic approaches become vitally important. Both the internal causal factors which are cognitively oriented and the external environmental factors which are behavioristically oriented become important. In other words, the social learning approach that incorporates both cognitive and behavioristic concepts is an appropriate conceptual framework for an organizational behavior model that will help understand, predict, and control.

An S-O-B-C model

An S-O-B-C model was developed to identify the major variables in organizational behavior and show how they relate to one another. The letters stand for Stimulus—Organism—Behavior—Consequence. Based on a social learning framework, this model recognizes the interactive nature of environmental (S and C), intrapersonal, cognitive (O), and behavioral (B) variables. In a strictly behavioristic approach, a three-variable model consisting of antecedent cues or stimuli (S), behaviors (B), and consequences (C) is typically used. However, when the human organism (O), representing cognitive mediating processes, is included, as in a social learning approach, then the four-term model results. Unlike the more limited S-B-C behavioristic model, which emphasizes the need to identify observable contingencies (S and C) for the prediction and control of behavior (B), or the O-B model, which says that internal cognitions (O) lead to behavior (B), the expanded S-O-B-C model recognizes the interactive nature of both the environment (S and C) and the person's cognitions (O) in determining behavior.

With the S-O-B-C model the antecedent cues or discriminative stimuli (S), the behavior itself (B), and the consequence (C) can be either overt (external and observable) or covert (internal and nonobservable). This, of course, represents a significant departure from more traditional behavioristic approaches that, at least implicitly, have recognized only overt variables. Once again, however, it should be remembered that the S-O-B-C model does not abandon the emphasis on behavior or the principles of the operant approach; it merely expands the group of variables to include cognitive mediating processes and covert as well as overt contingencies and behaviors. It is felt that this S-O-B-C model best identifies the relevant variables and shows how they are related in order to accomplish the goals of understanding, prediction, and control of human behavior in organizations.

Figure 3-2 graphically shows the S-O-B-C model. The variables are briefly identified and the interactive relationship among all the variables is indicated. The following sections will break out these variables for further identification and discussion, but it must be remembered that in reality they are interacting and are reciprocal in nature.

The S variable   The S variable in the model stands for the stimulus or, more broadly, the environmental situation. Common stimuli include lights, sounds, odors, pinpricks, and persons. In a strict S-R behavioristic interpretation, such stimuli (S) play the crucial role in eliciting behavior. Stimuli goad humans into action, interrupt what they are doing, and direct their choices. In this classical behavioristic view, the immediate stimulus object is the primary causal factor in behavior. In the operant view, the stimulus serves as the antecedent cue (*not* cause) for the behavior. However, it must also be remembered that the contingent consequence is also a type of

**Figure 3-2
The S-O-B-C model.**

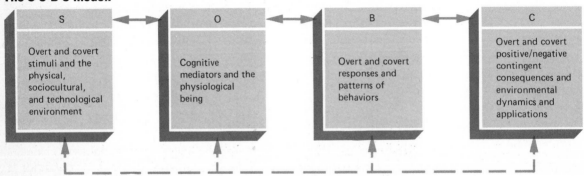

S	O	B	C
Overt and covert stimuli and the physical, sociocultural, and technological environment	Cognitive mediators and the physiological being	Overt and covert responses and patterns of behaviors	Overt and covert positive/negative contingent consequences and environmental dynamics and applications

environmental stimulus (R-S), and in the operant approach, behavior is a function of its consequences. In a social learning approach, this S variable can be an overt environmental event or a covert cue such as a goal or a subvocal reminder. Thus, the S variable in the S-O-B-C model is very comprehensive and all-encompassing in nature. When applied to organizational behavior, this S variable is primarily concerned with the macro, organizational environment. This organizational environment, which represents a macro perspective of organizational behavior, is given specific attention in Part 5 of this book.

The O variable The O variable in the model stands for the human organism and, more specifically, the cognitive mediating processes within the person. The use of the letter O to designate this variable is a fallback to the old S-O-R model of psychology, which recognized the organism with its accompanying cognitions as a mediating process between the stimulus and response. The inclusion of this O in the model gives recognition to the cognitive approach to behavior. The chapters on perception, personality, and motivation in Parts 2 and 3 of the book indicate its relative importance to the study of organizational behavior. It dominates the micro perspective of organizational behavior.

The B variable Perhaps the best way to describe the B variable (Behavior) is to state what it is and what it is not. Behavior is anything that a person does; it is not something that is done to a person. The nature of behavior can be clarified by analyzing two sets of examples. In the first set are five possible behaviors of an assembly line worker in a widget factory:

1. The worker started the machine.
2. The worker produced many widgets.
3. The worker did not produce many widgets.
4. The worker came to work late.
5. The worker came to work on time.

In these five instances the worker did something. Thus, according to the simple definition, these examples are forms of behavior. However, before jumping to this conclusion, a refinement is necessary. Each of the five examples is an outcome of the worker's behavior rather than a description of the actual overt (outward) or covert (inward) behavior. In understanding the behavioral variable, it is extremely important to separate the actual behavioral events from the outcomes of these events. The same five examples can be translated into more precise behavioral events in the following manner:

1. The worker pushed the button.
2. The worker moved his or her arms and hands very fast.
3. The worker moved his or her arms and hands very slowly.
4. The worker walked very slowly from the parking lot.
5. The worker walked very fast from the parking lot.

This second set of examples describes the specific, overt behavior, not the outcomes of the behavior. It must be remembered that not all behavior is overt. Subvocalizations or even a certain attitude could be considered to be forms of covert behavior. But these latter covert behaviors are internal events and thus are removed from direct observation and measurement. Therefore, although the existence of covert behaviors is acknowledged, organizational behavior mostly deals with the overt kinds.

Too often, both organizational behavior theorists and practicing managers forget that *motivation* or *leadership* are merely labels that are attached to hypothetical constructs. Behaviors are the only empirical reality and thus are the appropriate unit for analysis in the study and application techniques of organizational behavior. True, the hypothetical constructs such as motivation or leadership are important because they contribute to and help better explain, predict, and control *behavior*, but they should not be allowed to become ends in themselves. Most attention must be devoted to the *behavior* part of organizational behavior. Covert behaviors such as attitudes or satisfaction are not discussed specifically in this book. They are important dependent variables, especially in the motivational area, but these covert behaviors are not given whole chapters of discussion. Instead, this book gives performance behaviors and techniques for attaining these behaviors the most attention.

The C variable   Similar to the S variable in the model, the C variable is environmental in nature. It stands for Consequence. As the operant behavioristic approach points out, the person must operate on the environment in order to obtain a certain consequence. This is the contingent-consequence emphasis from modern behaviorism, but the C also includes broader-based dynamics (e.g., conflict) and applications (e.g., appraisal) as part of the environmental consequences of organizational behavior. The chapters in Parts 4 and 6 of the book relate to these important, broadly based consequences of organizational behavior.

The interactive nature of the variables   The social learning approach emphasizes the interactive nature of the environment-person-behavior variables. This is represented in the S-O-B-C model by the interacting double arrowheads between the variables and the feedback loops that connect all the variables as shown in Figure 3-2.

First is the interactive connection between S and O. This interactive process occurs between the situation and the person before behavior results. Merely placing the S and O together is not enough. As noted by one psychologist, "the situation is a function of the observer in the sense that the observer's cognitive schemes filter and organize the environment in a fashion that makes it impossible ever to completely separate the environment from the person observing it."[14] The interaction usually takes the form of the O's cognitive interpretation of the immediate S. This type of interaction can be thought of as the process of perception. However, this is only one simple form of interaction. In the S-O-B-C model the perceptual

[14]K. S. Bowers, "Situationism in Psychology: An Analysis and a Critique," *Psychological Review*, vol. 80, 1973, pp. 328–329.

process is part of the O, along with the other cognitive processes such as thinking. When the influence of the physiological being and personality and the greatly expanded conception of S are added, the complexity of the interaction between the S and O becomes clear. Yet in abstract, simplistic terms, the S↔O can be thought of as usually being the antecedent of behavior. This S↔O interaction should not be thought of as causing the behavior in the S-R sense. Instead, S↔O should be thought of as usually preceding the behavior, with the S serving as a cue for the behavior, the O as the mediating cognitive processes, and the ↔ as the complex interactive effect between the S and the O that leads to (*not* causes) the behavior.

The second important connection in the S-O-B-C model is the B↔C relationship. This is an outgrowth of the R-S relationship of the operant model in behavioristic psychology. One key to the connection between behavior and its consequence is the contingency concept. A contingent relationship is an "if-then" relationship. As used here, this simply means that the person's behavior is affected by its contingent consequences. *If* the person behaves a certain way, *then* a particular consequence will follow. Such contingent consequences can be used to predict and control behavior. This B↔C relationship will also interact and determine the S and O.

The feedback loops are also important to the model. These feedback loops, shown as the dashed lines in Figure 3-2, show that each variable affects and is affected by each of the other variables. In the simplest sense, these feedback loops can be thought of as social learning. For example, based on the consequences of behavior, the person's (O) perceptions and motives will be affected and situational cues (S) will become associated with or even change on the basis of certain consequences. However, just as the interaction between S and O involves more than perception, the feedback loops from C to O or S involve more than learning. There is a continuous interaction between the variables, and when the expanded nature of these variables is recognized, it is clear that organizational behavior is very complex indeed.

Obviously, the S-O-B-C model as presented in this chapter is only a "barebones" sketch of human behavior in organizations. It is hoped that as the remaining chapters of the book unfold, some of the fine points of the model will become clearer and some of the seemingly simplistic assumptions and unsupported statements will begin to make more sense. The purpose of this model, as with any model, is to identify the important variables and show how they relate to one another. Particularly with the field of organizational behavior, which is still developing and searching for a theoretical base, such a model is extremely important for structuring study and further development. Figure 3-3 places the major topics of the book into the S-O-B-C model.

The formal organization: The macro environment for organizational behavior

The S-O-B-C model shown in Figure 3-3 plugs the formal organization into S. The formal organization, of course, is the most important situational environment for the study of organizational behavior. Viewing the organization as a system, there are two subsystems that are especially important to

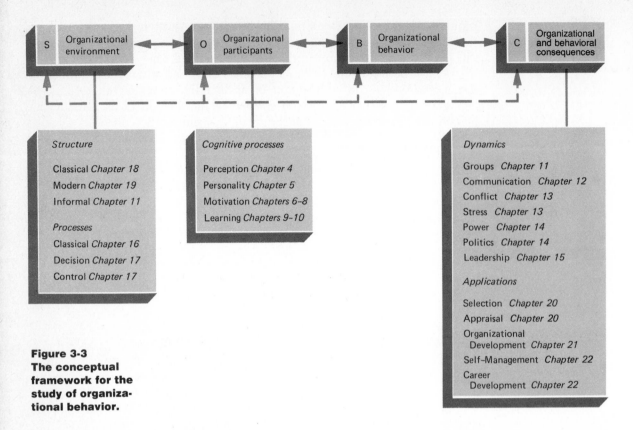

**Figure 3-3
The conceptual
framework for the
study of organiza-
tional behavior.**

the study of organizational behavior. The first, the structure, serves as the skeleton for the formal organization system. Structure allows the other management processes subsystem to operate. The bureaucratic model best represents the classical organization structure. Extensions and modifications of the bureaucratic model, such as centralization-decentralization, flat-tall, departmentation, and line-staff, also have an important role in classical organization structures. The modern structures of organization are based on behavioral, systems, and contingency theories and are designed to meet the challenges of growth, complexity, conflict, and change. Project, matrix, and freeform designs are examples of modern structural forms.

Interacting and interdependent with the organization structure are the management processes. Numerous designations are attached to the various processes, but most can be subsumed under decision making and control. These management processes are an integral subsystem of the formal organization system and, along with structure, constitute the macro environment in which organizational participants operate and behave.

Organizational participants

Organizational participants or employees (both managers and workers) are plugged into the O portion of the model. Analogous to thinking of the formal organization as the situation, these participants can be thought of as consisting of the cognitive processes. For example, analogous to the management processes of the formal organization are the participants' cognitive processes of perception, personality, and motivation. These processes are at the very heart of the micro study of organizational behavior. They are probably more vital than any other single part of the overall framework to the understanding of organizational behavior. However, just as separating the processes from the formal organization is largely an artificial construct, so is abstracting the cognitive processes from the totality of organizational behavior. Organizational participants constantly interact with the situation and the behavior itself and are not a collection of separate parts or processes.

Organizational and behavioral consequences

The study of the organizational environment and the organizational participant lead to a better *understanding* of organizational behavior. The study of the organizational and behavioral consequences can help to better predict and control organizational behavior. Again, the reader should be reminded that this is a highly simplified generalization. Cognitive and especially social learning theorists are beginning to provide ways to predict and control behavior, and behavioristically oriented theorists are certainly contributing to a better understanding of behavior. Nevertheless, the *emphasis* in the $S \leftrightarrow O$ is on understanding and in the $B \leftrightarrow C$ is on prediction and control.

Figure 3-3 indicates that certain dynamics and human resource management applications are especially relevant to the consequences portion of the model. The dynamics of groups, communication, conflict, stress, power, politics, and leadership are particularly important in the study of organizational behavior. The application of managerial techniques in the areas of selection, appraisal, organization development, self-management, and career development can provide feedback, leading to change in the organizational situation and, through learning, in the organizational participant and in the behavior itself. In other words, all the variables are in continuous interaction with one another and reciprocally determine one another.

SUMMARY

Everyone is concerned with human behavior. Yet philosophers, theologians, behavioral scientists, managers, and the person on the street have still not completely reached a true understanding of human behavior in general and organizational behavior in particular. All people think they are experts and are defensive about their views. The difference between the behavioral science approach and the other approaches is that behavioral scientists use the methods of science and take an understanding, rather than an evaluating, approach.

Some widely recognized frameworks include Sigmund Freud's psychoanalytic approach, the more philosophically based existentialist approach, the two major approaches from the behavioral sciences, the cognitive and behavioristic, and the newly emerging, more integrative, social learning approach. The cognitive model gives the human more "credit" and assumes that behavior is purposive and goal-oriented. Cognitive processes such as expectancy and perception help explain behavior. The behavioristic approach deals with observable behaviors and the environmental contingencies of the behavior. Classical behaviorism explained behavior in terms of S-R, whereas more modern behaviorism gives more emphasis to contingent consequences or R-S. The social learning approach emphasizes that the person, the environment, and the behavior itself are in constant interaction with one another and reciprocally determine one another.

The field of organizational behavior has the goals of understanding, prediction, and control. S-O-B-C is an eclectic model taken from both cognitive and behavioristic approaches but mainly based on the new social learning approach. This model can perhaps best meet the goals of organizational behavior. The $S \leftrightarrow O$ portion deals mainly with understanding and the $B \leftrightarrow C$ portion with prediction and control. If the organizational situation is substituted for S, the organizational participant for O, and the dynamics and applications are put into C, the model can serve as a conceptual framework for the study of organizational behavior. The parts of this framework provide the structure for the remaining chapters of the book.

QUESTIONS FOR DISCUSSION AND REVIEW

1. In your own words, identify and summarize the various frameworks for understanding human behavior.
2. How does the social learning approach differ from the cognitive approach? How does the social learning approach differ from the behavioristic approach?
3. Identify and explain the variables in the S-O-B-C model. How do these variables relate to each other?
4. What role do cognitive processes play in the S-O-B-C model?
5. What role does the environment play in the S-O-B-C model?

CASE:
CONCEPTUAL MODEL: DREAM OR REALITY?

Hank James has been section head for the accounting group at Yake Company for fourteen years. His boss, Mary Stein, felt that Hank was about ready to be moved up to the corporate finance staff, but it was company policy to send people like Hank to the University Executive Development Program before such a promotion was made. Hank became enrolled in the program and found that one of the first parts dealt with organizational behavior. Hank felt that with fourteen years of managing people, this would be a snap. However, during the lecture on organizational behavior the professor made some comments that really bothered Hank. The professor said,

Most managers know their technical job but do a lousy job of managing their people. One of the problems is that just because supervisors have a lot of experience with people, they think they are experts. The fact is that behavioral scientists are just beginning to scratch the surface of understanding human behavior. In addition, to effectively manage people we also have to somehow be able to better predict and control organizational behavior. There are some models that are just beginning to be developed that will hopefully help the manager better understand, predict, and control organizational behavior.

Hank was upset by the fact that this professor was apparently discounting the value of experience in managing people, and he could not see how a conceptual model that some professor dreamed up could help him manage people better.

1. Do you think Hank is justified in his concerns after hearing the professor? What role can experience play in managing people?
2. What is the purpose of a conceptual model such as the one presented in this chapter? How would you weigh the relative value of studying theories and research findings versus "school of hard knocks" experience for the effective management of people?
3. Using the S-O-B-C model presented in the chapter, how would you explain to Hank that this could help him better manage people in his organization?

CASE:
ANALYZING CLOWN BEHAVIOR

Ralph Baker was the company clown. He spent most of the day pulling practical jokes on co-workers and telling jokes and tall tales to anyone who would listen. His tall tales were becoming more unbelievable each day. Nobody took Ralph seriously, but most did admit that he kept them entertained and thought he was the funniest story teller in the whole office. While he did lighten up the day, many fellow workers felt that Ralph was not doing his share of the work. A few others were just tired of the sometimes inconsiderate practical jokes and stupid tall tales. For example, one day he hid the key to the file cabinet and told everyone that the boss had requested a certain file on the double. While you, as his immediate supervisor, think he is funny, you also know that you have to do something about Ralph's behavior.

1. How would you handle this problem employee?
2. Using the various frameworks for human behavior, how would you explain Ralph's behavior?
3. Plug this situation into the S-O-B-C model. Give examples from this incident for each of the variables in the model.
4. Is there any way that you could predict and/or control Ralph's behavior?

CASE:
A DUAL PROBLEM

At the Chemar Manufacturing Corporation everything seemed to be changing at a faster rate than ever before. At least, that is the way it seemed to Wes Dupree, one of the firm's managers. First Arnold Chemar, president and founder of the corporation, suffered a heart attack. That threw things into a turmoil for several months, since the president had almost run the corporation out of his hip pocket. Then, a few weeks after the founder returned to work, he suffered another major attack. The doctors told Mr. Chemar that he would have to retire. Any further strain brought on by the relentless pressures of work could prove fatal.

Grudgingly, the president agreed to step aside. In his place he appointed his son Randall. Randy, thirty-five, has been with the company for almost fifteen years. During his college years he worked for the firm during the summer months; upon graduation he took a full-time job with the company. Over the last thirteen years the elder Chemar had trained his son in some of the important managerial aspects of running a corporation. Randy had worked in every division in the company and was regarded as bright and quick to learn. Wes Dupree thought that the young man might do well in filling his father's shoes, although Wes admitted to himself that he wished Randy had had time for just a few more year's experience before assuming the helm.

One of the biggest problems facing Randy was a decision on the strategy the firm should follow in meeting competitive threats. It seems that over the last eighteen months three of Chemar's largest competitors had invested millions of dollars in the hope of obtaining a major technological breakthrough in a particular production process. If these firms succeeded, it could mean the loss of approximately 30 percent of Chemar's market share. On the other hand, if the corporation voted research and development funds to such a project, in the hope of keeping up with the competition, and the research proved to be a blind alley for everyone, Chemar would be in a weaker strategic position than any of them.

Meanwhile, within the corporation itself Wes Dupree and others had noticed a continual decline in work output. Actually the trend had started about three years ago and, at first, it was not very noticeable. Over time, however, production records indicated that there was indeed a gradual but constant decrease in average worker productivity. This development had been the major topic of discussion at the board meeting called just prior to Mr. Chemar's first heart attack. Thus Wes Dupree felt that Randy would have to be concerned with two major developments: one external to the firm, the other within the corporation itself.

At the first board meeting he convened, Randy had both of these topics on the agenda. Before deciding how to proceed on either, Randy recommended that the firm look into the use of consultants. "I'd like to get some outside experts in here to review our operations and give us their ideas on how we can meet both of these threats," he said. This was the first time the company had ever thought about bringing in outside people. Mr. Arnold Chemar had always preferred to handle corporate problems with inside resources. Nevertheless, the board agreed that this might be a good time to get an external point of view and the proposal was unanimously passed.

Two groups of consultants were brought in. The first was technically skilled and was asked to help Chemar deal with the external problem. The second group consisted of experts in organizational behavior. Mr. Dupree noted in examining their credentials that three of them were organizational behavior experts with strong backgrounds in the behavioral sciences. All had over five years of experience in the consulting field.

After a detailed study, the technical consultants recommended that Chemar not respond to the technology threat. Their reasoning was that the competition was playing a long shot and that if it paid off, Chemar could match the development within six months of the time that the other firms announced their breakthrough. Furthermore, the chance of success was small and the investment was far too large for a corporation the size of Chemar. Finally, the consultants noted that other large firms in the industry had not chosen to follow the lead of these three firms that were pumping all of their money into research and development. This was undoubtedly a sign that after examining the situation they felt it simply did not justify a special R and D effort. The board of directors was relieved to hear this news and promised that if someone would attain a major technological breakthrough, they would call the consultants back to advise them on how to proceed in meeting the competitive threat.

Meanwhile, in the case of the declining productivity, the picture was bleak. The behavioral consultants reported that there seemed to be a basic managerial problem in the handling of the work force. They noted in particular that there appeared to be a need for human resource training among the managerial force. This caused a great deal of concern among the board members.

When pressed to defend their conclusions, the consultants pointed out that the managerial staff seemed to have some arguable assumptions about the proper way to handle people. For example, a questionnaire survey filled out by the managers revealed that some of their assumptions about the workers included the following:

1. Most workers are basically lazy. They do not necessarily want to be lazy but what can they do? It's human nature that most people are like this.
2. Of all the things people want from their job, security is the most important.
3. Money is important but it is not the primary motivator.
4. People like boring jobs because they can handle them with little problem, thereby freeing themselves up for socializing with other workers.
5. Happy workers are productive workers.
6. Experience and a basic understanding of human nature will result in effective human resource management.

After reading over the list, most people on the board were confused. "What seems to be wrong with that list?" asked Wes Dupree. "It looks pretty good to me." The consultants admitted that number three was general enough to hold in most situations. However, the other assumptions were either erroneous or incomplete. "What are you trying to tell us?" asked Randy. The head of the consulting group phrased his answer this way: "Look, when you manage people there are many behavioral problems that you face. Some of these can be solved with 'gut feel,' while others require a more systematic approach. If human behavior were a simple process to understand, predict, and control you could take care of all your problems with common sense. However, it's a complex process that requires a very scientific approach. Today we are applying behavioral science concepts to the study of human beings in the work place. And do you know what we are finding? That armchair philosophy and common sense will take you only so far. If you want to know how to manage people effectively you have to learn the same way you learn anything else, with a vigorous logical approach. Most of the assumptions made by managers in the survey are erroneous because they are based on incomplete information or generalizations from a small sample to a large population. Now if you want to improve productivity in this plant you are going to have to train your managers in behavioral areas such as learning, perception, group dynamics, motivation, and leadership. You wouldn't let someone walk out onto the line and, using the knowledge he brings to the job with him, try to run an expensive, sophisticated piece of equipment, would you? Well, what makes you think you can manage an expensive, sophisticated human being with the knowledge the manager brings to the job?"

Randy found this line of reasoning both logical and fruitful. Therefore, he interrupted the consultant and asked him if his group could draw up a recommended program with behavioral objectives and a plan of action. The consultant promised to have this in the president's hands within two weeks.

1. Do you think that most organizations face technical and human problems as found in this firm? Which do you think is relatively more important today, the technical or the human element? Why?
2. Going through the list of assumptions derived from the survey, what possible errors are there in each assumption listed?
3. How can the study of organizational behavior help managers such as these do a better job? Explain.
4. What types of objectives and action plans would you expect the consultants to come up with? Be as specific as possible in your answer.

EXERCISE:

SYNTHESIS OF STUDENT AND IN-STRUCTOR NEEDS

Goals:

1. To "break the ice" in using experiential exercises
2. To initiate open communication between students and instructor regarding mutual learning goals and needs
3. To stimulate students to clarify their learning goals and instructional needs and to commit themselves to these
4. To serve as the first exercise in the "experiential" approach to management education

Implementation:

1. The class is divided into groups of four to six students each.
2. Each group openly discusses what members would like from the course and drafts a set of learning objectives and instructional aims. The group also makes up a list of learning/course objectives which they feel the instructor wants to pursue. (About twenty minutes.)
3. After each group has "caucused," a group spokesperson is appointed to meet with the instructor in an open dialogue in front of the class about course objectives.
4. The instructor meets with each group representative at the front of the classroom to initiate an open dialogue about the semester of learning. (About thirty minutes.) Several activities are carried out:
   a. Open discussion of the learning objectives of both students and instructor
   b. Recognition of the constraints faced by each party in accommodating these goals
   c. Identification of areas of goal agreement and disagreement, and feasible compromises
   d. Drafting a set of guidelines for cooperation between parties, designed to better bring about mutual goal attainment

EXERCISE:

WORK-RELATED ORGANIZA-TIONAL BEHAVIOR: IMPLICATIONS FOR THE COURSE

Goals:

1. To identify course topic areas from the participant's own work experience
2. To introduce experiential learning

Implementation:

Task 1: Each class member does the following:

1. Describes an experience in a past work situation that illustrates something about organizational behavior. (Some students have had only part-time work experience or summer jobs, but even the humblest job is relevant here.)
2. Explains what it illustrates about organizational behavior. (Time: Five minutes for individuals to think about and jot down notes covering these two points.)

Task 2: The class forms into triads and each triad does the following:

1. Member A tells his or her experience to B. Member B listens carefully and

paraphrases the story back to A and tells what it illustrates about organizational behavior. Member B must do this to A's satisfaction that B has understood fully what A was trying to communicate. Member C is the observer and remains silent during the process.

2. Member B tells his or her story to Member C, and A is the observer.
3. Member C tells his or her story to A, and B is the observer. (Time: Each member has about five minutes to tell his or her story and have it paraphrased back by the listener. The instructor will call out the time at the end of each five-minute interval for equal apportionment of "air time" among participants. Total time: fifteen minutes.)

Task 3:

Each triad selects one of its members to relate his or her incident to the class. The instructor briefly analyzes for the class how the related story fits in with some topic to be studied in the course, such as perception, motivation, communication, conflict, or leadership. The topic areas are listed in the table of contents of this book.

A MICRO PERSPECTIVE OF ORGANIZATIONAL BEHAVIOR: COGNITIVE PROCESSES AND PERSONALITY

PERCEPTION

IMPROVED PERCEPTION THROUGH DEEP SENSING*

John J. Byrne, chairman and chief executive officer of Government Employees Insurance Company, makes it a point to sit down with groups of fifteen or so of his employees representing differing levels of the company to conduct in-depth but informal discussion sessions. He feels that this arrangement leads to a clearer perception of exactly what is going on in the company. Mr. Byrne's approach is being used by an increasing number of organizations today and has been labeled *deep sensing.* This type of informal get together with employees at all levels gives top management officials a chance to interact with employees they would not normally meet. The goal is to build a greater understanding of the problems at all organizational levels and to foster upward communication. Organizations that have adopted deep sensing have found it very beneficial. Kaiser, Leeds and Northrup, Minnesota Power and Light, Lockheed, and General Electric, just to name a few, have found in it one means to build a better climate in the organization and to increase awareness and understanding at all organizational levels. Walter Heidt, director of manufacturing at Lockheed, indicated that this form of communication is one of the most powerful tools available to top management. Without good communications, perceptions can easily be distorted in organizations. Deep sensing seems to be one way to prevent this.

---

*Adapted from "Deep Sensing: A Pipeline to Employee Morale," *Business Week,* Jan. 29, 1979, pp. 124–128.

The last chapter indicated that cognitions are basically bits of information and the cognitive process involves the ways in which people process that information. In other words, the cognitive processes suggest that, like computers, humans are information processors. However, today's complex computers are very simple information-processing units when compared to *human information processing*. People's individual differences and uniquenesses are largely the result of the cognitive processes.

The S-O-B-C model presented in the last chapter indicates that the cognitive processes play an important mediational role (O) between the stimulus situation (S) and the behavior (B). Although there are a number of cognitive processes (imagination, perception, and even thinking) it is generally recognized that the perceptual process is most representative of the cognitive process that takes place between the situation and the behavior. The study of perception makes an important contribution to a better understanding of organizational behavior. For example, the observation that a department head may behave quite differently from her subordinate to the same top management directive can be better understood and explained by the perceptual process. In fact, some management writers give perception the major role in organizational behavior. They feel that behavior is largely a product of the way people perceive themselves and their world around them at any given moment.[1]

In this book, perception is but one variable to be considered in understanding organizational behavior. The environment (both antecedent and consequent) plus the other psychological processes (learning and motivation) and personality are also important. However, for the most part, although much of the material on perception is basic knowledge in the behavioral sciences, it has largely been overlooked or not translated for use by the organizational behavior field. All topics covered in this chapter are concerned with understanding organizational behavior and have many direct applications to organization and management practice.

The first major section presents a theoretical discussion of the general nature and significance of the perceptual process. The relationship between sensation and perception is clarified and some of the important perceptual subprocesses are discussed. The second section covers the various aspects of perceptual selectivity. Both external factors (intensity, size, contrast, repetition, motion, novelty, and familiarity) and internal ones (motivation, personality, and learning) are included. The third section discusses the role that the perceptual set plays in the workplace and presents the results and analysis of a specific perceptual study in industry. The next section is concerned with perceptual organization. The principles of figure-ground, grouping, constancy, and context are given primary emphasis. The last section focuses on social perception—the phenomena of attribution, stereotypes, and the halo effect.

---

[1]Anthony G. Athos and Robert E. Coffey, *Behavior in Organizations*, 2d ed., Prentice-Hall, Englewood Cliffs, N.J., 1975, p. 149.

THE NATURE AND IMPORTANCE OF PERCEPTION

Perception is a primary cognitive process. In terms of the S-O-B-C model presented in Chapter 3, perception is the cognitive process which involves the O selecting, organizing, and interpreting the S. The key to understanding perception is to recognize that it is a unique *interpretation* of the situation, not an exact *recording* of the situation. Stated more eloquently:

The cognitive map of the individual is not, then, a photographic representation of the physical world; it is, rather, a partial, personal construction in which certain objects, selected out by the individual for a major role, are perceived in an individual manner. Every perceiver is, as it were, to some degree a nonrepresentational artist, painting a picture of the world that expresses his individual view of reality.[2]

In short, perception is a very complex cognitive process that yields a unique picture of the world that may be quite different from reality.

Recognition of the difference between the perceptual world and the real world is vital to the understanding of organizational behavior. Harold Leavitt notes that "if one's concern as a supervisor or counselor or committee member is to try to effect some change in the behavior of other people, and if in turn people's present behavior is determined largely by their perceptions of their environments, then it is critical that one seek to understand their perceptions if one is to understand the circumstances under which their behavior might change."[3] He cites the example of the universal assumption made by managers that subordinates always want promotions when, in fact, many subordinates really feel psychologically *forced* to accept a promotion. Managers seldom attempt to find out, and sometimes subordinates themselves do not know, whether the promotion should be offered. In other words, the perceptual world of the manager is quite different from the perceptual world of the subordinate, and both may be very different from reality. If this is the case, what can be done about it from a management standpoint? The best answer seems to be that better understanding of the concepts involved should be developed. Direct applications and techniques should logically follow complete understanding. The rest of the chapter is devoted to providing a better understanding of the cognitive process of perception.

SENSATION VERSUS PERCEPTION

There is usually a great deal of misunderstanding about the relationship between sensation and perception. Berelson and Steiner make the following

---

[2]David Krech, Richard S. Crutchfield, and Egerton L. Ballachey, *Individual in Society*, McGraw-Hill, New York, 1962, p. 20.

[3]Harold J. Leavitt, *Managerial Psychology*, The University of Chicago Press, Phoenix Books, Chicago, 1958, p. 355.

profound statement: "(1) All knowledge of the world depends on the senses and their stimulation, but (2) the facts of raw sensory data are insufficient to produce or to explain the coherent picture of the world as experienced by the normal adult."[4] If this is true, then the study of perception should clarify the relationship between perception and sensation.

The senses

Psychologists are not in full agreement as to the differences and similarities between sensation and perception. The physical senses are considered to be vision, hearing, touch, smell, and taste. There are many other so-called sixth senses. However, none of these sixth senses is fully accepted. The five senses are constantly bombarded by numerous stimuli that are both outside and inside the human body. Examples of outside stimuli include light waves, sound waves, mechanical energy of pressure, and chemical energy from objects that smell and taste. Inside stimuli include energy generated by muscles, food passing through the digestive system, and glands secreting behavior-influencing hormones. These examples indicate that sensation deals chiefly with very elementary behavior that is largely determined by physiological functioning. In this way, the human being uses the senses to experience color, brightness, shape, loudness, pitch, heat, cold, odor, and taste.

Definition of perception

Perception is much more complex and much broader than sensation. The perceptual process involves a complicated interaction of selection, organization, and interpretation. Although perception largely depends upon the senses for raw data, the cognitive process may filter, modify, or completely change these data. A simple illustration may be seen by looking at one side of a stationary object, e.g., a statue or a tree. By slowly turning the eyes to the other side of the object, the person probably *senses* that the object is moving. Yet, the person *perceives* the object as stationary. The perceptual process overcomes the sensual process and the person "sees" the object as stationary. In other words, the perceptual process adds to, and subtracts from, the "real" sensory world. The following are some organizational examples which point out the difference between sensation and perception:

1. The purchasing agent buys a part that she thinks is best, not the part that the engineer says is the best.
2. A subordinate's answer to a question is based on what he heard the boss say, not on what the boss actually said.
3. The same worker may be viewed by one supervisor as a very good worker and by another supervisor as a very poor worker.
4. The same widget may be viewed by the inspector to be of high quality and by a customer to be of low quality.

---

[4]Bernard Berelson and Gary A. Steiner, *Human Behavior*, Harcourt, Brace & World, New York, 1964, p. 87.

5. The male chief executive officer of a large firm feels that women have an equal opportunity for advancement into top management, but the female assistant personnel manager feels there is no way she can break into top management's "good old boy" network.

6. The head engineer who tours the factory floor once a week in an electric cart feels this is a pleasant place to work, but a punch press operator thinks this place ranks right next to the state prison.

These are only representative of the thousands of everyday examples where perception plays a crucial part in organizational life.

Subprocesses in perception

The existence of several subprocesses gives evidence of the complexity and interactive nature of perception.[5] Figure 4-1 shows how these subprocesses relate to one another. The first important subprocess is the *stimulus* or *situation* that is present. Perception begins when a person is confronted with a stimulus or a situation. This confrontation may be with the immediate sensual stimulation or with the total physical and sociocultural environment. An example is the employee who is confronted with his supervisor or with the total formal organizational environment. Either one or both may initiate the workings of his perceptual process. In other words, this represents the S $\longleftrightarrow$ O in the model of Chapter 3.

In addition to the S $\longleftrightarrow$ O interaction are the internal cognitive processes of *registration, interpretation,* and *feedback.* During the registration phenomenon the physiological (sensory and neural) mechanisms are affected; the physiological ability to hear and see will affect perception. Interpretation is the most significant cognitive aspect of perception. The other psychological processes will affect the interpretation of a situation. For example, in an organization, employees' interpretations of a situation are largely dependent upon their learning and motivation and their personality. The fourth subprocess is feedback. Kimble and Garmezy explain that "most perceptual acts produce stimuli that are of value in interpreting the perceptual event."[6] An example would be the kinesthetic feedback (sensory impressions from muscles) that helps assembly line workers perceive the speed of materials moving by them on the line. An example of psychological feedback that may influence an employee's perception is the supervisor's raised eyebrow or a change in voice inflection. The behavioral termination of perception is the reaction or behavior, either overt or covert, which is necessary if perception is to be considered a behavioral event and thus an important part of organizational behavior. As a result of perception, an employee may move rapidly or slowly (overt behavior) or develop an attitude (covert behavior).

As shown in Figure 4-1, all of these perceptual subprocesses are compatible with the S-O-B-C model presented in Chapter 3. The stimulus or

---

[5]See Gregory A. Kimble and Norman Garmezy, *Principles of General Psychology,* 2d ed., Ronald, New York, 1963, p. 314.

[6]Ibid.

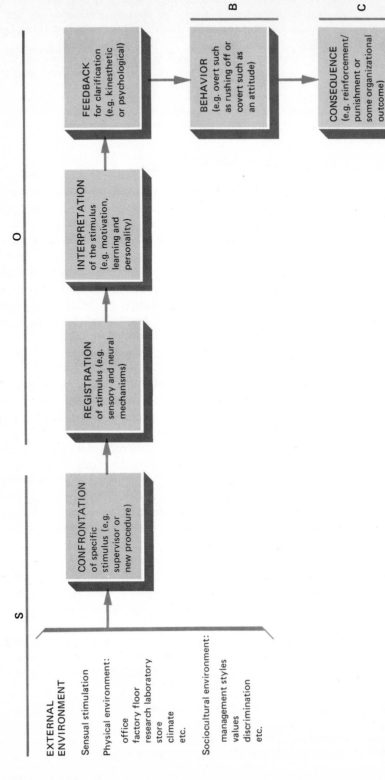

**Figure 4-1
The subprocesses of perception.**

environmental situation is part of the S; registration, interpretation, and feedback occur within the complex O; the resulting behavior is the B; and the consequences of this behavior make up the C. The subprocesses of registration, interpretation, and feedback are internal cognitive processes that are unobservable, but the situation, behavior, and consequence indicate that perception is indeed a behavioral process. Perceptual selectivity and organization, which are next discussed, play a key role in the internal cognitive aspects of perception.

PERCEPTUAL SELECTIVITY

There are numerous stimuli constantly confronting everyone all the time. At this very moment, the noise of the air conditioner or furnace, the sound of other people talking and moving, and outside noises from cars, planes, or street repair work are a few of the stimuli aimed at the hearing sense alone. There are literally hundreds of other stimuli affecting the other senses, plus the impact of the total environmental situation. With all this stimulation impinging upon people, how and why do they select out only a very few stimuli at a given time? Part of the answer can be found in the principles of perceptual selectivity.

External attention factors

Various external and internal attention factors affect perceptual selectivity. The external factors consist of outside environmental influences such as intensity, size, contrast, repetition, motion, and novelty and familiarity.

Intensity The intensity principle of attention states that the more intense the external stimulus, the more likely it is to be perceived. A loud noise, strong odor, or bright light will be noticed more than a soft sound, weak odor, or dim light. Advertisers use intensity to gain the consumer's attention. Examples include bright packaging and TV commercials that are slightly louder than the regular program. Supervisors may yell at their subordinates to gain attention. This last example also shows that other, more complex psychological variables may overcome the simple external variable. By speaking loudly, the supervisor may actually be turning the subordinates off instead of gaining their attention. These types of complications enter into all aspects of the perceptual process. As with the other psychological concepts, a given perceptual principle cannot stand alone in explaining complex human behavior. The intensity principle is only one small factor in the perceptual process, which is only a part of the cognitive processes, which are only a part of what goes into human behavior. Yet, for convenience of presentation and for the development of basic understanding, these small parts can be effectively isolated for study and analysis.

Size Closely related to intensity is the principle of size. It says that the larger the object, the more likely it will be perceived. The largest machine "sticks out" when personnel view a factory floor. The maintenance engineering staff may pay more attention to a big machine than to a smaller one, even though the smaller one costs as much and is as important to the operation. A 6-foot 4-inch, 250-pound supervisor may receive more attention from his subordinates than a 5-foot 10-inch, 160-pound supervisor. In advertising, a full-page spread is more attention-getting than a few lines in the classified section.

Contrast The contrast principle states that external stimuli which stand out against the background or which are not what people are expecting will receive their attention. Figure 4-2 demonstrates this perceptual principle. The black circle on the right appears much larger than the one on the left because of the contrast with the background circles. Both black circles are actually the same size. In a similar manner, plant safety signs which have black lettering on a yellow background or white lettering on a red background are attention-getting; and when the 6-foot 4-inch, 250-pound supervisor mentioned above is placed next to a 5-foot 4-inch, 130-pound supervisor, the smaller one will probably receive as much notice as the bigger one. A worker with many years' experience hardly notices the deafening noise on the factory floor of a typical manufacturing operation. However, if one or more of the machines should come suddenly to a halt, the person would immediately notice the silence.

The contrast principle can be demonstrated by the experience of some companies with training hard-core unemployed workers. In designing hard-core training programs, some firms have found that they have more success when they conduct the initial sessions in the unemployable person's own environment. The familiar location relieves some of the tension and creates a more favorable learning atmosphere. However, at some point the unemployable person must make the transition to the organization environment. A regular, quiet classroom in the organization does not seem to be

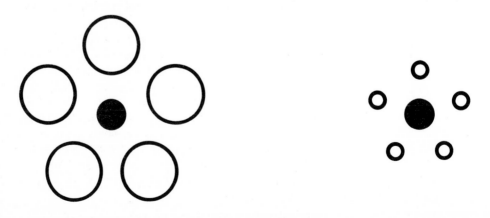

**Figure 4-2
The contrast principle of perception: Which black circle is larger?**

enough. One company learned that when the entire training of the hard-core trainees was conducted in a clean, quiet factory classroom, their subsequent performance was very poor. Fortunately, the company did not jump to the conclusion that the workers were "no good" or untrainable. Instead, through rational behavioral analysis, the company discovered that the poor performance was due to the extremely loud noises that occurred on the assembly line. The workers were not accustomed to the noise because their training had taken place under nice, clean, and quiet conditions. When placed on the noisy factory floor, the contrasting din drew all their attention and adversely affected their performance. To solve this problem, the company conducted the training sessions right next to the noisy factory floor. By the end of the training sessions, the workers were used to the noise and they performed very well when subsequently placed on the job.

Repetition   The repetition principle states that a repeated external stimulus is more attention-getting than a single one. The explanation is that "a stimulus that is repeated has a better chance of catching us during one of the periods when our attention to a task is waning. In addition, repetition increases our sensitivity or alertness to the stimulus."[7] Thus, a worker will generally "hear" better when directions for a dull task are given more than once. This principle partially explains why supervisors have to give directions over and over again for even the simplest of tasks. Workers' attention for a boring task may be waning and the only way they hear directions for the task is when the supervisors repeat themselves several times. Advertisers trying to create a unique image for a product which is undifferentiated from its competitors—such as aspirin, soap, and deodorant—rely heavily on repetitious advertising.

Motion   The motion principle says that people will pay more attention to moving objects in their field of vision than they will to stationary objects. Workers will notice materials moving by them on a conveyor belt but they may fail to give proper attention to the maintenance needs of the stationary machine next to them. In addition, the assembly line workers may devote their entire attention to the line of slowly moving materials they are working on and fail to notice the relatively nice working conditions (pastel-colored walls, music, and air conditioning). Advertisers capitalize on this principle by creating signs which incorporate moving parts. Las Vegas at night is an example of advertisement in motion.

Novelty and familiarity   The novelty and familiarity principle states that either a novel or a familiar external situation can serve as an attention getter. New objects or events in a familiar setting or familiar objects or events in a new setting will draw the attention of the perceiver. Job rotation is an example of this principle. Changing workers' jobs from time to time will tend to increase the attention they give to the task. Being a polisher one week

---

[7]Clifford T. Morgan and Richard A. King, *Introduction to Psychology*, 3d ed., McGraw-Hill, New York, 1966, p. 343.

and a painter the next week may not motivate workers, but it will increase their attention until they become accustomed to the new job. The same is true for the previously mentioned hard-core unemployed newly trained for their first job assignments. The work environment is a completely novel experience for them. If supervisors use familiar street jargon in communicating with the employees, they may receive more attention from them. However, once again, this approach could backfire unless properly handled.

Internal set factors

The concept of *set* is an important cognition in selectivity. It can be thought of as an internal form of attention getting and is largely based on the individual's complex psychological makeup. People will select out stimuli or situations from the environment that appeal to and are compatible with their learning and motivation and with their personality. Although these aspects are given specific attention in the next six chapters, a very brief discussion here will help in the understanding of perception.

Learning and perception Although interrelated with motivation and personality, learning may play the single biggest role in developing perceptual set. Read the phrase in the triangle below.

It may take several seconds to realize there is something wrong. Because of familiarity with the phrase from prior learning, the person is perceptually set to read "Turn off the engine." This illustration shows that learning affects set by creating an *expectancy* to perceive in a certain manner. As pointed out in Chapter 3, such expectancies are a vital element in the cognitive explanations of behavior. This view states simply that people see and hear what they expect to see and hear. This can be further demonstrated by pronouncing the following words very slowly:

M-A-C-T-A-V-I-S-H
M-A-C-D-O-N-A-L-D
M-A-C-B-E-T-H
M-A-C-H-I-N-E-R-Y

If the last word was pronounced "Mac-Hinery" instead of the more conventional "machinery," the reader was caught in a verbal response set.

There are many other illustrations that are commonly used to demonstrate the impact of learning on the development of perceptual set. Figure 4-3 is found in many introductory psychology textbooks. What is perceived in this picture? If one sees an attractive, apparently wealthy young woman, the perceiver is in agreement with about 60 percent of the people who see the

Figure 4-3
Ambiguous picture of a young woman and an old woman. (*Source:* Edwin G. Boring, "A New Ambiguous Figure," *American Journal of Psychology*, July 1930, p. 444. Also see Robert Leeper, "A Study of a Neglected Portion of the Field of Learning—The Development of Sensory Organization," *Journal of Genetic Psychology*, March 1935, p. 62. Originally drawn by cartoonist W. E. Hill and published in *Puck*, Nov. 6, 1915.)

picture for the first time. On the other hand, if an ugly, poor old woman is seen, the viewer is in agreement with about 40 percent of first viewers. Obviously, two completely distinct women can be perceived in Figure 4-3. Which woman is seen supposedly depends on whether the person is set to perceive young, beautiful women or old, ugly women. How did you come out?

How Figure 4-3 is perceived can be radically influenced by a simple learned experience. When first shown a clear, unambiguous picture of a beautiful young woman (Figure 4-4) and then shown Figure 4-3, the person will almost always report seeing the young woman in Figure 4-3. If the clear picture of the old woman is seen first (Figure 4-4) the viewer will subsequently report seeing the old woman in Figure 4-3.

In addition to the young woman–old woman example, there is a wide

Figure 4-4
Clear picture of the young and old woman. (*Source:* Robert Leeper, "A Study of a Neglected Portion of the Field of Learning—The Development of Sensory Organization," *Journal of Genetic Psychology*, March 1935, p. 62.)

Old woman

Young woman

variety of commonly used illusions that effectively demonstrate the impact of learned set on perception. An illusion may be thought of as a form of perception that badly distorts reality. Figures 4-5 and 4-6 show some of the most frequently used forms of perceptual illusion. The two three-pronged objects in Figure 4-5 are drawn contrary to common perceptions of such objects. In (a) of Figure 4-6, the length of the nose (from the tip to the X) is exactly equal to the vertical length of the face. In (b), the height of the hat is exactly equal to the width of the brim. Both shapes in (c) are exactly the same size, and in (d), the lines AX, CX, CB, and XD are of equal length.

Figure 4-7 brings out the role that learned set plays in perception even more strongly than Figure 4-6. The three men in Figure 4-7 are drawn exactly equal in height. Yet the men are perceived as of different heights because the viewer has learned that the cues found in the picture normally imply depth and distance. A lot of what the human "sees" in the world is a result of past experience and learning. Even though the past experience may not be relevant to the present situation, it is nevertheless used by the perceiver.

Perceptual set in the workplace

Perceptual set has many direct implications for organizational behavior. In organizational life, some employees have learned to perceive the world around them in the same way. For example, the single sentence "I cannot recommend this young man too highly" was reproduced and distributed to several managers in the same organization. Although this statement is ambiguous and unclear, without exception all the managers interpreted this to be a positive recommendation.[8] They had all learned to perceive this statement the same way—positive and favorable. In most cases, however, learning leads to extreme individual differences. For example, the young woman–old woman illustration demonstrates that the same stimulus may be perceived two completely different ways (young and beautiful or old and ugly) because of the way the individual is set to perceive. Numerous instances of this situation occur in a modern organization. Participants may perceive the same stimulus or situation in entirely different ways. A specific organizational example might be a poor output record in the production

---

[8]John Swanda, *Organizational Behavior*, Alfred, Sherman Oaks, Calif., 1979, p. 91.

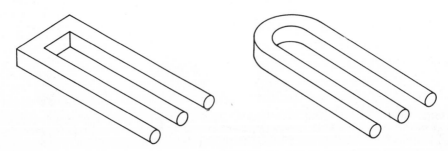

Figure 4-5
Common illusions.

department of a manufacturing plant. The engineer perceives the solution to this problem as one of improved machine design. The personnel manager perceives the solution as one of more training and better wage incentives. The department head perceives the solution to be more effective organizing, planning, and controlling. On the other hand, the workers may perceive the low output with pleasure because it is a way of "getting back" at their supervisor, whom they dislike. For the purpose of this discussion, it is not important who is right or wrong in this example; rather, the point is that all the relevant personnel perceive the *same* situation in completely *different* ways.

Another common example is the differences in perception that occur between the union and management. Stagner and Rosen believe that perceptual differences are a major explanation for industrial disputes. The same "facts" in a dispute are perceived quite differently by union members and by management.

Thus, to a union steward, the "fact" may be that a change in machine layout has created a safety hazard, whereas the foreman may deny that the safety hazard is a fact. Differences in job duties, calling for a pay increase, may seem obvious to workers, but the plant manager may honestly deny that any differences exist; and, for him, they do not exist.[9]

---

[9]Ross Stagner and Hjalmar Rosen, *Psychology of Union Management Relations*, Wadsworth, Belmont, Calif., 1965, p. 19.

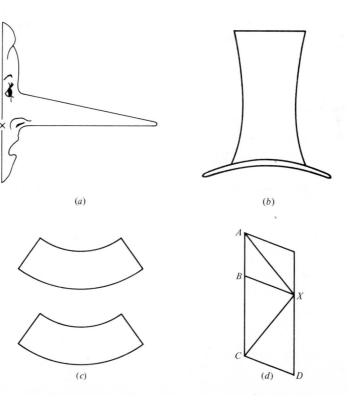

Figure 4-6 Common perceptual illusions. (These illusions are found in almost all introductory psychology textbooks. For example, see Gregory A. Kimble and Norman Garmezy, *General Psychology*, 2d ed., Ronald, New York, 1963, pp. 324–325. The face is from N. L. Munn and E. P. Johnson, *Student's Manual to Accompany Psychology*, 2d ed., Houghton Mifflin, Boston, 1951.)

(a)

(b)

(c)

(d)

A perceptual study in industry   Among the many instances of differences in perception in organization life, of particular relevance in recent years has been the black worker who comes from a different cultural and often disadvantaged educational background. This person is perceived in many completely different ways. One supervisor or white coworker may perceive a disadvantaged black worker as a no-good, defiant troublemaker who does not deserve a break. At the same time, another supervisor or white coworker may perceive the same black person as a decent human being who has been discriminated against and educationally deprived and is deserving of a break.

Using the facts regarding differing perceptions as a starting point, a survey was conducted to gather information through which to analyze how black workers are perceived by their managers.[10] The major finding of the study was that black workers currently on the job were generally perceived by their managers to be relatively good workers. This finding has interesting implications. If black workers are perceived as good workers, what is the problem? Why is the unemployment rate so much higher for blacks than for whites? Why are most blacks generally relegated to lower-level jobs? The answers to these complex questions may lie in how the word *qualification* is perceived.

What is the meaning of *qualification*? How is it perceived by white managers? How is it perceived by blacks? Although difficult to define operationally, "qualification" usually means an accepted quality, accom-

---

[10]Fred Luthans, "Training for Qualification: The Black Worker's Dilemma," *Training and Development Journal,* October 1968, pp. 3–7.

**Figure 4-7
The role that
learning plays in
perception.**

plishment, or level of standard which permits a person to perform accepta-
bly in a job. This elusive concept has been shown to be the single most
important concern of the entire business community when analyzing the
employment of blacks. For example, in an extensive American Management
Association study, it was found that in almost every survey response in
which the executive discussed the question of the employment of blacks, the
word "qualified" appeared as some part of the statement.[11] If managers
perceive the performance of their presently employed black workers
favorably, why are they so "hung up" on the black person's qualifications?
Has the staffing process found, chosen, and placed all so-called qualified
blacks? Or, as many blacks think, has "qualification" taken on the same
meaning as "law and order"? Both *qualification* and *law and order* are
righteous terms, but as far as many in the black community are concerned,
there are negative hidden meanings. For example, one interview study found
that black businessmen responded that *qualification* really meant "white,"
"establishment," "educated," and "ripoff."[12]

One purpose of the survey study was to attempt to determine how
managers really do perceive employee qualifications. The managers were
asked, in an open-ended question, to specify the two major factors holding
back the employment of blacks. Thus, the managers could express in their
own words what they meant by "qualification." The following shows the
three most frequently cited problems and summarizes the typical comments
regarding them.[13]

1. **Training (58 responses).** "It is much better to hire a skilled or trained person who
   is qualified for the job rather than to hire a black who is untrained. The biggest
   problem for blacks is lack of training."
2. **Education (44 responses).** "Those employers who try to hire black employees are
   faced with the very real problem of finding sufficiently qualified candidates. This
   is a problem of education. School counselors could put a greater effort into helping
   to keep black students in school at least through high school levels, and possibly
   help with expenses if the student would want additional education."
3. **Motivation and desire (40 responses).** "I have found that most black workers have
   plenty of ability, but my experience has shown these workers have a decided lack
   of desire."

Forty-four additional responses indicated that there were too few qualified
applicants but failed to give a particular reason for this situation. Lack of
dependability was mentioned by 17 managers, absenteeism and turnover by
9, and transportation difficulties by 6.

The conclusion from this study is that respondents seem to perceive
qualification to mean appropriate training, education, and motivation. It is
interesting to note that no one answered that prejudice or color of skin was
holding back the employment opportunities of blacks. The managers did not

[11]Jack G. Gourlay, "The Black Salaried Worker," *AMA Research Study 70*, American Management Association, New York, 1965, p. 12.

[12]Thomas A. DeCoster, John R. Swanda, Jr., and John P. Shilha, "Black Capitalism: Insights into
Interviewing," *Indiana Business Review*, January–February 1971, pp. 23–26.

[13]Luthans, op. cit., p. 5.

perceive, or at least were not willing to admit in a confidential questionnaire, that, for many blacks, "qualification" means being white, well educated, and highly skilled.

There are many obvious limitations to a study of this kind, but one in particular is that it assumes that all black workers make up a single entity. In truth, of course, each black employee is just as unique an individual as is each employee of any other color. Yet, in reality, this blanket perception does exist for members of minority races and to a large extent for women as well. Managers tend to discuss and perceive minority race members and women en masse instead of as a group of distinct, unique individuals whose skin happens to be a nonwhite color in the case of minority race members or whose gender happens to be female in the case of women employees. Hopefully, this blanket perception is disappearing. One way of accomplishing this is to recognize pluralistic values, styles, and standards in a truly nondiscriminatory, multicultural organizational environment.[14] As the upcoming generations, who will have different perceptual sets, replace the older generations, perhaps such an organizational environment can become a reality and the participants will have learned to have a new nondiscriminatory perception of others.

Motivation and perception   Besides the learned aspects of perceptual set, motivation also has a vital impact on perceptual selectivity. The primary motives of sex and hunger could be used to demonstrate the role that motivation plays in perception.

In traditional American culture, the sex drive has been largely suppressed, with the result being an unfulfilled need for sex. Accordingly, any mention of sex or a visual stimulus dealing with sex is very attention-getting to the average American. The picture of a scantily clad or naked female is readily perceived by the American male. On the other hand, as nudity becomes increasingly commonplace in magazines, motion pictures, live entertainment, and fashions, the female anatomy slowly begins to lose its appeal as an attention getter. In a culture where the female breasts are always exposed, such a sight draws no attention from the males of that culture. Analogously, however, if there is a great need for food in the culture, the mention, sight, or smell of food is given a great deal of attention.

The secondary motives also play an important role in developing perceptual set. A person who has a relatively high need for power, affiliation, or achievement will be more attentive to the relevant situational variables. An example is the worker who has a strong need for affiliation. When such a worker walks into the lunchroom, the table where several coworkers are sitting tends to be perceived and the empty table or the one where a single person is sitting tends to get no attention. Although very simple, the lunchroom example points out that perception may have an important impact on motivation as well as vice versa. This demonstrates once again the interrelatedness of these concepts.

---

[14]George Neely and Fred Luthans, "Using Survey Feedback to Achieve Enlightened AA/EEO," *Personnel*, October 1978, p. 19.

Another example is the role of motivation in the perception of the members of a top-management committee. One committee member may be self-oriented and perceive the problem being discussed as personally threatening. Another member may be interaction-oriented and perceive the same problem in terms of whether it is discussed in a relaxed, friendly way; the content is not important. A third member of the committee may be task-oriented and solely concerned with the content of the problem and bringing it to an immediate solution.[15] Chapter 6 will give detailed attention to the process of motivation, some of which is directly related to perception.

Personality and perception   Closely related to learning and motivation is the personality of the perceiving person, which affects what is attended to in the confronting situation. Leavitt reported on a senior executive whose biggest problem with young managers was their tendency to avoid making small, unpleasant decisions. The young managers did not pay attention to disciplining people, to digging through boring and repetitive records, or to writing unpleasant letters.[16] These annoying or boring tasks were not compatible with the personalities of the young managers. The tedious tasks were given attention by the older executive because his personality makeup had "hardened" over the years.

The growing generation gap recognized in recent years definitely contributes to differing perceptions. An example can be found in the perceptions of modern movies. Older people tend either to be disgusted or not to understand some of the popular movies of recent years, such as *Saturday Night Fever*. Those in the thirty-five to forty-five age group tend to perceive these movies as kind of "naughty but neat." The young, college-age people tend to perceive this type of movie as "where it's at." They tend to get neither "uptight" nor titillated over a movie like *Saturday Night Fever*. Of course, there are individual differences in all age categories, and the above example tends to stereotype (this is discussed later in the chapter) people by age. Yet it does show how personalities, values, and even age may affect the way people perceive the world around them.

PERCEPTUAL ORGANIZATION

The discussion of perceptual selectivity was concerned with the external and internal variables that gain an individual's attention. This section focuses on what takes place in the perceptual process once the information from the situation is received. This aspect of perception is commonly referred to as *perceptual organization*. An individual seldom perceives patches of color or light or sound. Instead, the person will perceive

---

[15]Bernard M. Bass and George D. Dunteman, "Behavior in Groups as a Function of Self, Interaction, and Task Orientation," *Journal of Abnormal and Social Psychology*, May 1963, pp. 419–428.

[16]Leavitt, op. cit., p. 31.

organized patterns of stimuli and identifiable whole objects. For example, when a male college student is shown a football, he does not normally perceive it as the color brown or as grain-leather in texture or as the odor of leather. Rather, he perceives a football which has, in addition to the characteristics named, a potential for giving the perceiver fun and excitement as either a participant or a spectator. In other words, the person's perceptual process organizes the incoming information into a meaningful whole.

Figure-ground

Figure-ground is usually considered to be the most basic form of perceptual organization. The figure-ground principle simply means that perceived objects stand out as separable from their general background. It can be effectively demonstrated as one is reading this paragraph. In terms of light-wave stimuli, the reader is receiving patches of irregularly shaped blacks and whites. Yet the reader does not perceive it this way. The reader perceives black shapes—letters, words, and sentences—printed against a white background. To say it another way, the reader perceptually organizes incoming stimuli into recognizable figures (words) that are seen against a ground (white page).

Another interesting figure-ground illustration is shown in Figure 4-8. At first glance, one probably perceives a jumble of black, irregular shapes against a white background. Only when the white letters are perceptually organized against a black background will the words FLY and TIE literally jump out with clarity. This illustration shows that perceptual selectivity will influence perceptual organization. The viewer is set to perceive black on white because of the black words (figures) throughout the book. However, in Figure 4-8 the reverse is true. White is the figure and black is the ground.

Perceptual grouping

The grouping principle of perceptual organization states that there is a tendency to group several stimuli together into a recognizable pattern. This

**Figure 4-8
Illustrations of
figure-ground.
(Sources: (a) Warner Brown and Howard Gilhousen, College Psychology,
Prentice-Hall, Englewood Cliffs,
N.J., 1949, p. 330;
(b) Jerome Kagan
and Ernest Havemann, Psychology:
An Introduction,
Harcourt, Brace &
World, New York,
1968, p. 166.)**

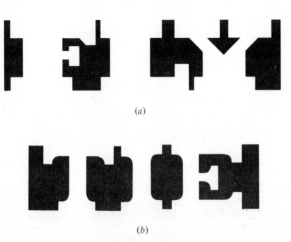

(a)

(b)

principle is very basic and seems to be largely inborn. There are certain underlying uniformities in grouping. When simple constellations of stimuli are presented to people, they will tend to group them together by closure, continuity, proximity, or similarity.

Closure   The closure principle of grouping is closely related to the gestalt school of psychology. A basic gestalt principle is that a person will sometimes perceive a whole when one does not actually exist. The person's perceptual process will close the gaps which are unfilled from sensory input. In the formal organization, participants may either see a whole where none exists or not be able to put the pieces together into a whole that does exist. An example of the first case is the department head who perceived complete agreement among the members of her department on a given project when, in fact, there was opposition from several members. The department head in this situation closed the existing gaps and perceived complete agreement when, in fact, it did not exist. An example of the other side of the coin is the adage of not being able to see the forest (whole) because of the trees (parts). High degrees of specialization have often resulted in functionally oriented managers losing sight of the whole organization's objectives. Specialists may get so caught up in their own little area of interest and responsibility that they lose sight of the overall goal. They cannot close their part together with the other parts to perceive the whole.

Continuity   Continuity is closely related to closure. Some psychologists do not even bother to make a distinction between the two grouping principles. However, there is a slight difference. Closure supplies *missing* stimuli and the continuity principle says that a person will tend to perceive *continuous* lines or patterns. This type of continuity may lead to inflexible, or noncreative, thinking on the part of organizational participants. Only the obvious, continuous patterns or relationships will be perceived. For example, a new design for some productive process or product may be limited to obvious flows or continuous lines. New, innovative ideas or designs may not be perceived. Continuity can greatly influence the systems design of an organizational structure.

Proximity   The principle of proximity or nearness states that a group of stimuli that are close together will be perceived as a whole pattern of parts belonging together. For example, several employees in an organization may be identified as a single group because of physical proximity. Several workers who work on a particular machine may be perceived as a single whole. If the output is low and the supervisor reports a number of grievances from the group, management may perceive all the workers on the machine as one troublemaking group when, in fact, some of the workers are loyal, dedicated employees. Yet, the fact remains that often departmental or work groups are perceived as a single entity because of physical proximity.

Similarity   The principle of similarity states that the greater the similarity of the stimuli, the greater is the tendency to perceive them as a common group. Similarity is conceptually related to proximity but in most

100

A MICRO PERSPECTIVE OF
ORGANIZATIONAL
BEHAVIOR: COGNITIVE
PROCESSES AND
PERSONALITY

cases is stronger than proximity. In an organization, all employees who wear blue (white) collars may be perceived as a common group when, in reality, each blue(white-) collar worker is a unique individual. Similarity also applies to minorities and women as discussed earlier. There is a tendency to perceive minority and women employees as a single group.

Perceptual constancy

Constancy is one of the more sophisticated forms of perceptual organization. It gives a person a sense of stability in a changing world. Constancy permits the individual "to interpret the kaleidoscopic variability of proximal stimuli in such a manner that these same stimuli more or less accurately reflect the constancies of the real world—the stability and unchangeability of objects and people, the consistency of the three-dimensionality of our everyday world."[17] Learning plays a much bigger role in the constancy phenomenon than in figure-ground or grouping phenomena.

The size, shape, color, brightness, and location of an object are fairly constant regardless of the information received by the senses. It has been pointed out that "perceptual constancy does not result from ignoring any particular cue; it results from responding to *patterns* of cues."[18] These patterns of cues are for the most part learned, but each situation is different and there are interactions between the inborn and learned tendencies within the entire perceptual process.

If constancy were not at work, the world would be very chaotic and disorganized for the individual. An organizational example would be the worker who must select a piece of material or a tool of the correct size from a wide variety of materials and tools at varying distances from a work station. Without perceptual constancy, the sizes, shapes, and colors of objects would change as he or she moved about and would make the job almost impossible.

Perceptual context

The highest, most sophisticated form of perceptual organization is context. It gives meaning and value to simple stimuli, objects, events, situations, and other persons in the environment. The principle of context can be simply demonstrated by the well-known doodles shown in Figure 4-9 (answers are found in Footnote 19). The visual stimuli by themselves are meaningless. Only when the doodles are placed in a verbal context do they take on meaning and value to the perceiver.

The macro organizational environment provides the primary context in which workers and managers do their perceiving. Thus, a verbal order, a

---

[17]Merle J. Moskowitz and Arthur R. Orgel, *General Psychology*, Houghton Mifflin, Boston, 1969, p. 168.

[18]Howard H. Kendler, *Basic Psychology*, 2d ed., Appleton-Century-Crofts, New York, 1968, p. 162.

[19]Answers to doodles in Figure 4-9 are (a) the start of a "rat race"; (b) two mice in a beer can; (c) a column of ants marching through spilled whiskey.

memo or new policy, a suggestion, a raised eyebrow, or a pat on the back takes on unique meaning and value when placed in the context of the work organization. Organizational structure (discussed in Chapters 18 and 19) and processes (Chapters 16 and 17) form the major context in which organizational participants perceive.

Perceptual defense

Closely related to context is perceptual defense. A person may build a defense (block or refusal to recognize) against stimuli or situational events in the context that are personally or culturally unacceptable or threatening. Accordingly, perceptual defense may play an influential role in understanding union-management or supervisor-subordinate relationships.

Although there is some conflicting evidence, most studies verify the existence of a perceptual defense mechanism. Two examples are the classic studies by Bruner and Postman,[20] who found barriers to perceiving personally threatening words, and by McGinnies,[21] who discovered identification thresholds for critical, emotionally toned words. In a classic study more directly relevant to organizational behavior, Haire and Grunes describe how people may react with a perceptual defense that is activated in them when they are confronted with a fact inconsistent with a preconceived notion.[22] In this study, college students were presented with the word *intelligent* as a characteristic of a factory worker. This was counter to their perception of

[20]Jerome S. Bruner and Leo Postman, "Emotional Selectivity in Perception and Reaction," *Journal of Personality*, September 1947, pp. 69–77.

[21]Elliott McGinnies, "Emotionality and Perceptual Defense," *Psychological Review*, September 1949, pp. 244–251.

[22]Mason Haire and Willa Freeman Grunes, "Perceptual Defenses: Processes Protecting an Organized Perception of Another Personality," *Human Relations*, vol. 3, no. 4, 1950, pp. 403–412.

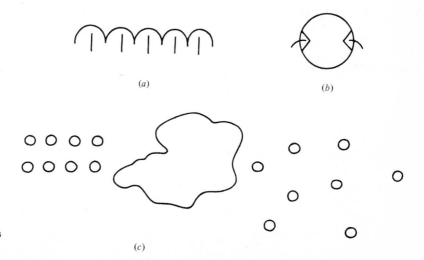

Figure 4-9 Doodles: Illustration of the role that context plays in perception.

102

A MICRO PERSPECTIVE OF
ORGANIZATIONAL
BEHAVIOR: COGNITIVE
PROCESSES AND
PERSONALITY

factory workers, and they built defenses in the following ways:

1. *Denial.* A few of the subjects denied the existence of intelligence in factory workers.
2. *Modification and distortion.* This was one of the most frequent forms of defense. The pattern was to explain away the perceptual conflict by joining intelligence with some other characteristic, e.g., "He is intelligent, but doesn't possess initiative to rise above his group."
3. *Change in perception.* Many of the students changed their perception of the worker because of the intelligence characteristic. The change, however, was usually very subtle, e.g., "cracks jokes," became "witty."
4. *Recognition, but refusal to change.* A very few subjects explicitly recognized the conflict between their perception of the worker and the characteristic of "intelligent" that was confronting them. For example, one subject stated, "The traits seem to be conflicting . . . most factory workers I have heard about aren't too intelligent."[23]

From this study, the general conclusion is that people may learn to avoid perceiving certain conflicting, threatening, or unacceptable aspects of the context.

The above and other relevant experiments have been summarized into three general explanations of perceptual defense:

1. Emotionally disturbing information has a higher threshold for recognition (i.e., we do not perceive it readily) than neutral or nondisturbing information. This is why a chain of events may be seen differently by those who are not personally involved than by those who are involved, so that warning signs of trouble are often not seen by those who will be most affected by the trouble.
2. Disturbing information and stimuli are likely to bring about substitute perceptions which are distorted to prevent recognition of the disturbing elements. In this way the manager can perceive that his workers are happy when actually they are disgruntled. Then when a grievance committee is formed or a strike takes place, he cannot perceive his "happy" workers participating willingly and concludes that it is because they have fallen victim to some agitator and that things in the shop are still basically fine.
3. Emotionally arousing information actually does arouse emotion even though the emotion is distorted and directed elsewhere. Kicking the cat, snarling at the wife and kids, cutting someone off for trying to pass you on the right while driving home, or browbeating an underling all offer a sense of relief and are good substitutes for perceiving that the people "upstairs" think you are an idiot.[24]

Such findings as the above help explain why some people, especially supervisors and subordinates in an organization, have a "blind spot." (They do not "see" or they consistently misinterpret certain events or situations.)

SOCIAL PERCEPTION

Although context and perceptual defense are closely related to social perception, this section gives recognition to social perception per se. The

---

[23]Ibid., pp. 407–411.

[24]David J. Lawless, *Organizational Behavior*, Prentice-Hall, Englewood Cliffs, N.J., 1979, p. 85.

social aspects of perception are given detailed coverage because they play such an important role in organizational behavior. Social perception is directly concerned with how one individual perceives other individuals. Formal organization participants are constantly perceiving one another. Managers are perceiving workers, workers are perceiving managers, line personnel are perceiving staff personnel, staff personnel are perceiving line personnel, superiors are perceiving subordinates, subordinates are perceiving superiors, and on and on. There are numerous complex factors which enter into such social perception, but the primary factors are found in the psychological processes and personality.

Characteristics of perceiver and perceived

A summary of research findings on some specific characteristics of the perceiver and the perceived reveal a profile of the perceiver as follows:

1. Knowing oneself makes it easier to see others accurately.
2. One's own characteristics affect the characteristics one is likely to see in others.
3. People who accept themselves are more likely to be able to see favorable aspects of other people.
4. Accuracy in perceiving others is not a single skill.[25]

These four characteristics greatly influence how a person perceives others in the environmental situation.

There are also certain characteristics of the person being perceived which influence social perception. Research has shown that:

1. The status of the person perceived will greatly influence others' perception of him.
2. The person being perceived is usually placed into categories to simplify the viewer's perceptual activities. Two common categories are status and role.
3. The visible traits of the person perceived will greatly influence the perception of him.[26]

These characteristics of the perceiver and the perceived suggest the extreme complexity of social perception. Organizational participants must realize that their perceptions of others are greatly influenced by characteristics of themselves and characteristics of the other person. For example, if the manager feels good about himself and the other person is physically attractive, pleasant and comes from the home office, then he will likely perceive this other person in a positive, favorable manner. On the other hand, if the manager is down on herself and the other person is an arrogant, unattractive salesman, she will likely perceive this other person in a negative, unfavorable manner. Such attributions that people make of others play a vital role in their social perceptions and resulting behavior.

---

[25]Sheldon S. Zalkind and Timothy W. Costello, "Perception: Some Recent Research and Implications for Administration," *Administrative Science Quarterly*, September 1962, pp. 227–229.

[26]Ibid., p. 230.

104

A MICRO PERSPECTIVE OF
ORGANIZATIONAL
BEHAVIOR: COGNITIVE
PROCESSES AND
PERSONALITY

Attribution

Attribution simply refers to how a person explains the cause of another's or of his or her own behavior. In recent years attribution theories have been playing an increasingly important role in work motivation and leadership.[27] These attribution theories of motivation and leadership will be covered in Chapters 7 and 15. Applied to social perception, attribution is the search for causes (attributes) in making interpretations of other persons or of oneself. For example, what the manager attributes the cause of a subordinate's behavior to will affect the manager's perception of and the resulting behavior toward the subordinate. If the subordinate's outstanding performance is attributed to a new machine or engineering procedure, the perception and resulting treatment will be different from that resulting if the performance is attributed to ability and drive. The same is true of attributions made of one's own behavior. Perceptions and thus behaviors will vary depending on whether internal, personal attributions or external, situational attributions are made. In other words, the type of causal attributions one makes greatly affect perception and, as the later discussions in motivation and leadership will indicate, there is growing evidence that this attributional process and the form it takes seem to greatly affect the resulting organizational behavior.

Stereotyping

In addition to attribution, there are two other important areas of social perception that are especially relevant to the understanding of organizational behavior. These are the common errors or problems that creep into social perception called stereotyping and halo effect.

The term *stereotype* refers to the tendency to perceive another person (hence social perception) as belonging to a *single* class or category. Besides this categorization, a stereotype also implies general agreement on the attributed traits and the existence of a discrepancy between attributed traits and actual traits.[28]

The word *stereotype* is derived from the typographer's word for a printing plate made from previously composed type. In 1922, Walter Lippmann applied the word to perception. Since then, stereotyping has become a frequently used term to describe perceptual errors. In particular, it is employed in analyzing ethnic prejudice. Not commonly acknowledged is the fact that stereotyping may attribute favorable or unfavorable traits to the person being perceived. Social psychologists explain that "stereotyping is

[27]For example, see: Bobby J. Calder, "An Attribution Theory of Leadership," in Barry M. Staw and Gerald R. Salancik (eds.), *New Directions in Organizational Behavior*, St. Clair Press, Chicago, 1977, pp. 179–204; and T. R. Mitchell, J. R. Larson, and S. G. Green, "Leader Behavior, Situational Moderators, and Group Performance: An Attributional Analysis," *Organizational Behavior and Human Performance*, vol. 18, 1977, pp. 254–268.

[28]Paul F. Secord and Carl W. Backman, *Social Psychology*, 2d ed., McGraw-Hill, New York, 1974, pp. 20–30.

not simply the assignment of favorable or unfavorable traits to a class of persons as a function of whether the observer has a positive or negative attitude toward the person category. Most stereotypes have both favorable and unfavorable traits, and more prejudiced individuals assign both in greater degree."[29] Most often a person is put into a stereotype because the perceiver knows only the overall category to which the person belongs. However, because each individual is unique, the real traits of the person will generally be quite different from those the stereotype would suggest.

Stereotyping greatly influences social perception in today's organizations. Common stereotyped groups include managers, supervisors, union members, minorities, women, white- and blue-collar workers, and all the various functional and staff specialists, e.g., accountants, salespeople, computer programmers, and engineers. There is a consensus about the traits possessed by the members of these categories. Yet in reality there is often a discrepancy between the agreed-upon traits of each category and the actual traits of the members. In other words, not all engineers carry calculators and are coldly rational, nor are all personnel managers do-gooders who are trying to keep workers happy. On the contrary, there are individual differences and a great deal of variability among members of these groups. In spite of this, other organization members commonly make blanket perceptions and behave accordingly. For example, in one research study it was found that individuals will both perceive and be perceived according to whether they are identified with a union or a management group. "Thus, 74 percent of the subjects in the managerial group chose the word 'honest' as a description of Mr. A, *when he was identified as a manager.* The same managerial subjects, however, chose the word 'honest' to describe Mr. A only 50 percent of the time when he was identified as a representative of the union."[30] There are numerous other research studies and common, everyday examples which point out the stereotyping that occurs in organizational life.

Halo effect

The *halo error* in social perception is very similar to stereotyping. Whereas in stereotyping the person is perceived according to a single category, under the halo effect the person is perceived on the basis of one trait. Halo is often discussed in performance appraisal when a rater makes an error in judging a person's total personality and/or performance on the basis of a single trait such as intelligence, appearance, dependability, or cooperativeness. Whatever the single trait is, it may override all other traits in forming the perception of the person. Examples of halo effect are the extremely attractive woman secretary who is perceived by her male boss as being an intelligent, good performer, when, in fact, she is a poor typist and quite dense, and the

---

[29]Ibid., p. 30.

[30]Mason Haire, "Role-Perception in Labor-Management Relations: An Experimental Approach," *Industrial and Labor Relations Review,* January 1955, p. 208.

106

A MICRO PERSPECTIVE OF
ORGANIZATIONAL
BEHAVIOR: COGNITIVE
PROCESSES AND
PERSONALITY

good typist who is also very bright but who is perceived by her male boss as a "secretary," not as a potential manager with the ability to cope with important responsibilities. One study noted three conditions where the halo effect is most marked: (1) when the traits to be perceived are unclear in behavioral expressions; (2) when the traits are not frequently encountered by the perceiver; and (3) when the traits have moral implications.[31]

Many research studies have pointed out how halo effect can influence perception. For example, one study found that when two persons were described as having identical personalities except for one trait—the character qualities in one list included the trait *warm* and in the other list, the trait *cold*—two completely different perceptions resulted.[32] In other words, one trait blinded the perceiver to all other traits in the perceptual process. Another study also documented the impact of the halo effect on employee perceptions in a company that was in receivership. Although the company paid relatively high wages and provided excellent working conditions and at least average supervision, the employees did not perceive these favorable factors. The insecurity produced an inverse halo effect so that insecurity dominated over the pay and positive conditions of the job.[33] The results of this study make the point that "when there's one important 'rotten' attitude, it can spoil the 'barrel' of attitudes."[34] As with all the other aspects of the psychological process of perception discussed in this chapter, the halo effect has important implications for the study and eventual understanding of organizational behavior.

SUMMARY

Perception is an important mediating cognitive process. Through this complex process, persons make interpretations of stimulus situations they are faced with. Both selectivity and organization go into perceptual interpretations. Externally, selectivity is affected by intensity, size, contrast, repetition, motion, novelty, and familiarity. Internally, perceptual selectivity is influenced by the individual's motivation, learning, and personality. After the stimulus situation is filtered by the selective process, the incoming information is organized into a meaningful whole. Figure-ground is the most basic form of perceptual organization. Another basic form is the grouping of constellations of incoming stimuli by closure, continuity, proximity, and similarity. The constancy, context, and defensive aspects of perceptual

[31]Jerome S. Bruner and Renato Tagiuri, "The Perception of People," in Gardner Lindzey (ed.), *Handbook of Social Psychology*, Addison-Wesley, Cambridge, 1954, p. 641.

[32]S. E. Asch, "Forming Impressions of Personalities," *Journal of Abnormal and Social Psychology*, July 1946, pp. 258–290.

[33]Byron A. Grove and Willard A. Kerr, "Specific Evidence on Origin of Halo Effect in Measurement of Employee Morale," *Journal of Social Psychology*, August 1951, pp. 165–170.

[34]Timothy W. Costello and Sheldon S. Zalkind, *Psychology in Administration*, Prentice-Hall, Englewood Cliffs, N.J., 1963, p. 35.

organization are more complex. The social context in particular plays an important role in understanding human behavior in organizations.

QUESTIONS FOR DISCUSSION AND REVIEW

1. Do you agree with the opening observation that people are human information processors? Why?
2. How does sensation differ from perception?
3. Give some examples of the external factors that affect perceptual selectivity.
4. Explain how perceptual constancy works.
5. What does stereotyping mean? Why is it considered to be a perceptual problem?
6. What effect can the perceptual process have on organizational behavior?

CASE:
SPACE
UTILIZATION

Sherman Adder, assistant plant manager for Frame Manufacturing Company, was chairman of the ad hoc committee for space utilization. The committee was made up of the various department heads in the company. The plant manager of Frame had given Sherman the charge to see if the various office, operations, and warehouse facilities of the company were being optimally utilized. The company was beset by rising costs and the need for more space. However, before okaying an expensive addition to the plant, the plant manager wanted to be sure that the currently available space was being utilized properly.

Sherman opened up the first committee meeting by reiterating the charge of the committee. Then Sherman asked the members if they had any initial observations to make. The first to speak was the office manager. He stated, "Well, I know we are using every possible inch of room that we have available to us. But when I walk out into the plant I see a lot of open spaces. We have people piled on top of one another, but out in the plant there seems to be plenty of room." The production manager quickly replied, "We do not have a lot of space. You office people have the luxury facilities. My supervisors don't even have room for a desk and a file cabinet. I have repeatedly told the plant manager we need more space. After all, our operation determines whether this plant succeeds or fails, not you people in the front office pushing paper around." Sherman interrupted at this point and said, "Obviously we have different interpretations of the space utilization around here. Before further discussion I think it would be best if we have some objective facts to work with. I am going to ask the industrial engineer to provide us with some statistics on plant and office layouts before our next meeting. Today's meeting is adjourned."

1. What perceptual principles are evident in this case?
2. What concept was brought out when the production manager labeled the office personnel a bunch of "paper pushers"? Can you give other organizational examples of this concept?
3. Do you think that Sherman's approach to getting "objective facts" from statistics on plant and office layout will affect the perceptions of the office and production managers? How does such information affect perception in general?

CASE:
QUELLING A RIOT

Training police to handle or quell a riot normally includes a session or two on the importance of accurately perceiving what is happening within an unruly crowd. This need for accurate perception has resulted from several true incidents where instigators of riots deliberately attempted to provoke police into acting in a violent manner. It has been shown in several riots that what the police perceived as a threat to their lives was really nothing more than a deliberate attempt to provoke them with harmless acts or objects. For example, crumpled paper has been mistaken as a rock in the fist of an angry rioter. The sound of a thrown light bulb breaking has been confused with a gun discharging. A protruding stick being carried by a protester has been confused with the barrel of a rifle from a distance. All these possible misperceptions could lead and in some cases have led to violence and death. Training the police in accurate perception can be a life or death matter.

1. If you were given the responsibility of training police in improving their perceptual skills to avoid the problems identified above, how would you go about it? What perceptual principles would have applicability?
2. Can police work also benefit from understanding social perception areas such as stereotyping or halo effect? How?

PERSONALITY

THE GAMESMAN PERSONALITY
FOR CORPORATE SUCCESS*

Washington psychoanalyst Michael Maccoby recently published a book called *The Gamesman.* This book was the result of six years of study of 250 managers in a dozen elite business firms. He concludes from this work that there are four dominant personality types in today's successful organizations. He labels these personalities the craftsman, the jungle fighter, the company man, and the gamesman. The craftsman is concerned with his or her own technical specialty and with doing a high-quality job. Maccoby points out that, unfortunately, the craftsman is too concerned with details to have a total organizational perspective. The jungle fighter's personality is very aggressive; such people will attempt to succeed at any cost and will openly attack anyone who keeps them from attaining goals. Company men attempt to be very conservative and will protect themselves and the company at all costs. This sort of individual does not have a risk-taking personality and will hurt the company in the long run through missed opportunities. The gamesman, according to Maccoby, is the ideal person to run a company. He or she balances risk taking with security. The gamesman likes to assume responsibility and to take calculated risks, and has a winning mentality.

*Adapted from "Age of the Gamesman," *Time,* Feb. 14, 1977, pp. 57–58.

110

A MICRO PERSPECTIVE OF
ORGANIZATIONAL
BEHAVIOR: COGNITIVE
PROCESSES AND
PERSONALITY

Whereas the last chapter, on perception, represents the cognitive processes that are important to the study of organizational behavior, this chapter represents the micro perspective from the *whole person*, personality standpoint. Organizational participants operate as a whole, not as a series of distinct parts. To make a very simple analogy, the various psychological processes may be thought of as pieces of a jigsaw puzzle and personality as the completed puzzle picture. However, one psychologist warns:

Analogies are often misleading and many psychologists would say that the jigsaw concept may be inadequate. Perhaps it is better to consider the individual aspects of a person's makeup as bricks and personality as the whole house, built of bricks but held together with cement.[1]

As indicated in the quote, personality is probably more accurately portrayed as something over and above the psychological building blocks. Contrary to mathematical logic, personality seems to be a case where the whole is greater than the sum of the parts. This, of course, has implications from gestalt psychology discussed in Chapter 2 and the synergistic effect in systems analysis discussed in the organizational theory chapters.

The discussion of personality in this chapter is aimed at improving understanding of the complexities of today's employees. Such understanding is vital to the study and analysis of organizational behavior. Similar to the previous chapter on perception, this chapter offers only a few *direct* applications of its content to the management of human resources. It attempts to be more education- than applications-oriented, and it serves as the natural conceptual conclusion to the second part of the book, which examines organizational behavior from a micro perspective.

The first section of the chapter defines and clarifies the concept of personality. The next section is devoted to personality development and includes discussions of some well-known theories on stages of development, formulated by Freud, Erikson, Piaget, and Argyris. The third section breaks down the determinants of personality development into biological, cultural, family, social, and situational categories. Some of the more important research findings on these determinants of personality are included, and the socialization process is given detailed attention because it is especially relevant to organizational behavior. The last section gives a brief overview of the major theories of personality structure. Particular attention is given to the psychoanalytic, type, trait, self, and social theories.

THE DEFINITIONAL CONTROVERSY

Over forty years ago Gordon Allport found no less than fifty different definitions of personality. He categorized these definitions into five areas and labeled them as follows:

1. *Omnibus.* These definitions view personality as the "sum total," "aggregate," or "constellation" of properties or qualities.

---

[1]D. E. James, *Introduction to Psychology*, Constable, London, 1968, p. 219.

2. *Integrative and configurational.* Under this view of personality, the organization of personal attributes is stressed.

3. *Hierarchical.* These definitions specify the various levels of integration or organization of personality.

4. *Adjustment.* This view emphasizes the adjustment (adaptation, survival, and evolution) of the person to the environment.

5. *Distinctiveness.* The definitions for this category stress the uniqueness of each personality.[2]

Drawing on these five approaches, Allport offered his own definition of personality: "Personality is the dynamic organization within the individual of those psychophysical systems that determine his unique adjustments to his environment."[3]

Unfortunately, Allport's analysis did not lead to universal agreement on the meaning of personality. Much of the controversy can be attributed to the fact that laypersons and behavioral scientists define personality from different perspectives. Laypersons tend to equate personality with social success (good, popular, or "a lot of personality") and to describe personality by a single dominant characteristic (strong, weak, shy, or polite). When it is realized that more than 4,000 words in the dictionary can be used to describe personality this way, the definitional problem becomes staggering. The academicians, on the other hand, take a different perspective. For example, the descriptive-adjective approach used by the layperson plays only a small part. However, scholars cannot agree on a definition of personality because they operate from different theoretical bases. As long as there is disagreement on the theory of personality, there will be disagreement on its definition.

THE COMPREHENSIVE MEANING OF PERSONALITY

The word *personality* has an interesting derivation. It can be traced to the Latin words *per sonare*, which translates as "to speak through." The Latin term was used to denote the masks worn by actors in ancient Greece and Rome. This Latin meaning is particularly relevant to the contemporary analysis of personality. Common usage of the word *personality* emphasizes the role which the person (actor) displays to the public. The academic definitions of personality are concerned more directly with the person (actor) than with the role played. Probably the most meaningful approach would be to include both the person and the role, as Floyd Ruch does in his definition. He states that the human personality includes:

1. External appearance and behavior or social stimulus value
2. Inner awareness of self as a permanent organizing force
3. The particular pattern or organization of measurable traits, both "inner" and "outer"[4]

---

[2]Gordon W. Allport, *Personality*, Henry Holt, New York, 1937, pp. 43–47.

[3]Ibid., p. 48.

[4]Floyd L. Ruch, *Psychology and Life*, 6th ed., Scott, Foresman, Chicago, 1963, p. 353.

112

A MICRO PERSPECTIVE OF
ORGANIZATIONAL
BEHAVIOR: COGNITIVE
PROCESSES AND
PERSONALITY

More recently, Walter Mischel has emphasized the need to recognize the person-situation *interaction,* i.e., the social learning aspects of personality.[5] As Chapters 2 and 3 pointed out, such a social learning interpretation seems to be the most comprehensive and meaningful to the overall study of human/organizational behavior. Thus, in addition to the three points made above by Ruch, a comprehensive discussion of personality must include the uniqueness of each situation (rather than the commonality assumed by the more traditional approaches to personality) and any measure of personality must attempt to assess the person-situation interaction. Mischel notes that "Individuals show far less cross-situational consistency in their behavior than has been assumed by trait-state theories. The more dissimilar the evoking situations, the less likely they are to produce similar or consistent responses from the same individual."[6] In summary, in this book *personality* will mean how people affect others and how they understand and view themselves, as well as their pattern of inner and outer measurable traits, and the person-situation interaction.

How people affect others primarily depends upon their external appearance (height, weight, facial features, color, and other physical aspects) and behavior (vulgar, friendly, courteous, and so on). The role concept is closely tied to these aspects of personality. A very large, friendly worker will have a different impact on other people than a very small, courteous manager. Obviously, all the ramifications of perception enter into these aspects of personality.

People's attempts to understand themselves are called the *self-concept* in personality theory. The self is a unique product of many interacting parts and may be thought of as the personality viewed from within. The last part of the chapter analyzes this self-concept in more detail.

The pattern of measurable traits adds an important dimension to the understanding of the human personality. As explained by Ruch, the traits are

. . . *dimensions* of personality because they can be measured on a mathematical *continuum.* . . . The basic problem in describing a given individual is not deciding which traits he does or does not possess, but finding *how much* of each trait he possesses and, equally important, how the traits *interact* in the total pattern of his personality.[7]

The trait theories of personality are covered in the last part of the chapter.

The person-situation interaction dimension of personality extends the trait approach. Each situation, of course, is different. The differences may seem to be very small on the surface, but when filtered by the person's cognitive mediating processes, they can lead to quite large, subjective differences and diverse behavioral outcomes. Thus, this last dimension suggests that people are not static, acting the same in all situations, but

---

[5]Walter Mischel, "Toward a Cognitive Social Learning Reconceptualization of Personality," *Psychological Review,* vol. 80, 1973, pp. 252–283.

[6]Walter Mischel, *Personality and Assessment,* Wiley, New York, 1968, p. 177.

[7]Ruch, op. cit., p. 354.

instead are ever changing and flexible. For example, employees can change depending on the particular situation they are in interaction with. Even everyday work experience can change people. The sections in this chapter dealing with the socialization process and the situation are relevant to this important person-situation interaction. The last section, on personality theories, also covers the social learning approach.

In summary, the personality is a very diverse and complex psychological concept. It incorporates most everything studied in this book and more. As defined above, personality is concerned with external appearance and behavior, self, measurable traits, and situational interactions. Probably the best concluding statement on the meaning of personality was given many years ago by Kluckhohn and Murray when they said that to some extent, a person's personality is like all other people's, like some other people's, like no other people's.[8]

THE DEVELOPMENT OF PERSONALITY

Study of and research on the development of personality has traditionally been an important area of behavioral analysis. It is concerned with "the processes by which children gradually acquire patterns of overt behavior, thinking, problem solving, and above all, the motives, emotions, conflicts, and ways of coping with conflicts that will go to make up their adult personalities."[9]

The development approach is actually a form of personality theory but, in contrast to most personality theories, it is highly research-oriented. Modern developmental psychology does not get into the argument of heredity versus environment or maturation versus learning. As previously pointed out, the human system consists of both physiological *and* psychological interacting parts. Therefore, heredity, environment, maturation, and learning *all* contribute to the human personality.

The study of personality development can be divided into two separate but closely allied approaches. One approach attempts to identify specific physiological and psychological stages that occur in the development of the human personality. The other approach has tried to identify the important determinants of personality. The "stages" approach has been theoretical in nature, whereas the search for major determinants has been more empirically based.

There are many well-known stage theories of personality development. Most deal with psychosocial development rather than directly with personality development. As with most aspects of personality, there is little agreement among psychologists about the exact stages. In fact, a growing number of today's psychologists contend there are *no* identifiable stages. Their argument is like the Mischel argument for the importance of person-

[8]Clyde Kluckhohn and H. A. Murray, "Personality Formation: The Determinants," in C. Kluckhohn and H. A. Murray (eds.), *Personality*, Knopf, New York, 1948, p. 35.

[9]Jerome Kagan and Ernest Havemann, *Psychology*, Harcourt, Brace & World, New York, 1968, p. 536.

114

A MICRO PERSPECTIVE OF
ORGANIZATIONAL
BEHAVIOR: COGNITIVE
PROCESSES AND
PERSONALITY

situation interactions: Personality development is a continuous process and the sequence is based solely upon the learning opportunities available. The opposing view, which supports stages in personality development, is summarized by Mischel as follows: "Socialization is not a haphazard accumulation of bits of behavior but entails, instead, some orderly development. That is true at least to the degree that some complex social behavior patterns are sequential."[10]

Freudian stages

Once again, Sigmund Freud is found in the vanguard. Although the analysis of stages of development can be traced as far back as the ancient Greeks, it was Freud who first formulated a meaningful stage theory. He felt that a child progresses through four identifiable stages of psychosexual development: oral, anal, phallic or oedipal, and genital. These stages were believed to be the main driving forces behind the personality.

To most persons, the Freudian stages often seem silly or even bizarre. In addition, modern psychologists are generally not in agreement with Freud's theory of stages. However, they do give Freud credit for providing some valuable insights and for initiating the meaningful study of personality development. The major disagreement centers on Freud's terminology and the degree to which he carried the stages, rather than on the possibility that he was totally wrong. For example, with regard to Freud's choice of words, Mischel notes:

Without having at hand a suitable set of learning concepts and terms for personality development, Freud relied on his own preference for a "body language": he preferred to say "oral" rather than "dependent," "anal" rather than "compulsive," "genital" rather than "mature."[11]

Unfortunately, when one assesses Freud's contribution to the understanding of personality development, the sexually oriented terms seem to overshadow the underlying concepts.

Neo-Freudian stages

Besides the controversy on terminology, the major disagreement with Freud is the heavy emphasis he placed on the sexual and biological factors in the developing personality. This criticism seems to be more legitimate. Among others, Erik Erikson felt that relatively more attention should be given to the social rather than the sexual adaptations of the individual. He identified eight psychosocial stages:[12]

---

[10]Walter Mischel, *Introduction to Personality*, Holt, New York, 1971, p. 227.

[11]Ibid., p. 43.

[12]Erik Erikson, *Childhood and Society*, 2d ed., New York, 1963. Also see Mischel, op. cit., pp. 39–41.

Stage of development	Age
1. Mouth and senses	0–1
2. Eliminative organs and musculature	1–2
3. Locomotion and the genitals	3–5
4. Latency	6–puberty
5. Puberty and adolescence	
6. Early adulthood	
7. Young and middle adulthood	
8. Mature adulthood	

Erikson asserted that a psychosocial crisis occurs within each of the above stages, and in order to have a normal, fulfilling personality, each crisis should be optimally resolved. Probably the most widely known crisis identified by Erikson is the identity experience of adolescents. He believes that the optimum outcome of this teenage crisis is the reintegration of past with present goals. For purposes of the study of organizational behavior, the most relevant stage is that of the young and middle adult. Typical organizational participants in the midst of their productive years are in this stage. In Erikson's thinking, the crisis that this person faces is one of generativity versus stagnation. The best outcome for personality fulfillment would be an attitude of *production* and concern with the world and future generations. Put another way, according to Erikson young and middle-aged adults who solve their psychosocial crises by being productive will develop the healthiest personalities. The employing organization should permit and take advantage of this productivity. This type of analysis provided by Erikson has especially important implications for career planning. Chapter 22 will draw from this analysis in its discussion of career development.

Erikson's approach is representative of the neo-Freudian stage theories. As indicated by the stages he identified, he did not totally reject, but rather changed the emphasis of, modified, and extended the ideas of Freud.

Cognitive stages

The cognitive stage theories of personality development make a more complete break with Freudian ideas. The work of the Swiss psychologist Jean Piaget probably best represents the cognitive stages approach.[13] In contrast to Freud, Piaget was convinced that the conscious, not the instinctive unconscious, was the critical variable in the developing personality. It is sometimes said that whereas Freud discovered the unconscious, Piaget "discovered" the conscious. In addition to the break from Freud, Piaget is often credited with being the first to offer a successful challenge to the prevailing behaviorist perspective in modern American child psychology.

[13]Jean Piaget, "The General Problems of the Psychobiological Development of the Child," in J. M. Tanner and Bärbel Inhelder (eds.), *Discussions on Child Development*, International Universities Press, New York, 1960, pp. 3–27.

116

A MICRO PERSPECTIVE OF
ORGANIZATIONAL
BEHAVIOR: COGNITIVE
PROCESSES AND
PERSONALITY

He based his theories and extensive research (30 books and 100 articles) on children as subjects, whereas the behaviorists seldom used children as subjects in their research. He felt that the behavioristic approach to learning was too narrow and superficial. He felt that learning was more broadly concerned with development and would only occur when the child had the necessary cognitive structures for assimilating new information.

Piaget identified four major stages of cognitive or intellectual development:

Stage of development	Age
1. Sensorimotor	0–2
2. Preoperational	2–7
3. Concrete operational	7–11
4. Formal operational	11 and above

In the initial stage, infants acquire knowledge or cognition about their surrounding environment through simple, sensorimotor manipulations. When only a few months old, children begin to repeat acts which produce reward or some other interesting outcome. As children approach two years of age, they start to solve simple problems and to realize they are in a world of objects separate from themselves that they can control and affect. Thus, at about age two children's intellectual capacities shift from a strict sensorimotor level to more of a conceptual or operational level. It is during this preoperational stage that children begin to use symbols and language in their thought processes and to develop a concept of class or category.

At about age seven children enter the concrete stage of cognitive development. They are now able to understand concepts such as conservation, which can be simply demonstrated as follows:

Water is first poured into two identical, flat containers. Children in either the preoperational or concrete-operational stages will readily acknowledge that the two containers contain equal amounts of water. Then the water in one of the flat containers is poured into a tall container *in front of the child*. When asked which container has more water, children in the preoperational stage will generally say the tall container, but children who are in the concrete stage will say that there is the same amount of water in both the flat and tall containers.

This demonstration indicates that only children who have reached the concrete stage of operational development will understand concepts such as conservation (the mass of an object remains constant no matter how much the form changes).

Empirical research has generally given support to the stages identified by Piaget. Recent studies have implied that certain social and political attitudes may be dependent upon the stage of cognitive development. Such findings have significant implications for organizational behavior. For instance, determining organizational participants' stages of cognitive development may greatly help in explaining their behavior.

The final formal operational stage of cognitive development is most relevant to the study of organizational behavior. This is the developmental stage reached by most of the mature, intelligent adults found in today's organizations. Organizational participants in this stage of conceptualization need not depend upon the manipulation of concrete objects. They have the capacity symbolically to analyze, reason, imagine, and evaluate events. However, it must be remembered that the cognitive stages cannot be totally equated with personality stages any more than can Freud's psychosexual stages. Both the cognitive and psychosexual stage theories only partially contribute to the understanding of the complex human personality.

Immaturity to maturity

In a departure from the strict stage approach, Chris Argyris has identified specific dimensions of the human personality as it develops. Argyris proposes that the human personality, rather than going through precise stages, progresses along a continuum from immaturity as an infant to maturity as an adult. However, at any age, people can have their degree of development plotted according to the seven dimensions shown in Table 5-1.

Argyris carefully points out that this model does not imply that all persons reach or strive for all dimensions on the mature end of the continuum. He further explains:

1. The seven dimensions represent only one aspect of the total personality. Much also depends upon the individual's perception, self-concept, and adaptation and adjustment.
2. The seven dimensions continually change in degree from the infant to the adult end of the continuum.
3. The model, being only a construct, cannot predict specific behavior. However, it does provide a method of describing and measuring the growth of any individual in the culture.
4. The seven dimensions are based upon latent characteristics of the personality which may be quite different from the observable behavior.[14]

In contrast to the stage theories of Freud, Erikson, and Piaget, Argyris's

---

[14]Chris Argyris, *Personality and Organization*, Harper, New York, 1957, pp. 51–53.

Table 5–1

THE IMMATURITY-MATURITY CONTINUUM

Immaturity characteristics	Maturity characteristics
Passivity	→ Activity
Dependence	→ Independence
Few ways of behaving	→ Diverse behavior
Shallow interests	→ Deep interests
Short-time perspective	→ Long-time perspective
Subordinate position	→ Superordinate position
Lack of self-awareness	→ Self-awareness and control

Source: Adapted from Chris Argyris, *Personality and Organization*, Harper, New York, 1957, p. 50.

118

A MICRO PERSPECTIVE OF
ORGANIZATIONAL
BEHAVIOR: COGNITIVE
PROCESSES AND
PERSONALITY

immaturity-maturity model of personality is specifically directed to the study and analysis of organizational behavior. He assumes that the personalities of organizational employees can be generally described by the mature end of the continuum. This being the case, in order to obtain full expression of their personalities, the formal organization should allow for activity rather than passivity, independence rather than dependence, long- rather than short-time perspective, occupation of a position higher than that of peers, and expression of deep, important abilities.[15] Argyris argues that too often the exact opposite occurs. The mature organizational participant becomes frustrated, anxious, and in conflict with the modern formal organization. In other words, Argyris sees a *basic incongruence* between the needs of the mature personality and the nature of the formal organization. This incongruency premise is an important cornerstone for the entire conceptualization of person-organizational structure interaction that was discussed in the organizational behavior model in Chapter 3. It is also particularly relevant to Chapter 13, on conflict and stress.

MAJOR DETERMINANTS OF PERSONALITY

What determines personality? Of all the complexities and unanswered questions in the study of human behavior, this question may be the most difficult. The problem lies in the fact that the cognitive and psychological processes, plus many other variables, *all* contribute to personality. However, for ease of study and analysis, the determinants of personality can perhaps best be grouped in five broad categories: biological, cultural, family, social, and situational.

Biological contributions

The study of the biological contributions to personality can be divided into several major approaches: heredity, the brain, biofeedback, and physical stature.

The role of heredity   The impact of heredity on personality is a very active but still unsettled area of understanding. One problem is that geneticists face a major obstacle in gathering information scientifically on the human being. Animal scientists can conduct highly controlled breeding experiments, but geneticists studying human heridity cannot. Through research on animals, it has been clearly shown that both physical and psychological characteristics can be transmitted through heredity.[16] However, in the case of humans, who cannot be subjected to the necessary controls, the evidence is much less conclusive. Although studies of twins permit some control over the critical variables, they have generally proved to be

---

[15]Ibid., p. 53.

[16]Louis Kaplan, *Foundations of Human Behavior*, Harper & Row, New York, 1965, p. 24.

inadequate.[17] Yet, despite these problems, with the recent breakthroughs in genetics, e.g., discovery of the double-helix model of DNA, there are potential ways of altering and controlling behaviors. This is called *genetic engineering*. Genetics experts feel that some aspects of the human personality are at least partly affected by heredity. For example, one list contains such items as strength of sex drive, aggressiveness, sensitivity, verbal and mathematical abilities, musical ability, the craving for alcohol and drugs, and intelligence as being at least partly determined by genetic endowment.[18] Especially the impact of heredity on intelligence has created much controversy. The *Wall Street Journal* reported that the heredity versus environmental impact on IQ is "the most furious controversy to rock the educational world since the days of John Dewey 70 years ago."[19] Geneticists have been joined by some educational psychologists such as Arthur Jensen in claiming that intelligence is largely inherited. This, of course, has implications for racial differences, which adds emotional fuel to the controversy. The major issue of the controversy is how intelligence is measured. Until this is fully answered, the controversy and emotional debates will continue. In the meantime, there seems little doubt that the role of heredity in behavior will receive increased attention in the coming years.

The role of the brain   The second biological approach is to concentrate on the role that the brain plays in personality. Like the geneticists, the physiologists have been unable to supply precise information on the contributions of the brain, but also, as in genetics, some promising inroads are being made. The most recent and exciting possibilities come from the work done with electrical stimulation of the brain (ESB) and split-brain psychology. Although both approaches are somewhat faddish, there are enough preliminary results so far to indicate potential promise.

To date, ESB has been conducted primarily on animal subjects. Electrodes are implanted in the animal's brain. Depending upon the area that is stimulated, either a pleasurable or a painful sensation is experienced. In rats, about 60 percent of the brain has been determined to be neutral, 35 percent pleasurable, and 5 percent painful. Several years ago a spectacular demonstration of ESB was conducted by José Delgado. He implanted a radio-controlled electrode in the pleasure area of a bull's brain. When stimulated, the bull could be stopped in the middle of a ferocious charge.[20]

Work with ESB on human subjects is just beginning; the research results are, in general, similar to those on animals. There seem to be definite pleasurable and painful areas in the human brain. This being true, it may be possible physically to manipulate personality through ESB. Some business

---

[17]Ibid., pp. 25–26.

[18]Charles R. Shaw, *When Your Child Needs Help,* New York, 1972.

[19]Jerry E. Bishop, "The Argument over Heredity and I.Q.," *Wall Street Journal,* June 20, 1973, p. 14.

[20]José Delgado, *Physical Control of the Mind,* Harper & Row, New York, 1969, pp. 166–168.

120

A MICRO PERSPECTIVE OF
ORGANIZATIONAL
BEHAVIOR: COGNITIVE
PROCESSES AND
PERSONALITY

firms are reportedly investigating ESB as a method of reducing executive tensions and stimulating creative thinking.[21] Publicity on ESB research has resulted in some controversy, including such far-out notions as the possibility that future people may possess a little button that literally "turns them on" or "off" depending on their mood, the possibility that the basic human personality can be altered by ESB, and that there may be some diabolical plot afoot to take over the world with ESB.

Research so far indicates that it is not possible to substitute one entire personality for another through ESB. Instead, ESB seems to work in a manner similar to hypnosis. It can give pleasure or pain, and it seems to influence some of the conscious and unconscious characteristics of the personality, but it cannot alter the basic personality structure. As far as someone's using ESB to take over the world, one doctor who works with ESB notes, "Anyone influential enough to get an entire population to consent to having electrodes placed in its heads would already have achieved his goal without firing a single volt."[22]

Split-brain (right versus left) psychology is closely related to ESB and is probably more popular, but has less research backup. The split-brain fad was carried over to the management field when Henry Mintzberg wrote a widely read article, "Planning on the Left Side and Managing on the Right." He went so far as to declare, "Which hemisphere of one's brain is better developed may determine whether a person ought to be a planner or a manager."[23] This and other articles in popular management and psychology literature have generated considerable interest among industrial training and development personnel. Workshops and training sessions are based on split-brain psychology.

Split-brain psychology is the subject of a controversy that can be traced back to the classic mind-body dualism debate in psychology: Are the mind and body separate entities, or is the mind simply a function of the physical being? Work done on ESB suggests that there are clearly identifiable portions of the physical brain that control "mind" functions such as emotion and aggression. There is also enough evidence to indicate the right hemisphere of the brain may have functions such as those listed in the right column of Table 5-2 and the left hemisphere may have the functions listed in the left column of the table. But these are still open for further research, and assertions such as the following are exaggerated, according to some researchers:[24]

1. Statements by Marshall McLuhan, the widely known communications expert, that "bureaucracy is left hemisphere. . . . The generation gap of the 1960s was a conflict between right-hemisphere kids and left-hemisphere parents"

---

[21]*Newsweek*, June 12, 1971, p. 65.

[22]Ibid., p. 67.

[23]Henry Mintzberg, "Planning on the Left Side and Managing on the Right," *Harvard Business Review*, July-August 1976, p. 49.

[24]Ron Zemke, "Right Brain vs. Left Brain: How to Sort Fact from Fiction," *Training HRD*, January, 1978, p. 30.

Table 5–2

SUMMARY OF CHARACTERISTICS AND DIMENSIONS ATTRIBUTED TO THE LEFT AND RIGHT BRAIN HEMISPHERES

Left hemisphere (right side of body)	Right hemisphere (left side of body)
Speech/verbal	Spatial/musical
Logical, mathematical	Holistic
Linear, detailed	Artistic, symbolic
Sequential	Simultaneous
Controlled	Emotional
Intellectual	Intuitive, creative
Dominant	Minor (quiet)
Worldly	Spiritual
Active	Receptive
Analytic	Synthetic, gestalt-oriented
Reading, writing, naming	Facial recognition
Sequential ordering	Simultaneous comprehension
Perception of significant order	Perception of abstract patterns
Complex motor sequences	Recognition of complex figures

Source: Adapted from Robert J. Trotter, "The Other Hemispheres," *Science News,* Apr. 3, 1976, p. 219.

2. The suggestion made by some educators that truth, beauty, justice, and love are rooted in the right brain

3. Some dream experts' claim that dreaming is the function of the right brain

4. Claims by media experts that newspapers and magazines are left-brain media and television is a right-brain medium

5. Claims that invention is a right-brain function and production is a left-brain function.

In an attempt to separate the fiction from facts, a comprehensive analysis of the existing knowledge about right brain–left brain points out the following:[25]

1. The brain has more than a right side and a left side. It could just as easily be depicted from front to back or top to bottom.

2. The right side of the brain is not idle but is simply less active when the person is doing something linear. The evidence appears to show that every mental operation requires many parts of the brain to be active.

3. There may be important sex-linked differences and hormonal-balance differences which account for many of the things now being attributed to the split brain.

As the discussion of the split brain indicates, there are more questions raised than answers provided. Yet few would disagree with the idea that the brain certainly holds many unlocked secrets for the future understanding of personality and behavior in general.

Biofeedback Similar to the work on the brain have been some of the widely publicized and spectacular results of biofeedback training (BFT).

---

[25]Daniel Goleman, "Split-Brain Psychology: Fad of the Year," *Psychology Today,* October 1977, pp. 89–90, 149–151.

122

A MICRO PERSPECTIVE OF
ORGANIZATIONAL
BEHAVIOR: COGNITIVE
PROCESSES AND
PERSONALITY

Until recently, physiologists and psychologists felt that certain biological functions such as brainwave patterns, gastric secretions, and fluctuations in blood pressure and skin temperature were beyond conscious control. Now some scientists believe that these involuntary functions can be consciously controlled through biofeedback. In BFT the individual learns the internal rhythms of a particular body process through electronic signals fed back from equipment that is wired to the body area (e.g., skin, brain, or heart). From this biofeedback the person can learn to control the body process in question. A very simple example of biofeedback would be to hold a thermometer between the index finger and thumb. If the person watches the thermometer and concentrates and thinks very hard about the finger and thumb getting warmer, the temperature may begin to rise.

It is now generally recognized that BFT has several medical applications, for example, it may be used to alleviate migraine headaches by diverting blood from the throbbing region to other parts of the body; cerebral palsy patients have learned to control muscle spasms by listening to clicks from a feedback machine wired to their body; people with dangerously irregular heart rhythms have learned to modify them by watching blinking lights that tell them when the heart is functioning properly; and, on the lighter side, a person can control an electric train through brain waves.[26] Such applications have become so popular that the implication is that there has been uniform success. Such is not the case. Researchers have found BFT to have mixed results.[27] Many individuals who have tried BFT are unable to control the process in question or fail to experience the intended benefits. Most behavioral scientists are still taking a wait-and-see approach to BFT. For example, Hilgard and Bower note that "the evidence to date suggests that 'alpha control' may be little more than inexplicit control of eye-movement or eye-focusing," but they do add that "despite these critical remarks, it should be noted that this research has been significant in altering our conceptions of self-control, awareness, and the nature of 'private events.'"[28] More research is needed on biofeedback before any definitive conclusions can be drawn. But its potential impact could be extremely interesting for the future.

Physical characteristics and rate of maturing Besides the brain and biofeedback, another biologically based approach is to analyze the effects of physical characteristics and rate of maturing on personality. Despite the tremendous potential offered by the study of genetics, the brain, and biofeedback, this approach has already proved to be a significant contributor to the study of personality. An individual's external appearance, said to be a vital ingredient of the personality, is biologically determined. The fact that a person is tall or short, fat or skinny, handsome or ugly, or black or white will

---

[26]*Newsweek*, Oct. 14, 1974, pp. 76–77.

[27]Thomas B. Mulholland, "Occipital Alpha Revisited," *Psychological Bulletin*, September 1972, pp. 176–182; and D. A. Paskewitz and M. T. Orne, "Visual Effects on Alpha Feedback Training," *Science*, vol. 181, 1973, pp. 360–363.

[28]Ernest R. Hilgard and Gordon H. Bower, *Theories of Learning*, 4th ed., Prentice-Hall, Englewood Cliffs, N.J., 1975, pp. 559–560.

influence the person's effect on others and, this in turn, will affect the self-concept.

There are entire theories of personality based upon body build. Sheldon's classic theory, which correlated certain body builds (endomorphic, mesomorphic, and ectomorphic) with specific personality traits, is an example. However, most modern psychologists do not go so far as Sheldon in emphasizing the importance of physical attributes. There are too many exceptions for such a theory to be meaningful. On the other hand, practically all would agree that physical characteristics have at least some influence on the personality. The prevailing attitude is expressed by one psychologist as follows: "A child's physical characteristics may be related to his approach to the social environment, to the expectancies of others, and to their reactions to him. These, in turn, may have impacts on personality development."[29] This same reasoning is applied to the rate of maturation. A rapidly maturing boy or girl will be exposed to different physical and social situations and activities than will a slowly maturing child. This differing rate of maturation will be reflected in the personality.

Cultural contribution

Traditionally, cultural factors are usually considered to make a more significant contribution to personality than biological factors. The learning process plays an important role in personality development. Often, however, in discussions that stress either the cognitive or reinforcement aspects of this process, nothing is mentioned about what is learned—the *content*. Yet, in terms of personality development, the content is probably as important as the process. Culture is the key concept in analyzing the content of learning. The prevailing culture pretty much dictates *what* a person will learn.

As indicated in Chapter 2, culture is a major tenet of anthropology. Anthropologists, using cross-cultural analysis, have clearly demonstrated the important role that culture plays in the development of the human personality. The methods by which an infant is fed and is toilet-trained, and makes the transition from adolescence to adulthood are all culturally determined. As indicated by the discussion of the stage theories, such cultural events contribute significantly to the personality. The culture largely determines attributes toward independence, aggression, competition, and cooperation. One psychologist noted:

Each culture expects, and trains, its members to behave in the ways that are acceptable to the group. To a marked degree, the child's cultural group defines the range of experiences and situations he is likely to encounter and the values and personality characteristics that will be reinforced and hence learned.[30]

For example, Western cultures generally reward a person for being indepen-

---

[29]Paul H. Mussen, *The Psychological Development of the Child,* Prentice-Hall, Englewood Cliffs, N.J., 1963, pp. 60–61.

[30]Ibid., p. 62.

124

A MICRO PERSPECTIVE OF
ORGANIZATIONAL
BEHAVIOR: COGNITIVE
PROCESSES AND
PERSONALITY

dent and competitive while Oriental cultures do not. It follows that a person reared in a Western culture has a different personality from a person reared in an Oriental culture. A person who is biologically of Western descent but is brought up in an Oriental culture will have an Oriental type of personality, and vice versa.

Despite the importance of the cultural contribution to personality, a linear relationship cannot be established between personality and a given culture. One problem stems from the existence of numerous subcultures within a given culture. For example, the Protestant ethic may be an overall value of Western culture. However, there are extreme differences among socioeconomic classes, ages, and geographic regions. The point is that it is wrong to assume that all workers or managers in Western societies possess the Protestant ethic. On the other hand, this does not rule out the fact that culture affects personality. The difficulty comes when broad generalizations are made. When analyzing organizational behavior, the *relevant* cultural impact must be recognized. Workers are not influenced by the same culture as managers are, and technical, skilled workers are affected by a different culture than unskilled workers. These and many other differences must be taken into account when analyzing the impact of culture on organizational behavior.

Contribution from the family

Whereas the culture generally prescribes and limits what a person can be taught, it is the family, and later the social group, which selects, interprets, and dispenses the culture. Thus, the family probably has the most significant impact on early personality development; later, the socialization process takes over.

The parents play an especially important part in the identification process which is important to the person's early development. Usually, the parent of the same sex as the child will serve as the model for the child's identification. The process can be examined from three different perspectives.

First, identification can be viewed as the similarity of behavior (including feelings and attitudes) between child and model.
Second, identification can be looked at as the child's motives or desires to be like the model.
Third, it can be viewed as the process through which the child actually takes on the attributes of the model.[31]

From all three perspectives, the identification process is fundamental to the understanding of personality development.

A substantial amount of empirical evidence indicates that the overall home environment created by the parents, in addition to their direct influence, is critical to personality development. For example, children with

---

[31]Mischel, *Personality and Assessment,* op. cit., p. 312.

markedly institutional upbringing (orphans) or children reared in a cold, unstimulating home are much more likely to be socially and emotionally maladjusted than children raised by parents in a warm, loving, and stimulating environment. The key variable in this case does not seem to be the parents per se, but rather the type of atmosphere that is generated for the child. As explained by Mussen:

> Children between the ages of four and six from democratic homes are more stable, less argumentative, more sensitive to praise and blame, more socially successful, and more considerate than children from authoritarian homes. Overattention or overindulgence at home also leads to many kinds of maladaptive, infantile behavior—for instance, crying easily, dawdling, lack of independence and persistence, withdrawal, and high dependence on adults.[32]

Clinical case histories of maladjusted children and adults also show the important role that the parents play. The most common element in histories of maladjusted persons is friction between their mother and father.[33]

Research study on parental influence A classic study by James Abegglen effectively points up the impact of the parents on the personalities of very successful executives.[34] He conducted a detailed case study of twenty executives who had risen from a lower-class childhood to hold top-ranking positions with business firms. Data were accumulated from interviews which at first focused on personal and job histories and then on the use of eight thematic apperception cards (pictures from which subjects report what they see). It was found that fifteen of the twenty executives, while children, had what Abegglen called a separation trauma with their fathers. Two fathers had died during the childhood of the subjects, two subjects had lived with their mothers following a divorce, six of the fathers had been in severe business and financial difficulties, and in five cases the fathers were seriously ill. The fathers were blamed by the sons for the hardships suffered by the family. They were described as inept, sometimes hostile, and usually inadequate. The mother, on the other hand, was generally viewed as being economically and morally stable but not "motherly" in the sense of affectionate.

The results obtained by Abegglen indicate that a classic Freudian reaction formation had taken place. The normal positive identification process between father and son had been blocked. Instead, the son negatively identified with his father and strove to be the opposite from him. This negative identification seemed to be a major motivating force throughout the son's life. The high needs for achievement and low needs for affiliation exhibited by the subjects can be traced back to the negative identification in childhood. Thus, the father and mother (who transmitted

---

[32]Mussen, op. cit., pp. 72–73.

[33]Ibid., p. 73.

[34]James C. Abegglen, "Personality Factors in Social Mobility: A Study of Occupationally Mobile Businessmen," *Genetic Psychology Monographs*, August 1958, pp. 101–159.

126

A MICRO PERSPECTIVE OF
ORGANIZATIONAL
BEHAVIOR: COGNITIVE
PROCESSES AND
PERSONALITY

values that were conducive to upward striving) seemed to have had a great deal of influence on the personalities of this group of business executives.

The Abegglen study has potentially significant implications for the study of organizational behavior. For instance, the case histories of organizational participants might provide much insight into their behavior. Yet, as with most studies of this nature in the behavioral sciences, broad generalizations or grandiose conclusions are unwarranted. One organizational behavior expert, in evaluating the Abegglen study, cautions,

> Intriguing as Abegglen's findings are, it must be remembered that they were drawn from a small and highly select group. He has demonstrated that an early reaction-formation can lead to a lifelong pattern of achievement striving and upward mobility; but so can other kinds of psychological relationships. Sons who are disappointed in their fathers are not destined to corner the market in successful careers![35]

Birth-order data Siblings (brothers and sisters) also contribute to personality. So far, studies of birth order have produced some very interesting but inconclusive results. Studies by social psychologists have found that firstborn and only children in a family have a stronger need to affiliate than do children born later. The conclusion drawn from one such research study is that "firstborn children, at least in our society, are probably more anxious, more dependent on others, especially in anxious situations; and more inclined to go along with the group than are other children."[36] There is other research evidence, although it is far from being conclusive, that indicates firstborns may be more serious, less carefree, and more likely to be a problem than later-borns.[37]

Staunch advocates of birth-order data claim it is possible to describe major personality characteristics based solely upon position in the family constellation. For example, Toman gives specific personality sketches for the oldest and youngest brother of one or more brothers (OBB and YBB, respectively); and the oldest and youngest brothers of sisters (OBS and YBS, respectively). These four types have equivalent female counterparts for a total of eight combinations. Toman even makes suggestions, based upon empirical data, as to the kind of worker each type will be. For example, he states that the OBB is a good worker and independent; YBB fakes independence and tends to be an irregular worker; the OBS, who is also said to be a "true ladies' man" who adores women, is a responsible worker; and the YBS, who is adored and loved by women, is not a very regular or systematic worker but is capable of great accomplishments.[38] On the surface, there seems to be a great deal of truth to these descriptions and possible implications for management. For example, if found to correlate with employment variables, birth order may take on added significance in the

[35]Saul W. Gellerman, *Motivation and Productivity*, American Management Association, New York, 1963, p. 147.

[36]Bernard Berelson and Gary A. Steiner, *Human Behavior*, Harcourt, Brace & World, New York, 1964, p. 74.

[37]Ibid., p. 73.

[38]Walter Toman, "Birth Order Rules All," *Psychology Today*, December 1970, pp. 46–49.

selection process. At the present time, however, birth-order data, like astrology charts, make a lot of surface sense but need much more scientific research before any definitive conclusions can be drawn.

Socialization process

Besides the biological, cultural, and family influences on personality, there is increasing recognition given to the role of other relevant persons, groups, and especially organizations, which greatly influence an individual's personality. This is commonly called the socialization process. It is especially relevant to organizational behavior because the process is not confined to early childhood, taking place rather throughout one's life. In particular, evidence is accumulating that socialization may be one of the best explanations for why employees behave the way they do in today's organizations. For example, Edgar Schein notes, "It is high time that some of our managerial knowledge and skill be focused on those forces in the organization environment which derive from the fact that organizations are social systems which do socialize their new members. If we do not learn to analyze and control the forces of organizational socialization, we are abdicating one of our primary managerial responsibilities."[39]

Socialization involves the process by which a person acquires, from the enormously wide range of behavioral potentialities that are open to him or her starting at birth, those behavior patterns that are customary and acceptable according to the standards of, initially, the family, and later the social group and the employing organization.[40] Thus, socialization starts with the initial contact between a mother and her new infant. After infancy, other members of the immediate family (father, brothers, sisters, and close relatives or friends), then the social group (peers, school friends, and members of the work group) play influential roles, and of particular interest is Schein's idea that the organization itself also contributes to socialization. He points out that the process includes only the learning of those values, norms, and behavior patterns which, from the organization's/work group's point of view, are necessary for any new organization member to learn. He suggests that areas such as the following are the focus of organization socialization:

1. The basic *goals* of the organization
2. The preferred *means* by which those goals should be attained
3. The basic *responsibilities* of the member in the role which is being granted to him by the organization
4. The *behavior patterns* which are required for effective performance in the role
5. A set of rules or principles which pertain to the *maintenance of the ideality and integrity* of the organization[41]

Accordingly, the organization member must learn things like not to drive a

---

[39]Edgar H. Schein, "Organizational Socialization and the Profession of Management," in David Kolb, Irwin Rubin, and James McIntyre, *Organizational Psychology: A Book of Readings*, Prentice-Hall, Englewood Cliffs, N.J., 1971, pp. 14–15.

[40]Mussen, op. cit., p. 65.

[41]Schein, op. cit., p. 3.

128

A MICRO PERSPECTIVE OF
ORGANIZATIONAL
BEHAVIOR: COGNITIVE
PROCESSES AND
PERSONALITY

Ford if he or she is working for Chevrolet, not to criticize the company in public, and not to wear the wrong kind of clothes or be seen in the wrong kind of place.[42]

Recent studies have indicated that socialization is important not only to new organization members but also in the superior-subordinate relationship, and when personnel switch jobs (e.g., move from a line to a staff position) or are promoted.[43] Van Maanen also suggests specific socialization strategies such as formal or informal, individual or collective, sequential or non-sequential, or fixed or variable, which will lead to different outcomes for the individual and the organization.[44] For example, a company may use a sequential socialization strategy to groom a person for a top management position by first rotating him or her through a series of relevant functional specialties. Another organization, say a government agency, may take someone with political power from the rank and file and make him or her the head of the agency. This nonsequential strategy will result in different personal (i.e., the personality will be affected) and organizational outcomes. Such deliberate socialization strategies have tremendous potential impact on human resource management and organizational effectiveness.

More immediate situational considerations

The socialization process is obviously concerned with the situational impact on personality and thus falls in line with a social learning perspective. The cultural and family impact is more concerned with the historical nature of personality development. Both the cultural/family and socialization processes are important to personality, but it should also be recognized that the immediate situation may in the final analysis predominate. As the S-O-B-C model in Chapter 3 showed, it is the situation interacting with the human being, including the individual's personality, that are vital antecedents to behavior. An example is the worker whose developmental history has shaped a personality which incorporates a high need for power and achievement. When placed in a highly bureaucratized work situation, this individual may become frustrated and behave apathetically and/or aggressively. Thus, on the surface this worker appears to be lazy and/or a troublemaker. Yet the developmental history would predict that the individual would be a very hard worker, striving to get ahead. The countless potential combinations of the situation and the human being make it virtually impossible always to predict accurately from the developmental history alone the ways in which the personality will be behaviorally expressed. The interaction is too complex, and when the role of consequences is included, it becomes obvious that the developmental aspects of

---

[42]Ibid.

[43]John Gabarro, "Socialization at the Top—How CEO's and Subordinates Evolve Inter-personal Contracts," *Organizational Dynamics*, Winter 1979, pp. 3–23.

[44]John Van Maanen, "People Processing: Strategies of Organizational Socialization," *Organizational Dynamics*, Summer 1978, pp. 19–36.

personality by themselves do not provide a means of understanding, predicting, and controlling human behavior.

Research on the immediate situational impact   A very dramatic study by Stanley Milgram gives support to the important role that the immediate situation plays in the human personality. He conducted a series of tightly controlled experimental studies that used almost a thousand adult subjects.[45] These subjects were not students, ranged from twenty to fifty years of age, and came from a wide variety of occupations (unskilled, skilled, white-collar, sales, business, and professional). Each experimental session consisted of a naive subject, an accomplice, and the experimenter. The experimenter explained that the subject would be part of a learning experiment to test the effect of punishment on memory. After a rigged drawing on roles to be played, the naive subject always became the "teacher" and the accomplice became the "learner" in the experiment. The learner (experimenter's accomplice) was then taken to the next room and strapped into a sinister-looking "electric chair," which the subject could see through a glass partition. The experimenter carefully explained that the "teacher" (naive subject) would administer increasing levels of shock to the learner whenever a mistake was made. The shock generator had clearly marked voltage levels that ran from 15 to 450 volts, and printed descriptions that ranged from "Slight Shock" to "Danger: Severe Shock." To convince the naive subjects of the authenticity of the shock device, they were given a real shock from the 45-volt switch.

For control purposes, accomplices' responses to the shocks were broadcast from a premade tape, and of course they did not actually receive any shocks. Starting with what the subject believed to be a 75-volt shock, the "learner" began to grunt and moan. As the succeeding shocks increased in voltage, the cries became louder and more desperate. The "learner" pleaded with the "teacher" to have mercy and to stop the experiment. Whenever the "teacher" (subject) would hesitate to administer more shock, the experimenter would prod him or her on by saying, "You have no other choice, you must go on!" Finally, the "learner" could give no more answers and the naive subject was told by the experimenter to give the maximum voltage shock. Contrary to common expert opinion, almost two-thirds of the subjects went ahead and administered what they thought was a very dangerous, severe shock that might even lead to death. Milgram, who was obviously disturbed by his findings, stated:

With numbing regularity good people were seen to knuckle under the demands of authority and perform actions that were callous and severe. Men who are in everyday life responsible and decent were seduced by the trappings of authority, by the control of their perceptions, and by the uncritical acceptance of the experimenter's definition of the situation, into performing harsh acts.[46]

---

[45]Stanley Milgram, "Some Conditions of Obedience and Disobedience to Authority," *Human Relations*, February 1965, pp. 57–76.

[46]Ibid., p. 75.

130

A MICRO PERSPECTIVE OF
ORGANIZATIONAL
BEHAVIOR: COGNITIVE
PROCESSES AND
PERSONALITY

Implications of the Milgram study Compared to the developmental aspects of personality, relatively little attention has been given to the situational impact. Yet Milgram's research suggests the very powerful role that the immediate situation may play in the human personality. In fact, he calls for a theory that would provide a definition and typology of situations. He believes that if such guidance were available, certain definable properties of situations could be transformed into psychological forces in the individual.[47] In other words, studying the situational determinants may be of as much value as studying case histories. To prove the point, Milgram put leading advocates of the case history approach to the test. Forty psychiatrists from a prestigious medical school were asked to predict the behavior of the subjects in the shock experiment. The highly trained experts did a very poor job. They estimated that only about one tenth of 1 percent of the subjects would administer maximum shock, when in fact almost 63 percent did so.

The Milgram research certainly does not completely rule out the importance of the developmental aspects of personality. Rather, it demonstrates that the immediate situation may potentially have a very big impact on the behavioral expression of the personality, even to the point where it seems to override what one would predict on the basis of the developmental history. The experimenter in the Yale psychological laboratory where the studies were conducted produced a situation where people violated their moral codes. They were obedient to scientific authority. When the setting was moved to a run-down commercial building under the guise of Research Associates of Bridgeport, the percentage of those who obeyed to the end dropped to 48 percent.

The results of Milgram's studies have produced a strong emotional reaction from academicians and the public. Critics claim that Milgram was unethical, and they doubt that the subjects really believed that they were administering such a severe shock. Milgram answers the first charge by saying that every precaution was taken and all subjects were carefully debriefed. He supported those who disobeyed and assured those who obeyed that their behavior was perfectly normal and that other subjects had shared their conflicts. Follow-up questionnaires found that almost everyone said the experiment had been worthwhile and only 1 percent of the subjects were sorry they had participated. As for the charge questioning the validity of the study, Milgram has data from direct observation, interviews, and questionnaires to support his claim that subjects accepted the experiment at face value. He feels that not one subject suspected the deception.

In a more recent book, *Obedience to Authority*, Milgram expounds on some of his original findings and discusses the follow-up on the modifications and variations. The following summarizes some of the finer points and variations in obedience to authority:

1. Obedience decreases when the ("learner") is in the same room as the "teacher," and decreases further when the teacher must touch the "learner" directly to

---

[47]Ibid.

administer the shock. The modern state, of course, is designed for impersonality, where switches can be pulled and bombs dropped without anyone ever seeing the victim.

2. Obedience drops sharply when the experimenter is absent. To commit acts they would otherwise consider immoral, people must have authority behind them.

3. Obedience drops when the subject is in a group of rebellious peers. Rebels awaken the subject to the possibility of disobedience and, in this case, to its benign results. The group offers social support for the decision to disobey.

4. By contrast, obedience increases when the subject is merely an accessory to the crime, when he does not have to pull the shock lever himself. In this case, thirty-seven subjects out of forty stay in the experiment to the end.[48]

The findings of Milgram's study have implications for explaining the behavior during some of the highly publicized war atrocities (for example, at Auschwitz in World War II and My Lai in the Vietnam war). In fact, the studies are sometimes called the "Eichmann experiments" after the Nazi war criminal Adolf Eichmann. Some of the anxieties of Milgram and the implications of the study have also been captured in a fictionalized television drama, *The Tenth Level*. Besides the emotional impact the studies have on people, Milgram's work does have significant implications for understanding organizational behavior. Although this chapter has been primarily concerned with the impact of the situation on personality, in the broader sense the Milgram study reinforces the importance that the situation also has on overall human behavior. As stated by Milgram,

A situation exerts an important press on the individual. It exercises constraints and may provide push. In certain circumstances it is not so much the kind of person a man is, as the kind of situation in which he is placed, that determines his actions.[49]

Once again the person-situation interaction surfaces as an important, but often overlooked, dynamic in the understanding of human behavior.

THEORIES OF PERSONALITY

So far, the discussion has centered on the meaning and development of personality, but realistically, of course, these factors cannot be separated from the general theory of personality. However, for the purposes of this chapter, it is convenient to separate them.

Just as all people have their own definition of personality, practically all laypersons and scholars have their own theory of personality. The diversity is attributable to the extreme complexity of the unique, whole person conceptualization of the personality. Because of the wide range of opinion, it is difficult to organize a meaningful discussion. However, the most logical breakdown seems to be into psychoanalytic, type, trait, self, and social theories of personality.

---

[48]See *Psychology Today*, June 1974, p. 77.

[49]Milgram, op. cit., p. 72.

132

A MICRO PERSPECTIVE OF
ORGANIZATIONAL
BEHAVIOR: COGNITIVE
PROCESSES AND
PERSONALITY

Psychoanalytic theories

Sigmund Freud has been presented as one of the foremost pioneers in many areas of psychological thought, and personality theory is no exception. Freud's theory, based upon the concepts of id, ego, and superego and discussed in detail in Chapter 3, is historically the most significant and probably the best-known theory of the structure of personality. But as in the case of his ideas about personality development, the id, ego, and superego theory served only as a point of departure for further refinement, modification, and extension. The work of Carl Jung, one of Freud's colleagues, is an example.

Usually classified as a neo-Freudian, Jung carried Freud's concept of the unconscious one step further. He believed that a collective unconscious exists in the personality which is deeper and more unknown to the person than the personal unconscious conceived by Freud. Jung went so far as to say that the collective unconscious includes the cumulative experiences of *all* past generations, even those of primitive ancestors. Perhaps a more significant contribution than the concept of the collective unconscious (which is thought-provoking and novel but which relies heavily on mysticism rather than on science) is his work on introversion and extroversion. Jung felt that these two opposing attitudes or modes of reaction exist in every person but that one will dominate the other.

Many colleagues and contemporaries of Freud besides Jung contributed historically important psychoanalytic ideas about personality theory. In addition, all the other historical schools (structuralism, functionalism, behavioralism, and gestaltism) made contributions. Yet, Freud's theory of personality has had the greatest and most long-lasting impact.

Type theories

The type theories represent an attempt to put some degree of order into the chaos of personality theory. Both layperson and scholar would feel more comfortable if they could place personalities into clearly identifiable categories. This is a basic aim of any scientific endeavor. The search for personality types has generally taken one of the following three approaches:

1. The physique or body-type theories have concentrated on determining a relationship between features of the face or body and personality. Sheldon's body types, mentioned in the discussion of the biological determinants of personality development, is the most widely known body-type theory.
2. The physiological theories have concentrated on the relationship between body chemistry or endocrine balance and personality. Typically, certain chemical substances are correlated with temperament.
3. The third way to type personalities is in terms of behavior or psychological factors. Jung's introvert and extrovert types are an example. However, as Jung himself pointed out, the introvert-extrovert typology turns out to be more in the nature of a continuum than discretely separate types.

The continuum reference made by Jung generally applies to the other type theories as well. They tend to oversimplify the very complex human personality. It is doubtful that any truly meaningful personality type theories can ever be developed.

Trait theories

Another approach to putting some degree of order into personality theory has been the search for identifiable traits. A personality trait can be defined as an "enduring attribute of a person that appears consistently in a variety of situations."[50] In combination, such traits distinguish one personality from another. The two most widely known trait theories come from the classic work of Gordon Allport and Raymond Cattell.

Allport's trait theory Allport bases his theory on the distinction between common traits and personal dispositions. Common traits are used to compare people. For example, the theoretical, economic, esthetic, social, political, and religious categories in Allport's *Scale of Values Test* are primarily used for comparison purposes. However, besides the common traits, there are traits which are completely unique. These unique traits Allport calls *personal dispositions*. They can be cardinal (most pervasive), central (unique and limited in number), or secondary (peripheral). Allport's emphasis on personal dispositions is a departure from the more traditional common-trait approach. He gives more recognition to the complexity and uniqueness of the human personality.

Cattell's trait theory Cattell takes a different approach than Allport. As was pointed out in the introductory discussion in this chapter, many thousands of words can be used to describe personality. By eliminating overlapping meanings, Cattell was able to come up with 171 words that can be used to describe personality traits. He then made a distinction between what he called *surface traits* and *source traits*. He determined thirty-five surface traits by finding clusters of traits that correlated. Some examples are wise-foolish, affectionate-cold, sociable-seclusive, and honest-dishonest. Such traits lie on the surface of the personality and are largely determined by the underlying source traits. Using factor analysis, Cattell was able to determine twelve source traits. Examples include affectothymia (good nature and trustfulness) versus sizothymia (critical and suspicious attitudes); ego strength (maturity and realism) versus emotionality and neuroticism (immaturity and evasiveness); dominance versus submissiveness; and surgency (cheerfulness and energy) versus desurgency (depressed and subdued feelings).[51]

The value of trait theories Overall, the trait theories seem to make more sense than the type theories. The type theories unrealistically attempt to

[50]Gregory A. Kimble, Norman Garmezy, and Edward Zigler, *General Psychology*, 4th ed., Ronald, New York, 1974, p. 298.

[51]Raymond B. Cattell, *The Scientific Analysis of Personality*, Aldine, Chicago, 1965. First published in 1965 by Penguin, Baltimore.

134

A MICRO PERSPECTIVE OF
ORGANIZATIONAL
BEHAVIOR: COGNITIVE
PROCESSES AND
PERSONALITY

place personalities into discrete, discontinuous categories. The trait theories, on the other hand, give recognition to the continuity of personalities. The trait theorists have also contributed personality tests and factor-analysis techniques to the behavioral sciences. The major drawback of these theories is that they are very descriptive rather than analytical and are a long way from being comprehensive theories of personality.

Self theories

The psychoanalytic, type, and trait theories represent the more traditional approaches to explaining the complex human personality. Of the many other theories, the two that have received the most recent emphasis and that are probably most relevant to the study of organizational behavior are the self and social theories of personality. They seem to hold the most promise for better personality theory.

Elements of the self-concept   Self theories attempt to integrate the various parts of the personality structure into a meaningful whole. Carl Rogers is most closely associated with this approach. He defined the self or self-concept as an "organized, consistent conceptual gestalt composed of perceptions of the characteristics of the 'I' or 'me' and the perceptions of the relationships of 'I' or 'me' to others and to various aspects of life, together with the values attached to these perceptions."[52] The distinction made between "I" and "me" is vitally important to the understanding of the self-concept.

The "I" is the *personal* self, the self that one believes oneself to be and strives to be. It consists of the individual's psychological processes (perception, learning, and motivation) which, in combination, result in a unique whole.

The "me" represents the *social* self. The "me" is the way a person appears to others and the way this person thinks he or she appears to others. The "me" is explained in more explicit terms as follows:

When I know what other people expect, I can try to integrate myself with the social situation by being a "normal" person in that situation as this is defined by others. This part of me is the part I want to and find myself willing to set forth in my behavior or what, because it is my habitual way, I want to be. The role that I play is therefore a reflection of my inner self. . . . It is also a mirror image of what I believe others expect from me. . . .[53]

This explanation points out that the "me" is closely tied to the role expectations that others have of the self.

Impact of the self-concept   The self-concept (both "I" and "me") gives the individual a sense of meaningfulness and consistency. Gellerman notes

---

[52]Carl R. Rogers, "A Theory of Therapy, Personality, and Interpersonal Relationships, as Developed in the Client-centered Framework," in S. Koch (ed.), *Psychology: A Study of Science*, vol. 3, McGraw-Hill, New York, 1959, p. 200.

[53]Henry P. Knowles and Borje O. Saxberg, *Personality and Leadership Behavior*, Addison-Wesley, Reading, Mass., 1971, p. 78.

that "the average individual is not particularly well acquainted with himself, so to speak, but he remains quite faithful to his not-so-accurate image of himself and thereby acquires some consistency."[54] People's self-concepts will also have a direct effect on their behavior. Thus, in analyzing organizational behavior, it would be beneficial to remember that because each self-concept is unique, the application of various reinforcement, motivation, task design, and leadership techniques will have different effects on different people. For example, monetary reward for performance, a security-oriented motivation technique, routine job design, or an authoritarian leadership style applied to a worker with a self-concept of independence, intelligence, security, and confidence, may be ineffective. On the other hand, the same reward for performance, motivational technique, task design and leadership style applied to a worker with a self-concept of dependence, unintelligence, insecurity, and indecisiveness may be effective. This simple example points out the potential applicability that the self theory of personality may have to the study of organizational behavior and the need for contingency application of reinforcement, motivation, task design, and leadership techniques.

Social theories

As the discussions of the definition, socialization process, and the immediate situational impact pointed out, the social learning framework, as outlined in Chapters 2 and 3 and which will be given further attention in Chapters 9 and 22, can be a useful theoretical framework for personality. The person-situation interaction that is emphasized by social learning can serve as a theoretical foundation for personality. For example, the work done by Schein on socialization or Milgram on obedience to authority indicates that the social situation is as important, if not more important, than the individual's traits in determining how a person will behave. "It has therefore become evident that it is more productive to analyze and study the cognitive and social learning conditions that seem to foster or undermine the behavioral personality response to a given stimulus. Understanding of the mediation processes is, then, the same as understanding the personality of an individual."[55] Table 5-3 demonstrates how this social learning approach to personality could be used to analyze organizational behavior. In essence, in this view personality becomes a mediational process between the situation and the behavior. Personality is considered to be part of the "O" in the S-O-B-C conceptual model for organizational behavior.

SUMMARY

Personality represents the "whole person" concept. It includes perception, learning, motivation, and more. Definitionally, people's external appearance

---

[54]Gellerman, op. cit., p. 184.

[55]H. Randolph Bobbitt, Jr., Robert H. Breinholt, Robert H. Doktor, and James P. McNaul, *Organizational Behavior*, 2d ed., Prentice-Hall, Englewood Cliffs, N.J., 1978, p. 204.

136

A MICRO PERSPECTIVE OF
ORGANIZATIONAL
BEHAVIOR: COGNITIVE
PROCESSES AND
PERSONALITY

Table 5–3

AN EXAMPLE OF A SOCIAL LEARNING ANALYSIS OF ORGANIZATIONAL BEHAVIOR

Organization member views relationships between the behavior of certain individuals (e.g., top management) and outcomes of the behaviors (i.e., the degree to which the behavior is reinforced). →	These relationships are learned as a result of those observations and perceptions. →	After learning the relationships between these behaviors and their outcomes, the organizational participant engages in behaviors which, according to these learned cognitions, will enable him or her to achieve desired outcomes. (For example, if the participant wishing to achieve organizational success sees that the president of the company behaves in a certain way in order to achieve success, the participant is likely to behave in the same manner.)

The eventual development of (1) learned behaviors that lead to desired outcomes; (2) increased value for the stimuli and objects associated with the reinforced behaviors as a result of secondary reinforcement processes.

Source: Adapted from Abraham K. Korman, *Organizational Behavior,* Prentice-Hall, Englewood Cliffs, N.J., 1977, p. 286.

and behavior, inner awareness of self, pattern of measurable traits, and the person-situation interaction make up their personalities. Classic stage theories of personality development by Freud, Erikson, and Piaget make significant contributions, but the seven-dimension continuum of immaturity-maturity by Argyris is of more relevance to the study of organizational behavior. Determining the inputs into personality may be the most complex and difficult task in the study of human behavior, but a comprehensive approach would have to include biological, cultural, family, socialization, and immediate situational factors.

A universally accepted personality theory does not currently exist. The historically significant theories were dominated by the psychoanalytic ideas of Freud. The traditional type and trait theories attempted to put some order into the existing diversity. Both approaches made a contribution but fell far short of providing an overall theory of personality. The type theories unrealistically tried to force personalities into discrete, discontinuous categories, and the trait theories were helpfully descriptive but not meaningfully analytical. The more recent self and social theories try to integrate the various complex parts of the personality into a more meaningful whole. The self-concept seems to have a chance for unifying personality theory but a social learning view that is just emerging may be most relevant for organizational behavior analysis and explanation.

QUESTIONS FOR DISCUSSION AND REVIEW

1. Critically analyze the statement that "the various psychological processes could be thought of as pieces of a jigsaw puzzle and personality as the completed puzzle picture."
2. What is the comprehensive definition of personality? Give brief examples of each of the major elements.
3. What are the various factors in the biological contributions to personality? The cultural contributions? The family contributions? The socialization contributions? The immediate situational contributions?
4. How do the type theories differ from the trait theories?
5. What are the major elements of the self-concept? How can this analysis contribute to a better understanding of organizational behavior?
6. What is the focus of a social theoretical approach to personality? Why is such an approach so relevant to organizational behavior?

CASE: CHEERLEADER VERSUS ACTIVIST

Liz Schmit grew up in a Midwestern town of 25,000 people. She was the third generation of the Schmit family in this town. Her grandparents, who had come from Germany, were retired, but they took care of her younger brother and her whenever her mother and dad had to go some place—like a wedding or a funeral. Neither of Liz's parents had attended college, but once her father took an IQ test and scored almost in the genius category. Her parents always encouraged her to do well in school and saved their money so she could go to State University. Liz also worked during the summer to save money for college. She did very well academically in high school and was a varsity cheerleader. She went on to State University, joined a sorority, majored in English, graduated with honors, and took a job with Landis and Smith Advertising Agency. Liz, now thirty-seven years old, has been with L&S for fifteen years and has a good work record.

One of Liz's co-workers is Todd Long. Todd grew up in a suburb of Los Angeles. His parents both attended U.C.L.A., and he had seen his grandparents, who were retired military people, only a few times. While growing up, Todd's parents were gone a lot. His mother had arranged for babysitters while she finished her degree at U.C.L.A. It was always assumed that when Todd graduated from high school he too would go on to U.C.L.A. Todd was not particularly active in extracurricular activities but graduated in the top 10 percent of his high school class. At U.C.L.A. he majored in journalism and was very active in the student movement in the late 1960s. Upon graduation he cut his hair and went to work for L&S. Todd, now 32, has been employed by L&S for ten years and has a very good work record.

The job of copy editor is now open, and Liz and Todd are the two top

138

A MICRO PERSPECTIVE OF
ORGANIZATIONAL
BEHAVIOR: COGNITIVE
PROCESSES AND
PERSONALITY

candidates. The head of L&S, Stacy McAdams, made it clear that "this job requires a good personality. He or she will be in contact with all the people in the office, and we need someone who can get along well with others and still be able to coordinate the work and meet our critical deadlines."

1. Based on the brief sketches of the two people in this incident, what do you think their personalities are like? Use the determinants of personality and give an example of each determinant that can be found in the incident.
2. Who do you think will get the job? You can discuss the male/female implications; but based solely upon personalities that you outlined in the first question, who do you think *would* get the job? Who do you think *should* get the job?
3. What does the boss mean by saying that a "good" personality is required? Is there such a thing? Do you feel that personality makes much of an input into these types of staffing decisions? Should it have an input? Why?
4. Do you think the socialization processes at L&S have completely overcome their biological, cultural, and family influences? Why or why not?

CASE:
PORTRAIT OF A BLACK LEADER

Several years ago in a very large midwestern city, there was a black man who had done much to unite local black leaders and black advocate groups, including violent street gangs. At the time there was a great deal of racial trouble in the area and a lot of hate on both sides, black and white. The city was characterized as a powder keg, ready to explode at any moment. The black leader had a strong commitment from most blacks in this city. If he had told them to riot in the streets and to bring the city to its knees economically, they would have done it without question. The power that comes from a normative commitment is very strong. But instead of channeling the efforts of blacks toward destructive, violent ends, he diligently worked toward a positive approach to improving the community and building bridges to the existing power structure. He emphasized the importance of education and jobs in improving conditions. He called upon black pride as the cornerstone of improving life for all of the city. After the destruction of the 1960s, hope grew and progress was made in the 1970s. While this leader still has not reached all his goals and there are still many frustrations and real problems to be solved, few would argue that things are as bad as when he started. This leader's name is Rev. Jesse Jackson.

1. How does the developmental versus social/situational impact on personality relate to the leader described in this case?
2. Do you think the socialization process affects leaders such as Jackson? Explain and give other examples.

CASE STUDY AND EXPERIENTIAL EXERCISES FOR PART 2

CASE:
PEOPLE DON'T CHANGE, OR DO THEY?

Paul Smith was a recruiter in the personnel department of a large organization. One day he was chatting with Dick Witte, a top manager. Paul was lamenting the fact that when he visited college campuses he had only fifteen minutes to talk with, and make a judgment about, a potential job candidate. "How can you decide in that short a period of time?" he asked. "I just hope the fellows I choose to come back here for follow-up interviews will meet with your approval." Dick assured him that they would, and the conversation went as follows:

"Don't let it worry you, Paul. You've got a knack for picking out good people. Besides, I know you can't allow anyone more than fifteen minutes with your busy schedule, and that doesn't give you a lot of time for making judgments. You know, though, I've often thought that it would be easier on interviewers if they talked to the neighbors of the interviewees who knew these people when they were kids."

"I don't think I follow you."

"Well, I'll bet you that if you knew a person as a kid and then met the person as an adult, you would find basically the same individual. I mean, the person wouldn't have changed very much at all."

"Do you really think so?"

"I'm positive of it. People just don't change."

"I'm not so sure that I agree with you, Dick. As people get older, they tend to do things differently from the way they did as children."

"Not quite. They might do things somewhat differently, but they would be predictable. I'm sure of it. For example, you take a kid who's a bookworm when he's seven or eight years old. The guy is going to be either a teacher or a librarian."

"Well, if that's true, why doesn't every kid become a doctor? At some stage they all seem to want to be one."

"Sure, but you have to distinguish between fleeting fancy and deep interest. I think this is possible to determine."

"Do you really think you can prove that?"

"You bet. I'll tell you what, get that yearbook from the shelf over there."

Paul did so and handed it to Dick.

"This is my high school yearbook. Now it's been almost twenty-five years since I graduated from high school, but I'll bet you that I can tell you what

140

A MICRO PERSPECTIVE OF
ORGANIZATIONAL
BEHAVIOR: COGNITIVE
PROCESSES AND
PERSONALITY

anyone in here is doing today if you just call out his name."

"Well, you might know just on the basis of the alumni get-togethers."

"If you'll take my word for it, I have never attended one of them. Furthermore, if you look at the address inside the cover, you'll see that the school is located on the other coast. Right after high school my folks moved here, and I haven't been back since. In fact, I never did see any of those guys again."

"All right, Dick. What do you think Frank Aaron is doing today? It says here that he liked chemistry and wanted to major in it at college."

"Don't take him because we have no way of checking. Choose someone with a rare name, and we'll call the city and try to locate him."

"All right, here's one. Theodore X. Culpepahr."

"Good choice. Old Teddy's father was a very successful mortician, but Teddy never seemed to express an interest in joining that business. As I remember him, he was always in school plays and loved to recite poetry."

"It says here that he wanted to major in English in college."

"I believe it. Now let's see. From what I remember of him he would be either an English teacher or the director of a local theater guild. I'll tell you what, I'll bet you that today he's teaching drama at a college somewhere on the coast."

"How can we find out?"

"With a name like that? Let's call information and see if he's still living in the same city. In any event, it shouldn't be too difficult to locate him."

The operator informed Dick that there was no one by the name of Theodore X. Culpepahr living in the city. Dick then asked her to give him the number of the Culpepahr mortuary. He placed a call there and asked for Teddy's father.

"Mr. Culpepahr? This is Dick Whitson. I was a high school classmate of Teddy's. I have a business trip scheduled for your area and I was just calling ahead to find out where Teddy was. I thought I might drop by and look him up."

"Well, he doesn't live here any more. He and his wife have a house about 100 miles up the shore."

"I see. Well tell me, what's he doing these days?"

"Oh he's teaching English composition and literature at a junior college."

"Well, isn't that great! Listen, tell him I called, won't you, and I'll try to get in touch with him sometime."

After hanging up, Dick turned back to Paul.

"What did I tell you? He's teaching English at a junior college. Now I'll concede that I was a little off, but not very much, right?"

"No, you were pretty accurate. However, I'm still not so certain that I hold with your theory concerning the fact that people don't change."

"Oh, heck, Paul. By the time people are five years old their futures are already spelled out. From there on they're just going through the motions of a prewritten script. If you want to find out about people, learn something of their early personality and environment. From there you can merely extrapolate."

1. What personality theory is Dick supporting when he is making his argument with Paul? If you were Paul, what personality theories would you suggest as alternatives to counter Dick's argument?

2. What kinds of perceptions does a recruiter like Paul form of a job applicant in a

fifteen-minute interview? What are some perceptual principles that will affect his impressions of candidates? Is there some way that recruiters could improve the accuracy of their perceptions?

3. How do you account for the fact that Paul seems to be doing a good job of recruiting good people? How do you account for the fact that Dick was fairly accurate in his prediction of what an old classmate was doing twenty-five years later?

EXERCISE:

THE EYE OF THE BEHOLDER

Goals:

1. To show how the same situation can be perceived in different ways by different people
2. To demonstrate that perception is influenced by a person's motives and personality

Materials required:

The film *The Eye of the Beholder* can be effectively used in this exercise. If this film is not available, the participants may be asked to put on a brief skit or role-play scene.

Implementation:

1. If the film is used, the participants are asked to answer the following questions with 5 (completely true), 4 (somewhat true), 3 (neutral or not relevant), 2 (somewhat incorrect), or 1 (incorrect):
   _____ a. Michael Gerrard is admired by the people who really know him well.
   _____ b. The cabdriver came very close to provoking violence in Gerrard.
   _____ c. The landlord sees Gerrard's personality quite accurately, even though the landlord is untactful.
   _____ d. Gerrard knows quite a bit about the profession of an artist, judging from his mannerisms and conversation.
   _____ e. Gerrard's behavior in the story would indicate that he is a well-adjusted man.
   _____ f. Michael Gerrard is a moody and unpredictable person.
   _____ g. If the girl in the nightclub had known more about Gerrard, she would *not* have consented to work for him as a model.
   _____ h. In view of Gerrard's behavior, I *would* recommend him for employment as an artist.
   (Note: If a skit or role-play is used, similar questions should be developed about it.)
2. After everyone has viewed the film and answered the questions, an average total is calculated for the class. Everyone can then see how they compare to the class average.
3. Each of the questions above and why the people answered the way they did can then be openly discussed. People may want to reveal their own motives and personality characteristics in terms of why they perceived the film the way they did.

EXERCISE:

SELF-PERCEPTION AND DEVELOPMENT OF THE SELF-CONCEPT

Goals:

1. For students to consider their own self-concept and to compare this with how they feel they are perceived by others
2. To explore how the self-concept in personality is formed largely on the basis of feedback received from others (the reality that we "mirror ourselves in others")
3. To stimulate student thinking about how management of human resources may involve perception and personality

Implementation:

1. Students are to take out a sheet of paper and fold it in half from top to bottom.
2. Head up the top with "How I See Myself." On the bottom put "How I Think Others See Me."
3. The students are to write down five one-word descriptions (adjectives) under each designation which, in their opinion, best describe how they perceive themselves and how others perceive them.
4. Students then share their two lists with their classmates (in dyads and triads, or the whole class) and discuss briefly. Each person may communicate what they are most proud of in themselves.
5. The instructor may participate in the exercise by sharing his or her list of adjectives.

MOTIVATION AND LEARNING: THE FOCUS OF THE MICRO APPROACH TO ORGANIZATIONAL BEHAVIOR

THE BASIC MOTIVATION PROCESS

WORKER DISCONTENT IS RISING*

The widely recognized Survey Research Center at the University of Michigan recently published the results of its four-year survey of the Quality of Employment in America. The results showed a marked decrease in the overall satisfaction that employees have with respect to their jobs. The researchers measured the attitudes of over 1500 workers in a wide variety of jobs and found a significant downward trend over the 1973 and 1969 survey results. Less than one-third of those responding indicated that they had good working conditions. In the 1973 survey almost 40 percent felt that they did. Also, in 1973 about half the workers felt that they had a job that was interesting, but in the latest survey this figure was down to 40 percent. Forty-five percent of the employees thought they had good pay and fringe benefits in 1973, but only a third now feel this way. Most important, almost a third of the employees in the recent survey felt that their skills were not being utilized well in their present job assignment.

These survey results point out a couple of interesting things concerning the present mood of people at work. Although not all employees are dissatisfied with their jobs and the way they are treated, and, in fact, other surveys even indicate a more positive outlook than is reported by the Michigan group, none can disagree that there is considerable room for improvement. The *trend* of the survey results is certainly in a downward direction. One could argue that jobs are becoming more boring, but it is true that the individuals who must do those jobs are becoming more educated and less satisfied with "the way things are." There is a new work force with increasing expectations and new demands. The management practices of the past, even the recent past, will not suffice for the present and future. There is a need to better understand the basic motivational processes of today's employees.

---

*Adapted from "A Warning that Worker Discontent is Rising," *Business Week,* June 4, 1979, pp. 152–153.

145

Motivation is a basic psychological process. Few would deny that it is the most important process in the micro approach to organizational behavior. Many people equate the causes of behavior with motivation. Chapter 3 and the two preceding chapters emphasized that the causes of behavior are much broader and more complex than can be explained by motivation alone. However, motivation should never be underrated. Along with perception, personality, and learning, it is presented here as a very important process in understanding behavior. Nevertheless, it must be remembered that motivation should not be thought of as the only explanation of behavior. It interacts with and acts in conjunction with other mediating processes and the environment. It must also be remembered that, like the other mediating processes, motivation cannot be seen. All that can be seen are behaviors. Motivation is a hypothetical construct that is used to help explain behavior; it should not be equated with the behavior.

This chapter presents motivation as a basic psychological process in human behavior. The more applied aspects of motivation are covered in the next two chapters. Approaches to job satisfaction and work motivation are given attention in Chapter 7, and some specific techniques to motivate workers and managers are found in Chapter 8, which deals with goal setting and job design. This chapter provides a necessary foundation for the theories and applications of work motivation.

The first section of the chapter traces the historical development of the study of motivation. A brief discussion of hedonism is followed by the major historical concepts: instincts, unconscious motivation, and drive theory. The second section clarifies the meaning of motivation by defining the relationship among its various parts. The need→drive→goal cycle is defined and analyzed. The rest of the chapter is devoted to an overview of the various types of human motives. The discussion is broken down into the three generally recognized categories of motives: primary, general, and secondary. The motives within the general and secondary categories are given major attention, and a summary of supporting research findings on these motives is included.

HISTORICAL DEVELOPMENT

The study of motivation can be traced back to the writings of the ancient Greek philosophers. More than twenty-three centuries ago, they presented hedonism as an explanation of human motivation. The concept of hedonism says that a person seeks out comfort and pleasure and avoids discomfort and pain. Many centuries later, hedonism was still a basic assumption in the prevailing economic and social philosophies of such famous men as Adam Smith, Jeremy Bentham, and John Stuart Mill. They all explained motivation in terms of people trying to maximize pleasure and minimize pain.

Early psychological thought was also influenced by the idea of hedonism. Psychologists in the 1800s and even in the early 1900s assumed that humans consciously and rationally strive for hedonistic pleasure and avoidance of pain. William James, who is often called the father of American psychology, was one of the first to question this assumption. In his classic

Principles of Psychology, he gave recognition to two additional important historical concepts in the study of motivation: instincts and unconscious motivation. Later, using the scientific perspective of early behaviorists, Clark Hull formulated the drive theory of motivation.

Instincts

James did not feel that the human is always consciously rational. He thought that much of human behavior is instinct-based. A partial list of the unlearned instincts that James believed influence behavior included crying, locomotion, curiosity, imitation, sociability, sympathy, fear of dark places, jealousy, and love. These and many other instincts were thought by James to be present in every person. William McDougall, the pioneering social psychologist, further developed the instinctual theory of behavior. In his social psychology book of 1908, he defined an instinct as "an innate disposition which determines the organism to perceive or to pay attention to any object . . . and to act or have an impulse to action which finds expression in a specific mode of behavior." The key assumption of those who advocated the instinctual approach was that there is an unlearned *predisposition* to behavior.

Starting in the 1920s, the instinctual view of human motivation came under heavy attack. In particular, the early behaviorists, who dealt with observable behavior in a purely scientific manner, completely disagreed with the theory of largely unobservable, almost mystical instinct. The other schools of thought also questioned some of the extreme instinctual views. This severe criticism has carried over so that today the term *instinct* is seldom used in academic discussions of human behavior. Although modern psychologists recognize that some human motives seem to be unlearned, they are not willing to accept the extreme instinctual views, especially the idea of predisposed behaviors that was advocated by James and McDougall.

There is too much evidence that humans do not have simplistic, innate predispositions toward behavior. Animals may have certain instincts of this kind, but humans do not. While some psychologists recognize a sucking instinct, most do not admit to the existence of any human instinct whatsoever. Instead, behavior is explained by complex cognitive and environmental interactions. As presented in Chapter 3, behavior consists of the interacting person (including cognitive processes)–environment–behavior dynamic. Instincts are an insufficient explanation for behavior because "(1) people differ in the strength of their motivational dispositions, and (2) at any one time the relevant behavior may not correspond to the strengths of the persisting dispositions."[1]

Unconscious motivation

Implicit in James's emphasis on instincts is the whole question of unconscious motivation. However, it was Sigmund Freud, not James, who openly

---

[1]Ernest R. Hilgard and Richard C. Atkinson, *Introduction to Psychology,* 4th ed., Harcourt, Brace & World, New York, 1967, p. 140.

recognized the importance of the unconscious and made it a vital part of the study of human motivation. In fact, many students of Freud argue that this recognition was his greatest contribution. In light of Freud's many significant contributions, this accolade indicates how important unconscious motivation can be to the study of human behavior.

The existence of unconscious motivation implies that humans are not consciously aware of all their desires. The presence of an unconscious explains why people cannot always verbalize their motivation to attain certain goals or even tell what their goals are. Freud uncovered this phenomenon while analyzing his clinical patients. He found that in many ways a person is like an iceberg: only a small part is conscious and visible, the rest is beneath the surface. This below-the-surface concept is the unconscious.

In contrast to their rejection of instincts, many contemporary psychologists accept the existence and importance of the unconscious. On the other hand, for the most part they do *not* agree with Freud's explanation of the unconscious. Like James, Freud attempted to equate unconscious motives with instincts. He felt that the unconscious motives are primarily sexual and aggressive in nature and, even though unconscious, that they greatly influence everyday behavior. He pointed out that these motives are revealed in dreams, slips of speech (the so-called Freudian slip), and lapses of memory.

The impact of unconscious motivation

The Freudian explanation of motivation has a devastating effect on human pride. People like to picture themselves as consciously rational and in complete control of their own behavior. Now, if Freud is right, this is an illusion. Is it true that sexual and aggressive motives locked in the mysterious unconscious determine people's behavior? In general such fears have been put to rest.

Psychologists generally recognize that a human possesses a degree of unconscious motivation, but not in the Freudian sense. Instead of the view that sexual and aggressive instincts dominate behavior, the more modern view is that normal behavior contains some consciously unexplainable motives, but that these are largely based on learning and not on instinct. For example, contemporary psychologists give reasons such as the following as to why all motives cannot be consciously explained:

1. Several drives and goals may be intertwined in any given bit of behavior; it is not always possible to identify correctly the motive or motives behind an act.
2. Habits of which the person is generally unaware may develop.
3. Some motives are formed under unpleasant circumstances and are repressed.[2]

The third point on repression is the most complex explanation of unconscious motivation. Repression was believed by Freud to be vital to under-

---

[2]Clifford T. Morgan and Richard A. King, *Introduction to Psychology*, 3d ed., McGraw-Hill, New York, 1966, p. 235.

standing abnormal personalities. A form of defense mechanism, repression disguises real motives by "perceiving them as different from what they really are, or by refusing to recognize them at all."[3]

Although instincts and the unconscious are important to a historical analysis of motivation, they play a relatively minor role in the modern study of motivation. On the other hand, although instincts are a dead issue, unconscious motivation is still open for discussion, debate, and more research. Currently, not much is known about the unconscious, but it may still prove to be an important element in improving understanding of human behavior. However, the major historical foundation for the study and understanding of motivation comes from Clark Hull's work on drive theory.

Early drive theories

The drive theories of motivation evolved from the dissatisfaction with the instinctual view of motivation. The drive theorists were greatly influenced by early behaviorists, who stressed the need for a scientific perspective. By the 1930s motivation was considered to be an important aspect of behavior, but no scientifically based theory could explain it. Clark Hull (1884–1952) was finally able to synthesize previous thinking into a scientifically based theory of motivation. Hull proposed that motivation was a product of drive and habit (Effort = D × H). The drive concept in particular was motivationally based. To Hull, drive was the energizing influence which determined the intensity of behavior. The habit concept reflected the behavioristic (learning) influence on Hull. Later, to counteract the emphasis given to the past by habit, Hull added the future-oriented concept of incentive to his equation (Effort = D × H × I). This incentive factor had cognitive properties and served as a forerunner of expectancy theories of motivation.

Hull's theory generated a tremendous amount of research in the 1940s and 1950s. Unfortunately, most of this research was conducted on rats in the laboratory, and few generalizations to human motivation are possible. Hull's students did extend the original concepts, but it is now generally recognized that most of Hull's concepts were wrong. Nevertheless, the scientific research tradition initiated by Hull and his followers, plus his emphasis on both the cognitive (drive and incentive) and learning (habit) aspects associated with motivation, are extremely important contributions to the modern study of motivation. Drive theory serves as a theoretical basis for the motivational cycle of needs→drives→goals.

The meaning of human motivation

Today, virtually all people—lay people and scholars—have their own definition of motivation. Usually one or more of the following words are included in the definition: desires, wants, wishes, aims, goals, needs, drives, motives, and incentives. Technically, the term *motivation* can be traced to the Latin word *movere* which means "to move." This meaning is evident in

---

[3]Ibid., p. 236.

the following comprehensive definition: "A motive is an inner state that energizes, activates, or moves (hence 'motivation'), and that directs or channels behavior toward goals."[4] A motive has also been described as follows: "A motive is a restlessness, a lack, a yen, a force. Once in the grip of a motive, the organism does something. It most generally does something to reduce the restlessness, to remedy the lack, to alleviate the yen, to mitigate the force."[5] The key to understanding motivation, it appears, lies in the meaning and relationship between needs, drives, and goals.

The motivation cycle

Figure 6-1 graphically depicts the motivation cycle. Needs set up drives to accomplish goals; this is what the basic process of motivation is all about. In a systems sense, motivation consists of three interacting and interdependent elements: needs, drives, and goals.

1. *Needs.* The best one-word definition of a need is *deficiency.* In the homeostatic sense, needs are created whenever there is a physiological or psychological imbalance. For example, a need exists when a cell in the body is deprived of food and water or when the human personality is deprived of other persons who serve as friends or companions.
2. *Drives.* With a few exceptions,[6] drives or motives (the two terms will be used interchangeably) are set up to alleviate needs. A drive can be simply defined as a deficiency with direction. The present definition is similar to Hull's use of the term: drives are action-oriented and provide an energizing thrust toward goal accomplishment. They are at the very heart of the motivational process. The examples of the needs for food and water are translated into the hunger and thirst drives, and the need for friends becomes a drive for affiliation.
3. *Goals.* At the end of the motivation cycle is the goal. A goal in the motivation cycle can be defined as anything which will alleviate a need and reduce a drive. Thus, attaining a goal will tend to restore physiological or psychological balance and will reduce or cut off the drive. Eating food, drinking water, and obtaining friends will tend to restore the homeostatic balance and reduce the corresponding drives. Food, water, and friends are the goals in these examples.

---

[4]Bernard Berelson and Gary A. Steiner, *Human Behavior,* Harcourt, Brace & World, New York, 1964, p. 240.

[5]Fillmore H. Sanford and Lawrence S. Wrightsman, Jr., *Psychology,* 3d ed., Brooks/Cole, Belmont, Calif., 1970, p. 189.

[6]The most frequently cited exception is the need for oxygen. A deficiency of oxygen in the body does not automatically set up a corresponding drive. This is a fear of high-altitude pilots. Unless their gauges show an oxygen leak or the increased intake of carbon dioxide sets up a drive, they may die of oxygen deficiency without a drive ever being set up to correct the situation. The same is true of the relatively frequent deaths of teen-agers parked in "lovers' lanes." Carbon monoxide leaks into their parked autos and they die from oxygen deficiency without its ever setting up a drive (to open the car door).

**Figure 6-1
The basic
motivation
process.**

NEEDS ⟶ DRIVES ⟶ GOALS
(Deprivation)   (Deprivation with direction)   (Reduction of drives)

Refinements of the motivation process

Before examining the individual motives, a couple of points about the basic motivation process need further refinement. First, it should be repeated that motivation, like perception and learning, is a hypothetical construct which is defined in terms of antecedent conditions and consequent behavior. No one has actually observed motivation or isolated it under a microscope. Motives such as hunger, sex, power, and achievement cannot be seen. Only the behavioral manifestations of these motives are observable. Restlessness, walking, running, and talking can be observed and so can eating food, drinking water, and winning a new friend. Yet, the corresponding motives can only be inferred from watching this behavior. As Sanford and Wrightsman note, "We can see [a person] seek a restaurant, we can see him eat, and we can see a decrease in restlessness. We infer, with considerable confidence, that a hunger motive was in full operation. But we have not directly observed hunger."[7]

Types of motivated behavior A point that needs emphasis is that motives can be expressed in several types of behavior. Kimble and Garmezy's description of three such types of motivated behavior[8] may be summarized thus:

1. *Consummatory behavior.* This is the most obvious form of motivated behavior because it directly satisfies the need in question. Examples of consummatory behavior with the corresponding drives would include eating (hunger), drinking (thirst), joining a small club (affiliation or status), and running for political office (power).

2. *Instrumental behavior.* This type of motivated behavior is instrumental in satisfying the need in question. Walking to the grocery store and joining the company bowling league are behavioral expressions of the hunger and affiliation motives. But this behavior is only instrumental in obtaining food and friends. The instrumental behavior does not directly satisfy the need as does consummatory behavior. A complicating factor is that the same behavior may be instrumental for one person but consummatory for another.[9]

3. *Substitute behavior.* This type of motivated behavior is the most complex and difficult to explain. The reason is that it is indirect or substitutive in nature and on the surface seems to have little relevance to the need in question. An example comes from the hunger study by Keys.[10] Much of the behavior of the semistarved human subjects in the study seemed to be substitute rather than consummatory or instrumental in obtaining food. Another example is the worker who has a strong affiliation need but produces above the informal performance norm. In a way, substitute behavior is a "black box" concept, i.e., it is known to be motivated behavior but it can't be fully explained.

The existence of instrumental and substitute behavior points up the

---

[7]Sanford and Wrightsman, op. cit., p. 191.

[8]Gregory A. Kimble and Norman Garmezy, *General Psychology*, 3d ed., The Ronald Press Company, New York, 1968, pp. 378–379.

[9]An example is sexual behavior. For a prostitute, sexual behavior may be instrumental in satisfying the hunger motive, but for the married couple, it may be consummatory.

[10]See A. Keys et al., *The Biology of Human Starvation*, vols. 1 and 2, The University of Minnesota Press, Minneapolis, 1950.

difficulty in trying to predict and control the behavior that will result from a given need. By the same token, it is impossible always to infer what motive is behind given observable behavior. In the earlier example, the man's eating behavior in the restaurant may or may *not* be based upon the hunger motive. Maybe he was having an extramarital affair (sex), and the restaurant provided an out-of-the-way meeting place. Another possibility is that the restaurant has a prestigious reputation and he wanted to be seen there (status). There are numerous other possible motives behind the eating behavior in the restaurant. Hilgard and Atkinson summarize five reasons for the difficulty in inferring motives from behavior:

1. The expression of human motives differs from culture to culture and from person to person within a culture.
2. Similar motives may be manifested through unlike behavior.
3. Unlike motives may be expressed through similar behavior.
4. Motives may appear in disguised forms.
5. Any single act of behavior may express several motives.[11]

Relationship among the variables Another complexity is the relationship among the variables in the motivation cycle. In Hull's formula for motivation there was a multiplicative relationship among drive, habit, and incentive. If any of the variables in Hull's formula was zero, e.g., there was no drive present, there would be no motivation. In the motivational cycle presented here, there is not such a multiplicative relationship among needs, drives, and goals. But drives will not be set up unless there is a need, and motivation involves—but not necessarily in a multiplicative relationship—all three variables. This, of course, indicates that motivation is extremely complex in nature and meaning. There is certainly not a simple relationship between motivation and behavior. Yet, despite this complexity, it is helpful to classify the various types of motives for study and analysis. For the purposes of this book, the primary, general, and secondary categories seem most appropriate.

PRIMARY MOTIVES

Psychologists do not totally agree on how to classify the various human motives, but, as was brought out in the discussion of instincts, they would acknowledge that some motives are unlearned and physiologically based. Such motives are variously called physiological, biological, unlearned, or primary. The last term is used here because it is more comprehensive than the other terms. The use of the term *primary* does not imply that this group of motives always takes precedence over the general and secondary motives.

Although the precedence of primary motives is implied in the motivation theories of Maslow and others,[12] there are many situations where general

---

[11]Hilgard and Atkinson, op. cit., pp. 141–142.

[12]See Abraham Maslow, *Motivation and Personality,* Harper, New York, 1954. His hierarchical theory of motivation is discussed in detail in Chapter 7.

and secondary motives predominate over primary motives. Common examples include celibacy among priests and fasting for a religious, social, or political cause. In both cases, learned secondary motives are stronger than unlearned primary motives. In this regard, Table 6-1 presents some interesting speculation as to what percentage of the population would perform varying degrees of antisocial acts in the face of starvation. The figure shows that scarcely anyone who was starving would murder someone in order to obtain food unless this person lived in a cannibalistic society. In this situation, under proper conditions, cannibals would kill other people and eat them without hesitation because they have learned that this is culturally acceptable. On the other hand, practically every hungry person in a noncannibalistic society would be willing to violate relatively unimportant societal values (to lie and cheat) in order to obtain food.

Two criteria are necessary in order for a motive to be included in the primary classification: It must be *unlearned*, and it must be *physiologically* based. Thus defined, the most commonly recognized primary motives include hunger, thirst, sleep, avoidance of pain, sex, and maternal concern. Some psychologists break the primary drives down into more finite catego-

Table 6–1

APPROXIMATE PERCENTAGE OF THE POPULATION SHOWING VARIOUS BEHAVIORS UNDER STARVATION CONDITIONS

Activities induced by starvation	Percentage of population succumbing to pressure of starvation
Cannibalism (in noncannibalistic societies)	Less than one third of 1 percent
Murder of members of the family and friends	Less than 1 percent
Murder of other members of one's group	Not more than 1 percent
Murder of strangers who are not enemies	Not more than 2 to 5 percent
Infliction of various bodily and other injuries on members of one's social group	Not more than 5 to 10 percent
Theft, larceny, robbery, forgery, and other crimes against property which have a clear-cut criminal character	Hardly more than 7 to 10 percent
Violation of various rules of strict honesty and fairness in pursuit of food, such as misuse of rationing cards, hoarding, and taking unfair advantage of others	From 20 to 99 percent depending upon the nature of the violation
Violation of fundamental religious and moral principles	Hardly more than 10 to 20 percent
Violation of less important religious, moral juridical, conventional, and similar norms	From 50 to 99 percent
Surrender or weakening of most of the aesthetic activities irreconcilable with food-seeking activities	From 50 to 99 percent
Weakening of sex activities, especially coitus	From 70 to 90 percent during prolonged and intense starvation
Prostitution and other highly dishonorable sex activities	Hardly more than 10 percent

Source: Pitirim A. Sorokin, *Man and Society in Calamity*, Dutton, Inc., New York, © 1942, p. 81. Renewal © 1970, by Helen P. Sorokin. Published by E. P. Dutton & Co., Inc., and used with their permission.

ries. For example, Berelson and Steiner use the following subclassifications for primary motives:

1. *Positive or supply motives.* This type is a direct result of homeostatic deficiency of the cells. Examples would be hunger, thirst, and sleep.
2. *Negative or avoidance motives.* This type results from the presence of physically harmful or potentially harmful noxious stimulation. An example would be pain.
3. *Species-maintaining motives.* This type results from the reproduction system that stimulates mating, produces children, and cares for the children. Examples would be sex and maternal.[13]

GENERAL MOTIVES

A separate classification for general motives is not always given. Yet, such a category seems necessary because there are a number of motives which lie in the gray area between the primary and secondary classifications. To be included in the general category, a motive must be unlearned but not physiologically based. Although not all psychologists would agree, the motives of competence, curiosity, manipulation, activity, and affection seem best to meet the criteria for this classification. An understanding of these general motives is important to the study of human behavior—especially in organizations. They are more relevant to organizational behavior than are the primary motives.

The competence motive

Robert W. White is most closely associated with the competence motive. He questioned the approaches to motivation that are based solely on the primary drives. For example, the primary drives cannot explain exploration, manipulation, and activity. White proposed a new conceptualization based upon the assumption that all organisms, animal or human, have a capacity to interact effectively with their environment. He called this common capacity *competence.* "It receives substantial contributions from activities which, though playful and exploratory in character, at the same time show direction, selectivity, and persistence in interacting with the environment."[14] Thus defined, the competence motive is the most inclusive general drive. The other general drives of curiosity, manipulation, and activity can be considered as more specific competence drives.

White built an entire theory of motivation around competence. He was convinced that people strive to have control or competence over their environment. People need to know what they are doing and to be able to make things happen. White determined that the critical age for competence development is between six and nine years old. During this age period, the

---

[13]Berelson and Steiner, op. cit., p. 242.

[14]Robert W. White, "Motivation Reconsidered: The Concept of Competence," *Psychological Review*, September 1959, p. 329.

children cut the apron strings and venture out into the world on their own. They develop needs to cross the street by themselves, to ride a bike, play baseball, roller-skate, and read. These needs are manifested by the drive for competence or mastery over the environment. The successes and failures that youngsters experience in this critical age period will have a lasting impact on the intensity of their competence motive.

This motive has interesting implications for job design in an organization. It says that people may be motivated by the challenge of trying to master the job or to become competent in the job. But once the job is mastered, which most highly specialized jobs in modern organizations are in a very short period of time, competence motivation will disappear. The discussion of job design in Chapter 8 draws from knowledge of the competence motive.

Curiosity, manipulation, and activity motives

Early psychologists noted that the animals used in their experiments seemed to have an unlearned drive to explore, to manipulate objects, or just to be active. This was especially true if monkeys were used as subjects and if they were placed in an unfamiliar or novel situation. These observations and speculations about the existence of curiosity, manipulation, and activity motives in monkeys were later substantiated through experimentation.[15] In this case, psychologists feel completely confident in generalizing the results of animal experiments to humans. It is generally recognized that human curiosity, manipulation, and activity drives are quite intense, and anyone who has reared or been around small children will quickly support this generalization.

Although these drives often get the small child into trouble, curiosity, manipulation, and activity, when carried forward to adulthood, can be very beneficial. If these motives are stifled or inhibited, the total society might become very stagnant. The same is true on an organizational level. If employees are not allowed to express their curiosity, manipulation, and activity motives, the organization will eventually suffer, given today's dynamic environment.

The affection motive

Love or affection is a very complex form of general drive. Part of the complexity stems from the fact that in many ways love resembles the primary drives and in other ways it is similar to the secondary drives. In particular, the affection motive is closely associated with the primary sex motive on the one hand and the secondary affiliation motive on the other. For this reason, affection is sometimes placed in all three categories of

---

[15]See Robert A. Butler, "Discrimination Learning by Rhesus Monkeys to Visual Exploration Motivation," *Journal of Comparative and Physiological Psychology*, vol. 46, 1953, pp. 95–98; and Robert A. Butler, "Incentive Conditions Which Influence Visual Exploration," *Journal of Experimental Psychology*, July 1954, pp. 19–23.

motives, and some psychologists do not even recognize it as a separate motive.

Affection merits specific attention because of its growing importance to the modern world. There seems to be a great deal of truth to the adages, "Love makes the world go around" and "Love conquers all." In a world suffering from intra- and interpersonal and national conflict and where quality of life and human rights are becoming increasingly important to modern society, the affection motive takes on added importance in the study of human behavior. It is given academic respectability mainly because of the extensive basic research done on primates by Harry F. Harlow at the University of Wisconsin.[16]

Harlow's findings suggest that monkeys have an intense, unlearned drive to receive warmth, comfort, and support. Through the years, Harlow has introduced many variations and refinements, but the same results continue to emerge. However, the big question remaining to be answered is whether a baby monkey's unlearned drive for warmth, comfort, and support can be generalized to apply to human love or affection. At this time such a generalization may not be justified. Yet, Harlow's findings provide some interesting insights and a sound beginning for the better understanding of the human motive for love.

SECONDARY MOTIVES

Whereas the general drives seem relatively more important than the primary ones to the study of human behavior in organizations, the secondary drives are unquestionably the most important. As a human society develops economically and becomes more complex, the primary, and to a lesser degree the general, drives give way to the learned secondary drives in motivating behavior. With some glaring exceptions that have yet to be eradicated, the motivations of people living in the economically developed Western world are not dominated by hunger or thirst. This situation is obviously subject to change; for example, the "population bomb" or the "energy crisis" may alter certain human needs. But for now, modern Western societies are largely populated by "men of full-blown human complexity, men who love and strive and hate and fight, men who create and destroy, men who shape the world and make human history."[17] In such a world, the learned secondary motives predominate.

Secondary motives are closely tied to the learning concepts that will be discussed in Chapter 9. In particular, the learning principle of reinforcement is conceptually and practically related to motivation. The relationship is obvious when reinforcement is divided into primary and secondary categories and is portrayed as incentives. Although some writers regard reinforcement and motivation as equivalent, they are treated separately in this book.

[16]See Harry F. Harlow, "The Nature of Love," *American Psychologist*, December 1958, pp. 673–685.

[17]Sanford and Wrightsman, op. cit., p. 208.

Once again, however, it should be emphasized that although the various behavioral concepts can be separated for study and analysis, in reality concepts like reinforcement and motivation do not operate as separate entities in producing human behavior. The interactive effects are always present.

A motive must be learned in order to be included in the *secondary* classification. Numerous important human motives meet this criterion. Some of the more important ones are power, achievement, and affiliation, or, as they are commonly referred to today, n *Pow*, n *Ach*, and n *Aff*. In addition, especially in reference to organizational behavior, security and status are also important secondary motives. Some scholars are also emphasizing that needs such as autonomy, n *Aut*, are also important to organizational behavior.[18]

The power motive

The power motive is discussed first because it has been formally recognized and studied for a relatively long time. The leading advocate of the power motive was Alfred Adler. In 1911, Adler officially broke his close ties with Sigmund Freud and proposed an opposing theoretical position. Where Freud stressed the impact of the past, and sexual, unconscious motivation, Adler substituted the future and a person's overwhelming drive for superiority or power. In Adler's words:

Now I began to see clearly in every psychical phenomenon the *striving for superiority*. . . . All our functions follow its direction; rightly or wrongly they strive for conquest, surety, increase. . . . Whatever premises all our philosophers and psychologists dream of—self preservation, pleasure principle, equalization—all these are but vague representations, attempts to express the great upward drive . . . *the fundamental fact of our life.*[19]

To explain the power need—the need to manipulate others or the drive for superiority over others—Adler developed the concepts of inferiority complex and compensation. He felt that every small child experiences a sense of inferiority. When this feeling of inferiority is combined with what he sensed as an innate need for superiority, the two rule all behavior. The person's life-style is characterized by striving to compensate for the feelings of inferiority which are combined with the innate drive for power.

Although modern psychologists do not generally accept the tenet that the power drive is inborn and so dominant, in recent years it has prompted renewed interest. The quest for power is readily observable in modern American society. The politician is probably the best example, and the Watergate scandal makes a fascinating study in the striving for and use of

---

[18]Thomas Harrell and Bernard Alpert, "The Need for Autonomy Among Managers," *Academy of Management Review,* April 1979, pp. 259–267.

[19]Alfred Adler, "Individual Psychology," translated by Susanne Langer, in Carl Murchison (ed.), *Psychologies of 1930,* Clark University Press, Worcester, Mass., 1930, pp. 398–399.

power in government and politics.[20] However, in addition to politicians, anyone in a responsible position in business, government, education, or the military may also exhibit a considerable need for power. It has significant implications for organizational leadership and the informal, political aspects of organizations. Chapter 14, "Power and Politics," will examine in detail the dynamics of power. It has emerged as one of the most important dynamics in the study of organizational behavior.

The achievement motive

Whereas recognition and discussion of the power motive have been going on for a long time, only very recently has there been any research activity. The opposite is true for the achievement motive. Although not having as long a history as the other motives, more is known about achievement than about any other motive because of the tremendous amount of research that has been devoted to it. The Thematic Apperception Test (TAT) has proved to be a very effective tool in researching achievement. The TAT can effectively identify and measure the achievement motive. The test works in the following manner:

One picture in the TAT shows a young man plowing a field while the sun is about ready to sink in the west. The person taking the test is supposed to tell a story about what he sees in the picture. By telling a story he will project his major motives. For example, the test taker may respond that the man in the picture is sorry the sun is going down because he still has more land to plow and he wants to get the crops planted before it rains. Such a response indicates high achievement. A low achiever might answer that the man is happy that the sun is finally going down so he can go into the house, relax, and have a cool drink.

The research approach to achievement has become so effective that it is often cited by psychologists as a prototype of how knowledge and understanding can be gained in the behavioral sciences.

Characteristics of high achievers

David C. McClelland, a Harvard psychologist, is most closely associated with study of the achievement motive and, as Chapter 14 will indicate, he is now doing considerable research on power as well. Beginning in 1947, McClelland thoroughly investigated and wrote about all aspects of n Ach (achievement).[21] Out of this extensive research has emerged a clear profile of the characteristics of the high achiever. Very simply, the achievement motive can be expressed as a desire to perform in terms of a standard of excellence, or to be successful in competitive situations. The specific characteristics of a high achiever can be summarized as follows:[22]

---

[20]Max Ways, "Watergate as a Case Study in Management," *Fortune*, November 1973, pp. 109–111, 196–201.

[21]David C. McClelland, et al., *The Achievement Motive*, Appleton-Century-Crofts, New York, 1953; and David C. McClelland, *The Achieving Society*, Van Nostrand, Princeton, N.J., 1961.

[22]For an expanded summary of the characteristics of the high achiever, see Saul W. Gellerman, *Motivation and Productivity*, American Management Association, New York, 1963, Chapter 12.

1. *Moderate risks.* Taking moderate risks is probably the single most descriptive characteristic of the person possessing high *n Ach*. On the surface it would seem that a high achiever would take high risks. However, once again research gives a different answer from common sense. The ring-toss game can be used to demonstrate risk-taking behavior. It has been shown that when ring tossers are told that they may stand anywhere they want to toss the rings at the peg, low and high achievers behave quite differently. Low achievers will tend to stand either very close and just drop the rings over the peg, or very far away and wildly throw the rings at the peg. In contrast, high achievers will almost always carefully calculate the exact distance from the peg that will challenge their own abilities. People with high *n Ach* will not stand too close because it would be no test of their ability simply to drop the ring over the peg. By the same token, they will not stand ridiculously far away because luck and not skill would determine whether the ring lands on the peg. In other words, low achievers take either a high or a low risk and high achievers take a moderate risk. This seems to hold true both for the simple children's game and for important adult decisions or activities.

2. *Immediate feedback.* Closely connected to high achievers' taking moderate risks is their desire for immediate feedback. People with high *n Ach* prefer activities which provide immediate and precise feedback information on how they are progressing toward a goal. Some hobbies and vocations offer such feedback and others do not. High achievers generally prefer hobbies such as woodworking or mechanics, which provide prompt, exact feedback, and they shy away from the coin-collecting type of hobby which takes years to develop. Likewise, the high achievers tend to gravitate toward, or at least are more satisfied in, job careers, such as sales or certain management positions, which are frequently evaluated by specific performance criteria. On the other side of the scale, high *n Ach* persons will generally not be found, or will tend to be frustrated, in research and development or teaching vocations where performance feedback is very imprecise, vague, and long-range.

3. *Accomplishment.* High achievers find accomplishing a task intrinsically satisfying in and of itself, or they do not expect or necessarily want the accompanying material rewards. A good illustration of this characteristic is money, but not for the usual reasons of wanting money for its own sake or for the material benefits that it can buy. Rather, high *n Ach* people look at money as a form of feedback or measurement of how they are doing. Given the choice between a simple task with a good payoff for accomplishment, other things being equal, high achievers generally choose the latter.

4. *Preoccupation with the task.* Once high achievers select a goal, they tend to be totally preoccupied with the task until it is successfully completed. They cannot stand to leave a job half finished and are not satisfied with themselves until they have given maximum effort. This type of dedicated commitment often reflects on their outward personalities, which frequently have a negative effect on those who come in contact with them. High achievers often strike others as being unfriendly and "loners." They may be very quiet and may seldom brag about their accomplishments. They tend to be very realistic about their abilities and do not allow other people to get in the way of their goal accomplishments. Obviously, with this type of approach high achievers do not always get along well with other people. Typically, high achievers make excellent salespersons but seldom good sales managers.

The four characteristics above have evolved out of McClelland's basic research over the years. Very recently, Jay Hall and his colleagues have reported the results of a comprehensive study that compared the managerial styles and methods of 16,000 high-, medium-, and low-achieving managers. The following are some of their major findings:[23]

1. Low n Ach managers are characterized by pessimistic outlooks and have a basic distrust of the intent and competence of their subordinates. High n Ach managers are the opposite. They are optimistic and view their subordinates favorably.
2. The manager's personal motivation is projected to his/her subordinates. Thus, high n Ach managers are concerned with aspects of the job that provide personal fulfillment; they talk to their subordinates about these things and attempt to structure the job so that their subordinates can receive such fulfillment. On the other hand, moderate achievers are mainly concerned with status symbols, low achievers with job security, and both try to motivate their subordinates the same way.
3. High n Ach managers readily use participative methods with subordinates, while moderate and low n Ach managers do not tend to involve their subordinates in the decision-making process.
4. High n Ach managers tend to be very open in their interactions and communications with others (both bosses and subordinates), while moderate achievers are preoccupied with their own ideas and feelings, and low achievers tend to avoid interacting and communicating altogether.
5. High achievers show concern for both people and production, whereas moderate achievers show high concern for production and low concern for people, and low achievers are mainly concerned with self-preservation and do not seem to care about people or production.

Some of these results do not really coincide with McClelland's profile of high and low achievers. For example, McClelland would maintain that high n Ach people tend to be loners and really do not genuinely like other people very much, whereas Hall's findings suggest that high n Ach managers tend to be very people-oriented. It must also be cautioned that Hall's findings tend to attribute all the popular notions of "good" management (e.g., job fulfillment, participation, open communication, duel concern for people and production) to the high n Ach manager, but to date it has not been demonstrated that this manager is indeed more effective in terms of actual performance.

Development of the achievement motive   Contrary to common belief, only about 10 percent of the population are actually high achievers. Similar to the other secondary motives, achievement seems to be developed at an early age. The child's independence training appears to be largely responsible for the development of achievement. One study empirically determined that the amount, timing, and type of independence that young children receive have the greatest impact on their later drive for achievement.[24] For instance, mothers of high achievers reported that they expected their children to obey traffic lights, entertain themselves, earn their own spending money, and choose their own clothes at a significantly younger age than did the mothers of low achievers. Another interesting finding was that mothers who gave physical rewards (hugging and kissing) for independence had sons

---

[23]The results are discussed in Ron Zemke, "What are High-Achieving Managers Really Like," Training/HRD, February 1979, pp. 35–36.

[24]M. R. Winterbottom, "The Relation of Childhood Training in Independence to Achievement Motivation," reported in McClelland et al., The Achievement Motive, op. cit., pp. 297–304.

who scored twice as high on the n Ach test as did the sons of mothers who did not give physical rewards for independence. An overall conclusion based on research investigating the development of achievement is that "the relatively demanding parent who clearly instigates self-reliance in the child and who then rewards independent behavior is teaching the child a need for achievement."[25]

Achievement and economic development   McClelland was not satisfied with just looking at the impact that achievement has on individual behavior. He broadened his research to encompass the effect that achievement motivation has on entire societies and the economic rise and fall of civilizations. His revealing studies of this broad area consistently find a positive relationship between the level of achievement motivation and the level of economic development of a given society.

Although there is a distinct time lag, a society whose populace generally exhibits high n Ach will experience economic growth and prosperity, whereas a society consisting of low achievers will economically decline and eventually collapse.[26] This conclusion is supported by many empirical studies. Typical was the study conducted on ancient Greece. The researchers determined the level of achievement of a given period in Greek history by examining the literature of the time. The economic activity was judged according to the areas of trade controlled by the Greeks. When the two variables were analyzed, it was found that a high level of achievement preceded a period of economic growth and a low achievement level was the forerunner of economic decline. A similar analytical approach has been applied to different periods of history and to a wide variety of societies around the world.

Achievement motivation in perspective   The full impact of the research findings on the achievement motive is yet to be felt. Probably the fundamental question is whether a high degree of achievement motivation is of beneficial value to an individual, organization, or society. Traditionally, high achievers have been portrayed as American folk heroes. Yet, from a "normal" personality standpoint, some of their characteristics are of questionable desirability. McClelland himself makes the following observations on his dealings with high achievers over the years:

Some psychologists think that because I've done so much on n Ach I must like the kind of people who have strong needs for achievement. I don't. I find them bores. They are not artistically sensitive. They're entrepreneurs, kind of driven—always trying to improve themselves and find a shorter route to the office or a faster way of reading their mail.[27]

Not only are high achievers not necessarily heroes, they also are not unique

---

[25]Sanford and Wrightsman, op. cit., p. 212.

[26]McClelland, *The Achieving Society,* op. cit.

[27]"To Know Why Men Do What They Do: A Conversation with David C. McClelland and T. George Harris," *Psychology Today,* January 1971, p. 36.

to American middle-class white males. McClelland shatters this myth by commenting as follows:

No, this is neither capitalist nor white, neither Western nor middle class. The Ethiopian people of the Gurage are fabulously high in n Ach. So are some tribes of American Indians, we've found, and the Biafran, or Ibo people. . . . Communist states like Poland and Russia now score very high in the achievement motive, and they seem to have passed it on to China. Why not? In Poland, for instance, plant managers work under a quota system for output that demands solutions to problems and provides very clear feedback.[28]

Under current societal values in this country, there seems little doubt that everyone needs a degree of achievement motivation to get along, but how much? The question becomes greatly amplified when applied to organizations and societies. Is n Ach the breakthrough for attaining objectives and economic development? Can an underdeveloped organization or entire country train its people to have high n Ach and become prosperous?

From psychoanalytic influence it has been generally assumed that motives such as achievement are developed only in childhood and, once they are formed, nothing much can be done to alter them. Some very interesting preliminary studies by McClelland have begun to undermine this traditional assumption. For the past decade McClelland and his research group have been attempting to develop achievement motivation in adults. Their achievement development course has four primary goals:

1. To teach participants how to think, talk, and act like a person with high achievement.
2. To stimulate participants to set higher, but carefully planned and realistic, work goals for themselves over the next two years.
3. To give the participants knowledge about themselves.
4. To create a group esprit de corps from learning about each other's hopes and fears, successes and failures, and from going through an emotional experience together, away from everyday life, in a retreat setting.[29]

So far, the achievement training has been given to executives in a large American firm and in several Mexican firms, businessmen in India, small and potential, mostly minority, entrepreneurs in Washington, D.C., rural areas of Oklahoma, Dallas, Seattle, and nine cities in a SBA (Small Business Administration) program. Although there are some inconsistencies, it has generally been shown that those who had taken the achievement course made more money, were promoted faster, and expanded their business faster than comparable people who had not taken the course or who had taken some other management course.[30] For example, in India a group of fifty-two entrepreneurs took the achievement-motivation course. Follow-ups were conducted over the next six to ten months on those who had completed the

---

[28]Ibid., p. 70.

[29]David C. McClelland, "That Urge to Achieve," *Think*, November–December 1966, p. 22.

[30]Ibid., and J. A. Timmons, "Black is Beautiful—Is it Bountiful?", *Harvard Business Review*, vol. 49, 1971, pp. 81–94.

training. Two-thirds of the subjects were unusually active in the post-training period. Some had actually started new businesses and others had investigated new product lines, had increased profits, or expanded their present organizations. For example, one banker became less conservative in his money-lending practices, and the owner of a small radio store opened a paint and varnish factory after completion of the training program. After a detailed analysis, McClelland concluded that the course appeared to have doubled the natural rate of unusual entrepreneurial activity in the group studied.[31] McClelland's most recent analysis of the impact of achievement motivation training on minority entrepreneurs in small businesses in a number of American cities concludes that there is

. . . impressive evidence that achievement motivation training significantly improves small-business performance provided there is some minimum of support from the economic infrastructure, in the form of available loans, market opportunities, and a labor force. . . . The type of business does not seem to matter: the training appears to be effective for manufacturing, retail, and service businesses.[32]

Thus, the results so far seem to indicate that achievement training can potentially play a role in getting disadvantaged Americans as well as underdeveloped countries into the mainstream of modern affluency. The potential for organization development also appears to be great. Whether such achievement training is right or wrong, good or bad, will be decided, it is hoped, by the persons affected.

The affiliation motive

Affiliation plays a very complex but vital role in human behavior. Sometimes affiliation is equated with social motives and/or group dynamics. As presented here, the affiliation motive is not so broad as is implied by the definition of social motives, nor so comprehensive nor complex as is implied by the definition of group dynamics. The study of affiliation is further complicated by the fact that some behavioral scientists believe that it is an unlearned motive. Their position is partially supported by the work of Harlow on the affection motive in monkeys. Few would debate that "some form of social contact appears necessary for the normal physical and personality development of the human infant; and total isolation is virtually always an intolerable situation for the human adult—even when physical needs are provided for."[33]

Autobiographical accounts of hermits, prisoners, and castaways support this conclusion on the importance of social interaction. The following pattern evolves from the reports of persons who have been deprived of other human beings:

---

[31]David C. McClelland, "Achievement Motivation Can be Developed," *Harvard Business Review*, November–December 1965, p. 20.

[32]David Miron and David C. McClelland, "The Impact of Achievement Motivation Training on Small Business," *California Management Review*, Summer 1979, p. 27.

[33]Berelson and Steiner, op. cit., p. 252.

1. The "pain" of isolation increases with time, but then decreases sharply.
2. Those who are isolated tend to think, dream, and occasionally hallucinate about people.
3. Isolates who keep occupied with distracting activities seem to suffer less than those who do not.[34]

Despite the evidence that suggests the inherent nature of affiliation, the majority of psychologists still classify the motive as one of the important secondary drives. In the few isolated cases where children have been taken away from human contact, for example, by being confined in an attic, the children do not express an affiliation drive. Such cases point to the fact that affiliation is probably learned; but because it is normally so intense, it appears on the surface to be an inherent human motive.

Research on the affiliation motive   In contrast to achievement, not much research has been done directly on affiliation. Although affiliation was formally recognized at the beginning of the century (for example, Trotter specifically mentioned gregariousness along with self-preservation, nutrition, and sex as the four most important instincts in the life of humans[35]), not much is really known about it even today. About the most promising effort so far is the classic research conducted by Stanley Schachter. One observation of the Schachter research is the following:

Schachter has pursued the affiliation motive further toward its origins than anyone else; yet it is clear that he has made only a beginning. In many ways his research raises more questions than it answers. Even so seemingly commonplace a trait as wanting to be with someone else turns out, on analysis, to be quite complex.[36]

"Misery loves company"   The best-known, most interesting, and potentially most significant research by Schachter was his study of the relationship between anxiety (fear) and affiliation.[37] The study was built around testing the folk hypothesis that misery loves company. Undergraduate females who did not know one another were used as subjects in the study. The experiment began by bringing Dr. Zilstein, a sinister-looking, stereotypical doctor from a horror movie, to the front of the room to talk to the women subjects. Behind the doctor was a conglomeration of devices containing many electric wires, knobs, and switches. The weird-looking doctor explained to the wide-eyed women that they were going to participate in an experiment that would test the effects of electric shock on human subjects. The terrified subjects found little consolation in the doctor's parting comment that although the shock would be quite painful, no permanent damage would result.

The purpose of the preliminaries in the experiment was to create fear in

---

[34]Stanley Schachter, *The Psychology of Affiliation*, Stanford, Stanford, Calif., 1959, pp. 6–8.

[35]W. Trotter, *Instincts of the Herd in Peace and War*, Macmillan, New York, 1916. His views were published in essay form ten years before publication of the book.

[36]Gellerman, op. cit., p. 115.

[37]Schachter, op. cit.

the subjects. Told that there would be a short delay while the electrical equipment was set up, the frightened subjects were asked whether they preferred to wait with the other subjects or by themselves. The results were overwhelmingly that the subjects would rather wait with the others. On the other hand, a control group of subjects who were not in the fear condition preferred to wait alone. Such a result substantiates that misery really does love company.

"Misery loves company that is miserable"   An important refinement of the misery study was then to divide the experimentally created miserable subjects into two groups. The members in one of the anxious groups were asked whether they preferred to wait alone or with other subjects in the same state, i.e., those who were also going to participate in the shock experiment. The other group of miserable subjects was given the choice of waiting alone or with some coeds in a different state, i.e., students who were waiting out in the hall to talk with their advisors. Some interesting results came out of this second phase of the study. A majority of the subjects in the first group chose to wait with other subjects in their same state. In contrast, not a single subject in the second group chose to wait with students not in their same state. This finding adds a qualification to the adage. Misery doesn't love just any company, misery only loves company that is miserable.

Analysis of results   Schachter suggests several possible explanations for the results of his misery study. Briefly, the logical reasons are as follows:

1. *Escape.* The subjects may have wanted to band together to formulate a plan for getting out of the terrifying experiment, the idea being that there is strength in numbers.
2. *Indirect anxiety reduction.* Possibly the subjects just wanted to get together to talk about the weather or whatever to get their minds off the upcoming ordeal.
3. *Cognitive clarity.* The subjects perhaps wanted to clarify in their own minds what the experiment was all about. For example, they may have wanted to make sure that Dr. Zilstein said that the shock would be extremely painful.
4. *Self-evaluation or social comparison.* It is possible that the subjects just wanted to see if everyone else in the experiment was as scared as they were. The subjects wanted to evaluate their own opinions and feelings.
5. *Direct anxiety reduction.* A final possibility is that the subjects merely wanted another miserable human being with them. They didn't have to talk abut escape, the weather, or what the experiment was about. Under this explanation, they didn't even have to look at the other subjects as they do in social comparison.

Each of the above statements represents a plausible explanation for the results of the misery study. However, to determine the best explanation more scientifically, Schachter carried his study one step further. When asking the subjects whether they wanted to wait alone or with others in the same state, he added a further choice variation. With some of the subjects he stipulated that they could communicate while waiting, and to others he stated that they could not communicate while waiting. The result of this phase was that being able to communicate or not made little difference to the subjects. The subjects did not care one way or the other if they could talk. Although they definitely wanted to wait with miserable counterparts, they did not necessarily want to talk and exchange ideas. This finding makes it possible to rule out escape, indirect anxiety reduction, and cognitive clarity as explanations for "misery loves company that is miserable." Each of these three goals requires verbal communication, but social comparison and direct anxiety reduction do not. Social comparison requires nonverbal communication, and direct anxiety reduction calls for no form of communication in the usual sense. The mere presence of another human being is all that is necessary for direct anxiety reduction. This is what Schachter thinks is the best explanation of why the subjects had an intense drive to affiliate.

Implications of the Schachter study   Relatively lengthy treatment has been given to Schachter's study because it contains some interesting implications for certain kinds of human behavior. For example, the misery study provides a scientifically based explanation of why people tend to group together during any kind of crisis situation. Another example is the problem faced by a military leader in combat. When his men come under enemy fire, there is always a tendency for them to bunch up, a formation that of course compounds the danger. The misery study also has direct implications for understanding human behavior in organizations. It provides some insights as to why workers join unions and contributes to the understanding of group dynamics and stress. To reduce their anxieties, which may have been created by a feeling of insecurity or a dead-end job, workers may be motivated to join with others who are in a similar miserable situation.

To draw too many generalizations from Schachter's research is at this time unwarranted. As the earlier quote noted, Schachter probably raises more questions than he answers. For example, studies relating affiliation with hunger come up with more complicated results. Affiliation tends to correlate positively with hunger up to a point, but then to taper off. Researchers have also found that anxiety created by embarrassing and normally inhibiting activities tends to decrease the affiliation motive. There are enough of these kinds of exceptions to stop one from generalizing that any strong drive will increase the affiliation drive. Although Schachter has made a good start and provides some interesting insights for human and organizational behavior, much more research on affiliation is badly needed. The chapters in Part 4 on the dynamics of organizational behavior, will provide further insights into the social interaction phenomena.

The security motive

Security is a very intense motive in a fast-paced, highly technological society such as is found in modern America. The typical American can be insecure in a number of areas of everyday living—being liable for payments on a car or house; keeping the lover's or spouse's affections; staying in school; getting into graduate, law, or medical school; or obtaining and/or keeping a good job. Job insecurity, in particular, has a great effect on organizational behavior.

On the surface, security appears to be much simpler than other secondary motives, for it is largely based on fear and is avoidance-oriented. One observation is that "the feeling involves being able to hold on to what one has, being sure that one will be able to fare as well in the future as in the past. Conversely, insecurity is a haunting fear that 'things may not last,' that one may lose what [one] now has."[38] Briefly, humans have a learned security motive to protect themselves from the contingencies of life and actively try to avoid situations which would prevent them from satisfying their primary, general, and secondary motives.

Complexity of the security motive　In reality, security is much more complex than it appears on the surface. There is the simple, conscious security motive described above, but there seems also to be another type of security motive that is much more complicated and difficult to identify. Gellerman notes that this special drive for security is largely unconscious but that it greatly influences the behavior of many people. He explains that "the hazards against which they seek to protect themselves are vague, pervasive, and fearsome; usually they have an underlying conviction that the environment is at best capricious and at worst malicious."[39] The simple, conscious security motive is typically taken care of by insurance programs, personal savings plans, and other fringe benefits at the place of employment. On the other hand, the more complex, unconscious security motive is not so easily fulfilled but may have a greater and more intense impact on human behavior. Although much attention has been given to the simple security motive, much more understanding is needed on the role of the unconscious, complex security motive.

Development of the security motive　Similar to the other secondary motives, the desire for security seems to be largely developed in childhood. The intensity of the security motive in adults largely depends upon their experiences as children. For example, people who have identified with security-conscious parents as children may carry their concern over to adulthood; or, as children, people may have been reared in an economic and social atmosphere of unpredictability which makes them very security-conscious as adults. Gellerman notes that a person whose security motive developed as a result of the latter childhood circumstances is apt to be an adult who is very likable, noncompetitive, patient, and slow to complain. "Other people tend not to expect too much of him and therefore seldom find fault with his work, and—what is more important—he is rather pleasant to have around."[40]

Another, essentially opposite, example of security development is the child who experiences overprotection and overindulgence. Under these conditions, the child grows up thinking that the world is a very nice place in

---

[38]Morgan and King, op. cit., p. 234.

[39]Gellerman, op. cit., p. 156.

[40]Ibid., p. 157.

which to live. This person feels that someone will grant every wish he or she makes and that no hard work or initiative is required. As an adult, this person tends to have an air of sublime assurance and an attitude of unruffled calm regardless of the pressure.[41]

Both the child who experiences the world as uncontrollable and the one who experiences it as benevolent will tend to have an intense security motive as an adult. These security-conscious individuals are most satisfied with, and tend to gravitate into, jobs which are secure, pleasant, and predictable. This type of analysis can contribute much to the better understanding of individual differences in organizational behavior.

The status motive

Along with security, the status or prestige motive is especially relevant to a dynamic society. The modern affluent person is often pictured as a status seeker. Such a person is accused of being more concerned with material symbols of status—the right clothes, the right car, the right address, and a swimming pool or an executive sandbox—than with the more basic, human-oriented values in life. Although the symbols of status are inferred to be a unique by-product of modern society, the fact is that status has been in existence since there have been two or more persons on the earth.

Determination of status Status can be simply defined as the *relative* ranking that a person holds in a group, organization, or society. Under this definition, any time two or more persons are together, a status hierarchy will evolve, even if it is an equal status. The symbols of status only attempt to represent the relative ranking of the person in the status hierarchy. The definition also corrects the common misconception that *status* means *high status*. Everyone has status, but it may be high or low depending on how the relative positions are ranked.

How are status positions determined? Why is one person ranked higher or lower than another? Secord and Backman say that status evolves from the capacity of people for rewarding those with whom they interact, the extent to which they are seen as receiving rewards, the types of costs they incur, and their investments (past history or background).[42] The sociologist Talcott Parsons summarizes several sources of status.[43]

1. *Membership in a family.* In previous eras, an individual could be born into a high-status (nobility) or low-status (serfs) family. Today, certain family names may still confer status in a locale but this is becoming less important than it once was.
2. *Personal qualities.* Physical characteristics (handsome or beautiful versus ugly) and personality may confer status. Age, race, and sex may also be determinants of status.
3. *Achievements.* Educational attainment (M.D. or Ph.D.) or professional accom-

[41]Ibid., pp. 157–158.

[42]Paul F. Secord and Carl W. Backman, *Social Psychology*, 2d ed., McGraw-Hill, New York, 1974, pp. 274–276.

[43]Talcott Parsons, *Essays in Sociological Theory*, rev. ed., Free Press, New York, 1964, pp. 75–76.

plishments (C.P.A. or C.L.U.) may be a source of status. A worker's skill or a person's athletic ability may also confer status.

4. *Possessions.* Material wealth such as a lot of money, real estate, or a yacht may be a source of status. These possessions can become status symbols.

5. *Authority and power.* Those who hold formal positions of authority and power in a company or a civic club or a crime ring may be given more status than those below them.

Each of the above factors is hedged by the words "may contribute to status" because, in the final analysis, status determination will always depend upon the prevailing cultural values and societal roles.

Status-determining factors generally have quite different meanings, depending on the values of a particular culture. An example of the impact of cultural values on status is the personal qualities of people. In some cultures, the older persons are, the higher is their status. However, in other cultures, once a person reaches a certain age, the status goes downhill. It must be remembered that such cultural values are highly volatile and change with the times and circumstances. There are also many subcultures in a given society which may have values different from the prevailing values of society at large and correspondingly different statuses.

Cultural roles have a big impact on status determination as well as on values. As indicated in Chapter 2's discussion of sociological concepts, a role represents expectations of a position. A level of status is accorded to each role in a society. Status is a significant input but is also inferred from roles such as those of parent or child, student or teacher, general or private, and manager or worker.

Development of the status motive The drive to attain higher status is fairly intense for most people. Like the other secondary motives, it seems to start developing at an early age. A frequent misconception is that the status-conscious person is always the Horatio Alger type who comes from a poverty-stricken background. Gellerman tries to dispel this notion by claiming that "it is not poverty itself but the individual's sense of justice—of whether his status is in line with what he deserves—that determines whether he will accept the status he was born to."[44] In other words, a person's specific background is important only to the extent that it affects the expectations of what his status should be. If people do not accept their present status, they will have a strong drive to attain a higher one and all the symbols that go with it.

Relation to level of aspiration The status motive is closely linked to what psychologists call the level of aspiration. This is the level at which people set their sights, their goals. For the high jumper in track and field it may be a 7-foot jump, or for the aspiring young executive it may be a salary of $50,000 per year. All the secondary motives have an input into what this level of aspiration will be, and the person's successes and failures will tend to raise or lower it. The level of aspiration can be translated into status

---

[44]Gellerman, op. cit., p. 153.

levels. The 7-foot high jumpers are a very high-status group among track and field athletes and their followers, and the same holds true for $50,000-a-year young executives.

SUMMARY

Motivation is a basic psychological process. The comprehensive understanding of motivation lies in the need-drive-goal sequence, or cycle. The basic process involves needs (deprivations) which set drives in motion (deprivations with direction) to accomplish goals (anything which alleviates a need and reduces a drive). The drives or motives may be classified into *primary*, *general*, and *secondary* categories. The primary motives are unlearned and physiologically based. Common primary motives include hunger, thirst, sleep, avoidance of pain, sex, and maternal concern. The general motives are also unlearned but are not physiologically based. Competence, curiosity, manipulation, activity, and affection are examples of general motives. Secondary motives are learned and are most relevant to the study of organizational behavior. The needs for power, achievement, affiliation, security, and status are major motivating forces in the behavior of organizational participants.

QUESTIONS FOR DISCUSSION AND REVIEW

1. Do humans have instincts? Explain your answer.
2. Briefly define the three classifications of motives. What are some examples of each?
3. What are the characteristics of high achievers?
4. What relevance does Schachter's research on the affiliation motive have for the study of organizational behavior?
5. How is status defined? What are some determinants of status?
6. What implications does the security motive have for modern human resource management?

CASE:
**STAR
SALESPERSON**

While growing up, Jerry Slate had always been rewarded by his parents for showing independence. When he started school, he was successful both inside and outside the classroom. He was always striving to be things like traffic patrolperson and lunch room monitor in grade school. Yet, his mother worried about him because he never got along well with other children his own age. When confronted with this, Jerry would reply, "Well, I don't need them. Besides, they can't do things as well as I can. I don't have time to help them, I'm too busy improving myself." Jerry went on to do very well in both high school and college. He was always at or near the top of his class academically and was a very good long-distance runner for the track teams in high school and college. In college he shied away from joining a fraternity and lived in an apartment by himself. Upon graduation he went to work for a large insurance company and soon became one of their top salespersons. Jerry was very proud of the fact that he had been one of the top five salespersons in six out of the eight years he was with the company.

At the home office of the insurance company, the executive committee that was in charge of making major personnel appointments was discussing the upcoming vacancy of the sales manager's job for the Midwest region. The personnel manager gave the following report:

Gentlemen and women, as you know, the Midwest region is lagging far behind our other regions as far as sales goes. We need a highly motivated person to take that situation over and turn it around. After an extensive screening process, I am recommending Jerry Slate be offered this sales manager position. As you know, Jerry has an outstanding record with the company and is highly motivated. I think he is the person for the job.

1. Do you agree with the personnel manager? Why or why not?
2. Based on Jerry's background, what motives discussed in the chapter would appear to be very intense in Jerry? What motive(s) would appear to be very low? Give specific evidence from the case for each motive.
3. What type of motivation is desirable for sales positions? What type of motivation is desirable for managerial positions?

CASE:
FROM MASTER POLITICIAN TO MR. OBNOXIOUS

Paul Kotter was hired several years ago to work as a liaison between his employer, a large advertising agency, and one of their major clients, an airline. Paul was a very motivated employee. He worked very hard at his job and amazed most of the staff with his "hustle." He made sure that all of the airline promotion campaigns were done on time and with his approval. Paul worked hard at building excellent working relationships with other departments he had to coordinate with and with key staff members throughout the agency. This coordination effort and informal network was an important factor in his success with the airline account. He was able to convince people to get his job done first. "That Paul is a master politician," one department head put it.

As a reward for his excellent performance, Paul was soon promoted to the position of vice president of transportation accounts. While the position itself was little more than expanding what he was already doing, the title was more important sounding and was given more as a way to impress external clients than really to mean anything "in-house." Paul, however, must not have understood this. In his new role, what had been masterful politicking now became vulgar power plays. Paul seemed to feel that the top management of the agency liked his style and had rewarded him accordingly. He really let loose on a few people in the agency and soon earned the nickname "Mr. Obnoxious." What people had been able to tolerate and even admire before, they could not stand now. Paul seemed to want to control, not work with, people to get the job done. Most important, the transportation accounts, which had been among the most profitable for the agency, were beginning to deteriorate.

1. What do you think Paul's major motives were? Find examples in the case of the need-drive-goal motivational process.
2. How do you explain that Paul went from master politician to Mr. Obnoxious? Did he really change?
3. If you were Paul's boss, what would you say to him?

WORK MOTIVATION

MOTIVATING CREATIVE TALENT*

According to managers in the creative industries, motivating their employees is a more difficult task than in other types of industries. They argue that when you are in an industry where artistic ability and not an established formula for success reigns, then greater attention must be given to motivate the artists to give their ability and opinions. For example, in the movie industry, a class A movie such as *The Godfather* cost over $6.8 million dollars to produce. *The Great Gatsby* had an initial cost of over $8 million dollars. The returns on each film were not proportional to their production cost. *The Godfather* netted $129 million dollars and *The Great Gatsby* only $24 million dollars. There is no discernable pattern. Only one in five movies ever makes a profit. In the record business only 5 percent of singles and 20 percent of albums return a profit. This sort of business relies on the artists' creative talents, and artists are very difficult to motivate. Corporate managers in the creative industries must contend with things such as a recent ad in *Variety* magazine, which condemned the ruination of artistic talents through the domination of large corporations in the entertainment industry. The ad ran shortly after the defection of five top-level executives from United Artists, a Transamerica subsidiary. There is a delicate balance between the larger corporate objectives and the fostering of a creative climate for the motivation of the artists. This makes motivating people in the creative industries a real challenge.

*Adapted from "Mastering Management in Creative Industries," *Business Week,* May 29, 1978, pp. 86–88.

The concept and applications of motivation are probably more closely associated with the field of organizational behavior than any other single topic covered in this book. The last chapter spelled out the basic motivational process and examined the major motives that lead to a better understanding of human behavior. This chapter uses these ideas as background information and is specifically concerned with work motivation. It is a step toward more direct application because work motivation has implications for the performance and satisfaction of organizational participants. The chapter first looks at traditional human relations approaches to motivation. The remainder of the chapter presents and analyzes the major content and process models of work motivation. Maslow's hierarchy of needs and Herzberg's two-factor theory are the two content models given the most attention. Alderfer's ERG theory is given as an extension of the Maslow model. In the process approach, the expectancy models of Vroom, and Porter and Lawler are given the most attention. Lawler's more recent refinement of the Porter-Lawler model is also discussed. Next, Adams's equity theory is presented and analyzed in the sense of adding to the better understanding of the cognitive processes of work motivation, and attribution theory and locus of control are examined as the newest approaches to work motivation. Particular attention is devoted to the research evidence supporting or not supporting each of these models and their implications for the actual practice of human resource management. The next chapter presents specific techniques, drawn from the theories presented in this chapter, to motivate workers and managers.

TRADITIONAL HUMAN
RELATIONS APPROACH TO MOTIVATION

The last chapter presented motivation as a basic psychological process consisting of needs, drives, and goals. Indirect attempts have been made to apply this elementary psychological process to the practice of management. Yet the traditional human relations approach to management generally failed to recognize the importance of this underlying psychological process. It sacrificed understanding of the variables and basic process involved for stopgap measures. The approach was based on three simple additive assumptions:

1. Personnel primarily are economically motivated and secondarily desire security and good working conditions. (A nonauthoritarian type of supervision is considered as part of conditions.)
2. Provision of the above rewards to personnel will have a positive effect on their morale.
3. There is a positive correlation between morale and productivity.

Such simplistic assumptions really didn't hurt anything, but as the introductory chapter pointed out, they didn't do much good either. Both research and actual experience have proven that these human relations assumptions fall way short of solving the complex problems facing today's management.

As the last chapter pointed out, people have diverse needs and although no one would argue against the importance of economic motives, it is not the be-all and end-all of work motivation. In addition, the human relations concept of morale turned out to be a very elusive concept. Seldom operationally defined, it became a catchall word and scapegoat for all the personnel problems facing management. If management could not explain a problem, it was a morale problem. Finally, as systematic research began to accumulate, the relationship between morale and productivity grew less clear. The positive correlation between them became more of an issue than an automatic assumption. Starting as far back as 1955, Brayfield and Crockett, in an extensive review of the literature up to that time, concluded that there was very little, if any, relationship between job satisfaction and performance.[1] About a decade later Victor Vroom analyzed the results of twenty studies and found a very low (.14) median correlation between satisfaction and performance.[2]

Today, the satisfaction-performance controversy still rages. Many articles in contemporary organizational behavior journals attempt to present evidence on the direction of causality between satisfaction and performance.[3] Three generally recognized points of view have emerged:

1. The view that satisfaction leads to performance, a position generally associated with early human relations concepts
2. The view that the satisfaction-performance relationship is moderated by a number of variables, a position which gained acceptance in the fifties and continues to be reflected in current research
3. The view that performance leads to satisfaction, a recently stated position[4]

Each of the above views currently has mixed support in theory and research, but one thing is certain. The human relations position was much too simplistic. The motivation to work is very complex, and the traditional explanations only began to scratch the surface. There are a number of internal and environmental variables that affect the motivation to work. The theories and research reviewed in this chapter take a definite step in the direction of better understanding.

MODERN THEORIES OF WORK MOTIVATION

As the number of human problems facing management began to mount, the limitations of the traditional human relations approach to motivation began

---

[1] A. H. Brayfield and W. H. Crockett, "Employee Attitudes and Employee Performance," *Psychological Bulletin*, vol. 52, 1955, pp. 396–424.

[2] Victor H. Vroom, *Work and Motivation*, Wiley, New York, 1964, p. 183.

[3] For example, see: Charles N. Greene and Robert E. Craft, Jr., "The Satisfaction-Performance Controversy—Revisited," in H. Kirk Downey, Don Hellriegel, and John W. Slocum, Jr., (eds.), *Organizational Behavior: A Reader*, West, St. Paul, 1977, pp. 187–201; and John M. Ivancevich, "High and Low Task Stimulation Jobs: A Causal Analysis of Performance-Satisfaction Relationships," *Academy of Management Journal*, June 1979, pp. 206–222.

[4] Donald P. Schwab and Larry L. Cummings, "Theories of Performance and Satisfaction: A Review," *Industrial Relations*, October 1970, p. 409.

to surface. Starting around the beginning of the 1960s, those concerned with work motivation started to search earnestly for a new theoretical foundation and to attempt to devise new techniques for application. As Chapter 1 indicated, some humanistic concerns served as a transition to the modern approach to work motivation. In particular, humanistic psychologist Abraham Maslow's hierarchy of needs was adapted to work motivation. Next came the two-factor theory of Frederick Herzberg. Instead of Maslow's five levels, Herzberg felt there were only two factors: hygiene/maintenance factors, and motivators. He emphasized the role of satisfaction and stimulated a great amount of research and controversy. Most recently, Clayton Alderfer reorganized the Maslow hierarchy into three groups of core needs: existence, relatedness, and growth (thus called the ERG model).

Because of the lack of research for the content approaches, Victor Vroom proposed an alternative theory of work motivation, based on expectancy. Since Vroom, there have been refinements of the expectancy model (by Porter and Lawler, and Lawler) and considerable interest in a related cognitive process approach called equity theory. Recently attention has focused on the potential contribution that attribution theory and locus of control can make to work motivation. Figure 7-1 graphically summarizes the theoretical streams for work motivation.

**Figure 7-1
Theoretical
development of
work motivation.**

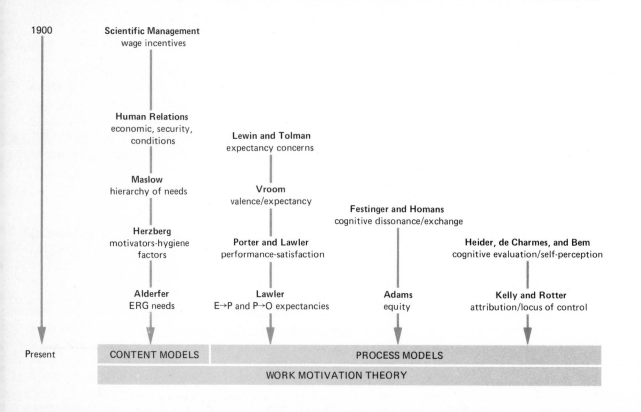

The figure shows four major lines of theoretical development. The content models go as far back as the turn of the century, when pioneering scientific managers such as Frederick W. Taylor, Frank Gilbreth, and Henry L. Gantt proposed sophisticated wage incentive models to motivate workers. Next came the human relations movement, and then the content models of Maslow, Herzberg, and Alderfer. More recent developments have come from process models. Most work has been done on expectancy-based process models, but recently, equity and attribution theories have received attention. These process models are cognitively based; there are other cognitive models that exist in psychology, but equity and attribution are the ones that have had the greatest influence on work motivation so far. Figure 7-1 purposely shows that at present there is a lack of integration or synthesis of the various models. At present a group of content models can be identified and a group of process models can be identified, but an overall theory of work motivation does not exist.

THE CONTENT THEORIES OF WORK MOTIVATION

The content theories of motivation attempt to determine what it is that motivates people at work. The content theorists are concerned with identifying the needs/drives that people have and how needs/drives are prioritized. They are concerned with the types of incentives or goals that people strive to attain in order to be satisfied and perform well. At first it was felt to be money only (scientific management) and then a little later it was felt to include working conditions, security, and perhaps a democratic style of supervision (human relations). More recently, the content of motivation has been deemed to be the so-called "higher-level" needs or motives, such as esteem and self-actualization (Maslow), responsibility, recognition, achievement, and advancement (Herzberg), and growth and personal development (Alderfer). A thorough understanding of the major content models contributes to the understanding of work motivation and leads to specific application techniques.

Maslow's hierarchy of needs

Although the last chapter discussed the most important primary, general, and secondary needs of humans, it did not relate them to a theoretical framework. Abraham Maslow, in a classic paper published in 1943, outlined the elements of an overall theory of motivation.[5] Drawing chiefly on his clinical experience, he thought that a person's motivational needs could be arranged in a hierarchical manner. In essence, he believed that once a given level of need became satisfied, it no longer served to motivate. The next higher level of need had to be activated in order to motivate the individual.

---

[5]A. H. Maslow, "A Theory of Human Motivation," *Psychological Review*, July 1943, pp. 370–396.

Maslow identified five levels in his need hierarchy (see Figure 7-2). They are, in brief, the following:

1. *Physiological needs.* The most basic level in the hierarchy, the physiological needs, generally corresponds to the unlearned primary needs discussed in Chapter 6. The needs of hunger, thirst, sleep, and sex are some examples. According to the theory, once these basic needs are satisfied, they no longer motivate. For example, a starving man will strive for a carrot held out in front of him. However, after he eats his fill of carrots and another carrot is held out, he will not strive to obtain it. Only the next higher level of needs will motivate him.

2. *Safety needs.* This second level of needs is roughly equivalent to the security need discussed in Chapter 6. Maslow stressed emotional as well as physical safety. The whole organism may become a safety-seeking mechanism. Yet, like the physiological needs, once these safety needs are satisfied, they no longer motivate.

3. *Love needs.* This third or intermediate level of needs loosely corresponds to the affection and affiliation needs covered in Chapter 6. Like Freud, Maslow seems guilty of poor choice of wording to identify his levels. His use of the word *love* has many misleading connotations, such as sex, which is actually a physiological need. Perhaps a more appropriate word describing this level would be *belongingness.*

4. *Esteem needs.* The esteem level represents the higher needs of humans. The needs for power, achievement, and status can be considered to be part of this level. Maslow carefully pointed out that the esteem level contains both self-esteem and esteem from others.

5. *Need for self-actualization.* This level represents the culmination of all the lower, intermediate, and higher needs of humans. People who have become self-actualized are self-fulfilled and have realized all of their potential. Self-actualization is closely related to the self-concept discussed in Chapter 5. In effect, self-actualization is the person's motivation to transform perception of self into reality.

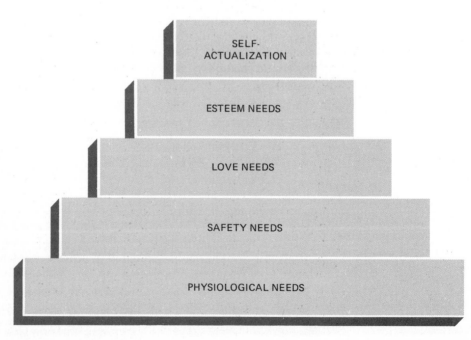

**Figure 7-2
Maslow's
hierarchy of needs.**

Maslow did not intend that his need hierarchy should be directly applied to work motivation. In fact, he did not delve into the motivating aspects of humans in organizations until about twenty years after he originally proposed his theory.[6] Despite this lack of intent on Maslow's own part, others, such as Douglas McGregor in his widely read book, *The Human Side of Enterprise* popularized the Maslow theory in management literature. The need hierarchy has had a tremendous impact on the modern management approach to motivation.

In a very rough manner, Maslow's need hierarchy theory can be converted into the content model of work motivation shown in Figure 7-3. If Maslow's estimates are applied to an organization example, the lower-level needs of personnel would be generally satisfied (85 percent of the basic needs and 70 percent of the security needs), but only 50 percent of the belonging needs, 40 percent of the esteem needs, and a mere 10 percent of the self-actualization needs would be met.

On the surface, the content model shown in Figure 7-3 and the estimated percentages given by Maslow seem logical and applicable to the motivation of humans in today's organizations. Maslow's need hierarchy has often been uncritically accepted by management textbooks and by practitioners. Unfortunately, the limited research that has been conducted lends little, if any, support to the theory. Maslow himself provided no research backup. About a decade after publishing his original paper, Maslow did attempt to modify his position by saying that gratifying the self-actualizing need of growth-motivated individuals can actually increase rather than decrease this need. He also hedged on some of his other original ideas, e.g., that higher needs

---

[6]A. H. Maslow, *Eupsychian Management*, Dorsey-Irwin, Homewood, Ill., 1965.

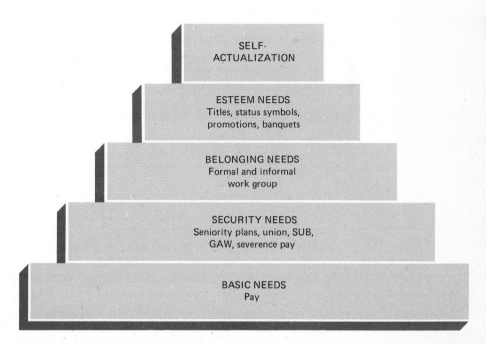

**Figure 7-3
A hierarchy of
work motivation.**

may emerge after the long deprivation or suppression of lower needs instead of only after the lower needs are satisfied.[7] He stressed that human behavior is multidetermined and multimotivated.

Despite Maslow's attempts to refine his need hierarchy theory, the direct attempts to test the theory have come up with at best inconclusive results. In one study of female clerks in an insurance company, it was concluded that the Maslow model is open to question as an overall theory of work motivation. However, the study did find the Maslow model to be a fairly reliable way of measuring priority needs of workers.[8] In another study, which gathered data from young managers at American Telephone and Telegraph over a five-year period, little support was found for the model when need changes were correlated with need strengths.[9] The researchers found from their annual interviews that the managers' needs changed, not in terms of prepotent need gratification as the Maslow model would predict, but rather because of developing career concerns. Based on this and other research, Hall claims that employees' needs change as they grow older and enter new career stages.[10] This interest in career development is given attention in Chapter 22. In another longitudinal study little support was found for the hypothesis that changes in satisfaction of needs in one level correlated negatively with changes in the importance of needs in the next higher level.[11] The most comprehensive review, by Wahba and Birdwell, also does not support the Maslow model.[12] They reviewed twenty-two studies and found two primary clusters of needs instead of Maslow's five, and they found no support for the contention that satisfaction of one level of need will be positively associated with the activation of the next higher level of needs. However, they did find in eighteen of the twenty-two studies that the strength of the self-actualization need was associated with a deprivation of that need.

The research studies cited above certainly make the point that Maslow is not the final answer in work motivation. Yet, the model does make a significant contribution in terms of making management aware of the diverse needs of humans at work. The number and names of the levels are not important nor, as the studies show, is the hierarchical concept. What is important is the fact that humans in the workplace have diverse motives, some of which are "high level." In other words, such needs as esteem and

[7]Also see Mahmoud A. Wahba and Lawrence G. Birdwell, "Maslow Reconsidered: A Review of Research on the Need Hierarchy Theory," *Proceedings of the Academy of Management*, 1973, pp. 514–520.

[8]Michael Beer, *Leadership, Employee Needs, and Motivation*, Ohio State University, College of Commerce and Administration, Bureau of Business Research, Monograph no. 129, Columbus, 1966, p. 68.

[9]Douglas T. Hall and Khalil E. Nougaim, "An Examination of Maslow's Need Hierarchy in an Organizational Setting," *Organizational Behavior and Human Performance*, February 1968, pp. 12–35.

[10]Douglas T. Hall, *Careers in Organizations*, Goodyear, Pacific Palisades, Calif., 1976.

[11]Edward E. Lawler and J. Lloyd Suttle, "A Causal Correlational Test of the Need Hierarchy Concept," *Organizational Behavior and Human Performance*, April 1972, pp. 265–287.

[12]Wahba and Birdwell, op. cit.

self-actualization are important to the content of work motivation. The exact nature of these needs and how they relate to motivation are not clear. To try to overcome some of the problems of the Maslow hierarchy, Alderfer has recently proposed a model containing three groups of needs. This model, called the ERG model, will be covered after the discussion of the Herzberg two-factor theory.

Herzberg's two-factor theory of motivation

Herzberg extended the work of Maslow and developed a specific content theory of work motivation. In the 1950s, he conducted a motivational study on about two hundred accountants and engineers employed by firms in and around Pittsburgh, Pennsylvania. He used the critical incident method of obtaining data for analysis. The professional subjects in the study were given the following directions by an interviewer:

Think of a time when you felt exceptionally good or exceptionally bad about your job, either your present job or any other job you have had. This can be either the "long-range" or the "short-range" kind of situation, as I have just described it. Tell me what happened.[13]

Responses obtained from this critical incident method were interesting and fairly consistent. Reported good feelings were generally associated with job experiences and job content. An example was the accounting supervisor who felt good about being given the job of installing new computer equipment. He took pride and was gratified in knowing that the new equipment made a big difference in the overall functioning of his department. Reported bad feelings, on the other hand, were generally associated with the surrounding or peripheral aspects of the job—the job context. An example of these feelings was related by an engineer whose first job was to keep tabulation sheets and manage the office when the boss was gone. It turned out that his boss was always too busy to train him and became annoyed when he tried to ask questions. The engineer said that he felt frustrated in this job context and that he felt like a flunky in a dead-end job. Tabulating these reported good and bad feelings, Herzberg concluded that job satisfiers were related to job content and job dissatisfiers were allied to job context. The satisfiers were labeled *motivators* and the dissatisfiers were called *hygiene factors*. Taken together, they became known as Herzberg's *two-factor theory of motivation*.

Herzberg's theory is closely related to Maslow's need hierarchy. The hygiene factors are preventive and environmental in nature, and they are roughly equivalent to Maslow's lower-level needs (see Table 7-1). These hygienic factors prevent dissatisfaction, but they do not lead to satisfaction. In effect, they bring motivation up to a theoretical zero level and are a necessary "floor" to prevent dissatisfaction, and they serve as a takeoff point

---

[13]Frederick Herzberg, Bernard Mausner, and Barbara Bloch Snyderman, *The Motivation to Work*, 2d ed., Wiley, New York, 1959, p. 141.

Table 7–1

HERZBERG'S TWO-FACTOR THEORY

Hygiene factors	Motivators
Company policy and administration	Achievement
Supervision, technical	Recognition
Salary	Work itself
Interpersonal relations, supervisor	Responsibility
Working conditions	Advancement

for motivation. By themselves, the hygiene factors do not motivate. Only the motivators (see Table 7-1) motivate humans on the job. They are roughly equivalent to Maslow's higher-level needs. According to the Herzberg theory, an individual must have a job with a challenging content in order to be truly motivated.

Herzberg's two-factor theory cast a new light on the content of work motivation. Up to this point, management had generally concentrated on the hygienic factors. When faced with a morale problem, the typical solution was higher pay, more fringe benefits, and better conditions. However, as pointed out earlier, this simplistic solution did not really work. Management is often perplexed because they are paying high wages and salaries, have an excellent fringe-benefit package, and great working conditions, but their employees are still not motivated. Herzberg's theory offers an explanation for this dilemma. By concentrating only on the hygienic factors, management is not motivating its personnel.

There are probably very few workers or managers who do not feel they deserved the raise they received. On the other hand, there are many dissatisfied workers and managers who did not get a large enough raise. This simple observation points out that the hygiene factors seem to be important in preventing dissatisfaction but do not lead to satisfaction. Herzberg would be the first to say that hygienic factors are absolutely necessary to maintain the human resources of an organization. However, as in the Maslow sense, once "the belly is full" of hygiene factors, which is the case in most modern organizations, dangling any more in front of employees will not motivate them. Only a challenging job which has the opportunities for achievement, recognition, responsibility, advancement, and growth will motivate personnel.

Criticism of Herzberg's theory

Although Herzberg's two-factor theory became very popular as a textbook explanation of work motivation and was widely accepted by practitioners in the 1960s, it came under heavy attack by most academicians. Victor Vroom was in the vanguard of the attack. In 1964, he stated that the two-factor conclusion was only one of many that could be interpreted from Herzberg's research findings. "One could also argue that the relative frequency with which job-content or job-contextual features will be mentioned as sources of satisfaction and dissatisfaction is dependent on the nature of the content and context of the work roles of the respondents."[14] Vroom cited the classic study of the assembly line worker, by Walker and Guest, to support his interpretation.[15] In response to this and other criticism, Herzberg cites the results of an impressive number and diversity of replications of his original Pittsburgh study which supported his position.[16] He included studies which were conducted on agricultural administrators, professional women, hospital maintenance personnel, nurses, manufacturing supervisors, food handlers, scientists, engineers, teachers, technicians, assemblers, accountants, military officers, and managers about to retire, plus cross-cultural studies conducted in Finland, Yugoslavia, Hungary, and Russia. He also obtained some support from those who analyzed the existing evidence from a wide variety of studies[17] and from further reexamination by himself and his colleagues.[18]

Analysis of the "Herzberg controversy"

The two keys to the "Herzberg controversy" lie in the different theoretical interpretations made and the research methodology that is used. For example, in one analysis no less than five different versions of the two-factor theory were identified.[19] Briefly summarized, these are:

1. Theory I states that all motivators combined contribute more to job satisfaction than to job dissatisfaction and that all hygienes combined contribute more to job dissatisfaction than to job satisfaction.
2. Theory II states that all motivators combined contribute more to job satisfaction than do all hygienes combined, and conversely, that the hygienes contribute more to job dissatisfaction than do the motivators.
3. Theory III states that each motivator contributes more to satisfaction than to dissatisfaction (and conversely, that each hygiene contributes more to dissatisfaction than to satisfaction).
4. Theory IV states that each principle hygiene contributes more to job dissatisfaction than does any motivator, and conversely, that each principal motivator contributes more to job satisfaction than does any hygiene.
5. Theory V states that only motivators determine job satisfaction and only hygienes determine job dissatisfaction.

This analysis then examined each of the five versions in light of existing research and concluded that Theories I and II have not been adequately tested to eliminate subjects' defensive biases and that Theories III, IV, and V,

---

[14]Vroom, op. cit., p. 128.

[15]Charles R. Walker and Robert H. Guest, *The Man on the Assembly Line,* Harvard, Cambridge, 1952.

[16]Frederick Herzberg, *Work and the Nature of Man,* World, Cleveland, 1966.

[17]Valerie M. Bockman, "The Herzberg Controversy," *Personnel Psychology,* Summer 1971, pp. 155–189.

[18]Benedict S. Grigaliunas and Frederick Herzberg, "Relevancy in the Test of Motivation-Hygiene Theory," *Journal of Applied Psychology,* February 1971, pp. 73–79.

[19]Nathan A. King, "A Clarification and Evaluation of the Two-Factor Theory of Job Satisfaction," *Psychological Bulletin,* July 1970, p. 18.

although supported by Herzberg-type studies, merely reflect experimenter biases and are thus invalid. A follow-up study of female office workers that specifically tested all five theories found no support for any of them.[20]

Inherent in the analysis of the five versions of the two-factor theory is the other key factor in the "Herzberg controversy"—the type of research methodology that is used. When researchers depart from the critical incident method used by Herzberg, they generally obtain results which are quite different from those the two-factor theory would predict.[21] These studies find that there is not always a clear distinction between factors that lead to satisfaction and those that lead to dissatisfaction. One study even used Herzberg's same methodology and obtained results different from what his theory would predict.[22] There seem to be job factors that lead to both satisfaction and dissatisfaction. These findings tend to invalidate a strict interpretation of the two-factor theory.

In spite of the seemingly legitimate criticism, few would question that Herzberg contributed substantially to the study of work motivation. He extended the Maslow need hierarchy concept and made it more applicable to work motivation. Herzberg also drew attention to the importance of job content factors in work motivation, which previously had been badly neglected and often totally overlooked. The job design technique of job enrichment is also one of Herzberg's contributions. Job enrichment is covered in detail in the next chapter. Overall, Herzberg added much to the better understanding of job content factors and satisfaction but, like his predecessors, fell short of a comprehensive theory of work motivation. His model describes only some of the content of work motivation; it does not adequately describe the complex motivational process of organizational participants.

Alderfer's ERG theory

A more recent extension of the Herzberg and, especially, Maslow content theories of work motivation comes from the work of Clayton Alderfer.[23] He formulated a need category model that was more in line with the existing empirical evidence. Similar to Maslow and Herzberg, he does feel that there

---

[20]L. K. Waters and Carrie Wherry Waters, "An Empirical Test of Five Versions of the Two-Factor Theory of Job Satisfaction," *Organizational Behavior and Human Performance*, February 1972, pp. 18–24.

[21]See Marvin D. Dunnette, John P. Campbell, and Milton D. Hakel, "Factors Contributing to Job Satisfaction and Job Dissatisfaction in Six Occupational Groups," *Organizational Behavior and Human Performance*, May 1967, pp. 143–174; C. L. Hulin and P. A. Smith, "An Empirical Investigation of Two Implications of the Two-Factor Theory of Job Satisfaction," *Journal of Applied Psychology*, October 1967, pp. 396–402; and C. A. Lindsay, E. Marks, and L. Gorlow, "The Herzberg Theory: A Critique and Reformulation," *Journal of Applied Psychology*, August 1967, pp. 330–339.

[22]Donald P. Schwab, H. William DeVitt, and Larry L. Cummings, "A Test of the Adequacy of the Two-Factor Theory as a Predictor of Self-report Performance Effects," *Personnel Psychology*, Summer 1971, pp. 293–303.

[23]Clayton P. Alderfer, *Existence, Relatedness and Growth: Human Needs in Organizational Settings*, Free Press, New York, 1972.

is value in categorizing needs and that there is a basic distinction between lower-order needs and higher-order needs.

Alderfer identified three groups of core needs: existence, relatedness, and growth (thus ERG theory). The *existence needs* are concerned with survival (physiological well-being). The *relatedness needs* stress the importance of interpersonal, social relationships. The *growth needs* are concerned with the individual's intrinsic desire for personal development. Figure 7-4 shows how these three groups of needs are related to the Maslow and Herzberg categories. Obviously they are very close, but the ERG needs do not have strict lines of demarcation.

Alderfer is suggesting more of a continuum of needs than hierarchical levels or two factors of prepotency needs. Unlike Maslow or Herzberg, he does not contend that a lower-level need has to be fulfilled before a higher-level need is motivating nor that deprivation is the only way to activate a need. For example, under ERG theory the person's background or cultural environment may dictate that the relatedness needs may take precedence over unfulfilled existence needs and the growth needs may increase in intensity the more they are satisfied.

To date, except for Alderfer's own empirical test,[24] there has been no direct research on ERG theory. Yet most contemporary analyses of work motivation tend to support the Alderfer theory over Maslow and Herzberg.[25] Overall, ERG seems to take some of the strong points of the earlier content theories but is less restrictive and limiting. The fact remains, however, that

---

[24]Clayton P. Alderfer, "An Empirical Test of a New Theory of Human Needs," *Organizational Behavior and Human Performance,* May 1969, pp. 142–175.

[25]Bronston T. Mayes, "Some Boundary Considerations in the Application of Motivation Models," *Academy of Management Review,* January 1978, pp. 51–52.

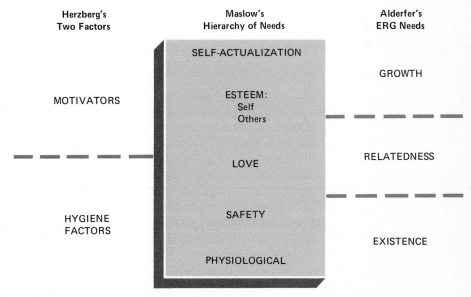

Figure 7-4 Relationship among Alderfer's ERG needs, Maslow's five-level hierarchy, and Herzberg's two factors.

the content theories in general lack explanatory power over the complexities of work motivation and, with the possible exception of the implications for job design of Herzberg's work, do not readily translate to the actual practice of human resource management.

THE PROCESS THEORIES OF WORK MOTIVATION

The content models attempted to identify what motivated people at work (e.g., self-actualization, responsibility, or growth); they tried to specify correlates of motivated behavior. The process theories, on the other hand, are more concerned with identifying the variables that go into motivation and, more importantly, how they relate to one another. As Figure 7-1 shows, the expectancy models make the most significant contribution to understanding the complex processes involved in work motivation. After these are examined, equity and attribution theories will also be presented and analyzed as major process models of work motivation.

Vroom's expectancy theory of motivation

The expectancy theory of work motivation has its roots in the cognitive concepts of pioneering psychologists Kurt Lewin and Edward Tolman, and in the choice behavior and utility concepts from classical economic theory. However, the first to formulate an expectancy theory directly aimed at work motivation was Victor Vroom in 1964. Contrary to most critics, Vroom proposed his expectancy theory as an alternative to the content models, which he felt were inadequate explanations of the complex process of work motivation. At least in academic circles, his theory has become a popular explanation for work motivation and has generated considerable research.

Figure 7-5 briefly summarizes the Vroom model. As shown, the model is built around the concepts of valence, instrumentality, and expectancy and is commonly called the VIE theory. The basic assumption is that "the choices made by a person among alternative courses of action are lawfully related to psychological events occurring contemporaneously with the behavior."[26]

Meaning of the variables   By *valence* Vroom means the strength of an individual's preference for a particular outcome. Other terms that might be substituted for valence include *value, incentive, attitude,* and *expected utility.* In order for the valence to be positive, the person must prefer attaining the outcome to not attaining it. A valence of zero occurs when the individual is indifferent toward the outcome; the valence is negative when the individual prefers not attaining the outcome to attaining it. Another major input into the valence is the *instrumentality* of the first-level outcome in obtaining a desired second-level outcome.

---

[26]Vroom, op. cit., pp. 14–15.

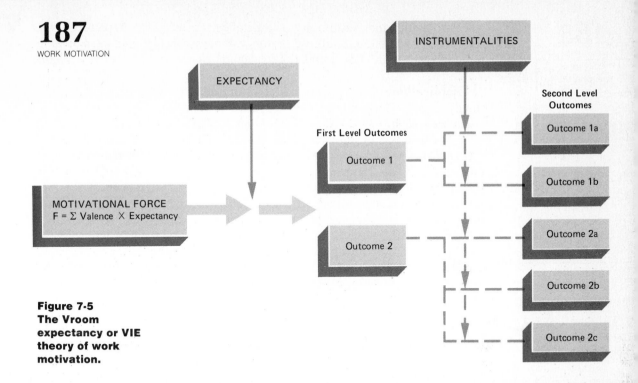

**Figure 7-5
The Vroom
expectancy or VIE
theory of work
motivation.**

For example, assume that an individual desires promotion and feels that superior performance is a very strong factor in achieving that goal. His first-level outcomes are then superior, average, or poor performance. His second-level outcome is promotion. The first-level outcome of high performance thus acquires a positive valence by virtue of its expected relationship to the preferred second-level outcome of promotion.[27]

In this example, the person would be motivated toward superior performance because of the desire to be promoted. The superior performance (first-level outcome) is seen as being instrumental in obtaining promotion (second-level outcome).

Another major variable in the Vroom motivational process is *expectancy*. Although at first glance the expectancy concept may seem to be the same as the instrumentality input into valence, it is actually quite different. "Expectancy differs from instrumentality in that it relates *efforts* to first-level outcomes where instrumentality relates first and second-level outcomes to each other."[28] In other words, expectancy is the probability (ranging from 0 to 1) that a particular action or effort will lead to a particular *first-level* outcome. *Instrumentality* refers to the degree to which a first-level outcome will lead to a desired *second-level* outcome. In summary, the

---

[27]J. G. Hunt and J. W. Hill, "The New Look in Motivation Theory for Organizational Research," *Human Organization,* Summer 1969, p. 104.
[28]Ibid.

strength of the motivation to perform a certain act will depend on the algebraic sum of the products of the valences for the outcomes (which include instrumentality) times the expectancies.

Implications of the Vroom model for organizational behavior   Vroom's theory departs from the content theories in that it depicts a process of cognitive variables that reflects individual differences in work motivation. It does not attempt to describe what the content is or what the individual differences are. Everyone has a unique combination of valences, instrumentalities, and expectancies. Thus, the Vroom theory indicates only the conceptual determinants of motivation and how they are related. It does not provide specific suggestions on what motivates organizational members, as did the Maslow, Herzberg, and Alderfer models.

Although the Vroom model does not directly contribute much to the techniques of motivating personnel in an organization, it is of value in understanding organizational behavior. For example, it can clarify the relationship between individual and organizational goals.

Thus instead of assuming that satisfaction of a specific need is likely to influence organizational objectives in a certain way, we can find out how important to the employees are the various second-level outcomes (worker goals), the instrumentality of various first-level outcomes (organizational objectives) for their attainment, and the expectancies that are held with respect to the employees' ability to influence the first-level outcomes.[29]

Suppose workers are given a certain standard for production. By measuring the workers' output, management can determine how important their various personal goals (second-level outcomes such as money, security, and recognition) are; the instrumentality of the organizational goal (the first-level outcome, such as the production standard) for the attainment of the personal goals; and the workers' expectancies that their effort and ability will accomplish the organizational goal. If output is below standard, it may be that the workers do not place a high value on the second-level outcomes; or they may not see that the first-level outcome is instrumental in obtaining the second-level outcomes; or they may think that their efforts will not be able to accomplish the first-level outcome. Any one, or a combination, of these possibilities Vroom feels will result in a low level of motivation to produce. The model is designed to help management understand and analyze the workers' motivation and identify some of the relevant variables; it does not provide specific solutions to motivational problems. Besides the application problem, the model also assumes, as did earlier economic theory, that people are rational and logically calculating. Such an assumption may be erroneous.

Research results on the Vroom model   To develop his model, Vroom depended largely upon prior research. Since the model has been proposed,

---

[29]Ibid., p. 105.

almost every issue of the academic journals in organizational behavior have reported the results of research on the expectancy model. Although not all studies directly test the Vroom model (some are more concerned with the Porter-Lawler type of model that is discussed next), some definite conclusions can begin to be drawn concerning its validity and predictability. One comprehensive analysis of the literature drew the conclusions that

1. In general, each variable pertinent to value/expectancy theory has been found to have significant predictive powers in some studies, but not in others.
2. The most consistently positive findings involve the expectancy that performance will result in extrinsic rewards, and that intrinsic satisfaction will result from the work itself. These variables show rather consistent, statistically significant associations (although usually of low or moderate magnitude) with effort and performance.
3. Weighting the expectancy that performance leads to rewards by the value placed on extrinsic rewards does not improve power of prediction over that obtained by using the unweighted expectancy that performance leads to rewards.
4. The theory is limited to conditions where subjects have the requisite ability, accurate role perceptions, and accurate perceptions of contingent rewards.
5. The better controlled the study (in longitudinal analyses and laboratory investigations) the more support will generally be shown for the theory. The superiority of such carefully controlled approaches over cross-sectional studies suggests that cross-sectional tests result in underestimates of the theory's predictive validity.[30]

In other words, there is some support, especially relative to the content theories, of the validity of the expectancy theory of motivation. On the other hand, even the most ardent supporters of this approach recognize that there are some conceptual and methodological problems.[31] Research is needed that more carefully and consistently measures the variables and that tests all the relevant variables and not just bits and pieces.

Importance of the Vroom model Probably the major reason Vroom's model has emerged as an important modern theory of work motivation and has generated so much research is that he does not take a simplistic approach. The content theories oversimplified human motivation. Yet the content theories remain extremely popular with practicing managers because the concepts are easy to understand and to apply to their own situations. On the otherhand, the VIE theory recognizes the complexities of work motivation, but it is relatively difficult to understand and apply. Thus, from a theoretical standpoint the VIE model seems to help appreciate the complexities of motivation, but it does not give managers much practical help in solving their motivational problems. This is not necessarily a criticism of the expectancy model per se because, as has been pointed out,

---

[30]Alan C. Filley, Robert J. House, and Steven Kerr, *Managerial Process and Organizational Behavior*, 2d ed., Scott, Foresman, Glenview, Ill., 1976, pp. 200–201. Also see: R. J. House, H. J. Shapiro, and M. A. Wahba, "Expectancy Theory as a Predictor of Work Behavior and Attitude: A Reevaluation of Empirical Evidence," *Decision Sciences*, December 1974, pp. 54–77.

[31]Terry Connolly, "Some Conceptual and Methodological Issues in Expectancy Models of Work Performance Motivation," *Academy of Management Review*, October 1976, pp. 37–47.

The expectancy model is just that: a model and no more. People rarely actually sit down and list their expected outcomes for a contemplated behavior, estimate expectancies and valences, multiply, and add up the total, unless, of course, they are asked to do so by a researcher. Yet people *do* consider the likely outcomes of their actions, do weigh and evaluate the attractiveness of various alternatives, and do use these estimates in coming to a decision about what they will do.[32]

The expectancy model is like marginal analysis in economics. Business persons do not actually calculate the point where marginal cost equals marginal revenue, but it is still a useful concept for the theory of the firm. The expectancy model attempts only to mirror the complex motivational process; it does not attempt to describe how motivational decisions are actually made or to solve actual motivational problems facing a manager.

The Porter-Lawler model:
Implications for performance and satisfaction

The introductory comments in the chapter pointed out the controversy that has existed since the human relations movement over the relationship between satisfaction and performance. The content theories implicitly assume that satisfaction leads to improved performance and that dissatisfaction detracts from performance. The Herzberg model is, at best, a theory of job satisfaction, but still it does not deal with the relationship of satisfaction to performance. The Vroom model also largely avoids the relationship between satisfaction and performance. Although satisfactions make an input into Vroom's concept of valence and the outcomes have performance implications, it was not until Porter and Lawler refined and extended Vroom's model (e.g., the relationships are expressed diagramatically rather than mathematically, there are more variables, and the cognitive process of perception plays a central role) that the relationships between satisfaction and performance was dealt with directly by a motivation model.

Porter and Lawler start with the premise that motivation (effort or force) does not equal satisfaction and/or performance. Motivation, satisfaction, and performance are all separate variables and relate in ways different from what was traditionally assumed. Figure 7-6 depicts the multivariable model used to explain the complex relationship that exists among motivation, performance, and satisfaction. As shown in the model, boxes 1, 2, and 3 are basically the same as the Vroom equation. It is important, however, that Porter and Lawler point out that effort (force or motivation) does not directly lead to performance. It is mediated by abilities/traits and role perceptions. More important in the Porter-Lawler model is what happens after the performance. The rewards that follow and how these are perceived will determine satisfaction. In other words, the Porter-Lawler model suggests—and this is a significant turn of events from traditional thinking—that performance leads to satisfaction.

---

[32]Lyman Porter, Edward E. Lawler, III, and J. Richard Hackman, *Behavior in Organizations*, McGraw-Hill, 1975, p. 58.

Variables in the Porter-Lawler model

Similar to the Vroom model, the Porter-Lawler model is an expectancy-based theory of motivation. The future-oriented expectancy theories emphasize the anticipation of response-outcome connections and depend heavily upon cognitive concepts such as value/valence and perception. Porter and Lawler explain their choice for the expectancy approach as follows:

> The emphasis in expectancy theory on rationality and expectations seems to us to describe best the kinds of cognitions that influence managerial performance. We assume that managers operate on the basis of some sort of expectancies which, although based upon previous experience, are forward-oriented in a way that does not seem to be as easily handled by the concept of habit strength.[33]

A clearer understanding of the model can be gained by a more detailed examination of the major variables in the model.

Effort   In the model, as in the daily language, "effort" refers to the amount of energy exerted by an employee on a given task. However, contrary to the common usage of the word, effort is not the same as performance. As used in the model, effort is more closely associated with motivation than with performance. The amount of effort depends upon the interaction

**Figure 7-6
The Porter-Lawler
motivation model.
(Source: Lyman W.
Porter and Edward
E. Lawler, III,
*Managerial
Attitudes and
Performance*,
Irwin, Homewood,
Ill., 1968, p. 165.
Used with
permission.)**

[33]Lyman W. Porter and Edward E. Lawler, III, *Managerial Attitudes and Performance*, Irwin, Homewood, Ill., 1968, pp. 12–13.

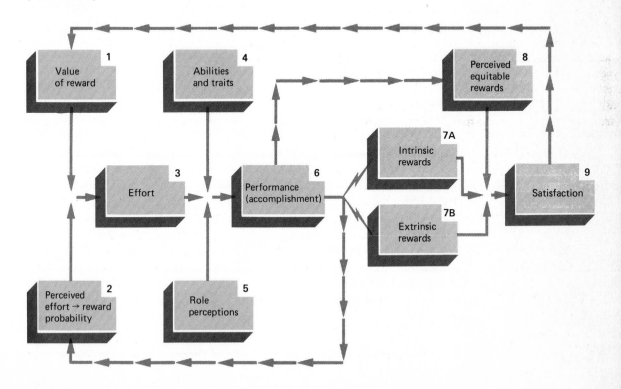

between the value of the reward and the perceived effort-reward probability. It is roughly equivalent to Vroom's use of the term *force*.

The value placed on a reward depends on its degree of attractiveness and desirability. Friendship, promotion, pay, recognition, and praise are assigned different values by different people. For example, one person may feel threatened and insecure with a promotion. The perceived effort-reward probability is the other major input into effort. This variable refers to the employees' perception of the probability that differential rewards depend upon differential amounts of effort. In interactive combination, these two variables (value of reward and perception of effort-reward probability) determine the amount of effort that will be exerted. If employees place a high value on a reward, and if they perceive a high probability that their effort will lead to this reward, then they will exert a great amount of effort. But, once again, it should be noted that this effort will not directly lead to a particular level of performance.

Performance Performance represents the pragmatic result that organizations are able to measure objectively. Effort precedes performance; the two cannot be equated. A discrepancy between effort and performance may result from the employees' abilities and traits and/or their role perceptions. Performance depends not only on the amount of effort exerted but also on the persons' abilities (e.g., job knowledge and skill) and the way they perceive the role they should take. The way the job is defined, the direction of efforts, and the level of effort thought to be necessary for effective performance all go into the role perception. In other words, even though the employees exert a great amount of effort, if they have little ability and/or an inaccurate role perception, the resulting performance may end up being ineffective. A good illustration would be the athletes who give a great deal of effort but, because of a lack of ability and/or because they perceive the situation incorrectly and misdirect that effort, turn out losers rather than winners. This ineffective performance occurred in spite of the amount of effort that was exerted by the athletes.

Rewards Initially, Porter and Lawler included only a single reward variable in their model. However, empirical testing showed that it should more accurately be divided into extrinsic and intrinsic categories. Chapter 9 will point out the difference between extrinsic and intrinsic rewards and the difficulty of operationalizing these concepts. As used in the Porter-Lawler model, both are desirable outcomes. However, Porter and Lawler feel that the intrinsic rewards are much more likely to produce attitudes about satisfaction that are related to performance. In addition, the perceived equitable rewards vitally affect the performance-satisfaction relationship. They reflect the fair level of rewards that the individual feels should be granted for a given level of performance. The perception of equitable rewards can be directly affected by self-rated performance, as indicated by the diagonally directed short arrows in the model in Figure 7-6.

Satisfaction As was pointed out, satisfaction is not the same as motivation. Satisfaction is an attitude, an internal cognitive state. Motivation is a process, and that is why the content models, especially Herzberg's, have more to do with satisfactions than with the complex process of motivation. In the content models, job satisfaction was deemed to be the sum of various content factors such as responsibility and growth potential. In Porter and Lawler's model, satisfaction is only one of the variables and is derived from the extent to which actual rewards fall short, meet, or exceed the person's perceived equitable level of rewards. Therefore, if actual rewards meet or exceed perceived equitable rewards, the individual will be satisfied. On the other hand, if actual rewards are below what is perceived to be equitable, the individual will be dissatisfied. This explanation of satisfaction makes two important departures from traditional thinking about satisfaction. First, the model recognizes that satisfaction is determined only in part by actual rewards received. It depends also on what a person feels the organization *should* reward for a given level of performance. Second, and of greater importance, the model recognizes satisfaction to be more dependent on performance than performance is on satisfaction. Only through the less direct feedback loops will satisfaction affect performance. This, of course, makes a 180-degree turn from the traditional analysis of the satisfaction-performance relationship.

Research on the Porter-Lawler model The model in Figure 7-6 was meant only to be the conceptual scheme to guide and structure a comprehensive research study that Porter and Lawler were conducting. They ran a correlational study that investigated the relationship between managerial attitudes toward pay and managerial performance. Based on the responses to 563 questionnaires filled out by managers in seven organizations, Porter and Lawler concluded that, taken as a whole, their model was validated by the study. They note that "those variables presumed to affect performance turned out to show relations to performance, and those variables presumed to result from performance also typically were related to performance."[34] Although they are careful to point out that the correlational study does not prove or show the direction of cause and effect, they are confident that the major hypothesis that performance causes satisfaction is supported by their data. Follow-up studies have generally substantiated this conclusion.[35]

Others have expressed concern that the relationship between performance and satisfaction is extremely complex and feel that the role of rewards

[34]Ibid., pp. 159–160.

[35]For example, see David G. Kuhn, John W. Slocum, Jr., and Richard B. Chase, "Does Job Performance Affect Employee Satisfaction?", *Personnel Journal*, June 1971, pp. 455–459 and 485; Jay R. Schuster, Barbara Clark, and Miles Rogers, "Testing Portions of the Porter and Lawler Model Regarding the Motivational Role of Pay," *Journal of Applied Psychology*, June 1971, pp. 187–195; and D. O. Jorgenson, M. D. Dunnette, and R. D. Pritchard, "Effects of the Manipulation of a Performance-Reward Contingency on Behavior in a Simulated Work Setting," *Journal of Applied Psychology*, vol. 57, 1973, pp. 271–280.

and moderating effects should be given more attention. For example, Greene and Craft conclude that "recent evidence is more indicative . . . that satisfaction and performance are covariants of a third (or more) variable(s)."[36] They stress that the administration of rewards is the most significant codeterminant and, in particular, that "(a) rewards constitute a more direct cause of satisfaction than does performance and (b) not satisfaction, but rewards based on current performance, cause subsequent performance."[37] Other moderating effects that have recently been shown to have an impact on the performance-satisfaction relationship included self-esteem[38] and task design.[39] Such interpretations have important implications for the actual practice of human resource management.

Implications for practice   Although the Porter-Lawler model is more applications-oriented than the Vroom model, it is still quite complex and has proved to be a difficult way to bridge the gap to actual management practice. To Porter and Lawler's credit, they have been very conscious of putting their theory and research into practice. They recommend that practicing managers should go beyond traditional attitude measurement and attempt to measure variables such as the values of possible rewards, the perceptions of effort-reward probabilities, and role perceptions.[40] These variables, of course, can help managers better understand what goes into employee effort and performance. Giving attention to the consequences of performance, Porter and Lawler also recommend that organizations should critically reevaluate their current reward policies. They stress that management should make a concentrated effort to measure how closely levels of satisfaction are related to levels of performance.[41] These types of recommendations have been verified in a few studies. For example, one study of piece-rate workers found that those with high effort-performance probability perceptions were significantly higher producers than those with low probability perceptions.[42] Such a finding could aid the actual practice of management. Some specifics of the reward applications can also be found in the recent book by Porter, Lawler, and Hackman.[43] The Porter-Lawler model has definitely made a significant contribution to the better understanding of work motivation and the relationship between performance and satisfaction, but, to date, it has not had much of an impact on the practice of human resource management. However, by stressing the reward implications,

---

[36]Greene and Craft, op. cit., p. 198.

[37]Ibid., p. 198.

[38]J. H. Kerr Inkson, "Self-Esteem as a Moderator of the Relationship Between Job Performance and Job Satisfaction," *Journal of Applied Psychology*, April 1978, pp. 243–247.

[39]Ivancevich, op. cit.

[40]Porter and Lawler, op. cit., p. 183.

[41]Ibid., pp. 183–184.

[42]Donald P. Schwab and Lee D. Dyer, "The Motivational Impact of a Compensation System on Employee Performance," *Organizational Behavior and Human Performance*, April 1973, pp. 215–225.

[43]Porter, Lawler, and Hackman, op. cit., especially Chap. 12.

especially the intrinsic-extrinsic distinction, there is a move away from a strictly cognitive view of work motivation and toward more of an operant, environmentally based view of motivation. Chapters 9 and 10 will discuss this view in detail.

The Lawler expectancy model: A refinement

Since the original Porter-Lawler model, Lawler has proposed several refinements on his own. In particular, he feels that there are actually two types of expectancies: the E→P and P→O expectancies. Both of these make an input into effort or motivation. There is a multiplicative relationship among the expectancy factors. The Lawler equation for motivation would be:

$$\text{Effort} = (E \rightarrow P) \times \Sigma \ [(P \rightarrow O)(V)]$$

Verbalized, this means that the effort→performance expectancy is multiplied by the sum of products of all performance→outcome expectancies times valences. Graphically, this equation can be represented in the model shown in Figure 7-7.

As shown in Figure 7-7, the first expectancy (E→P) is the person's estimate of the probability (from 0 to 1) of accomplishing the intended performance. The second expectancy (P→O) involves the person's estima-

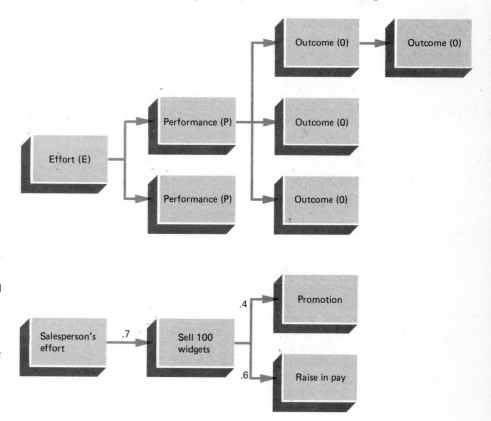

Figure 7-7
The Lawler
expectancy model
of motivation.
(*Source:* **Adapted**
from Edward E.
Lawler, III,
Motivation in Work
Organizations,
Brooks/Cole,
Monterey, Calif.,
1973, p. 50.)

tion (from 0 to 1) of the likelihood that performance will lead to particular outcomes. An example of an E→P expectancy (shown in Figure 7-7) would be the salesperson who estimates that there is a good probability (say, .7) of being able to sell 100 widgets. The outcomes of this level of performance (the P→O expectancies) may be a probability of .4 for a promotion or of .6 for a raise in pay.

Lawler feels that the single most important determinant of the E→P expectancy is the objective situation. In addition, the person's self-esteem, past experiences in similar situations, and communications from others are some of the major inputs into the person's perception of the situation. The person's perception of the P→O expectancies is influenced by many of the same things as the E→P expectancy. In addition, the attractiveness of outcomes, the belief of who controls the outcomes (the person himself or herself or others, which is known as *locus of control*, which is discussed after equity theory), and the E→P expectancy will all have an impact on the person's P→O expectancies.

This more complex expectancy model of work motivation is a step toward better understanding but compounds further the problems of translation into practice. Lawler himself does provide some insights into the use of the model to help explain how pay motivates behavior. After reviewing a number of studies, he concludes that:

1. Beliefs about the degree to which pay depends upon performance are positively related to job performance.
2. Where pay depends upon performance, statements about the importance of pay are related to job performance.
3. Job performance is most strongly related to a multiplicative combination of important attitudes and P→O beliefs.
4. P→O beliefs seem to be more strongly related to future performance than to either present or past performance.[44]

Despite these insights for the practical administration of pay plans, the fact remains, in Lawler's own words:

If we try to predict a person's behavior using our model, and if we gather complete data on all his or her perceptions of existing relationships, we still might predict behavior incorrectly because our model would be too complex to allow for valid predictions.[45]

Despite such self-criticism, there is value in the model. But, as was stated in the introductory part of the book, the goals of prediction and control may be more in the realm of the operant models that will be discussed in Chapters 9 and 10.

---

[44]Edward E. Lawler, III, *Pay and Organizational Effectiveness*, McGraw-Hill, New York, 1971, p. 139.

[45]Edward E. Lawler, III, *Motivation in Work Organizations*, Brooks/Cole, Monterey, Calif., 1973, p. 60.

Equity theory of work motivation

Equity theory has been around for just as long as the expectancy theories of work motivation. However, only recently has equity as a process of motivation received widespread attention in the organizational behavior field. As Figure 7-1 indicated, its roots can be traced back to cognitive dissonance theory, which will be discussed in Chapter 13, and exchange theory, which will be discussed in Chapter 11. As a theory of work motivation, credit for equity theory is usually given to J. Stacy Adams. Simply put, the theory argues that a major input into job performance and satisfaction is the degree of equity (or inequity) that people perceive in their work situation. In other words, it is another cognitively based motivation theory, and Adams depicts a specific process of how this motivation occurs.

Using the terminology of "person" (any individual for whom equity or inequity exists) and "other" (any individual with whom person is in a relevant exchange relationship or with whom person compares himself or herself), Adams states that, "Inequity exists for person whenever he perceives that the ratio of his outcomes to inputs and the ratio of other's outcomes to other's inputs are unequal."[46]

Schematically, inequity occurs when

$$\frac{\text{Person's outcomes}}{\text{Person's inputs}} < \frac{\text{other's outcomes}}{\text{other's inputs}}$$

$$\frac{\text{Person's outcomes}}{\text{Person's inputs}} > \frac{\text{other's outcomes}}{\text{other's inputs}}$$

$$\frac{\text{Person's outcomes}}{\text{Person's inputs}} = \frac{\text{other's outcomes}}{\text{other's inputs}}$$

Both the inputs and outputs of person and other are based upon the person's perceptions. Age, sex, education, social status, organizational position, qualifications, and how hard the person works would be examples of perceived input variables. Outcomes would primarily be rewards such as pay, status, promotion, or intrinsic interest in the job. In essence, the ratio is based upon the person's *perception* of what the person is giving (inputs) and receiving (outcomes) versus the ratio of what the relevant other is giving and receiving. This cognition may or may not be the same as someone else's observation of the ratios or the actual, realistic situation.

If the person's perceived ratio is not equal to the other's, he or she will strive to restore the ratio to equity. This "striving" to restore equity is used as the explanation of work motivation. The strength of this motivation is in direct proportion to the perceived inequity that exists. Adams suggests that such motivation may be expressed in several forms. To restore equity, the

[46]Stacy Adams, "Inequity in Social Exchange," in L. Berkowitz (ed.), *Advances in Experimental Social Psychology*, Academic Press, New York, 1965. Reprinted in Richard M. Steers and Lyman W. Porter, *Motivation and Work Behavior*, McGraw-Hill, 1975, p. 141.

person may alter the inputs or outcomes, cognitively distort the inputs or outcomes, leave the field, act on the other, or change the other.[47]

It is important to note that inequity does not come about only when the person feels cheated. For example, Adams has studied the impact that perceived overpayment has on inequity. His findings suggest that workers prefer equitable payment to overpayment. A worker on a piece-rate incentive system who feels overpaid will reduce his or her productivity in order to restore equity. More likely, however, is the case of people feeling underpaid (outcome) or overworked (input) in relation to others in the workplace. In the latter case there would be motivation to restore equity that may be dysfunctional from an organizational standpoint.

To date, research that has specifically tested the validity of Adams's equity theory has been fairly supportive. A recent comprehensive review found considerable laboratory research support for the "equity norm" (persons review the imputs and outcomes of themselves and others and if inequity is perceived, they strive to restore equity) but only limited support from more relevant field studies.[48] This review concludes that there are several methodological problems, and a definite need for more applied field research exists. Another comprehensive review of research on the way employees preceive their pay concludes the following about equity theory:[49]

1. Overpaid hourly or salaried employees will increase their contribution by producing more as a means of reducing inequity. There are mixed findings, but the better controlled studies show support for this proposition.
2. Overpaid piece-rate employees will produce higher quality and lower quantity than equitably paid employees. This is strongly supported by the findings.
3. Underpaid hourly or salaried employees will produce less to achieve a contribution-reward balance. There are mixed findings but at least some preliminary support exists.
4. Underpaid piece-rate employees will produce a high volume of low quality output because production of low quality output permits increasing rewards without substantially increasing contributions. There are only two studies that test this proposition but both support it.

Equity concepts are inherent in the integrative Porter-Lawler expectancy model discussed earlier. Perceived equitable rewards are a major input into employee satisfaction. Organ introduces equity and reciprocity also to defend the more traditional explanation of the relationship between satisfac-

---

[47]Ibid., pp. 144–151.

[48]Michael R. Carrell and John E. Dittrich, "Equity Theory: The Recent Literature, Methodological Considerations, and New Directions," *Academy of Management Review*, April 1978, pp. 202–210.

[49]Filley, House, and Kerr, op. cit., pp. 207–208. Also see: P. S. Goodman and A. Friedman, "An Examination of Adams' Theory of Inequity," *Administrative Science Quarterly*, vol. 16, 1971, pp. 271–288; and Charles S. Telly, Wendell L. French, and William G. Scott, "The Relationship of Inequity to Turnover Among Hourly Workers," *Administrative Science Quarterly*, March 1971, pp. 164–172. The latter study supports equity theory in regard to turnover while the others deal with compensation.

tion and performance.[50] He proposes that employees seek to reciprocate with their benefactors (the boss or perhaps a mentor). Thus, if they are satisfied, they will work hard for their benefactor, i.e., satisfaction leads to performance. This type of analysis begins to serve as a transition to the newly emerging attribution theory/locus of control explanation of work motivation.

Attribution theory and locus of control

Chapter 4, on perception, discussed the important role that attributions have for the cognitive processes of individuals. Recently, the attributions people make and the locus of control they perceive have emerged as important explanations of work motivation. Unlike the other motivation theories, attribution theory is more a theory of the relationship between person perception and interpersonal behavior than it is a theory of individual motivation. Kelly stresses that it is mainly concerned with the cognitive processes by which an individual interprets behavior as being caused by (or attributed to) certain parts of the relevant environment.[51] It is concerned with the "why" questions of motivation and behavior. Since most causes, attributes, or "whys" are not directly observable, the theory says people must depend upon cognitions, particularly perception. The attribution theorist assumes humans are rational and are motivated to identify and understand the causal structure of their relevant environment. It is this search for attributes that characterizes attribution theory.

Although attribution theory has roots in all the pioneering cognitive theorists' work (e.g., Lewin and Festinger), in de Charms' ideas on cognitive evaluation, and in Bem's notion of "self-perception," the theory's initiator is generally recognized to be Fritz Heider. Heider believed that both internal forces (personal attributes such as ability, effort, and fatigue) and external forces (environmental attributes such as rules or the weather) combine additively to determine behavior. He stressed that it is the *perceived*, not the actual determinants, that are important to behavior. People will behave differently if they perceive internal attributes than if they perceive external attributes. It is this concept of differential ascriptions that has very important implications for work motivation.

Using *locus of control*, work behavior may be explained by whether employees perceive their outcomes as controlled internally or externally. Employees who perceive internal control feel that they personally can influence their outcomes through their own ability, skills, or effort. Employees who perceive external control feel that their outcomes are beyond their own control; they feel that external forces control their outcomes. Important is that this perceived locus of control may have a differential impact on their performance and satisfaction. For example, studies by Rotter and his

---

[50]Dennis W. Organ, "A Reappraisal and Reinterpretation of the Satisfaction-Causes-Performance Hypothesis," *Academy of Management Review*, January 1977, pp. 46–53.

[51]H. H. Kelly, "Attribution Theory in Social Psychology," in D. Levine (ed.), *Nebraska Symposium on Motivation*, vol. 15, University of Nebraska Press, Lincoln, Nebr., 1967, p. 193. Also see Bernard Weiner, *Theories of Motivation*, Rand McNally, Chicago, 1972, Chap. 5.

colleagues suggest that skill versus chance environments differentially affect behavior.[52] In addition a number of studies have been conducted in recent years to test the attribution/locus of control model in work settings. One study found that internally controlled employees are generally more satisfied with their jobs, are more likely to be in managerial positions, and are more satisfied with a participatory management style than are employees who perceive external control.[53] Other studies have found internal managers to be better performers[54] and more considerate with subordinates.[55] The implication from these studies is that internal managers are better than external managers. However, such generalizations are not yet warranted because there is some contradictory evidence. For example, one study concluded that the ideal manager may have an external orientation because the results indicated that external managers were perceived as initiating more structure and consideration than internals.[56] This internal-versus-external argument carries over to the intrinsic versus extrinsic rewards controversy that has cropped up in recent years. Chapter 9 will discuss this argument and analyze the existing research.

Attribution theory and locus of control seems to hold a lot of promise for better understanding work motivation and predicting employee behavior. It also provides a framework for analyzing specific problem areas in human resource management. For example, Mitchell and his colleagues have developed the attribution model shown in Figure 7-8 to predict and analyze the supervisor's response to a subordinate's poor performance.[57] As shown there are two important links in such an analysis. In Link #1 the supervisor tries to determine the cause of the poor performance, i.e., an attribution is made. It is notable that such attributions are moderated by social and informational factors such as distinctiveness (how the subordinate performs on other types of tasks), consistency (how the subordinate performs on

[52]Julian B. Rotter, Shephard Liverant, and Douglas P. Crowne, "The Growth and Extinction of Expectancies in Chance Controlled and Skilled Tasks," *The Journal of Psychology*, July 1961, pp. 161–177.

[53]Terence R. Mitchell, Charles M. Smyser, and Stan E. Weed, "Locus of Control: Supervision and Work Satisfaction," *Academy of Management Journal*, September 1975, pp. 623–631.

[54]Carl R. Anderson, Don Hellriegel, and John W. Slocum, Jr., "Managerial Response to Environmentally Induced Stress," *Academy of Management Journal*, June 1977, pp. 260–272. The higher performance of externals was verified by the use of student subjects in a study by Carl R. Anderson and Craig Eric Schneier, "Locus of Control, Leader Behavior and Leader Performance Among Management Students," *Academy of Management Journal*, December 1978, pp. 690–698.

[55]M. W. Pryer and M. K. Distenfano, "Perceptions of Leadership, Job Satisfaction, and Internal-External Control Across Three Nursing Levels," *Nursing Research*, vol. 2, 1971, pp. 534–537.

[56]Douglas E. Durand and Walter R. Nord, "Perceived Leader Behavior as a Function of Personality Characteristics of Supervisors and Subordinates," *Academy of Management Journal*, September 1976, pp. 427–438.

[57]Terence R. Mitchell and Robert E. Wood, "An Empirical Test of an Attributional Model of Leaders' Responses to Poor Performance" in Richard C. Huseman (ed.), *Academy of Management Proceedings*, 1979, pp. 94–98; and Sam G. Green and Terence R. Mitchell, "Attributional Processes of Leaders in Leader-Member Interactions," *Organizational Behavior and Human Performance*, vol. 23, 1979, pp. 429–458.

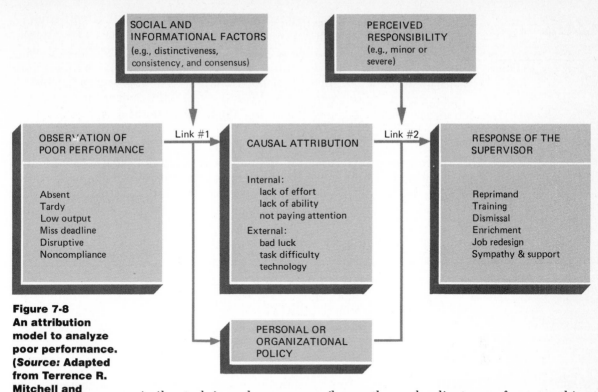

**Figure 7-8
An attribution model to analyze poor performance.** (*Source:* Adapted from Terrence R. Mitchell and Robert E. Wood, "An Empirical Test of an Attributional Model of Leaders' Responses to Poor Performance," in Richard C. Huseman (ed.), *Academy of Management Proceedings,* 1979, p. 94.)

similar tasks), and consensus (how other subordinates perform on this task).[58] Link #2 in the model suggests that the supervisor's response is determined by the type of attribution that is made. This relationship between attribution and response is moderated by the perceived responsibility (i.e., whether the poor performance results in minor or major problems).

An empirical test of the model using nursing supervisors in a hospital setting confirmed the researchers' predictions. Consensus, consistency, and distinctiveness did influence the supervisors' attributions; supervisors who made internal attributions of the problem behavior tended to respond in a more punitive manner; and supervisors made more internal attributions and responded more punitively when the problems were serious.[59] This type of research indicates that attribution theory and locus of control has potential for prediction as well as understanding and may be quite useful in the actual practice of human resource management.

Behavioristic implications for work motivation

As has been noted, the whole concept of motivation and the models discussed in this chapter are largely cognitively based. The refinements of the expectancy models do include rewards, and contingent consequences play an increasingly important role. However, it must be remembered that an

---

[58]Harold H. Kelly, "Attribution in Social Interaction," in E. E. Jones, et al. (eds.), *Attribution: Perceiving the Causes of Behavior,* General Learning Press, Morristown, N.J., 1972, pp. 1–26.

[59]Mitchell and Wood, op. cit.

operant learning perspective (discussed in Chapters 9 and 10) largely ignores the cognitive antecedents (for example, assignment of valences, determining expectancies, calculating input-output ratios, or making attributions), and instead concentrates on the impact that contingent consequences have on subsequent behavior. Instead of polarizing the two approaches (cognitive processes on the one extreme and contingent reinforcement on the other), there seems to be a need to bring these two approaches together and synthesize them. The Porter and Lawler model is a step in this direction, and the attribution theory and locus of control approach also has elements of both cognitive processes and reinforcement. But for now it should be remembered that the internal approach, as discussed in this chapter, is only one dimension of the micro perspective of organizational behavior. As was concluded at the end of the discussion of each model, the cognitive models, with the possible exception of the recently emerging attribution model, are a long way from the goals of prediction and especially control. Chapters 9 and 10 will present and analyze the external approach. The learning chapters, when combined with the motivational chapters, give a comprehensive look at the micro approach and can help fulfill all three goals: understanding, prediction, and control of organizational behavior.

SUMMARY

Work motivation and its dynamics were covered in this chapter. The simplistic human relations assumptions and approach have proved to be inadequate in terms of both theoretical explanation and the practice of human resource management. The modern approach to work motivation can be divided into content and process approaches. The Maslow, Herzberg, and Alderfer models attempt to identify specific content factors in the individual (in the case of Maslow and Alderfer) or in the job environment (in the case of Herzberg) that motivate employees. Although such a content approach has surface logic, is easy to understand, and can be readily translated into practice, the research evidence points out some definite limitations. There is very little research support for the theoretical basis and predictability for these models. The trade-off for simplicity sacrifices true understanding of the complexity of work motivation. On the positive side, however, the content models have given emphasis to important content factors that were largely ignored by the human relationists. In addition, the Alderfer model allows more flexibility and the Herzberg model is useful as an explanation for job satisfaction and a point of departure for job design.

The process theories provide a much sounder theoretical explanation of work motivation. The expectancy model of Vroom and the extensions and refinements provided by Porter and Lawler and Lawler help explain the important cognitive variables and how they relate to one another in the complex process of work motivation. The Porter-and-Lawler model also gives specific attention to the important relationship between performance and satisfaction. Porter and Lawler propose that performance leads to satisfaction, instead of the human relations assumption of the reverse. A growing research literature is somewhat supportive of these expectancy models, but conceptual and methodological problems remain. Unlike the content models, these expectancy models are relatively complex and difficult to translate into actual practice, and consequently they have generally failed to meet the goals of prediction and control of organizational behavior. More recently, in academic circles, equity theory and especially attribution theory and locus of control have received increased attention. These were presented, in the additive sense, for the better understanding of work motivation. Both process theories—the equity model, based upon perceived input-outcome ratios and the attribution theory, which ascribes internal or external causes to behavior—lend increased understanding to the complex cognitive process of work motivation but have the same limitation as the expectancy models for prediction and control in the practice of human resource management. Attribution theory and locus of control, as potentially important contributions to the cognitive development of work motivation theory may be able to overcome some of the application limitations of the process theories of work motivation and bring us closer to the goals of prediction and control.

QUESTIONS FOR DISCUSSION AND REVIEW

1. In your own words, briefly explain Maslow's theory of motivation. Relate it to work motivation and Alderfer's ERG model.
2. What is the major criticism of Herzberg's two-factor theory of motivation? Do you think it has made a contribution to the better understanding of motivation in the workplace? Defend your answer.
3. In Vroom's model, what do valence, expectancy, and force mean? How do these variables relate to one another and to work motivation? Give realistic examples.
4. In your own words, briefly explain the Porter-and-Lawler model of motivation. How do performance and satisfaction relate to one another? What is involved in Lawler's refinement?
5. Briefly give an example of an inequity that a manager of a small business may experience. How would the manager strive to attain equity in the situation you describe?
6. What is attribution theory? How can analysis of locus of control be applied to workers and managers?

CASE:
WHAT DO THEY WANT?

Mike Riverer is vice president of manufacturing and operations of a medium-sized pharmaceutical firm in the Midwest. Mike has a Ph.D. in chemistry but has not been directly involved in research and new-product development for twenty years. He was from the school of "hard knocks" when it came to managing operations, and he ran a "tight ship." The company did not have a turnover problem, but it was obvious to Mike and other key management personnel that the hourly people were only putting in their eight hours a day. They were not working anywhere near their full potential. Mike was very upset with the situation because, with rising costs, the only way that the company could continue to prosper was to increase the productivity of their hourly people.

Mike called in his personnel manager and laid it on the line. "What is it with our people anyway? Your wage surveys show that we pay near the top in this region, our conditions are tremendous, and our fringes choke a horse. Yet these people still are not motivated. What in the world do they want?" The personnel manager replied, "I have told you and the president time after time that money, conditions, and benefits are not enough. Employees also need other things to motivate them. Also, I have been conducting some random confidential interviews with some of our hourly people, and they tell me that they are very discouraged because, no matter how hard they work, they get the same pay and opportunities for advancement as their coworkers who are just scraping by." Mike then replied, "Okay, you are the motivation expert; what do we do about it? We *have* to increase their performance."

1. Explain the "motivation problem" in this organization in terms of the content models of Maslow, Alderfer, and Herzberg. What are the "other things" that the personnel manager is referring to in speaking of things besides money, conditions, and fringe benefits that are needed to motivate employees?
2. Explain the motivation of the employees in this company in terms of one or more of the process models. On the basis of the responses from the confidential interviews, what would you guess are some of the expectancies, valences, inequities, and attributions of the employees in this company? How about Mike? Do you think Mike is internally or externally controlled?
3. How would you respond to Mike's last question and statement if you were the personnel manager in this company?

CASE:
TOM, DICK, AND HARRY

You are in charge of a small department and have three subordinates—Tom, Dick, and Harry. The key to the success of your department is to keep these employees as motivated as possible. Here is a brief summary profile on each of these subordinates.

Tom is the type of employee that is hard to figure out. He has a much higher than average absenteeism record. He greatly enjoys his family (a wife and three small children) and thinks they should be central to his life. The best way to describe Tom is that he is kind of a throwback to the hippie generation and believes deeply in the values of that culture. As a result, the things that the company can offer him do little to really inspire him. He feels that the job is simply a means of financing his family's basic needs and little else. Overall, Tom does an adequate job and is very conscientious, but all attempts to get him to do more have failed. He has charm and is friendly, but he just is not "gung-ho" for the company. He is pretty much allowed to "do his own thing" as long as he meets the minimal standards of performance.

Dick is in many respects opposite from Tom. Like Tom, he is a likable guy, but unlike Tom, Dick responds well to the company's rules and compensation schemes and has a high degree of personal loyalty to the company. The problem with Dick is that he will not do very much independently. He does well with what is assigned to him, but he is not very creative or even dependable when on his own. He also is a relatively shy person who is not very assertive when dealing with people outside the department. This hurts his performance to some degree, because he can not immediately sell himself or the department to other departments in the company or to top management.

Harry, on the other hand, is a very assertive person. He will work for money and would readily change jobs for more money. He really works hard for the company but expects the company also to work for him. In his present job, he feels no qualms about working a sixty-hour week, if the money is there. Even though he has a family and is supporting his mother, he once quit a job cold when his employer didn't give him a raise on the premise that he was already making too much. He is quite a driver. A manager at his last place of employment indicated that, while he did do an excellent job for the company, his personality was so strong that they were glad to get rid of him. His former boss noted that Harry just seemed to be pushing all the time. If it wasn't for more money, it was for better fringe benefits; he never seemed satisfied.

1. Can you explain Tom, Dick and Harry's motivation by one or more of the work motivation models discussed in this chapter?
2. Using Alderfer's ERG theory, what group of core needs seems to dominate each of these three subordinates.
3. Using the attribution theory approach, what type of locus of control do you feel guides each of these three employees in his present job?

GOAL SETTING AND JOB DESIGN

JOB PRESSURE DAY*

June 15 was designated as "job pressure day" by the Communications Workers of America (CWA). The CWA demonstration was directed against the mammoth American Telephone and Telegraph Company (AT&T). This specially designated day probably is at least an indirect result of the increasing competition that AT&T is facing in recent years. The increased competition has led the company to react by implementing more precise measures of individual employee performance and the reexamination of the design of jobs. Consequently, supervisors have been putting considerable pressure on their people for higher levels of performance. The higher standards of performance and new job designs are being resisted by the employees. In addition, the employees claim that there are no provisions for job security in the drive for higher performance. The employees, through their union representatives, have aired their complaints in advertisements in major newspapers and now want to make their point more dramatically via the "job pressure day."

The company's retort is that there needs to be some criterion of performance or specific goals by which to judge individual employee performance. The CWA argues that the goals are too high, that they are unrealistic and the resulting pressure the supervisor places upon the employees creates an undesirable quality of work life. One of the complaints of the CWA is that the company is overly concerned with job performance issues and not enough with job security. The bottom line indicates that these differences could lead to a major impasse in the next collective bargaining session between CWA and AT&T.

*Adapted from "The Dissatisfaction at AT&T," *Business Week,* June 25, 1979, pp.91-96.

206

The preceding two chapters have been devoted to the basic motivational process and the various theoretical approaches to work motivation. In this chapter two of the more applied areas of motivation are examined: goal setting and job design. In recent years, relatively more research has been generated in these two areas than others in the field of organizational behavior. It is becoming increasingly clear that setting goals and appropriately designing jobs can have a positive impact on employee satisfaction and performance. More specifically, the emerging research seems to indicate that goal setting leads to improved performance and job redesign can have a beneficial impact on employee satisfaction. The purpose of this chapter is to give some of the background, review the related research, and spell out some of the specific applications for both goal setting and job design.

GOAL SETTING

Goal setting is often given as an example of how the field of organizational behavior should progress from a sound theoretical foundation to sophisticated research to the actual application of more effective management practice. There has been considerable theoretical development of goal setting, coming mainly from the cognitively based work of Edwin Locke and his colleagues. To test the theory, there has been considerable research in both laboratory and field settings on the various facets of goal setting. Finally, and important to an applied field such as organizational behavior, goal setting has become an effective tool for the practice of human resource management and an overall performance system approach in the form of management by objectives or MBO. As opposed to the work motivation theories discussed in the last chapter (e.g., content theories such as Maslow's hierarchy of needs, or process theories such as expectancy or exchange), goal setting can and is being successfully applied.

Theoretical background for goal setting

A 1968 paper by Locke is usually considered to be the seminal work on a theory of goal setting.[1] He gives considerable credit to Ryan[2] for stimulating his thinking on the role that intention plays in human behavior and also suggests that goal-setting theory really goes back to scientific management at the turn of the century. He credits its first exponent, Frederick W. Taylor, with being the "father of employee motivation theory."[3]

Although Locke argues that expectancy theories of work motivation originally ignored goal setting and were nothing more than "cognitive

---

[1]Edwin A. Locke, "Toward a Theory of Task Motivation and Incentives," *Organizational Behavior and Human Performance*, vol. 3, 1968, pp. 157–189.

[2]T. A. Ryan and P. C. Smith, *Principles of Industrial Psychology*, Ronald, New York, 1954 and T. A. Ryan, *Intentional Behavior*, Ronald, New York, 1970.

[3]Edwin A. Locke, "The Ubiquity of the Technique of Goal Setting in Theories of and Approaches to Employee Motivation," *Academy of Management Review*, July 1978, p. 600.

hedonism,"[4] his theoretical formulation for goal setting is very similar. He basically accepts the purposefulness of behavior which comes out of Tolman's cognitive theorizing (see Chapter 3) and the importance of values or valance and consequences. Thus, as in the expectancy theories of work motivation (see Chapter 7), *values* and *value judgments*, which he defines as the thing the individual acts upon to gain and/or keep, are important cognitive determinants of behavior. He then goes on to say that emotions or desires are the way the person experiences these values. In addition to values, *intentions* or *goals* play an important role as cognitive determinants of behavior. It is here, of course, where Locke's theory of goal setting goes beyond expectancy theory of work motivation. He feels that people strive to attain goals in order to satisfy their emotions and desires. Goals provide a directional nature to people's behavior and guide their thoughts and actions to one outcome rather than another. The individual then responds and performs according to these intentions or goals, even if the goal is not attained. The result of these responses are consequences, feedback or reinforcement. Figure 8-1 summarizes this goal-setting theory.

As previously noted, except for the concept of intention or goal, Locke's theory is very similar to the other process theories (most notably the Porter-Lawler expectancy model) of work motivation discussed in the last chapter. To Locke's credit, he does carefully point out that goal setting is not the only, nor necessarily the most important concept of work motivation. He recently noted that the concepts of need and value are the more fundamental concepts of work motivation and are, along with the person's knowledge and premises, what determine goals. In other words, Locke is an ardent supporter of the cognitive interpretation of behavior and is an outspoken critic of the environmentally based operant theory of behavior and its applications through organizational behavior modification.[5] Despite his plea for a complex cognitive interpretation of behavior, he maintains, "Goal setting is simply the most directly useful motivational approach in a *managerial* context, since goals are the most immediate regulators of human action and are more easily modified than values of sub-conscious premises."[6] It is this practical utility of goal-setting theory that has made it an

---

[4]Edwin A. Locke, "Personnel Attitudes and Motivation," *Annual Review of Psychology*, vol. 26, 1975, pp. 457–480 and pp. 596–598.

[5]See: Edwin A. Locke, "The Myths of Behavior Mod in Organizations," *Academy of Management Review*, October 1977, pp. 543–553 and Edwin A. Locke, "Resolved: Attitudes and Cognitive Processes Are Necessary Elements in Motivational Models," in Barbara Karmel (ed.), *Point and Counterpoint in Organizational Behavior*, Dryden Press, Hinsdale, Ill., 1980, pp. 19–42.

**Figure 8-1
Locke's goal
setting theory of
work motivation.**

[6]Locke, "The Ubiquity of the Technique of Goal Setting in Theories of and Approaches to Employee Motivation," op. cit., p. 599.

important contribution to the study and application of organizational behavior.

Research on the impact of goal setting

Locke's theory has generated considerable research. In particular, a series of laboratory studies by Locke and his colleagues and a series of field studies by Gary Latham and his colleagues have been carried out to test the linkage between goal setting and performance.[7] The results of this research generally show that both subjects in a lab experiment and actual employees in a field setting who set specific goals perform better than those who do not set goals or those who operate under some generalized goal condition such as "do your best." Furthermore, these studies have demonstrated that those individuals who set difficult goals perform better than those who set relatively easy goals. In addition to the Locke and Latham studies, more recent studies have generally verified these findings.[8]

Despite this relatively good body of research, as with any complex phenomena there still appear to be many important moderating variables in the relationship between goal setting and performance, and there are some contradictory findings. For example, a recent study by Latham and Saari found that a supportive management style had an important moderating effect and, contrary to the results of previous studies, specific goals did not lead to better performance than a generalized goal such as "do your best."[9] Despite some of these contrary findings, on balance there has been impressive support for the positive impact that setting specific, difficult goals has on performance. Not so clear is the impact that goal acceptance has on performance and the impact of goal setting on satisfaction. Although there has been an implicit assumption in applying goal setting that accepted goals will lead to better performance, the research findings have been mixed. One study found that there was no difference between the performance of groups who were simply assigned goals and the group which, through participation, accepted their goals.[10] A more recent study found that

---

[7]Locke, "Toward a Theory of Task Motivation and Incentives," op. cit., summarizes the lab studies, and Gary P. Latham and Gary A. Yukl, "A Review of the Research on the Application of Goal Setting in Organizations," *Academy of Management Journal*, vol. 18, 1975, pp. 824–845, summarizes the field studies.

[8]For example, see D. J. Campbell and D. R. Ilgen, "Additive Effects of Task Difficulty and Goal Setting on Subsequent Task Performance," *Journal of Applied Psychology*, vol. 61, 1976, pp. 319–324; G. P. Latham and L. M. Saari, "The Effects of Holding Goal Difficulty Constant on Assigned and Participatory Set Goals," *Academy of Management Journal*, March 1979, pp. 163–168, for supporting lab studies; J. S. Kim and W. C. Hamner, "The Effect of Goal Setting, Feedback and Praise on Productivity and Satisfaction in an Organizational Setting," *Journal of Applied Psychology*, vol. 61, 1976, pp. 48–57; and D. Dossett, G. P. Latham and T. R. Mitchell, "The Effects of Assigned Versus Participatively Set Goals, KR, and Individual Differences on Employee Behavior When Goal Difficulty Is Held Constant," *Journal of Applied Psychology*, vol. 64, 1979, pp. 291–298, for supporting field studies.

[9]Gary P. Latham and Lise M. Saari, "Importance of Supportive Relationships in Goal Setting," *Journal of Applied Psychology*, vol. 64, 1979, pp. 151–156.

[10]G. P. Latham and G. A. Yukl, "The Effects of Assigned and Participative Goal Setting on Performance and Job Satisfaction," *Journal of Applied Psychology*, vol. 61, 1976, pp. 166–171.

employee participation led to higher goals being set, which in turn leads to higher performance, but there was no significant difference between the performance of the participative- and the assigned-goal groups.[11] As in the studies reported in the last chapter on the impact of the expectancy models on employee satisfaction, studies on the impact of goal setting on employee satisfaction have shown positive, negative, and nonexistent relationships.[12] Although research on goal setting is off to a good start, as with other topics in organizational behavior, more research on the various facets of the topic are needed.

MBO: The application of goal setting to system performance

A logical extension of goal setting is the very popular, widely used, management-by-objectives or MBO approach to planning, control, personnel appraisal, and overall system performance. MBO has been around for over twenty-five years and thus preceded the theory and research on goal setting per se. MBO is usually attributed to Peter Drucker who coined the phrase and suggested that a systematic approach to setting of objectives and appraising by results would lead to improved organizational performance and employee satisfaction. Today, practically every large business firm and a growing number of nonbusiness organizations have implemented some form of MBO.

Not surprisingly, universal agreement does not exist among scholars and practitioners on exactly what is meant by MBO. One writer noted that MBO, like ice cream, comes in twenty-nine flavors.[13] Despite the variations, there is general agreement that MBO involves a series of systematic steps that follow a process similar to the one shown in Figure 8-2. A review of these steps will clarify the MBO approach.

Setting overall objectives MBO takes a from-the-top-down approach. If MBO is implemented on an organization-wide basis, the top management team gets together to formulate overall objectives. The usual procedure is first to identify key results areas in the organization. A key results area is one that has the greatest impact on the overall performance of the organization. It may be sales volume or market share, production output, or quality of service. After the key results areas are identified, measures of performance are determined. Objectives are always stated so that they can be objectively measured. Finally, the actual objectives are agreed upon (usually with input from all members of the top management staff but with final authority vested in the chief operating executive). These objectives are results-oriented and are stated in objective, measurable terms with target dates and accompanying action plans that propose how the objectives will be accomplished.

[11]G. P. Latham, T. R. Mitchell, and Dennis L. Dossett, "Importance of Participative Goal Setting and Anticipated Rewards on Goal Difficulty and Job Performance," *Journal of Applied Psychology*, vol. 63, 1978, pp. 163–171.

[12]See: Richard D. Arvey, H. Dudley Dewhirst, and Edward M. Brown, "A Longitudinal Study of the Impact of Changes in Goal Setting on Employee Satisfaction," *Personnel Psychology*, vol. 31, 1978, pp. 595–598, for a review of this literature.

[13]J. S. Hodgson, "Management by Objectives: The Experience of a Federal Government Department," *Canadian Public Administration*, vol. 16, 1973, pp. 422–431.

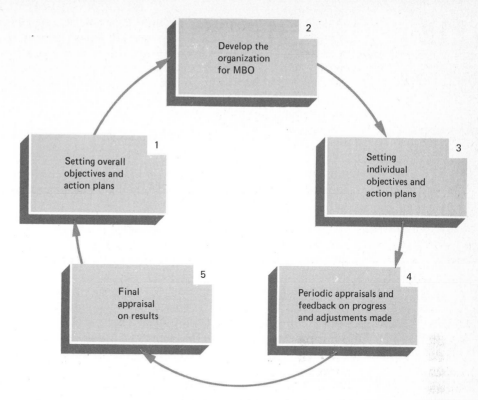

Figure 8-2
The MBO process.

Developing the organization for an MBO system After the overall objectives have been formulated, it is vital that the organization now be prepared to implement the system downward. What too often happens is that the chief executive, or someone who is close to the executive, gets sold on the idea of MBO. A memo to all personnel goes out that the organization will go onto an MBO system next Monday morning. This type of approach to implementing MBO is a sure way of ensuring that the program will not work. The people and the organization itself must be developed so that MBO can be successfully implemented. Such an organization development effort often involves using the techniques that will be discussed in Chapter 21. There may also be need for a reorganization to accommodate the MBO system. The needed development may take anywhere from a few weeks to several years, depending on the current stage of development of the human resources of the organization.

Setting individual objectives Once the overall objectives have been set and the organization is developed to the point of accommodating an MBO system, individual objectives are set. These individual objectives are determined by each superior-subordinate pair, starting at the top and going down as far as the system is to be implemented. The scenario for this process would be something like the following: The boss would contact each subordinate under him or her and say:

As you know, we have completed our MBO orientation and it is now time to set individual objectives. I would like you to develop by next Tuesday a proposed set of objectives for your area of responsibility. Remember that your set of objectives should be in line with the organization's overall objectives, which you have a copy of, and they should be able to contribute to the objectives of those that you interact with, namely, my objectives, the other units' objectives on your same level, and your subordinates' objectives. Your objectives should be stated in quantifiable, measurable terms and have a target date. I will also have some ideas and things written down that I think should be given top priority for your area of responsibility. We will sit down and have an open given-and-take session until we reach a mutually agreeable set of objectives for your area of responsibility.

Like the overall objectives, the set of individual objectives should also have action plans developed to spell out how the objectives are to be accomplished.

Appraisal by results So far, only the setting-of-objectives part of MBO has been discussed. However, these objectives play a vital role in the appraisal part of MBO. The individuals will be appraised on the basis of how they perform in accordance with the objectives that are set. These appraisals take place on both a periodic (at least every quarter in most MBO systems) and an annual basis. The appraisal sessions attempt to be diagnostic rather than purely evaluative. This simply means that the reasons why objectives were either attained or not attained are assessed in the sessions rather than punishments and rewards being given for failure or success in meeting objectives. Periodic reviews are conducted in order to evaluate progress toward the attainment of objectives, and they give the opportunity to make the necessary changes in objectives. Every organization is operating in such a dynamic environment that objectives set at the beginning of the period (usually the fiscal year) may be rendered obsolete in a few months because of changing conditions. Priorities and conditions are constantly changing, and these must be monitored in the periodic review sessions, and the needed changes must be made. Constant revision of the individual objectives and, to a lesser degree, the overall objectives makes MBO a living system that is adaptable to change. At the annual review session, overall diagnosis and evaluation are made according to results attained, and the system starts over again.

Critical analysis of MBO

Table 8-1 summarizes some of the generally recognized strengths and weaknesses of MBO systems. Such a list can serve as a beneficial guideline to more effective implementation. However, despite its widespread use and the relatively great amount of research conducted on goal setting per se, there has been practically no systematic research on the impact of MBO.

Although there are numerous descriptive articles on MBO[14] (e.g., they define the approach, suggest the steps for implementation, and analyze the

---

[14]For example, McConkie has a comprehensive summary of thirty-nine experts' descriptions of MBO. See: Mark L. McConkie, "A Clarification of the Goal Setting and Appraisal Processes in MBO," *Academy of Management Review,* January 1979, pp. 29–40.

Table 8–1

POTENTIAL ADVANTAGES AND PROBLEMS WITH MBO

Potential advantages	Potential problems
There can be improved short- and long-range planning.	The MBO program may be used as a whip, especially when it is closely tied to wage and salary programs.
MBO can provide a procedure for controlling work progress and results.	The MBO program may fail to receive continual top management commitment and support and may not reach the lower managerial levels.
There can be improved commitment to the organization because of increased motivation, loyalty, and participation of employees.	
MBO can lead to improved clarity of the manager's role and priorities.	There may be an overemphasis on production and productivity.
There can be improved communication—especially upward and horizontal.	Managers may not be adequately trained in the MBO process or in effective ways to coach and counsel subordinates.
	The MBO program may fail to provide adequate personal incentives to improve performance. The emphasis is only on the benefits to the organization and not the development of the participating managers.

Source: Adapted from John M. Ivancevich et al., "Goal Setting: The Tenneco Approach to Personnel Development and Managerial Effectiveness," *Organizational Dynamics*, Winter 1978, pp. 60–61.

advantages and disadvantages), to date only a couple of studies have used a control group design and hard performance data to analyze the impact of MBO on performance. One comprehensive study in an industrial setting did find that MBO had a favorable impact on several measures of qualitative and quantitative performance.[15] But a later study that evaluated MBO in a bank found no statistically significant differences between the experimental (those under MBO) and control group (those not under MBO) on several performance measures.[16] A very recently completed study examining the impact that MBO had on performance and satisfaction in a state government human services agency had somewhat, but not completely, supportive findings.[17] On the five measures of the quantity of performance, two showed statistically significant improvement and a combined measure was also significant. A matched control group (those not on the MBO system) showed no improvement in these measures over the same time period. Although a control group was not available for comparison, the MBO group did show significant improvement on all three measures of quality of performance.

---

[15]J. M. Ivancevich, "Changes in Performance in a Management by Objectives Program," *Administrative Science Quarterly*, vol. 19, 1974, pp. 563–574.

[16]J. P. Muczyk, "A Controlled Field Experiment Measuring the Impact of MBO on Performance Data," *Journal of Management Studies*, vol. 15, 1978, pp. 318–329.

[17]Kenneth R. Thompson and Fred Luthans, "The Effects of MBO on Performance and Satisfaction in a Public Sector Organization," presented at the 1980 Annual Meeting of the Academy of Management, Detroit, Michigan.

The MBO group also indicated a significant improvement in satisfaction with supervision but there was a nonsignificant change in job satisfaction.

With the few exceptions reported above, which have yielded mixed results, the other reported studies on the impact of MBO do not use control group designs and depend on questionnaires that attempt to tap the perceptions of performance improvement and managerial attitudes. After reviewing these latter types of studies on MBO, it was concluded, "This approach can improve managerial performance, managerial attitudes, and organizational planning. This research also indicates that MBO programs require considerable time and effort expenditures for successful adoption, and unless they are given adequate support and attention and are well integrated into the organization, they will fail or not live up to expectations."[18]

Thus, once again there is not enough research on overall MBO systems to draw any sound conclusions. But as the earlier discussion on goal setting pointed out, and the relatively great amount of research on participation and feedback has demonstrated (this will be covered in Chapter 10), research on the various subelements can be used to support MBO. There seems little question that MBO holds enough promise to continue its widespread applications. It is readily adaptable and can be used in conjunction with other modern human resource management techniques such as job enrichment, discussed next, and organizational behavior modification, which is examined in Chapter 10. MBO's greatest advantage is that it combines good, sound management techniques for decision making, communication, and control with basic behavioral requirements. Goal setting, feedback about performance, participative decision making, open two-way communication, and self-control are some of the very positive characteristics of MBO. This unique combination makes MBO worthy of careful consideration. Although there can be problems and more research is desperately needed, MBO, if carefully implemented and developed, seems to hold a great deal of promise for management in the future.

JOB DESIGN

Along with goal setting, job design has emerged as an important application area for work motivation and the study of organizational behavior. In many respects there have been parallel developments in goal setting and job design. Like goal setting, job design is based on an extensive and still growing theoretical base, has had considerable research attention in recent years, and is being widely applied to the actual practice of management.

Initially, the field of organizational behavior only paid attention to job enrichment approaches to job design. Now with *quality of work life*, or QWL, becoming a major societal issue in this country and throughout the world, job design has taken a broader perspective. Figure 8-3 summarizes the various dimensions of a comprehensive look at job design. Job enrichment

---

[18]Stephen J. Carroll, Jr. and Henry L. Tosi, Jr., *Management by Objectives*, Macmillan, New York, 1973, p. 16.

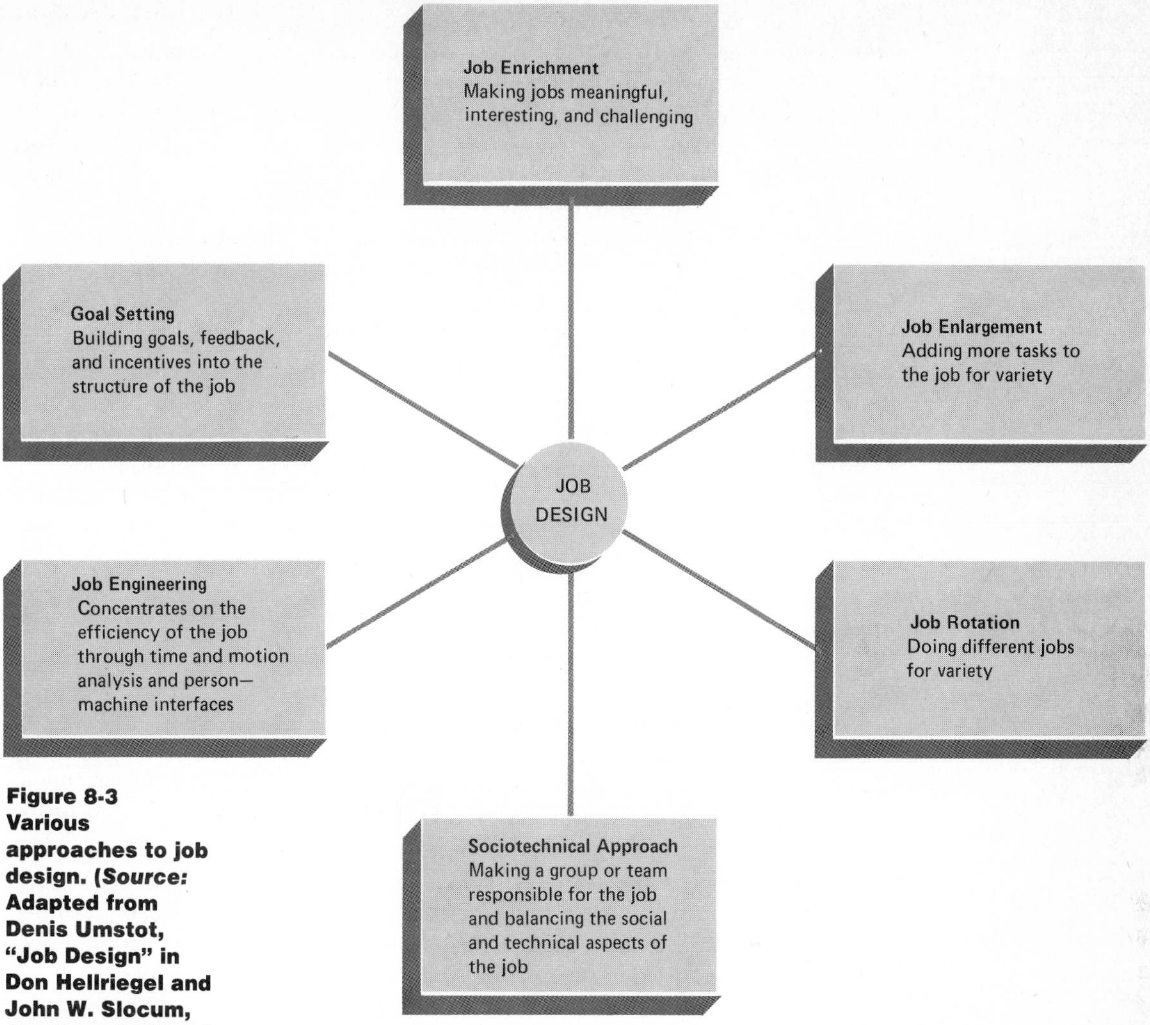
Job Enrichment
Making jobs meaningful, interesting, and challenging
Goal Setting
Building goals, feedback, and incentives into the structure of the job
Job Enlargement
Adding more tasks to the job for variety
JOB DESIGN
Job Engineering
Concentrates on the efficiency of the job through time and motion analysis and person—machine interfaces
Job Rotation
Doing different jobs for variety
Sociotechnical Approach
Making a group or team responsible for the job and balancing the social and technical aspects of the job

Figure 8-3 Various approaches to job design. (*Source:* Adapted from Denis Umstot, "Job Design" in Don Hellriegel and John W. Slocum, Jr., *Organizational Behavior*, 2d ed., West, St. Paul, 1979, p. 432.)

still dominates the job design literature in organizational behavior, but goal setting as discussed in this chapter is beginning to be linked to the design of jobs,[19] and the sociotechnical approach to job design is most closely associated with QWL. Job engineering, job enlargement, and job rotation are considered to have historical significance to job design, but are not in the current mainstream of job design research or application.

Background on job design

Job design concerns and approaches are usually considered to have begun with the scientific management movement at the turn of the century. Pioneering scientific managers such as Frederick W. Taylor, Frank Gilbreth,

[19]For example, see: Denis D. Umstot, Terrence R. Mitchell, and Cecil H. Bell, "Goal Setting and Job Enrichment: An Integrated Approach to Job Design," *Academy of Management Review*, October 1978, pp. 867–879.

Henry L. Gantt, and Harrington Emerson systematically examined jobs with techniques such as time and motion analysis. Their goal was to maximize human efficiency in jobs. Taylor suggested that task design might be the most prominent single element in scientific management. He described the scientific management approach to task design as follows: "This task specifies not only what is to be done but how it is to be done and the exact time allowed for doing it."[20] The scientific management approach evolved into what is now generally called job engineering. This industrial engineering approach is concerned with product, process, and tool design, plant layout, standard operating procedures, work measurement and standards, worker methods, and human-machine interactions. It has been the dominant form of job design analysis since the turn of the century and has gone hand-in-hand with automation in the 1950s and 1960s and cybernation (automatic feedback control mechanisms) and sophisticated computer systems in more recent times. Especially in blue-collar production jobs, but in an increasing number of white-collar jobs as well, jobs have become highly specialized (the employee does one or a very few tasks) and standardized (the employee does the task the same way every time).

The often cited example of the employee on the assembly line putting a nut on a bolt as the product moves by on the conveyor belt is all too common in today's manufacturing plants across the country. One young worker described his job in the technologically advanced Lordstown, Ohio, assembly plant of General Motors as follows: "There's a lot of variety in the paint shop. You clip on the color hose, bleed out the old color, and squirt. Clip, bleed, squirt, think; clip, bleed, squirt, yawn; clip, bleed, squirt, scratch your nose."[21] The same types of specialized jobs exist in banks, offices, hospitals, schools, and every other type of modern organizational setting. The general concensus was that these highly specialized, standardized jobs were very efficient and led to a high degree of control over workers. Up to recent times, few people questioned the engineering approach to job design. Top management could readily determine and see immediate cost savings from job engineering. But side effects on quality, absenteeism, and turnover were generally ignored.

Starting in the 1950s, some practicing managers around the country, such as the founder of IBM, Thomas Watson, became concerned about the impact of job engineering approaches to work and began implementing job enlargement and rotation programs. Essentially, the job enlargement programs horizontally loaded the job (expanded the number of operations performed by the worker, i.e., made the job less specialized), and the job rotation programs reduced boredom by switching people around to various jobs. Then, in the late 1960s and early 1970s, with the increasing concern over employee dissatisfaction and declining productivity—which was felt to be largely the result of so-called "blue-collar blues" and "white-collar woes"—there was an awakened interest in job design and it became the

---

[20]Frederick W. Taylor, *The Principles of Scientific Management*, Harper, New York, 1911.

[21]Barbara Garson, "Luddites in Lordstown," *Harper's*, June 1972, p. 69.

focus of attention for both academicians and practitioners of human resource management. Newspaper stories and TV news specials commonly had titles such as the following:

"Is the American Worker Alienated?"
"Today's Worker: Idealism's Gone"
"Is the Work Ethic Going out of Style?"
"Boredom Spells Trouble"

In particular, in a widely publicized special HEW task force report, *Work in America*, it was stated that "the productivity of the worker is low—as measured by absenteeism, turnover rates, wildcat strikes, sabotage, poor quality products, and a reluctance by workers to commit themselves to their work."[22] In addition, Gallup polls regularly reported that a majority of people responded that "they could produce more each day if they tried." A new look at job design seemed to provide a ready answer to the productivity problems and deteriorating human resources of organizations.

The reported successes of the early job enlargement programs,[23] plus the increasingly popular motivation theories of Maslow and Herzberg (discussed in the last chapter), led to the job enrichment movement in job design.

Job enrichment

Job enrichment represents an extension of the earlier, more simplified job rotation and job enlargement techniques of job design. Since it is a direct outgrowth of Herzberg's two-factor theory of motivation, the assumption is that in order to motivate personnel, the job must be designed to provide opportunities for achievement, recognition, responsibility, advancement, and growth. The technique entails "enriching" the job so that these factors are included. In particular, *job enrichment* is concerned with designing jobs that include a greater variety of work content; require a higher level of knowledge and skill; give the worker more autonomy and responsibility for planning, directing, and controlling his or her own performance; and provide the opportunity for personal growth and meaningful work experience. As opposed to job enlargement, which horizontally loads the job, job enrichment *vertically* loads the job (e.g., not necessarily more tasks to perform, but more responsibility and autonomy). Table 8-2 gives some specific examples of job enrichment.

Although Herzberg provided the necessary impetus for the development of job enrichment, M. Scott Meyers, formerly of Texas Instruments, and

---

[22]*Work in America*, Report of a Special Task Force to the Secretary of Health, Education, and Welfare, The MIT Press, Cambridge, 1973, p. xvi.

[23]Charles R. Walker, "The Problems of the Repetitive Job," *Harvard Business Review*, May 1950, pp. 54–58, reports on the IBM experience, and Maurice D. Kilbridge, "Reduced Costs Through Job Enlargement: A Case," *The Journal of Business*, October 1960, pp. 357–362, reports on the Maytag experience with job enlargement.

Table 8–2

EXAMPLES OF JOB ENRICHMENT

Old situation	Situation after job enrichment
Each employee rotated among all machines.	Each employee assigned to only two machines.
When machine failure occurred, operator called on maintenance group.	Each operator given training in maintenance; each conducts preventive and corrective maintenance on the two machines for which he or she is responsible.
Operator changes the slicing blade (the most important component of the machine) following a rigid rule contained in a manual.	Operator given authority to decide when to replace blade, based on own judgment.
Supervisor monitors operator and corrects unsatisfactory performance.	Performance feedback system developed that provides daily information on their work quality directly to operators.
Individuals perform specialized task on units passing by them.	Three- to five-person teams build entire unit.
Supervisor decides who should do what.	Team decides who should do what.
Inspectors and supervisor test output and correct performance.	Team conducts own quality audits.

Source: Ross A. Webber, *Management,* rev. ed., Irwin, Homewood, Ill., 1979, p. 82. These examples were provided to Webber by David R. Sirota, Wharton School, University of Pennsylvania.

Robert N. Ford of American Telephone and Telegraph assumed the role of proselytizers and implementers of the technique. The management at Texas Instruments (TI) undertook an extensive research study in an attempt to validate Herzberg's two-factor theory.[24] Satisfied with the outcome of this study, TI proceeded to enrich some of the jobs in the company. To implement the TI program, supervisors were trained to analyze subordinates' functions in terms of the potential for appealing to the hygiene or motivator factors. In addition, a formalized attitude measurement program structured around the motivation-hygiene factors was instituted for control purposes. At Texas Instruments, job enrichment became part of the management philosophy as well as a technique of job design.

The other leading advocate of job enrichment, Robert Ford, has been chiefly responsible for implementing the technique in the Bell System.[25] Taking a similar validation approach to that of Texas Instruments, Ford, on the basis of systematic evaluations, is convinced of the value of job enrichment. An often cited example of what can be accomplished with job enrichment is the Shareholder Relations Department of AT&T. After job enrichment was installed in this department of 120 correspondents, there was a 27 percent reduction in the termination rate and an estimated cost

[24]M. Scott Meyers, "Who Are Your Motivated Workers?" *Harvard Business Review,* January–February 1964, pp. 73–88.

[25]Robert N. Ford, *Motivation through the Work Itself,* American Management Association, New York, 1969.

savings of $558,000 over a twelve-month period.[26] Encouraged by this kind of result, Ford implemented job enrichment in many areas of the huge Bell System.

Criticism of job enrichment   As the last chapter pointed out, behavioral scientists have been critical of the Herzberg theory of work motivation practically since it was first formulated in the late 1950s. However, it is only in recent years that management writers in the literature aimed at practitioners have raised questions about the value of job enrichment.[27] Up to this time, both management professors and practitioners had generally accepted Herzberg's theme that "job enrichment pays off."[28] However, as the criticism of the two-factor theory began to grow and become more widely known, management professors and writers also started to question the effectiveness of job enrichment as a universally applicable technique of job design.

In general, the same criticisms leveled at the two-factor theory apply to job enrichment. However, of more direct consequence for management is that job enrichment may not be working out in actual practice as it was commonly thought to do. Even the "success stories" of job enrichment at Texas Instruments and Bell Telephone can be questioned. For example, a report to TI stockholders announced that the company aimed to have 10,000 employees involved in team-improvement efforts. On the surface, this looked very impressive, but as Mitchell Fein notes, the 10,000 figure represented only 16 percent of the total employment at Texas Instruments. Yet it is often falsely assumed that all TI personnel are on enriched jobs.[29] Not only is job enrichment not used throughout TI, but a survey of randomly selected large firms found only 5 of 125 respondents reported using any formal job enrichment.[30] In other words, job enrichment seemed to be talked about more than it is actually being used. Not only the extent of use but also the reported successes of job enrichment can be questioned. Reporting on the overall success of the AT&T job enrichment program, Ford himself stated, "Of the nineteen studies nine were rated 'outstandingly successful,' one was a complete 'flop,' and the remaining nine were 'moderately successful.'"[31] Obviously, when assessing the job enrichment impact at AT&T the operational definition of "success" becomes critical. It is also interesting to note a seldom cited comment by Ford. He stated:

No claim is made that these 19 trials cover a representative sample of jobs and people

---

[26]Robert Janson, "Job Enrichment: Challenge of the 70's," *Training and Development Journal*, June 1970, p. 7.

[27]For example see Thomas H. Fitzgerald, "Why Motivation Theory Doesn't Work," *Harvard Business Review*, July–August 1971, pp. 37–44; and William E. Reif and Fred Luthans, "Does Job Enrichment Really Pay Off?" *California Management Review*, Fall 1972, pp. 30–37.

[28]William J. Paul, Jr., Keith B. Robertson, and Frederick Herzberg, "Job Enrichment Pays Off," *Harvard Business Review*, March–April 1969, pp. 61–78.

[29]Mitchell Fein, *Approaches to Motivation*, unpublished paper, Hillsdale, N.J., 1970, p. 20.

[30]Fred Luthans and William E. Reif, "Job Enrichment: Long on Theory, Short on Practice," *Organizational Dynamics*, Winter 1974, p. 31.

[31]Ford, op. cit., p. 188.

within the Bell System. For example, there were no trials among the manufacturing or laboratory employees, nor were all operating companies involved. There are more than a thousand different jobs in the Bell System, not just the nine in these studies.[32]

Moreover, like other popular techniques, the failures are seldom reported. J. Richard Hackman, one of the most prolific researchers and writers on job design, concluded that job enrichment is probably failing at least as often as it is succeeding.[33]

Yet, despite this brief digression from bright optimism, Ford and many others have gone on to generalize that job enrichment has universal applicability to the problems facing modern human resource management. Unfortunately, this type of generalization does not seem entirely justified. To date, research evidence also indicates the following to be true:

1. There seems to be a substantial number of workers who are not necessarily alienated from work but are alienated from the middle class values expressed by the job enrichment concept. For these workers, job content is not automatically related to job satisfaction and motivation is not necessarily a function of job satisfaction. These "alienated from the middle class" workers are capable of finding need satisfaction outside the work environment. If they do experience satisfaction at work, it is not the result of job content or formal job design but instead, is due to their social interactions with other primary group members. Job enrichment may not motivate this type of worker.

2. For some workers improved job design (job enrichment) does not seem to be an even trade for the reduced opportunity for social interaction. The present job may be considered unpleasant and boring, but social isolation is completely unbearable.

3. The introduction of a job enrichment program may have a negative impact on many workers and result in feelings of inadequacy, fear of failure, and a concern for dependency. For many employees, low level competency, security, and relative independence are more important than the opportunity and potential for increased responsibility and growth in the enriched job.[34]

These points are not intended to deny the value of the enrichment technique, but they do show that, like the other application techniques discussed in this book, job enrichment is not a panacea for all job design problems facing modern management. Job enrichment is a valuable motivational technique, but management must use it selectively and give proper recognition to the complex human and situational variables. The new job characteristics models of job enrichment are beginning to do this.

The job characteristics approach to task design

To meet some of the criticism of the Herzberg approach to job enrichment (which he now prefers to call "orthodox job enrichment" or OJE[35]) a group of

[32]Ibid., p. 189.

[33]J. Richard Hackman, "On the Coming Demise of Job Enrichment," in E. L. Cass and F. G. Zumimer (eds.), *Man and Work in Society,* Van Nostrand, New York, 1975, p. 98.

[34]Reif and Luthans, op. cit., p. 36.

[35]Frederick Herzberg, "Orthodox Job Enrichment," in Louis E. Davis and James C. Taylor (eds.) *Design of Jobs,* 2d ed., Goodyear, Santa Monica, Calif., 1979, pp. 136–147.

researchers have begun to concentrate on the relationship that certain job characteristics or the job scope have with employee motivation and satisfaction. Drawing on the existing literature mainly in social psychology, in 1965 Professors Arthur Turner and Paul Lawrence of Harvard identified six task attributes that they felt were positively related to employee motivation and satisfaction: variety, autonomy, required interaction, optional interaction, knowledge and skill required, and responsibility.[36] They then constructed a Requisite Task Attribution (RTA) index to measure these job characteristics. They found that the RTA scores positively correlated with satisfaction and attendance of factory workers located in small towns, but for employees in urban settings satisfaction was inversely related to the scores on the RTA index and there was no relationship with absenteeism. In other words, the very first study on job characteristics indicate that there were moderating variables such as the sociocultural background of employees that seemed to effect the impact that job design had on outcome variables such as satisfaction and attendance. Subsequent research verified that sociocultural factors do moderate workers' reactions to the design of their jobs.[37]

Next, Professors J. Richard Hackman and Edward Lawler, based upon expectancy motivation theory, reconceptualized the Turner and Lawrence attributes into a job-based work motivation model. Based upon questionnaire data from employees in thirteen jobs in a telephone company, they derived the following six job attributes: variety, autonomy, task identity, feedback, dealing with others, and friendship opportunities.[38] In general, they found that the more employees perceived these attributes in their jobs, the more satisfied they were and their performance and attendance were better. However, like the earlier Turner and Lawrence study, they also found a strong moderating effect. Employees with strong needs for growth responded more favorably to jobs high in the attributes than employees with low growth needs.

Both the Turner and Lawrence and the Hackman and Lawler work provide an important background for the Hackman and Oldham model that has emerged in recent years as the most widely accepted job characteristics approach to job design measurement and application.

The Hackman-Oldham job characteristics model

Basing their work on the earlier Hackman-Lawler work, Richard Hackman and Greg Oldham developed the comprehensive model shown in Figure 8-4. This model recognizes that certain job characteristics contribute to certain psychological states and that the strength of employees' need for growth has

---

[36]Arthur N. Turner and Paul R. Lawrence, *Industrial Jobs and the Worker*, Harvard Graduate School of Business, Cambridge, 1965.

[37]Milton R. Blood and Charles L. Hulin, "Alienation, Environmental Characteristics, and Worker Responses," *Journal of Applied Psychology*, vol. 51, 1967, pp. 284–290 and Charles L. Hulin and Milton R. Blood, "Job Enlargement, Individual Differences, and Worker Responses," *Psychological Bulletin*, vol. 69, 1968, pp. 41–55.

[38]J. Richard Hackman and Edward E. Lawler, "Employee Reactions to Job Characteristics," *Journal of Applied Psychology*, vol. 55, 1971, pp. 259–286.

an important moderating effect. Table 8-3 summarizes what is meant by each of the job characteristics and psychological states.

In essence, the model says that certain job characteristics lead to critical psychological states. That is, skill variety, task identity, and task significance lead to experienced meaningfulness; autonomy leads to the feeling of responsibility; and feedback leads to knowledge of results. The more these three psychological states are present, the more employees will feel good about themselves when they perform well. Hackman states:

The model postulates that internal rewards are obtained by an individual when he *learns* (knowledge of results) that he *personally* (experienced responsibility) has performed well on a task that he *cares about* (experienced meaningfulness).[39]

He then goes on to point out that these internal rewards are reinforcing to employees, causing them to perform well. If they don't perform well they will try harder in order to get the internal rewards that good performance brings. He concludes:

The net result is a self-perpetuating cycle of positive work motivation powered by self-generated rewards. This cycle is predicted to continue until one or more of the three psychological states is no longer present, or until the individual no longer values the internal rewards that derive from good performance.[40]

An example of an enriched job according to the Hackman-Oldham job

---

[39]J. Richard Hackman, "Work Design," in J. Richard Hackman and J. Lloyd Suttle (eds.), *Improving Life at Work,* Goodyear, Santa Monica, California, 1977, p. 129.
[40]Ibid., p. 130.

**Figure 8-4
The Hackman-Oldham
job characteristics
model of work
motivation.
(*Source:* Adapted
from J. R.
Hackman and G. R.
Oldham,
"Motivation
Through the
Design of Work:
Test of a Theory,"
*Organizational
Behavior and
Human
Performance,* vol.
16, 1976, pp.
250–279.)**

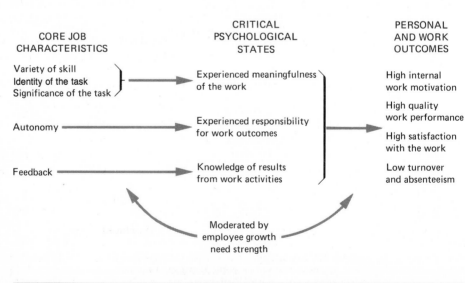

Table 8–3

SUMMARY OF THE DIMENSIONS IN THE HACKMAN-OLDHAM MODEL

Core job dimensions

1. *Variety of skill.* This refers to the degree to which the job requires the person to do different things and involves the use of a number of different skills, abilities, and talents.

2. *Identity of the task.* This involves a complete module of work, where the person can do the job from beginning to end with a visible outcome.

3. *Significance of the task.* This is concerned with the importance of the job. Does it have a significant impact on others—both internal and external to the organization?

4. *Autonomy.* This refers to the amount of freedom, independence, and discretion the person has in areas such as scheduling the work, making decisions, and determining how to do the job.

5. *Feedback.* This involves the degree to which the job provides the person with clear and direct information about job outcomes and performance.

Critical psychological states

1. *Experienced meaningfulness.* This is concerned with the extent to which the person experiences work as important, valuable, and worthwhile.

2. *Experienced responsibility.* This is concerned with the degree to which the individual feels personally responsible or accountable for the results of the work.

3. *Knowledge of results.* This involves the degree to which the person understands on a regular basis how effectively he or she is performing in the job.

Source: Adapted from David A. Nadler, J. Richard Hackman, and Edward E. Lawler, *Managing Organizational Behavior,* Little, Brown, Boston, 1979, pp. 81–82.

characteristics would be that of a surgeon. Surgeons must draw on a wide variety of skills and abilities; usually surgeons can readily identify the task because they handle patients from beginning to end (i.e., play a role in the diagnosis, perform the operation, and are responsible for postoperative care and follow-up); the job has life-and-death significance; there is a great deal of autonomy since the surgeon has the final word on all decisions concerning the patient; and there is clear, direct feedback whether the operation was sucessful or not. At the other extreme would be an assembly line worker in a blue-collar job or a clerk-typist in a white-collar job. All of the five core job dimensions would be low or nonexistent in the latter jobs.

There are several ways that the Hackman-Oldham model can be used to diagnose the degree of task scope that a job possesses. For instance, a manager could simply assess a particular job by clinically analyzing it according to the five core dimensions as was done in the example of the surgeon's job discussed above. Others have suggested a specific checklist which would include such items as the use of inspectors or checkers, labor pools, or narrow spans of control, to help pinpoint deficiencies in the core dimensions.[41] More systematically, Hackman and Oldham have developed a

---

[41]David Whitsett, "Where Are Your Enriched Jobs?" *Harvard Business Review,* January–February, 1975, pp. 74–80.

questionnaire called the Job Diagnostic Survey (JDS) to analyze jobs. The questions on this survey yield a quantitiative score that can be used to calculate an overall measure of job enrichment, or what is increasingly called job scope—to differentiate from Herzberg-type job enrichment. The formula for this motivating potential score (MPS) is the following:

$$\text{MPS} = \left[\frac{\text{Skill Variety} + \text{Task Identity} + \text{Task Significance}}{3} \right] \times \text{Autonomy} \times \text{Feedback}$$

Notice that the job characteristics of skill variety, task identity, and task significance are combined and divided by three, while the characteristics of autonomy and feedback stand alone. Also, since skill variety, task identity, and task significance are additive, any one or even two of these characteristics could be completely missing and the person could still experience meaningfulness, but if either autonomy or feedback were missing, the job would offer no motivating potential (MPS = O) because of the multiplicative relationships.

The JDS is a widely used instrument to measure task characteristics or task scope, but the research on the impact that the motivating potential of a job has on job satisfaction and performance is not that clear. Most of the support for the model comes from Hackman and his colleagues, who claim that people on enriched jobs (according to their characteristics as measured by the JDS) are definitely more motivated and satisfied and, although the evidence is not as strong, may have better attendance and performance effectiveness records.[42]

Emerging issues and applications of the task characteristics approach

The Hackman-Oldham model and their JDS measurement tool is the dominant task characteristics approach to job design, but there are also some models and measurement techniques that offer slight variations.[43] What is becoming increasingly clear to those who study the relationship between job scope and satisfaction or other outcomes is the importance of the employees' *perceptions* of the task characteristics and the role of *moderating variables*. For example, after reviewing the research literature, Aldag and Brief note:

Employees often react to their perceptions of the job's content, which do not necessarily coincide with the actual content of the job. Furthermore, the manager cannot directly change the job incumbent's perceptions and must instead attempt to alter the objective content of the job in order to influence employee perceptions.[44]

Recent studies have shown that perceptual assessments of task characteris-

[42]J. R. Hackman, G. R. Oldham, R. Janson, and K. Purdy, "A New Strategy for Job Enrichment," *California Management Review*, vol. 17, 1975, pp. 57–71.

[43]For example, see: H. P. Sims, Jr., A. D. Szilagyi, and R. T. Keller, "The Measurement of Job Characteristics," *Academy of Management Journal*, vol. 19, 1976, pp. 185–212.

[44]Ramon J. Aldag and Arthur P. Brief, *Task Design and Employee Motivation*, Scott Foresman, Glenview, Ill., 1979, p. 59.

tics vary with the individual's frame of reference and job attitudes.[45] Thus, the affect of the task design may have nothing to do with the objective characteristics of the job but, rather, with the individual's perception of the job design.

This concern with the impact of employee perceptions of task scope is closely related to the importance that contemporary researchers are also placing on moderating variables in the analysis of job design. The original work on job characteristics models (e.g., the Turner and Lawrence and the Hackman and Lawler models) and the most recent studies have begun to identify a number of important moderating effects on the job scope—job satisfaction relationship.[46] It is generally recognized, for example, that the need strength of the employee will have an important moderating effect on the relationships between job scope and job satisfaction.[47]

Figure 8-5 gives a comprehensive contingency model of job design that recognizes not only the job scope (simple or complex) and individual need strengths (high or low), but also the overall organizational design (organic or mechanistic). The contingency model shows that of the eight possible combinations, cells 2 and 7 have congruence among the three variables. In other words, the contingency guideline for practice would be, if there is a mechanistic organization and the employees have low growth needs, a simple, routine job design should be used; and if there is an organic design and employees have high growth needs, job enrichment should be used. The model would also predict that, because cells 1 and 8 have congruence between the variables, there would be poor performance and dissatisfaction. In cells 3 to 6 the variables are contradictory. For these cells, Porter, Lawler, and Hackman note:

> The prediction (which is not based firmly on existing theory or data) is that individuals will tend to respond to and act in accordance with *those cues which are congruent with their own need states.* Thus, high growth need individuals will tend to respond to cues provided by their jobs in cell 3 and to organizational cues in cell 5; low growth need people will tend to respond to the organization in cell 4 and to the job in cell 6.[48]

---

[45]Charles A. O'Reilly, G. Nicholas Parlette, and Joan R. Bloom, "Perceptual Measures of Task Characteristics: The Biasing Effects of Differing Frames of Reference and Job Attitudes," *Academy of Management Proceedings,* 1979, pp. 64–68.

[46]E. F. Stone, "The Moderating Effect of Work Related Values on the Job Scope–Job Satisfaction Relationship," *Organizational Behavior and Human Performance,* vol. 15, 1976, pp. 147–168; Daniel Ganster, "Individual Differences and Task Design: A Laboratory Experiment," *Organizational Behavior and Human Performance,* vol. 26, 1980, pp. 131–146; and Cathy J. Rudolf, Lawrence Peters, and Thomas Reynolds, "The Moderating Effect of Job Adaptation on the Job Scope Affective Response Relationship," *Academy of Management Proceedings,* 1979, pp. 69–73.

[47]E. F. Stone, R. T. Mowday, and L. W. Porter, "Higher Order Need Strengths as Moderators of the Job Scope–Job Satisfaction Relationship," *Journal of Applied Psychology,* vol. 62, 1977, pp. 466–471.

[48]Lyman W. Porter, Edward E. Lawler, and J. Richard Hackman, *Behavior in Organizations,* McGraw-Hill, New York, 1975, p. 310.

In any case, because of the contradictory relationship among the variables in cells 3 to 6, it is predicted that there will be poor performance and dissatisfaction.

The authors carefully point out that such "pure" categories as shown in Figure 8-5 seldom exist in reality and that it is more useful to think of the cells in the model as end points on a continuum. They also point out that, to date, there are only empirical research data to support the predictions of cells 1, 2, and 7. Yet despite the realistic limitations and the need for more empirical validation, this type of contingency model is indicative of the real progress that is being made in the applications area of job design.

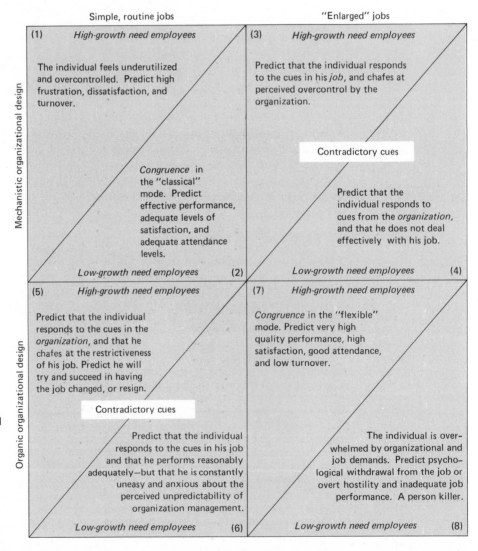

**Figure 8-5
Contingency model
of job design.
(Source: Lyman W.
Porter, Edward E.
Lawler, and J.
Richard Hackman,
Behavior in
Organizations,
McGraw-Hill, New
York, 1975, p. 309.
Used with
permission.)**

In addition to the contingency model, Hackman and his colleagues offer specific guidelines such as those shown in Figure 8-6 for changing and/or creating specific job characteristics. Such guidelines are making the job design area of organizational behavior popular and practical for more effective human resource management.

Quality of work life and sociotechnical design

So far, the discussion of job design has mainly revolved around the job enrichment approach and a micro perspective of the relationships between job characteristics or scope and employee satisfaction. The contingency model of Figure 8-5 added a more macro dimension with the impact of organization design. The concern for quality of work life (QWL) and the accompanying sociotechnical approach to job design also take a more macro perspective.

Unlike the job enrichment approach, QWL is not based on a particular theory nor does it advocate a particular technique for application. Instead, QWL is concerned with the overall climate of work. One recent analysis of QWL described it as "a process of joint decision making, collaboration and building mutual respect between management and employees."[49] The purpose is to change the climate at work so that the human-technological-organizational interface leads to a better quality of work life. Although how

---

[49]Deborah Shaw Cohen, "The Quality of Work Life Movement," *Training HRD*, January 1979, p. 24.

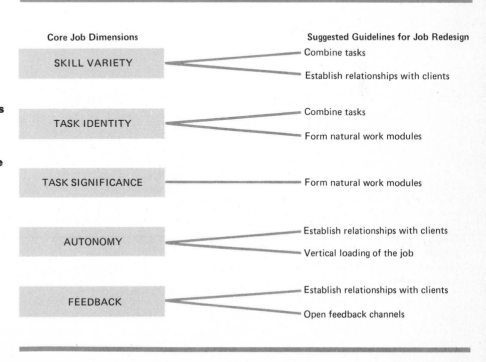

Figure 8-6
Specific guidelines for redesigning jobs for the more effective practice of human resource management. (*Source:* **Adapted from J. R. Hackman, G. Oldham, R. Janson, and K. Purdy, "A New Strategy for Job Enrichment,"** *California Management Review,* **vol. 17, no. 4, 1975, pp. 57–71.)**

Core Job Dimensions | Suggested Guidelines for Job Redesign

SKILL VARIETY — Combine tasks / Establish relationships with clients

TASK IDENTITY — Combine tasks / Form natural work modules

TASK SIGNIFICANCE — Form natural work modules

AUTONOMY — Establish relationships with clients / Vertical loading of the job

FEEDBACK — Establish relationships with clients / Open feedback channels

this is actually accomplished and exactly what is meant by a better *quality* of work life is unclear at present, there are a number of analyses and applications of the closely associated sociotechnical approach to job design.

Unlike the more general concept of QWL, the sociotechnical approach to job design (which is sometimes even equated with QWL) has a systems theoretical base.[50] In particular, the sociotechnical approach to job design is concerned with the interface between the technological system and the social system. In application this translates into the redesign of technological work processes and the formation of autonomous, self-regulating work groups or teams. A few widely publicized projects have used this approach.

The Volvo project The sociotechnical approach to job design has an international flavor, and although the Swedish automaker Saab pioneered the use of autonomous work groups to work on auto subassembly, the more widely publicized example is at a Volvo automobile plant in Sweden.[51] When Pehr Gyllenhammar took over as the head of Volvo, Sweden's largest employer, he was convinced that the very serious turnover and absenteeism problems were symtomatic of the values of their employees. Hand-in-hand with the emerging values of society as a whole, the Volvo employees were demanding more meaningful work—better pay and security, but also participation in the decision-making process and self-regulation. But the technological work process for making automobiles (i.e., the assembly line), did not allow such values to be expressed, and the results were turnover, absenteeism, and low-quality performance.

Taking a sociotechnical approach, under Gyllenhammar's leadership, technological changes were made to reflect more of a natural module of work rather than a continuous work flow, and autonomous work groups were formed. These groups consisted of five to twelve workers who elected their own supervisors, and scheduled, assigned, and inspected their own work. Group rather than individual piece rates were used and all group members made the same amount except for the elected supervisor. This sociotechnical approach (change the technological process and utilize autonomous, self-regulating work groups) was at first applied on a piecemeal basis around the company. Then, a few years ago, the new Kalmar assembly plant was completely redesigned along the lines of a sociotechnical approach. On the technological side, the conventional continuous assembly line was changed so that the work remained stationary. A special carrier was developed to transport the car to the various work groups. On the social side, about twenty-five groups made up of about twenty members each performed work on the various modules of an automobile (electrical, instrumentation, steering and controls, interior, etc.). These work teams organize any way they want and contract with management to deliver a certain number of

[50]Thomas G. Cummings, "Self-Regulating Work Groups: A Socio-Technical Synthesis," *Academy of Management Review,* July 1978, pp. 625–634.

[51]Pehr G. Gyllenhammar, *People at Work,* Addison-Wesley, Reading, Mass., 1977; and John M. Roach, "Why Volvo Abolished the Assembly Line," *Management Review,* September 1977, pp. 48–52.

products per day, e.g., brake systems installed or interiors finished. The workers have almost complete control over their own work, scheduling the pace of work and break times. Also important, these teams inspect their own work, and feedback is given to the group via a TV screen at the work station.

In line with more general quality of work life objectives, a more humane work climate was designed for this Volvo plant. The plant layout is set up to be very light and airy and have a low noise level. There are carpeted "coffee corners" where the groups take their breaks and they have well-equipped changing rooms.

After this approach to job design had been installed at Volvo, turnover and absenteeism were reduced, and quality of work life was reportedly improved. To date, however, no systematic analysis has demonstrated that causal inferences can be made. However, the Volvo top management feels that their new approach to job design has been successful. Only time and systematic evaluation will tell for sure whether this optimism is justified.

Other sociotechnical projects   Although the Volvo project is the most famous, a few companies in the United States have also tried a sociotechnical approach to job design. Probably the most widely reported example is the General Foods Topeka, Kansas plant which produces Gaines pet food. Similar to the Kalmar Volvo plant, this Topeka plant was technologically designed to be compatible with autonomous work groups. The groups were set up basically the same as those described at the Volvo plant. They had shared responsibility and worked for a coach rather than a supervisor. Status symbols such as parking privileges were abolished. Initially, the reports of this General Foods project were very favorable. The employees themselves expressed very favorable attitudes to this new approach to work, and management reported that after implementing the project, 35 percent fewer employees were needed to run the plant, quality rejects dipped to 92 percent below the industry norm, annual savings of $600,000 resulted from the reduction of variable manufacturing costs, and turnover dropped below the company average.[52] However, more recent reports do not paint such a rosy picture.[53] Some former employees at the Topeka plant indicate that the approach has steadily eroded. Apparently, some managers at the plant are openly hostile to the project because it undermined their power, authority, and decision-making flexibility.

Besides the General Foods project, General Motors, Wyerhauser, TRW, Rushton Mining, Harman International, Heinz, and Nabisco have reportedly initiated similar sociotechnical programs. Mainly based on testimonial evidence, these programs have supposedly resulted in savings from lower turnover, absenteeism, and accident rates; reduced supervision; better product and service quality; and more efficient working methods.[54] There have also been reportedly successful applications in public sector organiza-

---

[52]Richard E. Walton, "How to Counter Alienation in the Plant," *Harvard Business Review,* November–December 1972, p. 77.

[53]"Stonewalling Plant Democracy," *Business Week,* Mar. 28, 1977, pp. 78–81.

[54]Cohen, op. cit., p. 24.

tions such as the Tennessee Valley Authority and the city government of Jamestown, New York.[55] Obviously, with the conflicting reports coming out of the Topeka plant serving as a reminder, systematic evaluations are needed before any broad conclusions on the effectiveness of these sociotechnical programs can be drawn. But with the gathering societal support for the improvement of QWL, even to the point where it may be legislated in the near future,[56] there is no question but that the sociotechnical approach should and will play an increasingly important role in job design and the field of organizational behavior in general.

SUMMARY

This chapter has been concerned with two of the most important application areas to emerge in the field of organizational behavior and human resource management in recent years. The first part examined goal setting. Basing his approach on a cognitive perspective, Locke has developed a goal-setting theory of motivation. This theory emphasizes the important relationship between goals and performance. Laboratory and field studies have generally verified this relationship. An extension of the goal-setting approach is management by objectives or MBO. A total performance system, MBO is widely used, and, although more research is needed, this use seems justified.

Along with progress in the theory, research, and application of goal setting, there is progress in work being done on job design. Although the concern for designing jobs goes back to the scientific management movement at the turn of the century, the recent concern for the quality of work life (QWL) has lead to renewed interest and research on job design. The older job engineering and job enlargement and rotation approaches have given way to a job enrichment approach. Based primarily on the work of Herzberg, job enrichment has been popular (at least in the literature) but may be overly simplistic. The newest approach to job design tries to determine the important job characteristics that relate to psychological or motivational states that in turn relate to employee satisfaction and performance. Characteristics such as skill variety, task identity, task significance, autonomy, and feedback do seem to be related to employee satisfaction. But the way employees perceive these characteristics and the importance of moderating variables such as growth need strength are being shown to have an important impact on the job scope–job satisfaction and performance relationship. Emerging contingency models are beginning to account for these effects and also to recognize the impact of more macro-oriented variables such as organization structure and technology. More in line with this macro perspective and incorporating quality of work life concerns is the sociotechnical approach to job design. Sociotechnical projects at Volvo in Sweden and

[55]Ibid.

[56]Edward E. Lawler, "Should the Quality of Work Life be Legislated?" *Personnel Administrator*, January 1976, pp. 17–21.

General Foods and other companies in this country have reportedly been quite successful. Yet, as with the other techniques discussed in this book, more systematic research is needed for the future.

QUESTIONS FOR DISCUSSION AND REVIEW

1. In your own words, describe the theory behind goal setting. What has the research generally found in testing this theory?
2. Summarize the five basic steps of MBO. What have been the research findings on MBO?
3. Compare and contrast the engineering versus the enrichment approach to job design.
4. What are the core job characteristics in the Hackman-Oldham model? How do you calculate the motivating potential of a job? How would a professor's job and janitor's job measure up on these characteristics? Be specific in your answer.
5. Describe the sociotechnical project at Volvo. Would you rather work there or at the typical auto plant in this country? Why?
6. Considering that former employees at the General Foods plant indicate there may be some problems with sociotechnical design, what do you think the future holds for this type of approach? Do you think QWL will and should be legislated? Why?

CASE:
SPECIFIC GOALS FOR HUMAN SERVICE

Jackie Jordan is the regional manager of a state human services agency that provides job training and rehabilitation programs for deaf persons. Her duties include supervising counselors as well as developing special programs. One of the difficulties that Jackie had was with one of the project supervisors, Kathleen O'Shean. Kathleen was the coordinator of a three-year federal grant for a special project for the deaf. Kathleen had direct responsibility for the funds and the goals of the project. The federal agency that made the grant made continuance of the three-year grant conditional upon some "demonstrative progress" toward fulfilling the purpose of the grant. Jackie's problem with Kathleen was directly related to this proviso. She had repeatedly requested that Kathleen develop some concrete goals for the grant project. Jackie wanted these goals written in a specific, observable, and measurable fashion. Kathleen continually gave Jackie very vague, nonmeasurable platitudes. Jackie, in turn, kept requesting greater clarification, but Kathleen's response was that the work that was being done was meaningful enough and took all of her time. To take away from the work itself by writing these specific goals would only defeat the purpose of the grant. Jackie finally gave up and didn't push the issue further. One year later the grant was not renewed by the federal government because the program lacked "demonstrated progress."

1. Do you think Jackie was right in requesting more specific goals from Kathleen? Why or why not?
2. Do you think the federal government would have been satisfied with the goal-setting approach that Jackie was pushing as a way to demonstrate progress?
3. How would you have handled the situation differently if you were Jackie?

Kelly Sellers was really fed up with his department's performance. He knew that his people had a very boring job, and the way the technological process was set up left little latitude for what he had learned about vertically loading the job through job enrichment. Yet he was convinced that there must be some way to make it more interesting to do a dull job. "At least I want to find out for my people and improve their performance," he thought.

The employees in Kelly's department were involved in the assembly of small hair dryer motors. There were twenty-five to thirty steps in the assembly process depending upon the motor that was being assembled. The process was very simple, and currently each worker completed only one or two steps of the operation. Each employee had his or her own assigned work station and stayed at that particular place for the entire day. Kelly decided to try a couple of things to improve performance. First, he decided to organize the department into work groups. The members of each group could move the work stations around as they desired. He allowed each group to divide the tasks up as they saw fit. Next, Kelly decided to post each group's performance on a daily basis and to reward the group with the highest performance by giving them a "rubber chicken" award that they could display at their work benches. The production manager, after checking with engineering, reluctantly agreed to Kelly's proposal on a trial basis.

1. Do you think Kelly's approach to job redesign will work? Rate the core job dimensions from the Hackman-Oldham model of Kelly's employees before and after he redesigned their job. What could he do to improve these dimensions even more.

2. How do you explain the fact that Kelly felt he was restricted by the technological process, but he still redesigned the work? Is this an example of sociotechnical job redesign?

3. What if this experiment does not work out and the production manager forces Kelly to return to the former task design?

THE BASIC LEARNING PROCESS

LEARN TO PLUG THOSE EARS*

Managers at Beaunit Corporation, a textile spinning plant in North Carolina, were having difficulty getting their employees to comply with Occupational Safety and Health Administration's (OSHA) mandates on wearing hearing protection devices while doing noisy work. For example, in the carding department the employees were subject to 92 decibels for a period of seven hours per day, five days per week. This is way above OSHA standards, and failure to wear earplugs could lead to a fine to the company and termination of the errant employee. Yet most employees failed to wear the earplugs. The company was at a loss as to what to do. They hesitated to fire otherwise good employees, but they also didn't want to get in trouble with OSHA. The employees recognized that the noise levels were high, but they could not see the connection between the long-term loss-of-hearing effects of the noise condition and the short-term, seemingly no-impact results of not wearing protective earplugs. The result was that the company did little more than nag and harass the employees for not wearing earplugs.

A consulting firm specializing in operant conditioning approaches to behavioral management clearly pointed out to the employees a new direct connection between the wearing of earplugs and rewarding consequences. Each time supervisors observed employees wearing their earplugs they were instructed to give them positive comments, coffee, and donuts. In addition to the rewards, the percentage of those wearing earplugs was carefully recorded and posted on the department's bulletin board. The results of this approach were highly significant. Before this program was initiated, the percentage of those wearing earplugs was only about 15 percent; after the program was implemented, almost all employees started wearing the plugs. The employees had "learned" to associate wearing earplugs with positive consequences.

*Adapted from "Improving Safety Behavior" in Lawrence Miller, *Behavior Management,* Wiley, New York, 1978, pp. 44–51.

233

Along with motivation, learning has occupied a central role in the micro perspective of organizational behavior. Whereas motivation has been a more popular construct over the years in the field of organizational behavior, learning has been more dominant in the field of psychology. Only very recently has learning been given attention in the study of organizational behavior. Now a growing number of organizational behavior theorists and researchers believe that learning is the single most important concept in the study of human behavior, and few would challenge the statement that learning is involved in almost everything that everyone does. Learning definitely affects human behavior in organizations. There is little organizational behavior that is not either directly or indirectly affected by learning. For example, a worker's skill, a manager's attitude, a supervisor's motivation, and a secretary's mode of dress are all learned. Costello and Zalkind conclude:

Every aspect of human behavior is responsive to learning experiences. Knowledge, language, and skills, of course; but also attitudes, value systems, and personality characteristics. All the individual's activities in the organization—his loyalties, awareness of organizational goals, job performance, even his safety record—have been learned, in the largest sense of that term.[1]

Learning, of course, is also involved in the consequences of organizational behavior. The S-O-B-C model of Chapter 3 had feedback loops to and from all the variables. These feedback loops represent interactions, but also could be thought of as learning. The purpose of this chapter is to present an overview of the learning process and some of the basic principles which will contribute to the better understanding, prediction, and control of organizational behavior and will serve as a foundation for the application techniques in the next chapter.

The first section distinguishes among the types of learning and summarizes the major theoretical approaches. The next section presents the learning principles of acquisition-learning curves, extinction, spontaneous recovery, generalization, and discrimination. The reinforcement principle is given major attention in the third section. Included is a discussion of the law of effect, types of reinforcement, and schedules of reinforcement. The last section is devoted to the effect of punishment on learning and behavior.

TYPES AND THEORIES OF LEARNING

Learning is a term frequently used by a great number of people in a wide variety of contexts. Yet, despite its diverse use, academicians have generally recognized only one, or at most two, types of ways that behavior can be acquired or changed. Starting with the early behaviorists (e.g., John B. Watson and later B. F. Skinner), the most common explanation of learning

---

[1]Timothy W. Costello and Sheldon S. Zalkind, *Psychology in Administration*, Prentice-Hall, Englewood Cliffs, N.J., 1963, p. 205.

has been *direct*, noncognitively mediated, classical and operant conditioning. Most of the learning principles that have been developed over the years and the discussion in this chapter and the next are greatly influenced by this approach to learning. However, recognition of the interactive nature of human behavior and the role of cognitive contingencies that fall under the social learning theory described in Chapter 3, implies other explanations of learning. In particular, learning can also be explained by cognitively or noncognitively mediated vicarious or *modeling* processes and/or by cognitively or noncognitively mediated *self-control* processes.[2] These three types of learning—direct, modeling, and self-control—suggest that there are different theoretical bases for learning, and these will be drawn upon in the following sections.

The most basic purpose of any theory is to better explain the phenomena in question. When theories become perfected, they have universal application and should enable prediction and control. Thus, a perfected theory of learning would have to be able to explain all aspects of learning (how, when, and why), have universal application (for example, to children, college students, managers, and workers), and predict and control learning situations. To date, no such theory of learning exists. Although there is general agreement on some principles of learning, there is still disagreement on the theory behind it. This does not mean that no attempts have been made to develop a theory of learning. In fact, the opposite is true. The most widely recognized theoretical approaches follow the behavioristic and cognitive models discussed in Chapter 3 and the newly emerging social learning theory. An understanding of these three learning theories is important to the study of organizational behavior.

Connectionist, behavioristic theories of learning

The dominant and best-researched theory of learning comes out of the behavioristic school of thought in psychology. Most of the principles of learning discussed in this chapter and the applications discussed in the next chapter are based on operant or Skinnerian behaviorism.

The classical behaviorists such as Pavlov and Watson attributed learning to the association or connection between stimulus and response. The more modern behaviorists, in particular Skinner, give more attention to the role that consequences play in learning or the R-S (response-stimulus) connection. The emphasis on the connection (S-R or R-S) has led some to label these the "connectionist" theories of learning. The S-R deals with classical or respondent conditioning and the R-S with instrumental or operant conditioning. An understanding of these conditioning processes is vital to the study of learning.

Classical conditioning   Pavlov's classical conditioning experiment with dogs as subjects is undoubtedly the single most famous study ever

[2]Tim R. V. Davis and Fred Luthans, "A Social Learning Approach to Organizational Behavior," *Academy of Management Review*, April 1980, pp. 281–290.

conducted in the behavioral sciences. A simple surgical procedure permitted Pavlov to measure accurately the amount of saliva secreted by a dog. When he presented a piece of meat (unconditioned stimulus) to the dog in the experiment, Pavlov noticed a great deal of salivation (unconditioned response). On the other hand, when he merely rang a bell (neutral stimulus), the dog had no salivation. The next step taken by Pavlov was to accompany the meat with the ringing of the bell. After doing this several times, Pavlov rang the bell without the meat. This time, the dog salivated to the bell alone. The dog had become classically conditioned to salivate (conditioned response) to the sound of the bell (conditioned stimulus). This classical experiment was a major breakthrough and has had a lasting impact on the understanding of learning.

Pavlov went beyond the simple conditioning of the dogs to salivate to the sound of a bell. He next paired a black square with the bell. After a number of trials with this pairing, the dogs salivated to the black square alone. The original conditioned stimulus (bell) had become a reinforcing unconditioned stimulus for the new conditioned stimulus (black square). When the dogs responded to the black square, they became what is known as second-order conditioned. Pavlov was able to obtain no higher than third-order conditioning with his dogs.

Most behavioral scientists agree that humans are capable of being conditioned higher than the third order. The exact number is not important, but the potential implications of higher-order conditioning for human learning and behavior should be recognized.[3] For example, higher-order conditioning can explain how learning can be transferred to stimuli other than those used in the original conditioning. The existence of higher-order conditioning shows the difficulty of tracing the exact cause of a certain behavior. Another important implication concerns the principle of reinforcement. Higher-order conditioning implies that reinforcement can be acquired. A conditioned stimulus becomes reinforcing under higher-order conditioning. It substantiates, and perhaps offers a plausible explanation for, the secondary rewards which play such an important role in organizational behavior.

Classical conditioning experimentation has been a major source of support for the S-R theories of learning. Since Pavlov's original experiments in the 1880s, psychologists have classically conditioned everything from the flatworm to the human being. The overall conclusion from this vast amount of research is stated by Bass and Vaughn as follows:

In all probability, any response in an organism's behavioral repertoire can be conditioned if an unconditioned stimulus can be found that regularly produces the response and if this unconditioned stimulus can be paired in training with a conditioned stimulus.[4]

---

[3]Gregory A. Kimble and Norman Garmezy, *Principles of General Psychology*, 2d ed., Ronald, New York, 1963, p. 146.

[4]Bernard M. Bass and James A. Vaughan, *Training in Industry: The Management of Learning*, Wadsworth, Belmont, Calif., 1966, p. 15.

Despite the theoretical possibility of the widespread applicability of classical conditioning, most modern theorists agree that it represents only a very small part of total human learning. Skinner in particular felt that classical conditioning explained only respondent (reflexive) behaviors. These are the involuntary responses that are elicited by a stimulus. Skinner felt that the more complex, but common, human behaviors could not be explained by classical conditioning alone. He felt that most human behavior affects, or operates on, the environment. The latter type of behavior is learned through operant conditioning.

Operant conditioning Operant conditioning is primarily concerned with learning that occurs as a *consequence* of behavior. It is not concerned with the eliciting causes of behavior as is classical or respondent conditioning. The specific differences between classical and operant conditioning may be summarized as follows:

1. In classical conditioning, a change in the stimulus (unconditioned stimulus to conditioned stimulus) will elicit a particular response. In operant conditioning, one particular response out of many possible ones occurs in a given stimulus situation. The stimulus situation serves as a cue in operant conditioning. It does not elicit the response but serves as a cue for a person to emit the response. The critical aspect of operant conditioning is what happens as a consequence of the response. The strength and frequency of classically conditioned behaviors are mainly determined by the frequency of the eliciting stimulus (the environmental event that precedes the behavior). The strength and frequency of operantly conditioned behaviors are mainly determined by the consequences (the environmental event that follows the behavior).
2. During the classical conditioning process, the unconditioned stimulus, serving as a reward, is presented every time. In operant conditioning the reward will occur only if the organism performs the correct response. The organism must operate on the environment in order to receive a reward. The response is instrumental in obtaining the reward. Table 9-1 gives some simple examples of classical (S-R) and operant (R-S) conditioning.

Operant conditioning has a much greater impact on human learning than does classical conditioning. Operant conditioning also explains, at least in very general terms, much of organizational behavior. For example, it might be said that employees work eight hours a day, five days a week, in order to feed, clothe, and shelter themselves and their families. Working (conditioned response) is only instrumental in obtaining the food, clothing, and shelter. Some significant insights can be directly gained from this kind of analysis. The consequences of organizational behavior can change the environmental situation and largely affect subsequent employee behaviors. In other words, the analysis of the consequences of organizational behavior can help accomplish the goals of prediction and control.

In summary, it can be said that operant conditioning is the basis for modern behaviorism and consists of the following:

1. A series of assumptions about behavior and its environment
2. A set of definitions which can be used in objective, scientific description of behavior and its environment

Table 9–1

EXAMPLES OF CLASSICAL AND OPERANT CONDITIONING

Classical connection

	(S) Stimulus ⟶	(R) Response
The individual is:	stuck by a pin tapped below the kneecap shocked by electric current surprised by a loud sound	flinches lower leg flexes jumps/screams jumps/screams

Operant connection

	(R) Response ⟶	(S) Stimulus
The individual:	works talks to others enters a restaurant enters a library works hard	is paid meets more people obtains food finds a book receives praise and a promotion

3. A group of techniques and procedures for the experimental study of behavior in the laboratory
4. A large body of facts and principles which have been demonstrated by experiment[5]

These four points show that operant conditioning leads to a very comprehensive approach to the study of behavior. The next chapter will discuss in detail and apply to organizational behavior most of these aspects of operant conditioning.

Cognitive theories of learning

Edward Tolman was portrayed in Chapter 3 as a pioneering cognitive theorist. He felt that learning consisted of a *relationship between cognitive environmental cues and expectation*. He developed and tested this theory through controlled experimentation. He was one of the first to use the now famous white rat in psychological experiments. He found that a rat could learn to run through an intricate maze with purpose and direction toward a goal (food). Tolman observed that at each choice point in the maze, expectations were established. In other words, the rat learned to *expect* that certain cognitive cues associated with the choice point might eventually lead to food. If the rat actually received the food, the association between the cue and the expectancy was strengthened and learning occurred. In contrast to the S-R and R-S learning in the behaviorist approach, Tolman's approach could be depicted as S-S (stimulus-stimulus).

---

[5]G. S. Reynolds, *A Primer of Operant Conditioning*, Scott, Foresman, Glenview, Ill., 1975, p. 1.

Tolman's experiments proved to be embarrassing to the behavioristic learning theorists. For example, in his famous place-learning experiments he trained a rat to turn right in a "T" maze in order to obtain food. Then he started the rat from the opposite part of the maze and according to behavioristic theory the rat should turn right because of past conditioning. But, in Tolman's experiments the rat instead turned towards where the food had been placed. Tolman concluded that the rat's behavior was purposive, i.e., the rat formed a cognitive map to figure out how to get to the food. In other words, Tolman said that reinforcement was not a precondition for learning to take place. One stimulus led to another stimulus, or S-S, rather than the classical S-R or operant R-S explanation.

Tolman also conducted latent learning and transposition experiments to demonstrate that reinforcement was not needed for learning to occur. However, in time the behavioristic theorists were able to negate Tolman's results. By using more controlled experimental procedures they were able to verify their predictions. For example, when there were perfectly sterile conditions in the place-learning experiments, e.g., a bubble was placed over the maze and the runways were carefully scrubbed, etc., the rat turned right as conditioned instead of purposively going toward the food.

Even though most of Tolman's experiments have been discredited, he made a significant contribution to the development of learning theory. He forced the behaviorists to develop more complex explanations of behavior and pinpointed the need to consider cognitions at least as a possible mediating role between the stimulus environment and the behavior. This thinking has served as a transition and integrating mechanism leading toward social learning theory, which will be covered in the next section.

Besides being the forerunner of modern social learning theory, Tolman's S-S cognitive theory also had great impact on the early human relations movement. Industrial training programs in the 1940s and 1950s drew heavily on Tolman's ideas.[6] Programs were designed to strengthen the relationship between cognitive cues (supervision, organizational, and job procedures) and worker expectations (incentive payments for good performance). The theory was that the worker would learn to be more productive by building an association between taking orders or following directions and expectancies of monetary reward for this effort.

Today, the cognitive theories are still alive and well. The discussion of the motivation theories and techniques in the preceding three chapters are largely based on the cognitive approach. Expectations, attributions/locus of control, and goal setting (which are in the forefront of modern work motivation) are all cognitive concepts and represent the purposefulness of organizational behavior. More directly aimed at learning are the cognitively based selective learning theories.

In selective learning the person must not only associate stimulus and response and response and consequence experiences but must also determine which things to connect in the mind.[7] Under selective learning, the

---

[6] George S. Odiorne, *Training by Objectives*, Macmillan, New York, 1970.

[7] Norman R. F. Maier, *Psychology in Industry*, 3d ed., Houghton Mifflin, Boston, 1965, p. 379.

human chooses from a wide variety of possible learning mechanisms. For example, the individual does not have a simple choice, say, between classical and operant conditioning. Rather, selective learning involves a complex interaction among thinking, emotion, perception, and motivation. In other words, there are many cognitions that come into play in selective learning. As is true regarding the other theories of learning, there is no general agreement as to what exactly goes on in such a cognitive learning process, but whatever it is can be called *selective learning*. Other names attached to this complex cognitive type of learning include *insightful learning* and *perceptual learning*. The latter types give a slightly different emphasis, but they are all modern cognitive learning theories. Although controversy persists and knowledge is still inadequate, the cognitive learning theorists argue that a form of learning like selective learning does indeed take place, and that it is much more complex than merely strengthening stimulus-response or response-consequence connections.

Selective learning can be experimentally demonstrated by maze learning, or the term can be used to describe some of the very complicated learning tasks which occur in an organization. For example, an employee faced with a problem-solving type of situation may be using a selective learning process. Basic conditioning and the principles of learning are relegated to a supplementary role in selective learning. A worker faced with a job requiring a new skill, an office manager challenged by a new filing system, a systems analyst confronted by a new computer language, and a top executive who must explain the new budgeting system to the board of directors may be using the selective learning process to accomplish their relatively complex tasks.

Social learning theory

Chapter 3 introduced social learning theory. It was said that social learning theory combines and integrates both behavioristic and cognitive concepts and emphasizes the interactive nature of cognitive, behavioral, and environmental determinants. This social learning approach was used as the basis for developing the S-O-B-C conceptual framework for this book.

It is important to recognize that social learning theory is a *behavioral* theory and draws heavily from the principles of classical and operant conditioning. But equally important is the fact that social learning theory goes beyond classical and operant theory by recognizing that there is more to learning than direct learning via antecedent stimuli and contingent consequences. Social learning theory posits that learning can also take place via vicarious or modeling and self-control processes. Thus, social learning theory agrees with classical and operant conditioning processes but says they are too limiting.

Modeling process   The vicarious or modeling processes essentially involves observational learning. Almost forty years ago, Miller and Dollard suggested that learning need not result from discrete stimulus-response or response-consequence connections. Instead, learning can take place through imitating others. Albert Bandura is most closely associated with the modern view of modeling as an explanation of learning. He states:

> Although behavior can be shaped into new patterns to some extent by rewarding and punishing consequences, learning would be exceedingly laborious and hazardous if it proceeded solely on this basis. . . . it is difficult to imagine a socialization process in which the language, mores, vocational activities, familial customs and educational, religious and political practices of a culture are taught to each new member by selective reinforcement of fortuitous behaviors, without benefit of models who exemplify the cultural patterns in their own behavior. Most of the behaviors that people display are learned either deliberately or inadvertently, through the influence of example.[8]

He has done considerable research that demonstrates that people can learn from others.[9] This learning takes place in two steps. First, the person observes how others act and then acquires a mental picture of the act and its consequences (rewards and punishers). Then the person acts out the acquired image and if the consequences are positive, he or she will tend to do it again. If the consequences are negative, the person will tend not to do it again. This, of course, is where there is a tie-in with operant theory. But because there is cognitive, symbolic representation of the modeled activities instead of discrete response-consequence connections in the acquisition of new behavior, modeling goes beyond the operant explanation. In particular, Bandura concludes that modeling involves interrelated subprocesses such as *attention*, *retention*, and *motoric reproduction*, as well as reinforcement.

Modeling applications   There is a growing literature that suggests that modeling can be effectively applied to human resource management. A specific modeling strategy could be used to improve human performance. Such a strategy might include the following steps:

1. Precisely identify the goal or target behavior that will lead to performance improvement.
2. Select the appropriate model and modeling medium, i.e., live demonstration, training film, videotape, etc.
3. Make sure the employee is capable of meeting the technical skill requirements of the target behavior.
4. Structure a favorable learning environment which increases the probability of attention, participation, and ultimately, attainment of the target behavior.
5. Model the target behavior and carry out supporting activities such as role playing. Clearly demonstrate the positive consequences of the modeled target behavior.
6. Positively reinforce all progress of the modeled behavior.
7. Once achieved, maintain and strengthen the target behavior first with a continuous schedule of reinforcement and later with an intermittent schedule.[10]

---

[8]Albert Bandura, "Social Learning Theory," in J. T. Spence, R. C. Carson, and J. W. Thibaut, *Behavioral Approaches to Therapy*, General Learning Press, Morristown, N.J., 1976, p. 5.

[9]See Albert Bandura, *Social Learning Theory*, Prentice-Hall, Englewood Cliffs, N.J., 1977 for a summary of this research.

[10]Fred Luthans and Robert Kreitner, *Organizational Behavior Modification*, Scott, Foresman, Glenview, Ill., 1975, pp. 140–141.

Recent studies show that such modeling procedures can have a very favorable impact on industrial training programs.[11]

Besides modeling, social learning theory has important implications for self-control. This dimension of social learning is given detailed attention in Chapter 22. There seems little question that social learning theory is the type of comprehensive foundation that is necessary for the learning process and the understanding, prediction, and control of organizational behavior.

PRINCIPLES OF LEARNING

There are many widely recognized principles of learning. Although the cognitive and social learning theories are becoming increasingly important, the recognized principles of learning largely come out of classical and especially operant theories. For example, reinforcement is probably the single most important principle for explaining learning and predicting and controlling behavior. However, before reinforcement is examined in detail, other principles such as acquisition-learning curves, extinction, spontaneous recovery, generalization, and discrimination are briefly explored. Figure 9-1 summarizes some of these principles.

Acquisition-learning curves

Figure 9-1 clearly shows the principle of acquisition. There is a gradually increasing strength of response for each repeated trial. As represented, this applies mainly to classical conditioning, but operant conditioning also

---

[11]R. F. Burnaska, "The Effects of Behavior Modeling Training Upon Managers' Behaviors and Employees' Perceptions," *Personnel Psychology*, vol. 29, 1976, pp. 329–335; A. I. Kraut, "Developing Managerial Skills Via Modelling Techniques: Some Positive Research Findings—A Symposium," *Personnel Psychology*, vol. 29, 1976, pp. 325–369; and Gary P. Latham and Lise M. Saari, "Application of Social-Learning Theory to Training Supervisors Through Behavioral Modeling," *Journal of Applied Psychology*, vol. 64, 1979, pp. 239–246.

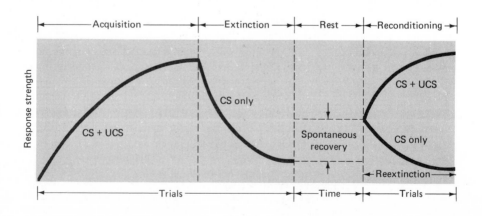

**Figure 9-1
Some principles of learning. (*Source:* Gregory A. Kimble, Norman Garmezy, and Edward Ziegler, *General Psychology*, 4th ed., copyright © 1974, Ronald, New York, p. 228. Used with permission.)**

follows an acquisition curve. The acquisition curve can be thought of as a learning curve, where the vertical axis represents measured performance and the horizontal axis represents the amount of practice or experience, which is usually expressed in time or number of trials. Figure 9-2 summarizes the four general types of learning curves.

Decreasing returns curve   The curve in (*a*) of Figure 9-2 is negatively accelerating and is commonly referred to as the *curve of decreasing returns*. The acquisition curve in Figure 9-1 is of this type. This curve shows the most common way in which acquisition takes place. The learning of most mental and motor tasks exhibits a decreasing returns pattern. There is an initial spurt of learning, which then begins to slow down and finally reaches a point where there is practically no learning progress. Learning to perform most of the specialized, routine-type jobs found in modern organizations would tend to follow the decreasing returns learning curve.

Increasing returns curve   The curve in Figure 9-2 (*b*) is essentially the opposite of (*a*). It shows a positively accelerating curve that produces

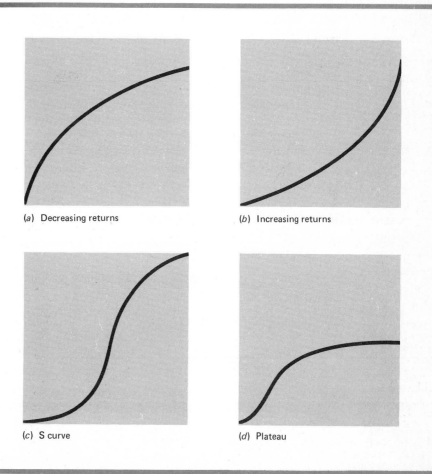

(*a*) Decreasing returns   (*b*) Increasing returns

(*c*) S curve   (*d*) Plateau

**Figure 9-2
Learning curves.**

increasing returns. The learning curve in (b) is rarer than the one in (a) and will usually occur only when a person is learning a completely unfamiliar mental or motor task. Many of the staff positions in an organization, e.g., engineers and marketing researchers, may experience an increasing return on certain tasks. The same holds true of workers learning very highly skilled lower-level jobs. In both cases, it has been found that initial learning may progress very slowly, but after a time, the learning will take giant strides.

S learning curve The learning curve in Figure 9-2(c) is commonly referred to as the S curve. This curve is really a combination of the decreasing and increasing returns curves. Theoretically, all learning would probably follow an S curve if the person brings absolutely no relevant experience to the learning situation. In reality, of course, this is not the case. An S curve would most likely result when a person attempts to learn a relatively difficult, unfamiliar task that requires insight. For example, learning many of the highly skilled jobs in a technical industry might follow the S pattern.

Learning plateau The curve in Figure 9-2 (d) shows the plateau principle of acquisition. Many learning situations seem to progress satisfactorily but then reach a point where nothing new is learned. This leveling off in learning is called a *plateau*. The learning of many relatively simple tasks follows this pattern. Most lower-level and "dead end" jobs in modern organizations have personnel who are in a learning plateau. Something must spur people on in order to get them on an accelerated path again. Behavioral techniques are needed to break organizational personnel out of plateau learning situations. Some of the techniques that can be used to change and accelerate learning behavior are covered in the next chapter.

Value of learning curves Not all human learning can be neatly fitted into one of the learning curves discussed here. On the other hand, the curves do represent in a general way the major patterns of acquisition, with the learning of certain types of tasks following certain types of curves. Psychologists have summarized the applicability of these curves to the learning of specific types of tasks as follows:

1. The more unfamiliar the task to be learned, the more likely it is that progress will be slow at the start and will then increase.
2. In most learning of complicated skills, there is at least one period, short or long, in which each new trial produces an improvement of equal size.
3. As we approach the ultimate limit of learning, progress slows down, and it takes many trials to produce even a small amount of improvement.[12]

Extinction

The principle of extinction is closely related to reinforcement. In classical conditioning, if the conditioned stimulus is not reinforced by the uncondi-

---

[12]Jerome Kagan and Ernest Havemann, *Psychology,* Harcourt, Brace & World, New York, 1968, p. 90.

tioned stimulus, the conditioned response will weaken and eventually disappear or become extinct. For example, in the Pavlov experiment, if the meat is withheld when the bell is rung, the drops of saliva will slowly decrease and will eventually become extinct with just the sound of the bell. In operant conditioning, if the response is not reinforced by the consequence, the response will become extinct. Thus, the extinction principle simply means that if a response is not reinforced, it will eventually disappear.

The principle of extinction has important implications for understanding and controlling human behavior. More detailed attention will be given to it in the discussion of reinforcement, but an example can demonstrate its impact. Workers may be continually rewarded, by bonus and praise, for learning a new skill in a training program. However, when the newly trained workers are placed on the job, they may never be rewarded for performing the skill. Their work record may slowly decline, and their newly acquired skill may even become extinct.

Besides occurring inadvertently the next chapter will show that it can be deliberately used as an effective strategy for decreasing undesirable behaviors as well. When a behavior is not reinforced (this does *not* mean punishing or ignoring the behavior but instead it means eliminating the reinforcer), the behavior will weaken and decrease in subsequent frequency. Such an extinction strategy does not have the side effect problems associated with punishment which are discussed later in the chapter. In other words, extinction has the same effect on behavior as does punishment, but without the problems of punishment. For example, suppose a supervisor wants to decrease the complaints from a subordinate. When the subordinate comes to the supervisor with a complaint, the supervisor could do one of three things: (1) give attention and listen carefully to the complaint, (2) chew the subordinate out for always complaining, or (3) not give attention nor listen to the complaint. The most likely extinction strategy would be the last one. The first is probably reinforcing and the second is probably punishing. If the third approach is used and the complaining behavior does decrease in subsequent frequency, the extinction strategy has worked. But as this example shows there is often a fine line between punishment and extinction.

Spontaneous recovery

Figure 9-1 shows another interesting learning principle, called *spontaneous recovery*. The graph in the figure indicates that if people experience a sequence of nonreinforced conditioned responses and then take a rest, immediately thereafter they will return to a more intense level of conditioned response even though no reinforcement has taken place. This jump in response strength following rest is called *the principle of spontaneous recovery*. This principle suggests that the conditioned response does not totally disappear during extinction, but instead is suppressed or becomes inhibited.

Figure 9-1 shows that, following spontaneous recovery, the slope of the relearning curve accelerates if the conditioned stimulus in classical or the response in operant conditioning is reinforced. In an analogous manner, the slope of the extinction curve also accelerates downward if there is no reinforcement. An example of spontaneous recovery occurring in an organizational situation would be the spurt in an employee's job performance immediately following his or her vacation or layoff. Management could take advantage of spontaneous recovery by consciously attempting to reinforce positive responses and nonreinforce undesirable responses immediately following the spurt in performance occurring after a rest. By doing this, management would be taking advantage of the steep relearning and extinction curves which follow spontaneous recovery.

Generalization

The common meaning of generalization is applicable to the learning principle of the same name. The generalization principle states simply, that a new, but similar, stimulus or stimulus situation will produce a response that is the same as that produced by the original stimulus. In classical conditioning, generalization occurs when a conditioned response that has been elicited by a conditioned stimulus is given a new but similar stimulus which produces the same conditioned response. The more the new stimulus is like the conditioned stimulus, the more probable it is that the new stimulus will produce the same conditioned response. This latter relationship is commonly called the *generalization gradient*, which is hypothetically depicted in Figure 9-3. Stimulus generalization can also occur in operant conditioning. A response that is reinforced in the presence of a certain cue

**Figure 9-3
A gradient for
generalization.
(Source: Bernard
M. Bass and
James A. Vaughan,
Training in
Industry: The
Management of
Learning,
Wadsworth,
Belmont, Calif.,
1966, p. 17.)**

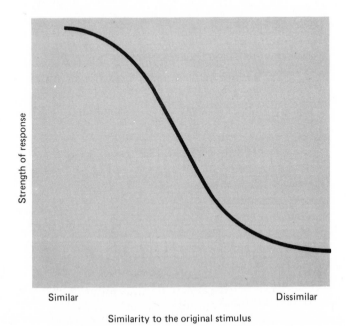

may generalize. Similar cues may cause the behavior to be emitted. In addition, response generalization may occur. For example, in a common Skinner box[13] if an animal's conditioned response of pressing the bar with its paw is prevented, a similar response, such as pushing the bar with its nose or tail, may take place. The latter response is an example of response generalization which is instrumental in obtaining the desired consequence.

The principle of generalization has important implications for human learning. Without generalization, the person would find it extremely difficult to adapt to any new situation. However, because of generalization, people do not have to completely relearn each of the new tasks or situations which constantly confront them. It allows the organizational participant to adapt to overall changing conditions and specific new or modified job assignments. The individual, no matter at what level in the organization, can borrow from past learning experiences to adjust more smoothly to new learning situations.

Besides the positive contributions that result from generalization, there are also certain negative implications for learning. Generalization may lead a person to counterproductive behaviors. For example, an accountant may make an entry in a similar, but incorrect, account in a management information report. This one error may lead the report reader to generalize to all accounting data and take erroneous actions. Another example of the possible negative impact of generalization is the case of hiring and training the hard-core unemployed. One or a few bad experiences may lead management to generalize that "they" are untrainable and poor risks. The one bad apple generalizes to the whole barrel. The implications of the word *they* point out the potentially harmful behavioral consequences that may result from stimulus generalization. The latter example also emphasizes the close relationship between the learning principle of generalization and the perceptual principles presented in Chapter 4. Once again, the difficulty is illustrated in isolating one psychological process for study without recognizing that it affects, and is affected by, the other psychological processes.

Discrimination

In recent times, the word *discrimination* has taken on the connotation of race prejudice. Technically, of course, the word has a much broader meaning. Applied to learning, discrimination is essentially opposite to generalization. Whereas generalization is a reaction to *similarities* of stimuli or responses, discrimination is a reaction to *differences,* as can be simply demonstrated by a Pavlovian type of experiment. A light can be added to the experiment of the dog being classically conditioned to the sound of a bell. If the experiment is set up so that the dog gets food only when the bell rings and the light is on, and he gets no food when the bell rings and the light is off, the dog will soon learn to discriminate between the two stimuli. The dog will respond only to the bell–light-on stimulus and not to the bell–light-off stimulus.

An example of the principle of discrimination operating in an organiza-

---

[13]This is a box containing a lever, which dispenses food and is widely used in learning experiments with animals.

tional situation is the supervisor who distinguishes between two equally productive workers. The supervisor responds positively to only one of the high producers, having learned to discriminate between them. One of the workers produces a great quantity of items but pays no attention to quality and has a lot of rejects. The other worker also produces a great quantity but has virtually no rejects as the result of being quality conscious. At first the supervisor may respond positively to both workers; but when the presence of the sloppy worker does not lead to desirable consequences for the supervisor's responses, the supervisor learns to discriminate between the two workers. Positive response is given only to the quality-conscious high producer. It is interesting to note that this discrimination may also modify the sloppy worker's behavior. If the worker is not reinforced by the supervisor for high-quantity–low-quality performance, the behavior will eventually become extinct. On the other hand, if no discrimination is made and the supervisor reinforces the high-quantity–low-quality performance, it will continue unabated.

In an analogous manner, discrimination also occurs in operant conditioning. A response that is reinforced in the presence of one stimulus situation but not in the presence of another will lead to stimulus discrimination. The behavior will be emitted only in the presence of the stimulus that led to a desirable consequence and will not be emitted when this stimulus is changed or absent. This leads to what is called *stimulus control*. Even though behavior is a function of its consequences in operant conditioning, the discriminative stimulus cue can control the behavior. Once again, this does *not* mean that this discriminative stimulus causes the behavior. Instead, it controls the behavior by serving as a cue to either emit or not emit the behavior.

Stimulus control also has many implications for organizational development. If environmental cues can be so arranged that participants emit more productive behaviors in an organization, many of the goals of organizational development can be accomplished. Chapter 21 is specifically devoted to organizational development.

THE REINFORCEMENT PRINCIPLE

Reinforcement has played a central role in the learning theories, concepts, and principles discussed thus far in the chapter. Most learning experts agree that reinforcement is the single most important principle of learning. Yet, there is much controversy over its theoretical explanation. The first major theoretical treatment given to reinforcement in learning and the theory that still dominates today is Thorndike's classic law of effect.

The law of effect

In Thorndike's own words, the law of effect is simply stated thus:

Of several responses made to the same situation, those which are accompanied or closely followed by satisfaction [reinforcement] . . . will be more likely to recur;

those which are accompanied or closely followed by discomfort [punishment] . . . will be less likely to occur.[14]

From a strictly empirical standpoint, most behavioral scientists, even those of a cognitive orientation, generally accept the validity of this law. It has been demonstrated time after time in highly controlled learning experiments and is directly observable in everyday learning experiences. Desirable or reinforcing consequences will increase the strength of a response and increase its probability of being repeated in the future. Undesirable or punishing consequences will weaken the strength of a response and decrease its probability of occurrence in the future. Despite the wide acceptance of this law, there is disagreement when it is carried a step further and used as an overall theory or an absolute requirement for learning.

As the discussion of cognitive learning theory indicated, Tolman and other critics of the requirement of reinforcement use such concepts as that of latent learning to make their point. For example, in latent learning experiments it was shown that rats running a maze that were reinforced after successful trials showed fewer errors than those rats who are not reinforced. However, once the rat was reinforced after a number of nonreinforced trials, there were very few if any errors. In other words, even though the nonreinforced rats were not as efficient, when they finally were reinforced they were more efficient. The explanation offered was that learning indeed takes place during the nonreinforcement trials and the reinforcement only makes it worthwhile. As did the place-learning experiments discussed earlier, these latent learning experiments proved to be embarrassing to the reinforcement theorists, but, also like the place-learning experiments, the behaviorists were eventually able to show under different experimental conditions, that such latent, nonreinforced learning did not occur.

Despite the theoretical controversy, few would argue against the importance of reinforcement to the learning process. Theoretical attempts besides the law of effect have generally failed to fully explain reinforcement. However, as with the failure to develop a generally accepted overall theory of learning, the lack of an accepted theory of reinforcement does not detract from its extreme importance. As one psychologist notes, "Controversies about theoretical issues are common in all sciences. The important point to understand is that, in spite of the fact that the nature of reinforcement is not fully comprehended, behavior nevertheless can be modified by controlling reinforcement."[15]

Definition of reinforcement

The term *reinforcement* is conceptually related to the psychological process of motivation, which was covered in the preceding chapters. There is a temptation to equate reinforcement with motivation. Although this is sometimes deliberately or nondeliberately done, this book treats them

---

[14]Edward L. Thorndike, *Animal Intelligence*, Macmillan, New York, 1911, p. 244.
[15]Howard H. Kendler, *Basic Psychology*, 3d ed., W. A. Benjamin, Menlo Park, Calif., 1974, p. 179.

separately. Motivation is a basic psychological process and is broader and more complex than is implied by the learning principle of reinforcement as used here. In addition, the need states that are so central to motivation are cognitive in nature; they are unobservable inner states. Reinforcement, on the other hand, is environmentally based. Reinforcers are external, environmental events that follow a response. In general terms, motivation is an internal explanation of behavior, and reinforcement is an external explanation of behavior. Thus, the perspectives and explanation of behavior from motivation and reinforcement are different.

An often cited circular definition of reinforcement says that it is anything the person finds rewarding. This definition is of little value because the words *reinforcing* and *rewarding* are used interchangeably but neither one is operationally defined. A more operational definition can be found by reverting back to the law of effect. With this law, reinforcement can be defined as anything that both increases the strength of response and tends to induce repetitions of the behavior that preceded the reinforcement.

Rewards, on the other hand, are simply the presentation of something that is subjectively deemed to be desirable. A reward is given by a person who thinks it is desirable. Reinforcement is functionally defined. Something is reinforcing only if it strengthens the response preceding it and induces repetitions of the response. For example, a manager may ostensibly reward an employee who found an error in a report by publicly praising the employee. Yet, upon examination it is found that the employee is embarrassed and harassed by co-workers, and error-finding behavior decreases in the future. In this example, the "reward" is *not* reinforcing. Even though there is this technical difference between a reward and a reinforcer, the terms are often used interchangeably and will be in this book.

Besides clearing up the differences between reinforcers and rewards, to better understand reinforcement it is necessary to make the distinctions between positive and negative, extrinsic and intrinsic, and primary and secondary reinforcers.

Positive and negative reinforcers

There is much confusion surrounding the terms *positive* and *negative reinforcement* and the terms *negative reinforcement* and *punishment*. First of all, it must be understood that reinforcement, positive or negative, strengthens the response and increases the probability of repetition. But the positive and negative reinforcers accomplish this impact on behavior in completely different ways. Positive reinforcement strengthens and increases behavior by the *presentation* of a desirable consequence. Negative reinforcement strengthens and increases behavior by the *termination* or *withdrawal* of an undesirable consequence. Figure 9-4 briefly summarizes the differences between positive and negative reinforcement, punishment and extinction. Giving praise to an employee for the successful completion of a task could be an example of a *positive* reinforcer (if this does in fact strengthen and subsequently increase this task behavior). On the other hand, a worker is *negatively* reinforced for getting busy when the supervisor walks through the area. Getting busy terminates being "chewed-out" by the supervisor.

Negative reinforcement is more complex than positive reinforcement but should not be equated with punishment. In fact, they have an opposite effect on behavior. Negative reinforcement strengthens and increases behavior while punishment weakens and decreases behavior. However, both are considered to be forms of negative control of behavior.[16] Negative reinforcement is really a form of social blackmail, because the person will behave a certain way or be punished. A discussion of escape and avoidance learning will help clarify this aspect of negative reinforcement.

Escape-avoidance learning:
A special case of negative reinforcement

A learning phenomenon which demonstrates the impact of negative reinforcement is escape-avoidance learning. It goes a step beyond simple conditioning by using negative reinforcement. A simple escape learning experiment involves shocking a rat in a Skinner box. Only pressing the bar will terminate the shock. The rat must learn to press the bar to escape the pain from the shock. Once escape is learned, avoidance can also be learned. In the Skinner box, a light may be timed to go on ten seconds before the shock is administered. The rat can learn to avoid the shock altogether by running over to press the bar whenever the bulb lights up.

Humans learn escape-avoidance in much the same way as the rat in the Skinner box. For example, workers in an organization may learn to escape a boring job with no challenge by forming into informal groups or by playing games during working hours. After the quitting whistle blows, the aversive situation stops and the employees return to being very active, serious-minded individuals. In another situation a worker may learn to avoid an unpleasant confrontation with a supervisor by knowing the time of day when the supervisor makes rounds. The worker is either conveniently gone or too busy to have any interaction with the supervisor, thus avoiding a punishing situation. People come to work on time to *avoid* being "chewed-out" by the boss. Supervisors get their reports in on time to *avoid* being punished by their boss. Middle managers conform to established policies to

---

[16]Luthans and Kreitner, op. cit., p. 112.

**Figure 9-4
Summary of the
operational
definitions of
positive and
negative
reinforcement,
punishment, and
extinction.**

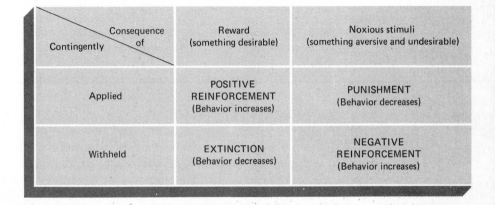

Contingently Consequence of	Reward (something desirable)	Noxious stimuli (something aversive and undesirable)
Applied	POSITIVE REINFORCEMENT (Behavior increases)	PUNISHMENT (Behavior decreases)
Withheld	EXTINCTION (Behavior decreases)	NEGATIVE REINFORCEMENT (Behavior increases)

avoid being punished by top management, and top management tries to look good on the balance sheet to *avoid* getting into trouble with the board of directors. In other words, organizational participants are exhibiting many avoidance behaviors and are under negative control. A major goal for organizational development would be somehow to turn this situation around so that organizational participants would perform appropriate behaviors because they are *positively* reinforced for doing so.

Extrinsic and intrinsic reinforcers

The distinction between extrinsic and intrinsic reinforcers is not as clear as the difference between positive and negative reinforcers. One recent study concluded that "among industrial and organizational psychologists in general, as well as those most likely to be reporting and reading motivational research, the concepts intrinsic and extrinsic convey a variety of divergent connotations. In no instance did a majority of the respondents agree on any particular definition of either of these terms."[17] Some of the representative definitions include the following:

Intrinsic rewards are those "mediated by the person himself" while extrinsic rewards are "externally mediated . . . mediated by someone other than the employee himself."[18]

Intrinsic factors are "those directly related to the actual performance of the job" and extrinsic factors are "those related to the environment in which the job is being performed."[19]

"All the intrinsic factors are internal *feelings*, while extrinsic factors are external situations."[20]

After an extensive review of such definitions and of the existing research on the two types of rewards, one researcher recently concluded that "this dichotomy of reward types, regardless of the specific criterion on which it is built, is not fruitful for understanding the nature of different work rewards."[21]

Obviously, there is a need for operational definitions of these terms if they are to be useful in the study of organizational behavior. In general, however, it can be said that an extrinsic reinforcer has no direct relationship with the behavior itself. It is external and often artificial. An example of how

[17]Lee Dyer and Donald F. Parker, "Classifying Outcomes in Work Motivation Research: An Examination of the Intrinsic-Extrinsic Dichotomy, *Journal of Applied Psychology*, August 1975, p. 457.

[18]E. L. Deci, "The Effects of Contingent and Non-Contingent Rewards and Controls on Intrinsic Motivation," *Organizational Behavior and Human Performance*, vol. 8, 1970, pp. 218–219.

[19]S. D. Saleh and T. G. Grygier, "Psychodynamics of Intrinsic and Extrinsic Job Orientation," *Journal of Applied Psychology*, vol. 53, 1969, p. 446.

[20]P. F. Wernimong, "A Systems View of Job Satisfaction," *Journal of Applied Psychology*, vol. 56, 1972, p. 173.

[21]Richard A. Guzzo, "Types of Rewards, Cognitions, and Work Motivation," *Academy of Management Review*, January 1979, p. 82.

extrinsic reward works would be the money given for a good idea in a suggestion plan. The money may reinforce a worker's putting suggestions into a box, but the money is not a natural outgrowth of this behavior. Intrinsic rewards, on the other hand, are a more natural consequence of a behavior. They create a cognitive expected relationship to the behavior itself. Organizational examples of intrinsic rewards include craftsmanship, successful completion of a difficult project, acquisition of a new skill, and performance up to capacity.[22]

The extrinsic and intrinsic concepts of reinforcement are closely related to the motivation process. For example, in an organization, money may be considered as a type of incentive in the motivation process or as an extrinsic reinforcer in the learning process. By the same token, giving a job challenge, growth, recognition, and responsibility may be considered types of motivators or intrinsic reinforcers. In general, the extrinsic reinforcers are more closely associated with the behavioristic approach and the intrinsic reinforcers are more associated with the cognitive approach. The humanistic and cognitive approaches stress the importance of the intrinsic over the extrinsic reinforcers. For example, Bass and Vaughan suggest four specific ways to make training more intrinsically rewarding to employees:

1. Stress the future utility or value of the activity or material to be learned.
2. Provide feedback during the learning experience, showing the extent to which the trainees are progressing toward the final training objectives.
3. Relate the learning activity to interesting, meaningful materials already studied outside the training program.
4. Maintain suspense as to the conclusion of a particular line of thought until all the relevant facts have been considered.[23]

The implication of the cognitive theorists is that the intrinsic reinforcers are more effective than the extrinsic. For example, Mitchell and Nebeker state that "a number of authors have presented data indicating that intrinsic factors are better motivators than extrinsic ones."[24] Edward Deci has even gone so far as to say that the use of extrinsic rewards will *decrease* intrinsic motivation. Basing his point of view on a series of laboratory studies and a peripheral field study,[25] he argues that people who are paid (extrinsic reward) to perform an interesting task will tend to attribute their behavior to external forces (i.e., have external locus of control) and the result will be a reduction in their intrinsic interest in the task. There has been considerable

---

[22]Costello and Zalkind, op. cit., p. 214.

[23]Bass and Vaughan, op. cit., p. 58.

[24]T. R. Mitchell and D. M. Nebeker, "Expectancy Theory Predictions of Academic Effort and Performance," *Journal of Applied Psychology*, vol. 57, 1973, p. 62.

[25]Deci, op. cit.; and E. L. Deci, "Effects of Externally Mediated Rewards on Intrinsic Motivation," *Journal of Personality and Social Psychology*, vol. 18, 1971, pp.105–115; and E. L. Deci, "Intrinsic Motivation, Extrinsic Reinforcement, and Inequity," *Journal of Personality and Social Psychology*, vol. 22, 1972, pp. 113–120. His generalizations from this research are found in E. L. Deci, *Intrinsic Motivation*, Plenum, New York, 1975 and E. L. Deci, "The Hidden Costs of Rewards," *Organizational Dynamics*, vol. 4, no. 3, 1976, pp. 61–72.

criticism of Deci's research methodology and conclusions.[26] Deci defends his position by contending that his critics are coming from a different theoretical base, i.e., the reinforcement-cognitive controversy.[27] But a recent comprehensive analysis reviewing both sides of the Deci controversy concludes, "The combined effects of these criticisms cast serious doubt on the accuracy of Deci's research and theorizing."[28] In any event, like many other areas in organizational behavior, the definitional problems need to be cleared up and more research is needed before any sound generalizations can be made concerning the impact that extrinsic rewards have on motivation.

Primary and secondary reinforcers

Besides making a distinction between extrinsic and intrinsic rewards, many discussions of learning divide reinforcement into primary and secondary categories. A primary reinforcer is innately satisfying to people and directly reduces their primary motivational drives. An example is the unconditioned stimulus of food in classical conditioning. The unconditioned stimulus is an unlearned reward for the organism. Primary rewards are largely used in simple learning situations. Food and candy are effective reinforcers in basic conditioning, such as in teaching children to do simple tasks or in behavior therapy for mental patients. In more complex human learning situations like those in modern organizations, secondary rewards are much more frequently used and are more effective than the primary rewards.

A secondary reinforcer results from previous association with a primary reinforcer. Whereas the primary reward is innately satisfying, the secondary reward must be learned. Starting in infancy, many neutral stimuli acquire reinforcing properties. A mother who feeds her infant milk (primary reward) soon becomes a secondary reinforcer herself. These learned secondary rewards play a vital role in understanding the more complex aspects of human behavior.

Numerous social stimuli serve as secondary reinforcers for human

---

[26]B. J. Calder and B. M. Staw, "Interaction of Intrinsic and Extrinsic Motivation: Some Methodological Notes," *Journal of Personality and Social Psychology*, vol. 31, 1975, pp. 76–80; Fred Luthans, Mark Martinko, and Thomas Kess, "An Analysis of the Impact of Contingent Monetary Rewards on Intrinsic Motivation," *Proceedings of the Midwest Academy of Management*, 1976, pp. 209–221; W. W. Notz, "Work Motivation and the Negative Effects of Extrinsic Rewards: A Review with Implications for Theory and Practice," *American Psychologist*, vol. 30, 1975, pp. 884–891; G. R. Salancik, "Interaction Effects of Performance and Money on Self-Perception of Intrinsic Motivation," *Organizational Behavior and Human Performance*, vol. 13, 1975, pp. 339–351; and W. E. Scott, "The Effects of Extrinsic Rewards on Intrinsic Motivation," *Organizational Behavior and Human Performance*, vol. 15, 1975, pp. 117–129.

[27]E. L. Deci, W. F. Cascio, and J. Krusell, "Cognitive Evaluation Theory and Some Comments on the Calder, Staw Critique," *Journal of Personality and Social Psychology*, vol. 31, 1975, pp. 81–85; and E. L. Deci, "Notes on the Theory and Metatheory on Intrinsic Motivation," *Organizational Behavior and Human Performance*, vol. 15, 1975, pp. 130–145.

[28]Larry E. Pate, "Cognitive Versus Reinforcement Views of Intrinsic Motivation," *Academy of Management Review*, July 1978, p. 510.

behavior.[29] Four of the more common forms relevant to organizational behavior are the following:

1. *Attention.* The mere visual stimulus of paying attention by looking at or responding to another human being is reinforcing. Managers giving their full attention to subordinates' ideas will reinforce participative behavior on the part of subordinates.
2. *Approval.* A visual stimulus of one person's affirmative nod or smile is reinforcing to another person. The same is true of a verbal stimulus indicating approval. A manager nodding his or her head or voicing approval of a suggestion from a subordinate would reinforce the subordinate's behavior.
3. *Affection.* Visual, verbal, and physical expressions of affections are an important form of reinforcement for human beings. A manager who expresses genuine affection for a subordinate will reinforce the subordinate's efforts to please the boss.
4. *Tokens.* Various types of tokens are probably the most consciously used type of secondary reinforcement for human behavior. Money is the best example. The adage "You cannot eat money" points out that money is not a primary reinforcer. Yet money remains an extremely important reinforcer, because many people believe that another adage, "Money will buy everything except possibly happiness," is true. Outstanding performance is reinforced by contingently administered raises and bonuses in an organization.

When each of these four secondary reinforcers is applied as a consequence and the behavior strengthens and increases, they are positive reinforcers. By the same token, their counterparts of lack of attention, disapproval, dislike, and docking of pay may act as negative reinforcers by strengthening and increasing behavior by their termination, or these can be punishing by their presentation. In the punishing case, presenting these as a consequence would weaken the behavior and decrease its subsequent frequency.

TECHNIQUES OF ADMINISTERING REINFORCEMENT

The preceding discussion was primarily concerned with the theoretical basis and categories of reinforcement. The role of reinforcement in the study of organizational behavior cannot be overemphasized. It plays a central role in human resource management areas such as training, appraisal, adaptation to change, and performance. Modification of certain specific aspects of organizational behavior, such as tardiness or participation, and overall organization development also depend upon reinforcement. Reinforcement will increase the strength of desired organizational behavior and the probability of its being repeated. As Bandura stated over a decade ago, "all behavior is inevitably controlled, and the operation of psychological laws cannot be suspended by romantic conceptions of human behavior, any more than indignant rejection of the law of gravity as antihumanistic can stop

---

[29]See Arthur W. Staats and Carolyn K. Staats, *Complex Human Behavior,* Holt, New York, 1963, p. 54.

people from falling."[30] Reinforcement is just such a law of psychology, and the research findings on its impact on organizational behavior can be summarized as follows:

1. Some type of reinforcement (reward or knowledge of successful performance) is necessary to produce change.
2. Some types of rewards are more effective for use in the organization than are others.
3. How fast learning takes place and also how lasting its effects will be is determined by the timing of reinforcement.[31]

The last point brings out the importance of administering reinforcement.

During the acquisition phase of classical conditioning experiments, every conditioned response is reinforced. This seldom occurs in reality. Human behavior in organizations or everyday life is generally reinforced on an intermittent or random basis. The exact pattern and timing of the reinforcement have a tremendous impact on the resulting behavior. In other words, how the reward is administered can greatly influence the specific organizational behavior that takes place. The four major techniques of administering rewards are fixed ratio, fixed interval, variable ratio, and variable interval.

Fixed ratio schedule

If a schedule is administered on a ratio basis, reinforcement is given after a certain *number* of responses. If the schedule is a fixed ratio, the exact number of responses is specified. A fixed ratio that reinforces after every response is designated as 1:1. The 1:1 fixed ratio is generally used in basic conditioning experiments, and almost every type of learning situation must begin with this schedule. However, as learning progresses, it is more effective to shift to a fixed ratio of 2:1, 4:1, 8:1, and even 20:1. To illustrate the extreme, Skinner was able to obtain responses from rats at a fixed ratio of 192:1.

Administering reward under a fixed ratio schedule tends to produce a high rate of response that is characterized as vigorous and steady. The person soon determines that reinforcement is based on the number of responses and performs the responses as quickly as possible in order to receive the reward. A common example of how the fixed ratio schedule is applied to industrial organizations is the piece-rate incentive system. Production workers are paid on the basis of how many pieces they produce (number of responses). Other things being equal, the worker's performance responses should be energetic and steady. In reality, of course, other things are not always equal, and a piece-rate incentive system may not lead to this type of behavior. Nevertheless, knowledge of the effects of the various methods of administering reward would be extremely valuable in analyzing employee-incentive systems.

---

[30]Albert Bandura, *Principles of Behavior Modification*, Holt, New York, 1969, p. 85.
[31]Costello and Zalkind, op. cit., p. 193.

Fixed interval schedule

The other most common way to administer reward is on a fixed interval basis. Under this schedule, reinforcement is given after a specified period of *time*, which is measured from the last reinforced response. The length of time that can be used by this schedule varies a great deal. In the beginning of practically any learning situation, a very short interval is required. However, as learning progresses, the interval can be stretched out. Skinner was able to make pigeons respond when rewards were as much as forty-five minutes apart, and more recently, experiments have successfully expanded the interval to several hours.

Behavior resulting from a fixed interval method of reinforcing is quite different from that exhibited by a fixed ratio. Whereas under fixed ratio there is a steady, vigorous response pattern, under fixed interval there is an uneven pattern that varies from a very slow, unenergetic response immediately following reinforcement to a very fast, vigorous response immediately preceding reinforcement. This type of behavior pattern can be explained by the fact that the person figures out that another reward will not immediately follow the last one. Therefore, the person may as well relax a little until it is time to be rewarded again. A common example of administering reward on a fixed interval schedule is the payment of employees by the hour, week, or month. Monetary reinforcement comes at the end of a period of time. In practice, however, even though people are paid by the hour, they receive their reward only weekly, biweekly, or monthly. Whether for pigeons or humans, this time interval is generally too long to be an effective form of reinforcement for the work-related behavior.

Variable or intermittent schedules

Both ratio and interval schedules can be administered on a variable or intermittent basis. This means that the reinforcement is given in an irregular or unsystematic manner. In variable ratio, the reward is given after a number of responses, but the exact number is randomly varied. When the variable ratio is expressed as some number, say 50, this means that on the *average* the organism is reinforced after 50 responses. However, in reality the ratio may randomly vary between 1:1 to 1:100. In other words, each response has a chance of being reinforced regardless of the number of reinforced or nonreinforced responses that have preceded it.

The variable interval schedule works basically the same as the variable ratio except that reward is given after a randomly distributed length of time rather than after a number of responses. A 50-minute variable interval schedule means that on the *average*, the individual is reinforced after 50 minutes, but the actual reinforcement may be given anywhere from a few seconds to several hours.

Behavior under variable schedules   Both variable ratio and variable interval schedules tend to produce stable, vigorous behavior. The behavior under variable schedules is similar to that produced by a fixed ratio schedule. Under the variable schedules, the person has no idea when reward is coming, so the behavior tends to be steady and strong. It logically follows that the variable schedules are very resistant to extinction.

Variable schedules are not very effective in highly controlled learning experiments and are seldom used. On the other hand, they are the way in which many real-life everyday learning situations are reinforced. Although primary reinforcers for humans are administered on a relatively fixed basis, e.g., food is given three times a day at mealtimes, and organization compensation plans are on either a fixed ratio or an interval basis, most of the other human behavior that takes place is reinforced in a highly variable manner. For example, practically all the social rewards are administered on a variable basis. Attention, approval, and affection are generally given as rewards in a very random fashion.

Examples of variable schedules   Variable reinforcement schedules play the most important role in most organizational behavior situations. Although piece-rate or day-rate payments for job performance appear on the surface to be fixed schedules, by paying on a biweekly or monthly basis, the supposedly fixed schedule becomes in reality no reinforcement for day-to-day job behaviors at all. Unfortunately, in most cases, all the weekly or monthly paycheck does is reinforce walking up to the pay window or opening the pay envelope. Consequently, organizational participants' job behaviors largely depend upon variably administered social rewards from supervisors and coworkers.

The variable schedule can be administered on a formal basis by an organization. The most common example is its application to the sales people who work on a commission. The salesperson's reinforcement (commission for a sale) is highly variable on either a ratio or an interval basis. The salesperson experiences a variable ratio when the commission depends upon the number of customers contacted, but a variable interval when it depends upon when the salesperson last called on the customer.

Administration of reinforcement in human resource management

The fixed ratio and interval and the variable ratio and interval are not the only methods of administering reward. Many other possible combinations exist. However, these four schedules are the way most employees in today's organizations are reinforced. These schedules greatly affect both the modification and extinction of organizational behavior. Staats and Staats note, "Not only do these intermittent schedules produce characteristically different rates of maintenance of the response, but, in addition, once reinforcement has been discontinued, different extinction rates are also produced."[32]

---

[32]Staats and Staats, op. cit., p. 65.

Much of the learning and resulting behavior of every worker, supervisor, salesperson, engineer, and executive is determined by when and how they are reinforced.

There is a growing research literature on the impact that continuous versus variable schedules have on employee performance. The problem is, however, that the results of job simulation studies conducted with student subjects in laboratory settings have different results than those studies using actual workers in a field setting. The lab studies found that the variable schedules led to better performance.[33] This verified what the operant learning theorists had been saying over the years. However, a couple of studies conducted on tree-planting crews found that the continuous schedules of reinforcement actually led to better performance.[34] Both the laboratory and, especially, the field studies had definite methodological problems that prevent any sound conclusions. A recent follow-up study of the tree-planting crews did try to eliminate some of the problems and still found that the employees as a whole performed better on the continuous schedule of reinforcement.[35] Yet despite this overall finding, the researchers recognize that some limitations still remain and that there are individual differences. For example, the inexperienced subjects worked better on a continuous schedule but the experienced workers did better on the variable schedule.

Although the research results on the application of schedules are not yet very clear, there are still some guidelines that can be given for effective human resource management. For example, the timing of the reward should be kept as close to the desired response as possible, not two weeks or a month away, as in the case of most of today's employees' paychecks. In addition, ratio schedules are generally more desirable than interval schedules because they tend to produce steady, strong responses, but as the discussion of the research indicated, specific guidance in the use of continuous versus variable schedules cannot yet be given. Although some types of employees may work better under continuous schedules, variable schedules may be better for other types of employees and certainly are more resistant to extinction. Understanding and then applying what is known about the administration of reinforcement can be of great assistance to

---

[33]G. A. Yukl, K. N. Wexley, and J. D. Seymore, "Effectiveness of Pay Incentives Under Variable Ratio and Continuous Reinforcement Schedules," *Journal of Applied Psychology*, vol. 56, 1972, pp. 19–23; and C. J. Berger, L. L. Cummings, and H. G. Heneman, III, "Expectancy Theory and Operant Conditioning Predictions of Performance Under Variable Ratio and Continuous Schedules of Reinforcement," *Organizational Behavior and Human Performance*, vol. 14, 1975, pp. 227–243.

[34]Gary A. Yukl and Gary P. Latham, "Consequences of Reinforcement Schedules and Incentive Magnitudes for Employee Performance: Problems Encountered in an Industrial Setting," *Journal of Applied Psychology*, vol. 60, 1975, pp. 294–298; and G. A. Yukl, G. P. Latham, and E. D. Pursell, "The Effectiveness of Performance Incentives Under Continuous and Variable Ratio Schedules of Reinforcement," *Personnel Psychology*, vol. 29, 1976, pp. 221–231.

[35]Gary P. Latham and Dennis L. Dossett, "Designing Incentive Plans for Unionized Employees: A Comparison of Continuous and Variable Ratio Reinforcement Schedules," *Personnel Psychology*, Spring 1978, 47–61.

modern human resource managers. In fact, one of the most important functions of all managers may well be the way they administer reinforcement to their people. The next chapter carries this discussion further by giving specific attention to behavioral-change strategies for modern human resource management.

THE EFFECT OF PUNISHMENT

Punishment is one of the most used but least understood and badly administered aspects of learning. Whether in rearing children or dealing with subordinates in a complex organization, parents and supervisors often revert to punishment instead of positive reinforcement in order to modify or control behavior. Punishment is commonly thought to be the reverse of reinforcement but equally effective in altering behavior. However, most psychologists discount this widely held view of punishment:

Reward tends to increase the probability of response's future occurrence; the effect of punishment cannot be said, unequivocally, to decrease its probability . . . If we are seeking a way to find punishment to be the opposite of reward, perhaps the answer can be found by saying the impact of reward on behavior is simple (it reinforces it); the impact of punishment on behavior is complex.[36]

In other words, punishment is a very complex phenomenon and must be carefully defined and used.

The definition of punishment

The meaning of *punishment* was mentioned in the discussion of extinction and negative reinforcement. To reiterate, punishment is anything which weakens behavior and tends to decrease its subsequent frequency. The punishment process is very close to extinction—both have the effect of decreasing the behavioral frequency—but technically there is a difference. Punishment usually consists of the *application* of an undesirable or noxious consequence but can also be defined as the *withdrawal* of a desirable consequence that is normally in the person's environment *before* the undesirable behavior occurs. Extinction, on the other hand, is the *withdrawal* of a desirable consequence that is contingent upon the person's behavior. The withdrawal of the desirable consequence under extinction occurs *after* the behavior is emitted. Thus, taking away certain organizational privileges from a manager who has a poor performance record could be thought of as punishing him or her, and moving a very friendly, talkative typist to another part of the office could be thought of as an extinction strategy for the receptionist's socializing behavior.

Regardless of the distinction between extinction and punishment, in order for punishment to occur, there must be a weakening and decrease in

---

[36]Costello and Zalkind, op. cit., p. 215.

the behavior which preceded it. Just because a supervisor gives a "tongue lashing" to a subordinate and thinks this is punishment, it is not necessarily that unless the behavior that preceded the "tongue lashing" weakens and decreases. In many cases when supervisors think they are punishing employees, they are in fact reinforcing them because they are giving attention, and attention tends to be very reinforcing. This explains the common complaint that supervisors often make: "I call Joe in, give him heck for goofing up, and he goes right back out and goofs up again." What is happening is that the supervisor thinks Joe is being punished, when operationally what is obviously happening is that the supervisor is reinforcing Joe's undesirable behavior by giving attention and recognition.

Administering punishment

Opinions on administering punishment range all the way from the one extreme of dire warnings never to use it to the other extreme that it is the only effective way to modify behavior. As yet, research has not been able to support either view completely. However, there is little doubt that the use of punishment tends to cause many undesirable side effects. Neither children nor adults like to be punished. The punished behavior tends to be only temporarily suppressed rather than permanently changed, and the punished person tends to get anxious or "up tight" and resentful of the punisher. The following summarizes some of the major difficulties in the use of punishment and some ways to more effectively administer it:

1. Punishment is effective in modifying behavior if it forces the person to select a desirable alternative behavior that is then reinforced.
2. If the above doesn't occur, then the behavior will be only temporarily suppressed and will reappear when the punishment is removed. Furthermore, the suppressed behavior may cause the person to become fearful and anxious.
3. Punishment is much more effective when applied at the time the undesirable behavior is actually performed than at a later time.
4. Punishment must be administered with extreme care so that it doesn't become a reward for undesirable behavior. The termination of punishment is reinforcing just as the termination of reinforcement is punishing.[37]

These four points should be considered when administering punishment in an organization. The persons administering punishment must always provide an acceptable alternative to the behavior that is being punished. If they do not, the undesirable behavior will tend to reappear and will cause fear and anxiety in the person being punished. The punishment must always be administered as close in time to the undesirable behavior as possible. Calling persons into the office to give them a reprimand for breaking a rule the week before is not effective. All the reprimand tends to do at this time is punish them for getting caught. It has little effect on the rule-breaking behavior. The fourth point above calls attention to the care that must be exercised so that what is intended as punishment does not in fact act

---

[37]Howard H. Kendler, *Basic Psychology*, 2d ed., Appleton-Century-Crofts, New York, 1968, pp. 290–291.

as a reward for the recipient. A supervisor who shouts at a worker may be rewarding this individual's position as the informal leader of a work-restricting group. The same is true of the example, given in the last section, of punishment turning into rewarding attention. It is very easy for supervisors or managers to use punishment but very difficult for them to effectively administer punishment so as to modify or change undesirable behavior. A simple rule of thumb for managers should be: Always attempt to reinforce instead of punish in order to change behavior. As discussed earlier, the use of an extinction strategy (nonreinforcement) is usually more effective in decelerating undesirable behaviors than is punishment, because the bad side effects do not accompany extinction. The next chapter will get into these behavioral-change strategies in more depth and will apply them more directly to human resource management.

SUMMARY

Learning is a major psychological process that has been largely neglected in the study of organizational behavior. It has not been generally recognized that there are different types of learning and different theoretical explanations of learning (behavioristic, cognitive, and social). Despite the controversy surrounding learning theory, there are many accepted principles of learning. Principles such as learning curves, extinction, spontaneous recovery, generalization, and discrimination are largely derived from experimentation and the analysis of classical and operant conditioning. Reinforcement is the single most important concept in the learning process and is most relevant to the study of organizational behavior. Based on the classic law of effect, reinforcement can be operationally defined as anything that increases the strength of response and that tends to induce repetitions of the behavior that preceded the reinforcement. Rewards may be positive or negative, extrinsic or intrinsic, or primary or secondary. They may be administered on a fixed ratio or interval, or on a variable ratio or interval basis. The effective administration of reinforcement and punishment may be one of the most critical challenges facing modern human resource management.

QUESTIONS FOR DISCUSSION AND REVIEW

1. Do you agree with the statement, "Learning is involved in almost everything that everyone does?" Explain.
2. What are the major dimensions of behavioristic, cognitive, and social learning theories?
3. What is the difference between classical and operant conditioning?
4. Apply three of the learning principles to the modern workplace.
5. What is the difference between positive and negative reinforcement? What is the difference between negative reinforcement and punishment?

6. What are some common forms of secondary reinforcers relevant to organizational behavior?

7. Why is the administration of reinforcement so vitally important to learning and management practice?

8. Make pro and con arguments for punishment.

CASE:
CONTRASTING STYLES

Henry Adams has been a production supervisor for eight years. He came up through the ranks and is known as a tough, but hard working, supervisor. Jerry Wake has been a production supervisor for about the same length of time and also came up through the ranks. Jerry is known as a nice, hard working guy. Over the past several years these two supervisors' sections have been head and shoulders above the other six sections on hard measures of performance (number of units produced). This is true despite the almost opposite approaches the two have taken in handling their workers. Henry explained his approach as follows:

The only way to handle workers is to come down hard on them whenever they make a mistake. In fact, I call them together every once in a while and give them heck whether they deserve it or not, just to keep them on their toes. If they are doing a good job, I tell them that's what they're getting paid for. By taking this approach, all I have to do is walk through my area, and people start working like mad.

Jerry explained his approach as follows:

I don't believe in that human relations stuff of being nice to workers. But I do believe that a worker deserves some recognition and attention from me if he or she does a good job. If people make a mistake, I don't jump on them. I feel that we are all entitled to make some errors. On the other hand, I always do point out what the mistake was and what they should have done, and as soon as they do it right I let them know it. Obviously, I don't have time to give attention to everyone doing things right, but I deliberately try to get around to people doing a good job every once in a while.

Although Henry's section is still right at the top along with Jerry's section in units produced, personnel records show that there has been three times more turnover in Henry's section than in Jerry's section, and the quality control records show that Henry's section has met quality standards only twice in the last six years but Jerry's has missed attaining quality standards only once in the last six years.

1. Both of these supervisors have similar backgrounds. On the basis of learning, how can you explain their opposite approaches to handling people?

2. What are some of the examples of punishment, positive reinforcement, and negative reinforcement found in this case? What schedule of reinforcement is Jerry using? If Jerry is using a reinforcement approach, how do you explain this statement, "I don't believe in that human relations stuff of being nice to people"?

3. How do you explain the performance, turnover, and quality results in these two sections of the production department?

CASE:
VOLUNTEERS CAN'T BE PUN- ISHED

Ann-Marie Jackson was the head of a volunteer agency in a large city. She was in charge of a volunteer staff of over twenty-five people. Weekly she would hold a meeting with this group in order to keep them informed and teach them the specifics of any new laws or changes in state and federal policies and procedures that might affect their work, and she would discuss priorities and assignments for the group. This meeting was also a time when members could share some of their problems and concerns for what they were personally doing and what the agency as a whole was doing. The meeting was scheduled to begin at 9 A.M. sharp every Monday. Lately, the volunteers have been filtering in every five minutes or so until almost 10 A.M. Ann-Marie felt she had to delay the start of the meeting until all the people arrived. The last few weeks the meetings haven't started until 10 A.M.; in fact, at 9 A.M. nobody has shown up. Ann-Marie cannot understand what has happened. She feels it is important to start the meetings right at 9 A.M. so it can be over by 10 or 10:30 and the whole morning isn't gone. On the other hand, she feels that her hands are tied because, after all, they are volunteers and she can't punish them or make them get to the meeting on time.

1. What advice would you give Ann-Marie? In terms of reinforcement theory explain what is happening here and what Ann-Marie needs to do to get the meetings started on time.
2. What learning theories (behavioristic, cognitive, and/or social) could be applied to Ann-Marie's efforts to teach her volunteers the impact of new laws and changes in state and federal policies and procedures?
3. How could someone like Ann-Marie use modeling to train her staff to do a more effective job?

CHAPTER 13

ORGANIZATIONAL
BEHAVIOR MODIFICATION

O.B. MOD. IN A FEDERAL AGENCY*

Pressures are increasing to improve performance and reduce costs in public sector agencies. The United States General Accounting Office (GAO) recently responded to these damands by implementing an organizational behavior modification (O. B. Mod.) program in the payroll and travel units. Supervisors in these units were essentially trained in the O.B. Mod. approach, which consists of *identifying* critical performance behavior; *measuring* the frequency of occurrence; *analyzing* the antecedents and consequences of the behavior; *intervening* with positive reinforcers and feedback; and *evaluating* to make sure performance is in fact improving. The results of this O.B. Mod. approach are very impressive. The six critical performance measures, e.g., number of vouchers audited or processing time, in the travel unit had a mean improvement of 78 percent. Where dollar amounts could be attached to the performance measures, this translated to annual cost savings in the payroll unit of $112,000; in the travel unit dollar savings were only relevant to one measure, but this amounted to a $35,000 reduction. The less quantifiable improvements attributed to the O.B. Mod. program included increased credibility, morale, and pride in the units, the removal of a crisis atmosphere, and a general shift to a positive work environment.

---

*Adapted from Craig E. Schneier, Robert Pernick, and David E. Bryant, Jr., "Improving Performance in the Public Sector Through Behavior Modification and Positive Reinforcement," *Public Personnel Management,* March–April 1979, pp. 101–110.

Chapter 3 introduced the environment-based behavioristic approach to organizational behavior. This approach emphasizes the important role that the environment plays in organizational behavior. In particular, the B-C (Behavior-Consequence) part of the S-O-B-C model of organizational behavior recognizes the importance of environmental consequences in the prediction and control of organizational behavior. The last chapter added some depth of understanding to this approach by explaining learning concepts, especially reinforcement. With the exception of these two chapters, the chapters in this part on motivation have been presented mainly from an internal, cognitive perspective.

This chapter is specifically devoted to an applied, environmental approach to the practice of human resource management. Observable behaviors and their direct impact on performance effectiveness are the focus of attention. The concepts and techniques presented in this chapter are not proposed as an alternative to the more traditional and widely accepted methods of human resource management presented in the other chapters. Instead, the suggested behavioral approach in this chapter is meant to supplement and to be used in combination with other approaches.

The first part of the chapter builds on the material that was given in Chapters 3 and 9. Background information on the use of organizational behavior modification, or more simply O.B. Mod., is given. Then almost the entire chapter is devoted to a fairly detailed explanation and analysis of this approach to human resource management. All the steps of O.B. Mod. (identify, measure, analyze, intervene, and evaluate) are given attention, but relatively more attention is given to the intervention strategies that can be used to change organizational behaviors. The last part of the chapter reports in detail some actual experiences and research findings on the application of O.B. Mod. in practicing organizations. Finally, some of the possible ethical implications are presented and analyzed.

BACKGROUND FOR O.B. MOD.

O.B. Mod. has its roots in modern behaviorism. Modern behaviorism stems from the significant distinction that B. F. Skinner made between respondent or reflexive behaviors, which are the result of classical conditioning, and operant behaviors, which are the result of operant conditioning (see Chapter 9 for a detailed discussion of the difference). In today's complex organizations, very few of the behaviors of participants are the result of classical conditioning; the mechanistic S-R type of behaviorism is of little value for analyzing or changing organizational behaviors. Operant conditioning is a much better basis for the pragmatic analysis and change of organizational behavior. Although a social learning approach as outlined in Chapters 3 and 9 has been suggested as a more comprehensive theoretical base for the understanding of organizational behavior and for application areas such modeling or self-management, the operant approach, with its premise that organizational behavior is a function of its consequences, can lead to the prediction and control of organizational behavior. Thus, O.B. Mod. is based on an operant approach to organizational behavior. The social-learning-based self-management technique will be covered in Chapter 22.

Behavior modification techniques

The basic principles of behavior modification were developed by Skinner and his colleagues mainly using lower animal subjects under highly controlled laboratory conditions. The application of Skinner's principles as a behavioral change strategy for humans had its beginnings in the mental health field. Through the systematic management of antecedent and consequent environments, clinical psychologists were able to dramatically change the behaviors of their patients (the mentally retarded, psychotics, and autistic children). For example, mentally retarded patients were systematically taught to take care of themselves, psychotically disturbed patients who had been silent for many years were shaped to the point where they carried on a conversation, and autistic children's self-destructive behaviors were eliminated. Such changes in behaviors were often attained with patients who had had years of traditional psychotherapeutic and medical treatments, with no noticeable effect. No one denies that behavior modification has had a tremendous impact on the treatment of mental patients in recent years.

The next major thrust of the application of Skinnerian behaviorism has been in education. In particular, behavior modification has been used in both classroom instruction techniques and child management problems. For example, it has been successfully used in the acquisition of language and other intellectual skills and in the modification of undesirable behaviors of problem children in a classroom. Many of today's teachers systematically manage their classroom environment to accelerate desirable behaviors and decelerate undesirable behaviors. Although the approach is still controversial, most would agree with the conclusion of one comprehensive review of the literature, "Operant Conditioning in the Classroom Setting," "It appears that the entry of the behavior modifiers into the public-school classroom has shown that the techniques and designs developed for behavioral control in the laboratory are applicable in natural settings."[1]

The application to organizational behavior and human resource management

The natural extension of the application of behavior modification from mental hospitals and classrooms would be to the more complex, less controlled environment of work organizations. Only recently has this been attempted. Although suggestions on the use of operant techniques in managing people can be found as far back as twenty years ago,[2] only in the

---

[1]Karl I. Altman and Thomas E. Linton, "Operant Conditioning in the Classroom Setting," *The Journal of Educational Research*, February 1971, reprinted in Roger Ulrich, Thomas Stachnik, and John Mabry (eds.), *Control of Human Behavior*, vol. 3, Scott, Foresman, Glenview, Ill., 1974, p. 86. This volume contains many other classic studies on the applications of behavior modification to education. The other two volumes contain applications to other settings.

[2]Owen Aldis, "Of Pigeons and Men," *Harvard Business Review*, July–August 1961, pp. 59–63.

last few years have systematic theory, research, and application of the operant approach to human resource management been attempted. In one of the first comprehensive articles in 1969, Walter Nord pointed to the fact that the work of Skinner had been almost completely ignored by the field of management. He suggested how the operant model could be applied to training and personnel development, job design, compensation, and organization design, and in a follow-up article he described how attendance may be improved.[3] Shortly after, Luthans and White suggested the direct application of behavior modification to human resource management in general, and Adam and Scott reported research results on the application of behavioral conditioning to quality control.[4] With this start, the theoretical underpinnings and practical applications for an operant, environmental approach to human resource management called "organizational behavior modification" or simply "O.B. Mod." has been developed.[5] By adding the word "organizational" to behavior modification, the distinction is made between the application to human resource management in work organizations and the more traditional applications to mental health and education.

Figure 10-1 briefly traces the theoretical paths of development. On one path is the development of behaviorism into behavior modification, and on the other is the development of the behavioral approach to management into organizational behavior. The combination of these two paths of development is *O.B. Mod.* The approach was introduced in the first edition of this book but was given only minor attention. The first comprehensive treatment of all aspects of O.B. Mod. (theory, research, and application) appeared in the book titled *Organizational Behavior Modification*, authored by Luthans and

---

[3]Walter R. Nord, "Beyond the Teaching Machine: The Neglected Area of Operant Conditioning in the Theory and Practice of Management," *Organizational Behavior and Human Performance,* November 1969, pp. 375–401 and Walter R. Nord, "Improving Attendance through Rewards," *Personnel Administration,* vol. 33, no. 6, 1970, pp. 37–41.

[4]Fred Luthans and Donald White, "Behavior Modification: Application to Manpower Management," *Personnel Administration,* July–August 1971, pp. 41–47 and E. E. Adam and William E. Scott, "The Application of Behavior Conditioning to the Problems of Quality Control," *Academy of Management Journal,* June 1971, pp. 175–193.

[5]See: Fred Luthans and Robert Kreitner, "The Role of Punishment in Organizational Behavior Modification (O.B. Mod.)," *Public Personnel Management,* May–June 1973, pp. 156–161; Fred Luthans and David Lyman, "Training Supervisors to Use Organizational Behavior Modification," *Personnel,* September–October 1973, pp. 38–44; Fred Luthans and Robert Ottemann, "Motivation vs. Learning Approaches to Organizational Behavior," *Business Horizons,* December 1973, pp. 55–62; Fred Luthans and Robert Kreitner, "The Management of Behavioral Contingencies," *Personnel,* July–August 1974, pp. 7–16; Fred Luthans and Mark Martinko, "An O.B. Mod. Analysis of Absenteeism," *Human Resource Management,* Fall 1976, pp. 11–18; Fred Luthans, "An Organizational Behavior Modification (O.B. Mod.) Approach to O.D.," *Organization and Administrative Sciences,* Winter 1975/1976, pp. 47–53; and Fred Luthans and Mark J. Martinko, *The Power of Positive Reinforcement: A Workbook on O.B. Mod.,* McGraw-Hill, New York, 1978. For comprehensive reviews of closely related approaches see: Donald M. Prue, Lee W. Frederiksen, and Ansley Bacon, "Organizational Behavior Management: An Annotated Bibliography," *Journal of Organizational Behavior Management,* Summer 1978, pp. 216–257; and Harold W. Bobb and Daniel G. Kopp, "Applications of Behavior Modification in Organizations: A Review and Critique," *Academy of Management Review,* April 1978, pp. 281–292.

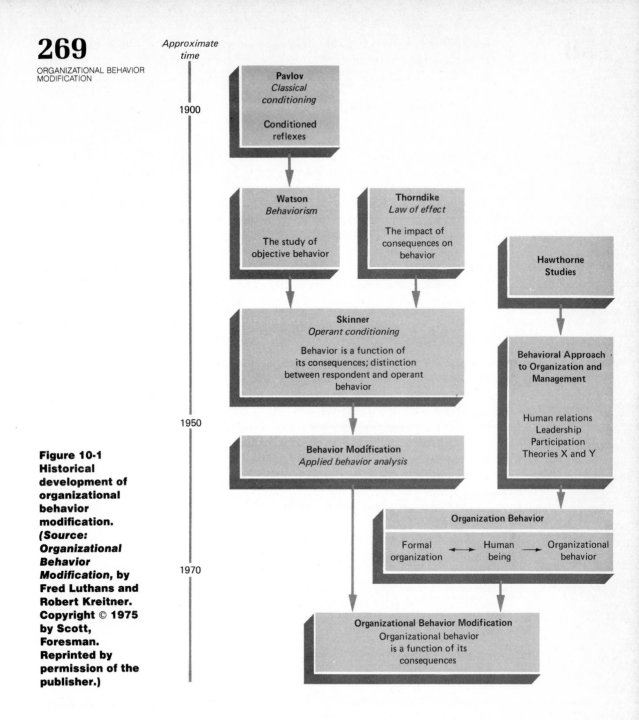

Figure 10-1 Historical development of organizational behavior modification. (Source: *Organizational Behavior Modification*, by Fred Luthans and Robert Kreitner. Copyright © 1975 by Scott, Foresman. Reprinted by permission of the publisher.)

Kreitner.[6] The rest of this chapter summarizes this approach to human resource management.

THE STEPS OF O.B. MOD.

As a specific approach to human resource management, O.B. Mod. can be portrayed as a five-step problem-solving model. Figure 10-2 shows this model. O.B. Mod. can be used in a step-by-step process to actually change performance-related behaviors of personnel in today's organizations. Again, the reader should be reminded that O.B. Mod. represents only one technique, but there are other techniques, such as goal setting and job enrichment discussed in Chapter 8 and the techniques discussed in the last part of the book, which can all be selectively used (desirably in a contingency framework) to effectively manage human resources. The following sections discuss the various steps of O.B. Mod.; then, experience with its application is reported and ethical implications are analyzed.

Step 1: Identification of critical behaviors

In this first step the critical behaviors that make a significant impact on performance (making or selling widgets, or service to clients or customers) are identified. In every organization, regardless of type or level, numerous behaviors are occurring all the time. Some of these behaviors have a significant impact on performance and some of them do not. The goal of the first step of O.B. Mod. is to identify the critical behaviors—the 5 to 10 percent of the behaviors that may account for up to 70 or 80 percent of the performance in the area in question.

Methods of identifying critical behaviors   The process of identifying the critical behaviors can be carried out in a couple of ways. One approach is to have the person closest to the job in question, the immediate supervisor or the actual jobholder, determine the critical behaviors. This goes hand in hand with using O.B. Mod. as a problem-solving approach for the individual manager. Its advantages are that the person who knows the job best can most accurately identify the critical behaviors, and, by participating, that person may be more committed to carrying the O.B. Mod. process to its successful completion.

Another approach to identifying critical behaviors would be to conduct a systematic *behavioral audit*. The audit would use internal staff specialists and/or outside consultants. The audit would systematically analyze each job in question, in the manner that jobs are analyzed in job analysis techniques commonly used in personnel administration. The advantages of the personal approach (where the jobholder and/or the immediate supervisor makes a vital input into the audit) can be realized by the audit. In addition, the

[6]Fred Luthans and Robert Kreitner, *Organizational Behavior Modification*, Scott, Foresman, Glenview, Ill., 1975.

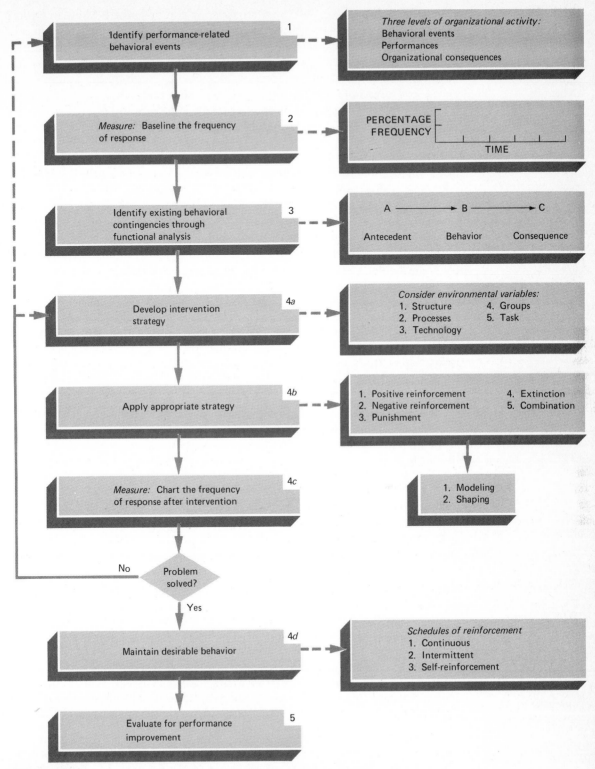

Figure 10-2
Steps in O.B. Mod. (*Source:* Fred Luthans and Robert Kreitner, "The Management of Behavioral Contingencies," *Personnel,* July–August 1974, p. 13.)

advantages of staff expertise and consistency can be gained. Such an audit approach has been successfully used in the widely publicized behavioral management program at Emery Air Freight.[7] Even if an outside audit identifies the critical behaviors, it is usually the supervisor of the area in question who performs the succeeding steps in O.B. Mod. In the future, if an entire organization sets up behavioral systems and takes an O.B. Mod. approach to total organization development,[8] there could be more involvement of staff specialists in the succeeding steps in O.B. Mod.

Guidelines for identifying critical behaviors   Regardless of the method used, there are certain guidelines that can be helpful in identifying critical behaviors. First, only observable, countable behaviors are included. An employee's "bad attitude" and someone who "goofs off all the time" are unacceptable. Attitudes and a lack of motivation are unobservable inner states of people. Only observables—behaviors that can be seen (e.g., absenteeism or attendance, tardiness or promptness, complaints or constructive comments, and doing or not doing a particular task or procedure that leads to quantity and/or quality outcomes) play a role in O.B. Mod. Something like "goofing off" is not acceptable because it is not operationally measurable. It could be broken down into observable, measurable behaviors such as not being at the work station, being tardy when returning from breaks, spending time at the water cooler, disrupting coworkers, and even flirting with the opposite sex. To be identified as a critical behavior there must be a positive answer to the questions (1) can it be seen? and (2) can it be measured?

Another helpful guideline for identifying critical behaviors is to work backward from an obvious performance deficiency. Just as not all behaviors contribute to performance, (e.g., complaining behavior may have nothing to do with performance), not all performance problems can be traced to behaviors. For example, the cause of poor performance of a production unit in a manufacturing organization may be faulty machinery or poorly trained workers (they do not know the proper procedures) or unrealistically high production standards. Each of these possible causes is not, at least directly, a behavioral problem. The same is true of the person who does not have the ability to produce at an acceptable level. This is a selection problem, not a behavioral problem. However, after noting the possibility of non-behaviorally-related performance problems, it should be emphasized that in general such problems are the exception rather than the rule. Most organizations are not having problems with their technology or the ability of their people, but they have many behaviorally related performance prob-

---

[7]"Performance Audit, Feedback, and Positive Reinforcement," *Training and Development Journal*, November 1972, pp. 8–13; and "At Emery Air Freight: Positive Reinforcement Boosts Performance," *Organizational Dynamics*, Winter 1973, pp. 41–50.

[8]An example of such a total organization development approach can be found in Luthans and Kreitner, *Organizational Behavior Modification*, op. cit., pp. 164–170, and Fred Luthans and Jason Schweizer, "How Behavior Modification Techniques can Improve Total Organizational Performance," *Management Review*, September 1979, pp. 43–50.

lems. Desirable performance-related behaviors need to be strengthened and accelerated in frequency, and undesirable performance-related behaviors need to be weakened and decelerated in frequency. Like the initial step in any problem-solving process, the critical behaviors must be properly identified or the subsequent steps of O.B. Mod. become meaningless for attaining the overall goal of performance improvement.

Step 2: Measurement of the behaviors

After the critical behaviors have been identified in Step 1, they are next measured. A baseline frequency is obtained by determining (either by observing and counting or by extracting from existing records) the number of times that the identified behavior is occurring under present conditions. Often this baseline frequency is in and of itself very revealing. Sometimes it is discovered that the behavior identified in Step 1 is occurring much less or much more frequently than anticipated. The baseline measure may indicate the problem is much smaller or bigger than was thought to be the case. In some instances the baseline measure may cause the "problem" to be dropped because its low (or high) frequency is now deemed not to need change. For example, attendance may have been identified in Step 1 as a critical behavior that needed to be changed. The supervisor reports that her people "never seem to be here." The baseline measure, however, reveals that there is 96 percent attendance, which is deemed to be acceptable. In this example, the baseline measure rules out attendance as being a problem. The reverse, of course, could also have occurred. Attendance may have been a much bigger problem than anticipated.

The purpose of the baseline measure is to provide objective frequency data on the critical behavior. A baseline frequency count is an operational definition of the strength of the critical behavior under existing conditions. Such precise measurement is the hallmark of any scientific endeavor, and it separates O.B. Mod. from more subjective human resource management approaches such as participation. Although the baseline is established before the intervention to see what happens to the behavior as a result of the intervention, it is important to realize that measures are taken post-intervention as well. Busy managers may feel that they do not have time to objectively record behavioral frequencies, but, at least initially, they must record them in order to effectively use the O.B. Mod. approach. The following discussion of tally sheets and charting point out how to minimize the problems associated with this second step of O.B. Mod.

Tally sheets A tailor-made tally sheet should be designed for each behavior. A piece of notebook paper usually is sufficient. Figure 10-3 shows a typical tally sheet. As shown, the tallies usually record behavioral frequencies in relation to time. The frequencies are usually broken down in a yes-no type of format, which greatly simplifies the job of the recorder. However, such an approach requires precise definitions of what constitutes a frequency. For example, say that the critical behavior is tardiness in returning from breaks. A decision must be made on what is considered tardy.

Say that it is decided (and this may be different from situation to situation) that five minutes or over is tardy. The observer/recorder then has a definite guideline in checking "yes" or "no" for frequency of tardiness behavior.

The time dimension on the tally sheet can also follow some specific guidelines to simplify the observer/recorder's job. With some behaviors, such as attendance or complaints, it may be feasible to record every occurrence. However, with many other critical behaviors it would be so time-consuming to record every frequency that it would be practically impossible. On behaviors of the latter type, time-sampling techniques can be effectively used. The approach is similar to the work-sampling techniques that have been successfully used by industrial engineers for years. An example of a time-sampling approach would be to randomly select a time per each working hour to observe the behavior. As in any sampling procedure, if the times are in fact random, confident generalizations can be made to the whole day.

Charting the behaviors The data collected on the tally sheets are transferred to a chart or graph like the one shown in Figure 10-4. As shown, the frequencies of behaviors are along the vertical and time is on the horizontal. Percentage rather than raw frequency is usually used. This usage again simplifies the recorder's job because it permits the recorder to miss a time or two during the day or even entire days without badly distorting the data.

Charting of critical behaviors is important to O.B. Mod. because it permits quick, accurate visual inspection of the frequency data. As Kreitner has noted,

**Figure 10-3
Typical tally sheet.**

	Monday		Tuesday		Wendesday		Thursday		Friday	
Times	Yes	No	Yes	No	Yes	No	Yes	No	Yes	No

Employee: _____ Behavior: _____

Position: _____ Supervisor: _____

In effect, behavior charts are mini behavioral experiments complete with "before" and "after" measures for control purposes. Baseline data collected under normal conditions later act as a standard for evaluating interventions. Baseline data help answer the pivotal question: Has the intervention strengthened, weakened, or not affected the target behavior?[9]

The role of the observer/recorder The role assumed by the observer/recorder can be important not only to the measurement step but to the credibility and ethics of the entire approach. As Chapter 2 pointed out, there is a real need for accurate, observational measures of organizational behavior. This is true not only in the O.B. Mod. approach but for gathering data for any research purpose in organizational behavior. Questionnaire and interview data were criticized in Chapter 2 as being highly reactive. However, the mere presence of an observer may also badly distort the behaviors being measured. For this reason, it is important that observational data be gathered as unobtrusively as possible.

Advocating the use of unobtrusive observational measures does not mean that hidden observers or hidden audio and/or video equipment should be used. Obviously, such practice gets into ethical and legal problems. With possibly a few exceptions (e.g., security), such hidden or deceptive approaches cannot be justified. On the other hand, straightforward observational techniques that use common sense can minimize the reactive effects of those being measured. The observer should be completely open to any questions that the person being observed may have. Most employees in modern organizations are not sensitive to being measured because industrial

---

[9]Robert Kreitner, "PM—A New Method of Behavior Change," *Business Horizons*, December 1975, p. 82.

**Figure 10-4
Charting critical
behaviors.**

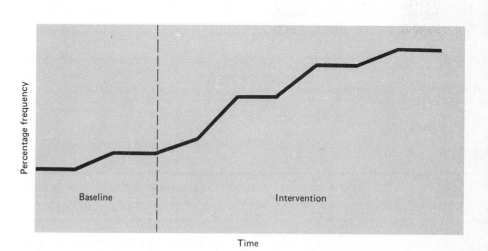

engineers and personnel specialists have been doing it for years. There have certainly been abuses of this in the past, but lessons have been learned and the abuses can be eliminated.

Much data on typical critical behaviors (e.g., absenteeism, quantity, and quality data) are already being gathered by other techniques. All that recorders have to do is retrieve these data; they do not have to intrusively intervene. Finally, self-reporting procedures can be employed to gather the data. Having people reinforced for honestly and accurately keeping records on their own targeted behaviors will eliminate the need for an observer/recorder. In the Emery Air Freight program of behavioral management such self-reporting was successfully used, and recent self-management studies (these will be covered in Chapter 22) depend on self-report data.[10]

Step 3: Functional analysis of the behavior

Once the critical behavior has been identified and a baseline measure is obtained, a functional analysis is performed. As Chapters 3 and 9 brought out, both the antecedent (the S in the S-O-B-C model) and the consequent (the C in the model) environments are vital to the understanding, prediction, and control of human behavior in organizations. In Table 10-1 a simple A-B-C functional analysis is shown. In an O.B. Mod. approach the "O" is dropped out of the functional analysis. Remember, in an operant approach, on which O.B. Mod. is based, congnitive mediating processes (represented by the "O") do not play a role. Such an omission may detract from the comprehensive understanding of organizational behavior and the analysis of modeling and self-control processes, but for the pragmatic application of O.B. Mod., an A-B-C functional analysis seems sufficient.[11] A four-term S-O-B-C functional analysis, which accounts for cognitive mediating processes (the "O") and covert as well as overt contingencies, seems more appropriate for the broader-based social learning approach to the overall understanding of organizational behavior (the conceptual model presented in Chapter 3), and for a behavioral self-management approach (the BSM technique described in Chapter 22).[12] In the A-B-C functional analysis used in O.B. Mod., A stands for antecedent, B is the performance behavior identified in Step 1, and C is the contingent consequence. Table 10-1 identifies some of the A's, B's, and C's for attendance and absenteeism. This

---

[10]"Performance Audit, Feedback, and Positive Reinforcement," op. cit.,; "At Emery Air Freight," op. cit.; and Fred Luthans and Tim R. V. Davis, "Behavioral Self-Management—The Missing Link in Managerial Effectiveness," *Organizational Dynamics*, Summer 1979, pp. 42–60.

[11]See Fred Luthans, "Resolved: Functional Analysis Is the Best Technique for Diagnostic Evaluation of Organizational Behavior," in Barbara Karmel (ed.), *Point and Counterpoint in Organizational Behavior*, Dryden Press, Hinsdale, Ill., 1980, pp. 48–60.

[12]See Tim R. V. Davis and Fred Luthans, "Leadership Reexamined: A Behavioral Approach," *Academy of Management Review*, April 1979, pp. 237–248; Fred Luthans and Tim R. V. Davis, "Operationalizing a Behavioral Approach to Leadership," in E. G. Miller (ed.), *Proceedings of the Midwest Academy of Management*, 1979, University of Michigan, Ann Arbor, pp. 144–155; and Tim R. V. Davis and Fred Luthans, "A Social Learning Approach to Organizational Behavior," *Academy of Management Review*, April 1980, pp. 281–290.

Table 10–1

AN EXAMPLE OF FUNCTIONAL ANALYSIS

Functional Analysis of Attendance Behavior(s)

A ——————————→ B ——————————→ C

Antecedent cue(s)	Behavior(s)	Consequence(s)
Awareness of any consequence	Going to bed on time	Reward programs
Advertising	Setting the alarm	Contingent time-off
Meetings	Waking up	Gifts/prizes
Memorandums	Getting dressed	Preferred jobs
Orientation	Getting children off to	Social
Bulletin board	school	Attention
Observation of any consequence	Leaving home	Recognition
Social status and pressure	Getting a baby-sitter	Praise
Temporal cues	Driving to work	Feedback
Special events	Reporting into work	Data on attendance
Weather		

Functional Analysis of Absenteeism Behavior(s)

A ——————————→ B ——————————→ C

Antecedent cue(s)	Behavior(s)	Consequence(s)
Illness/accident	Getting up late	Discipline programs
Hangover	Sleeping in	Verbal reprimands
Lack of transportation	Staying home	Written reprimands
Traffic	Drinking	Pay docks
No day-care facilities	Fishing/hunting	Layoffs
Family problems	Working at home	Dismissals
Company policies	Visiting	Social consequences from
Group/personal norms	Caring for sick child	co-workers
Seniority/age		Escape and avoidance of
Awareness/observation of		working
any consequence		Nothing

Source: Fred Luthans and Mark Martinko, "An Organizational Behavior Modification Analysis of Absenteeism," *Human Resources Management,* Fall 1976, p. 15.

functional analysis step of O.B. Mod. brings out the problem-solving nature of O.B. Mod. Both the antecedent cues to emit the behavior, and that sometimes control it, and the consquences that are currently maintaining the behavior must be identified and understood before an effective intervention strategy can be developed.

An example can demonstrate why the functional analysis is so important to O.B. Mod. In an actual case of an O.B. Mod. application, a production supervisor in a large manfacturing firm identified unscheduled breaks as critical behavior affecting the performance of his department. It seemed that his people were frequently wandering off the job; and when they were not tending their machines, time was lost—and irrecoverable production. When a baseline measure of this critical behavior was obtained, he was proved to be right. The data indicated that unscheduled breaks (defined as leaving the job for reasons other than taking a scheduled break or to obtain materials, etc.) were occurring in his department on a relatively frequent basis. The functional analysis was performed to determine the antecedent(s) and consequence(s) of the unscheduled break behavior. It was found that the clock served as the antecedent cue for the critical behavior. The workers in this department started work at 8 a.m.; at 10 a.m. they had their first scheduled break; they had lunch at 12. They started again at 1 p.m. and had a break at 3 p.m. and quit at 5 p.m. The functional analysis revealed that almost precisely at 9 a.m., 11 a.m., 2 p.m., and 4 p.m. the workers were leaving their jobs and going to the rest room. In other words, the clock served as a cue for them to take an unscheduled break midway between starting time and the first scheduled break, between the first scheduled break and lunch, between lunch and the scheduled afternoon break, and between the afternoon break and quitting time. The clock did not *cause* the behavior; it only served as a cue to emit the behavior. On the other hand, the behavior was under stimulus control of the clock because the clock dictated when the behavior would occur. The consequence, however, was what was maintaining the behavior. The critical behavior was a function of its consequences. The functional analysis revealed that the consequence of the unscheduled break behavior was escape from a dull, boring task (i.e., the unscheduled break behavior was being negatively reinforced) and/or meeting with coworkers and friends to socialize and have a cigarette (i.e., the unscheduled break behavior was being positively reinforced). Through this functional analysis the antecedents and consequences are identified so that an effective intervention strategy can be developed. The next section, on the intervention step, will reveal what the production supervisor actually tried in this case.

The functional analysis pinpoints one of the most significant practical problems of using an O. B. Mod. approach to change critical performance behaviors. Only the *contingent* consequences have an impact on subsequent behavior. The functional analysis often reveals that there are many competing contingencies for every organizational behavior. For example, a supervisor may be administering what he or she believes to be contingent punishment for the undesirable behavior of subordinates. However, what often happens is that the coworkers are providing a very rewarding consequence for the undesirable behavior. In many cases the persons who are supposedly being punished will allow the coworkers' rewards to be the contingent consequence, and their undesirable behavior will increase in subsequent frequency. In other words, the supervisor's punishment was not contingent; it had no impact on the subordinates' subsequent behavior. The functional analysis must make sure that the *contingent* consequences are identified, and the analyst must not be deluded by the consequences that on the surface appear to be affecting the critical behavior.

Step 4: Development of an intervention strategy

The first three steps in an O.B. Mod. approach are preliminary to the action step, the intervention. The goal of the intervention is to strengthen and accelerate desirable critical performance behaviors and/or weaken and decelerate undesirable critical performance behaviors. There are several strategies that can be used, but the main ones are positive reinforcement, punishment/positive reinforcement, and extinction/positive reinforcement.

Positive reinforcement strategy The last chapter devoted considerable attention to the concept of reinforcement. A *positive reinforcer* was defined as a consequence which strengthens the behavior and increases its subsequent frequency. It was also brought out that negative reinforcement (the termination or withdrawal of an undesirable consequence) has the same impact on behavior (strenghtens and increases subsequent frequency). Yet, positive and not negative reinforcement is recommended as an effective intervention strategy for O.B. Mod. The reason is that positive reinforcement represents a form of positive control of behavior while negative reinforcement and punishment represent forms of negative control of behavior. As Chapter 9 pointed out, negative reinforcement is actually a type of "blackmail" control of behavior; the person behaves in a certain way in order not to be punished. Most organizations today control participants in this manner. People come to work in order not to be fired and look busy when the supervisor walks by in order not to be punished. Under positive control, the person behaves in a certain way in order to receive the desired consequence. Under positive control people would come to work in order to be recognized for making a contribution to their department's goal of perfect attendance or would keep busy whether the supervisor was around or not in order to receive incentive pay or because they get self-reinforcement from doing a good job. Positive control through a positive-reinforcement intervention strategy is much more effective and long-lasting than negative control. It creates a much healthier and more productive organizational climate.

Identifying positive reinforcers The last chapter carefully pointed out that a reward becomes a positive reinforcer only if because of its presentation the behavior increases in subsequent frequency. Thus, some of the commonly used organizational rewards are not necessarily positive reinforcers. This is why it is so vitally important that the measures initiated in Step 2 be continued after the intervention. The objective measures are the only way to tell whether an intervention is in fact a positive reinforcer.

Chapter 9 presented the various conceptual categories of rewards (extrinsic/intrinsic and primary/secondary) and indicated the impacts that each tends to have on behavior. There are also available several techniques to help determine potential positive reinforcers.[13] The most accurate but often difficult-to-accomplish method of identifying positive reinforcers is to empirically analyze each individual's history of reinforcement. Knowledge of what a particular person likes and dislikes gained through experience can help in this regard, and, of course, empirical evidence post-intervention from the charting in Step 2 can be used to analyze the history of reinforcement. However, in cases where there is little or no experience with the individual prior to trying an intervention, several self-reporting techniques can be used.

The most straightforward technique is to simply ask what the person

---

[13]See: Luthans and Kreitner, *Organizational Behavior Modification*, op. cit., pp. 91–99.

finds to be rewarding. Although the person may not always tell the truth, it is nonetheless a logical point of departure for identifying potential reinforcers. Table 10-2 gives an example of the types of questions that could be asked employees to help identify potential reinforcers. Employees could fill out such a form when they are hired, or every year or so to help the manager find specific rewards for each employee.

A more formal approach is to use test instruments. For example, Blood developed an ipsative test which identifies the relative importance of several possible job-related reinforcers.[14] Another possible method of identifying reinforcers is the use of contingency questionnaires.[15] The latter tests measure perceived performance-outcome probabilities and can help identify the important outcomes (reinforcers) for employees. Still another way to help identify possible reinforcers is through self-selection techniques: the workers are allowed to select their own reinforcers from a variety of stated possibilities sometimes called "smorgasbords" or "menus."

Contrived reinforcers The various techniques discussed above can be used to help identify reinforcers for the positive reinforcement intervention strategy. Although reinforcers are highly individualized, research and experience have shown that there are several rewards that most organiza-

---

[14]Milton R. Blood, "Intergroup Comparisons of Intraperson Differences: Rewards from the Job," *Personnel Psychology*, Spring 1973, pp. 1–9.

[15]For example, see: H. Joseph Reitz, "Managerial Attitudes and Perceived Contingencies between Performance and Organizational Response," *Academy of Management Proceedings*, 1971, pp. 227–238.

Table 10–2

EXAMPLES OF QUESTIONS THAT COULD BE ASKED IN AN EMPLOYEE REINFORCER SURVEY

Employee reinforcer survey

1. In my free time my favorite activity is _____

2. I would like to visit _____

3. My favorite sports activity is _____

4. My favorite hobby is _____

5. Something that I really want to buy is _____

6. If I had fifty dollars to spend on myself right now I would _____

7. My job would be more rewarding if _____

8. If my manager would _____
   I would enjoy working here.

9. I would work harder if _____

10. The place that I most like to shop is _____

Source: Adapted from Lawrence M. Miller, *Behavior Management,* Wiley, New York, 1978, p. 149.

tional participants find positively reinforcing. These can be classified as contrived and natural rewards. The contrived rewards are those that are brought in from outside the natural work environment and generally involve costs for the organization over and above the existing situation.[16] Examples would include the consumables, manipulatables, visual/auditory reinforcers, and tokens found in Table 10-3. The two most widely used and effective contrived rewards would be money and feedback about performance.

The literature on the impact that feedback has on organizational participants was discussed in Chapter 8. Feedback played an important role in the Emery Air Freight program and was found to have a positively reinforcing impact on employee performance.[17] There is little question that despite the tremendous amount of data being generated by computerized information systems in modern organizations, individuals still receive very little, if any, feedback about their performance. People generally have an intense desire to know *how* they are doing, especially if they have some degree of achievement motivation (see Chapter 6). It is generally accepted that feedback enhances individual performance; that the more specific it is, the greater its impact; and the greater the delay between performance and feedback, the less the effect.[18] But there is some disagreement whether feedback per se is automatically reinforcing. Some studies have demonstrated that individual performance is directly related to the amount of feedback,[19] but recent comprehensive analyses point out the complexities of feedback and conclude that blanket generalizations about the reinforcing properties of feedback are too simplistic.[20] For example, after reviewing the existing research literature on feedback, Nadler concludes that its impact is contingent upon factors such as the nature of the feedback information, the process of using feedback, individual differences of the recipients of the feedback, and the nature of the task.[21] Despite such qualifications, a general guideline regarding feedback about performance is that it can be an effective reinforcement strategy for O.B. Mod. For example, the supervisor faced with

---

[16]Luthans and Kreitner, *Organizational Behavior Modification*, op. cit., p. 102.

[17]"Performance Audit, Feedback, and Positive Reinforcement," op. cit.; and "At Emery Air Freight," op. cit.

[18]R. B. Ammons, "Effects of Knowledge of Performance: A Survey and Tentative Theoretical Formulation," *Journal of General Psychology*, vol. 54, 1956, pp. 279–299; and J. Annett, *Feedback and Human Behavior*, Penguin, Baltimore, 1969.

[19]D. M. Cook, "The Impact on Managers of Frequency of Feedback," *Academy of Management Journal*, vol. 11, 1968, pp. 263–277; P. S. Hundal, "Knowledge of Performance as an Incentive in Repetitive Industrial Work," *Journal of Applied Psychology*, June 1969, pp. 224–226; and R. Anderson, R. Kulhavy, and T. Andre, "Feedback Procedures in Programmed Instruction," *Journal of Educational Psychology*, vol. 62, 1971, pp. 148–156.

[20]Daniel R. Ilgen, Cynthia D. Fisher, and M. Susan Taylor, "Consequences of Individual Feedback on Behavior in Organizations," *Journal of Applied Psychology*, vol. 64, 1979, pp. 349–371.

[21]David A. Nadler, "The Effects of Feedback on Task Group Behavior: A Review of the Experimental Research," *Organizational Behavior and Human Performance*, vol. 23, 1979, pp. 309–338.

Table 10–3

CLASSIFICATIONS OF ON-THE-JOB REWARDS

Contrived on-the-job rewards				Natural rewards	
Consumables	**Manipulatables**	**Visual and auditory**	**Tokens**	**Social**	**Premack**
Coffee-break treats	Desk accessories	Office with a window	Money	Friendly greetings	Job with more responsibility
Free lunches	Wall plaques	Piped-in music	Stocks	Informal recognition	Job rotation
Food baskets	Company car	Redecoration of work environment	Stock options	Formal acknowledgment or achievement	Early time off with pay
Easter hams	Watches	Company literature	Movie passes	Invitations to coffee/lunch	Work on personal project on company time
Christmas turkeys	Trophies	Private office	Trading stamps (green stamps)	Solicitations of suggestions	Use of company machinery or facilities for personal projects
Dinners for the family on the company	Commendations	Popular speakers or lecturers	Paid-up insurance policies	Solicitations of advice	Use of company recreation facilities
Company picnics	Rings/tie pins	Book club discussions	Dinner and theater tickets	Compliment on work progress	
After-work wine and cheese parties	Appliances and furniture for the home	Feedback about performance	Vacation trips	Recognition in house organ	
Beer parties	Home shop tools		Coupons redeemable at local stores	Pat on the back	
	Garden tools		Profit sharing	Smile	
	Clothing			Verbal or nonverbal recognition or praise	
	Club privileges				
	Special assignments				

Source: Fred Luthans and Robert Kreitner, *Organizational Behavior Modification*, Scott, Foresman, Glenview, Ill., 1975, p. 101. Used with permission.

the problem of his people taking unscheduled breaks that was cited earlier, used such a feedback intervention strategy. In that case, he could not change the antecedent cue (he could not change time) and he could not change the consequence by preventing his people from going to the bathroom. What he did do was calculate the exact cost for each worker in the unit (in terms of lost group piece-rate pay) every time any one of them took an unscheduled break. This information regarding the relatively significant amount of lost pay when any one of them took an unscheduled break was fed back to the employees in his unit. After this feedback intervention, staying on the job increased in frequency and taking unscheduled breaks dramatically decreased. The feedback pointed out the contingency that staying on the job meant more money. At least in this case, the money proved to be a more contingent consequence than the competing contingencies of social rewards with friends at the rest room and withdrawing from the boring job. The feedback in this case clarified the monetary contingency.

Money as a reinforcer   Despite the tendency in recent years to downgrade the importance of money as an organizational reward, there is ample evidence that money can be positively reinforcing for most people. The downgrading of money is partly the result of the motivation theories of Maslow and Herzberg plus the publicity from surveys which consistently place wages and salaries near the middle of the list of employment factors that are important to workers and managers. Although money was probably overemphasized in classical management theory and motivation techniques, the pendulum now has seemed to swing too far in the opposite direction. Money remains a very important but admittedly complex potential reinforcer.

In terms of Maslow's hierarchy, money is often equated only with the most basic level of needs. It is viewed in the material sense of buying food, clothing, and shelter. Yet money has a symbolic as well as an economic material meaning. It can provide power and status and can be a means to measure achievement. In the latter sense, money can be used as an effective positive-reinforcement intervention strategy.

Accepting the importance of money as a possible reinforcer does not mean that the traditional techniques for dispensing it are adequate. Starting with the scientific management movement at the turn of the century, numerous monetary incentive techniques have been developed. The payment schemes can be put into three broad categories:

1. *Base pay* or salary, which is given for a job regardless of how it is performed
2. *Variable pay*, which gives recognition to individual differences on the job
3. *Supplementary pay*, which is not directly related to the job or the individual[22]

The base-pay technique provides for minimum compensation for a particular job. Pay by the hour for workers and the base salary for managers are examples. The technique does not reward for above-average, or penalize

---

[22]Edwin B. Flippo and Gary Munsinger, *Management: A Behavioral Approach*, 3d ed., Allyn and Bacon, Boston, 1975, p. 334.

for below-average, performance, and it is largely controlled by the job rather than by the person performing the job. The variable-pay technique attempts to reward according to individual or group differences and is thus more human than job-controlled. Seniority variable-pay plans recognize age and length-of-service differentials, and merit and individual- or group-incentive plans attempt to reward contingently on performance. Incentive plans pay personnel according to piece rate, bonus, or profit sharing. Supplementary monetary techniques have nothing to do with the job or performance per se. The extensive fringe-benefit package received by employees in most modern organizations is an example.

Further refined and newly developed variable-pay or contingent-pay plans seem to be necessary to the effective use of money as a reinforcer. The base-and supplementary-pay plans are adequate for their intended purposes, but the variable-pay plans do not seem to have the desired effects. After an extensive review of relevant research, Hamner and Organ summarize the following problems with merit pay programs:[23]

1. *Pay is not perceived as being related to job performance.* For example, one survey of 600 managers found practically no relationships between their pay and their rated performance.
2. *Performance ratings are viewed as being biased.* Most employees feel that appraisals are based on subjective rather objective performance measures.
3. *The pay is not viewed as a reward.* Pay represents more than money to the employee. For example, conflicting reward schedules, perceived inequities, or threats to self-esteem may prevent a merit increase from becoming a reward.
4. *Those who administer merit pay are more concerned with employee satisfaction than with performance.* There should be variability in an effective pay plan, but many managers are overly concerned with the accompanying complaints.
5. *There is little trust or openness about merit increases.* For the merit pay plan to be effective, there must be an open climate where work and effort are valued and paid accordingly.
6. *Pay is viewed as the primary reinforcer and the job itself is ignored.* Feedback and pay systems must be designed both to get things done and to make the work enjoyable.

The above points indicate that incentive or merit pay plans are not a clear-cut way to contingently administer monetary rewards. The following guidelines are offered as a way to make money more effective as a reinforcer. The individual must believe:

1. Increased effort would lead to better performance.
2. Your employer can determine the improved performance.
3. Increased money will follow from this performance.
4. You would value the additional money because it would satisfy your needs.
5. You would not have to unduly sacrifice satisfaction of other needs for security, affiliation, and so on.[24]

---

[23]Clay Hamner and Dennis W. Organ, *Organizational Behavior*, Business Publications, Dallas, 1978, pp. 260–265.

[24]Ross A Webber, *Management*, Irwin, Homewood, Ill., 1975, p. 108.

Analyses of the role of money, such as those made above, are usually couched in cognitive terms. However, from these cognitive explanations it is very clear that the real key for assessing the use of money as a reinforcer is not necessarily whether it satisfies inner needs but rather how it is administered. In order for money to be an effective positive-reinforcement intervention strategy for O.B. Mod., it must be administered contingently on performing the critical behavior.

As the last chapter pointed out, about the only reinforcing function that pay currently has in organizations is to reinforce employees for walking up to a pay window or opening an envelope every two weeks or month. With the exception of some piece-rate incentive systems and commissions paid to salespersons, pay is generally not contingent on the performance of critical behaviors. One experimental study clearly demonstrated that money contingently administered can be an effective intervention strategy.[25] A contingently administered monetary bonus plan significantly improved the punctuality of workers in a Mexican division of a large United States corporation. It should be pointed out, however, that the mere fact that money was valued by the Mexican workers in this study does not mean that it would have the same impact on all workers. For example, in a society with an inflationary economy and nonmaterialistic social values, money may be much less likely to be a potential reinforcer for critical job behaviors. Money certainly cannot be automatically dismissed as a positive reinforcer, but, because of its complexity, it may also turn out to be a reward but not a reinforcer. Only post-intervention measurement will determine if in fact money is an effective positive reinforcer for the critical behavior in question.

Natural reinforcers   Besides the contrived rewards which most human resource managers tend to depend upon, there are a host of overlooked natural reinforcers available in every organizational setting. Potentially very powerful, these are the rewards that exist in the natural occurrence of events.[26] Table 10-3 categorized the natural rewards under social and Premack headings.

Social rewards such as recognition, attention, and praise tend to be very reinforcing for most people. In addition, few people become satiated (filled up) with social rewards. However, similar to the contrived rewards, the social rewards must be administered on a contingent basis. For example, a pat on the back or verbal praise that is randomly administered (as under the old human relations approach) may have more of a punishing, "boomerang" effect than a positive reinforcement effect. But genuine social rewards, contingently administered to the critical behavior, can be a very effective positive reinforcement intervention strategy. The added benefit of such a strategy in contrast to the use of contrived rewards is that the cost of social rewards to the organization is absolutely nothing.

---

[25]Jaime A. Hermann, Ana I. de Montes, Benjamin Dominguez, Francisco de Montes, and B. L. Hopkins, "Effects of Bonuses for Punctuality on the Tardiness of Industrial Workers," *Journal of Applied Behavioral Analysis*, Winter 1973, pp. 563–570.

[26]Luthans and Kreitner, *Organizational Behavior Modification*, op. cit., p. 103.

Premack rewards are derived from the work of psychologist David Premack.[27] Simply stated, the Premack principle is that high-probability behaviors can be used to reinforce low-probability behaviors. For example, if there are two tasks A and B, and the person prefers A over B, the Premack principle would say that the person should perform B first and then A. In this sequence, task A serves as a contingent reinforcer for completing task B, and the person will perform better on both tasks than if the sequence were reversed. In common practice, people often tend to do the task they like best first and put off the less desired task. This common sequence of doing things is in direct violation of the Premack principle and can contribute to ineffective performance.

As an O.B. Mod. intervention strategy, the Premack principle would suggest that a natural reinforcer could always be found. Certain job activities could always be used to reinforce other job activities. No matter how much employees dislike their jobs, there are going to be some things they like to do better than others. Premack sequencing would allow the more desired activities to reinforce less desired activities. The rewards listed under "Premack" in Table 10-3 can be used to reinforce the less desirable activities on a job.

Punishment/positive reinforcement strategy   The discussion so far has emphasized that the positive reinforcement strategy is the most effective intervention for O.B. Mod. Yet relistically it is recognized that in some cases the use of punishment to weaken and decelerate undesirable behaviors cannot be avoided. This would be true of something like unsafe behaviors that need to be immediately decreased. However, as was pointed out in Chapter 9, so many negative side effects accompany the use of punishment that it should be avoided if at all possible. Punished behavior tends to be only temporarily suppressed; e.g., if a supervisor reprimands a subordinate for some undesirable behavior, the behavior will decrease in the presence of the supervisor but will surface again when the supervisor is absent. In addition, a punished person becomes very anxious and uptight; reliance on punishment may have a disastrous impact on employee satisfaction. Perhaps the biggest problem with the use of punishment, however, is that it is very difficult for a supervisor to switch roles from punisher to positive reinforcer. Some supervisors/managers rely on punishment so much in dealing with their subordinates that it is almost impossible for them to effectively administer positive reinforcement. This is a bad situation for the management of human resources because the use of positive reinforcement is a much more effective way of changing organizational behavior. If punishment is deemed to be necessary, the desirable alternative behavior (e.g., safe behavior) should be positively reinforced at the first opportunity. By using this combination strategy, the alternative desirable behavior will begin to replace the undesirable behavior in the person's behavioral repertoire.

---

[27]David Premack, "Reinforcement Theory," in David Levine (ed.), *Nebraska Symposium on Motivation*, University of Nebraska Press, Lincoln, Nebr., 1965, pp. 123–180.

Punishment should never be used alone as an O.B. Mod. intervention. If punishment is absolutely necessary, it should always be used in combination with positive reinforcement.

Extinction/positive reinforcement A much more effective way to decrease undesirable behavior than by punishment is to use an extinction strategy. As the previous chapter pointed out, extinction has the same impact on behavior as punishment (although it does not act as fast), but extinction does not have the negative side effects of punishment. Punishment could be thought of as the application of a noxious or aversive consequence or the *deliberate withdrawal* of a positively reinforcing consequence that is already a part of the person's environment. Extinction involves the *withdrawal* of a desirable consequence that is contingent upon the person's behavior; this happens after the behavior is emitted. More simply, however, extinction can be defined as providing *no* consequence. Obviously, there is a fine line between extinction and the withdrawal of a positive-reinforcer type of punishment. In fact, there is such a fine distinction between the two that some behaviorists do not even deal with extinction. They simply operationally define anything which decreases behavior as punishment. But the important point for human resource management is that undesirable behavior can be decreased without the accompanying negative side effects of punishment. This can be done by making sure there is no consequence for the undesirable behavior, i.e., putting it on extinction.

In the functional analysis performed in Step 3 of O.B. Mod., the consequences maintaining the critical behavior were identified. The extinction strategy would eliminate those consequences of critical behaviors that were to be decelerated. For example, if complaining was the targeted behavior and the functional analysis revealed that the supervisor's attention to the complaining behavior was maintaining it, the extinction strategy would be to have the supervisor ignore the complaints—not give them any attention. The supervisor may be able to avoid the complainer. Walking away from the person when he starts to complain may be punishing; but if handled properly, i.e., in a nonobvious manner, it could be an extinction strategy without the negative side effects. Again, as with any intervention strategy, whether it was effective in reducing the behavior can be known only by what happened to the frequency measures post-intervention. Also, similar to the punishment strategy, extinction should be used only in combination with positive reinforcement. The desirable alternative behavior would be positively reinforced at the first opportunity. The positively reinforced behavior would begin to replace the undesirable behavior. In the example of the complaining behavior, when the person did not complain, the supervisor would notice and give attention to the person for constructive comments and noncomplaining behavior.

Because most organizational behaviors are being reinforced on intermittent schedules, which Chapter 9 pointed out are very resistant to extinction, the use of the extinction strategy may take time and patience. But as a long-range strategy for weakening undesirable behaviors and decelerating the frequency of occurrence, extinction can be effective. In general, the very simple rule of thumb to follow in employing an O.B. Mod. intervention strategy is to positively reinforce desirable behaviors and make sure undesirable behaviors are not reinforced. This simple guideline may have as big an impact on effective human resource management as any single thing the supervisor/ manager can do. But once again it should be pointed out that understanding and using the other concepts and techniques discussed in previous and following chapters are also necessary for the complex, challenging job of effective human resource management.

Step 5: Evaluation to assure performance improvement

A glaring weakness of most human resource management techniques is the absence of any systematic, built-in evaluation. For example, one comprehensive survey of 154 selected companies concluded that "most organizations are measuring *reaction* to training programs. As we consider the more important and difficult steps in the evaluation process (i.e., *learning, behavior,* and *results*) we find less and less being done, and many of these efforts are superficial and subjective."[28] In another survey, it was concluded that the typical firm that uses job enrichment "believes it has benefited from improvements in employee performance and job satisfaction but has made little effort to formally evaluate the effectiveness of the program, depending on impressions and anecdotal evidence, rather than quantifiable data, for its conclusions."[29] Such haphazard evaluations of human resource management techniques have led to credibility problems. Today all programs dealing with people, whether they are government welfare programs or human resource management programs, are under the pressure of accountability. Donald Campbell has labeled the current climate of accountability the "experimenting society."[30] Human resource managers no longer have the luxury of just trying something new and different and hoping they can improve performance. Today there is pressure for everything that is tried to be *proved* to have value. As with the validity of selection techniques which are currently under scrutiny, systematic evaluations of human resource management techniques should have been being done all along.

O.B. Mod. attempts to meet the credibility and accountability problems head-on by including evaluation as an actual part of the process. In this last step of the model, the need for four levels of evaluation (reaction, learning, behavioral change, and performance improvement) is stressed. The *reaction level* simply refers to whether the people using the approach and those having it used on them like it or not. If O.B. Mod. is well received, if there is a positive reaction to it, there is a better chance of its being used effectively.

---

[28]Ralph F. Cantalanello and Donald L. Kirkpatrick, "Evaluating Training Programs—The State of the Art," *Training and Development Journal,* May 1968, p. 9.

[29]Fred Luthans and William E. Reif, "Job Enrichment: Long on Theory, Short on Practice," *Organizational Dynamics,* Winter 1974, p. 33.

[30]Carol Tavris, "The Experimenting Society: A Conversation with Donald T. Campbell," *Psychology Today,* September 1975, pp. 47–56.

If it is not well received, there is little chance of its being used effectively. Reaction is obviously important to the evaluation of the O.B. Mod. technique. The second level is *learning*. This is especially important when first implementing an O.B. Mod. approach. Do the people using the approach understand the theoretical background and underlying assumptions and the meaning and reasons for the steps in the model? If they do not, the model will again tend to be used ineffectively. The third level is aimed at *behavioral change*. Are behaviors actually being changed? The charting of behaviors gives objective data for this level of evaluation. The fourth and final level, *performance improvement*, is the most important. The major purpose of O.B. Mod. is not to just receive a favorable reaction, learn the concepts, and change behaviors. The importance of these dimensions is mainly that they contribute to the overriding purpose, which is to improve performance. "Hard" measures (e.g., data on quantity and quality, turnover, absenteeism, customer complaints, employee grievances, length of patient stay, number of clients served, and rate of return on investment) and experimental methodology as discussed in Chapter 2 are used whenever possible to systematically evaluate the impact of O.B. Mod. on performance. The use of reversal and multiple-baseline designs as outlined in Chapter 2 is especially relevant to the evaluation of O.B. Mod. interventions.

EXPERIENCE WITH THE APPLICATION OF O.B. MOD.

As pointed out earlier, O.B. Mod. and related operant-based approaches to human resource management are relatively new. Several years ago, *Business Week* reported that a number of companies were either looking into or using behavior modification techniques, and more recently the same publication reported even greater popularity of this approach.[31] Table 10-4 summarizes the nature of the programs and the results obtained by some of the more than 100 companies who have reportedly used this technique.

The programs reported in Table 10-4 are all somewhat unique to the particular company and the consultant who implemented it. But there are also many similarities with the O.B. Mod. approach discussed so far. For example, the widely publicized Emery Air Freight program is similar to the O.B. Mod. approach in that critical performance-related behaviors are identified and then strengthened by positive reinforcement and feedback. In this company it was determined that a critical behavior was whether the dock workers were utilizing the air-freight containers to the fullest advantage. The containers have to be full in order for Emery to make money. Because the employees on this job were extensively trained and because they were constantly reminded of the importance of full containers, both management and the workers estimated that the containers were being

---

[31]"Where Skinner's Theories Work," *Business Week*, Dec. 2, 1972, pp. 64–65; and "Productivity Gains from a Pat on the Back," *Business Week*, Jan. 23, 1978, pp. 56–62. *Training Magazine* has also devoted a couple of issues (December 1976 and November 1978) to the use of behavior modification techniques in industry.

Table 10–4

SUMMARY OF SOME BEHAVIOR MODIFICATION PROGRAMS IN INDUSTRY

Company	Type of employees	Specific goals	Frequency of feedback	Reinforcers used	Results
Emery Air Freight	Entire work force	(a) Increase productivity (b) Improve quality of service	Immediate to monthly, depending on task	Previously only praise and recognition; others now being introduced	Cost savings can be directly attributed to program
Michigan Bell	Employees at all levels in operator services	(a) Decrease turnover and absenteeism (b) Increase productivity (c) Improve union-management relations	(a) Lower level—weekly and daily (b) Higher level—monthly and quarterly	(a) Praise and recognition (b) Opportunity to see oneself become better	(a) Attendance performance has improved by 50 percent (b) Productivity and efficiency have continued to be above standard in areas where positive reinforcement (PR) is used
Michigan Bell	Maintenance workers, mechanics, and first- and second-level supervisors	Improve: (a) Productivity (b) Quality (c) Safety (d) Customer-employee relations	Daily, weekly, and quarterly	(a) Self-feedback (b) Supervisory feedback	(a) Cost-efficiency increase (b) Safety improved (c) Service improved (d) No change in absenteeism (e) Satisfaction with superior & co-workers improved (f) Satisfaction with pay decreased
Connecticut General	Clerical employees and first-line supervisors	(a) Decrease absenteeism (b) Decrease lateness	Immediate	(a) Self-feedback (b) System feedback (c) Earned time off	(a) Chronic absenteeism and lateness have been drastically reduced (b) Some divisions refuse to use PR because it is "outdated"

Company	Employees	Objectives	Timing	Reinforcers	Results
General Electric	Employees at all levels	(a) Meet EEOC objectives (b) Decrease absenteeism and turnover (c) Improve training (d) Increase productivity	Immediate—uses modeling and role playing as training tools to teach interpersonal exchanges and behavior requirements	Social reinforcers (praise, rewards, and constructive feedback)	(a) Cost savings can be directly attributed to the program (b) Productivity has increased (c) Worked extremely well in training minority groups and raising their self-esteem (d) Direct labor cost decreased
Standard Oil of Ohio	Supervisors	Increase supervisor competence	Weekly over five-week (25-hour) training period	Feedback	(a) Improved supervisory ability to give feedback judiciously (b) Discontinued because of lack of overall success
Weyerhaeuser Company	Clerical, production (tree planters), and middle-level management and scientists	(a) To teach managers to minimize criticism and to maximize praise (b) To teach managers to make rewards contingent on specified performance (c) To use optimal schedule to increase productivity	Immediate—daily and quarterly	(a) Pay (b) Praise and recognition	(a) Using money, obtained a 33-percent increase in productivity with one group of workers, and 18-percent increase with a second group and an 8-percent decrease with a third group (b) Currently experimenting with goal setting and praise and/or money at various levels in organization (c) With a lottery-type bonus, the cultural and religious values of workers must be taken into account

Source: Adapted from W. C. Hamner and E. P. Hamner, "Behavior Modification on the Bottom Line," *Organizational Dynamics*, Spring 1976, pp. 12–24.

optimally utilized about 90 percent of the time. However, the performance audit team found the actual effective utilization to be 45 percent (this is essentially Step 2 of O.B. Mod.). Through feedback and social reinforcers this situation was quickly turned around. This same type of approach was successfully used in many other areas of the company and led to a reported $2-million savings to the company.[32] Unfortunately, such claims from the Emery program or the other outcomes shown in Table 10-4 are not (at least not reported in the literature) the result of systematic, methodologically sound evaluations. A comprehensive review of the training literature from 1967 to 1976 found *no scientific evaluations* of behavior modification as an industrial training technique.[33] To fill this void, O.B. Mod. is being systematically researched by the author of this text and his colleagues. The next section briefly summarizes this research to date.

Field research on O.B. Mod.

The initial study was conducted several years ago in a medium-sized, light manufacturing firm located in a large city. Two groups (experimental and control) of nine production-type supervisors were used in the study. The experimental group received training, essentially on the five steps, discussed earlier in this chapter, of the O.B. Mod. approach. The results showed that O.B. Mod. had a definite positive impact on reaction, behavior change, and performance. Learning was not evaluated in this study. Questionnaires administered to the trained supervisors indicated they liked the O.B. Mod approach, and the supervisors indicated their subordinates seemed to react positively. On the charts kept by each trainee (step 2) it was clearly shown that in all cases they were able to change critical behaviors. Examples of behavioral changes accomplished by the supervisors included decreasing the number of complaints, reducing the group scrap rate, decreasing the number of overlooked defective pieces, and reducing the assembly reject rate.[34] The most important result of the study, however, was the significant impact that the O.B. Mod. approach had on the performance of the supervisors' departments. By use of a pretest–post-test control group experimental design, it was found that the experimental group's (those supervisors who used O.B. Mod. in their departments) departments outperformed the control group's departments. Figure 10-5 shows the results. Statistical analysis revealed that the department production rates of supervisors who used O.B. Mod. increased significantly more than the department

---

[32]"Where Skinner's Theories Work," op. cit.; "Performance Audit, Feedback, and Positive Reinforcement," op. cit.; and "At Emery Air Freight," op. cit. There is also a widely viewed film on the Emery experience called "Business, Behaviorism, and the Bottom Line," CRM McGraw-Hill Films, Del Mar, Calif.

[33]William McGhee and William L. Tullar, "A Note on Evaluating Behavior Modification and Behavior Modeling as Industrial Training Techniques," *Personnel Psychology*, vol. 31, 1978, pp. 477–484.

[34]These examples are reported in detail including the charts, in Luthans and Kreitner, *Organizational Behavior Modification*, op. cit., pp. 153–157.

production rates of the control supervisors (those who were not using O.B. Mod.).[35]

A replication in a larger plant obtained almost identical results to those of the original study on all levels of evaluation (including learning). The following summarizes some typical cases of behavioral change that occurred in the production area of the larger manufacturing firm.

1. *Use of idle time.* One supervisor had a worker with a lot of idle time. Instead of using this time productively by helping others, the worker would pretend to look busy and stretch out the day. After getting a baseline measure and doing a functional analysis, the supervisor intervened by giving the worker social reinforcers (attention, praise, and recognition) contingent upon the worker's helping out at other jobs during idle time. Eventually the supervisor also reinforced the worker through more responsibility. This approach dramatically increased the worker's productive use of idle time.

2. *Low performer.* A production worker in one of the supervisor's departments was producing way below standard (80.3 percent of standard on a six-month baseline). The low performance was not deemed to be an ability, technical, training, or standards problem. After the functional analysis, the supervisor used an intervention of feedback and social reinforcers to increase the types of behaviors that

---

Robert Ottemann and Fred Luthans, "An Experimental Analysis of the Effectiveness of an Organizational Behavior Modification Program in Industry," *Academy of Management Proceedings*, 1975, pp. 140–142.

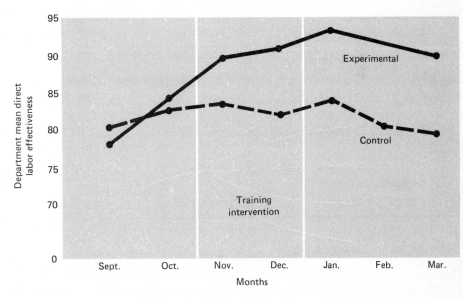

Figure 10-5 Performance results of experimental (those who received O.B. Mod. training) and control groups. (*Source:* Robert Ottemann and Fred Luthans, "An Experimental Analysis of the Effectiveness of an Organizational Behavior Modification Program in Industry," *Academy of Management Proceedings*, 1975, p. 141.)

would lead to higher output. This intervention resulted in a 93 percent performance level with no decrease in quality.

3. *Group quality.* One supervisor had a major problem with the quality of work in his department. The baseline measure verified this problem. After the functional analysis, the supervisor used feedback and social reinforcers on the group as a whole. Shortly after use of this intervention strategy the group attained the quality standard for the first time in three years.

4. *Group attendance.* Another supervisor felt he had an attendance problem in his department. The baseline measure revealed 92 percent attendence, which was not as big a problem as he had thought. However, he established the goal of 100 percent. After using daily feedback and social reinforcers on the group, 100 percent was attained very rapidly. An interesting anecdote told by the supervisor was that one of his workers was riding to work from a small town in a car pool early one morning when they hit a deer. The car was disabled by the accident. Co-workers who worked in other departments in the plant and rode in the car pool called relatives and went back home for the day. The worker in his department, however, because she did not want to spoil the 100 percent attendance record, hitchhiked to work by herself and made it on time.

5. *Problem with another department.* One supervisor felt the performance of his department was being adversely affected by the unrecoverable time of truck-lift operators who were not directly under his supervision. After obtaining baseline data and making a functional analysis, the supervisor decided to apply feedback and social reinforcers on the informal group leader and the supervisor of the truck-lift operators. This intervention substantially reduced the unrecoverable time affecting the operational performance of his department.

The five examples above are only representative of the type of behaviors that the supervisors using an O.B. Mod. approach were able to change. Cumulatively, such applied behavioral analysis and change were able to improve the overall performance of these supervisors' departments in both the original study and the follow-up.

More recently, the O.B. Mod. approach has been extended beyond first-line supervisory training to the total organizational development process and to nonmanufacturing organizations. The application of O.B. Mod. to total performance improvement was systematically evaluated in a small manufacturing plant.[36] It was implemented in three major phases. The first phase was primarily educational and consisted of training all three levels of management (first the owner/manager, then the four department heads, and finally the eight supervisors) in the principles of O.B. Mod., basically following the five-step model discussed in this chapter. The second stage involved a simulation/experiential approach. At first, the participants analyzed case studies and developed intervention strategies. Then, once both the participants and the researchers/trainers had developed confidence in the participants' skills, the participants applied O.B. Mod. principles to their own work areas in a manner similar to that already described in the first study. The third and final phase of the intervention involved the development of a total organizational performance management system. In this phase, all levels of management collaborated to identify key behaviors

---

[36]Fred Luthans and Jason Schweizer, op. cit., pp. 43–50.

and performance indexes. An organization-wide feedback system was then developed based on key behaviors and performance measures. In addition, programs for specific problem areas were developed.

The results of this comprehensive, *total organization* intervention indicated that there were significant improvements in both productivity and quality. In fact, *record* performance was attained. Statistical analyses demonstrated the significance of these changes and simple inspection of the graphical representation of the data shown in Figure 10-6 shows the impact that the O.B. Mod. program had in this company. The left-hand portion of the graph depicts the average levels and variability of both productivity and quality prior to the intervention. The next segment of the graph displays the effects of a contingent time-off intervention on productivity when no consequences were being applied to quality. As evidenced by the changes illustrated, productivity improved with the application of the contingent time-off consequences, while the quality level, for which consequences were not changed, remained about the same. The third segment then demonstrates the positive impact of the contingent application of social reinforcers on quality, while the productivity levels remained about the same. Finally, the last segment demonstrates improved levels of both quality and productivity under the control of the feedback system and contingent social reinforcement. Whereas the first study used a control group design, the multiple-

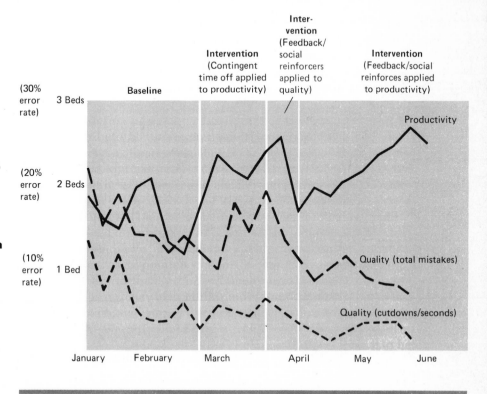

Figure 10-6
The impact of O.B. Mod. on the total performance improvement of a small factory.
(*Source:* Fred Luthans and Jason Schweizer, "How Behavior Modification Techniques Can Improve Total Organizational Performance," *Management Review,* September 1979, p. 49.)

baseline design (see Chapter 2 for a discussion of these research designs) was deemed to be more appropriate for the evaluation where the total organization was being impacted by the O.B. Mod. intervention. Such designs give considerable weight to the conclusion that the O.B. Mod. approach did indeed cause the total performance of this organization to improve.

Nonmanufacturing applications

The studies discussed above do provide considerable evidence that an O.B. Mod. approach can have a positive impact on employee performance, at least in relatively structured environments such as is found in most manufacturing plants. But what about less structured, nonmanufacturing organizations? Preliminary research indicates that similar results are possible in nonmanufacuturing organizations as well.

In a large hospital application, eleven supervisors from medical service, business, and operations units were given O.B. Mod. training in eight sessions over a two-month period.[37] During the O.B. Mod. training these hospital supervisors learned the principles of O.B. Mod. and used the five-step approach, i.e., they identified, measured, functionally analyzed, and intervened to change key performance behaviors of their subordinates, and then evaluated results in their respective areas of responsibility. The results of this program are shown in Table 10-5. Although the researchers were unable to employ an experimental design in this study (and therefore cause-and-effect conclusions are not warranted), the simple before-and-after analysis provides a rather convincing argument that the O.B. Mod. intervention was effective in modifying a broad range of performance-related behaviors in a hospital setting. The O.B. Mod. program seemed to effect both the quality and quantity performance measures. Moreover, the data indicates that each of the O.B.-Mod.-trained supervisors was successful in applying the intervention despite the wide variety of situations encountered.

In another nonmanufacturing organization, a somewhat different type of O.B. Mod. application was tried.[38] Instead of training supervisors to use an O.B. Mod. approach, the researchers themselves did the steps normally done by the supervisors. An experiment (an A-B-A compared to a control group, i.e., a true experimental design) was conducted in a major metropolitan department store. Critical performance behaviors of eighty-two retail clerks from sixteen randomly selected departments were identified. These behaviors included selling, stockwork, idle behaviors, absenteeism from the work station, and miscellaneous. Next, the baseline measure of these behaviors was obtained by observational/work sampling techniques. A detailed analysis was then conducted to determine the appropriate performance goals for these behaviors. For example, based upon job descriptions,

---

[37]Charles A. Snyder and Fred Luthans, "The Application of O. B. Mod. to Increase the Productivity of Hospital Personnel," *Personnel Administrator* (in press).

[38]Fred Luthans, Robert Paul, and Douglas Baker, "An Experimental Analysis of the Impact of a Contingent Reinforcement Intervention on Salespersons' Performance Behaviors," *Journal of Applied Psychology* (in press).

Table 10-5

PERFORMANCE MEASURES BEFORE AND AFTER AN O.B. MOD. TRAINING PROGRAM IN A LARGE HOSPITAL

Unit	Measure(s)	Pre-intervention	Post-intervention	Percent change
Emergency room clerks	Registration errors (per day)	19.16	4.58	76.1
Hardware engineer group, HIS	Average time to repair (minutes)	92.53	33.25	61.4
Medical records file clerks	Errors in filing (per person per audit)	2.87	0.078	97.3
Medical records	Complaints	8.0	1.0	875.0
Transcriptionists	Average errors	2.07	1.4	33.0
	Average output	2,258.0	2,303.33	2.0
Heart station	EKG procedures accomplished (average)	1,263.0	1,398.97	11.0
	Overdue procedures	7.0*	4.0	42.8
Eye clinic	Daily patient throughput	19.0	23.0	21.0
	Daily patient teaching documentation	1.0	2.8	180.0
	Protocols produced	0.0	2.0	200.0
Pharmacy technicians	Drug output (doses)	348.8	422.1	21.0
	Posting errors	3.67	1.48	59.7
	Product waste (percent)	5.8	4.35	25.0
Radiology echnicians	Average patient throughput (procedural)	3,849.5	4,049.0	5.0
	Retake rate (percent)	11.2	9.95	11.2
Patient accounting	Average monthly billings	2,561.0	3,424.5	33.7
Admitting office	Time to admit (minutes)	43.73	13.57	68.97
	Average cost	$ 15.05	$ 11.73	22.0
Data center operations	Systems log-on (time)	1.54	1.43	13.4

*Estimate.
All averages are arithmetic means.
Source: Charles A. Snyder and Fred Luthans, "The Application of O.B. Mod. to Increase the Productivity of Hospital Personnel," *Personnel Administrator* (in press).

organizational goals/policies, direct observations, and role plays, it was determined that (1) the salespersons, except when they had an excused absence, should be present in the department, within 3 feet of displayed merchandise, during assigned working hours; (2) when customers come to the department they should be offered assistance or acknowledged and promised immediate aid within five seconds; and (3) the display shelf should be filled to at least 70 percent capacity. The intervention consisted of contingently applying time-off with pay or equivalent cash and an opportunity to compete for a free vacation for two for attaining the performance goals. Observationally gathered behavioral data was collected during and after this intervention. For computational and graphic presentation, the selling, stockwork, and miscellaneous behaviors were collapsed into a single category, called "aggregate retailing behavior," and absence from the work station and idle time were also combined for this purpose. Figure 10-7 shows the results.

The baseline frequencies of these behaviors were not significantly

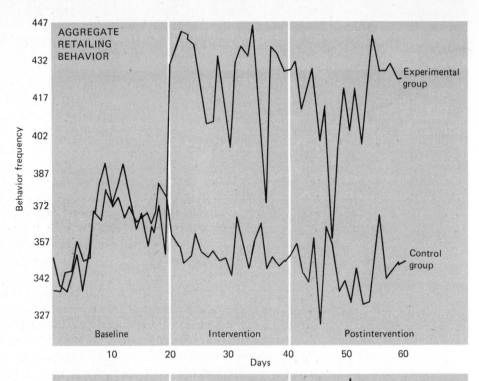

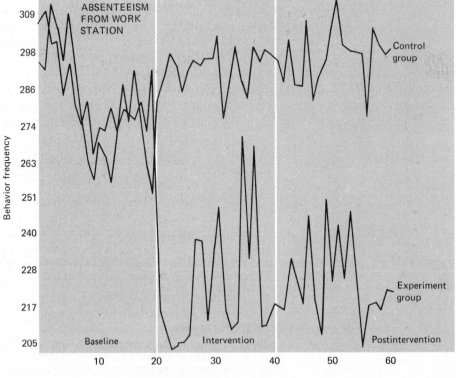

Figure 10-7 Results of a positive reinforcement intervention on salespersons' performance behavior. (*Source:* Fred Luthans, Robert Paul, and Douglas Baker, "An Experimental Analysis of the Impact of a Contingent Reinforcement Intervention on Salespersons' Performance Behaviors," *Journal of Applied Psychology* (in press).

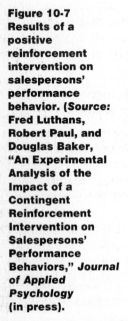

different, but immediately on the first day of the intervention the aggregate retailing behavior of the experimental group dramatically increased, and there was a huge decline in the average incidence of absence from the work station and idleness. As shown, this frequency maintained itself even after the intervention was withdrawn. This suggests that other more natural reinforcers in the environment and perhaps self-reinforcement had taken over.

Obviously, more research in more settings is needed before any definitive conclusions and broad generalizations about O.B. Mod. can be drawn. But, at least for now, O.B. Mod. does seem to hold considerable potential for the effective management of human resources.

ANALYSIS OF POSSIBLE ETHICAL ISSUES[39]

Skinner's theories in general and some of the behavior modification applications made in mental hospitals, clinics, classrooms, and especially prisons have generated emotional criticism and controversy. Surprisingly, this concern has not really carried over to the applications in human resource management. To be sure, there are some criticisms of an O.B. Mod. type of an approach in terms of theoretical orientation and its usefulness to practice,[40] but generally the ethics of the approach have not been unduly criticized. Nevertheless, there are probably many managers and potential managers who may feel uneasy about using an O.B. Mod. type of an approach. Although they may agree that it works, they still feel it is somehow wrong. Such concerns must be fully aired and constructively analyzed if O.B. Mod. is to be a viable human resource management approach now and in the future. The ethical problems must be anticipated and discussed rather than simply reacted to with emotion.

Popular criticism of behavior modification

Much of the popular criticism of Skinner's work revolves around his heavy dependence on the use of lower animals (especially the white rat) in developing the operant learning principles. The criticism that behavior modification tends to equate rats with humans is unfounded. The behaviorist would be the first to admit that rat and human behaviors are *not* the same. But at the same time they would point out that the *mechanism* of behavioral control is the same. From the operant perspective, all behaviors, animal and

---

[39]The author is indebted to Professor Robert Kreitner for many of the thoughts expressed in this section.

[40]For example, see: M. Hammer, "The Application of Behavior Conditioning Procedures to the Problems of Quality Control: Comment," *Academy of Management Journal,* December 1971, pp. 529–532; Fred Fry, "Operant Conditioning and O. B. Mod.: Of Mice and Men," *Personnel,* July–August 1974, pp. 17–24; W. F. Whyte, "Skinnerian Theory in Organizations," *Psychology Today,* April 1972, pp. 66–68; Edwin A. Locke, "The Myths of Behavior Mod in Organizations," *Academy of Management Review,* October 1977, pp. 543–553; and Patricia Cain Smith, "Resolved: Functional Analysis is the Best Technique for Diagnostic Evaluation of Organizational Behavior," in Barbara Karmel (ed.), op. cit., pp. 60–81.

human, depend on their consequences. The transition that behaviorism has made from animals to the mentally retarded to children to normal adults has been sufficiently demonstrated by both empirical research and practical application.

Besides the "applied ratamorphism" charge, another problem stems from the villainous portrayal of behavior control in popular literature, television, and the movies. The simple fact is that although the behavior control techniques portrayed in popular movies like *A Clockwork Orange* may be entertaining—if sinister manipulation and sadistic punishment can be called entertaining—and theoretically possible, they have nothing to do with the approach discussed in this chapter. Aversive conditioning and severe forms of punishment have no more chance of being used in human resource management than any other preposterous diabolical scheme.

Legitimate ethical concerns

Getting the popular and spectacular, but highly unreasonable ethical charges out of the way leaves the more legitimate ethical concerns surrounding control per se, particularly individual freedom and dignity, and the question of who controls the controllers. First of all it should be recognized that control of behavior has existed, exists now, and will continue to exist, regardless of whether it is purposeful or not. The primary concern should probably not be with control per se but instead with the beneficiary of the behavioral control. If behavioral control is misapplied for selfish purposes, the charge of being unethical seems legitimate. On the other hand, if the control is used for more effective management for the mutually beneficial consequences for both the person being controlled and the organization, it would seem to be on ethical ground.

The individual-freedom-and-dignity issue popularized by Skinner's book *Beyond Freedom and Dignity* largely boils down to a philosophical discussion of relative ethics. The O.B. Mod. approach, which emphasizes positive control and creating a reinforcing organization environment can increase rather than decrease an employee's freedom and dignity. This is especially true relative to the existing dependence on negative control found in most of today's organizations. The same can be said of the question of who controls the controllers. This is certainly not as big a problem in management application as it is in other applications. Whether in a public or private organization, the authority structure would always make the controller responsible to someone higher in the hierarchy. In addition, through countercontrol, subordinates can control their supervisors as well as be controlled by them. A major goal of O.B. Mod. is to create a mutually reinforcing environment so that participants may be self-reinforced for pursuing organizational objectives.

The charge of limited application and manipulation

Those who argue that organizational behavior modification can have only very limited application in a complex organizational setting must recognize that the underlying theory and mechanisms hold in very simple or in very complex environments. The previous section demonstrated how O.B. Mod. has been and can be applied in complex organizational settings. Certainly O.B. Mod. is not the only approach to effective human resource management, and there is a challenge for more research and broader application. This is why O.B. Mod. is exciting; it is relatively new in terms of application, and to date there is only preliminary research support, but it is built on a very well developed, sound theoretical base.

As far as being manipulative, the same charges could be made of the other techniques discussed in this book. O.B. Mod. seems to be no more and no less manipulative than other human resource management approaches. If anything, in O.B. Mod. the environmental contingencies are manipulated, not the individual, and positive control is suggested over the existing negative control of people at work.

A final word on ethical implications

Issues such as measuring on-the-job behaviors cannot be automatically dismissed. However, such measurement is certainly not new with O.B. Mod.—industrial engineers have been doing this since the turn of the century—and, as discussed earlier, there are ways of obtaining behavioral data without contaminating the data or compromising the individual's privacy. In the final analysis, the ethical answer to O.B. Mod. or any other technique lies in the professional integrity of the manager using the approach and the mutual organizational and individual beneficiaries. O.B. Mod. should in no way attempt to be secretive or manipulative. If O.B. Mod. is to be an effective human resource management approach, it must be completely ethical from a societal, organizational, and individual standpoint.

SUMMARY

This chapter uses the O.B. Mod. model as an approach to human resource management. The model consists of identifying critical performance-related behaviors; obtaining a baseline measure; functionally analyzing the antecedents and the consequences of the critical behavior; intervening by using a positive reinforcement strategy to accelerate desirable critical behaviors and an extinction strategy to decelerate undesirable critical behaviors; and evaluating to ensure performance improvement. This is an applied, environmentally based approach to organizational behavior rather than a cognitive, motivational approach. O.B. Mod. represents only one, but potentially a very powerful, approach to human resource management. It is given detailed attention so that the reader can gain some depth in an applied approach, but it should be recognized that the techniques covered in the other chapters are also important to effective human resource management in today's organizations.

QUESTIONS FOR DISCUSSION AND REVIEW

1. What are some methods that can be used to identify critical behaviors? What are some simple guidelines that can be used?
2. One of the quotes said, "In effect, behavior charts are mini behavioral experiments." Explain.
3. Why is positive reinforcement a more effective intervention strategy than punishment? What, if anything, is the difference between a punishment strategy and an extinction strategy?
4. What is the difference between contrived and natural rewards? Which is more effective to use as an O.B. Mod. intervention strategy? Why?
5. Briefly summarize the procedures and results of the manufacturing and nonmanufacturing studies reported in the chapter. How would you go about implementing and evaluating an O.B. Mod. approach in an organization you are familiar with? Be specific in your answer.
6. How, if possible, could you convince someone that an approach like O.B. Mod. is an ethical technique for human resource management?

CASE:
Up the Piece Rate

Larry Ames had successfully completed a company training program on O.B. Mod. He liked the approach and started using it on the workers in his department. Following the O.B. Mod. model, he identified several critical behaviors, measured and analyzed them, and used a positive reinforcement/extinction intervention strategy. His evaluation showed a significant improvement in the performance of his department. Over coffee one day he commented to one of the other supervisors, "This contingent reinforcement approach really works. Before, the goody-goody people up in personnel were always telling us to try to understand and be nice to our workers. Frankly, I couldn't buy that. In the first place I don't think there is anybody who can really *understand* my people—I certainly can't. More important, though, is that under this approach I am only nice *contingently*—contingent upon good performance. That makes a lot more sense, and my evaluation proves that it works." The other supervisor commented, "You are being reinforced for using the reinforcement technique on your people." Larry said, "Sure am. Just like the trainer said: 'Behavior that is reinforced will strengthen and repeat itself.' I'm so reinforced that I am starting to use it on my wife and kids at home, and you know what? It works there, too."

The next week Larry was called into the department head's office and told, "Larry, as you know, your department has shown a substantial increase in performance since you completed the O.B. Mod. program. I have sent our industrial engineer down there to analyze your standards. I have received her report and it looks like we will have to adjust your rates upward by 10 percent. Otherwise we are going to have to pay too much incentive pay. I'm sure you can use some of the things you learned in that O.B. Mod. program to break the news to your people. Good luck, and keep up the good work."

1. Do you think Larry's boss, the department head, attended the O.B. Mod. program? Analyze the department head's action in terms of O.B. Mod.

2. What do you think will be Larry's reaction now and in the future? How do you think Larry's people will react?

3. Given the 10 percent increase in standards, is there any way that Larry could still use the O.B. Mod. approach with his people? With his boss? How?

CASE:
A Tardiness Problem

You have been getting a lot of complaints recently from your boss on the consistent tardiness of your work group. The time sheet records indicate that your people's average start-up time is about ten minutes late. While you have never been concerned about the tardiness problem, your boss is really getting upset. He points out that the tardiness reduces the amount of production time and delays the start-up of the assembly line. You realize that the tardiness is a type of avoidance behavior, it delays the start of a very boring job. Your work group is very cohesive, each of the members will follow what the group wants to do. One of the leaders of the group is Carlos Lopez. He seems to spend a lot of time getting the group into trouble. You really want the group to come in on time, but you don't really want a confrontation on the issue because, frankly, you don't think it is that important to chance getting everyone upset with you. You decide to use an O.B. Mod. approach.

1. Trace through the five steps in the O.B. Mod. model to show how it could be applied to this tardiness problem. Make sure you are specific in identifying the critical performance behavior(s) and the antecedents and consequences of the functional analysis.

2. Do you think the approach you have suggested in your answer to Question 1 above will really work? Why or why not?

CASE:
Trouble Between Departments

Alice James is in charge of the human services division of a state welfare department and you are the personnel director. Lately, you have been concerned about the relations between the two departments. Alice, up to two years ago, had the full responsibility for hiring, training, and firing all the employees in her division. Then, with the increasing complexity of the personnel function and government regulations on equal opportunity in employment, the head of the welfare agency decided to centralize the personnel function and give the personnel director decision-making power over all personnel decisions. Since that directive, Alice has been relatively intolerant and upset with the personnel department as a whole and much of her wrath has been directed at you. Many times you have lost your temper and have really let her have it. The result of these emotional outbursts has been to worsen the situation and contribute to a greater sense of tension between the departments. Obviously, your emotional behavior has tended to reinforce Alice's contempt of the personnel department.

You have just completed a one week seminar on O.B. Mod. You think that you can use this approach to change Alice's behavior and smooth out the relationships between the departments.

1. Using the five-step O.B. Mod. model, how would you go about changing Alice's behavior and improving the relationship between personnel and the human services division? Be specific in your answer.

2. Do you think it is more difficult changing the kinds of behaviors mentioned in this case as opposed to quality and quantity types of performance behaviors as was done in the studies discussed in the chapter? Why or why not?

CASE STUDY AND EXPERIENTIAL EXERCISES FOR PART 3

CASE:
TROUBLE IN LORDSTOWN

In Lordstown, Ohio, General Motors has its only United States plant that turns out the Vega, a subcompact car. A description of the technology in the plant leads one into the realm of superlatives. For example, the assembly line is the most automated in the industry. It is also the fastest, having the capability to produce 100 cars an hour. The characteristics of the labor force are also somewhat special: the employees at the Vega plant are young (average age approximately twenty-four), long-haired, and bell-bottomed.

The plant was built with the hopes that it would be one of GM's most efficient. This did not happen. A couple of years after opening, the plant was experiencing the worst labor problems in the industry. Estimates placed GM's loss, from low productivity and shoddy quality at around $40 million. Everyone was careful not to call it sabotage, although some people were unsure of exactly what other term might better describe the situation. For example, someone deliberately set fire to an assembly line control box. The line had to be shut down. In addition, many of the cars, upon reaching the end of the line, were not ready to be delivered to the dealer's showroom. Instead, maintenance was needed. Some of the cars had slit upholstery, and others had scratched paint or dented bodies. It was not uncommon to find that bolts were either loose or missing. Wires under the hood were sometimes cut; turn signal switches were bent; ignition keys were broken off in the lock to prevent the car from being driven from the assembly line. Things got so bad that at one point the number of cars in the plant's repair lot exceeded the available space, there being room for no more than 2000 autos. As a result, the assembly line was stopped and the workers were sent home payless.

The trouble all began about eighteen months after the automated line went into operation. With many of the technical bugs worked out of the line and with the plant consolidated with an adjacent Fisher Body plant, the company laid off some of the workers. The union placed the number at 750, while the company claimed it was only half this number. In any event, the remaining workers began complaining that they were being expected to speed up their work so that they could assume the work of those who had been laid off. There were extra jobs to be done, and the remaining work force had to do them. The company did not give the complaints much attention. However, as the number of grievances grew, so did the number of new cars needing maintenance. Finally, the union, Local 1112, leaked a story to the press that GM was shipping defective Vegas to its dealers. The company immediately denied the charges, but the union members building the cars said that the charges were true. When interviewed on the CBS program "Sixty Minutes," they reiterated their claims.

The workers indicated that they were not interested in more money. At the time they were drawing around $4.50 an hour, plus $2.50 in fringe benefits. What they wanted was a redefinition of the work rules, the rehiring of some workers who were laid off, and the elimination of some of the extra work. They felt that they could not do all that was expected of them when there was an auto coming at them every thirty-six seconds. The company, meanwhile, pointed out that the additional chores were an attempt to make the job more meaningful and to alleviate the mind-numbing boredom that is often associated with doing just one task. The workers did not accept management's explanation of "job enrichment." They felt it was just a shield behind which GM was attempting to hide. The men said that they failed to see how a job could be enriched by giving someone two jobs to do thirty times an hour in contrast to his former work which called for doing one job sixty times an hour. They indicated that they wanted more time to do their single, simple job.

1. How do you explain the motivation of the employees at the Lordstown plant? What are their needs? Do any of the work motivation theories apply to them? How?
2. Do you think the company was really using job enrichment here? How would you rate the critical job characteristics (via the Hackman-Oldham model) of these assembly line jobs? How could you increase the motivating potential of these jobs? Do you think these workers would respond to an enriched job? How would you compare the Lordstown GM plant with the Volvo plant in Sweden?
3. Could an O.B. Mod. approach work at this Lordstown plant? What would be some examples of the five steps (identify, measure, analyze, intervene, and evaluate) that could be applied to increase the quantity and quality of performance at this plant?

EXERCISE:

MOTIVATION QUESTION-NAIRE

Goals:

1. To experience firsthand the concepts of one of the work motivation theories, in this case the popular Maslow hierarchy of needs
2. To get personal feedback on your opinions of the use of motivational techniques in human resource management

Implementation:

The following questions have seven possible responses.

Strongly agree	Agree	Slightly agree	Don't know	Slightly disagree	Disagree	Strongly disagree
+3	+2	+1	0	−1	−2	−3

Please mark one of the seven responses by circling the number that corresponds to the response that fits your opinion. For example: if you "Strongly agree," circle the number "+3."

Complete every item. You have about ten minutes to do so.

1. Special wage increases should be given to employees who do their jobs very well.
$\qquad$ +3 +2 +1 0 −1 −2 −3

2. Better job descriptions would be helpful so that employees will know exactly what is expected of them.
$\qquad$ +3 +2 +1 0 −1 −2 −3

3. Employees need to be reminded that their jobs are dependent on the Company's ability to compete effectively.
$\qquad$ +3 +2 +1 0 −1 −2 −3

4. Supervisors should give a good deal of attention to the physical working conditions of their employees.
$\qquad$ +3 +2 +1 0 −1 −2 −3

5. Supervisors ought to work hard to develop a friendly working atmosphere among their people.
$\qquad$ +3 +2 +1 0 −1 −2 −3

6. Individual recognition for above-standard performance means a lot to employees.
$\qquad$ +3 +2 +1 0 −1 −2 −3

7. Indifferent supervision can often bruise feelings.
$\qquad$ +3 +2 +1 0 −1 −2 −3

8. Employees want to feel that their real skills and capacities are put to use on their jobs.
$\qquad$ +3 +2 +1 0 −1 −2 −3

9. The company retirement benefits and stock programs are important factors in keeping employees on their jobs.
$\qquad$ +3 +2 +1 0 −1 −2 −3

10. Almost every job can be made more stimulating and challenging.
$\qquad$ +3 +2 +1 0 −1 −2 −3

11. Many employees want to give their best in everything they do.
$\qquad$ +3 +2 +1 0 −1 −2 −3

12. Management could show more interest in the employees by sponsoring social events after hours.
$\qquad$ +3 +2 +1 0 −1 −2 −3

13. Pride in one's work is actually an important reward.
$\qquad$ +3 +2 +1 0 −1 −2 −3

14. Employees want to be able to think of themselves as "the best" at their own jobs.
$\qquad$ +3 +2 +1 0 −1 −2 −3

Strongly agree	Agree	Slightly agree	Don't know	Slightly disagree	Disagree	Strongly disagree
+3	+2	+1	0	−1	−2	−3

15. The quality of the relationships in the informal work group is quite important. +3 +2 +1 0 −1 −2 −3

16. Individual incentive bonuses would improve the performance of employees. +3 +2 +1 0 −1 −2 −3

17. Visibility with upper management is important to employees. +3 +2 +1 0 −1 −2 −3

18. Employees generally like to schedule their own work and to make job-related decisions with a minimum of supervision. +3 +2 +1 0 −1 −2 −3

19. Job security is important to employees. +3 +2 +1 0 −1 −2 −3

20. Having good equipment to work with is important to employees. +3 +2 +1 0 −1 −2 −3

Scoring

1. Transfer the numbers you circled in the questionnaire to the appropriate places in the spaces below.

Statement no.	Score	Statement no.	Score
10	_____	2	_____
11	_____	3	_____
13	_____	9	_____
18	_____	19	_____
Total	_____	Total	_____
(Self-actualization needs)		(Safety needs)	

Statement no.	Score	Statement no.	Score
6	_____	1	_____
8	_____	4	_____
14	_____	16	_____
17	_____	20	_____
Total	_____	Total	_____
(Esteem needs)		(Basic needs)	

Statement no.	Score
5	_____
7	_____
12	_____
15	_____
Total	_____
(Belonging needs)	

2. Record your total scores in the following chart by marking an "X" in each row next to the number of your total score for that area of needs motivation.

	−12	−10	−8	−6	−4	−2	0	+2	+4	+6	+8	+10	+12
Self-actualization													
Esteem													
Belonging													
Safety													
Basic													

Low use   High use

By examining the chart you can see the relative strength you attach to each of the needs in Maslow's hierarchy. There are no right answers here, but most work motivation theorists imply that most people are mainly concerned with the upper level needs (i.e., belongingness, esteem, and self-actualization).

EXERCISE:

JOB DESIGN SURVEY

Goals:

1. To experience firsthand the job characteristics approach to job design, in this case through the Hackman-Oldham Job Diagnostic Survey (JDS)
2. To get personal feedback on the motivating potential of your present or past job and identify and compare its critical characteristics

Implementation:

1. Please describe your present job (or a job you have held in the past) as objectively as you can. Circle the number that best reflects the job.

    a. How much *variety* is there in your job? That is, to what extent does the job require you to do many different things at work, using a variety of your skills and talents?

1----------------2----------------3----------------4----------------5----------------6----------------7

Very little; the job requires me to do the same routine things over and over again.

Moderate variety

Very much; the job requires me to do many different things, using a number of different skills and talents.

b. To what extent does your job involve doing a *"whole" and identifiable piece of work?* That is, is the job a complete piece of work that has an obvious beginning and end? Or is it only a small part of the overall piece of work, which is finished by other people or by automatic machines?

```
1----------------2----------------3----------------4----------------5----------------6----------------7
```

| My job is only a tiny part of the overall piece of work; the results of my activities cannot be seen in the final product or service. | My job is a moderate-sized "chunk" of the overall piece of work; my own contribution can be seen in the final outcome. | My job involves doing the whole piece of work, from start to finish; the results of my activities are easily seen in the final product or service. |

c. In general, *how significant or important* is your job? That is, are the results of your work likely to significantly affect the lives or well-being of other people?

```
1----------------2----------------3----------------4----------------5----------------6----------------7
```

| Not very significant; the outcomes of my work are *not* likely to have important effects on other people. | Moderately significant. | Highly significant; the outcomes of my work can affect other people in very important ways. |

d. How much *autonomy* is there in your job? That is, to what extent does your job permit you to decide on *your own* how to go about doing the work?

```
1----------------2----------------3----------------4----------------5----------------6----------------7
```

| Very little; the job gives me almost no personal "say" about how and when the work is done. | Moderate autonomy; many things are standardized and not under my control, but I can make some decisions about the work. | Very much; the job gives me almost complete responsibility for deciding how and when the work is done. |

e. To what extent does *doing the job* itself provide you with information about your work performance? That is, does the actual *work* itself provide clues about how well you are doing—aside from any "feedback" coworkers or supervisors may provide?

```
1----------------2----------------3----------------4----------------5----------------6----------------7
```

| Very little; the job itself is set up so I could work forever without finding out how well I am doing. | Moderately; sometimes doing the job provides "feedback" to me; sometimes it does not. | Very much; the job is set up so that I get almost constant "feedback" as I work about how well I am doing. |

2. The five questions above measure your perceived skill variety, task identity, task significance, autonomy, and feedback in your job. The complete JDS uses several questions to measure these dimensions. But to get some idea of the motivating potential, use your scores (1 to 7) for each job dimension and calculate as follows:

$$MPS = \frac{\text{skill variety} + \text{task identity} + \text{task significance}}{3} \times \text{autonomy} \times \text{feedback}$$

Next, plot your job design profile and MPS score on the graphs below. These show the national averages for all jobs. Analyze how you compare and suggest ways to redesign your job.

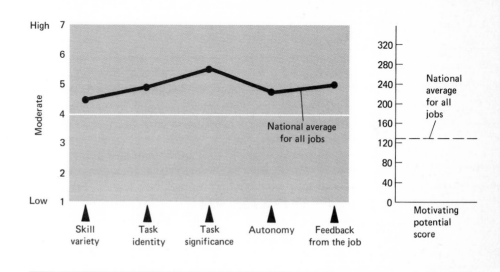

EXERCISE:

ROLE-PLAYING AND O.B. MOD.

Goals:

To experience the application of the O.B. Mod. approach to human resource management

Implementation:

This role-play situation involves two people: Allen, the supervisor of claims processing in a large insurance firm, and Francis, an employee in the department. One person will be selected to play the role of Allen and another will play Francis. The information and background for each of the participants follows. When the participants have carefully read their roles, the supervisor, Allen, will be asked to conduct a performance-related discussion with Francis. Those who are not playing one of the roles should carefully observe the conversation between Allen and Francis and provide the information requested below. The observers should not necessarily read the roles of Allen and Francis.

1. List those words, phrases, or sentences that Allen used that seemed particularly reinforcing.
2. List any words, phrases, or sentences used by Allen that may have been punishing.
3. List any suggestions that you have to improve Allen's future conversations with employees.
4. Using the steps of O.B. Mod. (identify, measure, analyze, intervene, and evaluate), how would you (or your group) improve the human performance in this claims department. Be as specific as you can for each step. You may have to fabricate some of the examples.

Role playing situation for Allen:

After reading the information below, you are to conduct a performance-related discussion with Francis in order to reward increased productivity.

You are the supervisor of twenty people in the claims processing department for a large insurance company. Several weeks ago, you established standards for claims processing and measured each employee's work output. One employee, Francis Nelson, had prarticularly low output figures and averaged less than 80 percent of standard during the baseline data collection period. Your target for rewarding Francis was an 85 percent average for a one-week period. During the first two weeks, Francis failed to meet this goal. Now, in the third week after you have decided to use this approach, Francis has achieved the new goal. Francis's performance is illustrated below.

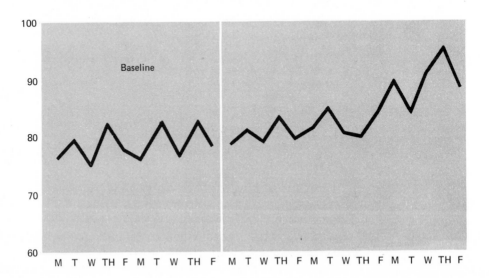

Role playing situation for Francis:

After reading the information below, you are to be interviewed by your supervisor concerning your performance.

You are Francis Nelson, an employee in the claims processing division of a large insurance company. Recently, your supervisor, Allen Parks, instituted a new system of measuring performance in the department. Most of the other employees have already discussed their performance with him, but for some reason Allen has not yet talked with you. Now this morning, Allen said he wanted to have a talk about your performance. You are somewhat anxious about what he will have to say. You know that you are not the best employee in the department but you do make your best effort. You hope that Allen will recognize this and not be too hard on you.

THE DYNAMICS OF ORGANIZATIONAL BEHAVIOR

CHAPTER 11

GROUP DYNAMICS

INFIGHTING AMONG THE MANAGEMENT GROUP*

Recently, Mario A. di Federico stepped down as President of Firestone. The huge rubber company has been hit with several critical events that have led to the turnover in the managerial staff. Over the last couple of years Firestone has lost fourteen of its twenty-four senior managers. The company's problems of product difficulties and illegal payoffs have been widely publicized. Not so publicized is the growing evidence that infighting among the top executive group has also taken its toll. Interdepartmental and personality conflicts within this group have created difficult situations, leading to a serious breakdown in coordination among departments. During the recent trouble with the radial 500 tires, several chief executives claimed they were totally uninformed of the gravity of the situation. Quick action and a unified management team would possibly have been able to minimize many of the difficulties the company had with the federal government and consumer groups. According to one executive, the lack of cohesion in management paralyzed the company's efforts to deal with the rubber strike a few years ago and has caused the company to lag behind others in needed diversification. The result is that about 80 percent of the net sales of Firestone has been in the tire market. Since this is a highly volatile market, this is a very questionable business strategy. Some insiders feel that the managerial infighting and instability have been a major cause of the "bottom line" problems of the company. From peak earnings of $165 million in 1973, the profit picture has steadily declined. In 1978 the company suffered a $148.3 million loss. Team cooperation and stability seem needed from the Firestone management group if the company is to survive, let alone prosper and grow, in the future.

*Adapted from "Firestone's Search for Stability," *Business Week,* July 9, 1979, pp. 44–49.

Parts 2 and 3 were devoted chiefly to the micro variables that input into organizational behavior. This part is more concerned with the dynamic nature of organizational behavior. This chapter approaches organizational behavior dynamics from the perspective of the group, informal roles, and organization. The first section examines the way groups are formed, the various types of groups, some of the dynamics and functions of groups, and the findings of research on groups. The second section discusses the committee as a particular, practical case of group dynamics. The positive and negative attributes of committees are analyzed, and special attention is devoted to the "groupthink" problem. The third and last section focuses on the dynamics of informal roles and organization. Managerial roles and the power and communication implications of the informal organization are stressed.

THE NATURE OF GROUPS

Chapter 2 introduced the group as an important unit of sociological analysis, which contributes much to the understanding of organizational behavior. This is especially true when the dynamics of the group are analyzed. Group dynamics is concerned with the interactions and forces among group members in a social situation. When the concept is applied to the study of organizational behavior, the focus is on the dynamics of members of formal or informal groups in the organization.

Just as there is no one definition of the group itself, there is no universal agreement on what is meant by group dynamics. Although Kurt Lewin popularized the term in the 1930s, through the years different connotations have been attached to it. One normative view is that group dynamics describes *how* a group *should* be organized and conducted. Democratic leadership, member participation, and overall cooperation are stressed. This view of group dynamics is given attention in Chapter 15. Another view of group dynamics is that it consists of a set of *techniques*. Here, role playing, brainstorming, buzz groups, leaderless groups, group therapy, sensitivity training, team building, transactional analysis, and the Johari window are equated with group dynamics. Some of these techniques are covered in Chapter 21, on organization development. A third view is the closest to Lewin's original conception. Group dynamics is viewed from the perspective of the internal nature of groups, how they form, their structure and processes, and how they function and affect individual members, other groups, and the organization.[1] The following sections are devoted to this third view of group dynamics.

The dynamics of group formation

Why do individuals form into groups? Before discussing some very practical reasons, it would be beneficial to examine briefly some of the major theories

---

[1] Joe Kelly, *Organizational Behaviour*, rev. ed., Dorsey-Irwin, Homewood, Ill., 1974, p. 306.

of group formation. The most basic theory explaining affiliation is *propinquity*. This interesting word simply means that individuals affiliate with one another because of spatial or geographical proximity. The theory would predict that students sitting next to one another in class, for example, are more likely to form into a group than students sitting at opposite ends of the room. In an organization, employees who work in the same area of the plant or office or managers with offices close to one another would more probably form into groups than those who are not physically located together. There is some research evidence to support the propinquity theory,[2] and on the surface it has a great deal of merit for explaining group formation. The drawback is that it is not analytical and does not begin to explain some of the complexities of group formation. Some theoretical and practical reasons need to be explored.

Theories of group formation   A more comprehensive theory of group formation than mere propinquity comes from George Homans. His theory is based on activities, interactions, and sentiments.[3] These three elements are directly related to one another. The more activities persons share, the more numerous will be their interactions and the stronger will be their sentiments; the more interactions among persons, the more will be their shared activities and sentiments; and the more sentiments persons have for one another, the more will be their shared activities and interactions. The Homans theory lends a great deal to the understanding of group formation and process. The major element is *interaction*. Persons in a group interact with one another, not in just the physical propinquity sense, but also to solve problems, attain goals, facilitate coordination, reduce tension, and achieve a balance.[4] Participants in an organization interacting in this manner tend to form into powerful groups.

There are many other theories that attempt to explain group formation. Most often they are only partial theories, but they are generally additive in nature. One of the more comprehensive is a *balance theory* of group formation proposed by Theodore Newcomb.[5] The theory states that persons are attracted to one another on the basis of similar attitudes toward commonly relevant objects and goals. Figure 11-1 shows this balance theory. Individual X will interact and form a relationship/group with Individual Y because of common attitudes and values toward Z. Once this relationship is formed, the participants strive to maintain a symmetrical balance between the attraction and the common attitudes. If an imbalance occurs, an attempt is made to restore the balance. If the balance cannot be restored, the relationship dissolves. Both propinquity and interaction play a role in balance theory.

---

[2]Leon Festinger, Stanley Schachter, and Kurt Back, *Social Pressures in Informal Groups: A Study of Human Factors in Housing*, Stanford, Stanford, Calif., 1963. First published by Harper in 1950.

[3]George C. Homans, *The Human Group*, Harcourt, Brace & World, New York, 1950, pp. 43–44.

[4]William G. Scott, *Organization Theory*, Irwin, Homewood, Ill., 1967, p. 83.

[5]Theodore M. Newcomb, *The Acquaintance Process*, Holt, New York, 1961.

The approach to group formation receiving the greatest recent emphasis is *exchange theory*.[6] Similar to its functioning as a work motivation theory, discussed in Chapter 7, exchange theory of groups is based upon reward-cost outcomes of interaction. A minimum positive level (rewards greater than costs) of an outcome must exist in order for attraction or affiliation to take place. Rewards from interactions gratify needs while costs incur anxiety, frustration, embarrassment, or fatigue. Propinquity, interaction, and common attitudes all have roles in exchange theory.

Practicalities of group formation   Besides the theoretical explanations for group formation, there are some very practical reasons for joining and/or forming a group. For instance, employees in an organization may form a group for economic, security, or social reasons. Economically, workers may form a group to work on a project that is paid for on a group-incentive plan or may form a union to demand higher wages. For security, joining a group provides the individual with a united front in combating indiscriminant, unilateral treatment. The adage that there is strength in numbers applies in this case. The most important practical reason why individuals join or form groups is, however, that groups tend to satisfy the very intense social needs of most people. Workers, in particular, generally have a very strong desire for affiliation. This need is met by belonging to a group. Research going as far back as the Hawthorne studies has found the affiliation motive to have a major impact on human behavior in organizations. Chapter 6 discussed this motive in detail.

Types of groups

There are numerous types of groups. The theories of group formation that were just discussed are partly based upon the attraction between two

[6]John W. Thibaut and Harold H. Kelley, *The Social Psychology of Groups*, Wiley, New York, 1959.

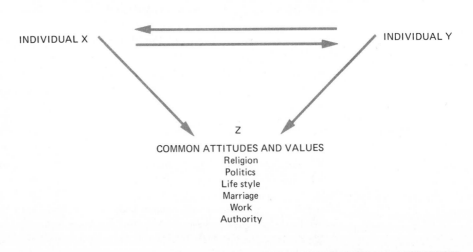

**Figure 11-1
A balance theory
of group formation.**

persons—the simple dyad group. Of course, in the real world groups are usually much more complex than the dyad. There are small and large groups, primary and secondary groups, membership and reference groups, in- and out-groups, and formal and informal groups. Each type has different characteristics and different effects on its members.

Primary groups   Charles H. Cooley was the first to define and analyze a primary group. In his book *Social Organization*, first published in 1909, he wrote, "By primary groups I mean those characterized by intimate, face-to-face association and cooperation. They are primary in several senses, but chiefly in that they are fundamental in forming the social nature and ideals of the individual."[7] Cooley's primary group concept was further developed and refined by George Homans. In Homans's classic book *The Human Group*, a group is described as "a number of persons who communicate with one another often over a span of time, and who are few enough so that each person is able to communicate with all the others, not at secondhand, through other people, but face-to-face."[8]

Often the terms *small group* and *primary group* are used interchangeably. Technically, there is a difference. A small group has to meet only the criterion of small size. Usually, no attempt is made to assign precise numbers, but the accepted criterion is that the group must be small enough for face-to-face interaction and communication to occur. In addition to being small, a primary group must have a feeling of comradeship, loyalty, and a common sense of values among its members. Thus, all primary groups are small groups but not all small groups are primary.

Two examples of a primary group are the family and the peer group. Initially, the primary group was limited to a socializing group, but then a broader conception was given impetus by the results of the Hawthorne studies. Work groups definitely have primary group qualities. Later, equally renowned studies, described in *Street Corner Society*, by William F. Whyte, and in *The American Soldier*, by Samuel Stouffer et al., further expanded the concept of the primary group.[9] These and many recent studies all point to the tremendous impact that the primary group has on individual behavior, regardless of context or environmental conditions.

Other types of groups   Besides primary groups, there are also other classifications of groups that are important to the study of organizational behavior. Two important distinctions are between membership and reference groups, and in- and out-groups. These differences can be described as follows:

Membership groups are those to which the individual actually belongs, while a

[7]Charles H. Cooley, *Social Organization*, Scribner, New York, 1911, p. 23. Originally published in 1909.

[8]Homans, op. cit., p. 1.

[9]See Fritz J. Roethlisberger and William J. Dickson, *Management and the Worker*, Harvard, Cambridge, 1945; W. F. Whyte, *Street Corner Society*, University of Chicago Press, Chicago, 1943 and 1955; and Samuel A. Stouffer et al., *The American Soldier*, Princeton, Princeton, N. J., 1949.

reference group is one with which he identifies or to which he would like to belong. . . . The in-group represents a clustering of individuals holding prevailing values in a society or, at least, having a dominant place in social functioning. . . . The out-groups are the conglomerates looked upon as subordinate or marginal in the culture.[10]

All these types of groups have relevance to the study of organizational behavior, but the formal and informal types are most directly applicable.

There are many formally designated groups and committees in the modern organization. Two very common examples are the command and task groups.[11] A command group consists of a superior and the immediate subordinates. The membership and structure of command groups are formally determined and are represented on the organization chart. The superior is granted formal authority over the other members of the command group. The task group is formally designed to work on a specific project or job. Its interaction and structure are formally designed to accomplish the task. Committees as a type of formal group are given detailed attention later in the chapter.

There are also numerous informal groups in the organization. Interest and friendship are common examples.[12] Although interest groups may also be formally designated, generally they are established on an informal basis according to common interests or attitudes in the manner described by Newcomb's balance theory. Common interests range from sports (an informal group gets together to bet on sports events) to hatred of management (an informal group unites to restrict output). Friendship groups are a more common kind of informal group. Persons join this type of group in the manner described by exchange theory—the rewards of the friendship group outweigh the costs. Organizational participants join and form friendship groups in order to satisfy their needs for affiliation. Most often, formal organizational arrangements do not satisfy the important social needs. The dynamics of informal groups are examined in more detail in the last part of the chapter.

Implications from research on group dynamics

Starting with the Hawthorne studies, there has been an abundance of significant research on groups that has implications for organizational behavior and management. Besides the Hawthorne studies, the widely known, classic studies that relate group dynamics to human performance in an organizational setting include the Lippitt and White leadership studies, which are covered in Chapter 15; the Coch and French study on overcoming

[10]Blair J. Kolasa, *Introduction to Behavioral Science for Business*, Wiley, New York, 1969, pp. 451–452.

[11]See Leonard R. Sayles, "Work Group Behavior and the Larger Organization," in *Research in Industrial Human Relations*, Industrial Relations Research Association, Publication no. 17, Harper, New York, 1957, pp. 131–145.

[12]Ibid.

resistance to change; Van Zelst's study of two groups of carpenters and bricklayers;[13] Trist and Bamforth's study of British coal mining;[14] and William F. Whyte's research of the restaurant industry.[15] In addition, there are numerous research studies on group dynamics which indirectly contribute to the better understanding of organizational behavior. Table 11-1 summarizes the research findings on the functions that groups can serve for both the organization as a whole and the individual organizational participant.

In addition to the somewhat general conclusions shown in Table 11-1, there are a number of studies in social psychology which seem to have particular relevance to organizational behavior. The work of social psychologist Stanley Schachter seems especially important for the application of group dynamics research to human resource management.[16]

The Schachter checkerboard study   Schachter and his associates tested the effect that group cohesiveness and induction had on productivity under

[13]Raymond H. Van Zelst, "Sociometrically Selected Work Teams Increase Production," *Personnel Psychology*, Autumn 1952, pp. 175–185.

[14]E. L. Trist and K. W. Bamforth, "Some Social and Psychological Consequences of the Longwall Method of Coal Getting," *Human Relations*, vol. 4, no. 1, 1951, pp. 3–38.

[15]William F. Whyte, *Human Relations in the Restaurant Industry*, McGraw-Hill, 1948.

[16]Stanley Schachter, Norris Ellertson, Dorothy McBride, and Doris Gregory, "An Experimental Study of Cohesiveness and Productivity," *Human Relations*, vol. 4, no. 3, 1951, pp. 229–239.

Table 11-1

SUMMARY OF RESEARCH ON THE IMPACT THAT GROUPS HAVE ON ORGANIZATIONAL AND INDIVIDUAL EFFECTIVENESS

The impact of groups on organizational effectiveness	The impact of groups on individual employee effectiveness
1. Accomplishing tasks that could not be done by employees themselves	1. Aiding in learning about the organization and its environment
2. Bringing a number of skills and talents to bear on complex, difficult tasks	2. Aiding in learning about one's self
3. Providing a vehicle for decision making that permits multiple and conflicting views to be aired and considered	3. Providing help in gaining new skills
4. Providing an efficient means for organizational control of employee behavior	4. Obtaining valued rewards that are not accessible by one's self
5. Facilitating changes in organizational policies or procedures	5. Satisfying important personal needs, especially needs for social acceptance and affiliation
6. Increasing organizational stability by transmitting shared beliefs and values to new employees	

Source: Adapted from David A. Nadler, J. Richard Hackman, and Edward E. Lawler, *Managing Organizational Behavior*, Little, Brown, Boston, 1979, p. 102.

highly controlled conditions. Women college students were used as subjects. *Cohesiveness* was defined as the average resultant force acting on members to remain in a group. The researchers assumed that by making the group appear attractive or not attractive, the subjects would correspondingly feel high or low cohesiveness. About half the subjects were told by the experimenter that they would be members of an extremely congenial group and that "there is every reason to expect that the other members of the group will like you and you will like them." The other half of the subjects were told by the experimenter that, because of scheduling difficulties, it was impossible to assemble a congenial group and that "there is no particular reason to think that you will like them or that they will care for you." In this manner, high- and low-cohesive groups were created by the experimenter.

All the subjects were told that their task was to make cardboard checkerboards. It was to be a three-person, assembly line operation consisting of cutting out pieces of cardboard, mounting and pasting them on heavier stock, and painting them through a stencil. For control purposes, all subjects were made cutters, but they thought they would pass on the cut boards to the other two members of their group (the paster and painter) in another room.

The subjects were informed that they could write notes to and would receive notes from their pasters and painters. Of course, the experimenter intercepted all the notes from the subjects and gave them prewritten notes. These notes were used to test the impact of positive and negative induction. In the first sixteeen minutes of the experiment, each subject received five notes from her nonexistent paster and painter that made no attempt to influence productivity. In the remaining sixteen minutes of the experiment, half the subjects who believed they were members of high cohesive groups and half the subjects who thought they were members of low cohesive groups received six positive notes. These notes urged increased production, for example, "Time's running out, let's really make a spurt—Paster." The other half of the high and low cohesive subjects received negative notes urging them to slow down production. An example of a negative note was: "Let's try to set a record—let's be the slowest subjects they ever had—Painter."

Through the manipulations of cohesiveness and induction just described, the following experimental groups were created:

1. High cohesive, positive induction (Hi Co, + Ind)
2. Low cohesive, positive induction (Lo Co, + Ind)
3. High cohesive, negative induction (Hi Co, − Ind)
4. Low cohesive, negative induction (Lo Co, − Ind)

Thus, the independent variables in the experiment were cohesiveness and induction and the dependent variable was productivity. Figure 11-2 summarizes the results. Although Schachter's experiment did not obtain a statistically significant difference in productivity between the high and low cohesive groups that were positively induced, a follow-up study which used a more difficult task did.[17]

---

[17]Leonard Berkowitz, "Group Standards, Cohesiveness, and Productivity," *Human Relations*, vol. 7, no. 4, 1954, pp. 509–519.

Implications of the Schachter study   The results of Schachter's study contain some very interesting implications for the study of organizational behavior. The "pitchfork" productivity curves in Figure 11-2 imply that highly cohesive groups have very powerful dynamics, both positive and negative, for human resource management. On the other hand, the low cohesive groups are not so powerful. However, of even more importance to human resource management is the variable of induction. Performance depends largely on how the high or low cohesive group is induced.

At least for illustrative purposes, leadership may be substituted for induction. If this is done, the key variable for the subjects' performance in the Schachter experiment becomes leadership. A highly cohesive group that is given positive leadership will have the highest possible productivity. On the other side of the coin, a highly cohesive group that is given poor leadership will have the lowest possible productivity. A highly cohesive group is analogous to a time bomb in the hands of management. The direction in which the highly cohesive group goes, breaking production records or severely restricting output, depends on how it is led. The low cohesive group is much safer in the hands of management. Leadership will not have a serious negative or positive impact on this group. However, the implication is that if management wishes to maximize productivity, it must build a cohesive group and give it proper leadership.

The above discussion does not imply that passing notes to college students cutting out checkerboards in a classroom laboratory setting can be made equivalent to managing human resources in the modern, complex organization. This, of course, cannot and should not be attempted. On the other hand, there are some interesting insights and points of departure for organizational behavior analysis that can come out of laboratory investigations such as Schachter's. For instance, the results of Schachter's study can be applied in retrospect to the work of Frederick W. Taylor or to the Hawthorne studies. Taylor accounted only for the *Hi Co, − Ind* productivity

**Figure 11-2
The "pitchfork"
results from the
Schachter
checkerboard
study. (*Source:*
Adapted from
Stanley Schachter
et al., "An
Experimental
Study of
Cohesiveness and
Productivity,"
Human Relations,
vol. 4, no. 3, 1951,
pp. 229–239.)**

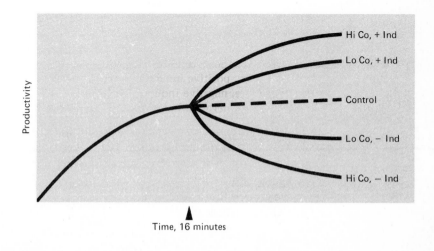

curve when he advocated "breaking up the group." If his scientific management methods could be considered as +*Ind*, the best productivity he could obtain would be that of the *Lo Co, + Ind*. In other words, in light of the Schachter study, Taylor's methods could only possibly yield second-best productivity. In the Hawthorne studies, both the relay room operatives and the bank wirers were highly cohesive work groups. As was brought out in Chapter 1, a possible explanation of why one highly cohesive work group (relay workers) produced at a very high level and the other highly cohesive group (bank wirers) produced at a very low rate is the type of induction (supervision) that was applied. The complex role that leadership plays in group dynamics is explored further in Chapter 15.

COMMITTEE ORGANIZATION

Any discussion of group dynamics within the context of organizational behavior would not be complete without thorough analysis of the committee form of organization. The committee is the most important type of formally designated group found in today's organizations. Unfortunately, these committees are often described in the following manner:

> A camel is a horse designed by a committee.
> The best committee is a five-person committee with four members absent.
> In a committee, minutes are taken but hours are wasted.
> A committee is a collection of the unfit appointed by the unwilling to perform the unnecessary.

These remarks are jokes, but they represent the widespread negativism attached to the committee form of organization.

Despite the attacks, all indications are that the use and perceived value of committees in organizations is still increasing. Most committees seem to serve as a focal point for the exchange of different viewpoints and information, but some are making major decisions. There is considerable evidence that the use of committees is directly related to the size of the organization. With today's organizations becoming increasingly large and complex, the committee form of organization will undoubtedly become more important and more widely used in the future.

The nature and functions of committees

There are many definitions of a committee. One general definition is: "A committee is a group of people who function collectively."[18] Another similar definition is: "A committee is a group of persons to whom, as a group, some matter is committed."[19] These and most other definitions stress the idea that

---

[18]Theo Haimann and William G. Scott, *Management in the Modern Organization*, Houghton Mifflin, Boston, 1970, p. 280.

[19]Harold Koontz and Cyril O'Donnell, *Management*, 6th ed., McGraw-Hill, New York, 1976, p. 403.

committees consist of groups that are formed to accomplish specific objectives. They can be conducted in either a formal manner (e.g., the finance committee) or an informal manner (e.g., the weekly staff meeting). Most often, committees have specified duties and authority. Some committees meet on an ad hoc basis to solve some specialized problem and then disband. Committees may be referred to as teams, commissions, boards, groups, or task forces.

Committees are found in all types of organizations. There is a myriad of committees in government, educational, religious, and business organizations. For example, the board of directors is a type of committee present in all corporate forms of organization. Other prevalent types in business are the finance, executive, operations, bonus, audit, and grievance committees. Although they are more frequent at the top of the pyramid, there is usually some type of formal committee on every level of the organization.

Committees perform many different functions. They may act in a service, advisory, coordinating, informational, or final decision-making capacity. In the decision-making function, a committee acts in a line capacity and is usually termed a *plural executive*. Many companies are moving toward the plural-executive concept rather than a single executive head. One top executive noted: "There is a tendency to include more than a single man in the role of chief executive in order to provide greater breadth. I suspect that this will become more and more popular in larger and more complex companies."[20] Union Carbide is typical of this trend. The company's major policies evolve from the office of the president. This office is composed of the president and three executive vice presidents. The quadrumvirate serves as the central point of management authority in the company. This type of group management is becoming increasingly common.

Positive attributes of committees

Committee action has many advantages over individual action. Perhaps the greatest attribute of the committee group is the combined and integrated judgment which it can offer. It is the adage that two heads are better than one. To speak optimistically, committee members bring with them a wide range of experience, knowledge, ability, and personality characteristics. This agglomeration lends itself to the tremendous amount of diverse knowledge that is required to solve modern organizational problems. Today's organizations also need an averaging of personalities and a source of creative ideas. The committee form of organization can contribute a great deal to these requirements; as is pointed out in Chapter 17's presentation of the group decision techniques of Delphi and the Nominal Group Technique (NGT), the interacting group may also inhibit individual creativity, but at least at some point the interactive, group dynamics effects as found in a committee can be beneficial to group problem solving.

Committees can be a very effective organizational device to help reduce conflict and promote coordination between departments and specialized

---

[20]"More Room at the Top?" *Dun's Review*, March 1967, p. 29.

subunits. Through committee discussion, each member can empathize with the others' purposes and problems. In effect, committees foster horizontal communication. An example is the interdepartmental meeting where each member receives information and insights about the others' departments. The production department is informed of delivery dates being promised by sales, and sales gets a firsthand look at the problems it may be creating for production scheduling and inventory. As the next chapter points out, the committee is about the only formalized vehicle for horizontal communication in most traditional forms of organization structure.

From a human standpoint, the biggest advantage of committees may be the increased motivation and commitment derived from participation. By being involved in the analysis and solution of committee problems, individual members will more readily accept and try to implement what has been decided. A committee can also be instrumental in human development and growth. Group members, especially the young and inexperienced, can take advantage of observing and learning from other members with much experience or with different viewpoints and knowledge. A committee provides the opportunity for personal development that individuals would never receive on their own.

Negative attributes of committees

The above discussion points out some definite advantages of committees. Traditionally, management theorists have stressed the negative aspects. The classical theorist Luther Gulick wanted to limit the use of committees to abnormal situations because he thought they were too dilatory, irresponsible, and time-consuming for normal administration.[21] The classical theorist Urwick was an even harsher critic. He listed no less than fourteen faults of committees, the main ones being that committees are often irresponsible, are apt to be bad employers, and are costly.[22] Thus, the classicists tended to emphasize the negative, but in the more modern view, committees have both positive and negative attributes.

One very practical disadvantage is that committees are indeed time-consuming and costly. Anyone who has participated in committee meetings can appreciate the satirical definition, cited earlier, that a committee takes minutes but wastes hours. The nature of a committee is that everyone has an equal chance to speak out, but this takes a great deal of time and time costs money. A $25,000-per-year manager costs almost $15 per hour. Therefore, a five-person committee of this caliber costs the organization $75 per hour. Added to this figure may be transportation, lodging, and staff backup costs.

Most often, cost is discussed with regard to committee versus individual

---

[21]Luther Gulick, "Notes on the Theory of Organization," in Luther Gulick and L. Urwick (eds.), *Papers on the Science of Administration*, Institute of Public Administration, New York, 1937, p. 36.

[22]Lyndall F. Urwick, *Committees in Organization*, reprint from the *British Management Review* by Management Journals, Ltd., 1933, p. 14; and *The Elements of Administration*, Harper & Row, New York, 1943, pp. 71–72.

action. Taking another approach, it can be argued that committees are actually *less* expensive when compared with a series of repetitious conferences. In terms of work hours, a committee meeting where a manager meets with five others for one hour represents six work hours. On the other hand, if the same executive meets for one hour with each of the five people individually, the expended time turns out to be ten work-hours. Assume that the executive makes $25,000 ($15 per hour) per year, and that the five others average $12,000 ($7 per hour). For the one-hour committee meeting the cost would be about $50, but for the five individual conferences the total cost would be about $110, over twice as much. The point of this elementary cost analysis is that one cannot automatically condemn all committees as being excessively expensive. The nature and purpose must be considered when assessing cost. Furthermore, it is difficult, if not impossible, to quantify for cost purposes the advantages of a committee in terms of member motivation and quality of decision or problem solution.

From an organizational standpoint, there are some potential problems inherent in committees. The most obvious is divided responsibility. Urwick made the analogy that a committee is like a corporation with "neither a soul to be damned nor a body to be kicked."[23] This is saying that in a committee, there is group or corporate but no individual responsibility or accountability. Thus, critics argue, the committee in reality turns out to have no responsibility or accountability. In fact, individuals may use the committee as a shield to avoid personal responsibility for bad decisions or mistakes. One solution to this problem is to make all committee members responsible, and another is to hold the chairman responsible. Both approaches have many obvious difficulties. For example, if the entire committee is held responsible for a wrong decision, what about the individual members who voted against the majority? Holding them accountable for the committee's decision could have disastrous effects on their morale, but holding only those who voted for a particular decision responsible would create an inhibiting effect that would destroy the value of committee action.

Besides being time-consuming and costly and having divided responsibility, committees may reach decisions that are products of excessive compromise, logrolling, and one-person or minority domination. The comment that the camel is a horse designed by a committee underscores this limitation. It represents the reverse of the advantages of integrated group judgment and the pooling of specialized knowledge. Where unanimity is either formally required or an informal group norm, the difficulties are compounded. The final decision may be so extremely watered down or "compromised to death" that the horse actually does turn out to be a camel. The strength of committee action comes through a synthesis and integration of divergent viewpoints, not through a compromise representing the least common denominator. One way to avoid the problem is to limit the committee to serving as a forum for the exchange of information and ideas. Another possibility is to let the chairperson have the final decision-making prerogative. Yet these solutions are not always satisfactory because when the

---

[23]Chris Argyris, *Leadership and Interpersonal Behavior*, Holt, New York, 1961, p. 331.

committee is charged with making a decision, considerable social skill and a willingness to cooperate fully must exist if good, quality decisions are to evolve.

"Groupthink": A major problem with committee action

A dysfunction of highly cohesive groups and committees that has received a lot of attention recently has been called "groupthink" by Irving Janis. He defines it as "a deterioration of mental efficiency, reality testing, and moral judgment that results from in-group pressures."[24] Essentially, groupthink results from the pressures on individual members to conform and reach consensus. Committees that are suffering from groupthink are so bent on reaching consensus that there is no realistic appraisal of alternative courses of action in a decision, and deviant, minority, or unpopular views are suppressed.

Janis has concluded that a number of historic fiascos by government policy-making groups (for example, Britain's do-nothing policy toward Hitler prior to World War II, the unpreparedness of U.S. forces at Pearl Harbor, the Bay of Pigs invasion of Cuba, and the escalation of the Vietnam War) can be attributed to groupthink. More recently, the Watergate affair can be explained as a product of groupthink.[25] For example, during the Senate hearing on Watergate, Herbert Porter, a member of Nixon's White House staff, answered in an interesting way the question, posed by Senator Howard Baker, of how he became so involved in the dirty tricks of the campaign. Porter said that he "was not one to stand up in a meeting and say that this should be stopped. . . . I kind of drifted along." When Baker asked what, if any, reason Porter had for getting in such a predicament, Porter replied: "In all honesty, because of the fear of the group pressure that would ensue, of not being a team player. . . . I felt a deep sense of loyalty to him [President Nixon] or was appealed to on that basis."[26]

Although historically notorious events such as Watergate can be used to dramatically point out the pitfalls of groupthink, it can commonly occur in committees in business firms or hospitals or any other type of organization. Table 11-2 summarizes some of the symptoms of groupthink that committees should recognize and then avoid if possible. For example, the first symptom leads to the so-called *risky shift phenomenon* of groups. Contrary to popular belief, research going back almost twenty years has shown that a group may make more risky decisions than the individual members would on their own.[27] This conclusion, of course, must be tempered by the values attached

---

[24]Irving L. Janis, *Victims of Groupthink*, Houghton Mifflin, Boston, 1972, p. 9.

[25]Stephen P. Robbins, *Organizational Behavior*, Prentice-Hall, Englewood Cliffs, N.J., 1979, pp. 208–209.

[26]*The Washington Post*, June 8, 1972, p. 20, as reported in Jerry B. Harvey, "The Abilene Paradox: The Management of Agreement," *Organizational Dynamics*, Summer 1974, p. 68 and also quoted in Robbins, op. cit., p. 204.

[27]The original research on risky shift goes back to a masters thesis by J.A.F. Stoner, *A Comparison of Individual and Group Decisions Involving Risk*, MIT, Sloan School of Industrial Management, Cambridge, Mass., 1961.

Table 11-2

SYMPTOMS OF GROUPTHINK

1. There is the illusion of *invulnerability*. There is excessive optimism and risk taking.
2. There are *rationalizations* by the members of the group to discount warnings.
3. There is an unquestioned belief in the group's *inherent morality*. The group ignores questionable ethical or moral issues or stances.
4. Those who oppose the group are *stereotyped* as evil, weak, or stupid.
5. There is *direct pressure* on any member who questions the stereotypes. Loyal members don't question the direction the group seems to be heading.
6. There is *self-censorship* of any deviation from the apparent group consensus.
7. There is the *illusion of unanimity*. Silence is interpreted as consent.
8. There are *self-appointed mindguards* who protect the group from adverse information.

Source: Adapted from Irving L. Janis, *Victims of Groupthink*, Houghton Mifflin, 1972, pp. 197–198.

to the outcomes, but most of the research over the years finds that groups take more risks than individuals acting alone.[28]

Such symptoms as this risky shift phenomenon and the others found in Table 11-2, should make groups take notice and be very careful that they do not slip into groupthink. To help overcome the potentially disasterous effects of groupthink, free expression of minority and unpopular viewpoints should be encouraged and legitimatized, and the pros and cons of each proposed alternative course of action should be thoroughly examined.[29]

THE DYNAMICS OF INFORMAL GROUPS

Informal groups play a significant role in the dynamics of organizational behavior. The major difference between formal and informal groups is that the formal group has officially prescribed goals and relationships whereas the informal one does not. Despite this distinction, it is a mistake to think of formal and informal groups as two distinctly separate entities. The two types of groups coexist and are inseparable. Every formal organization has informal groups and every informal organization eventually evolves some semblance of formal groups. As pointed out by Blau and Scott:

It is impossible to understand the nature of a formal organization without investigating the networks of informal relations and the unofficial norms as well as the formal hierarchy of authority and the official body of rules, since the formally instituted and the informally emerging patterns are inextricably intertwined. The distinction between the formal and the informal aspects of organization life is only an analytical one and should not be reified; there is only one actual organization.[30]

---

[28]The December 1971 issue of the *Journal of Personality and Social Psychology* contains a summary of research on group risk taking.

[29]Clarence W. Von Bergen, Jr. and Raymond J. Kirk, "Groupthink: When Too Many Heads Spoil the Decision," *Management Review*, March 1978, pp. 44–49.

[30]Peter M. Blau and W. Richard Scott, *Formal Organizations*, Chandler, San Francisco, 1962, p. 6.

Status, norms, and roles in informal groups

Informal groups largely evolve from the different status positions of the participants. There are four generally recognized status positions in a group:

1. Group leader
2. Member of the primary group
3. Fringe status
4. Out status[31]

Figure 11-3 depicts these status positions. Closely related to status are the norms and roles in informal groups in modern organizations.

With the exception of a single social act such as extending a hand upon meeting, the smallest units of analysis in group dynamics are norms and roles. Many behavioral scientists make a point of distinguishing between the two units, but conceptually they are very similar. *Norms* are the "oughts" of behavior. They are prescriptions for acceptable behavior determined by the group. A *role* consists of a pattern of norms; the use of the term in organizations is directly related to its theatrical use. A role is a position that can be acted out by an individual. The content of a given role is prescribed by the prevailing norms. Probably a role can best be defined as a position that has expectations evolving from established norms. One sociologist further refines the role concept by making this distinction: "As a pattern of *prescribed* behavior a role is a bundle of norms. As a pattern of *actual* behavior a role is one side of a set of social relationships."[32]

Informal managerial roles

Informal roles vary widely and are highly volatile. Table 11-3 summarizes some of the general informal roles that today's employees often assume. These role descriptions are not intended to be stereotypes or to imply that each organizational participant has only one role. The same person may have one role in one situation (a member of a middle management work group) and another role in another situation (informal leader of the dissident group on a new project).

Based on some important observational studies of managerial work, Henry Mintzberg has proposed that managers perform the three types of roles shown in Figure 11-4. The *interpersonal roles* arise directly from formal authority and refer to the relationship between the manager and others. By virtue of the formal position, the manager has a *figurehead role* as a symbol of the organization. Most of the time spent as a figurehead is on ceremonial duties such as greeting a touring class of students or taking an important customer to lunch. The second interpersonal role is called the *leader role*. In this role the manager uses his or her influence to motivate and encourage subordinates to accomplish organizational objectives. In the third type of interpersonal role the manager undertakes a *liaison role*. This role

[31]Haimann and Scott, op. cit., p. 432.

[32]Alan P. Bates, *The Sociological Enterprise*, Houghton Mifflin, Boston, 1967, p. 44.

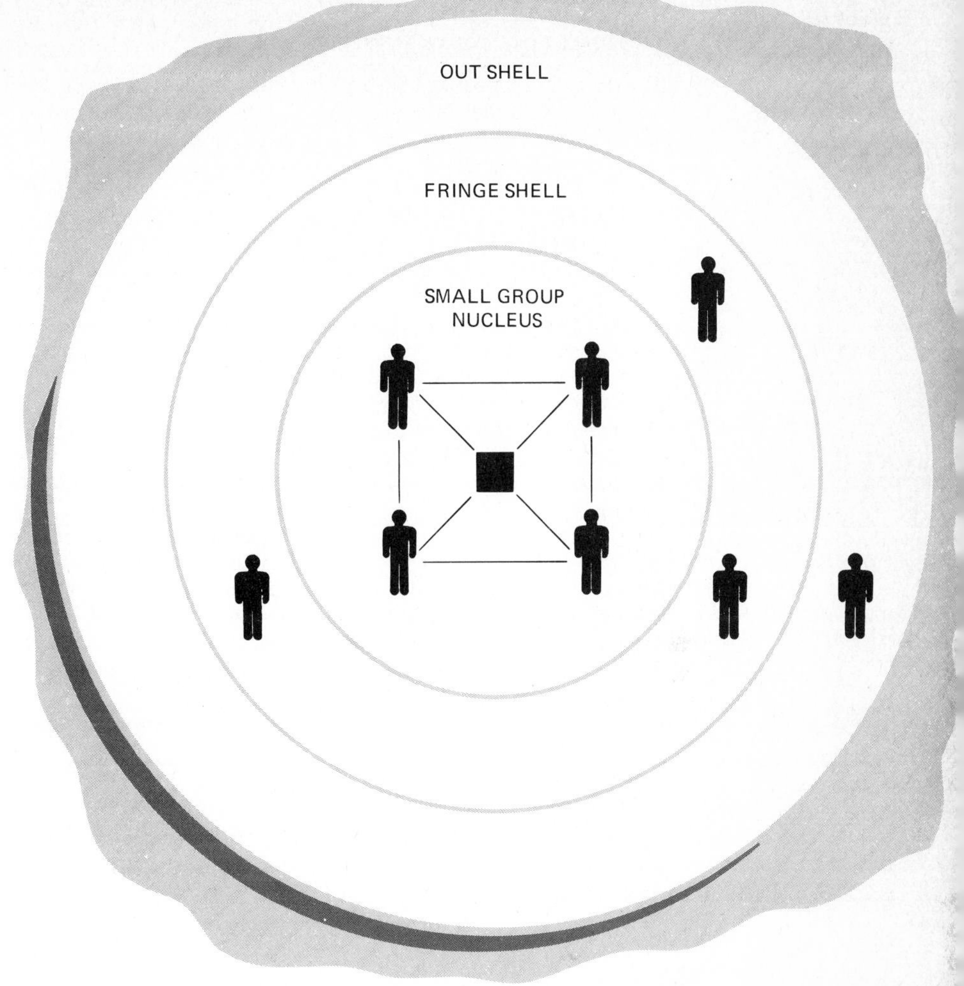

OUT SHELL

FRINGE SHELL

SMALL GROUP
NUCLEUS

**Figure 11-3
Relationship of
status positions in
an informal
organization.
(*Source:* Adapted
from Theo
Haimann and
William G. Scott,
*Management in the
Modern
Organization,*
Houghton Mifflin,
Boston, 1970, p.
433.)**

recognizes that managers often spend more time interacting with others outside their unit (with peers in other units or those completely outside the organization) than they do working with their own superiors and subordinates.

Besides the interpersonal roles flowing from formal authority, Figure 11-4 shows that managers also have important *informational* roles. Most observational studies find that managers spend a great deal of time giving and receiving information. As *monitor*, the manager is continually scanning the environment and probing subordinates, bosses, and outside contacts for information. As *disseminator*, the manager distributes information to key internal people, and as *spokesperson* the manager provides information to outsiders.

In the *decisional* roles the manager acts upon the information. In the *entrepreneur* role in Mintzberg's scheme, the manager initiates the development of a project and assembles the necessary resources. The *disturbance*

Table 11-3

INFORMAL ROLES OF EMPLOYEES

Task-oriented: those who have the role of "getting the job done" and known as those who "deliver the goods"

Technique-oriented: the masters of procedure and method

People-oriented: those who have the role of patron saint and good samaritan to people in need

Nay-sayers: those who counterbalance the "yes" persons, who have thick skins and can find fault with anything

Yea-sayers: those who counterbalance the nay-sayers, the "yes" persons who circumvent opposition

Rule-enforcers: the "people of the book" who are stereotype bureaucrats

Rule-evaders: the "operators," those who know how to get the job done "irrespective"

Rule-blinkers: the people who are not against the rules but don't take them seriously

Involved: those who are fully immersed in their work and the activities of the organization

Detached: slackers who either "go along for the ride" or "call it quits" at the end of regular hours

Regulars: those who are "in," who accept the values of the group and are accepted by the group

Deviants: those who depart from the values of the group—the "mavericks"

Isolates: the true "lone wolves," they are further from the group than deviants

Newcomers: they know little and must be taken care of by others; they are "seen but not heard"

Old-timers: those who have been "around" a long time and "know the ropes"

Climbers: those who are expected to "get ahead," not necessarily on the basis of ability but on the basis of potential

Stickers: those who are expected to stay put, who are satisfied with life and their position in it

Cosmopolitans: those who see themselves as members of a broader professional, cultural, or political community

Locals: those who are rooted to the organization and local community

Source: Adapted from Bertram M. Gross, *Organizations and Their Managing,* Free Press, New York, 1968, pp. 242–248.

handler, on the other hand, instead of being proactive like the entrepreneur is reactive to the problems and pressures of the situation. The disturbance handler is a crisis management type of role, for example, the employees are about to strike, or a major subcontractor is threatening to pull out. As *resource allocator* the manager decides who gets what in his or her department. Finally, the *negotiator* decisional role recognizes the time managers spend at all levels in the give-and-take of negotiating with subordinates, bosses, and outsiders. For example, a production manager may have to negotiate a grievance settlement with the union business agent, and a supervisor in a welfare department may have to negotiate certain benefit payments that one of the counselors wants to give a client.

These informal managerial roles suggested by Mintzberg get much closer to describing what managers really do than do the formally described and prescribed functions of managers. Mintzberg's work has definitely shed some important new light on the nature of managerial work.[33]

---

[33]See: Henry Mintzberg, *The Nature of Managerial Work,* Harper & Row, New York, 1973.

**Figure 11-4
Mintzberg's
managerial roles.
(Source: Adapted
from Henry
Mintzberg, "The
Manager's Job:
Folklore and Fact,"
Harvard Business
Review,
July–August 1975,
pp. 49–61.)**

Informal organization structures

Besides the informal roles that managers perform, the overall informal organization structure has important dynamics for the study of organizational behavior. The classic Milo study conducted by Melville Dalton remains the best illustration of the power of the informal organization.[34] Part (a) in Figure 11-5 represents the formal organization at Milo. Through the use of intimates, interviews, diaries, observation, and socializing, Dalton was able to construct the informal organization chart shown in (b) of Figure 11-5. This informal chart shows the actual power as opposed to the formally designated power and influence of the various managers at Milo.

As with the formal organization structures discussed in the next part of the book, the informal organization has both functions and dysfunctions. In contrast to formal organization analysis, the dysfunctional aspects of informal organization have received more attention than the functional. For example, conflicting objectives, restriction of output, conformity, blocking of ambition, inertia, and resistance to change are frequently mentioned dysfunctions of the informal organization.[35] More recently, however, organizational analysis has begun to recognize the functional aspects as well. For example, the following list suggests some practical benefits that can be derived from the informal organization:

[34]Melville Dalton, *Men Who Manage*, Wiley, New York, 1959.

[35]Ross Webber, *Management*, 2d ed., Irwin, Homewood, Ill., 1979, p. 118.

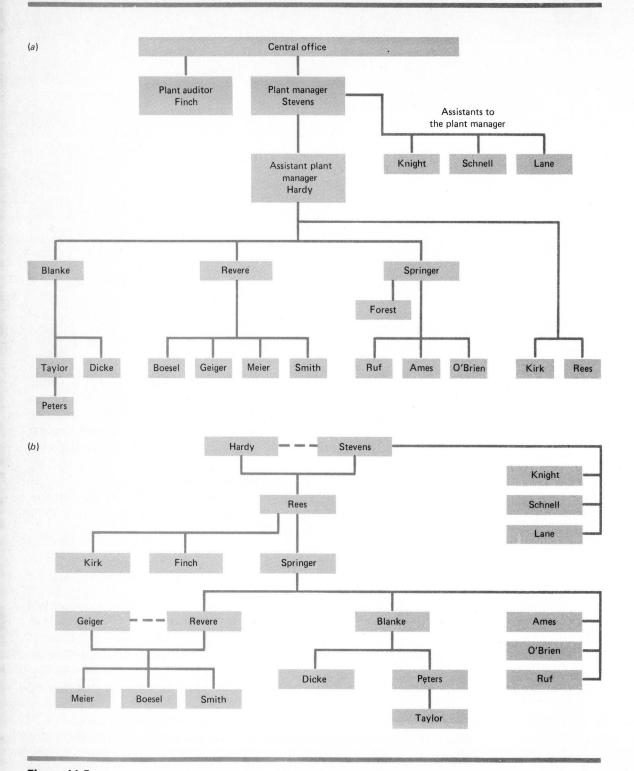

Figure 11-5
(a) A simplified formal organization chart of Milo. (b) An informal organization chart of Milo. (Source: Melville Dalton, *Men Who Manage*, Wiley, New York, 1959, pp. 21-22. Used with permission.)

1. It blends with the formal organization to make a workable system for getting the work done.
2. It lightens the workload of the formal manager and fills in some of the gaps of his abilities.
3. It gives satisfaction and stability to work groups.
4. It is a very useful channel of communication in the organization.
5. Its presence encourages a manager to plan and act more carefully than he would otherwise.[36]

Because of the inevitability and power of the informal organization, the functions should be exploited in the attainment of objectives rather than futilely combated by management. This is emphasized in the following statement:

It is folly for management to suppose that the functioning of the formal system alone can provide the entire range of satisfaction necessary for high spirit among employees. The informal organization has a positive contribution to make in this respect. As such, it should be nurtured by management.[37]

This is especially true with regard to the informal communication system of an organization.

Informal communication system

The term *grapevine* is commonly used to refer to the informal communication system in an organization. It can be traced back to the Civil War period when telegraph lines were strung from tree to tree like grapevines. Messages sent over this haphazard system often became garbled, and any false information or rumor that came along was therefore ironically said to come from the grapevine.[38] The negative connotation of the grapevine, carried over to modern times, seems to have the following pattern: The informal communication system is equated with the grapevine; the grapevine is equated with rumor; and rumor is viewed as being bad for the organization. In management practice, the next step in the above sequence is to interpret the informal system of communication as being bad for the organization. Although admittedly the informal system is often misused and has potential dangers, most organization theorists now agree that it also has many positive functions.

Negative and positive aspects of the grapevine The informal system of communication can be used to spread false rumors and destructive information, or it can effectively supplement the formal channels of communication discussed in the next chapter. It can quickly disseminate pertinent information that assists the formal systems to attain goals. However, whether the informal system has negative or positive functions for the organization

---

[36]Keith Davis, *Human Behavior at Work*, 5th ed., McGraw-Hill, New York, 1977, pp. 275–277.

[37]Haimann and Scott, op. cit., p. 435.

[38]Davis, op. cit., p. 278.

largely depends on the goals of the person doing the communicating. Like any communication system the entire informal system has a highly personal orientation and, as has been pointed out earlier, personal goals may or may not be compatible with organizational goals. The degree of compatibility that does exist will have a major impact on the effect that the grapevine has on organizational goal attainment. The negative viewpoint is expressed as follows:

There is very little that can be done to utilize the grapevine purposefully as a means of goal attainment. As a result, rumors probably do at least as much to subvert organizational goals as to foster them. They may well stir up dissension. They are contrary to fact.[39]

Research does not completely support this position. For example, one study of six companies analyzed the accuracy of thirty rumors which dealt with transfers, procedural changes, promotions, relocation, reorganization, profit sharing, retirement, pay raises, and union disaffiliation. Sixteen of these rumors proved to be groundless, nine turned out to be accurate, and five were partially accurate.[40] Thus, in this study, at least, only slightly more than half the rumors were false. Several other studies have found the grapevine to be even more accurate. Studies at a U.S. naval ordnance test station and a major public utility found about 80 percent accuracy.[41] In other words, it seems to be a mistake to equate the entire informal communication system with false rumors. A more logical criticism of informal communication is the following point made about irresponsibility.

Since the origin and direction of the flow of information on the grapevine is hard to pinpoint, it is difficult to assign responsibility for false information or morale-lowering rumors. The speed at which the grapevine is capable of transmitting information makes control of invalid messages troublesome.[42]

On the other hand, the speed factor mentioned above may also work to the advantage of the organization. Since the informal system is so personally based and directed, it tends to be much faster than the formal downward system of information flow. Important relevant information that requires quick responsive action by lower-level personnel may be more effectively handled by the informal system than by the formal system. As the next chapter will point out, the informal system is a major way that the necessary requirements for interactive and subordinate-initiated communication are accomplished. The formal horizontal and upward systems are often either inadequate or completely ineffective. The informal system is generally relied upon to coordinate the units horizontally on a given level and to provide

---

[39]John B. Miner, *Personnel Psychology*, Macmillan, New York, 1969, p. 259.

[40]Robert Hershey, "The Grapevine—Here to Stay but Not beyond Control," *Personnel*, January–February 1966, p. 64.

[41]Eugene Walton, "How Efficient Is the Grapevine," *Personnel*, vol. 28, 1961, pp. 45–49.

[42]Scott, op. cit., p. 172.

valuable upward information about subordinate performance, ideas, and attitudes.

Types of informal communication Since an informal organization structure will always coexist with a formal structure, there will be an informal communication system in every formal organization. Keith Davis has depicted the ways in which the informal communication networks may be arranged. Figure 11-6 shows four possible informal communication networks. The cluster chain, which research shows to be the most prevalent form of informal communication,

means that most people in management acted as passive receivers, and only a few (10 to 30 per cent in most cases) re-communicated the information originally to another person. . . . There was no established, consistent group of communicators, but some persons tended more than others to be active in communication.[43]

Management cannot directly establish a certain type of informal network, but it can indirectly influence the outcome of informal communication. Research has indicated certain predictable patterns of informal communication. For example:

1. People talk most when the news is recent.
2. People talk about things that affect their work.
3. People talk about people they know.
4. People working near each other are likely to be on the same grapevine.
5. People who contact each other in the chain of procedure tend to be on the same grapevine.[44]

---

[43]Keith Davis, "Communication within Management," *Personnel*, November 1954, p. 215.

[44]Ibid., p. 217.

**Figure 11-6
Informal
communication
networks in an
organization.
(*Source:* Adapted
from Keith Davis,
"Management
Communication
and the
Grapevine,"
*Harvard Business
Review*,
September–October
1953, p. 45.)**

SINGLE STRAND
(X communicates
with Y through
intervening
persons in a
strand.)

GOSSIP
(X nonselectively
communicates
with everyone.)

PROBABILITY
(X communicates
randomly with
others according
to the laws of
probability.)

CLUSTER
(X selectively
communicates
with those he
or she can
trust.)

Briefly, management must recognize that just as the informal organization is inevitable, so is the informal communication system. It should not be narrowly equated with false rumors. Rather, it should be recognized that the grapevine is accurate, it is fast, and it carries much information that is needed to supplement the formal systems of communication in an organization. Today's managers should attempt to manage and make use of the informal system to help them attain organization objectives.

SUMMARY

Groups represent an important dynamic input into organizational behavior. Group formation, types, and processes, and the dynamics of informal roles and organization, are all of particular relevance to the study of organizational behavior. Group formation can be theoretically explained by propinquity; as a relationship between activities, interactions, and sentiments; as a symmetrical balance between attraction and common attitudes; and as a reward-cost exchange. Participants in an organization also form into groups for very practical economic, security, and social reasons. Many different types of formal and informal groups are found in modern organizations. Command and task groups and all types of committees are common examples of formally designated groups. Committees in particular are playing an increasingly important role in modern organizations. Although they can be time-consuming, costly, and conducive to divided responsibility, excessive compromise, and groupthink, they can lead to improved decisions through combined and integrated judgment, reduce conflict, facilitate coordination, and increase motivation and commitment through participation.

Informal roles are being found increasingly useful for describing the true nature of managerial work. Informal structure coexists with every formal structure. The informal structure is not formally designated, but rather is determined by the various group-status positions and roles. Traditionally, only the dysfunctional aspects of informal organization have been emphasized. More recently, the functional aspects have also been recognized. A good example is the informal communication system, which can either spread false rumors and cause destructive conflict or become an effective supplement to the formal systems of communication. Management in the future must be able to understand and, when possible, take advantage of group dynamics and informal roles and organization.

QUESTIONS FOR DISCUSSION AND REVIEW

1. Briefly discuss the major theoretical explanations for group formation. Which explanation do you think is most relevant to the study of organizational behavior? Defend your choice.
2. What implications does the Schachter checkerboard study have for the study of organizational behavior?

3. How can the disadvantages of committees be overcome?
4. What are some of the major symptoms of groupthink? Can you give an example from your own experience where this may have happened?
5. Summarize some of the informal managerial roles suggested by Mintzberg. Do you think that these roles are descriptive of what managers really do? Why or why not?
6. What are some functions of the informal organization? What are some of the dysfunctions?

CASE:
THE SCHOOLBOY ROOKIE

Kent Sikes was a junior at State University. After spring semester he went back to his home town and took a summer job in the biggest factory in town. He was told to report to the warehouse supervisor the first day at work. The supervisor assigned him to a small group of men who were responsible for loading and unloading the boxcars that supplied the materials and carried away the finished goods of the factory.

After two weeks on the job, Kent was amazed how little work the men in his crew accomplished. It seemed that they were forever standing around and talking or, in some cases, even going off to hide when there was work to be done. Kent often found himself alone unloading a boxcar while the other members of the crew were off messing around some place else. When Kent complained to his coworkers, they made it very plain that if he did not like it he could quit, but if he complained to the supervisor he would be sorry. Although Kent was deliberately excluded from any of the crew's activities such as taking breaks together or a Friday afternoon beer after work at the tavern across the street, finally toward the end of the summer he went up to one of the older members of the crew and said, "What gives with you guys anyway? I am just trying to do my job. The money is good and I just don't give a hang about this place. I will be leaving to go back to school in a few weeks, and I wish I could have got to know you all better, but frankly I am sure glad I'm not like you guys." The old worker replied, "Son, if you were here as long as I have been, you would be just like us."

1. Using some of the theories, explain the possible reasons for the group formation of this work crew. What types of groups exist in this case?
2. Place this work group in the Schachter study. What role does the supervisor play in the performance of this group?
3. What are the major informal roles of the crew members and Kent? What status position did Kent have with the group? Why?
4. Why wasn't Kent accepted by the group? Do you agree with the old worker's last statement in the case? Why or why not?

CASE:
THE BLUE RIBBON COMMITTEE

Mayor Sam Small was nearing completion of his first term in office. He felt his record had been pretty good, except for the controversial issue of housing. He had been able to avoid doing anything so far and felt very strongly that this issue must not come to a head before the next election. The voters were too evenly divided on the issue, and he would lose a substantial number of votes no matter what stand he took. Yet with pressure increasing from both sides, he had to do something. After much distress and vacillation he finally came upon what he thought was an ideal solution to his dilemma. He would appoint a committee to study the problem and make some recommendations. To make sure that the committee's work would not be completed before the election came up, it was important to pick the right people. Specifically, Sam selected his "blue ribbon" committee from a wide cross section of the community so that, in Sam's words, "all concerned parties would be represented." He made the committee very large, and the members ranged from Ph.D's in urban planning to real estate agents to local ward committee persons to minority group leaders. He took particular care in selecting people who had widely divergent, outspoken, public views on the housing issue.

1. Do you think Sam's strategy of using this committee to delay taking a stand on the housing issue until after the election will work? Why or why not?
2. What are some of the important dynamics of this committee? Do you think they will arrive at a good solution to the housing problems facing this city?
3. Do you think this committee will suffer from groupthink?
4. What types of informal roles is Sam exhibiting? Do you think he is an effective manager? Do you think he is an effective politician? Is there a difference?

COMMUNICATION

COMMUNICATION BREAKDOWN AT BULOVA WATCH*

The Bulova Watch Company was in bad shape before the recent takeover by the Loews Company. The Loews management team was deeply concerned with what they perceived as an "incredible lack of communications." No branch of the company seemed to know what the other branch was doing. For example, during an orientation tour by the new management team, a shipment of 6000 watch assemblies (which amounted to ten days of production) arrived from Switzerland and no one was expecting it. The breakdown in communication seemed to be imbedded in the company like the separation of the divisions and plants into isolated groups. The Loews management team decided that the key to an improved profit picture for Bulova was in more effective organizational communication. They felt that this could best be accomplished through the recentralization of the decision-making capabilities. Steps were taken to ensure that this would happen. For example, there would be greater budgetary controls, and troubleshooters would ensure that upper-level management of the company were kept informed at all times what was happening out in the field. In addition, management would attempt to remedy the past communication difficulties through more extensive information gathering and precise interpretation at upper levels. The Loews people are hopeful that improved communications will lead to a reduction of the problems that Bulova has been suffering.

---

*Adapted from "After the Explosion in Bulova's Executive Suite," *Business Week,* June 4, 1979, pp. 108–110.

Communication is one of the most frequently discussed dynamics in the entire field of organizational behavior, but it is seldom clearly understood. In practice, effective communication is a basic prerequisite for the attainment of organizational goals, but it has remained one of the biggest problems facing modern management. Communication is an extremely broad topic and of course is not restricted to the organizational behavior field. Some estimates of the extent of its use go up to about three-fourths of an active human being's life, and even higher proportions of a typical manager's time.

Communication is often cited as being at the root of practically all the problems of the world. For example, some management writers have observed, "Perhaps it is true, as someone has suggested, that the heart of all the world's problems—at least of men with each other—is man's inability to communicate as well as he thinks he is communicating."[1] It is given as the explanation for lovers' quarrels, ethnic prejudice, war between nations, the generation gap, industrial disputes, and organizational conflict. These are only representative of the numerous problems which are attributed to ineffective communication. Obviously, this thinking can go too far. For example, a couple of management writers warn, "However important accurate communication may be, it is no panacea for all problems of conflict and lack of motivation."[2] While communication is recognized as a convenient scapegoat or crutch, the fact remains that the communication process is a very big problem in most human and organizational activities.

After a brief discussion of the historical treatment of the subject of communication in organizational behavior and management, a precise definition of communication is given. After a brief discussion of information theory and interpersonal communication, the organizational communication process is discussed. The Shannon-Weaver, Berlo, and transactional models are given particular attention. The last part of the chapter examines the three major types of communication as an important dynamic of organizational behavior: superior-subordinate, subordinate-initiated, and interactive communication. A *personal* as opposed to *linear* information flow perspective of communication is used throughout the chapter.

HISTORICAL BACKGROUND OF THE ROLE OF COMMUNICATION

Early discussions of management gave very little emphasis to communication. Although communication was implicit in the management function of command and the structural principle of hierarchy, the early theorists never fully developed or integrated it into management theory. At the same time, they did generally recognize the role of informal communication in relation

---

[1]Herbert G. Hicks and C. Ray Gullett: *The Management of Organizations*, 3d ed., McGraw-Hill, New York, 1976, p. 467.

[2]Edwin B. Flippo and Gary Munsinger, *Management*, 2d ed., Allyn and Bacon, Boston, 1975, p. 381.

to the problem of supplementing the formal, hierarchical channels. But Henri Fayol was about the only one who gave a detailed analysis and supplied a meaningful solution to the problem of communication.

Figure 12-1 shows how Fayol presented a simplified version of the formal organization. If the formal channels in this organization were strictly followed and F wanted to communicate with P, the communication would have to go through E—D—C—B—A—L—M—N—O—P and back again. In other words, F would have to go through a total of twenty positions. On the other hand, if F could lay a "gangplank" to P, it would, in the words of Fayol, "allow the two employees F and P to deal at one sitting, and in a few hours, with some question or other which via the scalar chain would pass through twenty transmissions, inconvenience many people, involve masses of paper, lose weeks or months to get to a conclusion less satisfactory generally than the one which could have been obtained via direct contact as between F and P."[3] This gangplank concept has direct implications for horizontal communication systems in modern formal organizations. Unfortunately, such classical insights were few and far between.

---

[3]Henri Fayol, *General and Industrial Management,* translated by Constance Storrs, Pitman, London, 1949, p. 35.

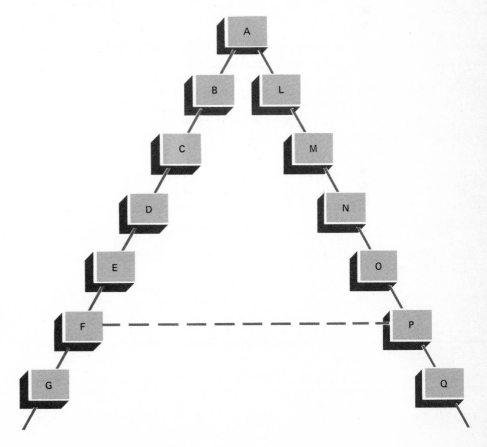

Figure 12-1 Fayol's gangplank concept. (*Source:* Henri Fayol, *General and Industrial Management,* translated by Constance Storrs, Pitman, London, 1949, p. 34.)

It was largely Chester Barnard in the late 1930s who meaningfully developed communication as a vital dynamic of organizational behavior. He was convinced that communication is the major shaping force in the organization. He ranked it with common purpose and willingness to serve as the three primary elements of the organization. To him, communication both makes the organization cooperative system dynamic and links the organization purpose to the human participants. Communication techniques, which he considered to be written and oral language, were deemed not only necessary to attain organization purpose but could also be a potential problem area for the organization. In Barnard's words, "The absence of a suitable technique of communication would eliminate the possibility of adopting some purposes as a basis of organization. Communication technique shapes the form and the internal economy of organization."[4]

Barnard also interwove communication into his concept of authority. He emphasized that meaning and understanding must occur before authority can be communicated from superior to subordinate. He listed seven specific communication factors which are especially important in establishing and maintaining objective authority in an organization. He believed them to be, in brief, the following:

1. The channels of communication should be definitely known.
2. There should be a definite formal channel of communication to every member of an organization.
3. The line of communication should be as direct and short as possible.
4. The complete formal line of communication should normally be used.
5. The persons serving as communication centers should be competent.
6. The line of communication should not be interrupted while the organization is functioning.
7. Every communication should be authenticated.[5]

Since the original contributions by Fayol and Barnard, the dynamics of communication has been one of, if not *the*, central concern of organizational behavior and management theorists. Except in the principles of those management textbooks that still rely heavily on a classical process framework, communication is given major attention. In addition, there has been a deluge of books and articles which deal specifically with interpersonal and organizational communication. Unfortunately, practically all of this vast literature gives only a surface treatment of the subject and is seldom based upon systematic research findings. One management writer sums up the literature on communication as being a bunch of twaddle.[6] Only recently have some insights begun to emerge on the true meaning of the communication process and especially on how it affects organizational behavior.

---

[4]Chester I. Barnard, *The Functions of the Executive*, Harvard, Cambridge, Mass., 1938, p. 90.

[5]Ibid., pp. 175–181.

[6]Saul W. Gellerman, *Management by Motivation*, American Management Association, New York, 1968, p. 41.

THE DEFINITION OF COMMUNICATION

The term *communication* is freely used by everyone in modern society, including members of the general public and organizational behavior scholars and management practitioners. In addition, as noted earlier, the term is employed to explain a multitude of sins both in the society as a whole and in work organizations. Despite this widespread usage, very few members of the general public and not a great many more management people can precisely define the term. Part of the problem is that communication experts have not agreed upon a definition themselves.

Most definitions of communication used in organizational behavior literature stress the use of symbols to transfer meaning of information.[7] Seemingly of more importance, however, is the fact that communication is a personal process that involves the exchange of behaviors. The personal aspects have been noted in no uncertain terms by one communications expert:

Let us understand clearly one thing about it: communication (*human* communication, at least) is *something people do*. It has no life of its own. There is no magic about it except what people in the communication relationship put into it. There is no meaning in a message except what people put into it. . . . To understand the human communication process one must understand how people relate to each other.[8]

In addition to its being a human process, another communication expert emphasizes the *behavioral* implications of communication by pointing out that "the only means by which one person can influence another is by the behaviors he performs—that is, the communicative exchanges between people provide the sole method by which influence or effects can be achieved."[9] In other words, the behaviors that occur in an organization are vital to the communication process. This personal and behavioral exchange view of communication takes many forms. The following definition points out the very comprehensive nature of communication in today's organizations.

By communication we mean the flow of material, information, perception, and understandings between various parts and members of an organization . . . all the methods, means, and media of communication (communication technology), all the channels, networks, and systems of communication (organizational structure), all the person-to-person interchange (interpersonal communication). . . . It includes all

---

[7]For example, see: Joe Kelly, *Organizational Behaviour*, rev. ed., Dorsey-Irwin, Homewood, Ill., 1974, p. 587; and Daniel K. Stewart, *The Psychology of Communication*, Funk & Wagnalls, New York, 1968, pp. 13–14.

[8]W. Schramm, "The Nature of Communications between Humans," in *The Process and Effects of Mass Communication*, W. Schramm and D. Roberts (eds.), University of Illinois Press, Chicago, 1971, p. 17.

[9]B. Aubrey Fisher, *Small Group Decision Making*, McGraw-Hill, New York, 1974, p. 23.

aspects of communication: up, down, lateral; speaking, writing, listening, reading; methods, media, modes, channels, networks, flow; interpersonnel, intraorganizational, interorganizational.[10]

Covering all these aspects of communication is beyond the scope of this chapter.

The following continuum can be used to identify the major categories of communication that are especially relevant to the study of organizational behavior.

Information theory	The organizational communication process	Interpersonal communication

On the one extreme is the technically very sophisticated information theory approach, and on the other extreme is the two-person or interpersonal communication approach. The middle ground is occupied by an organizational approach, which is the one taken by this chapter. A very brief overview of the information theory and interpersonal approaches is necessary to put the discussion of the organizational communication approach into proper perspective.

Information theory

Information theory is a strict, scientific approach to the study of communication. Deeply intertwined with the probability theory of mathematics, it is concerned primarily with the transmission aspects of the communication process. Specifically, the transmission concepts of encoder (sender) and decoder (receiver), in terms of both their functional roles and their contribution to the achievement of a given level of performance, are the distinguishing characteristics of information theory.[11]

The goal of information theory is to encode messages by taking advantage of their statistical nature and to use electrical signals to transmit messages over a given channel with minimum error.[12] Entropy, a statistical law of thermodynamics, further illustrates the information theory approach. This law states that there is a degree of randomness or error in any system; it will become disorganized over time. An example of trying to cope with entropy is given by the physicist who attempts to counteract it by developing control devices for heat machines. In a similar manner, information theorists recognize entropy in their analysis of a communication system; for example, they try to measure and control noise entropy that may arise from distractions, distortions, or the electrical static occurring when a message is transmitted over a communication system.

---

[10]George T. Vardaman and Carroll C. Halterman, *Managerial Control through Communication*, Wiley, New York, 1968, pp. 3–4.

[11]Robert G. Gallager, *Information Theory and Reliable Communication*, Wiley, New York, 1968, p. 1.

[12]See J. R. Pierce, *Symbols, Signals and Noise: The Nature and Process of Communication*, Harper, New York, 1961, p. 44.

Information theory has an unusual dual origin. The two founding fathers are usually considered to be Norbert Wiener and Claude Shannon. Separately, they outlined the basic concepts of information theory and cybernetics in 1948.[13] "To MIT's eminent mathematician, Norbert Wiener, goes the major credit for discovering the new continent and grasping its dimensions; to Claude Shannon of Bell Laboratories goes the credit for mapping the new territory in detail and charting some breathtaking peaks."[14] Thus, Wiener and Shannon were the first to emphasize communication from a mathematical perspective, and in so doing they developed cybernetics. Wiener coined the term *cybernetics* to cover information theory plus "the study of messages as a means of controlling machinery and society, the development of computing machines and other such automata, certain reflections upon psychology and the nervous system, and a tentative new theory of scientific method."[15] He derived the term from the Greek word *kubernetes*, which means "steersman" or "governor." His stated purpose for cybernetics was "to develop a language and techniques that will enable us indeed to attack the problem of control and communication."[16] Automatic feedback control mechanisms have been the primary technique used to attain this goal.

Much has happened since information theory and cybernetics were introduced by Wiener and Shannon. One information theorist has noted, "In the past twenty years, information theory has been made more precise, has been extended, and has been brought to the point where it is being applied in practical communication systems."[17] A great impetus to this development has come from computer technology and organizational systems analysis. Computers and systems go hand in hand with information theory and cybernetics. The impact that information theory has had on the study, analysis, and practice of organizational communication is somewhat analogous to the tremendous influence that quantitative techniques have had on management decision making. This perspective will be given further attention in the next part of the book, which takes a macro approach to the study of organizational behavior.

Interpersonal communication

The opposite extreme to information theory is the interpersonal approach to communication. Whereas information theory is mathematically oriented, interpersonal communication is behaviorally oriented. In the interpersonal approach, the major emphasis is on transferring information from one

---

[13]See Norbert Wiener, *Cybernetics, or Control and Communication in the Animal and the Machine*, Wiley, New York, 1948; and Claude E. Shannon, "The Mathematical Theory of Communication," *Bell System Technical Journal*, July and October 1948, reprinted in book form with a follow-up article by Warren Weaver, University of Illinois Press, Urbana, 1949.

[14]Francis Bello, "The Information Theory," *Fortune*, December 1953, p. 137.

[15]Norbert Wiener, *The Human Use of Human Beings*, 2d ed., rev., Doubleday, Garden City, N.Y., 1954, p. 15. Originally published in 1950 by Houghton Mifflin.

[16]Ibid., p. 17.

[17]Gallager, op. cit., pp. 1–2.

person to another. Communication is looked upon as a basic method of effecting behavior change, and it incorporates the psychological processes (perception, learning, and motivation) on the one hand, and language on the other. Listening sensitivity and nonverbal communications are also closely associated with this approach.

The often posed riddle that asks, "Is there a noise in the forest if a tree crashes to the ground but no one is there to hear it?" demonstrates some of the important aspects of interpersonal communication.[18] From a communications perspective the answer to the riddle is no. There are sound waves but no sound because no one perceives it. There must be both a sender and a receiver in order for interpersonal communication to take place. The sender is obviously important to communication, but so is the neglected receiver who gives feedback to the sender.

The importance of feedback cannot be overemphasized because effective interpersonal communication is highly dependent on it. The following comments on the interpersonal process points out the important role of feedback:

It permits expressive action on the part of one or more persons and the conscious and unconscious perception of such action. Perhaps one of the most important factors in this network is . . . feedback [which] is vital if the originator and receiver are to secure some level of effectiveness in the communication process.[19]

Another writer states that "the nub of the entire communication problem" is the following:

The sender, to be certain that his message will be accepted by the receiver, must be prepared to let the receiver influence him. He must even be prepared to let the receiver alter or modify the message in ways that make it more acceptable to the receiver. Otherwise it may not be understood, or it may not be accepted, or it may simply be given lip service and ignored.[20]

Table 12-1 summarizes some characteristics of effective and ineffective feedback for employee performance. The following list explains these characteristics in more detail:[21]

1. *Intention.* Effective feedback is directed toward improving job performance and making the employee a more valuable asset. It is not a personal attack and should not compromise the individual's feeling of self-worth or image. Rather, effective feedback is directed toward aspects of the job.
2. *Specificity.* Effective feedback is designed to provide recipients with specific information so that they know what must be done to correct the situation.

---

[18]Peter F. Drucker, *Management*, Harper & Row, New York, 1974, p. 483.

[19]Norman B. Sigband, *Communication for Management*, Scott, Foresman, Glenview, Ill., 1969, p. 8.

[20]Gellerman, op. cit., p. 46.

[21]Fred Luthans and Mark J. Martinko, *The Practice of Supervision and Management*, McGraw-Hill, New York, 1979, pp. 180–182.

Table 12-1

CHARACTERISTICS OF FEEDBACK FOR EFFECTIVE AND INEFFECTIVE INTERPERSONAL COMMUNICATION IN HUMAN RESOURCE MANAGEMENT

Effective feedback	Ineffective feedback
1. Intended to help the employee	1. Intended to belittle the employee
2. Specific	2. General
3. Descriptive	3. Evaluative
4. Useful	4. Inappropriate
5. Timely	5. Untimely
6. Employee readiness for feedback	6. Makes the employee defensive
7. Clear	7. Not understandable
8. Valid	8. Inaccurate

Source: Fred Luthans and Mark J. Martinko, *The Practice of Supervision and Management,* McGraw-Hill, New York, 1979, p. 183.

Ineffective feedback is general and leaves questions in the recipients' minds. For example, telling an employee that he or she is doing a poor job is too general and will leave the recipient frustrated in seeking ways to correct the problem.

3. *Description.* Effective feedback can also be characterized as descriptive rather than evaluative. It tells the employee what he or she has done in objective terms, rather than presenting a value judgment.

4. *Usefulness.* Effective feedback is information that an employee can use to improve performance. It serves no purpose to berate employees for their lack of skill if they do not have the ability or training to perform properly. Thus, the guideline is that if it is not something the employee can correct, it is not worth mentioning.

5. *Timeliness.* There are also considerations in timing feedback properly. As a rule, the more immediate the feedback, the better. This way the employee has a better chance of knowing what the supervisor is talking about and can take corrective action.

6. *Readiness.* In order for feedback to be effective, employees must be ready to receive it. When feedback is imposed or forced upon employees, it is much less effective.

7. *Clarity.* Effective feedback must be clearly understood by the recipient. A good way of checking this is to ask the recipient to restate the major points of the discussion. Also, supervisors can observe nonverbal facial expressions as indicators of understanding and acceptance.

8. *Validity.* In order for feedback to be effective, it must be reliable and valid. Of course, when the information is incorrect, the employee will feel that the supervisor is unnecessarily biased, or the employee may take corrective action which is inappropriate and only compounds the problem.

Besides feedback, other variables, such as trust, expectations, values, status, and compatibility, greatly influence the interpersonal aspects of communication. For example, there are research studies that show that people who do not trust one another do not communicate.[22] This finding, of

---

[22]For example, see Glen Mellinger, "Interpersonal Trust as a Factor in Communication," *The Journal of Abnormal and Social Psychology,* May 1956, pp. 304–309.

course, has significant implications for superior-subordinate relations in an organization. If the subordinate does not trust the boss, there will be ineffective communication. The same is true of the other variables mentioned. People perceive only what they expect to perceive; the unexpected may not be perceived at all. The growing generation gap can play havoc with interpersonal communication; so can status differentials and incompatibilities of any sort. Giving attention to and doing something about these interpersonal variables can spell the difference between effective and ineffective communication.

Interpersonal communication plays a central role in organizational communication and is directly relevant to the study of organizational behavior. It is not given further attention in this chapter but, as indicated earlier, it is really a major portion of Parts 2 and 3 and of the chapters that follow in this part.

ORGANIZATIONAL COMMUNICATION

The organizational approach to communication represents the middle ground between information theory on the one hand and interpersonal communication on the other. Traditionally, the organization structure was viewed as a network over which there were linear information flows. For example, one observation noted that the organization structure provides the

paths of inputs that form intricate circuits of communication. An organizational communication network is analogous to a telephone system: information flows in certain restricted patterns or paths through the entire system.[23]

Especially in classical organization structures, communication consisted simply of the following:

1. Instructions and commands to do or not do are always communicated down the chain of command, and only from one person to others directly below him in the hierarchy.
2. Reports, inquiries, and requests are always communicated up the chain of command, and only to the one person directly above the communicator in the hierarchy.
3. Subgroups do not communicate directly with other subgroups at their level on the chart, but instead communicate up the chain of command until the message arrives at an office where both subgroups share a supervisor, then down the chain of command to the recipient subgroup.
4. The staff plays the role of communication gadfly—i.e., it is given free rein to collect and disseminate nonauthoritative information in its role as an extension of the boss.[24]

---

[23]Hicks and Gullett, op. cit., p. 488.

[24]Eugene Walton, *A Magnetic Theory of Organizational Communication*, U.S. Naval Ordinance Test Station, China Lake, Calif., 1962.

This traditional conception of organizational communication has been very influential through the years, but it has also been very limiting. One view interestingly notes that the purely structural view of organizational communication is like a bikini: "What it reveals is interesting, but what it conceals is vital."[25] The vital part that is concealed by this view is the dynamic, personal aspect of organizational communication.

The Shannon-Weaver model of organizational communication

One of the first widely accepted comprehensive models of the communication process was the Shannon and Weaver model. Since they were information theorists, the model stressed the transmission of information. Figure 12-2 shows this model. The major parts of the model can be summarized as follows:

1. *Information source.* This is the logical beginning of the communication process. The source consists of raw information and includes some form of intent and purpose on the part of the sender. Accounting, statistics, and computer data are examples of raw information which must be given meaning and purpose in the information source.
2. *Transmitter.* The transmitter encodes the data into a message and sends it on to the receiver. The major form of encoding is language, which can be defined as any systematic pattern of signs, symbols, or signals. The raw data from the source are encoded into a meaningful language, e.g., the accounting, statistics, and computer data are translated into a message. This message is then transmitted by means of sound waves, electrical impulses, light waves, or marks on pieces of paper.
3. *Noise.* Noise is any interference that takes place between transmission and reception. It can be electrical static, semantic problems with the language, or deliberate distortion of the message. Noise is a "black box" concept. Any communication problem that cannot be fully explained can be categorized as noise.
4. *Receiver.* Under this step of the model, the communication has passed from the

**Figure 12-2
A model of the communication process. (*Source:* Claude E. Shannon and Warren Weaver, *The Mathematical Theory of Communication,* The University of Illinois Press, Urbana, 1949, pp. 5 and 98.)**

[25]Philip K. Tompkins, "Organizational Communication: A State-of-the-Art Review," in G. Richetto (ed.), *Conference on Organizational Communication,* George C. Marshall Space Flight Center, Huntsville, Ala., 1967.

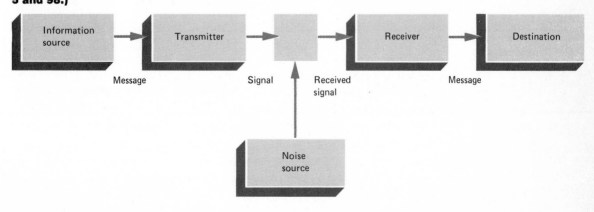

Information source → Transmitter → (Message) (Signal) → Received signal → Receiver → (Message) → Destination

Noise source

sender side of the process to the receiver side. Decoding of the message now takes place. An interpretation must be made and understanding must be gained of the accounting, statistical, or computer information. Besides knowledge requirements, perception and listening enter the reception phase of the process model.

5. *Destination.* Just as the information source is a requirement for the communication process to begin, a destination is necessary in order for the process to be completed. In the organization, the accounting, statistical, or computer information is most likely destined to go to line managers to assist them in accomplishing their unit's objectives or to top managers for use in evaluating performance.

Although the Shannon-Weaver model extended the classical structural approach to organizational communication by recognizing that it was a process, it still stressed linear information flows and was too static. As was pointed out in the discussion of the definition, communication involves behaviors; it is a personal process. For example, receiver acceptance and expectations are vital to organizational communication. Merely sending and receiving information, i.e., transmission, is a necessary but insufficient condition for communication to take place in an organization.

The Berlo dynamic process model

The first widely recognized model that presented communication as a dynamic, interactive process was proposed by David Berlo. He countered the linear, step-by-step information approach with the following ideas:

If we accept the concept of process, we view events and relationships as dynamic, on-going, ever-changing, continuous. When we label something as a process, we also mean that it does not have *a* beginning, *an* end, a fixed sequence of events. It is not static, at rest. It is moving. The ingredients within a process interact; each affects all the others.[26]

Figure 12-3 summarizes the Berlo model.

Organizational communication as a transactional process

Contemporary theory and research have extended the Berlo dynamic process. For example, some communication experts now present communication as a transactional process. The prefix "trans-" (meaning "mutually" and "reciprocally") is stressed instead of "inter-" (meaning "between"). These experts state that in the process approach to communication, "All persons are engaged in sending (encoding) and receiving (decoding) messages *simultaneously*. Each person is constantly *sharing* in the encoding and decoding process, and each person is *affecting* the other."[27] This perspective, of course, is in line with the social learning approach to organizational

---

[26]David Berlo, *The Process of Communication*, Holt, New York, 1960, p. 24.

[27]John R. Wenburg and William W. Wilmont, *The Personal Communication Process*, Wiley, New York, 1973, p. 5.

behavior, which was outlined in Chapter 3. The reciprocal determinism of social learning is very similar to what is called here a dynamic, transactional approach to communication. Such an approach is a much more accurate and useful way of viewing communication than is the more limiting linear information flow perspective of communication. The remainder of this chapter assumes the perspective of this dynamic, transactional view of organizational communication.

SUPERIOR-SUBORDINATE COMMUNICATION

Traditionally, one of the dominant themes of organizational communication has been the so-called "downward" system. However, when a dynamic, transactional perspective replaces a linear information flow perspective, the downward system is more accurately portrayed as superior-subordinate communication. There are personal linkages, not just information flows, in the downward system.

The purposes and methods of superior-subordinate communication

Katz and Kahn have identified five general purposes of superior-subordinate communication in an organization:

1. To give specific task directives about job instructions
2. To give information about organizational procedures and practices
3. To provide information about the rationale of the job
4. To tell subordinates about their performance
5. To provide ideological-type information to facilitate the indoctrination of goals[28]

In the past and also to a large extent today, most organizations have concentrated on and accomplished only the first two of these purposes. In general, superior-to-subordinate communication on job performance and the rationale-ideological aspects of jobs have been badly neglected. After an extensive review of the research literature, one communications expert

**Figure 12-3
The Berlo model of communication. (*Source:* Adapted from David K. Berlo, *The Process of Communication,* Holt, New York, 1960, pp. 30–32.)**

[28]Daniel Katz and Robert L. Kahn, *The Social Psychology of Organizations,* Wiley, New York, 1966, p. 239.

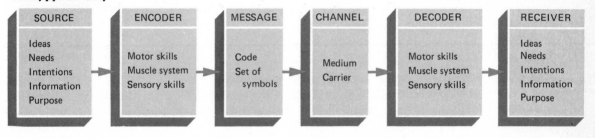

SOURCE	ENCODER	MESSAGE	CHANNEL	DECODER	RECEIVER
Ideas Needs Intentions Information Purpose	Motor skills Muscle system Sensory skills	Code Set of symbols	Medium Carrier	Motor skills Muscle system Sensory skills	Ideas Needs Intentions Information Purpose

concludes that "widespread ineffectiveness is the rule, probably because of a variety of causes."[29]

A communication system that only gives specific directives about job instructions and procedures and fails to provide information about job performance or rationale-ideological information about the job has a negative organizational impact. This type of downward orientation promotes an authoritative atmosphere which tends to inhibit the effectiveness of the upward and horizontal systems of communication. Communicating the rationale for the job, the ideological relation of the job to the goals of the organization, and information about job performance to employees can, if properly handled, greatly benefit the organization. As Katz and Kahn point out, "If a man knows the reasons for his assignment, this will often insure his carrying out the job more effectively; and if he has an understanding of what his job is about in relation to his subsystem, he is more likely to identify with organizational goals."[30] This does not imply that management should tell assembly line workers that their jobs are extremely important to the success of the company, that the company would fold without their putting on a bolt right or welding a fender properly. Obviously, this type of communication can backfire. The workers would justifiably reason: "Who are they trying to kid? My job isn't *that* important. It is just another hypocritical con job by management." What is meant is that providing *full* information about the job, its ramifications for the rest of the organization, and the quality of the employee's performance in it should be an important function of superior-subordinate communication.

Traditional downward communication systems rely on many types of media to disseminate information. Some examples of written media are organizational handbooks, manuals, magazines, newspapers, and letters sent to the home or distributed on the job; bulletin board items, posters and information displays; and standard reports, descriptions of procedures, and memos. Examples of oral media utilized in the system include direct verbal orders or instructions from superiors, speeches, meetings, closed-circuit television sets, public address systems, and telephones. In addition, computerized information systems are becoming a major contributor in the downward flow of communication.

The numerous types of media give an indication of the avalanche of information that is descending on personnel from the downward system. Quality of information has often been sacrificed for quantity. Some organizations have tried to solve their downward communication problems by creating special departments whose goals are to make information reports more readable, to process information faster, and to prune information reports for brevity.[31] Besides the quantity and quality difficulties, much of

---

[29]Tompkins, op. cit., p. 9.

[30]Katz and Kahn, op. cit., p. 242.

[31]"The Crisis in Corporate Controls," *Dun's Review*, July 1963, p. 61. Also see: "An Avalanche," an illustrative case based upon the above, in Fred Luthans, *Cases, Readings, and Review Guide for Principles of Management*, Wiley, New York, 1969, p. 137.

downward communication becomes lost, distorted, misinterpreted, or ignored by organizational participants. One study of the communication efficiency of 100 representative business and industrial firms found:

There is tremendous loss of information—37 percent—between the Board of Directors and the Vice-Presidential level. General supervisors got 56 percent of the information; plant managers 40 percent; and general foremen received only 30 percent of what had been transmitted downward to them. An average of only 20 percent of the communication sent downward through the five levels of management finally gets to the worker level.[32]

These problems point out that just because there is a very active downward flow of information, it does not mean that it is accurate or that it is received, understood, or accepted by subordinates.

Toward more effective superior-subordinate communication

To improve the effectiveness of superior-subordinate communication, more attention must be given to the receiver and to the use of multimedia techniques. After reviewing the literature, Tompkins notes:

The studies seem to suggest that management is ill-advised to depend on one-message campaigns or upon the written medium alone. Communication effectiveness can better be achieved by careful analysis of the intended receiver, by use of a combination of media and methods (giving the oral medium prominence), by careful monitoring of feedback, and by a continual effort to communicate.[33]

Most studies show that combined oral and written methods are most effective and that oral only is better than written only.

The biggest problem, however, is ignoring the importance of the receiver. This problem, of course, is symptomatic of taking a linear (in this case downward) information flow perspective as opposed to a dynamic perspective. After an extensive review of the literature, Donald Roberts concludes that the downward flow of information can affect receivers in the following ways:

1. People's interpretations of communications follow the path of least resistance.
2. People are more open to messages which are consonant with their existing image, their beliefs, and values.
3. Messages which are incongruent with values tend to engender more resistance than do messages which are incongruent with rational logic.
4. To the extent that people positively value need fulfillment, messages which facilitate need fulfillment are more easily accepted than messages which do not.
5. As people see the environment changing, they are more open to incoming messages.

---

[32]Ralph G. Nichols, "Listening Is Good Business," *Management of Personnel Quarterly,* Winter 1962, p. 4.

[33]Tompkins, op. cit., p. 9.

6. The total situation affects communication; a message interpreted as congruent in one situation may be interpreted as incongruent in another.[34]

If managers understand these impacts of communication on subordinates and do something about it, communication can become more effective. There is a series of recent studies indicating that if subordinates do get needed information (i.e., if superior-subordinate communication is effective), they perform better as individuals and in groups.[35]

SUBORDINATE-INITIATED COMMUNICATION

Just as the downward system becomes superior-subordinate communication from a dynamic, personal perspective, the upward system becomes subordinate-initiated communication in the dynamic, personal view. In the traditional view, the classical organization structure formally provided for vertical information flows, downward and upward. However, in practice, except for feedback controls, the downward system completely dominated the upward system. Whereas the downward system is highly directive—giving orders, instructions, information, and procedures—the upward system is characteristically nondirective in nature. While bureaucratic authority facilitates a directive atmosphere, a free, participative supervisory approach is necessary for subordinate-initiated communication. Traditionally, bureaucratic authority has prevailed over the more participative styles, with the result that subordinate-initiated communication has often been outwardly stifled, badly misused, or conveniently ignored by management.

Research on subordinate-initiated communication

Research has generally verified the ineffectiveness of subordinate-initiated communication in organizations. One study asked the managers of twenty-four industrial plants to rank the ten most important morale factors of any employee group. The workers were then asked to do the same thing. Interestingly, the managers named the following bottom three factors: in the eighth place, full appreciation of work done; in the ninth, feeling "in" on things; and in the lowest place, sympathetic help on personal problems. The workers, on the other hand, ranked these same three factors as the first, second, and third most important.[36] The fact that the managers were

---

[34]Donald F. Roberts, "The Nature of Communication Effects," in Wilbur Schramm and Donald F. Roberts (eds.), *The Process and Effects of Mass Communication*, rev. ed., University of Illinois Press, Urbana, Ill., 1971, pp. 368–371.

[35]Charles A. O'Reilly, "Supervisors and Peers as Information Sources, Group Supportiveness, and Individual Performance," *Journal of Applied Psychology*, vol. 62, 1977, pp. 632–635; and Charles A. O'Reilly and Karlene H. Roberts, "Task Group Structure, Communication, and Effectiveness in Three Organizations," *Journal of Applied Psychology*, vol. 62., 1977, pp. 674–681.

[36]Nichols, op. cit.

completely wrong about the morale factors gives evidence that there was no effective communication from the workers to the managers.

In another study, fifty-eight superior-subordinate pairs, representing all functional areas from upper management levels of five companies, were interviewed to determine the extent of mutual understanding and agreement on four factors of the subordinates' jobs: (1) duties, (2) requirements, (3) future changes, and (4) obstacles. After analyzing statistical results, the researchers concluded that "[the subordinate] and his boss do not agree, or differ more than they agree, in almost every area. Also, superior and subordinate very often disagree about priorities—they simply don't see eye to eye on which are the most important and the least important tasks for the subordinate."[37] Once again these results do not speak very highly of the effectiveness of subordinate-initiated communication. Even when subordinates do communicate upward, the content is often meaningless because they send up only what they think the boss wants to hear or reports that are distorted or manipulated so that they contain only information that makes the subordinates look good. "Full and objective reporting is difficult, regardless of the organizational situation; no individual is an objective observer of his own performance and problems."[38]

Methods of improving the effectiveness of subordinate-initiated communication

The hierarchical structure is about the only formal method that the classical approach used to communicate upward and, as has been pointed out, in practice this has not worked out well. Other techniques and channels for subordinate-initiated communication are necessary.[39] The following are some possible ways to promote more effective subordinate-to-superior communications:

1. *The grievance procedure.* Provided for in most collective bargaining agreements, the grievance procedure allows employees to make an appeal upward beyond their immediate superior. It protects individuals from arbitrary action by their direct superior and encourages communication about complaints.
2. *The open-door policy.* Taken literally, this means that the superior's door is always open to subordinates. It is a continuous invitation for subordinates to come in and talk about anything that is troubling them. Unfortunately, in practice the open-door policy is more fiction than fact. The boss may slap the subordinate on the back and say, "My door is always open to you," but in many cases both the subordinate and the boss know the door is really closed. It is a case where the adage that actions speak louder than words applies.
3. *Counseling, attitude questionnaires, and exit interviews.* The personnel depart-

---

[37]Norman R. F. Maier, L. Richard Hoffman, John J. Hooven, and William H. Read, *Superior-Subordinate Communication in Management*, American Management Association, New York, 1961, p. 9.

[38]Katz and Kahn, op. cit., p. 246.

[39]Flippo and Munsinger, op. cit., pp. 389–392.

ment can greatly facilitate subordinate-initiated communication by conducting nondirective, confidential counseling sessions, periodically administering attitude questionnaires, and holding meaningful exit interviews for those who leave the organization. Much valuable information can be gained from these forms of communication.

4. *Participative techniques.* Participative-decision techniques can generate a great deal of communication. This may be accomplished by either informal involvement of subordinates or formal participation programs such as the use of junior boards, union-management committees, and suggestion boxes. There is also empirical research evidence indicating that participants in communication networks are generally more satisfied with their jobs, are more committed to their organizations, and are better performers than those who are not involved in the communication process.[40]

5. *The ombudsperson.* A largely untried but potentially significant technique to enable management to obtain more subordinate-initiated communication is the use of an ombudsperson. The concept has been used primarily in Scandinavia to provide an outlet for persons who have been treated unfairly or in a depersonalized manner by large, bureaucratic government. It has more recently gained popularity in American state governments, military posts, and universities. Although it is just being introduced in a few business organizations, if set up and handled properly, it may work where the open-door policy has failed. As business organizations become larger and more depersonalized, the ombudsperson may fill an important void that exists under these conditions.

Overall, subordinates can supply basically two types of information: first, personal information about ideas, attitudes, and performance, and second, more technical feedback information about performance, a vital factor for the control of any organization. The personal information is generally derived from what subordinates tell their superiors. Some examples of such information are:

1. What the persons have done
2. What those under them have done
3. What their peers have done
4. What they think needs to be done
5. What their problems are
6. What the problems of the unit are
7. What matters of organizational practice and policy need to be reviewed[41]

The other type of upward information, feedback for control purposes, is necessary if the organization is to survive. As has been pointed out, "Decision centers utilize information feedback to appraise the results of the organization's performance and to make any adjustments to insure the accomplishment of the purposes of the organization."[42] The role that

---

[40]Karlene H. Roberts and Charles A. O'Reilly, "Some Correlations of Communication Roles in Organizations," *Academy of Management Journal*, March 1979, pp. 42–57.

[41]Katz and Kahn, op. cit., p. 245.

[42]William G. Scott and Terence R. Mitchell, *Organization Theory*, rev. ed., Irwin, Homewood, Ill., 1972, p. 147.

feedback communication plays has already been stressed at the beginning of the chapter. Its role in the control process is covered in Chapter 17.

INTERACTIVE COMMUNICATION IN ORGANIZATIONS

The classical hierarchical organization structure gives formal recognition only to vertical communication. Nevertheless, most of the classical theorists saw the need to supplement the vertical with some form of horizontal system, as Fayol did with his gangplank concept. Horizontal communication is required to make a coordinated effort in achieving organizational goals. The horizontal requirement becomes more apparent as the organization becomes larger, more complex, and more subject to dramatic change. The modern organization designs that will be discussed in Chapter 19, the free form and matrix, recognize this need by formally incorporating horizontal flows into the structure. However, as with vertical (downward and upward) flows in the organization structure, the real key to horizontal communication is found in people and behaviors. Because of the dynamic, personal aspects of communication, the *interactive* seems more appropriate than *horizontal*. The horizontal flows of information (even in a matrix structure) are only part of the communication process that takes place across an organization.

The extent and implications of interactive communication

Most management writers today stress the important but overlooked role that interactive communication plays in organizations. In most cases the vertical communication process overshadows the horizontal. For example, one observational study found that 17 percent of the total communications of a line-production manager in one plant were sent horizontally and 22 percent were received from a horizontal source. In another plant in the same study, 41 percent of the production manager's communications were sent horizontally and 40 percent were received from a horizontal source.[43] Obviously, the exact amount of horizontal communication is highly contingent upon the situation. One potentially significant research finding is that the nature of the productive or technological process will influence the type of communication that occurs. For example, the researcher found that communications of first-line supervisors were mainly horizontal because of the mechanized, assembly line nature of their work.[44] The assembly line type of operation discouraged and even inhibited vertical communication, but it encouraged horizontal communication. The reason is that an assembly line job is highly structured and largely dependent upon the speed of the line. Thus, there is

---

[43]Henry A. Landsberger, "The Horizontal Dimension in Bureaucracy," *Administrative Science Quarterly*, December 1961, p. 315.

[44]Richard L. Simpson, "Vertical and Horizontal Communication in Formal Organizations," *Administrative Science Quarterly*, September 1959, p. 195.

little need for directives, instructions, or orders from above, but there is a necessity to communicate along the line to get the job done.

Just as in other aspects of organizational communication, there are many behavioral implications contained in the interactive process. Communication with peers, i.e., those persons of relatively equal status on the same level of an organization, provides needed social support for an individual. People can more comfortably turn to a peer for social support than they can to those above or below them. The result can be good or bad for the organization. If the support is couched in terms of task coordination to achieve overall goals, interactive communication can be good for the organization. On the other hand, "if there are no problems of task coordination left to a group of peers, the content of their communication can take forms which are irrelevant to or destructive of organizational functioning."[45] In addition, interactive communication among peers may be at the sacrifice of vertical communication. Persons at each level, giving social support to one another, may freely communicate among themselves but fail to communicate upward or downward.

The purposes and methods of interactive communication

Just as there are several purposes of vertical communication in an organization, there are also various reasons for the need for interactive communication. Basing his inquiry on several research studies, a communications scholar has summarized four of the most important purposes for interactive communication:

1. *Task coordination.* The department heads may meet monthly to discuss how each department is contributing to the system's goals.
2. *Problem solving.* The members of a department may assemble to discuss how they will handle a threatened budget cut; they may employ brainstorming techniques.
3. *Information sharing.* The members of one department may meet with the members of another department to give them some new data.
4. *Conflict resolution.* Members of one department may meet to discuss a conflict inherent in the department or between departments.[46]

The examples for each of the major purposes of interactive communication are mainly departmental or interdepartmental meetings. Such meetings and the system of committees that exist in most organizations have been the major methods of interactive communication. In addition, most organizations' procedures require written reports to be distributed across departments. The quantity, quality, and human implications discussed in relation to the vertical communication process are also inherent in the traditional methods of interactive communication.

Because of the failure of the classical structures to meet the needs of interactive communication, the informal organization and groups have filled

---

[45]Katz and Kahn, op. cit., p. 244.

[46]Gerald M. Goldhaber, *Organizational Communication*, William C. Brown, Dubuque, Iowa, 1974, p. 121.

the void. Informal contacts with others on the same level are a primary means of interactive communication. The last chapter explored some of the dynamics of informal and group communication.

SUMMARY

At every level of modern society, communication is a problem. One of the problems when applied to organizations has been the failure to recognize that communication involves more than just linear information flows: it is a dynamic, personal process that involves behavior exchanges. Knowledge of both information theory and interpersonal approaches is a necessary background for understanding organizational communication.

A purely structural view of organizational communication is no longer adequate. The Shannon-Weaver model was the first to recognize that communication is a process, but the Berlo model added a dynamic interactive dimension. The contemporary view is that communication is a dynamic personal process. The three major dimensions of organizational communication from this perspective are superior-subordinate, subordinate-initiated, and interactive processes. Each has varied purposes and methods. The downward system is generally adequate in the superior-subordinate process, but better techniques are needed to improve the upward and horizontal systems. All three processes in organizations can greatly benefit from increased attention given to the dynamic, personal aspects of communication.

QUESTIONS FOR DISCUSSION AND REVIEW

1. Explain Fayol's "gangplank" concept. What are some of its advantages and disadvantages?
2. Compare and contrast the information theory and the interpersonal approaches to communication.
3. Why is feedback so important to communication? What are some guidelines for the effective use of feedback?
4. What are some of the major purposes and methods of supervisor-subordinate communication?
5. What are some techniques for improving subordinate-initiated communication?
6. What are the major purposes and methods of interactive communication?

CASE:
DOING MY
OWN THING

Rita Lowe had worked for the same boss for eleven years. Over coffee one day, her friend Sara asked her, "What is it like to work for old Charlie?" Rita replied, "Oh, I guess it's okay. He pretty much leaves me alone. I more or less do my own thing." Then Sara said, "Well, you've been at that same job for eleven years. How are you doing in it? Does it look like you will ever be promoted? If you don't mind me saying so, I can't for the life of me see that what you do has anything to do with the operation." Rita replied, "Well, first of all, I really don't have any idea of how I am doing. Charlie never tells me, but I've always taken the attitude that no news is good news. As for what I do and how it contributes to the operation around here, Charlie mumbled something when I started the job about being important to the operation, but that was it. We really don't communicate very well."

1. Analyze Rita's last statement, "We really don't communicate very well." What is the status of superior-subordinate communication in this work relationship? Katz and Kahn identified five purposes of the superior-subordinate communication process. Which ones are being badly neglected in this case?
2. It was said in this chapter, that communication is a dynamic, personal, process. Does the situation described verify this contention? Be specific in your answer.
3. Are there any implications in this situation for subordinate-initiated communication and for interactive communication? How could feedback be used more effectively?

CASE:
BAD BRAKES

Michelle Adams was the maintenance supervisor of a large taxicab company. She was very concerned because the cabdrivers were not reporting potential mechanical problems. Several months previously she had implemented a preventive maintenance program. This program depended upon the drivers filling out a detailed report when they suspected any problem. But this was not happening. On a number of occasions a cab left the garage with major problems that the previous driver was aware of but had not reported. Calling out the field repair teams to fix the breakdown was not only costing the company much time and trouble, but it was in some cases very unsafe and created a high degree of customer ill will. The drivers themselves suffered from a loss of fares and tips, and in some cases their lives were endangered by these mechanical failures. After many verbal and written threats and admonishments, Michelle decided to try a new approach. She would respond directly to each report of a potential mechanical problem sent in by a driver with a return memo indicating what the maintenance crew had found wrong with the cab and what had been done to take care of the problem. In addition, the personal memo thanked the driver for reporting the problem and encouraged him or her to report any further problems with the cabs. In less than a month the number of field repair calls had decreased by half and the number of turned-in potential problem reports had tripled.

1. In communications terms, how do you explain the success of Michelle's follow-up memos to the drivers?
2. Explain and give examples of the three communications systems in this company (i.e., superior-subordinate, subordinate-initiated, and interactive)?

CONFLICT AND STRESS

COMPANIES WITH EXECUTIVE STRESS*

The prestigious Cornell University Medical School is on record as stating that conflict and stress constitute "one of the most debilitating medical and social problems in the United States today." This problem is especially relevant to modern organizational life. Remember that people spend about half of their adult waking life in the organization that employs them. An increasing number of organizations are attempting to combat conflict and stress by implementing specialized programs. For example, some companies have called on the famous Menninger Foundation which has been offering its services to counsel and help solve conflict and stress problems of executives for more than twenty years. Clients such as International Business Machines, Chase Manhattan Bank, and Continental Illinois Bank have all implemented formal programs to aid their executives in coping with organizational conflict and stress. Lately, organizations have also begun to develop programs of their own. For example, Hughes Aircraft, Connecticut General Insurance, and Xerox currently have conflict and stress reduction programs in operation.

What is involved in these programs? The typical approach is to develop techniques for measuring conflict and stress in each individual and then to offer specific ways to deal with the problem before it becomes a physical or mental health problem or before the person quits. The Menninger program depends considerably on biofeedback. In this approach, individuals are taught how to measure their own pulse rate, skin temperature, and muscle tension; they then learn how to relax and keep these under control. In addition to biofeedback, systematic exercise programs are being used to reduce tension, along with specific approaches in how to deal with stressful situations. Training for the latter includes role-playing exercises, simulations, and other personal involvement techniques. Companies that have implemented these programs claim that they have had considerable success. They justify the time and cost of the programs in terms of the debilitating effects that conflict and stress can have on the performance and turnover of their personnel.

---

*Adapted from "How Companies Cope with Executive Stress," *Business Week,* Aug. 21, 1978, pp. 107–108.

From an international, societal, organizational, group, interpersonal, or intraindividual point of view, the dynamics and ramifications of conflict and stress are becoming increasingly important. In the study of organizational behavior, conflict and stress have "arrived" as an important topic area. Conflict and stress are sometimes treated separately and the two terms are sometimes used interchangeably.

A recent extensive review of the literature notes the extreme diversity of the definitions of and approaches to conflict:

Conflict has been defined as the condition of objective incompatibility between values or goals, as the behavior of deliberately interfering with another's goal achievement, and emotionally in terms of hostility. Descriptive theorists have explained conflict behavior in terms of objective conflict of interest, personal styles, reactions to threats, and cognitive distortions. Normative recommendations range over the establishment of superordinate goals, consciousness raising, selection of compatible individuals, and mediating conflict.[1]

Stress, on the other hand, has just recently emerged as a topic area for organizational behavior. Stress has some of the same characteristics as conflict but is usually associated with more physiological outcomes. The following comprehensive definition reflects this physiological emphasis:

Stress is defined by a set of circumstances under which an individual cannot respond adequately or instrumentally to environmental stimuli, or can so respond only at the cost of excessive wear and tear on the organism—for example, chronic fatigue, tension, worry, physical damage, nervous breakdown, or loss of self-esteem.[2]

With the surge of interest and concern of contemporary society for physical fitness and the quality of life, stress takes on increased importance in the field of organizational behavior. For example, a recent study found:

1. The average employee sees himself or herself physically fit and in good health.
2. From the standpoint of objective coronary risk, the average employee is in unsatisfactory shape.
3. The average employee engages in no regular vigorous exercise.
4. The average employee is strongly interested in modifying his or her coronary risk factors.[3]

In this chapter, conflict is given major attention, but the term is often used interchangeably with *stress*. In particular, the intraindividual aspect is directly relevant to both conflict and stress. The other units of analysis, interpersonal and organizational, are more oriented to conflict per se rather

[1]Ralph H. Kilmann and Kenneth W. Thomas, "Four Perspectives on Conflict Management: An Attributional Framework for Organizing Descriptive and Normative Theory," *Academy of Management Review*, January 1978, pp. 59–60.

[2]W. Clay Hamner and Dennis W. Organ, *Organizational Behavior*, Business Publications, Dallas, Tex., 1978, p. 193.

[3]Robert Kreitner, Steven D. Wood, and Glenn M. Friedman, "Just How Fit Are Your Employees?" *Business Horizons*, August 1979, pp. 44–45.

than stress. The first section then examines conflict and stress from the perspective of the individual. Intraindividual concepts such as frustration, goal conflict, and role conflict and ambiguity are initially given attention, and then interpersonal conflict is discussed within the framework of the Johari window. Strategies for conflict resolution are presented. Next, conflict from the perspective of the organization is discussed. Some of the major assumptions and strategies in the management of organizational conflict are included in this discussion.

INTRAINDIVIDUAL ASPECTS OF CONFLICT AND STRESS

A smooth progression of the need-drive-goal motivational cycle (discussed in Chapter 6) and fulfillment of one's role expectations do not always occur in reality. Within every individual there are usually (1) a number of competing needs and roles; (2) a variety of different ways that drives and roles can be expressed; (3) many types of barriers which can occur between the drive and the goal; and (4) both positive and negative aspects attached to desired goals. These complicate the human adaptation process and often result in conflict and stress. Intraindividual forms of conflict and stress can be analyzed in terms of the frustration paradigm, goals, and roles.

Conflict and stress from frustration

Frustration occurs when a motivated drive is blocked before reaching a desired goal. Figure 13-1 illustrates what happens. The barrier may be either overt (outward, physical) or covert (inward, mental-sociopsychological). An example of a frustrating situation might be that of the thirsty person who comes up against a stuck door and is prevented from reaching a water fountain. Figure 13-2 illustrates this simple frustrating situation. Frustration

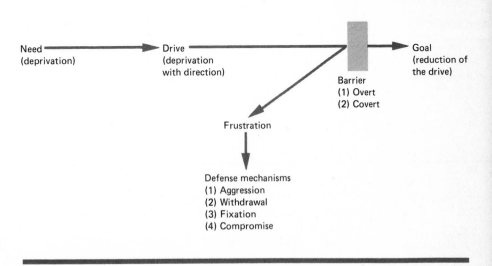

**Figure 13-1
A simple model of
frustration.**

normally triggers defense mechanisms in the person. Traditionally, psychologists felt that frustration always led to the defense mechanism of aggression. On becoming frustrated, it was thought that a person would react by physically or symbolically attacking the barrier. In the example in Figure 13-2, the person would react by kicking and/or cursing the jammed door.

More recently, aggression has come to be viewed as only one possible reaction. Frustration may lead to any of the defense mechanisms used by the human organism. Although there are many such mechanisms, they can be summarized into four broad categories: aggression, withdrawal, fixation, and compromise. In the illustration of Figure 13-2, backing away from the door and pouting would be an example of withdrawal; pretending the door is not jammed and continually trying to open it would be an example of fixation; and substituting a new goal (a cup of coffee already in the room) or a new direction (climbing out the window) would be an example of compromise.

Although the thirsty person frustrated by the stuck door is a very uncomplicated example, the same frustration model can be used to analyze more complex behavior. One example would be a black individual who comes from a disadvantaged educational and economic background but who still has intense needs for pride and dignity. A goal that may fulfill the individual's needs is meaningful employment. The drive set up to alleviate the need and accomplish the goal would be to search for a good job. The black person in this example who meets barriers (prejudice, discrimination, lack of education, and nonqualification) may become frustrated. Possible reactions to this frustration may be aggression (riot or hate), withdrawal (apathy and unemployment), fixation (pretending the barriers do not exist and continuing to search unsuccessfully for a good job), or compromise

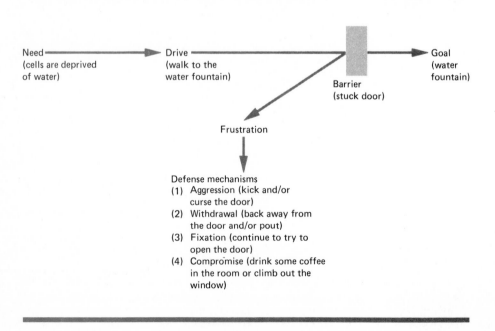

**Figure 13-2
A simple example
of frustration.**

(finding expression of pride and dignity in something other than a good job, such as in a militant group).

The frustration model can be useful in the analysis not only of behavior in general but also of specific aspects of organizational behavior. Table 13-1 summarizes some behavioral reactions to frustration that may occur in the

Table 13-1

EXAMPLES OF REACTIONS TO FRUSTRATION

Adjustive reactions	Psychological process	Illustration
Compensation	Individual devotes himself to a pursuit with increased vigor to make up for some feeling of real or imagined inadequacy	Zealous, hard-working president of the Twenty-Five-Year Club who has never advanced very far in the company hierarchy
Conversion	Emotional conflicts are expressed in muscular, sensory, or bodily symptoms of disability, malfunctioning, or pain	A disabling headache keeping a staff member off the job, the day after a cherished project has been rejected
Displacement	Redirecting pent-up emotions toward persons, ideas, or objects other than the primary source of the emotion	Roughly rejecting a simple request from a subordinate after receiving a rebuff from the boss
Fantasy	Daydreaming or other forms of imaginative activity provide an escape from reality and imagined satisfactions	An employee's daydream of the day in the staff meeting when he corrects the boss's mistakes and is publicly acknowledged as the real leader of the industry
Identification	Individual enhances his self-esteem by patterning his own behavior after another's, frequently also internalizing the values and beliefs of the other; also vicariously sharing the glories or suffering in the reversals of other individuals or groups	The "assistant-to" who takes on the vocabulary, mannerisms, or even pomposity of his vice president boss
Negativism	Active or passive resistance, operating unconsciously	The manager who, having been unsuccessful in getting out of a committee assignment, picks apart every suggestions that anyone makes in the meetings
Projection	Individual protects himself from awareness of his own undesirable traits or unacceptable feelings by attributing them to others	Unsuccessful person who, deep down, would like to block the rise of others in the organization and who continually feels that others are out to "get him"
Rationalization	Justifying inconsistent or undesirable behavior, beliefs, statements, and motivations by providing acceptable explanations for them	Padding the expense account because "everybody does it"

Table 13-1

EXAMPLES OF REACTIONS TO FRUSTRATION

Adjustive reactions	Psychological process	Illustration
Reaction-formation	Urges not acceptable to consciousness are repressed and in their stead opposite attitudes or modes of behavior are expressed with considerable force	Employee who has not been promoted who overdoes the defense of his boss, vigorously upholding the company's policies
Regression	Individual returns to an earlier and less mature level of adjustment in the face of frustration	A manager having been blocked in some administrative pursuit busies himself with clerical duties or technical details more appropriate for his subordinates
Repression	Completely excluding from consciousness impulses, experiences, and feelings which are psychologically disturbing because they arouse a sense of guilt or anxiety	A subordinate "forgetting" to tell his boss the circumstances of an embarrassing situation
Fixation	Maintaining a persistent nonadjustive reaction even though all the cues indicate the behavior is not an appropriate response to the problem	Persisting in carrying out an operational procedure long since declared by management to be uneconomical as a protest because the employee's opinion wasn't asked
Resignation, apathy, and boredom	Breaking psychological contact with the environment; withholding any sense of emotional or personal involvement	Employee who, receiving no reward, praise, or encouragement, no longer cares whether or not he does a good job
Flight or withdrawal	Leaving the field in which frustration, anxiety, or conflict is experienced, either physically or psychologically	The salesman's big order falls through and he takes the rest of the day off; constant rebuff or rejection by superiors and colleagues pushes an older worker toward being a loner and ignoring what friendly gestures are made

Source: Timothy W. Costello and Sheldon S. Zalkind, *Psychology in Administration: A Research Orientation,* Prentice-Hall, Englewood Cliffs, N.J., © 1963, pp. 148–149. Reprinted by permission.

formal organization. These examples generally imply that there is a negative impact on the individual's performance and on the organization as a result of frustration. Although research indicates this is generally true, it cannot be automatically assumed. There are some cases where frustration may actually result in a positive impact on individual performance and organizational goals. An example is the worker or manager who has high needs for competency and achievement and has a self-concept that includes confidence in being able to do a job well. A person of this type who is frustrated on the job may react in a traditional defensive manner, but the frustration may result in improved performance. The person may try harder to overcome the barrier or may overcompensate, or the new direction or goal sought may be more compatible with the organization's goals. In addition, it should be remembered that defense mechanisms per se are not bad for the individual. They play an important role in the psychological adjustment process and are "unhealthy" only when they dominate the individual's personality. Reactions to frustration are also influenced by external factors. For example, group norms, such as those that exist in a professional setting, may dictate that the accepted reaction to frustration is to try harder to overcome the barriers.[4] Obviously, examples such as the above are the exceptions, but they do point out that, in certain situations, frustration can lead to positive as well as negative organizational behavior. However, in general, a major goal of management should be to eliminate the barriers (imagined, real, or potential) that are or will be frustrating to employees.

Goal conflict

Another common source of conflict for an individual is a goal which has both positive and negative features, or two or more competing goals. Whereas in frustration a single motive is blocked before the goal is reached, in goal conflict two or more motives block one another. For ease of analysis, three separate types of goal conflict are generally identified:

1. *Approach-approach* conflict, where the individual is motivated to approach two or more positive but mutually exclusive goals.
2. *Approach-avoidance* conflict, where the individual is motivated to approach a goal and at the same time is motivated to avoid it. The single goal contains both positive and negative characteristics for the individual.
3. *Avoidance-avoidance* conflict, where the individual is motivated to avoid two or more negative but mutually exclusive goals.

To varying degrees, each of these forms of goal conflict exists in the modern organization.

Approach-approach conflict   This type of goal conflict probably has the least impact on organizational behavior. Research from the behavioral sciences concludes that "the choice between two positive goals naturally becomes more difficult and takes longer when they are seen of equal value, but in any case it remains relatively easy to make a selection."[5] For example, if both personal and organizational goals are attractive to organizational participants, they will usually make a choice rather quickly and thus eliminate their conflict. A more specific example would be the young person who is faced with two excellent job opportunities or the executive who has the choice between two very attractive offices in which to work. Such

---

[4]See: Abraham K. Korman, *Industrial and Organizational Psychology*, Prentice-Hall, Englewood Cliffs, N.J., 1971, pp. 170–171.

[5]Bernard Berelson and Gary A. Steiner, *Human Behavior*, Harcourt, Brace & World, New York, 1964, p. 271.

situations often cause the person some anxiety but are quickly resolved and the person does not "starve between two haystacks."

Approach-approach conflict can be analyzed in terms of Leon Festinger's well-known theory of cognitive dissonance.[6] In simple terms, dissonance is the state of psychological discomfort or conflict created in people when they are faced with two or more goals or alternatives to a decision. Although these alternatives occur together, they do not belong or fit together. The theory states that the person experiencing dissonance will be highly motivated to reduce or eliminate it and will actively avoid situations and information which would likely increase it. For example, the young person faced with two equally attractive job opportunities would experience dissonance. According to Festinger's theory, this young person would actively try to reduce the dissonance. The individual may cognitively rationalize that one job is really better than the other one, and once the choice is made be sincerely convinced that it was the right choice and actively avoid any evidence or argument to the contrary.

Approach-avoidance conflict This type of goal conflict is most relevant to the analysis of organizational behavior. Normally, organizational goals have both positive and negative aspects for organizational participants. Accordingly, the organizational goal may arouse a great deal of conflict within a person and may actually cause the person to vacillate anxiously at the point where approach equals avoidance.

Figure 13-3 shows some possible gradients for approach and avoidance.

---

[6]Leon Festinger, *A Theory of Cognitive Dissonance*, Stanford, Stanford, Calif., 1957.

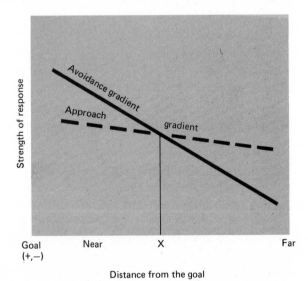

**Figure 13-3
Gradients of ap-
proach-avoidance
conflict.**

X represents the point of maximum conflict where the organism may come to a complete stop and vacillate. In order for the organism to progress beyond X, there must be a shift in the gradients so that there is a greater strength of response for approach than for avoidance. The slopes of the gradients shown in Figure 13-3 approximate those obtained from animals who are first trained to approach food at the end of a runway and are then shocked while feeding there. "The pull toward a positive goal increases with nearness, but only slightly; while the tendency to retreat from a negative goal rises very steeply as it is approached."[7]

The approach-avoidance gradients for humans will not always resemble that found in Figure 13-3. The slopes may be different for different people and different goals. In general, however, it is safe to assume that the positive aspects of a given organizational goal are stronger and more salient at a distance (in time and/or space) than are the negative aspects. On the other hand, as a person gets nearer to the goal, the negative aspects become more pronounced, and at some point the individual may hesitate or fail to progress any further. For example, managers engaged in long-range planning typically are very confident of a goal (plan) they have developed for the future. Yet, as the time gets near to commit resources and implement the plan, the negative consequences seem to appear much greater than they did in the developing stage. The manager or managers involved may reach the point where approach equals avoidance. The result is a great deal of internal conflict and stress which may cause indecision, ulcers, or even neurosis. Such conflict and its aftermath are very common among decision makers and people in responsible positions in modern, complex organizations. The following almost unbelievable health report on executives in one randomly selected successful firm is indicative of the situation.[8]

1. *Executive vice president,* aged fifty, had had three attacks and a stroke. He was retired on full pay and shortly afterward committed suicide.
2. *Treasurer* trembles each time the president talks to him and has developed a skin disease.
3. *Employee relations director* feels he cannot live up to the job, has had a nervous breakdown, and is under constant treatment by a psychiatrist.
4. *Vice president marketing* had had a heart attack while playing with his children after "a record game of golf."
5. *Vice president planning* had become a manic-depressive and had to be moved to another location—to a "soft job."
6. *Vice president finance* had been fired after a disagreement with the president; he had overdrawn on his charge accounts with local firms because of the pressure his wife had been exerting on him to live beyond his means.
7. *Director of purchasing* suddenly dropped dead of a heart attack.
8. *Regional manager* suddenly dropped dead of a heart attack.

Obviously, the above is not necessarily representative of all executive personnel, but it does make the point that the stress and internal conflict in

---

[7]Berelson and Steiner, op. cit., p. 273.

[8]Ernest Dale and Lyndall Urwick, *Staff in Organization,* McGraw-Hill, New York, 1960, pp. 17–18.

executives are certainly more severe than in the population as a whole. On the other hand, the approach-avoidance type of conflict can often be resolved in the same manner as cognitive dissonance, or the gradients may be shifted by the individual so that either the positive or the negative aspects clearly predominate.

Avoidance-avoidance conflict   Analogous to approach-approach conflict, this type of conflict does not have a great deal of impact on organizational behavior. Avoidance-avoidance conflict is usually easily resolved. A person faced with two negative goals may not choose either of them and may simply leave the situation. If this can be done, the conflict is quickly resolved. In some situations, however, the person is unable to leave. This would be true of persons in nonvoluntary organizations, such as inmates in a prison, patients in a hospital, or draftees in the armed services. To a lesser extent, most personnel in modern organizations are also restricted from leaving. An example is the worker who detests his supervisor and has too much pride to accept unemployment compensation. This worker cannot easily resolve his avoidance-avoidance conflict in a time when jobs are very scarce.

Goal conflict in perspective   All three types of goal conflict might in certain instances benefit the organization. Approach-approach conflicts can be mildly distressing for a person but represent the best of two worlds. Approach-avoidance conflicts arising over organizational goals may force very careful planning and forecasting of exact positive and negative outcomes. Even avoidance-avoidance may stimulate the person involved to examine and try to solve the problems causing the conflict and stress. Yet, on balance, except for approach-approach conflicts, management should attempt to resolve goal conflicts. In particular, a major management effort should be devoted to building compatibility, not conflict, between personal and organizational goals.

Role conflict and ambiguity

The concept of role has been pointed out as a basic unit of analysis in the behavioral sciences. Closely related to the concept of norms (the "oughts" of behavior), *role* was defined in Chapter 11 as a position that has expectations evolving from established norms. Persons living in a contemporary Western society assume a succession of roles throughout life. A typical sequence of social roles would be that of child, son or daughter, teen-ager, college student, boyfriend or girlfriend, spouse, parent, and grandparent. Each of these roles has recognized expectations which are acted out like a role in a play.

Besides progressing through a succession of roles such as those just mentioned, the adult in modern society fills numerous other roles at the same time. It is not uncommon for the adult middle-class male to be simultaneously playing the roles of husband, father, provider, son (to elderly parents), worker or manager, student (in a night program), coach of a Little

League baseball team, church member, member of a social club, bridge partner, poker club member, officer of a community group, and weekend golfer. Although all the roles which individuals bring into the organization are relevant to their behavior, in the study of organizational behavior the organizational role is the most important. Roles such as assembly line worker, clerk, supervisor, salesperson, engineer, systems analyst, department head, vice president, and chairperson of the board often carry conflicting demands and expectations. The classic example of an organizational role in constant conflict and ambiguity is that of the first-line supervisor.

Role conflict and ambiguity in supervisors The first-line supervisor is often described as the person in the middle. One set of expectations of this role is that the supervisor is part of the management team and should have the corresponding values and attitudes. A second set of expectations is that the supervisor came from, and is still part of, the workers' group and should have their values and attitudes. Still a third set of expectations is that supervisors are a separate link between management and the work force and should have their own unique set of values and attitudes. Conflict arises because supervisors themselves, like the workers and managers, do not know which set of expectations they should follow.

The typical supervisor often experiences intrarole as well as interrole conflict. Intrarole conflict is inherent in the following description of the supervisor's job: "It is thus abundantly clear that the foreman's job necessitates a 'management slant.' But at the same time, he should be able to see the job from the worker's point of view."[9] This dual membership in both the management and rank-and-file groups is a source of anxiety and intrarole conflict. The interrole conflict on the other hand, is candidly expressed by one supervisor as follows: "the supervisor is a 'bumping post.' . . . He's a 'bumping post' because he's in the middle; he has to take it from both ends; and those running the place don't give him any credit for it."[10]

The first-line supervisor obviously represents the extreme case of organizational role conflict. Yet to varying degrees, depending on the individual and the situation, every other position in the modern organization also experiences both intrarole and interrole conflict. Staff engineers are not sure of their real authority. The clerk in the front office does not know whether to respond to a union organizing drive. The examples are endless. The question is not whether role conflict and ambiguity exist—they do, and they seem inevitable. Rather, the key to organizational analysis is to determine how role conflict can be resolved or effectively managed. Recent research has found that role conflict is significantly related to areas such as participation in decision making and organizational structure variables such

---

[9]John P. Foley, Jr., and Anne Anastasi, *Human Relations and the Foreman*, National Foremen's Institute, Chicago, 1951, p. 25.

[10]William F. Whyte and Burleigh Gardner, "The Position and Problems of the Foreman," *Applied Anthropology*, Spring 1945, p. 19.

as supervisory span of control, span of subordination, and formalization.[11] Such findings suggest specific ways (e.g., more participation or more formalized rules and procedures) in which human resource managers could reduce the role conflict and ambiguity of their people.

Role conflict: the lesser of two evils   Filley and House conclude, after an extensive review of research literature on organizational role conflict, that it has undesirable consequences but may be the lesser of two evils.[12] An example would be the classic interrole conflict between the staff engineer and the line supervisor. This conflict could easily be resolved by granting the engineer final decision-making authority. Yet, this "solution" to role conflict may create more problems than it solves. In this situation, from the perspective of organizational goals, it is probably preferable to have interrole conflict rather than to have formal decision-making authority lie with the staff engineer. Filley and House also report that research indicates that the extent of the undesirable effects from role conflict depends upon four major variables:

1. Awareness of role conflict
2. Acceptance of conflicting job pressures
3. Ability to tolerate stress
4. General personality makeup[13]

Role conflict cannot be wished or completely planned away. As with the other forms of individual conflict and stress already discussed, the approach that management should take is to recognize the existence of role conflict, attempt to understand its causes and ramifications, and then try to manage it as effectively as possible.

INTERPERSONAL CONFLICT

Besides the intraindividual aspects of conflict and stress, the interpersonal aspects of conflict are also an important dynamic of organizational behavior. The interrole conflict discussed in the last section certainly has interpersonal implications, and so does organizational conflict, discussed in the next section. But this section is specifically concerned with analyzing the conflict that can result when two or more persons are interacting with one another. Kelly notes, "Conflict situations inevitably are made up of at least two individuals who hold polarized points of view, who are somewhat intolerant of ambiguities, who ignore delicate shades of grey, and who are quick to jump to conclusions."[14] He goes on to state that conflict occurs in a group

[11]James H. Morris, Richard Steers, and James C. Koch, "Influence of Organization Structure and Role Conflict and Ambiguity for Three Occupational Groupings," *Academy of Management Journal,* March 1979, pp. 58–71.

[12]Alan C. Filley and Robert J. House, *Managerial Process and Organizational Behavior,* Scott, Foresman, Glenview, Ill., 1969, p. 315.

[13]Ibid.

[14]Joe Kelly, *Organizational Behaviour,* rev. ed., Dorsey-Irwin, Homewood, Ill., 1974, p. 563.

setting when members are faced with a novel problem or task; when new values are imported from the social environment into the group; or when members' extragroup roles are different from their intragroup roles. Yet, even though these and many other examples indicate the inherent conflict found when people interact in groups or on a one to one basis, its presence does not necessarily imply a negative impact for organizational behavior. Citing Georg Simmel's classic essay called "Conflict," Lewis Coser explains:

> Groups require disharmony as well as harmony, dissociation as well as association, and conflicts within them are by no means altogether disruptive factors. Group formation is the result of both types of processes. Far from being necessarily dysfunctional, a certain degree of conflict is an essential.[15]

This positive view of interactive conflict found in groups can also be taken when analyzing conflict from the perspective of individuals and the organization.

Besides from the perspective of the group, insight of interpersonal conflict can be gained from examining some different ways that the "self" interacts with others.

The Johari window

One increasingly popular framework for analyzing the dynamics of the interaction between self and others is the Johari window. Developed by Joseph Luft and Harry Ingham (thus the name *Johari*), this model can be used to analyze interpersonal conflict. As Figure 13-4 shows, the model helps identify several interpersonal styles, shows the characteristics and results of these styles, and suggests ways of interpreting the conflicts that may develop between self and others.

In simple terms, the self can be thought of as "me" and others can be thought of as "you" in two-person interaction. There are certain things that the person knows about himself or herself and certain things that are not known. The same is true of others. There are certain things the person knows

---

[15]Lewis Coser, *The Functions of Social Conflict,* Free Press, Glencoe, Ill., 1956, p. 31.

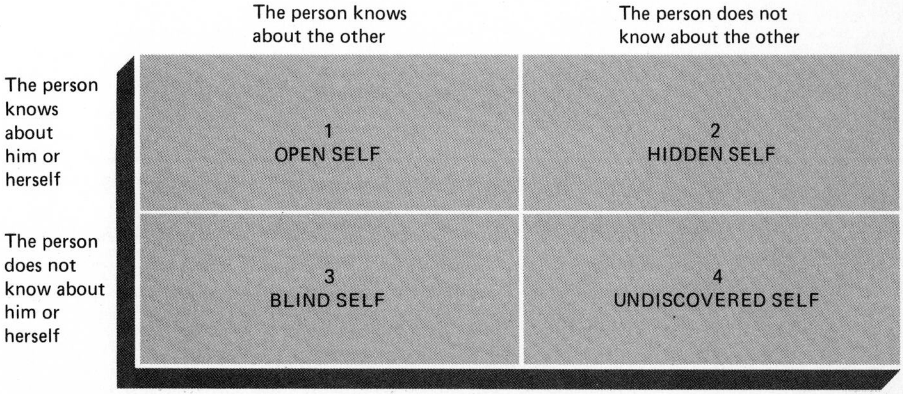

**Figure 13-4
The Johari
window. (*Source:*
Adapted from
Joseph Luft, "The
Johari Window,"
*Human Relations
Training News,* vol.
5, no. 1, 1961, pp.
6–7.)**

	The person knows about the other	The person does not know about the other
The person knows about him or herself	1 OPEN SELF	2 HIDDEN SELF
The person does not know about him or herself	3 BLIND SELF	4 UNDISCOVERED SELF

about the other and certain things that are not known about the other. The following summarizes the four cells in the Johari window:

1. *Open self.* In this form of interaction the person knows about himself or herself and about the other. There would generally be openness and compatibility and little reason to be defensive. This type of interpersonal relationship would tend to lead to little, if any, interpersonal conflict.
2. *Hidden self.* In this situation the person understands himself or herself but does not know about the other person. The result is that the person remains hidden from the other because of the fear of how the other might react. The person may keep his or her true feelings or attitudes secret and will not open up to the other. There is potential interpersonal conflict in this situation.
3. *Blind self.* In this situation the person knows about the other but not about himself or herself. The person may be unintentionally irritating to the other. The other could tell the person but may be fearful of hurting the person's feelings. As in the "hidden self," there is potential interpersonal conflict in this situation.
4. *Undiscovered self.* This is potentially the most explosive situation. The person does not know about himself or herself and does not know about the other. In other words, there is much misunderstanding, and interpersonal conflict is almost sure to result.

The Johari window only points out possible interpersonal styles. It does not necessarily describe but rather helps analyze possible interpersonal conflict situations.

One way of decreasing the "hidden self" and increasing the "open self" is through the processes of self-disclosure. By becoming more trustful of the other and disclosing information about oneself, the potential for conflict may be reduced. On the other hand, such self-disclosure is a risk for the individual, and the outcome must be worth the cost. To decrease the "blind self" and at the same time increase the open self, the other must give and the person must use feedback. The National Training Laboratory (NTL) recommends seven guidelines for providing feedback for effective interpersonal relations:

1. Be descriptive rather than judgmental.
2. Be specific rather than general.
3. Deal with things that can be changed.
4. Give feedback when it is desired.
5. Consider the motives for giving and receiving feedback.
6. Give feedback at the time the behavior takes place.
7. Give feedback when its accuracy can be checked with others.[16]

Following these seven guidelines can help decrease the potential for interpersonal conflict.

Strategies for interpersonal conflict resolution

In addition to the self-disclosure and feedback approaches to interpersonal conflict reduction, there are three basic strategies, called according to the outcomes lose-lose, win-lose, and win-win.

---

[16]*National Training Laboratories' Summer Reading Book,* NTL Institute for Applied Behavioral Science, Bethel, Maine, 1968.

Lose-lose A lose-lose approach to conflict resolution is where both parties lose. It has been pointed out that this approach can take several forms.[17] One of the more common approaches is to compromise or take the middle ground in a dispute. A second approach is to pay off one of the parties in the conflict. These payments often take the form of bribes. A third approach is to use an outside third party or arbitrator. A final type of lose-lose strategy appears when the parties in a conflict resort to bureaucratic rules or existing regulations to resolve the conflict. In all four of these approaches, both parties in the conflict lose. It is sometimes the only way that conflicts can be resolved, but it is generally less desirable than the win-lose or, especially, the win-win strategy.

Win-lose A win-lose strategy is a very common way of resolving conflict in American society. In a competitive type of culture, as is generally found in America, one party in a conflict situation attempts to marshal its forces to win, and the other party loses. The following list summarizes some of the characteristics of a win-lose situation:

1. There is a clear we-they distinction between the parties.
2. Parties direct their energies toward each other in an atmosphere of victory and defeat.
3. Parties see the issue from their own point of view.
4. The emphasis is on solutions rather than on the attainment of goals, values, or objectives.
5. Conflicts are personalized and judgmental.
6. There is no differentiation of conflict-resolving activities from other group processes, nor is there a planned sequence of those activities.
7. The parties take a short-run view of the issues.[18]

Examples of win-lose strategies can be found in superior-subordinate relationships, line-staff confrontations, union-management relations, and many other conflict situations found in today's organizations. The win-lose strategy can have both functional and dysfunctional consequences for the organization. It is functional in the sense of creating a competitive drive to win and it can lead to cohesiveness and esprit de corps among the individuals or groups in the conflict situation. On the dysfunctional side, a win-lose strategy ignores other solutions such as a cooperative, mutually agreed-upon outcome; there are pressures to conform which may stifle a questioning, creative atmosphere for conflict resolution; and highly structured power relationships tend to emerge rapidly. The biggest problem, however, with a win-lose strategy is that someone always loses. Those who suffer the loss may learn something in the process, but losers also tend to be bitter and vindictive. A much healthier strategy is to have both parties of a conflict situation win.

Win-win A win-win strategy of conflict resolution is probably the most desirable from a human and organizational standpoint. Energies and

---

[17]Alan C. Filley, Robert J. House, and Steven Kerr, *Managerial Process and Organizational Behavior,* 2d ed., Scott, Foresman, Glenview, Ill., 1976, pp. 166–167.

[18]Ibid., p. 167.

creativity are aimed at solving the problems rather than beating the other party. It takes advantage of the functional aspects of win-lose and eliminates many of the dysfunctional aspects. The needs of both parties in the conflict situation are met and both parties receive rewarding outcomes. A review of the relevant literature revealed that "win-win decision strategies are associated with better judgments, favorable organization experience, and more favorable bargains."[19] Although it is often difficult to accomplish a win-win outcome of an interpersonal conflict, this should be a major goal of the management of conflict.

ORGANIZATIONAL CONFLICT

So far, this chapter has concentrated on intraindividual and interpersonal conflict. This type of conflict can take place within the organizational setting, and that is why it is so important to the study of organizational behavior. However, now attention is directed at organizational conflict per se, but it must be remembered that both intra- and interpersonal conflict are inherent in organizational conflict.

Structural conflict

Individuals in the organization have many conflicting organizational cross-pressures operating on them. The following examples indicate the sources of potential conflict:

The boss wants more production; subordinates want more consideration. Customers demand faster deliveries; peers request schedule delays. Consultants suggest change; subordinates resist change. The rule book prescribes a formula; the staff says it will not work.[20]

More conceptually, it has been suggested that there are four causes of organizational conflict: (1) an incompatible goals situation, (2) the existence of incompatible means or incompatible resource allocations, (3) a problem of status incongruities, and (4) a difference in perceptions.[21] These sources of organizational conflict result largely from the dynamics of individual and group interactions and psychological processes.

In the classical organization there are four structural areas where conflict is most pronounced:

1. *Hierarchical conflict.* There may be conflict among the various levels of the

---

[19]Ibid., p. 177.

[20]Bernard M. Bass and Edward C. Ryterband, *Organizational Psychology*, 2nd. ed., Allyn and Bacon, Boston, 1979, pp. 377–379.

[21]Joseph A. Litterer, "Managing Conflict in Organizations," *Proceedings of the 8th Annual Midwest Management Conference*, Southern Illinois University, Business Research Bureau, 1965. Reprinted in Max S. Wortman and Fred Luthans, *Emerging Concepts in Management*, Macmillan, 1969, pp. 192–194.

organization. The board of directors may be in conflict with top management, middle management may be in conflict with supervisory personnel, or there may be general conflict between management and the workers.

2. *Functional conflict.* There may be conflict among the various functional departments of the organization. Conflict between the production and marketing departments in an industrial organization is a classic example.

3. *Line-staff conflict.* There may be conflict between the line and staff. It often results from situations where staff personnel do not formally possess authority over line personnel.

4. *Formal-informal conflict.* There may be conflict between the formal and informal organizations. For example, the informal organization's norms for performance may be incompatible with the formal organization's norms for performance.

The hierarchical, functional, and line-staff forms of organizational conflict will be covered extensively in Chapter 18. The dynamics of the formal-informal conflict situation were analyzed in Chapter 11.

Modern organization design (covered in Chapter 19) also contains potential conflict situations. The project and matrix organizations in particular have structurally created conflict. The project manager with responsibility but no authority and the manager in a matrix structure with a functional boss and a project boss present two obvious conflict situations. But the existence of conflict in modern organization design also indicates that it can be healthy. In some cases the modern designs may actually try to promote conflict to benefit the organization.

The role of conflict in today's organizations

Traditionally, the approach to organizational conflict was very simple and optimistic. It was based on the following assumptions:

1. Conflict is by definition avoidable.
2. Conflict is caused by troublemakers, boat rockers, and prima donnas.
3. Legalistic forms of authority such as "going through channels" or "sticking to the book" are emphasized.
4. Scapegoats are accepted as inevitable.[22]

Management relied on formal authority and classical organization restructuring to solve their "conflict problem." Individual managers often became hypocritical in order to avoid conflicts from above or below. They developed blind spots to the existence of conflict, created ingenious delaying tactics to avoid conflict, and reverted to the extensive use of defense mechanisms as pseudosolutions to conflict.[23]

Starting with the wide acceptance of the Argyris thesis that there is a basic incongruency between the needs and characteristics of adult, mature employees and the requirements of the modern formal organization, the behavioral approach to management began to reexamine its assumptions about conflict. Today, conflict has become one of its most vital subjects. This

[22]Kelly, op. cit., p. 555.
[23]Bass and Ryterband, op. cit., pp. 376–377.

development has, at least indirectly, been caused by the overall societal concern with conflict, on national, organizational, group, and individual bases. The outcome has been a new set of assumptions about conflict, which are almost the exact opposite of the traditional assumptions. Some of the new assumptions about conflict are the following:

1. Conflict is inevitable.
2. Conflict is determined by structural factors such as the physical shape of a building, the design of a career structure, or the nature of a class system.
3. Conflict is integral to the nature of change.
4. A minimal level of conflict is optimal.[24]

Based on these assumptions, the management of organizational conflict has taken several approaches.

Strategies for managing organizational conflict

Pondy has identified three major conceptual approaches to managing organizational conflict:[25]

1. *Bargaining approach.* This model of conflict deals with interest groups who compete for limited resources. The strategy to resolve the conflict revolves around either the attempt to increase the pool of available resources or to decrease the demands of the competing parties.
2. *Bureaucratic approach.* This model of conflict deals with the vertical, authority relationships in a hierarchical structure. Conflict occurs when superiors attempt to control subordinates, and they resist such control. The strategy to resolve the conflict is to substitute impersonal bureaucratic rules for personal control.
3. *Systems approach.* Whereas the bargaining model emphasizes the problems of competition and the bureaucratic model is concerned with the difficulties of control, the systems model is about coordination problems. Specifically, the systems approach deals with the lateral or horizontal relationships between functions (e.g., marketing and production) of an organization. There are two main strategies to reduce functional conflict and attain coordination. First, reduce goal differentiation by modified incentive or by proper selection, training, or assignment procedures. Second, reduce functional interdependence by reducing dependence on common resources, by reducing pressures for consensus, and by loosening up schedules or introducing buffers (e.g., inventories or contingency funds).

Each of the above approaches provides a conceptual basis for managing conflict. On a more practical level, the following steps have been suggested for more effective management of conflict:

1. Perceiving/experiencing unacceptable conflict,
2. Diagnosing the sources of the conflict, and
3. Intervening.[26]

---

[24]Kelly, op. cit., p. 555.

[25]Louis R. Pondy, "Organizational Conflict: Concepts and Models,"*Administrative Science Quarterly*, September 1967, pp. 296–320.

[26]Kilmann and Thomas, op. cit., p. 60.

Intervention can take several forms. Representative are Litterer's three basic strategies.[27] First, buffers can be erected between conflicting parties. The classic example of this strategy was described by Whyte in his classic study of the restaurant industry. To reduce the conflict between the cooks and runners which was caused by status incongruency—the runners were giving orders to the higher-status chefs—the runners were told to place their order slips on a hook. This hook created a buffer between the conflicting parties and the conflict was reduced. A second strategy is to help the parties in the conflicting situation develop better insights into themselves and how they affect others. The organizational development techniques discussed in Chapter 21 can be used to implement this strategy. A third strategy is to redesign the organization structure in order to reduce the conflict. This, of course, was the major strategy taken by the traditional approach to the management of conflict. However, besides trying to reduce conflict, the new approach also tries to contain it and, if at all possible, use it to obtain the objectives of the organization. As Pondy has stated, "Conflict is not necessarily bad or good, but must be evaluated in terms of its individual and organizational functions and dysfunctions. In general, conflict generates pressures to reduce conflict, but chronic conflict persists and is endured under certain conditions, and consciously created and managed by the politically astute administrator."[28]

Conflict can lead to innovation and change; it can energize people to activity, develop protection for something else in the organization (in the divide-and-conquer sense), and be an important element in the systems analysis of the organization.[29] Such factors indicate that conflict can be managed to work for, rather than against, goal attainment in the modern organization.

SUMMARY

The dynamics of conflict and stress plays an increasingly important role in the analysis and study of organizational behavior. Although conflict and stress are defined a bit differently (stress is more associated with physiological problems), they are generally treated interchangeably in this chapter. The chapter views conflict and stress from an intraindividual perspective and conflict from interpersonal and organizational perspectives. Frustration, goal conflict, and role conflict and ambiguity are the major conceptual categories of intraindividual conflict. Frustration occurs when goal-directed behavior is blocked. Goal conflict can come about from approach-approach, approach-avoidance, or avoidance-avoidance situations. Role conflict and ambiguity results from a clash in the expectations of the various roles possessed by an individual. Interpersonal conflict was examined within the framework of the Johari window styles (open, hidden, blind, and undiscovered) and of the

---

[27]Litterer, op. cit., p. 195.

[28]Pondy, op. cit., p. 320.

[29]Litterer, op. cit., p. 192.

three major strategies of interpersonal conflict resolution (lose-lose, win-lose, win-win). The broader organizational perspective of conflict can be found in both the classical (hierarchical, functional, line-staff, and formal-informal) and modern (project and matrix) structures. Traditionally, the management of organizational conflict was based on simplistic assumptions. Formal authority and classical restructuring were used in attempts to eliminate it. The more modern approach is to assume the inevitability of conflict, recognize that it is not always bad for the organization, and try to manage it effectively rather than merely try to eliminate it.

QUESTIONS FOR DISCUSSION AND REVIEW

1. What, if anything, is the difference between conflict and stress?
2. What is frustration? What are some of its manifestations? How can the frustration model be used to analyze organizational behavior?
3. Explain approach-avoidance conflict. Give a realistic organizational example of where it may occur.
4. In an organization, when may role conflict be the lesser of two evils?
5. Briefly summarize the four "selfs" in the Johari window. What implications does each have for interpersonal conflict?
6. How do the traditional assumptions about organizational conflict differ from the modern assumptions? What implications do these new assumptions have for the management of conflict?

CASE:
DRINKING UP
THE PAYCHECK

James Emery was the father of four children. He had been raised in a hard-working immigrant family. Needs for achievement and power were developed while growing up. Now he found himself in a low-paying, dead-end, assembly line job with a large manufacturing firm. It was all he could do to get through the day, so he started daydreaming on the job. On payday he would often go to the tavern across the street and generally spend a lot of money. The next day he would not only be hung over but would become very depressed because he knew that his wife could not make ends meet and his children often went without the basic essentials.

One day he could not take it any longer. At first he thought of going to his boss for some help and advice, but he really did not understand himself well enough, and he certainly did not know or trust his boss enough to openly discuss his problems with him. Instead he went to his union steward and told him about his financial problems and how much he hated his job. The steward told James exactly what he wanted to hear. "This darn company is the source of all of your problems. The working conditions are not suited for a slave, let alone us. The pay also stinks. We are all going to have to stick together when our present contract runs out and get what we deserve—better working conditions and more money."

1. Explain James's behavior in terms of the frustration model.
2. Cite a specific example of role conflict in this case.
3. What style from the Johari window can explain James's relationship with his boss? With his union steward?
4. What type of conflict resolution strategy is the union steward suggesting? Do you think the real problems facing James are working conditions and pay? Why or why not?
5. What, if anything, can be done to help the James Emerys of the world? Keep your answer in terms of human resource management.

CASE: ARRESTING THE NEIGHBOR'S KID

Barney Kohl was a police officer assigned to the juvenile department of a large city. Part of the oath that Barney took was to uphold the law consistently for all people. The scope of his job included investigation of youth drug traffic, alcoholism, and vandalism. Barney was also involved in the community outreach program, which worked to build greater understanding and cooperation between the police department and the youth of the community.

While working on the night shift during the summer, Barney ran into one of the most difficult, if not dangerous, problems he had ever faced. While on patrol, he received a radio report to investigate some possible vandalism at a junior high school. Upon reaching the scene he found five youths, aged twelve to fifteen, engaged in malicious acts of vandalism. They were throwing rocks through the windows and had splashed paint against the walls. After calling backup units, he proceeded to run down and arrest the vandals. He was successfully holding the group at bay and was waiting for the backup unit to arrive when he noticed one of the offenders was his neighbor's son. The city had a parents' responsibility law where the parents were financially liable for the damage caused by their child's actions. The damage looked as if it would be considerable, probably running into the thousands of dollars. Barney knew his neighbor couldn't afford the costs because he was crippled and out of work. He also knew this incident would lead to great problems in their family and, of course, would place a great strain on his own and his family's relationship with the neighbors.

1. What kind of conflict is this police officer experiencing? What should he do?
2. How do you explain the boys' behavior in terms of the frustration model?
3. If you were asked to conduct a training seminar for police officers on the management of conflict, what topics would you cover? What strategies would you suggest?

CHAPTER 14

POWER AND POLITICS

FROM POLITICAL RUBBER-STAMPING TO LEGITIMATIZED POWER*

The bankruptcy of the Penn Central Transportation Company precipitated several suits filed by investors against the directors of the company. The result was over $10 million dollars in out-of-court settlements and an awakened awareness of the responsibilities that outside (nonmanagement) board members have to the stockholders of a company. Heretofore, outside directors had often been appointed—and they had accepted—for political reasons. It looked good to have a respected attorney or member of the financial community on the board. These outside members rarely became actively involved in the internal affairs of the company and relied only upon the information provided by its management team. The Penn Central disaster and the resulting suits woke up many outside board members of corporations around the country to the importance of their fiduciary responsibility to the owners and creditors. Now, many boards of directors have begun to exercise the important powers granted by law. For example, it is current modus operandi of many boards for outside board members to work with independent audit teams to ensure that investments are protected and the company is being run in a responsible manner. Individual executives and whole management teams have found themselves relieved of their services if they do not comply with the board's wishes. Before the Penn Central case, outside board members were usually passive, uninterested observers of the actions of the internal top management team. Now, however, companies such as General Automation and Itel have let top executives go when they failed to comply with the board's desires. The replacement of political rubber-stamping with legitimatized power of the board of directors seems to restore a more realistic balance in corporations between ownership (the investors) and control (internal management).

---

*Adapted from "End of the Director's Rubber Stamp," *Business Week,* Sept. 10, 1979, pp. 72–83.

386

Over the years, groups, informal organization, communication, conflict and stress, and leadership have received considerable attention as important dynamics of organizational behavior; power and politics, however, have been largely ignored. Yet it is becoming clear, and anyone who has spent any time in a formal organization can readily verify, that organizations are highly political and power is the name of the game. Power and politics must be brought "out of the closet" and recognized as an important dynamic in organizational behavior. The other topics in this book are obviously important to organizational behavior, but the following quote by a manager who was explaining how he got ahead in his company highlights the importance of power and politics:

When I was a salesman, I heard that my company was going in for a new line of synthetics. I pulled a few strings, got myself transferred to the division that would handle the new product. When the division began to expand, I was in the catbird seat.[1]

The first part of the chapter defines what is meant by power and politics and describes how the two concepts are related to one another. The next part concentrates on the various classifications of power. Particular attention is given to the French and Raven classification of sources of power. After examining some of the research results on the French and Raven power types, attention is given to some contingency approaches (for example, the influenceability of the target and overall and managerial contingency models of power). The last section is concerned with organizational politics. Particular attention is given to a political perspective of power in today's organizations and to some specific political strategies for its acquisition.

THE MEANING AND RELATIONSHIP OF POWER AND POLITICS

Although the concepts in the field of organizational behavior seldom have universally agreed upon definitions, power and politics may have even more diverse definitions than most. Almost every author who writes about power defines it differently. Going way back, for example, the famous pioneering sociologist Max Weber defined power as "the probability that one actor within a social relationship will be in a position to carry out his own will despite resistance."[2] Recently, Walter Nord defined power as "the ability to influence flows of the available energy and resources towards certain goals as opposed to other goals. Power is assumed to be exercised only when these goals are at least partially in conflict with each other."[3] Every writer in

---

[1]From Auren Uris, *Turn Your Job into a Successful Career*, Simon & Schuster, New York, 1967.

[2]A. M. Henderson and Talcott Parsons (trans. and ed.), *Max Weber, The Theory of Social and Economic Organization*, Free Press and Falcon's Wing Press, 1947, p. 152.

[3]Walter R. Nord, "Dreams of Humanization and the Realities of Power," *Academy of Management Review*, July 1978, p. 675.

between has defined power a little differently. Robbins supplies one of the most detailed, and perhaps most understandable, definitions as follows:

When we discuss power, we mean the ability to affect and control anything that is of value to others. If A has power over individual or group B, then A can influence certain actions of B so that the outcome is preferable to the self-interest of A. Therefore, power requires two or more people—an exerciser and a subject. Power also disregards intent. Whether A *wants* to have control over B is irrelevant. . . . Finally, power may exist but not be used. It is a capacity or potential.[4]

Usually, definitions of power are intertwined with the concepts of authority and influence. For example, all three definitions above use the word influence in describing power, the pioneering theorist Chester Barnard defined power in terms of "informal authority," and many modern organizational sociologists define authority as "legitimate power."[5] These distinctions among concepts need to be cleared up in order to understand power.

The distinctions among power, authority, and influence

In Chapter 6 the power motive was defined as the need to manipulate others and have superiority over them. Extrapolating from this definition of the need for power, power itself can be defined as *an ability to get an individual or group to do something—to get the person or group to change in some way.* The person who possesses power has the ability to manipulate or change others. Such a definition of power distinguishes it from authority and influence.

Authority legitimatizes power. Authority is the *right* to manipulate or change others. Power need not be legitimate. In addition, the distinction must be made between top-down classical, bureaucratic authority and Barnard's concept of bottom-up authority based upon acceptance. In particular, Barnard defined authority as "the character of a communication (order) in a formal organization by virtue of which it is accepted by a contributor to or 'member' of the organization as governing the action he contributes."[6]

Such an acceptance theory of authority is easily differentiated from power. Grimes notes, "What legitimizes authority is the promotion or pursuit of collective goals that are associated with group consensus. The polar opposite, power, is the pursuit of individual or particularistic goals associated with group compliance."[7]

Influence is usually conceived of as being narrower in scope than power. It involves the ability of a person to alter another person or group in specific

---

[4]Stephen P. Robbins, *Organizational Behavior*, Prentice-Hall, Englewood Cliffs, N.J., 1979, p. 263.

[5]A. J. Grimes, "Authority, Power, Influence and Social Control: A Theoretical Synthesis," *Academy of Management Review*, October 1978, p. 725.

[6]Chester I. Barnard, *The Functions of the Executive*, Harvard, Cambridge, Mass., 1938, p. 163.

[7]Grimes, op. cit., p. 726.

ways, such as in their satisfaction and performance. Influence is more closely associated with leadership than is power, but both obviously are involved in the leadership process. Thus, authority is different from power because of its legitimacy and acceptance, and influence is narrower than power, but is so conceptually close that the two terms can be used interchangeably.

The above discussion points out that an operational definition for power is lacking, and this vagueness is a major reason power has been largely ignored in the study of organizational behavior. Hicks and Gullett point out the problems with the study of power when they say, "Because power is not well understood, is often extremely subtle or obscure, springs from multiple sources, is highly dynamic, has multiple causes and effects, is multidimensional, and is particularly difficult—if not impossible—to quantify, positivists have tended to ignore it."[8] Yet, especially when it is linked to the emerging concern for organizational politics, the study of power can greatly enhance the understanding of organizational behavior.

The role and relationship of organizational politics

Organizational participants have always known the importance of organizational politics. But it has only become a topic of study in organizational behavior recently. There are a number of definitions of organizational politics. In academic discussions, the term politics refers to the structure and process of the use of authority and power to effect definitions of goals, directions, and other major parameters of the organization.[9] More formally, politics has been defined as "the management of influence to obtain ends not sanctioned by the organization or to obtain sanctioned ends through nonsanctioned influence means."[10] In the more practitioner-oriented literature, the discussion of politics usually refers to pragmatic ways to get ahead in an organization. This view is reflected in Robbins's definition of organizational politics as "any behavior by an organization member that is self-serving."[11]

The view taken in this chapter is that organizational politics are an important dynamic of organizational behavior, especially in relation to the acquisition of power. The political strategies for career advancement are given some attention in the last chapter, which deals with self-management and career development. For now, however, the perspective taken is similar to Schoonmaker's view:

Politics does not mean shirking work, apple polishing, or joining the right clubs; nor

---

[8]Herbert G. Hicks and C. Ray Gullett, *Organizations: Theory and Behavior*, McGraw-Hill, New York, 1975, p. 238.

[9]G. Wamsley and M. Zald, *The Political Economy of Public Organizations*, Heath, Lexington, Mass., 1973, p. 18.

[10]Bronston T. Mayes and Robert W. Allen, "Toward a Definition of Organizational Politics," *Academy of Management Review*, October 1977, p. 675.

[11]Robbins, op. cit., p. 403.

is it a legitimate excuse for not getting ahead (although many people use politics as an alibi). These things are part of politics, but politics is a much more general phenomenon that involves the distribution of power and strategies for obtaining and retaining it. Politics is always concerned with power. . . . [12]

Power and politics are closely intertwined and are treated accordingly in this chapter.

SOURCES AND TYPES OF POWER

Over the years sociologists and social psychologists have devoted considerable attention to classifying the various sources of power. The most widely recognized and researched classifications are those of French and Raven, Etzioni, and McClelland.

The French and Raven classifications of power

Any discussion of power usually begins and sometimes ends with the five categories of the sources of power identified by social psychologists John French and Bertram Raven.[13] Describing and analyzing these five types of power (reward, coercive, legitimate, referent, and expert) serves as a necessary foundation and point of departure for the entire chapter. Most of the examples and applications to organizational behavior come from these five types of power.

Reward power This source of power depends on the person having the ability and resources to reward others. In addition, the target of this power must value these rewards. In an organizational context, managers have many potential rewards such as pay increases, promotions, favorable work assignments, more responsibility, new equipment, praise, feedback, and recognition available to them. In operant terms, this means the manager has the power to administer positive reinforcers. In expectancy terms this means that the person has the power to provide positive valences and the other person perceives this ability. To understand this source of power more completely, it must be remembered that the recipient holds the key. If managers offer subordinates what they think is a reward (e.g., a promotion with increased responsibility), but subordinates do not value it (e.g., they are insecure or have family obligations that are more important to them than a promotion) then managers do not really have reward power. By the same token, managers may not think they are giving a reward to subordinates (they calmly listen to chronic complainers) but if subordinates perceive this as rewarding (the managers are giving them attention by intently listening to

[12]Alan N. Schoonmaker, *Executive Career Strategy*, American Management Association, New York, 1971, p. 99.

[13]John R. P. French, Jr., and Bertram Raven, "The Bases of Social Power," in *Studies in Social Power*, D. Cartwright (ed.), Institute for Social Research, Ann Arbor, Mich., 1959.

their complaining), they nevertheless have reward power. Also, managers may not really have the rewards to dispense (they may say that they have considerable influence with top management to get their people promoted, but actually they don't), but as long as their people think they have it, they do indeed have reward power.

Coercive power This source of power depends on fear. The person with coercive power has the ability to inflict punishment or aversive consequences on the other person or, at least, to make threats that the other person believes will result in punishment or undesirable outcomes. This form of power has contributed greatly to the negative connotation that power has for the layperson. As David Kipnis states in his book *The Powerholders*, "Of all the bases of power available to man, the power to hurt others is possibly most often used, most often condemned, and most difficult to control."[14]

Although coercive power is most commonly thought of in terms of physical force or perhaps the use of a weapon, it can also take more subtle forms. Kipnis points out, "Individuals exercise coercive power through a reliance upon physical strength, verbal facility, or the ability to grant or withhold emotional support from others. These bases provide the individual with the means to physically harm, bully, humiliate, or deny love to others."[15]

In an organizational context, managers frequently have coercive power in that they can fire or demote subordinates or dock their pay, although unions have certainly stripped some of this power away over the years. Management can also directly or indirectly threaten an employee with these punishing consequences. In operant terms, this means the person has the power to administer punishers or negatively to reinforce (terminate punishing consequences, which is a form of negative control). In expectancy terms, this means that power comes from the expectation on the part of the other persons that they will be punished if they do not conform to the powerful person's desires. For example, there is fear of punishment if they do not follow the rules, directives, or policies of the organization. It is probably this fear that gets most people to come to work on time and look busy when the boss walks through the area. In other words, much of organizational behavior may be explained in terms of coercive power rather than reward power.

Legitimate power This power source, identified by French and Raven, stems from the internalized values of the other persons which give the legitimate right to the agent to influence them. The others feel they have the obligation to accept this power. It is almost identical to what is usually called authority and is closely aligned with both reward and coercive power because the person with legitimacy is also in a position to reward and

---

[14]David Kipnis, *The Powerholders*, University of Chicago Press, Chicago, 1976, pp. 77–78.
[15]Ibid.

punish. However, legitimate power is unlike reward and coercive power in that it does not depend on the relationships with others but rather on the position or role that the person holds. For example, people obtain legitimacy because of title (captain or doctor) or position (oldest in the family or officer of a corporation) rather than their personalities or how they affect others.

Legitimate power can come from three major sources. First, the prevailing cultural values of a society, organization, or group determine what is legitimate. For example, in some societies, the older people become, the more legitimate power they possess. The same may be true for certain physical attributes, sex, or vocation. In an organizational context, managers generally have legitimate power because employees believe in private property law values and in the hierarchy where higher positions have been designated to have power over lower positions. The same holds true for certain functional positions in an organization. An example of the latter would be engineers who have legitimacy in the operations area of a company while accountants have legitimacy over financial matters. The prevailing values within a group also determine legitimacy. For example, in a street gang the toughest member may have legitimacy while in a work group the union steward may have legitimacy.

Secondly, people can obtain legitimate power from the accepted social structure. In some societies there is an accepted ruling class. But an organization or a family may also have an accepted social structure that gives legitimate power. For example, when blue-collar workers accept employment from a company they are in effect accepting the hierarchical structure and granting legitimate power to their supervisors.

A third source of legitimate power can come from being designated as the agent or representative of a powerful person or group. Elected officials, a chairperson of a committee, or a member of the board of directors of a corporation or a union or management committee would be examples of this form of legitimate power.

Each of these forms of legitimate power creates an obligation to accept and be influenced. But, in actual practice, there are often problems, confusion, or disagreement about the range or scope of this power. One author points out these problems as follows:

An executive can rightfully expect a supervisor to work hard and diligently; may he also influence the supervisor to spy on rivals, spend weekends away from home, join an encounter group? A coach can rightfully expect his players to execute specific plays; may he also direct their life styles outside the sport? A combat officer can rightfully expect his men to attack on order; may he also direct them to execute civilians whom he claims are spies? A doctor can rightfully order a nurse to attend a patient or observe an autopsy; may he order her to assist in an abortion against her will?[16]

These gray areas point to the real concern that many people have in contemporary society regarding the erosion of traditional legitimacy. These uncertainties also point to the complex nature of power.

---

[16]H. Joseph Reitz, *Behavior in Organizations*, Irwin, Homewood, Ill., 1977, p. 468.

Referent power　This type of power comes from the feeling or desire on the part of the other persons to identify with the agent wielding power. Others want to identify with the powerful person, regardless of the outcomes. The others grant the person power because he or she is attractive and has desirable resources or personal characteristics.

Advertisers take advantage of this type of power when they use celebrities, such as movie stars or sports figures, to do testimonial advertising. The buying public identifies with (finds attractive) certain famous people and grants them power to tell them what product to buy.

Timing is an interesting aspect of the testimonial advertising type of referent power. Only professional athletes who are in season (e.g., baseball players in the summer and early fall, football players in the fall and early winter, or basketball players in the winter and early spring) are used in the advertisements, because then they are very visible, in the forefront of the public's awareness, and consequently have referent power. Out of season the athlete is forgotten and has little referent power. Exceptions, of course, are the handfull of superstars (e.g. Joe Namath, Pete Rose, or O. J. Simpson) who transcend seasons and have referent power all year long, and even after they have retired.

Other subtle characteristics and personal traits may give one person referent power and someone else, who may be equally in the public eye, no such power. Examples can again be drawn from sports, where some interesting matchups in terms of referent power would be Muhammad Ali versus Joe Frazier, Billie Jean King versus Chris Evert, and Arnold Palmer versus Jack Nicklaus. Although all of these are gifted athletes and are or were at the top of their respective sports, few would argue that Ali, King, and Palmer would have more referent power than their counterparts. The reasons for this are not always clear, because especially in the case of Ali, the personal traits exhibited seem to run counter to prevailing cultural values.

In an organizational setting, referent power is much different than the other types of power discussed so far. For example, managers with referent power must be attractive to subordinates so that subordinates want to identify with these managers, regardless of whether they later have the ability to reward or punish or whether they have legitimacy. In other words, the manager who depends on referent power must be personally attractive to subordinates.

Expert power　The last source of power identified by French and Raven is based on the extent to which others attribute knowledge and expertise to the power seeker. Experts are perceived to have knowledge or understanding only in certain well-defined areas. All the sources of power depend on the target's perceptions, but expert power may be even more dependent on this than the others. In particular, the target must perceive the agent to be credible, trustworthy, and relevant before expert power is granted.

Credibility comes from having the right credentials, i.e., the person must really know what he or she is talking about and be able to show tangible evidence of this knowledge. For example, if Kurt Thomas gave an aspiring young gymnast some advice on how to do a new trick on the parallel bars, he would be closely listened to—he would be granted expert power. The reason

Kurt Thomas would have expert power in this case is because he is so knowledgeable about gymnastics. His evidence for this credibility is that he is a national champion and the first American gymnast ever to win an all-around gold medal in the world championships. If Kurt tried to give advice in basketball or on how to manage a corporation, he would have no credibility in these areas, and thus would have no expert power. For gymnastics "groupies," however, Kurt may have general referent power (i.e., he is very attractive to them) and they would be influenced by what he has to say on any subject—basketball or corporate management.

Besides athletics, credibility is also important to expert power in areas such as foreign affairs or in the conduct of a business. For example, the major reason Henry Kissinger had so much power in government several years ago was because of his expertise in foreign affairs. A Harvard professor, he "wrote the book," so to speak, on international relations. Therefore, he was perceived by foreign and domestic government officials as being very knowledgeable and thus was granted considerable power by them.

In organizations, staff specialists have expert power in their functional areas, but not outside. For example, engineers are granted expert power on production matters but not on personnel or public relations problems. The same holds true for other staff experts such as computer technologists or accountants. In one company, a staff accountant with twenty years of experience was the only one who really understood the general accounting system. As described by Robbins:

It caused considerable discomfort for the controller, since he was solely dependent on this long-standing employee (let us call him A.J.) in areas pertaining to general accounting. The area supervisor was a young college graduate with little experience in how the system worked. In addition, no other employee except A.J. had performed all the general accounting functions. By reason of his expertise, A.J. had made himself almost irreplaceable *and powerful.*[17]

As already implied, however, expert power is highly selective and, besides credibility, the agent must also have trustworthiness and relevance. By trustworthiness it is meant that the person seeking expert power must have the reputation of being honest and straightforward. In the case of Kissinger, events such as the scandal of Nixon's corrupt administration and Kissinger's role in getting the Shah of Iran into this country undoubtedly eroded his expert power in the eyes of the American public. He still has unquestionable knowledge about foreign affairs, but he has lost expert power because he may no longer be trustworthy. In addition to credibility and trustworthiness, a person must have relevance and usefulness to have expert power. Going back to the earlier example, if gymnast Kurt Thomas gave advice on world affairs or Henry Kissinger gave advice on gymnastics, it would be neither relevant nor useful and they would therefore have no expert power in these areas.

It is evident that expertise is the most tenuous type of power, but

---

[17]Robbins, op. cit., p. 265.

managers, and especially staff specialists, who seldom have the other sources of power available to them, often have to depend upon their expertise as their only source of power. As organizations become increasingly technologically complex and specialized, the expert power of organization members at all levels may become more and more important.

It must also be remembered that French and Raven did recognize that there may be other sources of power, but the ones they identified were considered to be the major ones. They also point out that the five sources are interrelated (for example, the use of coercive power by managers may reduce their referent power), and the same person may exercise different types of power under different circumstances and at different times. The latter point has recently led to some contingency models of power in organizations. But before this contingency approach is presented, the research on the French and Raven classification of sources of power will be reviewed.

Research on the French and Raven power scheme

There has been some research devoted to the French and Raven categories of power. One review of several studies that directly tested the bases of power found that coercive power induces greater resistance than reward power; users of reward power are liked better than those depending on coercive power; conformity to coercive power increases with the strength of the potential punishment; as the legitimacy of a punishing act increases, the conformity increases; and expertness on one task increases the ability to exert influence on a second task.[18] However, the reviewer does point out that the interdependence of the bases of power may contaminate the findings.

Of more direct relevance to organizational behavior are the studies that have related the bases of a manager's power or control to satisfaction and performance. On the basis of five organizational studies (branch office, college, insurance agency, production work units, and utility company work group) the following conclusions were drawn concerning each of the French and Raven bases of power.[19]

1. *Expert power* was most strongly and consistently correlated with satisfaction and performance.
2. *Legitimate power* along with expert power was rated as the most important basis for complying with a supervisor's wishes but was an inconsistent factor in organizational effectiveness.
3. *Referent power* was given intermediate importance as a reason for complying and in most cases was positively correlated with organizational effectiveness.
4. *Reward power* was also given intermediate importance for complying but had inconsistent correlations with performance.
5. *Coercive power* was by far the least prominent reason for complying and was actually negatively related to organizational effectiveness.

[18]John Schopler, "Social Power," in *Advances in Experimental Social Psychology*, vol. 2, Leonard Berkowitz (ed.), Academic, New York, 1965, pp. 177–218.

[19]Jerald G. Bachman, David G. Bowers, and Philip M. Marcus, "Bases of Supervisory Power: A Comparative Study in Five Organizational Settings," in *Control in Organizations*, Arnold S. Tannenbaum (ed.), McGraw-Hill, New York, 1968, p. 236.

These findings relate to employee satisfaction and performance; another recent review of both the empirical and theoretical literature concludes the following in relation to the management of people at work:[20]

1. *Expert power.* This type of power is closely related to a climate of trust, thus the manager's influence can be internalized by subordinates, i.e., there will be attitudinal conformity and internalized motivation on the part of subordinates. Also, since expert power is fairly impersonal and more directly concerned with task performance, it can be effective under conditions of low task visibility and may eliminate or at least diminish the need for surveillance.

2. *Legitimate power.* This type of power can be depended on initially, but continued reliance on it may create problems such as the following:
   a. It can aggravate the feelings of powerlessness and create dissatisfaction, resistance, and frustration among employees.
   b. If it does not coincide with knowledge-based power, there may be ineffective utilization of human resources with resulting negative effects on productivity.
   c. It may be inconsistent with modern employee quality of work life values of meaningful involvement and participation in organizational affairs.
   d. Dependence on it may lead to only minimum compliance and simultaneously to increases in resistance.

3. *Referent power.* Since this type of power is emotional in nature it can lead to enthusiastic and unquestioning trust, compliance, loyalty, and commitment from subordinates. Like expert power, employees would be more internally motivated and would not require direct surveillance. However, some possible limitations are that this type of commitment is not always needed, and that it may even hurt the performance of routine tasks. It could also lead to highly personal, selfish gains and manipulation of subordinates.

4. *Reward power.* The use of this power carries all the implications of the concept of reinforcement that were discussed in Chapters 9 and 10. In other words, the use of rewards can directly influence the frequency of employee performance behaviors. In addition, however, dependence on this type of power may have limitations such as the following:
   a. Tangible rewards such as pay or promotions are generally in very short supply or nonexistent to managers, especially in unionized organizations.
   b. They may have only a short-run impact.
   c. In many instances the rewards available to managers are not really valued by the employees.
   d. The use of rewards can lead to a dependent relationship where the subordinates feel manipulated and become dissatisfied.

5. *Coercive power.* Coercion, also carries all the implications that were discussed under punishment in Chapters 9 and 10. Although coercion may lead to temporary compliance by subordinates, it produces the undesirable side effects of frustration, fear, revenge, and alienation. This, in turn, may lead to poor performance, dissatisfaction, and turnover. Unlike the use of expert and referent power, both reward and coercive power require considerable surveillance of employees.

The conclusion to be drawn from research so far is that the nonformal bases of power (expert and referent) impact most favorably on organizational

---

[20]Y. K. Shetty, "Managerial Power and Organizational Effectiveness: A Contingency Analysis," *Journal of Management Studies*, May 1978, pp. 178–181.

effectiveness. However, such a conclusion should be interpreted with caution because, like most of the motivation and leadership studies, the studies on power are almost all based on questionnaire responses and may reflect the cultural values of the respondents instead of the actual uses of power in an organization. A study by Patchen, which generally substantiates the findings reported above, warns, "It is possible that some respondents were reluctant to talk about such modes of influence (as rewards and coercion)."[21] The challenge for the future will be to use other measures in the research of power and take into consideration situational differences as will be discussed next.

Contingency approaches to the French and Raven power sources

As with other areas of organizational behavior and management, contingency approaches to power are beginning to emerge. Some authors have summarized the research literature into contingency statements such as the following:

1. The greater the professional orientation of group members, the greater relative strength referent power has in influencing them.
2. The less effort and interest high-ranking participants are willing to allocate to a task, the more likely are lower-ranking participants to obtain power relevant to this task.[22]

Besides these overall contingency observations, there is increasing recognition of the fact that power is a two-way street. The influence target is an important variable in the power relationship. The characteristics of influence targets (i.e., their influenceability) have an important moderating impact on the types of power that can be successfully used. An examination of these characteristics of the target and some overall contingency models are presented next.

Influenceability of the targets of power Most discussions of power imply a unilateral process of influence from the agent to the target. It is becoming increasingly clear, however, that power involves a reciprocal relationship between the agent and the target, which is in accordance with the overall social learning perspective taken in other chapters of the book. The power relationship can be better understood by examining some of the characteristics of the target. The following characteristics have been identified as being especially important to the influenceability of targets:[23]

1. *Dependency.* The greater the targets' dependency on their relationship to agents (e.g., when a target cannot escape a relationship, perceives no alternatives, or values the agent's rewards as unique), the more targets are influenced.

---

[21]Martin Patchen, "The Locus and Basis of Influence on Organizational Decisions," *Organizational Behavior and Human Performance*, April 1974, p. 216.

[22]Robbins, op. cit., p. 276.

[23]Adapted from Reitz, op. cit., pp. 473–476.

2. *Uncertainty.* Experiments have shown that the more uncertain people are about the appropriateness or correctness of a behavior, the more they are susceptible to be influenced to change that behavior.

3. *Personality.* There have been a number of research studies to show the relationship between personality characteristics and influenceability. Some of these findings are obvious (for example, people who cannot tolerate ambiguity or are highly anxious are more susceptible to influence or those with high needs for affiliation are more susceptible to group influence), but some are not (for example, both positive and negative relationships have been found between self-esteem and influenceability).

4. *Intelligence.* There is no simple relationship between intelligence and influenceability. For example, highly intelligent people may be more willing to listen, but, because they also tend to be held in high esteem, they also may be more resistant to influence.

5. *Age.* Social psychologists have generally concluded that susceptibility to influence increases in young children up to about age eight or nine and then decreases with age until adolescence where it levels off.

6. *Culture.* Obviously, the cultural values of a society have a tremendous impact on the influenceability of its people. For example, some cultures, such as Western cultures, emphasize individuality, dissent, and diversity, which would tend to decrease influenceability, while others, such as many Oriental cultures, emphasize cohesiveness, agreement, and uniformity, which would tend to promote influenceability.

These individual differences in targets greatly complicate the effective use of power and point up the need for contingency models.

An overall contingency model for power Many other contingency variables in the power relationship besides the target could be inferred from the discussion of the various types of power, for example, credibility and surveillance. All these variables can be tied together and related to one another in an overall contingency model.

The classic work on influence processes, by social psychologist Herbert Kelman, can be used to structure an overall contingency model of power. Figure 14-1 shows such a model. It recognizes that there are several sources of power that input into three major processes of power.

According to the model, the target will *comply* in order to gain a favorable reaction or avoid a punishing one from the agent. This is the process that most supervisors in work organizations must rely upon. But in order for compliance to work, the supervisor must be able to reward and punish (i.e., have control over the means to their subordinates' ends) and keep an eye on subordinates (i.e., the supervisor must have surveillance over subordinates).

People will *identify,* not in order to obtain a favorable reaction from the agent as in compliance, but because it is self-satisfying to do so. But in order for the identification process to work, the agent must have referent power—be very attractive to the target—and be salient. For example, a research study by Kelman found that students were initially greatly influenced by a speech given by a very handsome star athlete, i.e., they identified with him. However, when the students were checked six months after the speech they were not influenced. The handsome athlete was no longer salient, i.e., he was no longer in the forefront of their awareness, and his words carried no influence. Except for the handful of superstars, athletes are soon forgotten and have no power over their even most avid fans. Once they have graduated or are out of season, they lose their salience and, thus, their power.

Finally, people will *internalize* because of compatibility with their own value structure. But, as Figure 14-1 shows, in order for people to internalize, the agent must have expert or legitimate power (credibility) and, in addition, be relevant. Obviously, this process of power is most effective. Kelman, for example, found that internalized power had a lasting impact on his subjects.

The notorious Patty Hearst kidnapping case a few years ago is an example of how this model could be used to analyze power. Without getting into the specific details of the case, it is generally known that she was forcibly kidnapped by the radical SLA (Symbionese Liberation Army), held captive by the SLA or stayed of her own free will for several months, and was finally arrested and put on trial. In terms of the power model, the defense attorneys for Patty would argue the compliance point of view: she was forcibly held captive and made the propaganda statements and participated in robberies in order to not get punished or killed by her captors. The state prosecutor would counter this premise with the fact that surveillance, at least physical surveillance, was not always present. They would argue from the perspective of internalization. She may have been forcibly taken, but then she found her captors to have expert and legitimate power (they had credibility for her) and their values were consistent with her own. The latter explanation would suggest that she was a willing participant in the robberies and should be found guilty as charged. In reality, however, maybe the best explanation of her behavior according to the model would be identification.

Figure 14-1 An overall contingency model of power. (*Source:* Adapted from Herbert C. Kelman, "Compliance, Identification, and Internalization: Three Processes of Attitude Change," *Journal of Conflict Resolution*, March 1958, pp. 51–60.)

Required Sources of Power	Process of Power	Target's Influenceability	Required Conditions
Reward / Coercive / Means-ends-control	Compliance	Wants to gain a favorable reaction; avoid a punishing one from the agent	The agent must have surveillance over the target
Referent / Attractiveness	Identification	Finds a self-satisfying relationship with the agent. Wants to establish and maintain a relationship with the agent	The agent must have salience; the agent must be in the forefront of the target's awareness
Expert / Legitimate / Credibility	Internalization	Goes along with the agent because of consistency with internal values	The agent must have relevance

The process of compliance was initially at work, but after a while she found her captors to have referent power, i.e., they were attractive to her. During the months of her captivity she identified with her captors. When she was finally arrested she gave the raised clenched fist sign of her captors. But after she had been incarcerated for a short while her captors lost their salience and therefore their power over her. She then went back to being a nice rich girl, denounced the SLA, and married her bodyguard. All of this, of course, is pure speculation, but it does point out how the model could be used to analyze a very complex situation involving power and resultant behavior.

A contingency model of managerial power and organizational effectiveness When directly applied in an organization and management context, the important variables for a contingency approach to power would include the manager, the subordinate, and the organization itself. In addition to the dynamics of the power sources of the manager, the influenceability of the subordinate, and the dynamics of the organizational environment, Shetty pinpoints several specific manager, subordinate, and organizational characteristics that he deems to be especially important to a contingency analysis of managerial power. Figure 14-2 summarizes this contingency model.

Shetty is careful to point out that the contingency factors identified in his model are not exhaustive but are intended to be representative of some of the more important research findings on managerial power. To take an example from each contingency factor, he cites relevant research findings and makes statements such as the following:[24]

1. Authoritarian managers would tend to emphasize legitimate power to achieve predictable behavior rather than to tolerate the ambiguity they perceive to be inherent in the use of expert and referent power.

---

[24]Shetty, op. cit., pp. 181–184.

**Figure 14-2
A contingency model of the French and Raven power types.** (*Source:* Adapted from Y. K. Shetty, "Managerial Power and Organizational Effectiveness: A Contingency Analysis," *Journal of Management Studies,* May 1978, p. 184.)

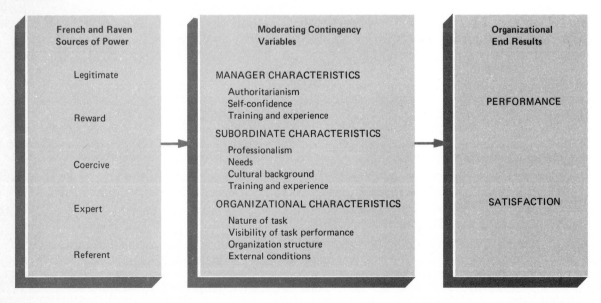

2. Employees who are basically concerned with their physiological and security needs would tend to be satisfied with legitimate and reward power.

3. In matrix organizations, where project managers lack position power, they must rely on personality, persuasive ability, and negotiation to influence functional team members.

Other contingency statements can also be drawn from the identified characteristics in the model.

Regarding the effective use of power in today's organizations, Shetty draws two overall conclusions. "First, the successful manager is one who is aware of the existence of multiple sources of power in work situations. Second, the effectiveness of power types depends on the nature of managerial, subordinate, and organizational variables."[25]

Other classifications of power

So far, the discussion of power has revolved around the French and Raven categories. The reason this classification is given so much attention is because it is very comprehensive and widely accepted. Obviously, there are many other classification schemes of power in organizations. Two of the most relevant to the study and understanding of the dynamics of organizational behavior are the work of Etzioni and McClelland.

Etzioni's analysis of power A widely recognized social scientist, Amitai Etzioni has proposed a type of contingency analysis of power in organizations.[26] Figure 14-3 shows the two factors he identified as being most relevant to organizational power: (1) The types of power that organizations and their managers try to use in order to influence their members; and (2) The types of involvement that organizations and their managers expect and seek to generate among their members.

Thus, unlike French and Raven, who identified five types of power,

---

[25]Ibid., p. 186.

[26]Amitai Etzioni, *A Comparative Analysis of Complex Organizations*, Free Press, New York, 1961; and Amitai Etzioni, "Organizational Control Structure," in James C. March (ed.), *Handbook of Organizations*, Rand McNally, Chicago, 1965.

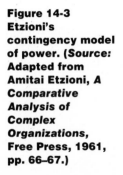

Figure 14-3 Etzioni's contingency model of power. (Source: Adapted from Amitai Etzioni, A Comparative Analysis of Complex Organizations, Free Press, 1961, pp. 66–67.)

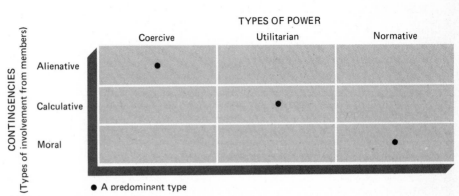

Etzioni feels the following three best represent the types of organizational power:

1. *Coercive*. This type of power forces the organization members to follow specific courses of action. It is very similar to the French and Raven definition of coercive power; a prison organization is an example of coercive power in operation.
2. *Utilitarian*. This is a contingent reward type of power. The subordinate must perform as expected in order to be rewarded. Most business organizations are at least supposed to operate under this type of power.
3. *Normative*. Under this type of power organization members obey because they want to be part of the organization. It is similar to the French and Raven referent power category; an example would be a religious organization.

These three types of power are each separate, distinct ways that managers would use to obtain compliance from subordinates. However, the effectiveness of these power sources depends on the type of involvement the organization has from its members. An *alienation* involvement is characterized by highly negative, often hostile feelings by organization members. Under a *calculative* involvement, organization members have a self-seeking, rational, personal-gain attitude. *Moral* involvement is characterized by highly positive feelings of self denial by organization members.

As shown in Figure 14-3, the three types of power and the three types of involvement yield nine possible combinations. Fortunately, in most organizations the type of power that is used and the type of involvement of its members are already compatible. For example, prisons (which have alienative members) depend on coercive power, business firms (which have calculative employees) depend on utilitarian power, and religious organizations (which have moral members) depend on normative power. Etzioni suggests that, in order to be effective, managers should not deviate from this model. They should use the type of power that is compatible with their organizational environment (which he mainly defines in terms of subordinate involvement). In other words, a manager of a business firm (which has calculative employees) should not attempt to use coercive power because the employees would become dissatisfied, reduce their productive effort, and possibly quit. By the same token, if the business manager depended upon normative power, employees would tend to ignore him or her and nothing would get done. Such contingency guidelines for the use of power have definite implications for the discussion of leadership in the next chapter.

McClelland's two faces of power Whereas both French and Raven's and Etzioni's work has much relevance for the dynamics of organizational behavior, David McClelland has, as Chapter 6 pointed out, done considerable work on the impact of the motivational need for power (what he calls n Pow) on organizational power. He also is convinced that there are two major types of power, one negative and one positive.

Over the years, power has often had a negative connotation. The commonly used term *power hungry* reflects this negative feeling about power. According to McClelland, power:

is associated with heavy drinking, gambling, having more aggressive impulses, and collecting "prestige supplies" like a convertible or a Playboy Club Key. People with this personalized power concern are more apt to speed, have accidents, and get into physical fights. If . . . possessed by political officeholders, especially in the sphere of international relations, the consequences would be ominous.[27]

McClelland feels that this negative use of power is associated with *personal power*. He feels that it is primitive and does indeed have negative consequences.

The contrasting "other face" of power identified by McClelland is *social power*. It is characterized by a "concern for group goals, for finding those goals that will move men, for helping the group to formulate them, for taking some initiative in providing members of the group with the means of achieving such goals, and for giving group members the feeling of strength and competence they need to work hard for such goals."[28] In this definition of social power, the manager may often be in a precarious position of walking a fine line between an exhibition of personal dominance and the more socializing use of power.

As the discussion of power and achievement motives in Chapter 6 indicated, McClelland is beginning to accumulate evidence that seems to indicate that managers who use social power may be the most effective. His data shows that the successful manager has four discernible power-related characteristics:

Firstly he believes in an authority system, that the institution is more important than the individuals in it. Secondly, he likes to work and he likes the discipline of work, which leads to orderly management. Thirdly, he is altruistic in that he will sacrifice his own self-interest for the welfare of the company and does this in some obvious way that everybody can see. And fourthly, he believes in justice above everything else, that people must have even-handed treatment.[29]

McClelland's position on the importance of power to successful management is in direct opposition to the more humanistic (McGregor's, Maslow's, or Likert's) positions, which emphasize the importance of democratic values and participative decision-making. But regardless of the controversy surrounding the definition and classification of power be it by French and Raven, Etzioni, or McClelland, it is clear that power is inevitable in today's organizations. One of Adolf Berle's several "laws" of power is that power invariably fills any vacuum in human organization.[30] How power is used and what type of power is used will vitally affect human performance and organizational goals. In French and Raven's terms, the use of expert and

[27]David C. McClelland, "The Two Faces of Power," *Journal of International Affairs*, vol. 24, no. 1, 1970, p. 36.

[28]Ibid., p. 41.

[29]"McClelland an Advocate of Power," *International Management*, July 1975, pp. 27–28.

[30]Adolf A. Berle, *Power*, Harcourt, Brace & World, New York, 1969, p. 37.

referent power in organizations may be more effective than traditionally used legitimate and coercive power. In McClelland's terms, social power may be of greater value to the organization than is traditionally used personal power. Research gives some indication that such conclusions are valid. But once again, the use of the various types of power depends on the situation. Thus, the contingency models of power seem to be a healthy development in the analysis and normative prescriptions of the use of power in today's organizations.

POLITICAL IMPLICATIONS OF POWER

As the introductory part of the chapter pointed out, power and politics are very closely related concepts. A popular view of organizational politics is how one can pragmatically get ahead in an organization. Another view, however, deals with the acquisition of power. In this latter view, power and politics become especially closely intertwined. A recognition of the political realities of power acquisition in today's organizations and an examination of some specific political strategies for acquiring power are of particular interest for understanding the dynamics of organizational behavior.

A political perspective of power in organizations

As Chapter 18 will discuss in detail, the classical organization theorists portrayed organizations as highly rational structures where authority meticulously followed the chain of command and managers had legitimatized power. The discussion in Chapter 11 of informal managerial roles and organization portrayed another, more realistic, view of organizations. It is this more realistic view of organizations where the importance of the political aspects of power comes to the forefront.

Walter Nord has recently tried to dispel some of the dreams of ideal, rationally structured and humanistic organizations by pointing out some of the stark realities of political power. He suggests four postulates of power in organizations that help focus in on the political realities:

1. Organizations are composed of coalitions which compete with one another for resources, energy, and influence.
2. Various coalitions will seek to protect their interests and positions of influence by moderating environmental pressures and their effects.
3. The unequal distribution of power itself has non-humanizing effects.
4. The exercise of power within organizations is one very crucial aspect of the exercise of power within the larger social system.[31]

In other words, the political power game is very real in today's organizations. But, like other aspects of organizational dynamics, politics is not a simple process; it can vary from organization to organization and even from one subunit of the organization to another.

---

[31]Nord, op. cit., pp. 675–677.

Recent research on organizational politics has identified several areas that are particularly relevant to the degree to which organizations are political rather than rational. Miles has summarized these areas as follows:[32]

1. *Resources.* There is a direct relationship between the amount of politics and how critical and scarce the resources are. Also, politics will be encouraged when there is an infusion of new, "unclaimed" resources.
2. *Decisions.* Ambiguous decisions, decisions on which there is lack of agreement, and uncertain, long-range strategic decisions lead to more politics than do routine decisions.
3. *Goals.* The more ambiguous and complex the goals become, the more politics there will be.
4. *Technology and external environment.* In general, the more complex the internal technology of the organization, the more politics there will be. The same is true of organizations operating in turbulent external environments.
5. *Change.* A reorganization or a planned organization development (OD) effort (see Chapter 21 on various OD techniques) or even an unplanned change brought about by external forces, will all encourage political maneuvering.

The above implies that some organizations and subunits within the organization will be more political than others. By the same token, however, it is clear that most of today's organizations meet the above requirements for being highly political. That is, they have very limited resources; make ambiguous, uncertain decisions; have very unclear yet complex goals; have increasingly complex technology; and are undergoing drastic change. This existing situation facing organizations makes them more political and the power game becomes increasingly important. Miles states, "In short, conditions that *threaten* the status of the powerful or *encourage* the efforts of those wishing to increase their power base will stimulate the intensity of organizational politics and increase the proportion of decision-making behaviors that can be classified as political as opposed to rational."[33] The next section presents some of these political strategies for power acquisition.

SPECIFIC POLITICAL STRATEGIES FOR POWER ACQUISITIONS

Once it is understood and accepted that contemporary organizations are in reality largely political systems, then some very specific strategies can be identified to help organization members more effectively acquire power.

For over twenty years, various political strategies for gaining power in organizations have been suggested. Table 14-1 gives a representative summary of these strategies. Some modern organization theorists take more analytical approaches than most of the strategies suggested in Table 14-1, and they depend more on concepts such as uncertainty in their political strategies for power. For example, Perrow suggests creating a fiction of

---

[32]Robert H. Miles, *Macro Organizational Behavior*, Goodyear, Santa Monica, Calif., 1980, pp. 182–184.

[33]Ibid., p. 182.

Table 14-1

POLITICAL STRATEGIES FOR ATTAINING POWER IN ORGANIZATIONS

Taking counsel
Maintaining maneuverability
Promoting limited communication
Exhibiting confidence
Controlling access to information and persons
Making activities central and nonsubstitutable
Creating a sponsor-protegé relationship
Stimulating competition among ambitious subordinates
Neutralizing potential opposition
Making strategic replacements
Committing the uncommitted
Forming a winning coalition
Developing expertise
Building personal stature
Employing trade-offs
Using research data to support own point of view
Restricting communication about real intentions
Withdrawing from petty disputes

Source: Adapted from Robert H. Miles, *Macro Organizational Behavior,* Goodyear, Santa Monica, Calif., 1980, pp. 174–175.

uncertainty and steering the organization into areas of uncertainty you can manage,[34] while Pfeffer's strategies include managing uncertainty, controlling resources, and building alliances.[35]

One of the more comprehensive and relevant lists of strategies for modern managers comes from DuBrin.[36] A closer look at his suggested strategies provides important insights into power and politics in modern organizations.

Maintain alliances with powerful people   As has already been pointed out, the formation of coalitions (alliances) is critical to the acquisition of power in an organization. An obvious coalition would be with members of other important departments or with members of upper-level management. Not so obvious but as important would be to form an alliance with the boss's secretary or staff assistant, i.e., someone who is close to the powerful person.

Embrace or demolish   Machiavellian principles can be applied as strategies in the power game in modern organizations. One modern management writer has applied these principles to modern corporate life.

---

[34]Charles Perrow, "Departmental Power and Perspectives in Industrial Firms," in Mayer N. Zald (ed.), *Power in Organizations*, Vanderbilt, Nashville, Tenn., 1970.

[35]Jeffrey Pfeffer, "Power and Resource Allocation in Organizations," in Barry M. Staw and Gerald R. Salancik (eds.), *New Directions in Organizational Behavior*, St. Clair Press, Chicago, 1977, pp. 255–260.

[36]These strategies are discussed fully in DuBrin, op. cit., pp. 158–163, who, in turn, abstracted them from the existing power and politics literature.

For example, for corporate takeovers, he draws on Machiavelli to give the following advice:

> The guiding principle is that senior men in taken-over firms should either be warmly welcomed and encouraged or sacked; because if they are sacked they are powerless, whereas if they are simply downgraded they will remain united and resentful and determined to get their own back.[37]

Divide and rule   This widely known political and military strategy can also apply to the acquisition of power in a modern organization. The assumption, sometimes unwarranted, is that those who are divided will not form coalitions themselves. For example, in a business firm the head of finance may generate conflict between marketing and production in hopes of getting a bigger share of the limited budget from the president of the company.

Manipulation of classified information   The observational studies by Mintzberg[38] and others have clearly demonstrated the importance of obtaining and disseminating information. The politically astute organization member carefully controls this information in order to gain power. For example, the purchasing agent may reveal some new pricing information to the design engineer before an important meeting. Now the purchasing agent has gained some power because the engineer owes him a favor.

Make a quick showing   This is a strategy to look good on some project or task right away in order to get the right people's attention. Once this positive attention is gained, then power is acquired to do other, usually more difficult and long-range, projects.

Collect and use IOU's   This strategy says that the power seeker should do other people favors but it should be made clear that they owe something in return and will be expected to pay up when asked. The "Godfather" in the famous book and movie of that name very effectively used this strategy to gain power.

Fabianism—avoid decisive engagement   This is a strategy of going slow and easy—an evolutionary rather than a revolutionary approach to change. By not "ruffling feathers" the power seeker can slowly but surely become entrenched and gain the cooperation and trust of others.

Camel's head in the tent   This simply means to progress one step at a time instead of trying to push a whole major project or reorganization attempt. One small change can be a foothold that the power seeker can use as a basis to get other, more major, things accomplished.

---

[37]Anthony Jay, *Management and Machiavelli*, Holt, New York, 1967, p. 6.

[38]Henry Mintzberg, *The Nature of Managerial Work*, Harper & Row, New York, 1973.

Things must get worse before they get better   This strategy uses the reverse of "no news is good news." That is to say, bad news gets attention. For example, many deans in large universities can only get the attention of central administration and the board of regents/trustees when their college is in trouble, for example, if their accreditation is threatened. Only under these crisis conditions can they get the necessary funding to move their college ahead.

Take counsel with caution   Finally, this suggested political strategy is more concerned with how to keep rather than to acquire power. Contrary to the traditional prescriptions concerning participative management, this suggests that at least some managers should avoid "opening up the gates" to their subordinates in terms of shared decision making. The idea here is that allowing subordinates to participate and to have this expectation may erode the power of the manager.

A final word on power and politics

Obviously, the strategies discussed above are only representative, not exhaustive, of the possible politically based strategies for acquiring power in organizations. Perhaps even more than for many of the other topics covered in the book, there is little research backup for these ideas on power and, especially, politics. One thing, however, is certain—modern, complex organizations tend to create a climate that promotes power seeking and political maneuvering. It is a fact of modern organizational life, and hopefully in the future research will be forthcoming that will help managers understand better the dynamics, meaning, and successful application of power and politics.

SUMMARY

This chapter has examined one of the most important and realistic dynamics of organizational behavior—power and politics. *Power* and *politics* have a number of different meanings. Power can be distinguished from authority and influence, but most definitions subsume all three concepts. Most of the attention on power over the years has been devoted to the French and Raven classification of power types: reward, coercive, legitimate, referent, and expert. Recently, some contingency models for power have been developed, which take into consideration the influenceability of the targets of power (i.e., their dependency, uncertainty, personality, intelligence, age, and culture). Overall contingency models are also beginning to emerge. Closely related to the contingency models of the French and Raven power types are the views of power of Etzioni and McClelland. Etzioni contingently relates his coercive, utilitarian, and normative types of power to the type of involvement of members in an organization (i.e., alienative, calculative, or moral). McClelland's two faces of power are negative personal and positive social.

Politics is very closely related to power. This chapter gave particular attention to a political perspective of power in modern organizations, in terms of resources, decisions, goals, technology, external environment, and change, and to strategies for the acquisition of power. Some specific political strategies are to maintain alliances with powerful people, embrace or demolish, divide and rule, manipulate classified information, make a quick showing, collect and use IOU's, Fabianism—avoid decisive engagement, camel's head in the tent, things must get worse before they get better, and take counsel with caution. Above all, it should be remembered that both power and politics represent the realities of modern organizational life. The study of these important dynamics can significantly improve the understanding of organizational behavior.

QUESTIONS FOR DISCUSSION AND REVIEW

1. How would you define power in your own words? How does power differ from authority? From influence?
2. Identify, briefly summarize, and give some realistic examples of each of the French and Raven power types.
3. Using the contingency model of power, what would be your major argument for defending Patty Hearst? What would be your major argument for prosecuting her? Explain.
4. Identify, briefly summarize, and give some realistic examples of the Etzioni model of power.
5. In the chapter it is stated: "The political power game is very real in today's organizations." Explain in terms of the discussion in the chapter and any firsthand experience you have had to verify this statement.
6. Identify three or four of the political strategies that are discussed in the chapter. Explain how these might actually help someone to acquire power in a modern organization.

CASE:
THE DALEY MACHINE

Former Mayor Richard Daley of Chicago is generally considered to have been one of the most powerful politicians of the last several decades. He had the power to affect national, state, and, of course, local politics. He had control over a political machine consisting of virtually thousands of city and county employees. In addition, he developed close personal friendships with many senators and even U.S. Presidents over his nearly two decades in office. Daley had a certain flair about him that convinced people around him and the voters that he had a way to keep Chicago in line—to make it the "big city that works." Daley had amazing command of minute facts and information, which made him appear very knowledgeable about the history of particular issues and the current operations of various relatively detailed portions of the city and county operations. When Daley spoke out on an issue, the general public and his coworkers would pay attention because he had the facts and the muscle to back him up. People did respect him, even those who did not like his style, for he did much to improve and maintain the downtown area of Chicago as a lively center.

Since his death, several popular books that have closely analyzed the man and his methods have concluded that he was a very effective politician.

1. On the basis of the information given in the case and of what you know about Daley, what type of power do you think he had? Explain.
2. How did he mix power and politics? What political strategies in the chapter would apply to politicians in general? Could some of them backfire?
3. Do you think Daley would have been an effective business executive? Why or why not?

CASE:
THROWING AWAY A GOLDEN OPPORTUNITY

Roger Allen was a man on the move. Everyone in the firm felt that someday he would be company president. To listen to his boss, Harry Walden, it was only a matter of time before Roger would be at the helm.

The current president of the firm was a marketing person. She had worked her way up from field salesperson to president by selling both the product and herself to customers and company alike. In a manner of speaking, the marketing department was the "well-oiled" road to the top. Roger was the number one salesperson and, according to the grapevine, was due to get Harry Walden's job when the latter retired in two years. However, Roger was not sure that he wanted to be vice president of marketing. Another slot was opening up in foreign sales. Roger knew nothing about selling to Europe, but this was the firm's first venture outside the United States, and he thought he might like to give it a try. He talked to Harry about it, but the vice president tried to discourage him. In fact, Harry seemed to think that Roger was crazy to consider the job at all. "Kid," he said, "that's no place for you. Things are soft and cozy back here. You don't have to prove yourself to anyone. You're the number one boy around here. Just sit tight and you'll be president. Don't go out and make some end-runs. Just keep barreling up the middle for four yards on each carry and you'll score the big touchdown." Roger was not convinced. He thought perhaps it would be wise to discuss the matter with the president herself. This he did. The president was very interested in Roger's ideas about international marketing. "If you really think you'd like to head up this office for us, I'll recommend you for the job."

After thinking the matter over carefully, Roger decided that he would much rather go to Europe and try to help establish a foothold over there than sit back and wait for the stateside opening. He told his decision to Harry. "Harry, I've talked to the president, and she tells me that this new opening in foreign sales is really going to get a big push from the company. It's where the action is. I realize that I could sit back and take it easy for the next couple of years, but I think I'd rather have the international job." Harry again told Roger that he was making a mistake. "You're throwing away a golden opportunity. However, if you want it, I'll support you."

A week later, when the company selected someone else from sales to head the international division, Roger was crushed. The president explained the situation to him in this way: "I thought you wanted the job and I pushed for you. However, the other members of the selection committee voted against me. I can tell you you certainly didn't sell Harry very strongly on your idea. He led the committee to believe that you were really undecided about the entire matter. In fact, I felt rather foolish telling them how excited you were about the whole thing, only to have Harry say he talked to you since that time and you weren't that sure at all. When Harry got done, the committee figured you had changed your mind after talking to me and they went on to discuss other likely candidates."

1. Who had power in this organization? What type of power did Harry Walden have?
2. Do you think Roger played company politics well? If so, why didn't he get the international sales job?
3. At this point, what would you do if you were Roger? What political strategies could he use?

LEADERSHIP PROCESSES AND STYLES

A PRESIDENTIAL LEADERSHIP VOID?*

There have been some doubts about the adequacy of Presidential leadership in the United States in the last decade. Some feel there has been an actual "crisis" in leadership in the United States. There is the feeling that the past few Presidents have not shown a sufficient amount of leadership to meet the needs of the country. In this leadership void, Congress has taken several steps to limit the powers of the President. For example, during the 1970s, legislation was passed such as the War Powers Act, which requires congressional approval of armed action that the President orders, and the Budget and Impoundment Control Act, which prevents the President from withholding approval to allocate funds authorized and appropriated by Congress. In addition, congressional action such as the Watergate and impeachment hearings and the utilization of the legislative veto have, according to many political scientists, been the direct result of the lack of faith and confidence in the leadership abilities of the Presidents of the 1970s.

---

*Adapted from "The Great Congressional Power Grab," *Business Week,* Sept. 11, 1978, pp. 90–99.

This chapter is an appropriate conclusion to the dynamics of organizational behavior part of the book. There is a close relationship— a dynamic relationship— among groups, communications, conflict and stress, power and politics, and leadership. The first half of the chapter deals with the classical background and major theoretical perspectives of leadership. Particular attention is devoted to the newer contingency, path-goal, and social learning theories of leadership. The second half of the chapter presents and analyzes various styles of leadership and supervision. Particular attention is given to the work of Blake and Mouton, Reddin, Likert, and Vroom and Yetton.

THE BACKGROUND AND CLASSIC STUDIES ON LEADERSHIP

Leadership has probably been written about, formally researched, and informally discussed more than any other single topic. Throughout history, it has been recognized that the difference between success and failure, whether in a war, a business, a protest movement, or a basketball game, can be largely attributed to leadership. Yet, despite all the attention given to it and its recognized importance, leadership still remains pretty much of a "black box" or unexplainable concept. It is known to exist and to have a tremendous influence on human performance, but its inner workings and specific dimensions cannot be precisely spelled out. Despite these inherent difficulties, a review of some of the widely known classic studies on leadership can help set the stage for the analysis of modern theories and styles of leadership.

Iowa leadership studies

A pioneering leadership study conducted in the late 1930s by Ronald Lippitt and Ralph K. White under the general direction of Kurt Lewin at the University of Iowa has had a lasting impact. Lewin is recognized as the father of group dynamics and as an important cognitive theorist. In the initial studies, hobby clubs for ten-year-old boys were formed. Each club was submitted to three different styles of leadership— authoritarian, democratic, and laissez faire. The authoritarian leader was very directive and allowed no participation. This leader tended to give individual attention when praising and criticizing but tried to be friendly or impersonal rather than openly hostile. The democratic leader encouraged group discussion and decision. He tried to be "objective" in his praise or criticism and to be one of the group in spirit. The laissez faire leader gave complete freedom to the group; he essentially provided no leadership.

Under experimental conditions, the three leadership styles were manipulated to show their effects on variables such as satisfaction and frustration-aggression. Controls in the experiment included the following:

1. *Characteristics of the boys.* All the boys had about the same intelligence and social behaviors.

2. *Types of activities performed.* Each of the clubs made similar things, such as masks, model airplanes, murals, and soap carvings.
3. *The physical setting and equipment.* The experiments were conducted in the same rooms and used identical equipment for all the clubs.
4. *The physical characteristics and personality of the leader.* The leaders assumed a different style as they shifted every six weeks from group to group.[1]

These controls were employed so that the experimenters could state with some degree of assurance that the styles of leadership were causing the changes in the dependent variables of satisfaction and frustration-aggression.

Results of the studies Some of the results were clear-cut and others were not. One definite finding was the boys' overwhelming preference for their democratic leader. In individual interviews, nineteen of the twenty boys stated they liked the democratic leader better than the authoritarian leader. Interestingly, the only boy who preferred the autocratic leader was the son of an army officer stationed with the university ROTC unit. The boy commented that the leader who had the authoritarian role "was the strictest, and I like that a lot."[2] The other nineteen boys did not consider strictness a virtue. They said the autocrat "didn't let us do what we wanted to do," or "we just had to do things; he wanted us to get it done in a hurry."[3] They liked the democratic leader because "he never did try to be the boss, but we always had plenty to do."[4] The boys also chose the laissez faire leader over the autocratic one in seven out of ten cases. For most of the boys, even confusion and disorder were preferable to strictness and rigidity.

Unfortunately, the effects that styles of leadership had on productivity were not directly examined. The experiments were primarily designed to examine patterns of aggressive behavior. However, an important by-product was the insight that was gained into the productive behavior of a group. For example, the researchers found that the boys subjected to the autocratic leader reacted in one of two ways: either aggressively or apathetically. By filming and recording detailed observations, Lippitt's original 1937 study found that hostility was thirty times as frequent in the autocratic as in the democratic group. Also, aggression ("hostility" and "joking hostility") was eight times as prevalent. In a second experiment performed a year later, one of five autocratic groups had the same aggressive reaction. The other four had extremely nonaggressive, "apathetic" patterns of behavior. Both the aggressive and apathetic behaviors were deemed to be reactions to the frustration caused by the autocratic leader. The researchers also pointed out that the apathetic groups exhibited outbursts of aggression when the

---

[1] All specific references made to the styles-of-leadership study are drawn from Kurt Lewin, Ronald Lippitt, and Ralph K. White, "Patterns of Aggressive Behavior in Experimentally Created 'Social Climates,'" *Journal of Social Psychology,* May 1939, pp. 271–276.

[2] Ibid., p. 284.

[3] Ibid.

[4] Ibid.

autocratic leader left the room or when a transition was made to a freer leadership atmosphere. The laissez faire leadership climate actually produced the greatest number of aggressive acts from the group. The democratically led group fell between the one extremely aggressive group and the four apathetic groups under the autocratic leaders.

Implications of the studies Sweeping generalizations on the basis of the Lippitt and White studies are dangerous. Preadolescent boys making masks and carving soap are a long way from adults working in a complex, formal organization. Furthermore, from the viewpoint of modern behavioral science research methodology, many of the variables were not controlled. Nevertheless, these leadership studies have extremely important historical significance. They were the pioneering attempts to determine, experimentally, what effects styles of leadership have on a group. As with the Hawthorne studies, the Iowa studies are too often automatically discounted or at least deemphasized because they were experimentally crude. The values of the studies were that they were the first to analyze leadership from the standpoint of scientific methodology and, more important, they showed that different styles of leadership can produce different, complex reactions from the same or similar groups.

Ohio state leadership studies

In 1945, the Bureau of Business Research at Ohio State University initiated a series of studies on leadership. An interdisciplinary team of researchers from psychology, sociology, and economics developed and used the Leader Behavior Description Questionnaire (LBDQ) to analyze leadership in numerous types of groups and situations.[5] Studies were made of Air Force commanders and members of bomber crews; officers, noncommissioned personnel, and civilian administrators in the Navy Department; manufacturing supervisors; executives of regional cooperatives; college administrators; teachers, principals, and school superintendents; and leaders of various student and civilian groups.

The Ohio State studies started with the premise that no satisfactory definition of leadership existed. They also recognized that previous work had too often assumed that "leadership" was synonymous with "good leadership." The Ohio State group was determined to study leadership, regardless of definition or of whether it was effective or ineffective.

In the first step, the LBDQ was administered in a wide variety of situations. In order to examine how the leader was described, the answers to the questionnaire were then subjected to factor analysis. The outcome was amazingly consistent. The same two dimensions of leadership continually emerged from the questionnaire data. They were *consideration* and *initiating structure*. For example, one of the first studies conducted by Halpin and

---

[5]Ralph M. Stogdill and Alvin E. Coons (eds.), *Leader Behavior: Its Description and Measurement*, Ohio State University, Bureau of Business Research, Columbus, 1957.

Winer examined fifty-two bomber crews.[6] The leadership behaviors of the commanders were described on the questionnaire by 300 crew members. It was found that consideration accounted for 49.6 percent of the common-factor variance. This consideration factor meant that a friendly, trusting, respectful, and warm relationship existed between the bomber commander and his crew. Close behind consideration was the dimension of initiating structure. This factor accounted for 33.6 percent of the common-factor variance. *Initiating structure* meant that the leader organized and defined the relationship between himself and the members of his crew. "He tends to define the role which he expects each member of the crew to assume, and endeavors to establish well defined patterns of organization, channels of communication, and ways of getting jobs done."[7] Combined, consideration and initiating structure accounted for 83.2 percent of the common-factor variance in this study.

The same two factors were found in many follow-up studies encompassing many kinds of leadership positions and contexts. The researchers carefully emphasize that the studies show only *how* leaders carry out their leadership position. Initiating structure and consideration are very similar to the time-honored military commander's functions of mission and concern with the welfare of the men. In simple terms, the Ohio State factors are task or goal orientation (initiating structure) and recognition of individual needs (consideration). The two dimensions are separate and distinct from one another.

The Ohio State studies certainly have value for the study of leadership. They were the first to point out and emphasize the importance of *both* task direction and consideration of individual needs in assessing leadership. This two-dimensional approach lessened the gap between the strict task orientation of the scientific management movement and the human relations emphasis which was popular up to that time. However, on the other side of the coin, in the rush for empirical data on leadership, the great dependence on questionnaires in the Ohio State studies to generate data about leadership behaviors may not have been justified. Only recently have the validity of these instruments been questioned. For example, Schriesheim and Kerr concluded after a review of the existing literature that "the Ohio State scales cannot be considered sufficiently valid to warrant their continued uncritical usage in leadership research."[8] In addition to the validity question is the almost unchallenged belief that these indirect questionnaire methods are in fact measuring leadership *behaviors* instead of simply measuring the questionnaire respondent's behavior and/or perceptions and attitudes about leadership. A multiple measures approach, especially observation tech-

---

[6]Andrew W. Halpin and B. James Winer, "A Factorial Study of the Leader Behavior Descriptions," in ibid., pp. 39–51.

[7]Ibid., pp. 42–43.

[8]Chester A. Schriesheim and Steven Kerr, "Theories and Measures of Leadership: A Critical Appraisal of Current and Future Directions," in James G. Hunt and Lars L. Larson (eds.), *Leadership: The Cutting Edge*, Southern Illinois University Press, Carbondale, 1977, p. 22.

niques, seem needed for the future. The discussion later in the chapter will further explain this need for a behavioral emphasis in leadership studies, and its accompanying observation measurement techniques.

Early Michigan studies on leadership styles

At about the same time the Ohio State studies were being conducted, the Office of Naval Research granted a contract to the University of Michigan Survey Research Center. The purpose of the grant was to determine the "principles which contribute both to the productivity of the group and to the satisfaction that the group members derive from their participation."[9] To accomplish this objective, a study was initiated in 1947 at the home office of the Prudential Insurance Company in Newark, New Jersey.

The Michigan group tried to avoid the methodological difficulties of other pioneering research such as the Hawthorne studies. The researchers were particularly critical of the failure of the Hawthorne studies to develop quantitative measures for variables affecting supervisors and workers. In the Prudential study, systematic measurement was made of the perceptions and attitudes of supervisors and workers. These variables were then related to measures of performance. The research design also included a high degree of control over nonpsychological variables that might influence morale and productivity. Thus, certain factors, such as type of work, working conditions, and work methods, were controlled.

Twelve high-low productivity pairs were selected for examination. Each pair represented a high-producing section and a low-producing section, with the other variables, such as type of work, conditions, and methods, being the same in each pair. Nondirective interviews were conducted with the 24 section supervisors and 419 clerical-type workers. Results showed that supervisors of high-producing sections were significantly more likely

1. To receive general, rather than close, supervision from their supervisors;
2. To like the amount of authority and responsibility they have in their jobs;
3. To spend more time in supervision;
4. To give general, rather than close, supervision to their employees; and
5. To be employee-oriented, rather than production-oriented.[10]

The low-producing section supervisors had essentially opposite characteristics and techniques. They were found to be close, production-centered supervisors. Another important, but sometimes overlooked, finding was that employee satisfaction was *not* directly related to productivity.

The general, employee-centered supervisor, described above, has been the standard-bearer for the traditional human relations approach to leadership. The results of the Prudential studies are always cited when human

---

[9]Rensis Likert, "Foreword," in Daniel Katz, Nathan Maccoby, and Nancy C. Morse, *Productivity, Supervision and Morale in an Office Situation,* University of Michigan, Survey Research Center, Ann Arbor, 1950.

[10]Ibid., p. 62.

relations advocates are challenged to prove their theories. The studies have been followed up with hundreds of similar studies in a wide variety of industrial, hospital, governmental, and other organizations. Thousands of employees, performing unskilled to highly professional-scientific tasks, have been analyzed. In 1961, Rensis Likert, the director of the Institute for Social Research of the University of Michigan, presented the results of the years of research in *New Patterns of Management*.[11] Although there were some variations and refinements, the "new patterns" were essentially the same as those found in the Prudential studies. More recently, Likert has stressed his "system 4" leadership style approach which is covered later in the chapter.

THEORIES OF LEADERSHIP

The Iowa, Ohio State, and Michigan studies are three of the historically most important leadership studies for the study of organizational behavior. Unfortunately, they are still heavily depended upon, and leadership research has not surged ahead from this relatively auspicious beginning. Before analyzing the current status of leadership research, it is important to look at the theoretical development that has occurred through the years.

There are several distinct theoretical bases for leadership. At first, leaders were felt to be born, not made. This so-called "great man" theory of leadership implied that some individuals were born with certain traits that allowed them to emerge out of any situation or period of history to become a leader. This evolved into what is now known as the "trait theory" of leadership. Another approach was to give greater attention to followers. The trait approach is mainly concerned with identifying personality traits of the leader. Dissatisfied with this approach, and stimulated by research such as the Ohio State studies, researchers switched their emphasis from the individual leader to the group being led. In the group approach, leadership is viewed more in terms of the leader's behavior and how such behavior affects and is affected by the group of followers.

Finally, in addition to the leader and the group, the situation began to receive increased attention in leadership theory. The situational approach was initially called *Zeitgeist* (a German word meaning "spirit of the times"); the leader is viewed as a product of the times, the situation. The person with the particular qualities or traits that a situation requires will emerge as the leader. Such a view has much historical support as a theoretical basis for leadership and serves as the basis for today's situational, and now, contingency, theories of leadership.

More recently, some of the expectancy concepts of motivation that were discussed in Chapter 7 began to be adapted to leadership. Called the path-goal theory of leadership, this modern approach is a step toward synthesizing motivational and leadership concepts.

Finally, analogous to developments throughout the field of organizational behavior, a behaviorally oriented social learning approach to leadership

---

[11]Rensis Likert, *New Patterns of Management*, McGraw-Hill, New York, 1961.

has been proposed.[12] This comprehensive theory emphasizes the reciprocal determinism among the leader (including his or her cognitions), the environmental situation (including followers and macro variables), and the behavior itself. The following will examine in detail these major theoretical bases of leadership.

Trait theories of leadership

The scientific analysis of leadership started off by concentrating on leaders themselves. The vital question that this theoretical approach attempted to answer was, what characteristics or traits make a person a leader? The earliest trait theories, which can be traced back to the ancient Greeks and Romans, concluded that leaders were born, not made. The "great man" theory of leadership said that a person was born either with or without the necessary traits for leadership. Famous figures in history, for example Napoleon, were said to have had the "natural" leadership abilities to rise out of any situation to be a great leader.

Eventually, the "great man" theory gave way to a more realistic trait approach to leadership. Under the influence of the behavioristic school of psychological thought, the fact was accepted that leadership traits are not completely inborn but can also be acquired through learning and experience. Attention turned to the search for universal traits possessed by leaders. Numerous physical, mental, and personality traits were researched from about 1930 to 1950. The results of this voluminous research effort were generally very disappointing. Only intelligence seemed to hold up with any degree of consistency. One summary of leadership research found intelligence in ten studies, initiative in six, extroversion and sense of humor in five, and enthusiasm, fairness, sympathy, and self-confidence in four.[13] When combined with studies on physical traits, the conclusion seems to be that leaders are bigger and brighter than those being led, but not too much so.

When the trait approach is applied to organizational leadership, the result is even cloudier. One of the biggest problems is that all managers think they know what the qualities of a successful leader are. As noted by one author,

This optimistic if somewhat naïve attitude springs from the belief that a manager is a person who has some of the following characteristics (which and how many depends upon the prejudices of the individual making the selection): analytical, intelligent, not too bright, keen, enthusiastic, aggressive, capable of maintaining smooth interpersonal relationships, persuasive, dominant, personally acceptable, tactful, extroverted, well-balanced, needing to succeed, ambitious, etc.[14]

---

[12]Fred Luthans, "Leadership: A Proposal for a Social Learning Theory Base and Observational and Functional Analysis Techniques to Measure Leader Behavior," in James G. Hunt and Lars L. Larson (eds.), *Crosscurrents in Leadership*, Southern Illinois University Press, Carbondale, 1979, pp. 201–208.

[13]Joe Kelly, *Organizational Behaviour*, rev. ed., Irwin, Homewood, Ill., 1974, p. 363.

[14]Ibid., pp. 363–364.

Obviously, almost any adjective can be used to describe a successful leader. Recognizing these semantic limitations and realizing that there is no cause-and-effect relationship between observed traits and successful leadership, Keith Davis summarizes four of the major traits which seem to have an impact on successful organizational leadership:[15]

1. *Intelligence.* Research generally shows that the leader has higher intelligence than the average intelligence of his followers. Interestingly, however, the leader cannot be exceedingly much more intelligent than his followers.
2. *Social maturity and breadth.* Leaders tend to be emotionally stable and mature and to have broad interests and activities. They have an assured, respectful self-concept.
3. *Inner motivation and achievement drives.* Leaders have relatively intense motivational drives of the achievement type. They strive for intrinsic rather than extrinsic rewards.
4. *Human relations attitudes.* Successful leaders recognize the worth and dignity of their followers and are able to empathize with them. In the terminology of the Ohio State leadership studies leaders possess consideration, and in the Michigan studies terminology, they are employee- rather than production-centered.

The above represents only one among many possible lists of important organizational leadership traits. Although one can find some research evidence to support the traits on Davis's list and others, to date none are conclusive. Research findings do not begin to agree on which traits are generally found in leaders or even which ones are more important than others. Similar to the trait theories of personality, the trait approach to leadership has provided some descriptive insight but has little analytical or predictive value.

Group and exchange theories of leadership

The group theories of leadership have their roots in social psychology. Classic exchange theory, in particular, serves as an important basis for this approach. Discussed in Chapters 7 and 11, this simply means that the leader provides more benefits/rewards than burdens/costs for followers. There must be a positive exchange between the leader and followers in order for group goals to be accomplished. Chester Barnard applied such an analysis to managers and subordinates in an organizational setting almost a half century ago. More recently, Hollander and Julian have articulated the social exchange view of leadership as follows:

The person in the role of leader who fulfills expectations and achieves group goals provides rewards for others which are reciprocated in the form of status, esteem, and heightened influence. Because leadership embodies a two-way influence relationship, recipients of influence assertions may respond by asserting influence in return. . . . The very sustenance of the relationship depends upon some yielding to influence on both sides.[16]

---

[15]Keith Davis, *Human Behavior at Work*, 4th ed., McGraw-Hill, New York, 1972, pp. 103–104.

[16]Edwin P. Hollander and James W. Julian, "Contemporary Trends in the Analysis of Leadership Processes," *Psychological Bulletin*, vol. 71, 1969, pp. 387–397. Reprinted in Richard M. Steers and Lyman W. Porter, (eds.), *Motivation and Work Behavior*, McGraw-Hill, New York, 1975, p. 349.

The above quote emphasizes that leadership is an exchange process between the leader and followers and also involves the sociological concept of role expectations. Social psychological research can be used to support the exchange and role concepts applied to leadership. In addition, the original Ohio State studies and follow-up studies through the years, especially the dimension of giving consideration to followers, gives support to the group perspective of leadership. A thorough review of research indicated that leaders who take into account and support their followers have a positive impact on attitudes, satisfaction, and performance.[17]

Equally important are a few recent studies that indicate followers/subordinates may actually affect leaders as much as leaders affect followers/subordinates. For example, Greene found that when subordinates were not performing very well the leaders tended to emphasize initiating structure but when subordinates were doing a good job leaders increased their emphasis on consideration.[18] In a lab study Barrow found that group productivity had a greater impact on leadership style than leadership style had on group productivity.[19] In other words, such studies seem to indicate subordinates affect leaders and their behaviors as much as leaders and their behaviors affect subordinates. This, of course, is the premise of a social learning approach to leadership. However, before this approach is presented, the currently popular situational and path-goal theories are examined.

Situational theories of leadership

After the trait approach proved to fall short of being an adequate overall theory of leadership, attention turned to the situational aspects of leadership. Starting in the 1940s, social psychologists began the search for situational variables that impact on leadership roles, skills, and behavior and on followers' performance and satisfaction. Numerous situational variables were identified, but no overall situational theory pulled it all together. Then, about fifteen years ago, Fred Fiedler proposed a widely recognized situation-based model for leadership effectiveness. A brief review of his research techniques and findings is necessary to fully understand his contingency theory of leadership effectiveness.

ASO and LPC scores   Fiedler developed a unique operational technique to measure leadership style. Measurement is obtained from scores that indicate the Assumed Similarity between Opposites (ASO) and Least Preferred Coworker (LPC). ASO calculates the degree of similarity between leaders' perceptions of their most and least preferred coworkers. The more widely used LPC calculates the degree to which the leaders favorably

---

[17]Alan C. Filley, Robert J. House, and Steven Kerr, *Managerial Process and Organizational Behavior,* 2d ed., Scott, Foresman, Glenview, Ill., 1976, pp. 219–222.

[18]Charles N. Greene, "The Reciprocal Nature of Influence Between Leader and Subordinate," *Journal of Applied Psychology,* vol. 60, 1975, pp. 187–193.

[19]J. C. Barrow, "Worker Performance and Task Complexity as Causal Determinants of Leader Behavior Style and Flexibility," *Journal of Applied Psychology,* vol. 61, 1976, pp. 433–440.

perceive their worst coworkers. The two measurements, which can be used interchangeably, relate to leadership style in the following manner:

1. *The human relations or "lenient" style* is associated with the leader who does not discern a great deal of difference between the most and least preferred coworkers (ASO) or who gives a relatively favorable description of the least preferred coworker (LPC).
2. *The task-directed or "hard-nosed" style* is associated with the leader who perceives a great difference between the most and least preferred coworkers (ASO) and gives a very unfavorable description of the least preferred coworker (LPC).

Fiedler's findings   Through the years the performance of both laboratory groups and numerous real groups (basketball teams, fraternity members, surveying teams, bomber crews, infantry squads, open-hearth steel employees, and farm-supply service employees) was correlated with the leadership styles described above. The results were somewhat encouraging, but no simple relationships between leadership style as determined by the leaders' ASO and LPC scores and group performance developed. Eventually, Fiedler concluded that more attention would have to be given to situational variables. He became convinced that leadership style in *combination* with the situation determines group performance.

Fiedler's contingency model of leadership

To test the hypothesis he had formulated from previous research findings, Fiedler developed what he called a *contingency model of leadership effectiveness*. This model contained the relationship between leadership style and the favorableness of the situation. Situational favorableness was described by Fiedler in terms of three empirically derived dimensions:

1. The *leader-member relationship,* which is the most critical variable in determining the situation's favorableness;
2. The degree of *task structure,* which is the second most important input into the favorableness of the situation; and
3. The leader's *position power* obtained through formal authority, which is the third most critical dimension of the situation.[20]

Situations are favorable to the leader if all three of the above dimensions are high. In other words, if the leader is generally accepted by followers (high first dimension), if the task is very structured and everything is "spelled out" (high second dimension), and if a great deal of authority and power is formally attributed to the leader's position (high third dimension), the situation is very favorable. If the opposite exists (if the three dimensions are low), the situation will be very unfavorable for the leader. Fiedler was convinced that the favorableness of the situation in combination with the leadership style determines effectiveness.

Through the manipulation of research findings, Fiedler was able to

---

[20]Fred E. Fiedler, *A Theory of Leadership Effectiveness,* McGraw-Hill, New York, 1976, pp. 143–144.

discover that under very favorable *and* very unfavorable situations, the task-directed or "hard-nosed" type of leader was most effective. However, when the situation was only moderately favorable or unfavorable (the intermediate range of favorableness), the human relations or lenient type of leader was most effective. Figure 15-1 summarizes this relationship between leadership style and the favorableness of the situation.

Why is the task-directed type of leader successful in very favorable situations? Fiedler offered the following explanation:

In the very favorable conditions in which the leader has power, informal backing, and a relatively well-structured task, the group is ready to be directed, and the group expects to be told what to do. Consider the captain of an airliner in its final landing approach. We would hardly want him to turn to his crew for a discussion on how to land.[21]

As an example of why the task-oriented leader is successful in a highly unfavorable situation, Fiedler cited

the disliked chairman of a volunteer committee which is asked to plan the office picnic on a beautiful Sunday. If the leader asks too many questions about what the group ought to do or how he should proceed, he is likely to be told that "we ought to go home."[22]

---

[21]Ibid., p. 147.
[22]Ibid.

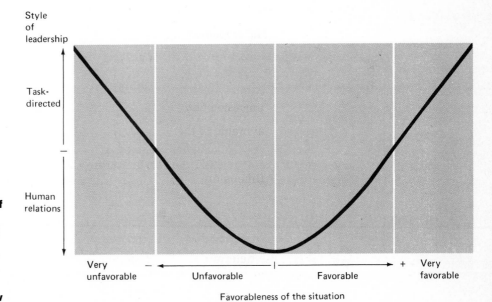

**Figure 15-1
Fiedler's model of
leadership.
(*Source:* Adapted
from Fred E.
Fiedler, *A Theory
of Leadership
Effectiveness,*
McGraw-Hill, New
York, 1967, pp.
142–148.)**

The leader who makes a wrong decision in this highly unfavorable type of situation is probably better off than the leader who makes no decision at all. Figure 15-1 shows that the human relations leader is effective in the intermediate range of favorableness. An example of such situations is the typical committee or a unit which is staffed by professionals. In these situations, the leader may not be wholly accepted by the other members of the group, the task may be generally vague and not completely structured, and little authority and power may be granted to the leader. Under such circumstances, the model predicts that a human relations, lenient type of leader will be most effective.

Research support for the contingency model   As is true of any widely publicized theoretical development, Fiedler's model has stimulated a great deal of research. Not surprisingly, the results are mixed and a controversy has been generated. Fiedler and in particular his students have provided almost all the support for the model over the years. For example, to defend the validity of his theory, he cites thirty studies in a wide variety of teams and organizations, e.g., Navy teams, chemical research teams, shop departments, supermarkets, heavy machinery plant departments, engineering groups, hospital wards, public health teams, and others, and concludes that "the theory is highly predictive and that the relations obtained in the validation studies are almost identical to those obtained in the original studies."[23] With one exception, which Fiedler explains away, he maintains that the model correctly predicted the correlations that should exist between LPC scores of the leader (which determines the style) and performance in relation to the identified favorableness of the situation. As predicted, his studies show that in very unfavorable and very favorable situations, there is a negative correlation between the leader's LPC score and performance (i.e., the task-oriented leader performs best). In a moderately favorable and moderately unfavorable situation, there is a positive correlation between the leader's LPC score and performance (i.e., the human relations–oriented leader is more effective). Although he recognizes that there is increasing criticism of his conclusions, in his most recent publication he maintains that, "methodologically sound validation studies have on the whole provided substantial support for the theory."[24]

Critical analysis of the contingency model   Although there is probably not as much criticism of Fiedler's work as there is, for example, of Herzberg's motivation theory, a growing number of leadership researchers do not wholly agree with Fiedler's interpretations or conclusions. For example, Graen and his colleagues and Ashour initially raised some criticisms of the

---

[23]Fred Fiedler and Martin M. Chemers, *Leadership and Effective Management*, Scott, Foresman, Glenview, Ill., 1974, p. 83.

[24]Fred E. Fiedler and Linda Mahar, "The Effectiveness of Contingency Model Training: A Review of the Validation of Leader Match," *Personnel Psychology*, Spring 1979, p. 46.

procedures and statistical analysis of the studies used to support the validity of the model.[25] More recently, Schriesheim and his colleagues have been especially critical of the reliability and validity of the LPC instrument.[26] Fiedler[27] and his colleagues[28] have answered these criticisms of LPC to their satisfaction, but the fact remains that this questionnaire measure (and others such as those developed at Ohio State and Michigan) do have problems and may be a major reason why leadership understanding and predictability has not progressed as fast as it was once thought it would. As Korman took care to point out:

> The need for better measurement in leadership theory is a matter of prime necessity. Measurement and theory go hand-in-hand and the development of one without the other is a waste of time for all concerned. . . . The point is *not* that adequate measurement is "nice." It is *necessary, crucial,* etc. Without it, we have nothing.[29]

It may well be that there has been an overdependence on the LPC type of measure for leadership theory and research.

In addition to the reliability and validity questions, there is also the criticism of Fiedler's extension of the model to the actual practice of human resource management. Based on the model, Fiedler suggests that management would be better off engineering positions so that the requirements fit the leader instead of the more traditional way of selecting and developing leaders to fit into existing jobs.[30] With this in mind, Fiedler and his colleagues then developed a self-programmed training manual (called *Leader Match*), which includes a series of questionnaires that identify the person's leadership style (LPC) and the situational dimensions of their job (task structure, leader-member relations, and position power).[31] Then the

[25]George Graen, D. Alvares, J. B. Orris, and J. A. Martella, "Contingency Model of Leadership Effectiveness: Antecedent and Evidential Results," *Psychological Bulletin,* vol. 74, 1970, pp. 285–296; George Graen, James B. Orris, and Kenneth M. Alvares, "Contingency Model of Leadership Effectiveness: Some Experimental Results," *Journal of Applied Psychology,* June 1971, pp. 196–201; and Ahmed Ashour, "The Contingency Model of Leadership Effectiveness: An Evaluation," *Organizational Behavior and Human Performance,* June 1973, pp. 339–355.

[26]Schriesheim and Kerr, op. cit., and Chester A. Schriesheim, Brendan D. Bannister, and William H. Money, "Psychometric Properties of the LPC Scale: An Extension of Rice's Review," *Academy of Management Review,* April 1979, pp. 287–290.

[27]Fred E. Fiedler, "A Rejoinder to Schriesheim and Kerr's Premature Obituary of the Contingency Model," in Hunt and Larson, op. cit., 1977, pp. 45–51.

[28]Robert W. Rice, "Reliability and Validity of the LPC Scale: A Reply," *Academy of Management Review,* April 1979, pp. 291–294.

[29]Abraham K. Korman, "Contingency Approaches to Leadership: An Overview," in James G. Hunt and Lars L. Larson (eds.), *Contingency Approaches to Leadership,* Southern Illinois University Press, Carbondale, 1974, p. 194.

[30]Fred E. Fiedler, "Engineer the Job to Fit the Manager," *Harvard Business Review,* September–October 1965, pp. 115–122.

[31]Fred E. Fiedler, Martin M. Chemers, and Linda Mahar, *Improving Leadership Effectiveness: The Leader Match Concept,* Wiley, New York, 1976.

trainee is given a series of short problems with several alternate solutions. The trainee is taught (based on feedback compatible with the contingency model) ways to diagnose the situation so as to change it and optimize the leader style–leader situation match. Most of the support for this model has come from Fiedler and his students/colleagues. After a review of five studies conducted in civilian organizations and seven conducted in military settings, Fiedler concluded that all twelve studies yielded statistically significant results supporting *Leader Match* training.[32] He claims that these studies also support "the contested point that leaders are able to modify their leadership situations to a degree sufficient to increase their effectiveness."[33]

Overall, there seems little question that Fiedler has provided one of the major breakthroughs for leadership theory and practice. Further research should put Fiedler's contingency approach on firmer ground, especially research leading to an understanding of what behavior is actually represented by the LPC response and specifying how the situational moderators will change as the leader exerts influence on subordinates.[34] Also, more research is needed on *Leader Match* training before it can effectively guide the future practice of human resource management. But at least Fiedler has done and continues to do considerable empirical research,[35] and he has set an important precedent for the development of empirically based contingency models. Fiedler's ideas certainly do not represent the ultimate in leadership theory, research, and practice, but he has made a lasting contribution to this field.

Path-goal leadership theory

The other most widely recognized theoretical development for leadership studies besides the contingency approach is the path-goal theory derived from the expectancy framework of motivation theory. This is a healthy development because leadership is closely related to work motivation on the one hand (discussed in Chapter 7) and power on the other (discussed in the previous chapter). Any theory that attempts to synthesize the various concepts seems to be a step in the right direction.

Although Georgopoulos and his colleagues at the University of Michigan's Institute for Social Research used path-goal concepts and terminology almost twenty-five years ago in analyzing the impact of leadership on performance, the modern development is usually attributed to Martin Evans

[32]Fiedler and Mahar, op. cit.

[33]Ibid., p. 61.

[34]Filley, House, and Kerr, op. cit., p. 261.

[35]Besides the recent Fiedler and Mahar, op. cit., on *Leader Match*, Fiedler departs from his almost exclusive use of the LPC instrument by reporting data that suggests that leader experience and intelligence (i.e., traits) may have differential effects on unit performance depending upon the amount of interpersonal stress (a new contingency variable) felt by the leader. See: Fred E. Fiedler, "Organizational Determinants of Managerial Incompetence," in Hunt and Larson, op. cit. 1979, pp. 11–22.

and Robert House, who wrote separate papers on the subject.[36] In essence, the path-goal theory attempts to explain the impact that leader behavior has on subordinate motivation, satisfaction, and performance. The House version of the theory incorporates four major types or styles of leadership.[37] Briefly summarized, these are:

1. *Directive leadership.* This style is similar to the Lippitt and White authoritarian leader. Subordinates know exactly what is expected of them and specific directions are given by the leader. There is no participation by subordinates.
2. *Supportive leadership.* Self-explanatory; the leader is friendly and approachable and shows a genuine human concern for subordinates.
3. *Participative leadership.* This leader asks for and uses suggestions from subordinates but still makes the decisions.
4. *Achievement-oriented leadership.* This leader sets challenging goals for subordinates and shows confidence in them to attain these goals and perform well.

This path-goal theory—and here is how it differs in one respect from Fiedler's contingency model—suggests that these various styles can be and actually are used by the same leader in different situations.[38] Two of the situational factors that have been identified so far are the personal characteristics of subordinates and the environmental pressures and demands facing subordinates. With respect to the first situational factor, the theory asserts:

Leader behavior will be acceptable to subordinates to the extent that the subordinates see such behavior as either an immediate source of satisfaction or as instrumental to future satisfaction.[39]

And with respect to the second situational factor, the theory states:

Leader behavior will be motivational (e.g., will increase subordinate effort) to the extent that (1) it makes satisfaction of subordinate needs contingent on effective performance, and (2) it complements the environment of subordinates by providing the coaching, guidance, support, and rewards which are necessary for effective performance and which may otherwise be lacking in subordinates or in their environment.[40]

Using one of the four styles contingent upon the situational factors as outlined above, the leader attempts to influence subordinate's perceptions and motivate them, which in turn leads to their role clarity, goal expectan-

---

[36]Basil S. Georgopoulos, Gerald M. Mahoney, and Nyle W. Jones, "A Path-Goal Approach to Productivity," *Journal of Applied Psychology*, December 1957, pp. 345–353; Martin G. Evans, "The Effect of Supervisory Behavior on the Path-Goal Relationship," *Organizational Behavior and Human Performance*, May 1970, pp. 277–298; and Robert J. House, "A Path-Goal Theory of Leader Effectiveness," *Administrative Science Quarterly*, September 1971, pp. 321–338.

[37]Robert J. House and Terence R. Mitchell, "Path-Goal Theory of Leadership," *Journal of Contemporary Business*, Autumn 1974, pp. 81–97.

[38]Ibid.

[39]Ibid., in Steers and Porter, op. cit., p. 386.

[40]Filley, House, and Kerr, op. cit., p. 254.

cies, satisfaction, and performance. This is specifically accomplished by the leader as follows:

1. Recognizing and/or arousing subordinates' needs for outcomes over which the leader has some control
2. Increasing personal payoffs to subordinates for work-goal attainment
3. Making the path to those payoffs easier to travel by coaching and direction
4. Helping subordinates clarify expectancies
5. Reducing frustrating barriers
6. Increasing the opportunities for personal satisfaction contingent on effective performance[41]

In other words, by doing the above the leader attempts to make the path to subordinate's goals as smooth as possible. But to accomplish this path-goal facilitation, the leader must use the appropriate style contingent on the situational variables present. Figure 15-2 summarizes this path-goal approach.

As is true of the expectancy theory of motivation, there has been a recent surge of research on the path-goal theory of leadership. So far, the research has concentrated on only parts of the theory rather than on the entire theory. For example, a sampling of the research findings indicates:[42]

1. Studies of seven organizations have found that *leader directiveness* is (1) positively related to satisfactions and expectancies of subordinates engaged in ambiguous tasks, and (2) negatively related to satisfactions and expectancies of subordinates engaged in clear tasks.
2. Studies involving ten different samples of employees found that *supportive*

---

[41]House and Mitchell, op. cit., in Steers and Porter, op. cit., pp. 385–386.

[42]Filley, House, and Kerr, op. cit., pp. 256–260.

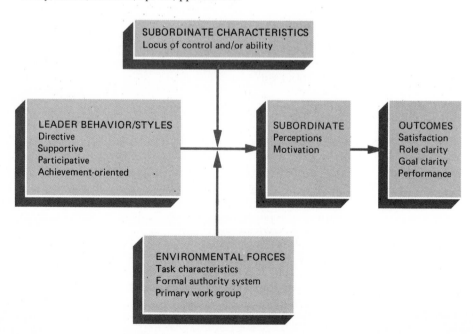

**Figure 15-2
Summary of
path-goal
relationships.**

leadership will have its most positive effect on satisfaction for subordinates who work on stressful, frustrating, or dissatisfying tasks.

3. In a major study in an industrial manufacturing organization, it was found that in nonrepetitive ego-involving tasks, employees were more satisfied under *participative leaders* than under nonparticipative leaders.

4. In three separate organizations it was found that for subordinates performing ambiguous nonrepetitive tasks, the higher the *achievement orientation of the leader,* the more subordinates were confident that their efforts would pay off in effective performance.

The more recent reviews of the research on path-goal theory are not as supportive as the above. For example, Schriesheim and DeNisi note that only a couple of hypotheses have really been drawn from the theory, which means that it may be incapable of generating meaningful predictions.[43] Another note of pessimism offered by these reviewers is that only one of the two hypotheses has received consistent empirical support. The hypothesis that the higher the task structure (repetitiveness) of the jobs performed by subordinates, the higher will be the relationship between supportive leader behavior/style and subordinate satisfaction has generally been substantiated by research. On the other hand, the second hypothesis—that the higher the task structure, the lower the correlation between instrumental (directive) leader behavior and subordinate satisfaction—has received at best mixed research support. Schriesheim and DeNisi then report results of their own research, which indicates that the path-goal theory is capable of producing meaningful and testable predictions beyond the two task structure hypotheses.[44]

Overall, the path-goal theory, like the other theories presented in this and other chapters, seems to need more research, but it certainly warrants further attention in the coming years. Unlike the Fiedler contingency theory, "the path-goal approach not only suggests what type of leadership style may be most effective in a given situation but also attempts to explain why it is most effective."[45] In other words, the path-goal theory, like the expectancy theory in work motivation, may help better explain the complexities of the leadership process.

A social learning approach to leadership

Despite a relative degree of acceptance of the contingency and path-goal theories of leadership and the great (at least relative to other areas in organizational behavior) amount of research that has been conducted, few would disagree today that leadership is still in trouble. Leadership is currently being attacked on all fronts—in terms of theories relating to it,

[43]Chester A. Schriesheim and Angelo DeNisi, "Task Dimensions as Moderators of the Effects of Instrumental Leader Behavior: A Path-Goal Approach," *Academy of Management Proceedings,* 1979, p. 103. Also see: Schriesheim and Kerr, op. cit.

[44]Ibid., pp. 103–105.

[45]H. Randolph Bobbitt, Jr., Robert Breinholt, Robert H. Doktor, and James P. McNaul, *Organizational Behavior,* 2d ed., Prentice-Hall, Englewood Cliffs, N.J., 1978, p. 277.

research methods for studying it, and applications.[46] In spite of this mounting criticism, with only a couple of possible exceptions[47] very few new ideas or alternatives are being offered. For example, John Miner was very critical of leadership theory and then proposed that it be dropped altogether;[48] and after their scathing review of existing questionnaire methods used in leadership research, Schriesheim and Kerr offer no alternative methods.[49] The time seems ripe for new thinking and a new theory, new research methods, and new applications for leadership studies. A social learning approach may best meet this challenge.[50]

Just as social learning theory was shown in Chapter 3 to provide the basis for an overall conceptual model for organizational behavior,[51] social learning theory can provide a model for the continuous, reciprocal interaction among the leader (including his or her cognitions), the environment (including subordinates/followers and macro variables), and the behavior itself. These interactions are shown in Figure 15-3. This would seem to be a comprehensive and viable theoretical foundation for understanding leadership.[52] Any of the other theoretical approaches, standing alone, seem too limiting. For example, the one-sided, cognitively based trait theories suggest leaders are causal determinants that influence subordinates independent of subordinates' behaviors or the situation. The contingency theories are a step in the right direction, but even they for the most part have a unidirectional conception of interaction, where leaders and situations somehow combine to determine leadership behavior. Even those leadership theories which claim to take a bidirectional approach (either in the exchange sense between the leader and subordinate/group or in the contingency sense between the leader and situation) actually retain a unidirectional view toward leadership behavior. In these theories, the causal input into the

---

[46]Representative of the critical analysis of modern leadership theory and research would be Korman, op. cit., pp. 189–195; Charles N. Greene, "Disenchantment with Leadership Research: Some Causes, Recommendations, and Alternative Directions," in Hunt and Larson, op. cit., 1977, pp. 57–67; Schreisheim and Kerr, op. cit.; and Barbara Karmel, "Leadership: A Challenge to Traditional Research Methods and Assumptions," *Academy of Management Review*, July 1978, pp. 475–482.

[47]Some new theoretical developments include: Robert J. House, "A 1976 Theory of Charismatic Leadership," in Hunt and Larson, op. cit., 1977, pp. 189–207; William E. Scott, Jr., "Leadership: A Functional Analysis," in Hunt and Larson, op. cit., 1977, pp. 84–93; and Henry P. Sims, "The Leader as a Manager of Reinforcement Contingencies: An Empirical Example and a Model," in Hunt and Larson, op. cit., 1977, pp. 121–137.

[48]John B. Miner, "The Uncertain Future of the Leadership Concept: An Overview," in James G. Hunt and Lars L. Larson (eds.), *Leadership Frontiers*, the Comparative Administration Resources Institute, Kent State University, 1975, pp. 197-208.

[49]Schriesheim and Kerr, op. cit.

[50]See: Luthans, op. cit.; Fred Luthans and Tim R. V. Davis, "Operationalizing a Behavioral Approach to Leadership," *Proceedings of the Midwest Academy of Management*, 1979, pp. 144–155; and Tim R. V. Davis and Fred Luthans, Leadership Reexamined: A Behavioral Approach," *Academy of Management Review*, April 1979, pp. 237–248.

[51]Also see: Tim R. V. Davis and Fred Luthans, "A Social Learning Approach to Organizational Behavior," *Academy of Management Review*, April 1980, pp. 281–290.

[52]See: Luthans, op. cit. for an expanded discussion.

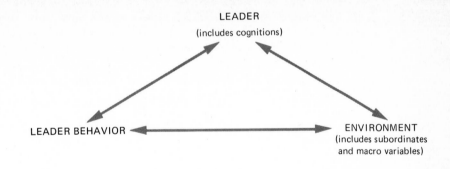

Figure 15-3
A social learning approach to leadership. (*Source:* Adapted from Albert Bandura,
***Social Learning Theory,* Prentice-Hall, Englewood Cliffs, N.J., 1977; and Fred**
Luthans, "Leadership: A Proposal for a Social Learning Theory Base and Observa-
tional and Functional Analysis Techniques to Measure Leader Behavior," in
James G. Hunt and Lars L. Larson (eds.), ***Crosscurrents in Leadership,* Southern**
Illinois University Press, Carbondale, 1979, p. 205.)

leader's behavior is the result of the interdependent exchange, but the behavior itself is ignored as a leadership determinant.

Obviously, the focus of a social learning approach, and what distinguishes it from the other approaches, is the role of leadership *behavior* and the *continuous, reciprocal interaction* among all the variables. With this as the focus of attention, the alternative research methods and application techniques for leadership naturally follow. As Kerlinger has noted, "observations must be used when the variables of research studies are interactive and interpersonal in nature."[53] Thus, there is a need for observational measures of leadership behaviors in naturalistic settings. The pilot work on the development of a Leader Behavior Observation System (LBOS) has been completed,[54] and now research is being conducted to attempt to build an internally and externally valid observation instrument that can be at least an effective supplement, if not an alternative, to the more traditional questionnaire methods used in leadership research.

As far as leadership application for the social learning approach, the four term contingency S-O-B-C (situation-organism-behavior-consequence) model introduced in Chapter 3 can be used by leaders to perform a functional analysis. Unlike the more limited A-B-C (antecedent-behavior-consequence) functional analysis used in O.B. Mod. (see Chapter 10), the variables in the S-O-B-C functional analysis can be either overt as in the operant view or covert as recognized in the social learning view, and, of course, recognition is given to the role of cognitive mediating processes by the insertion of the O. The successful application of this S-O-B-C functional

[53]Fred N. Kerlinger, *Foundations of Behavioral Research,* Holt, New York, 1973, p. 554.

[54]Terry L. Maris and Fred Luthans, "The Leader Behavior Observation System: An Alternative to Questionnaire Measures," working paper, University of Nebraska, Lincoln, 1980.

analysis to human resource management "depends upon the leader's ability to bring into awareness the overt or covert antecedent cues and contingent consequences that regulate the leader's and subordinate's performance behavior."[55] More specifically, in this leadership application, the subordinates are actively involved in the process, and together with the leader they concentrate on their own and each other's *behaviors*, the environmental contingencies (both antecedent and consequent) and their mediating cognitions. Some examples of this approach would be the following:

1. The leader becomes acquainted with the macro and micro variables that control his/her own behavior.
2. The leader works with the subordinate to discover the personalized set of behavioral contingencies that regulate the subordinate's behavior.
3. The leader and the subordinate jointly attempt to discover ways in which they can manage their individual behavior to produce more mutually reinforcing and organizationally productive outcomes.[56]

In such an approach, the leader and the subordinate have a negotiable, interactive relationship and are consciously aware of how they can modify (influence) each other's behavior by giving or holding back desired rewards.

Although work has been done on the theoretical development of a social learning approach to leadership, research and application are just getting under way.[57] Only time will tell whether it will hold up as a viable alternative approach to leadership. However, because of its growing importance as a theoretical foundation for the fields of psychology and organizational behavior as a whole and because it recognizes the interactive nature of all the variables of previous theories, a social learning approach to leadership would seem to have potential for the future.

LEADERSHIP STYLES

The classic leadership studies discussed at the beginning of the chapter and the various leadership theories all have direct implications for what style the manager or supervisor uses in human resource management. The word *style* is roughly equivalent to the *way* in which the leader influences followers. The following discussion will first explore the implications for leadership style of the classic studies and the theories, and then it will present the most recent approaches that deal directly with style.

Style implications of the classic studies and the modern theories

Chapter 1 discussed the major historical contributions to the study of organizational behavior. Most of this discussion has had indirect or direct

---

[55]Davis and Luthans, "Leadership Reexamined," op. cit., p. 244.

[56]Ibid., p. 245.

[57]See Fred Luthans and Tim R. V. Davis, "Behavioral Self-Management: The Missing Link in Managerial Effectiveness," *Organizational Dynamics*, Summer 1979, pp. 42–60.

implications for leadership style. For example, the Hawthorne studies were interpreted in terms of their implications for supervisory style. Also relevant is the classic work done by Douglas McGregor where his Theory X represents the old, authoritarian style and his Theory Y represents the enlightened, humanistic style of leadership. The studies discussed at the beginning of this chapter are directly concerned with style. The Iowa studies analyzed the impact of autocratic, democratic, and laissez faire styles, and the studies conducted by the Michigan group found the employee-centered supervisor to be more effective than the production-centered supervisor. The Ohio State studies identified consideration (a supportive type of style) and initiating structure (a directive type of style) as being the major functions of leadership. The trait, group, and social learning theories have indirect implications for style, and the human relations and task-directed styles play an important role in Fiedler's contingency theory. The path-goal conceptualization depends heavily upon directive, supportive, participative, and achievement-oriented styles of leadership. A rough approximation of the various styles derived from the studies and theories discussed so far can be incorporated into the continuum shown in Table 15-1. For ease of presentation, the styles listed may be substituted for the expressions "boss-centered" and "subordinate-centered" used by Tannenbaum and Schmidt in their classic leadership continuum shown in Figure 15-4. The verbal descriptions and the relationship between authority and freedom found in Figure 15-4 give a rough representation of the characteristics of the various styles of leadership. This depiction can serve as background for a more detailed examination of the specific application of styles to the practice of human resource management.

Managerial grid styles

One very popular approach to identifying leadership styles of practicing managers is Robert R. Blake and Jane S. Mouton's managerial grid. Figure 15-5 shows that the two dimensions of the grid are concern for people along the vertical axis and concern for production along the horizontal. These two dimensions are of course equivalent to the consideration and initiating structure functions identified by the Ohio State studies and the employee-centered and production-centered styles used in the Michigan studies.

Table 15-1

SUMMARY CONTINUUM OF LEADERSHIP STYLES DRAWN FROM THE CLASSIC STUDIES AND THEORIES OF LEADERSHIP

Boss-centered	**Subordinate-centered**
Theory X ⟵⟶	Theory Y
Autocratic ⟵⟶	Democratic
Production-centered ⟵⟶	Employee-centered
Close ⟵⟶	General
Initiating structure ⟵⟶	Consideration
Task-directed ⟵⟶	Human relations
Directive ⟵⟶	Supportive
Directive ⟵⟶	Participative

The five basic styles identified in the grid represent varying combinations of concern for people and production. The 1,1 manager has minimum concern for people and production; this style is sometimes called the "impoverished" style. The opposite is the 9,9 manager. This individual has maximum concern for both people and production. The implication is that the 9,9 is the best style of leadership, and Blake and Mouton have recently stated in no uncertain terms, "There should be no question about which leadership style is the most effective. It's that of the manager whom we call, in the terminology of the Managerial Grid, a 9,9 team builder."[58] The 5,5 manager is the "middle-of-the-roader," and the other two styles represent the extreme concerns for people (1,9, "country club" manager) and production (9,1, "task" manager). A manager's position on the grid can be determined by a questionnaire developed by Blake and Mouton and can play an important role in organization development (OD). Chapter 21 will discuss this grid approach to OD and analyze the research findings.

Reddin's three-dimensional model

Blake and Mouton's grid identifies the style of a manager but does not directly relate it to effectiveness. William J. Reddin, a Canadian professor and consultant, has added the third dimension of effectiveness to his model. Besides incorporating the effectiveness dimension, he also builds in the situational impact on the appropriate style. Figure 15-6 shows the relatively elaborate 3-D leader effectiveness model.

[58]Robert Blake and Jane S. Mouton, "Should You Teach There's Only One Best Way to Manage?" *Training HRD*, April 1978, p. 24.

**Figure 15-4
A continuum of leadership behavior. (Source: Robert Tannenbaum and Warren H. Schmidt, "How to Choose a Leadership Pattern,"** *Harvard Business Review,* **March–April 1958, p. 96. Used with permission.)**

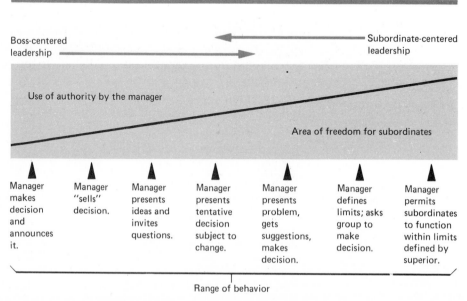

Boss-centered leadership

Subordinate-centered leadership

Use of authority by the manager

Area of freedom for subordinates

| Manager makes decision and announces it. | Manager "sells" decision. | Manager presents ideas and invites questions. | Manager presents tentative decision subject to change. | Manager presents problem, gets suggestions, makes decision. | Manager defines limits; asks group to make decision. | Manager permits subordinates to function within limits defined by superior. |

Range of behavior

The center grid in Figure 15-6 represents the four basic leadership styles. These are essentially the same as the styles first identified by the Ohio State studies and used by Blake and Mouton in their grid. Reddin goes beyond the Blake and Mouton grid in saying that each of the four styles can be effective or ineffective, depending on the situation. The four styles on the upper right are effective (they achieve the output requirements of the manager's job and attain the goals of the position) and the four styles on the lower left are ineffective. Very briefly, these eight styles can be summarized as follows:[59]

Effective styles

1. *Executive.* This style gives a great deal of concern to both task (task-oriented, or TO) and relationships (RO). A manager using this style is a good motivator, sets high standards, recognizes individual differences, and utilizes team management.
2. *Developer.* This style gives maximum concern to relationships (RO) and minimum concern to the task (TO). A manager using this style has implicit trust in people and is mainly concerned with developing them as individuals.
3. *Benevolent autocrat.* This style gives maximum concern to the task (TO) and

---

[59]William J. Reddin, "Managing Organizational Change," *Personnel Journal,* July 1969, p. 503.

**Figure 15-5
The managerial grid. (Source: Robert R. Blake and Jane S. Mouton, "Managerial Facades," Advanced Management Journal, July 1966, p. 31. Used with permission.)**

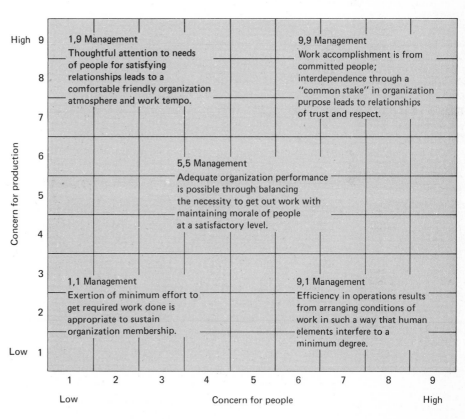

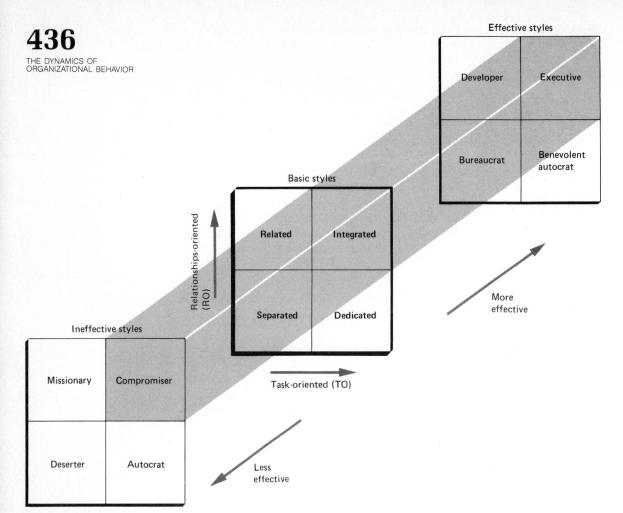

**Figure 15-6
Reddin's 3-D model
of leadership
effectiveness.
(*Source:* Adapted
from W. J. Reddin,
*Managerial
Effectiveness*,
McGraw-Hill, New
York, 1970, p. 230.
Used with
permission.)**

minimum concern to relationships (RO). A manager using this style knows exactly what he or she wants and how to get it without causing resentment.

4. *Bureaucrat.* This style gives minimum concern to both task (TO) and relationships (RO). A manager using this style is mainly interested in the rules and wants to maintain and control the situation by their use and is seen as conscientious.

Ineffective styles

1. *Compromiser.* This style gives a great deal of concern to both task (TO) and relationships (RO) in a situation that requires only emphasis on one or neither. This style of manager is a poor decision maker; the pressures affect him or her too much.

2. *Missionary.* This style gives maximum concern to people and relationships (RO) and minimum concern to the task (TO), where such behavior is inappropriate. This manager is typically the "do-gooder" who values harmony as an end in itself.

3. *Autocrat.* This style gives maximum concern to the task (TO) and minimum concern to the relationships (RO), where such behavior is inappropriate. This manager has no confidence in others, is unpleasant, and is interested only in the immediate job.

4. *Deserter.* This style gives minimum concern to task (TO) and relationships (RO) in a situation where such behavior is inappropriate. This manager is uninvolved and passive.

Reddin has developed a sixty-four-item forced-choice test that managers can take to identify their styles. It has become a very popular technique to use in training programs and executive development seminars. The test can help managers make a self-diagnosis of their strengths and weaknesses. It is emphasized that a style per se can be effective or ineffective depending on the situation. Reddin's 3-D approach incorporates three theoretical bases (traits, group, and situation) and stresses that the manager should have an adaptive style that leads to effectiveness.

Likert's four systems of management

Both the Blake and Mouton and Reddin 3-D approaches are highly descriptive and at this time lack empirically validated research backup. In contrast, Rensis Likert proposes four basic systems or styles of organizational leadership evolved from the many years of research by the Michigan group. Table 15-2 summarizes these four styles, called systems.

The manager who operates under a system 1 approach is very authoritarian and actually tries to exploit subordinates. The system 2 manager is also authoritarian but in a paternalistic manner. This benevolent autocrat keeps

Table 15-2

LIKERT'S SYSTEMS OF MANAGEMENT LEADERSHIP

Leadership variable	System 1 (exploitive autocratic)	System 2 (benevolent autocratic)	System 3 (participative)	System 4 (democratic)
Confidence and trust in subordinates	Has no confidence and trust in subordinates	Has condescending confidence and trust, such as master has to servant	Substantial but not complete confidence and trust; still wishes to keep control of decisions	Complete confidence and trust in all matters
Subordinates' feeling of freedom	Subordinates do not feel at all free to discuss things about the job with their superior	Subordinates do not feel very free to discuss things about the job with their superior	Subordinates feel rather free to discuss things about the job with their superior	Subordinates feel completely free to discuss things about the job with their superior
Superiors seeking involvement with subordinates	Seldom gets ideas and opinions of subordinates in solving job problems	Sometimes gets ideas and opinions of subordinates in solving job problems	Usually gets ideas and opinions and usually tries to make constructive use of them	Always asks subordinates for ideas and opinions and always tries to make constructive use of them

Source: Adapted from Rensis Likert, *The Human Organization,* McGraw-Hill, New York, 1967, p. 4. Used by permission.

strict control and never delegates to subordinates, but he or she "pats them on the head" and "does it for their best interests." The system 3 manager uses a consultative style. This manager asks for and receives participative input from subordinates but maintains the right to make the final decision. The system 4 manager uses a democratic style. This manager gives some direction to subordinates but provides for total participation and decision by consensus and majority.

To give empirical research backup on which style is most effective, Likert and his colleagues asked thousands of managers to describe, on an expanded version of the format shown in Table 15-2, the highest- and lowest-producing departments with which they have had experience. Quite consistently, the high-producing units are described according to systems 3 and 4, and the low-producing units fall under systems 1 and 2. This response occurs irrespective of the manager's field of experience or whether the manager is in a line or staff position.[60]

The impact of intervening variables and time   An important refinement of Likert's work is the recognition of three broad classes of variables that affect the relationship between leadership and performance in a complex organization.[61] Briefly summarized, these are:

1. *Causal variables.* These are the independent variables that determine the course of developments and results of an organization. They include only those variables that are under control of management; e.g., economic conditions are *not* causal variables in this sense. Examples would include organization structure and management's policies and decisions and their leadership styles, skills, and behavior.
2. *Intervening variables.* These reflect the internal climate of the organization. Performance goals, loyalties, attitudes, perceptions, and motivations are some important intervening variables. They affect interpersonal relations, communication, and decision making in the organization.
3. *End-result variables.* These are the dependent variables, the outcomes of the organization. Examples would be productivity, service, costs, quality, and earnings.

Likert points out that there is not a direct cause-and-effect relationship between, for example, leadership style (a causal variable) and earnings (an end-result variable). The intervening variables must also be taken into consideration. For example, moving to a system 1 style of management may lead to an improvement in profits but a deterioration of the intervening variables (i.e., attitudes, loyalty, and motivation decline). In time, these intervening variables may lead to a decrease in profits. Thus, although on the surface it appeared that system 1 was causing profits, because of the impact on the intervening variables, in the long run system 1 may lead to a decrease in profits. The same can be said for the application of a system 4 style. In the short run, profits may dip; but because of the impact on intervening variables, there may be an increase in profit over time. Obviously, the time

---

[60]Rensis Likert, *The Human Organization*, McGraw-Hill, New York, 1967, pp. 3 and 11.

[61]Ibid., pp. 26 and 29.

lag between intervention and the impact on end-result variables becomes extremely important to Likert's scheme. Based upon some research evidence, Likert concludes that, "Changes in the causal variables toward System 4 apparently require an appreciable period of time before the impact of the change is fully manifest in corresponding improvement in end-result variables."[62]

An example of time lag Likert's "time lag" helps explain the following relatively common sequence of events. A system 1 manager takes over an operation and immediately gets good performance results. In the meantime, however, the intervening variables are declining. Because the system 1 manager is getting results, he is promoted. A system 4 manager now takes over the operation. Because of the time lag, the intervening variables, which were affected by the system 1 manager, now start to impact on performance. Under the system 4 manager, performance starts to decline but the intervening variables start to improve. However, top management sees that when the system 4 manager took over, performance started to decline. The system 4 manager is replaced by a system 1 manager to "tighten up" the operation. The intervening variables affected by the system 4 manager now start to affect performance and the cycle repeats. Figure 15-7 depicts this situation. In other words, the cause-and-effect relationships that appear on the surface may be very misleading because of the time-lag impact of the intervening variables. As in the example, top-management evaluations often credit the wrong manager (the system 1 manager in this case) for improving performance and unjustly blame the wrong manager (the system 4 manager in the example) for poor performance. Some organizations may be guilty of this

---

[62]Ibid., pp. 80–81.

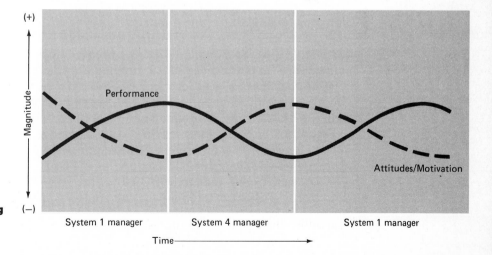

Figure 15-7 Hypothetical example depicting Likert's time lag impact of intervening variables on performance.

never-ending cycle of rewarding and punishing the wrong managers because of the time lag effect of intervening variables.

Analysis of Likert's approach Likert and his colleagues are still actively involved in further development, research, and application of the system 4 style of management. For example, some predictive models have been developed to forecast what impact current causal and intervening variables have on future outcome variables such as profit. In his latest book, coauthored with his wife, he describes and gives case studies of how system 4 can lead to a win-win resolution of organizational conflict.[63] In addition, the survey instruments that he and his colleagues at Michigan's Institute for Social Research developed are still being widely used in the diagnostic phase of organizational development. These will be covered in Chapter 21. The concept and practice of human resource accounting, which Likert has helped develop and of which he is a leading advocate, are also closely tied into this approach. Chapter 17 will cover this important development for managerial control.

One of the major criticisms of Likert's work concerns its overdependence on survey questionnaire measures for gathering data to develop the theory and application of system 4 management. Sole dependence on Likert scale (continuums of dimensions as shown in Table 15-2) questionnaire responses is not enough. As has been pointed out a number of times in this book, there is increasing criticism of data gathered only by questionnaires and interviews. Multiple measures of behaviorally oriented variables in organizations are needed. More use of archival information (existing records kept by every organization for other use, for example, government reports, personnel records, and performance data) and data gathered through observation are needed. Although ethical standards must always be maintained, subject awareness must be minimized to increase the reliability and validity of data that are gathered for research purposes. Both questionnaires and interviews have a great deal of subject awareness or intrusiveness. Archival analysis and some naturalistic observational techniques minimize subject awareness and are called *unobtrusive measures*.[64] Not only Likert's work but much of the other research reported in this book is based upon indirect questionnaire measures. What is needed is to supplement these measures with other measures such as observations and archival data. As Chapter 2 pointed out, the use of multiple measures increases tremendously the chance of getting better, more accurate, and more valid data.

Another problem inherent in Likert's scheme besides the real and potential measurement problems is the implication of the universality of the system 4 approach. Although Likert points out that "differences in the kind of work, in the traditions of the industry, and in the skills and values of the employees of a particular company will require quite different procedures

---

[63]Rensis Likert and Jane Gibson Likert, *New Ways of Managing Conflict*, McGraw-Hill, New York, 1976.

[64]Eugene J. Webb, Donald T. Campbell, Richard D. Schwartz, and Lee Sechrest, *Unobtrusive Measures: Nonreactive Research in the Social Sciences*, Rand McNally, Chicago, 1966.

and ways to apply appropriately the basic principles of system 4 management,"[65] he still implies that system 4 will *always* be more effective than system 1. Proponents of situational/contingency leadership theories and their research findings would, of course, counter this generalization.

The Vroom-Yetton normative model

The Blake and Mouton, Reddin, and Likert approaches to leadership are all directly or by implication prescriptive. In addition, they try in varying degrees to take into consideration the situation (Blake and Mouton and Likert in passing, and Reddin as a vital part of his approach). But none of these approaches spell out exactly *how* a manager should act or what decision should be made in a given situation. Vroom and Yetton attempt to provide a specific, normative model (how decisions "ought" to be made in given situations) that a leader could actually use in making effective decisions.[66]

The Vroom-Yetton model was first developed several years ago and has since been modified. The latest model contains five leadership styles, seven situation dimensions, fourteen problem types, and seven decision rules. The leadership styles consist of variations on autocratic, consultative, and group styles and the situational dimensions are of two general types: (1) the way in which problems affect the quality and acceptance of a decision, and (2) the way in which the problems affect the degree of participation. The seven situational dimensions are stated in the form of yes-no questions and the answers can quickly diagnose the situation for the leader.

Vroom and Yetton use a decision tree to relate the situation to the appropriate leadership style. Figure 15-8 shows the approach. The seven situational questions are listed at the top. Starting at the left, the manager would answer each question above the box in the decision tree until it led to the appropriate style. In this way the manager could determine the appropriate style based on the given situation. Vroom and Yetton also point out that the fourteen problem types (the combinations of the seven situational variables, listed as 1 through 14 in the decision tree) could actually have more than one acceptable leadership style. In order to be acceptable, the style must meet the criteria of seven decision rules that protect quality and acceptance. If more than one style remains after the test of both quality and acceptance (and many do), the third most important aspect of a decision—the amount of time—is used to determine the single style that ought to be used in the given situation. The styles shown at the ends of the various branches on the decision tree reflect the single best style that should be used in light of the way the situation was diagnosed by answers to the questions at the top.

The Vroom-Yetton model is a fitting conclusion to the discussion of

[65]Rensis Likert, *The Human Organization*, op. cit., p. 192.

[66]Victor H. Vroom and Philip W. Yetton, *Leadership and Decision-Making*, University of Pittsburgh Press, Pittsburgh, Pa., 1973, chap. 3.

leadership in this chapter. The progression has been from theory to styles to specific prescription. Several studies have tested this model.[67] Most of this research has been done by Vroom and his colleagues and they do provide some evidence that the model is valid. However, a recent critique that closely examined the methodology used in these studies led the reviewer to seriously question the validity of the model.[68] Specifically, the dependence on self-report data in these studies is a weakness. For example, managers

Figure 15-8
Vroom-Yetton
normative
leadership model.
(*Source:* Adapted
from Victor H.
Vroom, "A New
Look at
Managerial
Decision Making,"
Organizational
***Dynamics*, vol. 1,**
no. 4, 1973, pp. 67
and 70.)

[67]For example, see T. E. Hill and N. Schmitt, "Individual Differences in Leadership Decision Making," *Organizational Behavior and Human Performance*, vol. 19, 1977, pp. 353–367; A. G. Jago, "A Test of Spuriousness in Descriptive Models of Participative Leader Behavior," *Journal of Applied Psychology*, vol. 63, 1978, pp. 383–387; and V. H. Vroom and A. G. Jago, "On the Validity of the Vroom-Yetton Model," *Journal of Applied Psychology*, vol. 63, 1978, pp. 151–162.

[68]R. H. George Field, "A Critique of the Vroom-Yetton Contingency Model of Leadership Behavior," *Academy of Management Review*, April 1979, pp. 249–257.

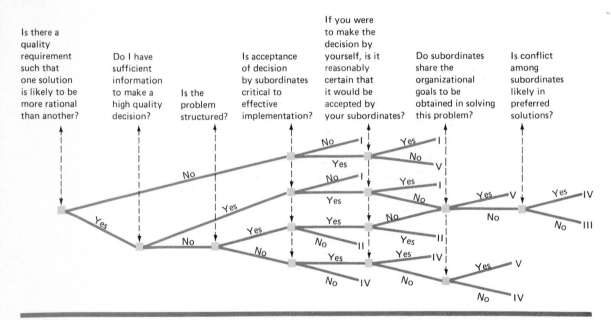

I You solve the problem or make the decision yourself, using information available to you at that time. **II** You obtain the necessary information from your subordinate(s), then decide on the solution to the problem yourself. You may or may not tell your subordinates what the problem is in getting the information from them. The role played by your subordinates in making the decision is clearly one of providing the necessary information to you, rather than generating or evaluating alternative solutions. **III** You share the problem with relevant subordinates individually, getting their ideas and suggestions without bringing them together as a group. Then *you* make the decision that may or may not reflect your subordinates' influence. **IV** You share the problem with your subordinates as a group, collectively obtaining their ideas and suggestions. Then *you* make the decision that may or may not reflect your subordinates' influence. **V** You share a problem with your subordinates as a group. Together you generate and evaluate alternatives and attempt to reach agreement (consensus) on a solution. Your role is much like that of a chairperson. You do not try to influence the group to adopt "your" solution and you are willing to accept and implement any solution that has the support of the entire group.

going through training and development programs are simply asked to recall a problem they have encountered and to indicate which of the five styles in the model they used to solve the problem. In addition, managers are given standardized problem cases and are asked which style from the model could best be used to solve it. Such methods, of course, have a number of internal validity problems (experimenter effect and social desirability effect) and external validity problems (the use of standardized cases in a training situation may not generalize to the real world). In addition to the validity problems of the model, it may also have limited utility for two major reasons:

First, it is not as parsimonious as other models of leader decision process choice. *Second*, it deals with only one aspect of leader behavior, that of selecting different decision processes for different problem situations.[69]

Therefore, despite the surface logic of the model and the fact that it does give precise answers to practicing managers, the research conducted so far is far from sufficient to validate it and justify its use in actual practice. On the other hand, its attempt to bridge the gap from theory to practice may be a step in the right direction and it can serve as a prototype for the actual practice of contingency management.

SUMMARY

This chapter presented and analyzed various theoretical and practical aspects of leadership. The classic research studies on leadership set the stage for the theoretical development of leadership. The trait theories concentrate on the leaders themselves but, with the possible exception of intelligence, really do not come up with any agreed traits of leaders. The group theories emphasize the importance of the followers, but these are also only partial theories. Today, the widely recognized theories of leadership are situationally based. In particular, Fiedler's contingency model makes a significant contribution to leadership theory and potentially to the practice of human resource management. The path-goal approach is also an important contribution to leadership theory. It incorporates expectancy motivation concepts. Both the Fiedler and path-goal approaches have generated a growing body of research on leadership dimensions, but there are still problems. A social learning approach that incorporates the leader, the situation, and the behavior itself is proposed as a possible alternative. This approach emphasizes the importance of behavior and the continuous, interacting nature of all the variables in leadership.

There are many style implications in both the classic leadership studies and the modern theories. Blake and Mouton's managerial grid, Reddin's 3-D model, and Likert's four systems focus attention directly on leadership

---

[69]Ibid., p. 256.

styles. Each of these is of value in relation to the actual practice of human resource management. The grid and 3-D models are valuable mainly to let managers describe their styles, and Likert's work has implications for organizational effectiveness. Likert's recognition of intervening variables and their time lag effects has significant implications for practice. Finally, the Vroom and Yetton model attempts to prescribe exactly what style to use in a given situation. All of these approaches to style need more and better research in order to make meaningful contributions to the actual practice of human resource management in the future.

QUESTIONS FOR DISCUSSION AND REVIEW

1. Briefly summarize the findings of the three classical leadership studies.
2. How do the group theories differ from the trait theories of leadership?
3. What are the three critical situational variables identified by Fiedler? If these are very favorable, what is the most effective style to use?
4. In simple terms, what is the path-goal theory of leadership? What is the leader's function in this conceptualization?
5. What are the three variables in the social learning approach to leadership? How do they relate to one another? How can this approach be applied to the practice of human resource management?
6. Briefly identify the major styles from Blake and Mouton's grid, from Reddin's 3-D model, and from Likert's four systems. Which are more effective or less effective?

CASE:

IF IT IS GOOD ENOUGH FOR US, IT IS GOOD ENOUGH FOR THEM

Jesse White was a training specialist for the personnel department of a large company. His boss, Rose O'Brien, called him in one day and said that she had just come back from an executive committee meeting. She had been given the charge of developing a leadership training program for all middle management personnel in the firm. She told Jesse that he would be in charge of the project. Jesse wanted to know what the objectives of the program were supposed to be. Rose replied that the top management of the company were concerned that the styles that they were using now and in the past were not being used by the middle managers. For example, the executive vice president was concerned that the younger lower/middle managers were too idealistic about how to treat people. The others had all agreed with this observation. Then the vice president for finance added that it was their styles that had taken this company to the top of the industry, and if it was good enough for them it should be good enough for the middle managers. Rose then said, "I have to follow orders, so what I would like you to do is first get a good understanding of the modern theoretical basis for leadership. Then find out what styles of leadership the president and the vice presidents are using in their present jobs. Based upon the theory and what you find out about their present styles, design a program that I can present to the executive committee for middle management leadership training."

1. Do you agree with the approach outlined by Rose to set up the training program? If you were Jesse, what would be some important theoretical considerations that would

go into your program? What techniques would you use to determine the top managers' present styles?

2. Based on the comments of the executive vice president and the vice president for finance, what styles do you feel you would find for the top managers? For the middle managers? How would you be able to justify a program that was different from the styles of the top managers?

3. Using the Blake and Mouton, Reddin, or Likert approach to style, describe some of the details and implications of your leadership program.

CASE:
THE PUPPET

Rex Justice was a long-term employee of the Carfax Corporation, and for the last several years he had been a supervisor in the financial section of the firm. He was very loyal to Carfax and worked hard to follow the company policies and procedures and the orders of the managers above him. In fact, the upper level management staff thought very highly of him; they could always count on Rex meeting any sort of demand that the company placed on him. He was valued and well liked by all the top managers. His employees in the financial section had the opposite opinion of Rex. They felt that he was too concerned with pleasing the upper-level brass and not nearly enough with meeting the needs and concerns of the employees in his department. For example, they felt that Rex never really pushed hard enough for a more substantial slice of the budget. Relative to other departments in the company, they felt they were underpaid and overworked. Also, whenever one of them went to Rex with a new idea or suggestion for improvement he always seemed to have five reasons why it couldn't be done. There was considerable dissatisfaction in the department and everyone thought that Rex was just a puppet for management. Performance was beginning to suffer because of his style of leadership. Upper-level management seemed to be oblivious to the situation in the finance section.

1. How would you explain Rex's leadership style in terms of one or more of the theories discussed in the chapter?

2. What advice would you give Rex to improve his leadership style?

CASE STUDY AND EXPERIENTIAL EXERCISES FOR PART 4

CASE:
THE DYNAMICS OF TRIVIA

C. Northcote Parkinson has been well known for a number of years for his various "laws"—described tongue in cheek—governing organizations and their management.[1] For example, there is Parkinson's law of the rising pyramid, which states that work expands to fill the time available for its completion. Another of Parkinson's laws is that expenditures will rise to meet income. The role that Parkinson has played in contemporary management thought has been that of the gadfly. As in the fairy tale, while all others contend that the king's wardrobe is impeccable, he delights in shouting, "The king has no clothes," thereby exposing the naked truth.

The typical management committee is one of many topics to which he has addressed himself. Parkinson likes to point out that the only individuals who truly understand high finance are either those who are millionaires or those who have nothing. The first can comprehend a million dollars because they have it. Of the second, namely economics professors and applied mathematicians, Parkinson says, "A million dollars is at least as real as a thousand, they having never possessed either sum."[2] All other individuals fall between these two extremes. They understand what a thousand dollars is but know nothing of millions. These assumptions led Parkinson to formulate his law of triviality. This law states that the time people consume on any committee agenda item will be in inverse relation to the proportion of the sum involved. The example Parkinson uses to support his law is that of a management group preparing to discuss the purchase of an atomic reactor. The treasurer presents his report in the following language:

The estimate for the Atomic Reactor is before you, sir, set forth in Appendix H of the subcommittee's report. You will see that the general design and layout has been approved by Professor McFission. The total cost will amount to $10,000,000. The contractors, Messrs. McNab and McNash, consider that the work should be completed by April, 1959. Mr. McGee, the consulting engineer, warns us that we should not count on completion before October, at the earliest. In this view he is supported by Dr. McHeap, the well-known geophysicist, who refers to the probable need for piling at the

---

[1]C. Northcote Parkinson, *Parkinson's Law,* Houghton Mifflin, Boston, 1957, p. 2. This case is drawn from this source.

[2]Ibid., p. 24.

lower end of the site. The plan of the main building is before you—see Appendix IX—and the blueprint is laid on the table. I shall be glad to give any further information that members of the committee may require.[3]

The chairperson of the meeting thanks the treasurer for his very "lucid" explanation of the plan and then invites the members to present their points of view.

The truth of the matter is that most of the managers present are unable to say anything substantive because they lack the technical knowledge needed to discuss the subject intelligently. For example, four of them do not know what a reactor is, including the chairperson. Of the rest, some are unsure of why the reactor is being built, while others are completely in the dark regarding whether or not $10 million is an accurate figure for such an undertaking.

Only two of the managers attempt to speak out. The rest remain mute so no one will discover what they do not know. The first to speak is a Ms. Isaacson, who expresses her feeling about the contractors, McNab and McNash. Isaacson feels that Messrs. David and Goliath would have done a bang-up job on the reactor. Having nicely straddled the fence on an issue about which it is too late to do anything, Isaacson asks for her observations to be entered in the minutes. This is done. Having obtained her goal of building a bridge in her rear should anything go wrong with the present plan, Ms. Isaacson moves to the sidelines.

The other manager who ponders speaking out is Mr. Brickworth. Of all the managers present, Brickworth is by far the most competent to speak on the issue. First, he distrusts the estimate of $10 million. He feels that for a figure to come out in such nice round numbers makes it automatically suspect. He also has some questions about the mechanics of the construction. In addition, Dr. McHeap, the geophysicist mentioned by the treasurer, rings a bell in Brickworth's mind.

He wonders if this is not the same man who was sued just last year by the Trickle and Driedup Oil Corporation. He just does not know where to begin. On the other hand, he realizes that if he says anything, he may be opening a Pandora's box. For example, if he starts questioning the construction aspects of the reactor, he may find it necessary to refer to the blueprints. However, he is unsure of whether the other managers are capable of reading blueprints. Thus, to allude to the blueprints might make them look foolish. The same would be true if he started explaining the function of a reactor. Some of the members might think he was preaching to them. Thus, Brickworth decides that it is best to head for the sidelines without getting involved. This he does by announcing he has "no comment" to make.

Having exhausted conversation on the issue, the chairperson calls for a vote and the group agrees to build the reactor. When all is said and done, it has taken the group approximately two and a half minutes to spend $10 million.

Moving on to the next item on the agenda, the chairperson asks for discussion regarding an estimate that has been received to build a bicycle shed for use by the clerical staff. The cost involved is $2350. The committee members now come to life. Not only do they feel they did not carry their own

---

[3]Ibid., pp. 25–26.

weight on the reactor vote, but now they see something about which they are qualified to speak. Everyone wants in on the act. Mr. Softleigh questions whether the roof should be aluminum. Would asbestos not be cheaper, he asks? Mr. Holdfast believes galvanized iron would be an even better substitute, while simultaneously questioning whether the shed cannot be constructed for under $2000. Mr. Daring suggests abandoning the entire project, feeling that if the shed is built for the employees they will want garages next. And so it goes. For three-quarters of an hour the debate rages over the materials and the cost.

Finally, the group resolves the issue and pushes on to another agenda item: the serving of refreshments at the Joint Welfare Committee meetings. The cost of these refreshments is $4.75 monthly. Now the members really get into the act. Each has something to say and is eager to respond to the comments made by fellow managers. In all, an hour and a quarter is spent on the $57 annual charge. Thus, concludes Parkinson, there is an inverse relationship between the cost of an item and the amount of time spent on it by committees.[4]

1. Briefly, how are each of the major topics discussed in this part of the book (groups, informal organization, communication, conflict, stress, power, politics, and leadership) reflected in this case?
2. Do you think the dynamics of real world management decision making and relationships are like what Parkinson describes in this case? Can you give any examples of your own to support your answer?
3. Do you think the decisions made in this case will help or hurt this company?
4. Can you give any specific suggestions or techniques from the chapters studied in this part for improving the process described?

EXERCISE:

GROUPS AND CONFLICT RESOLUTION

Goals:

1. To compare individual versus group problem solving and decision making
2. To analyze the dynamics of groups
3. To demonstrate conflict and ways of resolving it

Implementation:

1. Divide any number of people into small groups of four or five.
2. Take about fifteen minutes for individual responses and thirty minutes for group consensus.
3. Each individual and group should have a worksheet. Pencils, flip chart (newsprint or blackboard), marker pens, or chalk may also be helpful to the groups.

Process:

1. Each individual has fifteen minutes to read the story and answer the eleven questions about the story. Each person may refer to the story as often as needed but may not

---

[4]Ibid., pp. 24–32.

confer with anyone else. Each person should circle "T" if the answer is clearly true; "F" if the answer is clearly false; or "?" if it isn't clear from the story whether the answer is true or false.

2. After fifteen minutes each small group makes the same decisions using group consensus. No one should change his or her answers on the individual questions. The ground rules for group decisions are:

   a. Group decisions should be made by consensus. It is illegal to vote, trade, average, flip a coin, etc.

   b. No individual group member should give in only to reach agreement.

   c. No individual should argue for his own decision. Instead, he should approach the task using logic and reason.

   d. Every group member should be aware that disagreements may be resolved by facts. Conflict can lead to understanding and creativity if it does not make group members feel threatened or defensive.

3. After thirty minutes of group work, the exercise leader should announce the correct answers. Scoring is based on the number of correct answers out of a possible total of eleven. Individuals are to score their own individual answers, and someone should score the group decision answers. The exercise leader should then call for:

   a. The group-decision score in each group

   b. The average individual score in each group

   c. The highest individual score in each group

4. Responses should be posted on the tally sheet. Note should be taken of those groups in which the group score was (1) higher than the average individual score (2) higher than the best individual score. Groups should discuss the way in which individual members resolved disagreements and the effect of the ground rules on such behavior. They may consider the obstacles experienced in arriving at consensus agreements and the possible reasons for the difference between individual and group decisions.

The story:

A businessman had just turned off the lights in the store when a man appeared and demanded money. The owner opened a cash register. The contents of the cash register were scooped up, and the man sped away. A member of the police force was notified promptly.

Statements about the story:

1. A man appeared after the owner had turned off his store lights.	T	F	?
2. The robber was a man.	T	F	?
3. A man did not demand money.	T	F	?
4. The man who opened the cash register was the owner.	T	F	?
5. The store owner scooped up the contents of the cash register and ran away.	T	F	?
6. Someone opened a cash register.	T	F	?
7. After the man who demanded the money scooped up the contents of the cash register, he ran away.	T	F	?
8. While the cash register contained money, the story does *not* state *how much*.	T	F	?
9. The robber demanded money of the owner.	T	F	?
10. The story concerns a series of events in which only three			

persons are referred to: the owner of the store, a man who demanded money, and a member of the police force.   T   F   ?

11. The following events in the story are true: someone demanded money, a cash register was opened, its contents were scooped up, and a man dashed out of the store.   T   F   ?

Tally Sheet

GROUP NUMBER	GROUP SCORE	AVG. INDIVIDUAL SCORE	BEST INDIVIDUAL SCORE	GROUP SCORE BETTER THAN AVG. INDIV.?	GROUP SCORE BETTER THAN BEST INDIV.?

EXERCISE:
POWER AND POLITICS

Goals:

1. To gain some insights into your own power needs and political orientation

2. To examine some of the reasons people strive for power and what political strategies can be used to attain it

Implementation:

Directions: Answer each question below with "mostly agree" or "mostly disagree," even if it is difficult for you to decide which alternative best describes your opinion.

	Mostly agree	*Mostly disagree*
1. Only a fool would correct a boss's mistakes.	_____	_____
2. If you have certain confidential information, release it to your advantage.	_____	_____
3. I would be careful not to hire a subordinate with more formal education than myself.	_____	_____
4. If you do somebody a favor, remember to cash in on it.	_____	_____

5. Given the opportunity, I would cultivate friendships with powerful people.

6. I like the idea of saying nice things about a rival in order to get that person transferred from my department.

7. Why not take credit for someone else's work? They would do the same to you.

8. Given the chance, I would offer to help my boss build some shelves for his or her den.

9. I laugh heartily at my boss's jokes, even when they are not funny.

10. I would be sure to attend a company picnic even if I had the chance to do something I enjoyed more that day.

11. If I knew an executive in my company was stealing money, I would use that against him or her in asking for favors.

12. I would first find out my boss's political preferences before discussing politics with him or her.

13. I think using memos to zap somebody for his or her mistakes is a good idea (especially when you want to show that person up).

14. If I wanted something done by a coworker, I would be willing to say "If you don't get this done, our boss might be very unhappy."

15. I would invite my boss to a party at my house, even if I didn't like him or her.

16. When I'm in a position to, I would have lunch with the "right people" at least twice a week.

17. Richard M. Nixon's alleged bugging of the Democratic headquarters would have been a clever idea if he hadn't been caught.

18. Power for its own sake is one of life's most precious commodities.

19. Having a high school named after you would be an incredible thrill.

20. Reading about job politics is as much fun as reading an adventure story.

Interpretation of scores:

Each statement you check "mostly agree" is worth one point toward your power and political orientation score. If you score 16 or over, it suggests that you have a strong inclination toward playing politics: A high score of this nature would also suggest that you have strong needs for power. Scores of 5 or less would suggest that you are not inclined toward political maneuvering and that you are not strongly power driven.

The customary caution is again in order. This questionnaire is designed primarily to encourage you to introspect about the topic of power and politics. The questionnaire lacks the scientific validity of a legitimate, controlled test.

EXERCISE:

LEADERSHIP QUESTION-NAIRE

Goal:

To evaluate oneself in terms of the leadership dimensions of task orientation and people orientation

Implementation:

1. Without prior discussion, fill out the Leadership Questionnaire. Do *not* read the rest of this until you have completed the test.
2. In order to locate yourself on the Leadership-Style Profile Sheet, you will score your own questionnaire on the dimensions of task orientation (T) and people orientation (P).
3. The scoring is as follows:
   a. Circle the item number for items 8, 12, 17, 18, 19, 30, 34, and 35.
   b. Write the number 1 in front of a *circled item number* if you responded S (seldom) or N (never) to that item.
   c. Also write a number 1 in front of *item numbers not circled* if you responded A (always) or F (frequently).
   d. Circle the number 1's which you have written in front of the following items: 3, 5, 8, 10, 15, 18, 19, 22, 24, 26, 28, 30, 32, 34, and 35.
   e. *Count the circled number 1's.* This is your score for the level of your concern for people. Record the score in the blank following the letter P at the end of the questionnaire.
   f. *Count the uncircled number 1's.* This is your score for your concern for the task. Record this number in the blank following the letter T.
4. Next look at the Leadership Style Profile Sheet on p. 454 and follow the directions.

Variations:

1. Participants can predict how they will appear on the profile prior to scoring the questionnaire.
2. Paired participants already acquainted can predict each other's scores. If they are not acquainted, they can discuss their reactions to the questionnaire items to find some bases for this prediction.
3. The leadership styles represented on the profile sheet can be illustrated through role playing. A relevant situation can be set up, and the "leaders" can be coached to demonstrate the styles being studied.
4. Subgroups can be formed of participants similarly situated on the shared leadership scale. These groups can be assigned identical tasks to perform. The work generated can be processed in terms of morale and productivity.

LEADERSHIP QUESTIONNAIRE

Name _____   Group _____

Directions: The following items describe aspects of leadership behavior. Respond to each item according to the way you would most likely act if you were the leader of a work group. Circle whether you would most likely behave in the described way: always (A), frequently (F), occasionally (O), seldom (S), or never (N).

A F O S N   **1.** I would most likely act as the spokesperson of the group.
A F O S N   **2.** I would encourage overtime work.
A F O S N   **3.** I would allow members complete freedom in their work.
A F O S N   **4.** I would encourage the use of uniform procedures.
A F O S N   **5.** I would permit the members to use their own judgment in solving problems.
A F O S N   **6.** I would stress being ahead of competing groups.
A F O S N   **7.** I would speak as a representative of the group.
A F O S N   **8.** I would needle members for greater effort.
A F O S N   **9.** I would try out my ideas in the group.
A F O S N   **10.** I would let the members do their work the way they think best.
A F O S N   **11.** I would be working hard for a promotion.
A F O S N   **12.** I would tolerate postponement and uncertainty.
A F O S N   **13.** I would speak for the group if there were visitors present.
A F O S N   **14.** I would keep the work moving at a rapid pace.
A F O S N   **15.** I would turn the members loose on a job and let them go to it.
A F O S N   **16.** I would settle conflicts when they occur in the group.
A F O S N   **17.** I would get swamped by details.
A F O S N   **18.** I would represent the group at outside meetings.
A F O S N   **19.** I would be reluctant to allow the members any freedom of action.
A F O S N   **20.** I would decide what should be done and how it should be done.
A F O S N   **21.** I would push for increased production.
A F O S N   **22.** I would let some members have authority which I could keep.
A F O S N   **23.** Things would usually turn out as I had predicted.
A F O S N   **24.** I would allow the group a high degree of initiative.
A F O S N   **25.** I would assign group members to particular tasks.
A F O S N   **26.** I would be willing to make changes.
A F O S N   **27.** I would ask the members to work harder.
A F O S N   **28.** I would trust the group members to exercise good judgment.
A F O S N   **29.** I would schedule the work to be done.
A F O S N   **30.** I would refuse to explain my actions.
A F O S N   **31.** I would persuade others that my ideas are to their advantage.
A F O S N   **32.** I would permit the group to set its own pace.
A F O S N   **33.** I would urge the group to beat its previous record.
A F O S N   **34.** I would act without consulting the group.
A F O S N   **35.** I would ask that group members follow standard rules and regulations.

T _____   P _____

T-P LEADERSHIP STYLE PROFILE SHEET

Name _____   Group _____

Directions: To determine your style of leadership, mark your score on
the *concern for task* dimension (T) on the left-hand arrow below. Next,
move to the right-hand arrow and mark your score on the *concern for
people* dimension (P). Draw a straight line that intersects the P and T
scores. The point at which that line crosses the *shared leadership* arrow
indicates your score on that dimension.

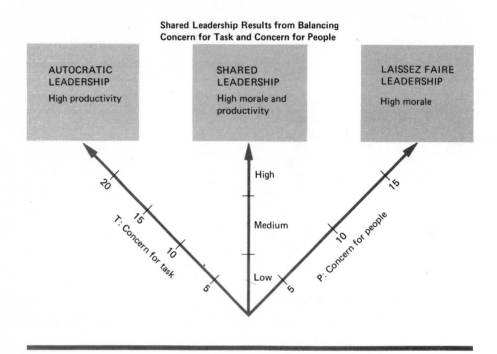

Shared Leadership Results from Balancing
Concern for Task and Concern for People

AUTOCRATIC
LEADERSHIP

High productivity

SHARED
LEADERSHIP

High morale and
productivity

LAISSEZ FAIRE
LEADERSHIP

High morale

THE MANAGEMENT PROCESSES AND ORGANIZATION THEORY: A MACRO PERSPECTIVE OF ORGANIZATIONAL BEHAVIOR

MANAGEMENT PROCESSES

A FRUSTRATED GROUP MANAGER*

John Doughtery had a successful career with Arnold Products, Inc., rising to vice president and general manager of the Cole Division. Then three years ago he changed jobs for a big raise in pay and what he thought was a better management challenge. He became group vice president of industrial products for AFT Industries. In his previous job he had full command over all the management processes, i.e., he had a major input into strategic plans, was responsible for making key decisions, and was a major force in shaping the controls of the division. He took pride in the fact that during the last five years under his management, sales had more than doubled, reaching $130 million, and profits had tripled. Now, three years later at AFT, he is very frustrated and is beginning to question whether he made the right career decision. To an outside consultant John has identified several causes of his frustration. For example, his decision latitude has not expanded and in some ways is actually narrower than it was in his previous job. Although he is nominally responsible for five divisions with sales of a half a billion dollars, because of the wide diversity of the products, technology, and markets, the key decisions and strategies are made at the division level, not at his higher group level. His management role is unclear. All he knows is that his responsibility and authority are completely out of balance. He feels responsible for the various divisions under him (in fact his bonus depends on their performance), yet he does not really feel he can give the divisional managers direct orders or take specific corrective action. More than once, the CEO has bypassed him and gone directly to his division managers on important matters. John feels this undercuts his authority and makes his job more difficult and frustrating. With certain positions at least, such as in a group executive position held by John Doughtery, the classic management processes are not always clearly defined and executed.

*Adapted from James H. Ransom, "The Group Executive's Job: Mission Impossible?" *Management Review,* March 1979, pp. 9–10.

457

458

THE MANAGEMENT
PROCESSES AND
ORGANIZATION THEORY:
A MACRO PERSPECTIVE OF
ORGANIZATIONAL BEHAVIOR

So far the chapters in the book have progressed from very micro-oriented individual variables of organizational behavior (perception, personality, motivation, and learning) to dynamic, more group-oriented variables of organizational behavior (communication, conflict and stress, power and politics, and leadership). In this part of the book a macro—management and organization—perspective of organizational behavior is taken. Thus, an inductive approach (specific micro perspective to a more general macro perspective) is followed in the study of organizational behavior. The initial chapter in this macro-oriented part of the book is concerned with the general management processes.

The management field is generally recognized to be much broader than, and has been an identifiable academic discipline much longer than, the field of organizational behavior. Figure 16-1 shows how the theoretical orientations of management have changed through the years and how organizational behavior fits into the management picture. In the last few years, however, many organizational behavior theorists, as well as curriculum designers in schools of business, are beginning to subsume the management processes

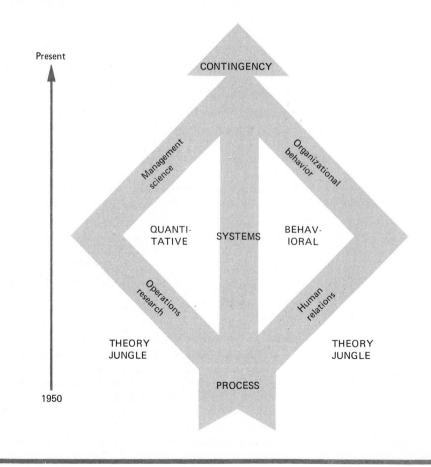

**Figure 16-1
The approaches to management and their relationships through time.
(*Source:* Fred Luthans, "The Contingency Theory of Management: A Path Out of the Jungle," *Business Horizons*, June 1973, p. 69. Used with permission.)**

under organizational behavior. This, of course is the approach taken here. In particular, this chapter gives most attention to the classical principles and the dynamic processes of management. Then, following the model in Figure 16-1, the more recent developments in the quantitative, systems, and contingency approaches to management are briefly summarized. The major thrust of this chapter is to provide a management framework for the behavior of organizational participants. The management processes have many indirect implications for the better understanding, prediction, and control of human behavior in organizations.

CLASSICAL MANAGEMENT PRINCIPLES

The pioneering theorists in the management field first attempted to identify universal management functions and then to establish fundamental principles. Henri Fayol is most closely associated with this classical approach. He first presented his views at the International Mining and Metallurgical Congress held in 1900.[1] However, it was not until 1949 that his book *General and Industrial Management* was translated into English and became part of the mainstream of American management theory.[2]

Fayol identified five functions of management: planning, organizing, command, coordination, and control. Other pioneering management theorists offered essentially the same functions but gave them slightly different names. For example, in 1937 Luther Gulick described the management process as POSDCORB. This acronym stands for planning, organizing, staffing, directing, coordinating, reporting, and budgeting.[3] More recently, managerial processes have served as the conceptual framework for widely used principles of management textbooks. George Terry uses planning, organizing, actuating, and controlling, and Koontz and O'Donnell use planning, organizing, staffing, directing, and controlling.[4]

After determining appropriate names to attach to the various management functions, the classical theorists attempted to formulate universal principles. In his *Elements of Administration*, Lyndall Urwick listed twenty-nine such principles.[5] Figure 16-2 summarizes them. They include most of the concepts in the classical approach. However, the four principles that emerge as most representative of the classical approach and are most relevant to organizational behavior are: (1) unity of command; (2) equal

---

[1] For a discussion of Fayol's early work, see Henry H. Albers, *Principles of Management*, 4th ed., Wiley, New York, 1974, pp. 23–24.

[2] Henri Fayol, trans. by Constance Storrs, *General and Industrial Management*, Pitman, London, 1949.

[3] Luther Gulick, "Notes on the Theory of Organization," in Luther Gulick and Lyndall Urwick (eds.), *Papers on the Science of Administration*, Institute of Public Administration, New York, 1937, p. 13.

[4] George Terry, *Principles of Management*, 6th ed., Irwin, Homewood, Ill., 1972; and Harold Koontz and Cyril O'Donnell, *Management*, 6th ed., McGraw-Hill, New York, 1976.

[5] Lyndall Urwick, *The Elements of Administration*, Harper, New York, 1943.

460

THE MANAGEMENT
PROCESSES AND
ORGANIZATION THEORY:
A MACRO PERSPECTIVE OF
ORGANIZATIONAL BEHAVIOR

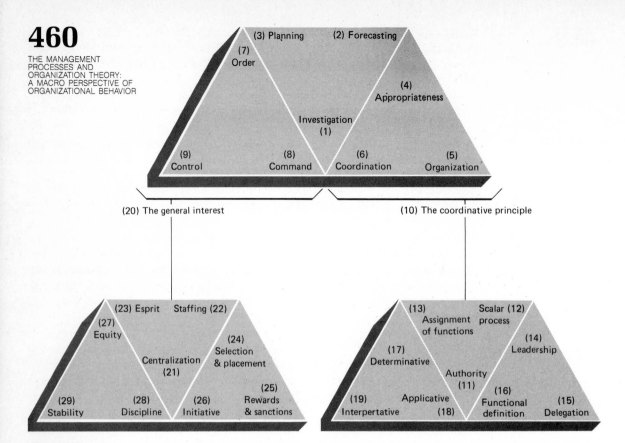

**Figure 16-2
Urwick's elements
of administration.
(Source: Adapted
from Lyndall
Urwick, *The
Elements of
Administration*,
Harper & Row,
New York, 1943, p.
119.)**

authority and responsibility; (3) limited span of control; and (4) delegation of routine matters.

Unity of command

The principle of unity of command states that each participant in the formal organization should be responsible to, and receive orders from, only one superior. Fayol stressed this principle above all others. He felt that if it is violated, "authority is undermined, discipline is in jeopardy, order disturbed and stability threatened."[6] The principle is closely associated with military organization.

An interesting contrast to unity of command is the scientific management pioneer Frederick W. Taylor's concept of functional foremanship. Taylor proposed that an individual worker be directly responsible to, and take orders from, as many as five different superiors. Each supervisor was a specialized expert in one function of the operation. Taylor was convinced that this inverted organizational arrangement would lead to maximum productivity. In "Shop Management," he advocated the functional plan as follows:

---

[6]Fayol, op. cit., p. 24.

Throughout the whole field of management the military type of organization should be abandoned, and what may be called the "functional type" substituted in its place. . . . If practicable, the work of each man in the management should be confined to the performance of a single leading function.[7]

Fayol answered Taylor's functional idea of management in these words:

For myself I do not think that a shop can be well run in flagrant violation of [unity of command]. Nevertheless, Taylor successfully managed large-scale concerns. How, then, can this contradiction be explained? I imagine that in practice Taylor was able to reconcile functionalism with the principle of unity of command. . . . I think it dangerous to allow the idea to gain ground that unity of command is unimportant and can be violated with impunity.[8]

Other classical theorists, such as Urwick, have also emphasized the importance of unity of command over functionalization.[9] The solution to the dilemma is usually found in the more modern concept of *staff*, which is discussed in Chapter 18.

Equal authority and responsibility

Equal authority and responsibility is a time-honored management principle. It means that if managers are charged with the responsibility of accomplishing a given task, they must be given the commensurate authority to carry it out. An example is supervisors who are given the responsibility of keeping within a given budget. According to the principle, they should also have the authority to influence every item in the budget. If they do not have influence, say, over certain overhead items, these items should be divorced from their responsibility. Some of the newer responsibility-accounting techniques discussed in the next chapter are a direct reflection of this classical principle.

Urwick emphatically states:

To hold a group or individual accountable for activities of any kind without assigning to him or them the necessary authority to discharge that responsibility is manifestly both unsatisfactory and inequitable. It is of great importance to smooth working that at all levels authority and responsibility should be coterminous and coequal.[10]

The principle is complicated by the staff concept. Moreover, committee management and dual and functional authority structures also severely test the applicability of this classical principle. In Chapter 19 the project and

---

[7]Frederick W. Taylor, "Shop Management," in *Scientific Management*, Harper, New York, 1947, p. 99. Original copyright held by Taylor in 1911.

[8]Fayol, op. cit., pp. 69–70.

[9]For example, see Lyndall Urwick, *The Load on Top Management—Can It Be Reduced?* Urwick, Orr, London, 1954, p. 28.

[10]Urwick, *The Elements of Administration*, op. cit., p. 46.

462

THE MANAGEMENT
PROCESSES AND
ORGANIZATION THEORY:
A MACRO PERSPECTIVE OF
ORGANIZATIONAL BEHAVIOR

matrix organization structures will be shown to complicate equal authority and responsibility even further.

Limited span of control

Span of control is defined as the number of subordinates directly reporting to a superior. Even in antiquity, there was concern over the proper span of control. An interesting passage in the Bible, Book of Exodus, Chapter 18, relates "Moses sat to judge the people: and the people stood by Moses from the morning unto the evening." Jethro, Moses' father-in-law, viewed this with a critical eye. He noted the span-of-control implications of Moses' methods and warned him, "The thing thou doest is not good. Thou will surely wear away, both thou, and this people that is with thee: for the thing is too heavy for thee; thou are not able to perform it thyself alone." Jethro then proposed an organization with a much more limited span of control. Moses heeded the advice and "chose able men out of all Israel, and made them heads over the people, rulers of thousands, rulers of hundreds, rulers of fifties, and rulers of tens."

The classical process theorists were in general agreement with Jethro that there should be a limited number of subordinates reporting to a superior. They even made the fatal mistake of attaching precise numbers to the optimum span. A military management expert, Sir Ian Hamilton, a British general in World War I, is given credit for one of the first systematic analyses of span of control. After thoroughly studying military units, he concluded that each span should range between three and six subordinates. He reasoned that the average human brain can effectively handle only three to six other brains, and that "the nearer we approach the supreme head of the whole organization, the more we ought to work towards groups of three; the closer we get to the foot of the whole organization (the Infantry of the Line) the more we work towards groups of six."[11]

Hamilton's ideas on limiting the span were perpetuated by other classical theorists such as V. A. Graicunas. A management consultant, Graicunas figured out a mathematical formula that gave the exact number of relationships in a span of control. He emphasized that the number of social relationships was more crucial to analyzing span of control than merely the number of subordinates. For example, the simple organization in Figure 16-3 shows six different relationships but only two subordinates. Graicunas calculated the number of relationships as follows:

1. X to Y and X to Z are two direct-single relationships.
2. X to Y, with Z present, and X to Z, with Y present, are two direct-group relations.
3. Finally, Z to Y and Y to Z are two cross-relationships.

The total of the direct-single, direct-group, and cross-relationships in Figure 16-3 comes to six.

Under the formula provided by Graicunas, the number of relationships

---

[11]Sir Ian Hamilton, *The Soul and Body of an Army*, Doran, New York, 1921, p. 230.

in a span of control increases at a tremendous rate. For instance, twelve subordinates under a superior yield over 20,000 relationships, and twenty subordinates result in over 10 *million* relationships. The implication that Graicunas was trying to show is obvious. Twenty thousand or ten million relationships would be an impossible burden for effective management. Armed with this type of logic, the classical theorists concluded. "No superior can supervise directly the work of more than five or, at the most, six subordinates whose work interlocks."[12]

Delegation of routine matters

The classical principle of delegation states that decisions should be made at as low an organization level as possible. Accordingly, top management should not be making decisions on routine matters that could be effectively handled by first-line supervision. Once again, this principle can be traced to ancient times. The passage from Exodus, cited earlier, also contains a directive for delegation. "And they judged the people at all seasons: the hard cases they brought unto Moses, but every small matter they judged themselves." This, of course, also hints of Frederick Taylor's exception principle, which stated that managers should control by giving attention to the exceptions. All classical theorists advocated delegation but recognized that it was not easily accomplished. Mooney and Reiley noted, "One of the tragedies of business experience is the frequency with which men, always efficient in anything they personally can do, will finally be crushed and fail under the weight of accumulated duties that they do not know and cannot learn how to delegate."[13]

The major reason it takes courage to delegate is that delegation does not absolve one from responsibility. The fear of being ultimately responsible may prevent delegation. Fayol recognized the existence of this fear but condemned it. He stated:

Responsibility is feared as much as authority is sought after, and fear of responsibility paralyses much initiative and destroys many good qualities. A good leader should possess and infuse into those around him courage to accept responsibility.[14]

---

[12]Urwick, *The Elements of Administration*, op. cit., pp. 52–53.

[13]James D. Mooney and Alan C. Reiley, *Onward Industry!*, Harper, New York, 1931, p. 39.

[14]Fayol, op. cit., p. 22.

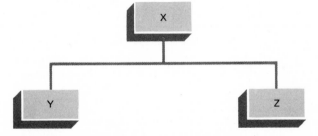

Figure 16-3 Simple organization structure.

464

THE MANAGEMENT
PROCESSES AND
ORGANIZATION THEORY:
A MACRO PERSPECTIVE OF
ORGANIZATIONAL BEHAVIOR

One way of solving the delegation-responsibility question would be as Fayol suggested—with executive courage and leadership. Another approach would be to change the attitude of superiors regarding the capabilities of their subordinates. If one assumes that people are basically lazy, must be closely controlled, and do not want responsibility, i.e., Douglas McGregor's famous Theory X, it is only logical that the superior would be reluctant to delegate. On the other hand, if one believes that people react in the way they are treated, work better under self-control, and will actually thrive under the challenge of responsibility, i.e., McGregor's famous Theory Y, delegation becomes much easier. The classical theorists never really addressed themselves to this type of behavioral analysis. Nevertheless, from a behavioral standpoint, delegation is undoubtedly the most forward-thinking classical principle.

A critique of the classical approach

The classical approach has been vehemently attacked by the other schools of management thought. The critics ask the legitimate question, what progress has been made since Fayol's perceptive analysis at the beginning of the century? To be sure, Fayol made a very significant, if not the most significant, contribution to an overall theory of management. However, since Fayol, the classical theorists seem excessively concerned with semantic problems of what to call the functions for example, "directing" or "commanding," "budgeting" or "planning," and "reporting" or "controlling." Furthermore, the sacred principles have generally turned out to have neither empirical validity nor universal applicability.

Universal truths?   Perhaps the most legitimate criticism of the classical theorists was that they passed off their ideas as universal truths. Each "principle" has been empirically shown not to be applicable to *all* organizational situations. In fact, in some cases the principles even contradict one another. An example is span of control. Numerous surveys have revealed that highly successful organizations have spans that would cause classical theorists to shudder. Mason Haire, a behaviorally oriented theorist, calls Graicunas's analysis of social relationships "just plain silly." He explains, "Making the superior responsible in any direct sense for all the relationships between and among his subordinates seems to extend unduly the functions of the executive."[15]

Herbert A. Simon, a well-known management theorist and recent Nobel Prize winner, was one of the early critics of the universal, classical principles. A major portion of his book *Administrative Behavior* was devoted to discounting the classical principles of specialization, hierarchy, and limited span of control.[16] He noted that unity of command is often inconsistent with specialization and cited the following cases:

[15]Mason Haire, "Biological Models and Empirical Histories of the Growth of Organizations," in Mason Haire (ed.), *Modern Organization Theory: A Symposium of the Foundation for Research on Human Behavior,* Wiley, Inc., New York, 1959, p. 295.

[16]Herbert A. Simon, *Administrative Behavior,* 2d ed., Macmillan, New York, 1957, pp. 20–36.

For example, if an accountant in a school department is subordinate to an educator, and if unity of command is observed, then the finance department cannot issue direct orders to him regarding the technical, accounting aspects of his work. Similarly, the director of motor vehicles in the public works department will be unable to issue direct orders on care of motor equipment to the fire truck driver.[17]

After a detailed analysis, Simon concluded that the classical principles "cannot be more than proverbs."[18] In more recent years the situational or contingency approach to management has evolved to directly counter the universal principles approach. The last section of this chapter spells out what is involved in this new contingency approach.

Lack of behavioral sensitivity in the classical approach In addition to the criticism aimed at universality, fault is also found with the classicists' lack of behavioral sensitivity. The classical theorists are accused of making too simple and mechanistic assumptions. The following summarizes the classical assumptions concerning what top management must do to be successful. It need only:

1. Know what it wants done;
2. Arrange a structure in which the various tasks are exactly dovetailed;
3. Provide for coordination through common superiors or some other formal arrangement;
4. Issue the necessary orders down through the chain of command; and
5. See that each person is held accountable for his part of the work.[19]

The classicists assumed that if these conditions were met, there would be a smooth-running organization. Any minor obstacles could be overcome by management leadership. In reality, of course, things are not quite this simple. One major reason is the extreme complexity of the human being. For instance, there are motivation and behavior problems that may be compounded, instead of solved, by the classical principles. For example, one of the best-known organizational behavior theorists, Chris Argyris, notes that "the formal organizational principles make demands of relatively healthy individuals that are incongruent with their needs. Frustration, conflict, failure, and short time perspective are predicted as resultants of this basic incongruency."[20] Such dynamics were discussed in Chapter 13 on conflict and stress.

Defense of the classical principles Defenders of the classical principles accuse their critics of not fully understanding their content or intent. For example, Harold Koontz claims that the Argyris analysis is a classic case of misunderstanding and misapplication. He states, "Argyris has simply proved that wrong principles badly applied will lead to frustration; and

---

[17]Ibid., p. 24. Also see Herbert A. Simon, "Decision Making and Administrative Organization," *Public Administration Review*, Winter 1944, pp. 16–30.

[18]Ibid., p. 44.

[19]Ernest Dale, *Management: Theory and Practice*, 3d ed., McGraw-Hill, New York, 1973, p. 176.

[20]Chris Argyris, *Personality and Organization*, Harper, New York, 1957, p. 74.

466

THE MANAGEMENT
PROCESSES AND
ORGANIZATION THEORY:
A MACRO PERSPECTIVE OF
ORGANIZATIONAL BEHAVIOR

every management practitioner knows this to be true!"[21] There is no doubt that those who argue against the classical approach carefully select the principles they use to demonstrate their points. This is especially true of unity of command and limited span of control. Equal authority and responsibility and delegation are often conveniently overlooked when condemning classical ideas.

The classical approach is still widely used and staunchly defended by practitioners and academicians. For example, in a survey conducted by the American Management Association, medium and large-sized companies were asked what management concepts were particularly useful to them. A great majority responded with one or more of the classical principles. Almost half the large companies stated that they had found the principle of equal authority and responsibility of value, and more than two-thirds mentioned one or more of the classical principles.[22] Harold Koontz, among others, has defended these principles. In his noted article "The Management Theory Jungle" he wrote:

Those who feel that they gain caste or a clean slate for advancing a particular notion or approach often delight in casting away anything which smacks of management principles. Some have referred to them as platitudes, forgetting that a platitude is still a truism and a truth does not become worthless because it is familiar.[23]

Some of the defense of the classical approach seems completely justified. However, part of the problem is delineating what is to be included as classical and what is not. A blanket criticism of all classical principles merely because they are old and familiar is neither logical nor desirable. On the other hand, the defenders must face up to the question of whether the classical principles are still relevant and applicable to organizations in the 1980s and beyond. One necessary modification is to make the management processes more dynamic. The following section presents such a dynamic approach.

A dynamic process

To argue over the naming or the number of management functions and to search for universal principles is certainly of limited value to the study of organizational behavior. However, the management process, whatever the exact names of the functions or the nature of the principles, can serve a useful purpose in the study of organizational behavior if the static classical approach is made more dynamic. The basic purpose of any theory is to better understand the given phenomenon or concept. To better understand the management processes, dynamism must replace the static nature of the

---

[21]Harold Koontz, "The Management Theory Jungle," *Academy of Management Journal*, December 1961, p. 185.
[22]Ernest Dale, *Organization*, American Management Association, New York, 1967, p. 41.
[23]Koontz, op. cit., p. 184.

classical approach. One step toward making the process framework more dynamic is to incorporate feedforward and feedback communication. Henry Albers suggests such a dynamic process, which consists of decision making, communication, and control.[24] Figure 16-4 summarizes this approach.

A manager occupying a position involving a superior-subordinate relationship makes various kinds of decisions. Planning, organizing, and coordination are some general examples. If the process stopped at this stage, it would be only a static approach. It would not differ from the classical approach except for its combining of the functions under the general classification of decision making. To make the static model dynamic, there must be a systems integration of feedforward and feedback communication. Once managers make planning decisions or other kinds of decisions, they must communicate them forward to subordinates. Types of feedforward communication range from the lifting of an eyebrow to a sophisticated, computerized information system monitoring inputs. After receiving the communication, the subordinate performs. To complete the dynamic process, feedback communication about subordinate performance must be obtained by the manager. Types of feedback vary from simple observation to the profit and loss statement. Using feedback communication, the manager makes a control decision. If feedback indicates that planning or organizing decisions are not being carried out in actual practice, the decision to alter the original plan or organization may be made. Another decision may be to motivate or reinforce subordinates by involving them through more partici-

---

[24]Albers, op. cit., pp. 43–45.

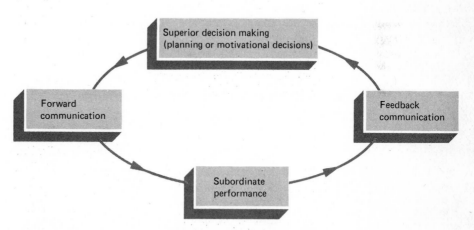

Figure 16-4
The dynamic management process. The dynamic management process begins with planning decisions setting forth previously nonexistent behavioral norms. These norms are then communicated to subordinate personnel. Performance information is relayed back to the superior, who may make motivational or control decisions if behavior is not in accord with the norms of the planning decisions. (*Source:* Henry H. Albers, *Principles of Management*, 3d ed., Wiley, New York, 1969, p. 90. Used with permission.)

468

THE MANAGEMENT
PROCESSES AND
ORGANIZATION THEORY:
A MACRO PERSPECTIVE OF
ORGANIZATIONAL BEHAVIOR

pation in the decision-making process or providing them feedback about individual performance. Such control decisions are then communicated forward, and the entire process continually repeats itself. Normally, the dynamic process occurs in the sequence described. However, Albers points out that there are exceptions. For example, "Decisions involving motivation are often made without regard to particular plans. Some plans are not activated by the communication function because they may not now be pertinent."[25]

The dynamic process approach described above seems to lead to effective understanding of what management is all about. Presenting the processes of decision making, communication, and control in a dynamic systems framework provides insights into the quantitative, the behavioral, and, most directly, the systems approaches to management. Such a dynamic process can also be incorporated into the contingency approach and, overall, is more relevant to the study of organizational behavior.

THE QUANTITATIVE APPROACH

As shown in Figure 16-1, the modern quantitative approach is often referred to as *management science*. It focuses primarily on the management processes from the perspective of mathematical models and quantitative techniques. Frederick Taylor's scientific management was a forerunner, but mathematical techniques and operations research (OR) models best represent the modern quantitative approach.

Mathematical techniques

There is little question that mathematical techniques have made an important contribution to the practice of management in the last several years. Most of the math techniques take the form of models, which fall more appropriately under the heading of operations research, covered in the next section. This section is more directly concerned with general mathematical techniques.

Applied rather than pure mathematics is most relevant to management decision making. Statistical probability can be particularly effective when applied to the risk type of decision. Many managers have only a limited amount of empirical information or experience on the basis of which to make a choice. The exact amount of information depends upon the thoroughness of the data gathering and real-world constraints. The degrees of information and experiences available to managers can be represented by the certainty, risk, and uncertainty types of decisions. Mathematical techniques can be analyzed with reference to these three categories.

Certainty Certainty decisions are very simple because for each alternative there is a certain outcome. Although certainty decisions are fairly

---

[25]Ibid., p. 44.

common for lower-level managers, mathematics does not help much in making them. The traditional techniques of habit, standard operating procedures, and classical structure are just as effective. In some certainty decisions where there are numerous alternatives to choose from, however, calculus and certain mathematical programming techniques can be of assistance.

Risk   Risk decisions are more difficult to make than certainty decisions. There is only limited information and experience, and there are many possible outcomes for each alternative. Most important management decisions at middle and upper levels are risk decisions. The traditional methods break down when applied to these decisions. It is with risk decisions that the mathematical technique of probability makes its biggest contribution.

Two types of probability can be applied to risk decisions, objective statistical probability and subjective probability. Objective statistical probability is a precise mathematical technique that permits the decision maker to calculate possible outcomes and make inferences. The probability calculation is based upon past experience. Tossing a coin provides a simple example of the method and has implications for statistical probability.

A person tosses an unbiased, balanced coin 100 times. The outcome of the 100 tosses is 50 heads and 50 tails. With this experience, the decision maker will assign a probability of .5 that, on the 101st toss, the coin will show a head (or a tail).

The coin tossing example represents an ideal situation for the manager. Unfortunately, most management decision makers in a modern organization do not have so much or such relevant experience as does the coin tosser. Furthermore, the coin tosser can be pretty sure that half the time the hundred-first toss will be heads. Yet if he gets several tails in a row, it will take little time and effort on his part to toss the coin 100 more times and to end up with fifty heads. In other words, it may take a great number of outcomes in order for the probability to work itself out. Typically, management decision makers must place all their eggs in one basket, the next outcome. They do not have the time or resources to let the probability work itself out. In short, objective statistical probability has certain realistic constraints which cannot and should not be overlooked. Yet, despite the limitations, statistical probability, when properly applied and interpreted, has proved to be a very effective tool in helping managers make risk decisions.

Besides utilizing the calculation of objective statistical probability, many decision makers rely on subjective probability assignment. This represents more of an educated guess than a mathematical computation as to what the outcome of a decision will be. Basing their judgment on some type of experience, managers will formally or informally guess what the probable outcome of choosing a given alternative will be. Obviously, relying too heavily on subjective probability assignments can become very risky. Many social and behavioral factors can also enter into subjective probability.

470

THE MANAGEMENT
PROCESSES AND
ORGANIZATION THEORY:
A MACRO PERSPECTIVE OF
ORGANIZATIONAL BEHAVIOR

Nevertheless, subjective probability is more effective than reliance on chance alone.

Uncertainty Uncertainty decisions are the most complex type of decision. No meaningful experience or probability of outcomes can be assigned for extreme cases of uncertainty. It follows that mathematical techniques are useless in true cases of uncertainty. However, when decisions lie between risk and uncertainty, certain mathematical techniques can be applied. Two of the more common are minimax analysis and Bayes' procedure. Under minimax, the decision maker attempts to calculate the worst outcome that can possibly occur for each alternative. In Bayes' procedure the decision maker utilizes the concept of expected value and assumes that each possible outcome has an equal chance of occurring. These techniques show some potential promise, but by and large, mathematics is most useful when applied to risk, not certainty or uncertainty, decisions.

Operations research modeling techniques

Operations research (OR) has become almost synonymous with the quantitative approach to management, but it is practically as broad in scope as mathematics. Frederick Taylor's scientific management was the forerunner of OR, but its recognized beginning was during World War II. OR differs from scientific management in taking a broader perspective and in making more extensive use of mathematically based models. Iconic (scaled reproductions) or analogue (one set of properties to represent another set) models can be used, but generally OR models are symbolic or mathematical in nature.

Applications of OR Specific applications of OR include inventory, resource allocation, and waiting line problems. In the certainty type of inventory situations. Economic Order Quantity (EOQ) models are very precise and lead to optimum results. On the other hand, where the inventory variables are less certain (risk and uncertainty), only a satisficing (one that is satisfactory or good enough), rather than a maximizing, solution can be obtained through operations research.

Resource-allocation problems are especially adaptable to the more sophisticated mathematical models. Every organization operates with limited resources. The management problem is one of allocating the given resources properly so as to attain the desired objectives. Linear programming is widely used for this purpose. It utilizes simultaneous algebraic equations to represent allocation variables. Some of the more common variables include machine capacities, storage space, and transportation routes. Solutions to the equations give the optimum allocations according to the algebraic statement of the payoff criterion. The effectiveness of linear programming depends on the degree to which the decisional problem is linear. Recently, effective nonlinear models have also been developed.

Queuing models are used to help solve waiting line problems. A service type of operation that faces an irregular demand will produce situations where there are lax periods and periods when there is overcrowding and waiting in line. Examples include maintenance on machinery, trucks at a loading dock, customers at a supermarket, students at registration, and patients in a hospital emergency room. Waiting time is costly to the organization. Costs are incurred from the time wasted by those standing in line and by personnel who have nothing to do during slack periods. Queuing models which incorporate mathematical techniques allocate time, personnel, and equipment. The model will also determine priorities and assign probabilities to minimize the costs of waiting. To help solve the more complex waiting problems, managers have turned to simulation techniques for more satisfactory results.

Quantitative approach in perspective

Operations research and the quantitative approach as a whole should not be thought of as a panacea for all the problems of management. Henry H. Albers cautions, "Operations research like other innovations in human history, has had its share of zealots proclaiming the dawn of a new management order. Executives should be wary of attempts to make operations research sound as though miracles were somehow possible through the magic of higher mathematics."[26] Despite the potential oversell of the quantitative approach, there is little question that it has made a substantial contribution to more effective certainty and risk types of decisions, especially in the management processes of planning and control. The quantitative approach does provide more and better alternatives for management decision making. When constructing a model of the decisional problem under consideration, management is forced to make a logical analysis which stresses goals and measures of effectiveness. However, it must be remembered that these techniques only aid the decision maker. The quantitative approach is not the whole of management but, instead, provides very effective techniques for certain management problems.

THE SYSTEMS APPROACH

The systems approach to management, currently very popular, often gives the impression of being extremely new and different. The truth is that systems theory is not new at all. A systems viewpoint has been developed and used in the natural and physical sciences for years.[27] Moreover, systems concepts were indirectly utilized, to varying degrees, by management pioneers such as Frederick W. Taylor. His analysis of human-machine interactions is one example. Operations research and information theory, initiated in the late 1940s, also incorporated a systems viewpoint. However,

---

[26]Ibid., p. 388.

[27]A classic article specifically using the term *systems theory* appeared three decades ago in Ludwig von Bertalanffy, "General Systems Theory: A New Approach to the Unity of Science," *Human Biology*, December 1951, pp. 302–312. The paper was originally presented at the 47th Annual Meeting of the American Philosophical Association, Eastern Division, Dec. 29, 1950.

472

THE MANAGEMENT
PROCESSES AND
ORGANIZATION THEORY:
A MACRO PERSPECTIVE OF
ORGANIZATIONAL BEHAVIOR

the emphasis given today to the direct study, analysis, and operation of management as a system is relatively new.[28]

In 1956, Kenneth Boulding wrote a now famous article titled "General Systems Theory: The Skeleton of Science."[29] It described the general nature and purpose of and needs for a systems approach to all scientific phenomena. Boulding felt there was a need for a systematic, theoretical framework which would describe general relationships of the empirical world. He carefully pointed out that the purpose of General Systems Theory (GST) is not "to establish a single, self-contained 'general theory of practically everything' which will replace all the special theories of particular disciplines."[30] Rather, the goal is to reach a happy medium between the "specific that has no meaning and the general that has no content. . . . It is the contention of the General Systems Theorists that this optimum degree of generality in theory is not always reached by the particular sciences."[31] This viewpoint has been adopted by the systems approach to management.

Levels of systems

Under a GST approach there are recognized levels of systems complexity. Boulding classified nine such levels.[32]

1. The most basic level is the static structure. It could be termed the level of *frameworks*. An example would be the anatomy of the universe.
2. The second level is the simple dynamic system. It incorporates necessary predetermined motions. This could be termed the level of *clockworks*.
3. The next level would be a cybernetic system characterized by automatic feedback control mechanisms. This could be thought of as the level of the *thermostat*.
4. The fourth level is called the "open system." It is a self-maintaining structure and is the level where life begins to differentiate from nonlife. This is the level of the *cell*.
5. The fifth level can be termed the genetic-societal level. It is typified by the *plant* and occupies the empirical world of the botanist.
6. The next is the *animal* system level, which is characterized by increased mobility, teleological behavior, and self-awareness.
7. The seventh level is the *human* level. The major difference between the human level and the animal level is the human's possession of self-consciousness.
8. The next level is that of *social organizations*. The important unit in social organization is not the human per se but rather the organizational role that the person assumes.
9. The ninth and last level is reserved for *transcendental* systems. This allows for ultimates, absolutes, and the inescapable unknowables.

---

[28]Albers, op. cit., 1st ed., 1961, presented the management process from a systems viewpoint, but the 1963 book by Richard A. Johnson, Fremont E. Kast, and James E. Rosenzweig, *The Theory and Management of Systems*, McGraw-Hill, New York, is probably the most widely known approach which specifically analyzed management from a systems viewpoint.

[29]Kenneth Boulding, "General Systems Theory: The Skeleton of Science," *Management Science*, April 1956, pp. 197–208.

[30]Ibid., p. 197.

[31]Ibid.

[32]Ibid., pp. 202–205.

At present, varying degrees of knowledge exist at each of these levels. Each level is more developed than the one preceding it. For example, much knowledge exists at the static level; most disciplines have very good descriptive static models. However, even this first level is not completely developed (e.g., the theory of cataloging and indexing is still not complete). In each succeeding level in the hierarchy, there is more and more incompleteness. In fact, beyond the second level, comprehensive theoretical models are very rare. At the very complex human and social organization levels, Boulding felt twenty-five years ago that there are not even the rudiments of meaningful theoretical systems. This is changing with the development of the recent theories of organizational behavior.

Application of systems analysis

As a fundamental principle, the systems approach is quite basic. It simply means that everything is interrelated and interdependent. A system is composed of elements that are related and dependent upon one another and that, when in interaction, form a unitary whole. Thus, by definition, almost any phenomenon can be analyzed or presented from a systems viewpoint. Biological, physical, economic, and cultural-social systems are examples.

As an approach to management, "systems" encompasses both general and specialized systems and closed and open analysis. A general systems approach to the management process can be concerned with formal organization and technical, sociopsychological, and philosophical concepts. Specific management systems analysis includes areas such as organization structure, job design, accounting, computerized information, and planning and control mechanisms. Actual occupational positions are occupied by systems analysts, who are in great demand by all types of up-to-date organizations.

In theorizing, observing, and analyzing, either a closed- or open-systems approach can be taken. A closed-systems perspective is closed-loop. No external input is recognized. Such a closed-systems approach is relatively easy to accomplish with the proper assumptions and a commonsense philosophy. Katz and Kahn write that the use of this approach requires two major assumptions, namely:

. . . that the location and nature of an organization are given by its name; and that an organization is possessed of built-in goals—because such goals were implanted by its founders, decreed by its present leaders, or because they emerged mysteriously as the purposes of the organization system itself.[33]

The second approach is to apply an open-systems concept in the development of an original theory and design and then to implement it in practice. Katz and Kahn depict the organization as an energetic input-output system that is flagrantly open in its interaction with the environment. The common characteristics of all open systems are the following:[34]

---

[33]Daniel Katz and Robert L. Kahn, *The Social Psychology of Organizations*, Wiley, New York, 1966, p. 14.

[34]Ibid., pp. 19–29.

474

THE MANAGEMENT
PROCESSES AND
ORGANIZATION THEORY:
A MACRO PERSPECTIVE OF
ORGANIZATIONAL BEHAVIOR

1. The *input of energy* from the environment
2. The *through-put* or transformation of the imported energy into some product form
3. The *exporting of the product* back into the environment
4. A *reenergizing of the system* from sources in the environment
5. *Negative entropy,* which helps the system survive by importing more energy from the environment than is expended
6. The *feedback* of information which helps the system maintain a steady state or homeostasis
7. The tendency for *differentiation* and elaboration because of subsystem dynamics and the relationship between growth and survival
8. The existence of *equifinality* whereby the system can reach the same final state from different initial conditions and by different paths of development

In modern management analysis, both closed- and open-systems approaches are taken. However, the classical theorists recognized only a closed-systems viewpoint; they did not design and implement from an open-systems standpoint. Only the closed-systems aspects of existing organizations were sometimes emphasized by the classical theories. This closed-systems approach concentrated on internal relationships and consistency, which were represented by principles such as unity of command, span of control, and equal authority and responsibility. The closed-systems approach ignores effects of the environment. The more recent open-systems approach recognizes the input of the environment but does not functionally relate it to management processes that lead to goal attainment. The contingency approach to management attempts to do the latter and takes up where the open-systems approach leaves off.

THE CONTINGENCY APPROACH

Theorists of the classical, quantitative, and systems approaches to management have not integrated the environment and often assume that their concepts and techniques have universal applicability. For example, the classical theorist often assumes that strategic planning applies to all situations; the quantitative expert generally feels that linear programming can be used under all conditions; and the systems advocate tends to emphasize the need for computerized information flows in all situations. On the other hand, practicing managers are finding out that a particular concept or technique from the various approaches just does not work effectively in their situation. The theorists accuse practitioners of not applying the concept or technique properly and the practitioners accuse the theorists of being unrealistic. The contingency approach does incorporate the environment and attempts to bridge this existing theory-practice gap.[35]

---

[35]See: Fred Luthans, *Introduction to Management: A Contingency Approach*, McGraw-Hill, 1976. This book, especially Chapter 2, contains an expanded discussion of all aspects of contingency management. For a more sophisticated treatment of contingency management, see: Fred Luthans and Todd I. Stewart, "A General Contingency Theory of Management," *Academy of Management Review*, April 1977, pp. 181–195.

The *if-then* management contingency

A contingent relationship can be thought of simply as an *if-then* functional relationship. The "if" represents environmental variables and the "then" represents the management variables. For example, *if* prevailing social values are oriented toward nonmaterialistic, free expression and the organization employs professional personnel in a high technology operation, *then* a participative, open leadership style would be most effective for goal attainment. On the other hand, *if* prevailing social values are oriented toward materialism and obedience to authority and the organization employs unskilled personnel working on routine tasks, *then* a strict, authoritarian leadership style would be most effective for goal attainment. In order for such contingency relationships to be part of contingency management and serve as effective guidelines for practitioners, they must be empirically validated. In addition, although the environment variables are usually independent and the management concepts and techniques are usually dependent, the reverse can also occur. In some cases management variables are independent and the environment variables are dependent. For example, *if* a very participative, open leadership style is instituted by top management, *then* personnel will respond by exhibiting self-control and responsible social values. Although it is recognized that it is possible for management concepts and techniques to affect the environment in the systems interaction sense, contingency management generally treats the environment as independent (the "if's") and the management concepts and techniques as dependent (the "then's").

A framework for general contingency management

Figure 16-5 summarizes a simple if-then conceptual framework for contingency management. As shown, the environmental variables are along the horizontal axis of the matrix and the management variables are along the vertical. Maximum goal attainment is ensured with this two-dimensional matrix. The cells in the matrix represent an empirically derived data base of functional relationships. Thus, if a diagnosis reveals a certain situation (one or a combination of the "ifs"), then it would be contingently related to the appropriate management technique leading to goal attainment. The empirically derived functional relationships would be obtained from research and would be stored in the cells of the matrix.

To date, of course, this contingency management approach represented by the two-dimensional matrix is only a theoretical framework. To begin to operationalize such an approach, a three-dimensional model as shown in Figure 16-6 seems necessary. The third dimension recognizes different levels of performance effectiveness. Thus, depending on the extent of the data base (information stored in the cells of the matrix, which is derived from research), if any two variables are known, the third can be predicted. In other words, in an identifiable situation where the manager wants to maximize performance, the matrix would reveal what management techniques and approaches should be used. Or, given a certain situation and the application

476

THE MANAGEMENT
PROCESSES AND
ORGANIZATION THEORY:
A MACRO PERSPECTIVE OF
ORGANIZATIONAL BEHAVIOR

of a certain management technique, the matrix could predict what level of performance would result.

Such an approach to contingency management as depicted by the three-dimensional matrix is dependent upon the ability to diagnose the situation and the extent and accuracy of the data base. Whether this can ever be done or not in any meaningful way is still being debated. However, it should be pointed out that as far as diagnosing the environment, the survey techniques being developed in economics, technological forecasting, market research, and organization development could be equally applicable to contingency management. And as far as the data base is concerned, the contingency-based models and research in the areas of task design (covered in Chapter 8), leadership (Chapter 15), and organization structure (Chapter 19) could already make a substantial contribution, and other areas are also beginning to make contributions. Obviously, a major challenge for the future would be to fill in the numerous gaps that currently exist in the data base.

Realistically to operationalize the contingency framework would require the use of computer modeling and simulation techniques and analysis. For example, computer programming would be needed to allow environmental input into a stored data base that would then output specific recommendations for the actual practice of management. Preliminary work by Stewart

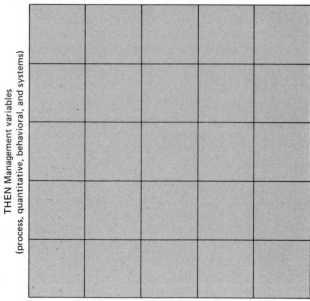

**Figure 16-5
A conceptual framework for contingency management. (Source: Fred Luthans, Introduction to Management: A Contingency Approach, McGraw-Hill, New York, 1976, p. 48. Used with permission.)**

THEN Management variables
(process, quantitative, behavioral, and systems)

IF Environment variables
(external—social, technical, economic, politcal/legal)
(internal—structure, processes, technology)

and Luthans indicates that this computer-assisted capability is definitely possible to accomplish.[36] Only time will tell, but contingency management certainly seems to offer considerable promise for the future of both management theory and practice.

SUMMARY

Management pioneers such as Henri Fayol and Lyndall Urwick initiated the search for a theoretical base for management. This classical approach identified certain functions of management and universal principles such as unity of command, equal authority and responsibility, limited span of control, and delegation of routine matters. The breakdown of the universality assumption and a lack of behavioral sensitivity have led to much criticism of the classical approach. A more dynamic approach incorporating decision making, feedforward and feedback communication, and control leads to

---

[36]Todd I. Stewart and Fred Luthans, "Operationalizing the Contingency Management Framework by the Use of Computer Programming and Information Systems Analysis," working paper, Department of Management, University of Nebraska, Lincoln, 1980.

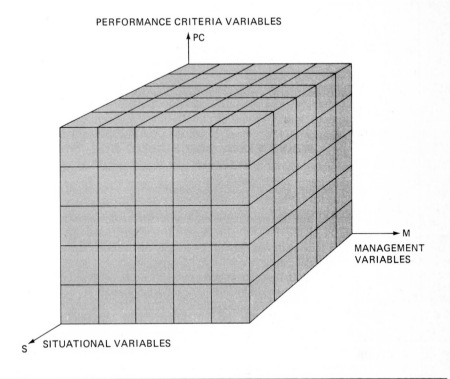

**Figure 16-6
A three-dimensional general contingency framework.
(Source: Fred Luthans and Todd I. Stewart, "A General Contingency Theory of Management,"** *Academy of Management Review,* **April 1977, p. 189.)**

478

THE MANAGEMENT
PROCESSES AND
ORGANIZATION THEORY:
A MACRO PERSPECTIVE OF
ORGANIZATIONAL BEHAVIOR

better understanding of the management processes. The quantitative approach uses mathematical and operations research techniques to solve decision problems. This approach forces logical analysis and generates decision alternatives but is not the whole of management. Systems is the most recently established approach to management and can be viewed from a general systems theory standpoint or a systems analysis standpoint. A systems approach stresses the interrelatedness and interdependency of the parts with the whole. The open-systems perspective recognizes the input of the external environment and serves as a point of departure for contingency management. The contingency approach has emerged out of the dissatisfaction with the universality assumption and the need to incorporate the environment into management theory and practice. The contingency approach uses "if-then" functional relationships where the "if's" represent environmental variables and the "then's" consist of management concepts and techniques that lead to goal attainment. A two-dimensional matrix can be an effective conceptual framework for contingency management, but to operationalize the approach a third dimension reflecting different levels of performance is needed. Preliminary research and development indicates that such an approach can potentially contribute to the more effective practice of management.

QUESTIONS FOR DISCUSSION AND REVIEW

1. Which theoretical approach to management do you believe is the best? Defend your choice.
2. Are the classical process approach and the accompanying principles of any value to management today? Why or why not?
3. Explain the systems approach in your own words.
4. What is contingency management? How can it contribute to the theory and practice of management?

CASE:
KNOW IT FOR THE TEST, BUT DO IT THE OLD WAY

Tom James, the manager of a large supermarket, was taking an organizational behavior course in the evening program at the local college. The professor had given an interesting but disturbing lecture the previous night on the various approaches to the management processes. Tom had always thought that management involved just planning, organizing, and controlling. Now this professor was saying that management could also be thought of as quantitative models, systems theory and analysis, and even something called *contingency relationships.* Tom had always considered himself a good manager, and his record with the supermarket chain proved it. He thought to himself, "I have never used operations research models, thought of my store as an open system, or developed or utilized any contingency relationships. By doing a little planning ahead, organizing the store, and making sure things got done, I have been a successful manager. That other stuff just does not make sense. All that professor was trying to do was complicate things. I guess I'll have to know it for the test, but I'm sticking with my old plan-organize-and-control approach to managing my store."

1. Critically analyze Tom's reasoning.
2. If you were the professor and you knew what was going through Tom's mind, what would you say to Tom?
3. Explain, if possible, how each of the approaches discussed in the chapter could apply to the management of a supermarket.

CASE:
A HAND-TIED MANAGER

Henry Steed was a trainmaster for a large railroad. A trainmaster is assigned the responsibility of supervising the movement of trains over a particular region. His main job is to make sure the train is on schedule. When it's not, the blame is placed right on his shoulders. Yet Henry does not have the responsibility for the maintenance of the roadbed nor for engine assignments for the particular trains. He has received a lot of criticism lately from his boss because the trains in the region have not been maintaining their schedules. Often the trains have stalled on Big Deer Hill, located in the south end of his region. Henry gets upset at the criticism he is getting and feels that the blame really lies in the poor condition of the track: the engineer cannot approach the hill at sufficient speed to be able to get the train over the hill. Another problem is that the engines that are assigned to the trains on this run do not have sufficient horsepower to make the grade without stalling. The end result is that trains must wait until additional engines can be found to push the freight trains over the grade. This situation is greatly affecting the productivity of the division and top management says that things had better change and soon. Henry is at a loss as to what to do. He feels his hands are tied and he can't properly exercise his managerial functions.

1. Do you agree with Henry? Is there anything he can do to solve the problem?
2. Use the various approaches to management to explain and help solve this manager's problem.

DECISION MAKING
AND CONTROL

CALCULATORS FOR DECISION MAKING AND CONTROL*

Recently, a lightning storm started a fire in the Kootenai National Forest in Montana. The U.S. Forest Service sent, as part of the fire-fighting package, several hand-held calculators. The calculators had specific memory chips containing programs that could predict the fire's path, based on diverse variables such as the current fire intensity, rate of current speed, and wind direction. The Forest Service aimed to give valuable information to those who are on the scene fighting the fire. The problem heretofore had been the difficulty in finding out information about the fire and then using that information to plot where equipment and personnel should be allocated to maximize their effectiveness. Conditions on the scene would change relatively quickly negating the effectiveness of the "main fire command" in decision making and control. The calculators proved to be a big help to those on the scene in making timely, accurate decisions. Decisions that before had taken several hours to make were now being made in minutes. The success of the Kootenai experiment led the Forest Service to purchase an additional 2000 calculators for future fire fighting uses. The Forest Service is convinced that this tool can improve decision making and control.

---

*Adapted from "Customizing the Calculator," *Business Week,* Aug. 6, 1979, p. 66.

In this chapter the important management processes of decision making and control are given attention. A process is any action which is performed by management to achieve organizational objectives. Thus, decision making and control are managerial processes because they are actually performed by managers. They are also organizational processes because they transcend the individual manager to have an effect on organizational goals. These two management and organization processes are a vital part of the organization system and have extremely important behavioral implications. First, the overall nature of the decision process and various types of decisions are explored. This is followed by a discussion of behavioral models and of the implications of decision making and some behavioral and computer-based decision techniques. The last half of the chapter is devoted to control. After clearing up some misconceptions about control, the process is carefully defined and its basic elements are emphasized. The last part gives specific attention to the behavioral implications of control.

THE NATURE OF DECISION MAKING

Decision making is almost universally defined as *choosing between alternatives*. It is closely related to all the traditional management functions. For example, when a manager plans, organizes, and controls, he or she is making decisions. The classical theorists, however, did not generally present decision making this way. Fayol and Urwick were concerned only with the decision process to the extent that it affects delegation and authority, while Frederick W. Taylor alluded to the scientific method only as an ideal approach to making decisions. Like most other aspects of modern organization and management theory, the beginning of a meaningful analysis of the decision-making process can be traced to Chester Barnard. In *The Functions of the Executive*, Barnard gave a comprehensive analytical treatment of decision making and noted, "The processes of decision . . . are largely techniques for narrowing choice."[1]

Steps in the decision process

Most discussions of the decision process break it down into a series of steps. For the most part, the logic can be traced to the ideas on the stages of thinking developed by John Dewey early in the twentieth century. Dewey outlined three stages of judgment which are analogous to the decision process. "First, there must be a controversy consisting of opposite claims regarding the same objective situation. Second, there must be a process of defining and elaborating these claims. Finally, a decision is made which closes the matter in dispute and serves as a rule or principle for the future."[2]

Herbert A. Simon, probably the best-known and most widely quoted

---

[1]Chester I. Barnard, *The Functions of the Executive*, Harvard, Cambridge, 1938, p. 14.

[2]John Dewey, *How We Think*, Heath, Boston, 1933, p. 120.

482

THE MANAGEMENT
PROCESSES AND
ORGANIZATION THEORY:
A MACRO PERSPECTIVE OF
ORGANIZATIONAL BEHAVIOR

decision theorist, conceptualizes three major phases in the decision-making process. These are:

1. *Intelligence activity.* Borrowing from the military meaning of intelligence, this initial phase consists of searching the environment for conditions calling for decision.
2. *Design activity.* In this second phase, inventing, developing, and analyzing possible courses of action takes place.
3. *Choice activity.* The third and final phase is the actual choice, selecting a particular course of action from those available.[3]

Another comprehensive approach to decision making is systems analysis. Figure 17-1 shows the five steps which Elbing feels affect the management decision maker:

1. A manager inevitably experiences feelings of disequilibrium and regards some situations as problem situations, whether or not he has a clear, rational basis for his identification.
2. His response to the disequilibrium necessarily involves an assumption about the underlying cause, or a diagnosis of the situation, whether or not his diagnosis is rational, systematic, and explicit.
3. His response to the disequilibrium necessarily includes a definition of the problem to be solved, whether his definition of the problem is ambiguous or clear, sound or unsound, explicit or implicit.
4. His response constitutes a selection of method and solution, whether by conscious design or not.
5. Finally, his response also constitutes his implementation of his choice, whether or not it actually leads to the solution of the problem.[4]

Whether expressed in the very simple terms used by Dewey or in more complex systems terms such as those of Elbing, there seem to be identifiable, preliminary steps leading to the choice activity in decision making. The steps become more realistic when they are put into a time framework: "(1) *the past,* in which problems develop, information accumulates, and the need for a decision is perceived; (2) *the present,* in which alternatives are found and the choice is made; and (3) *the future,* in which decisions are carried out and evaluated."[5] Thus, decision making is a dynamic process and what the

**Figure 17-1
Elbing's
decision-making
process. (*Source:
Alvar O. Elbing,
Behavioral
Decisions in
Organizations,
Scott, Foresman,
Glenview, Ill.,
1970, p. 13.*)**

---

[3]Herbert A. Simon, *The New Science of Management Decision,* Harper & Row, New York, 1960, p. 2.

[4]Alvar O. Elbing, *Behavioral Decisions in Organizations,* Scott, Foresman, Glenview, Ill., 1970, p. 13.

[5]Dalton E. McFarland, *Management Principles and Practices,* 4th ed., Macmillan, New York, 1974, p. 262.

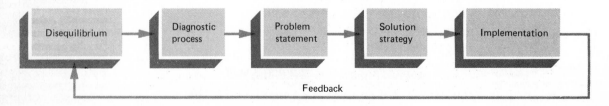

steps are called is not really important. The essential point is that decision making is composed of a series of dynamically related steps.

The scope of the decision process

Decision making incorporates most of the traditional management functions. For example, some management writers equate the process with planning,[6] and others classify planning, motivating, and controlling under decision making.[7] Simon goes all the way and treats decision making as being the same as managing. He states, "In treating decision making as synonymous with managing, I shall be referring not merely to the final act of choice among alternatives, but rather to the whole process of decision."[8] Some theorists have even gone beyond the realm of management to equate decision making with thinking. This idea is implied in Donald W. Taylor's statement that "decision making is that thinking which results in the choice among alternative courses of action."[9]

In this chapter, decision making is interpreted as encompassing the traditional management function of planning and as somewhat similar to problem solving. Problem solving is any goal-directed activity that must overcome some type of barrier to accomplish the goal. Thus defined, problem solving is somewhat broader than decision making, but conceptually it is not so important for the purposes of this chapter. One management writer explains that while the problem-solving process is a significant generator of decision-making behavior, its importance can be overstressed. "For example, overemphasis on problem solving leads to exaggerating the need for getting answers, whereas it may often be more important to find the right question than the right answer."[10] Although these differences do exist between problem solving and decision making, the terms can generally be used interchangeably.

Types of management decisions

There are many types of organization and management decisions. The two most widely recognized classifications include personal and organizational decisions and basic and routine decisions.

Personal and organizational decisions Once again, Chester Barnard was in the vanguard of analyzing, or at least making a point about, the difference between personal and organizational decisions. In his opinion,

---

[6]William H. Newman, Charles E. Summer, and E. Kirby Warren, *The Process of Management*, 3d ed., Prentice-Hall, Englewood Cliffs, N.J., 1972, p. 243.

[7]Henry H. Albers, *Principles of Management*, 4th ed., Wiley, 1974, pp. 43–44.

[8]Simon, op. cit., p. 1.

[9]Donald W. Taylor, "Decision Making and Problem Solving," in James G. March (ed.), *Handbook of Organizations*, Rand McNally, Chicago, 1965, p. 48.

[10]McFarland, op. cit., p. 286.

484

THE MANAGEMENT
PROCESSES AND
ORGANIZATION THEORY:
A MACRO PERSPECTIVE OF
ORGANIZATIONAL BEHAVIOR

the basic difference is that "personal decisions cannot ordinarily be delegated to others, whereas organization decisions can often if not always be delegated."[11] Thus, the manager makes organizational decisions that are aimed at organizational goals and personal decisions that attempt to achieve personal goals. In reality, it is often difficult or even impossible to separate these two aspects of a management decision. Sometimes personal and organizational decisions are compatible and will facilitate each other's goal attainments and sometimes they are incompatible and impede each other's goal attainment.

Basic and routine decisions   Another common way to classify types of decisions is as basic or routine. One writer states, "Basic decisions are those which are unique, one-time decisions involving long-range commitments of relative permanence or duration, large investments, and a degree of importance such that a mistake would seriously injure the organization."[12] Examples of basic decisions in a business firm include decisions which deal with things like plant location, organization structure, wage negotiations, product line, and vertical integration. In other words, most top management policy decisions can be considered basic decisions.

Routine decisions are at the opposite extreme to the basic decisions. They are the everyday, highly repetitive management decisions which by themselves have little impact on the overall organization. However, taken together, the routine decisions play a tremendously important role in the success of an organization. Among examples of routine decisions are an accountant making a decision on a new entry, a production supervisor deciding what the new tool room procedures will be, a personnel manager hiring a new worker, and a salesperson deciding on what territory to cover. Obviously, a very large proportion (most experts estimate about 90 percent) of the decisions made in an organization are of the routine variety. However, the exact proportion of the basic to routine types depends on the level of the organization at which the decisions are made. For example, a first-line supervisor makes practically all routine decisions, whereas the chairperson of the board makes very few routine decisions but many basic decisions.

Classifying decisions into basic and routine categories does not imply that there is a clear distinction between the two. Actually, the difference is only a matter of degree. Basic and routine should be thought of as the two extremes on a continuum. Besides the many organization factors, there are also many personal factors that will determine whether a decision is basic or routine. Experience, motivation, and personality may have a bearing on which type of decision will be made. A lower-level manager faced with a normally routine decision may turn it into a basic decision which has a long-lasting impact on the entire organization.

---

[11]Barnard, op. cit., p. 188.
[12]McFarland, op. cit., p. 268.

BEHAVIORAL IMPLICATIONS OF DECISION MAKING

Why does a decision maker choose one alternative over another? The answer to this question involves decision rationality and behavioral decision models. These are given attention in the following sections.

Decision rationality

Means-ends is the most often used definition of rationality in decision making. If appropriate means are chosen to reach desired ends, the decision is said to be rational. However, there are many complications to this simple test of rationality. To begin with, it is very difficult to separate means from ends because an apparent end may be only a means for some future end. This idea is commonly referred to as the *means-ends chain* or *hierarchy*. Simon points out that "the means-end hierarchy is seldom an integrated, completely connected chain. Often the connection between organization activities and ultimate objectives is obscure, or these ultimate objectives are incompletely formulated, or there are internal conflicts and contradictions among the ultimate objectives, or among the means selected to attain them."[13]

Besides the complications associated with the means-ends chain, it may be that the concept is even obsolete. For example, using open-systems analysis, it has been conceded that disturbances in an equilibrium may actually set up nonrational, goal-seeking behavior.[14] Decision making relevant to the national economy supports this position. Decision makers who seek to make seemingly rational adjustments in the economic system may in fact produce undesirable, or at least unanticipated, end results. Simon also warns that a simple means-ends analysis may have inaccurate conclusions. The following three points should help in avoiding the inherent problems of means-ends analysis:

First, the ends to be attained by the choice of a particular behavior alternative are often incompletely or incorrectly stated through failure to consider the alternative ends that could be reached by selection of another behavior.
Second, in actual situations a complete separation of means from ends is usually impossible.
Third, the means-end terminology tends to obscure the role of the time element in decision making.[15]

One way to clarify means-ends rationality is to attach appropriate qualifying adverbs to the various types of rationality. Thus, *objectively* rational can be applied to decisions that maximize given values in a given

---

[13]Herbert A. Simon, *Administrative Behavior*, 2d ed., Macmillan, New York, 1957, p. 64.

[14]David W. Miller and Martin K. Starr, *The Structure of Human Decisions*, Prentice-Hall, Englewood Cliffs, N.J., 1967, pp. 43–44.

[15]Simon, *Administrative Behavior*, op. cit., p. 65.

486

THE MANAGEMENT
PROCESSES AND
ORGANIZATION THEORY:
A MACRO PERSPECTIVE OF
ORGANIZATIONAL BEHAVIOR

situation. *Subjectively* rational might be used if the decision maximizes attainment relative to knowledge of the given subject. *Consciously* rational might be applied to decisions where adjustment of means to ends is a conscious process. A decision is *deliberately* rational to the degree that the adjustment of means to ends has been deliberately sought by the individual or organization. A decision is *organizationally* rational to the extent that it is aimed at the organization's goals, and *personally* rational if the decision is directed to the individual's goals.[16]

Models of decision-making behavior

There are many descriptive models of rationality-of-choice behavior. In effect, these have become models for much of management decision behavior. The models attempt to describe theoretically and realistically how practicing managers make decisions. In particular, the models strive to determine to what degree management decision makers are rational. The models range from complete rationality, as in the case of the *economic* model, to complete irrationality, as in the case of the *social* model. Figure 17-2 summarizes on a continuum the two major extremes and the in-between Simon model. These models deal specifically with management decision behavior, whereas the various models discussed in Chapter 3 were more concerned with the overall nature of human behavior.

Economic model   The classical economic model—the entrepreneur of classical economics—is perfectly and completely rational in every way. Regarding the entrepreneur's decision-making activities, the following conditions are assumed:

1. The decision will be completely rational in the means-ends sense.
2. There is a complete and consistent system of preferences which allow a choice among the alternatives.
3. There is complete awareness of all the possible alternatives.
4. There are no limits to the complexity of computations that can be performed to determine the best alternatives.
5. Probability calculations are neither frightening nor mysterious.[17]

---

[16]Ibid., pp. 76–77.

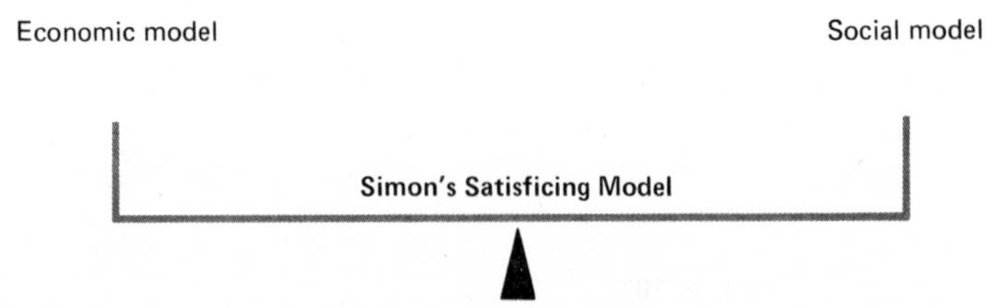

Economic model   Social model

Simon's Satisficing Model

**Figure 17-2
The continuum of
management
decision-making
behavior.**

With this almost infallible ability, the economic person always strives to maximize decisions. In the business firm, decisions will be directed to the point of maximum profit where marginal cost equals marginal revenue (MC = MR).

Most economists do not claim that this depiction is a realistic descriptive model of modern management decision-making behavior. They use this economic model primarily for certain theoretical analyses. For example, one economist points out that the model is "not, as so many writers believe, designed to explain and predict the behavior of real firms; instead it is designed to explain and predict changes in observed prices as effects of particular changes in conditions."[18] On the other hand, some aspects of the model can be useful in describing actual decision-making behavior. For example, a survey of "excellently managed" firms found that short views, innovative sensitivity, marginal costing, and marginal pricing were all common attitudes among the respondents.[19] But except for the few indirect exceptions, the economic model is not realistically descriptive of management decision-making behavior. The major criticism has been summarized as follows:

The theory of the choosing mechanism in economics is completely uninformative on internal structure. The postulates of rationality and goal are given, and behavior is contingent upon environmental or external factors. Economic man, therefore, is an automaton, stripped bare of any of the human characteristics that all real men possess.[20]

Social model   At the opposite extreme from the economic model is the social model of psychology. Sigmund Freud presented humans as bundles of feelings, emotions, and instincts, with their behavior guided largely by their unconscious desires. Obviously, if this were an accurate description, people would not be capable of making rational management decisions.

Although most contemporary psychologists would take issue with the Freudian description of humans, almost all would agree that social influences have a significant impact on decision-making behavior. Furthermore, social pressures and influences may cause managers to make irrational decisions. The well-known conformity experiment by Solomon Asch demonstrates human irrationality.[21] His study utilized several groups of seven to nine subjects each. They were told that their task was to compare the length of lines. All except one of the "subjects" in each group had

---

[17]Ibid., p. xxiii.

[18]Fritz Machlup, "Theories of the Firm: Marginalist, Behavioral, Managerial," *American Economic Review*, March 1957, p. 9.

[19]James S. Earley, "Marginal Policies of 'Excellently Managed' Companies," *American Economic Review*, March 1956, p. 66.

[20]Joseph W. McGuire, *Theories of Business Behavior*, Prentice-Hall, Englewood Cliffs, N.J., 1964, p. 181.

[21]Solomon E. Asch, "Opinions and Social Pressure," *Scientific American*, November 1955, pp. 31–35.

488

THE MANAGEMENT
PROCESSES AND
ORGANIZATION THEORY:
A MACRO PERSPECTIVE OF
ORGANIZATIONAL BEHAVIOR

prearranged with the experimenter to give clearly wrong answers on twelve of the eighteen line-judgment trials. About 37 percent of the 123 naive subjects yielded to the group pressures and gave incorrect answers to the twelve test questions. In other words, more than a third of the experimental subjects conformed to a decision they knew was wrong.

If over one-third of Asch's subjects conformed under "right and wrong," "black and white" conditions of comparing the length of lines, a logical conclusion would be that the real, "gray" world is full of irrational conformists. It takes little imagination to equate Asch's lines with the alternatives of a management decision. There seems to be little doubt of the importance of social influence in decision-making behavior.

There is still much to be learned of the impact of social pressures on decision-making behavior. Certainly, the completely irrational person depicted by Freud is too extreme a case to be useful. On the other hand, as the chapters in this book point out, there is little question of the important role that human behavior does play in management decision making. Some management behavior is irrational but still very realistic. For example, the author and a colleague recently completed two studies that showed that subjects in both laboratory and field settings who did not have computer experience were more influenced in their choice activities by information presented on computer printout paper than they were by information presented on regular stenographic paper.[22] On the other hand, for those subjects with computer experience, the reverse was true. In other words, decision makers are influenced in their choice activities even by what type of format the information is presented to them on. Managers without computer experience may be in awe of the computer and place more value on computer-generated information than is justified, while those with computer experience may be highly skeptical and may underrate the importance of computer-generated information.

Simon's satisficing model   To present a more realistic alternative to the classical economic model, Herbert Simon proposed what he called "administrative man." He felt that management decision-making behavior could best be described as follows:

1. In choosing between alternatives, managers attempt to satisfice or look for the one which is satisfactory or "good enough." Examples of satisficing criteria would be share of the market, adequate profit, and fair price.
2. They recognize that the world they perceive is a drastically simplified model of the real world. They are content with this simplification because they believe the real world is mostly empty anyway.
3. Because they satisfice rather than maximize, they can make their choices without first determining all possible behavior alternatives and without ascertaining that these are in fact all the alternatives.

---

[22]Fred Luthans and Robert Koester, "The Impact of Computer-Generated Information on the Choice Activity of Decision Makers," *Academy of Management Journal*, June 1976, pp. 328–332; and Robert Koester and Fred Luthans, "The Impact of the Computer on the Choice Activity of Decision Makers: A Replication with Actual Users of Computerized MIS," *Academy of Management Journal*, June 1979, pp. 416–422.

4. Because they treat the world as rather empty, they are able to make decisions with relatively simple rules of thumb or tricks of the trade, or from force of habit. These techniques do not make impossible demands upon their capacity for thought.[23]

In contrast to the economic man, Simon's administrative man tries to be rational and maximizing, but he ends up satisficing because he does not have the ability to maximize. The case against maximizing behavior has been summed up by noting that objectives are dynamic rather than static; information is seldom perfect; there are obvious time and cost constraints; alternatives seldom lend themselves to quantified preference ordering; and the effect of environmental forces cannot be disregarded.[24] Simon's model recognizes these limitations. The economic model's assumptions are viewed as unrealistic. But in the final analysis, the difference between the economic model and Simon's model is one of relative degree because, under some conditions, satisficing approaches maximizing, whereas in other conditions satisficing and maximizing are very far apart.

There are many economic, social, and organizational variables which influence the degree to which satisficing becomes maximizing. An example of an economic variable is market structure. The more competitive the market, the more satisficing may approach maximizing. In an agricultural products market situation, satisficing will by necessity become maximizing. A generalization made by economists is that "in perfectly competitive conditions the more nearly a firm approaches the profit maximum the greater are its chances of survival."[25] Thus, it appears that in order to survive in a competitive market situation, the decision maker must make maximizing decisions. In an oligopolistic market situation, e.g., the auto and steel industries, satisficing is quite different from maximizing. Oligopolistic firms can still survive on the basis of adequate profit or share of the market. They do not have to operate at the point where marginal cost equals marginal revenue, and, in fact, they may be unavoidably prevented from maximizing.

Besides the economic market constraints, there are many socially based obstacles which prevent maximization in practice. Some of these social barriers are not consciously recognized by the management decision maker. Examples are resistance to change, desire for status, concern for image, and just plain stupidity. On the other hand, the decision maker may in some cases consciously avoid maximizing. Examples of the latter behavior include decisions which discourage competitive entry or antitrust investigation, restrain union demands, or maintain consumer goodwill.

From an organizational standpoint, there are also formal structural barriers to maximization. The next two chapters will point out both the functional *and* dysfunctional aspects of organization structure. For instance,

---

[23]Simon, *Administrative Behavior,* op. cit., pp. xxv–xxvi.

[24]E. Frank Harrison, *The Managerial Decision-making Process,* Houghton Mifflin, Boston, 1975, p. 69.

[25]J. H. Davies, "Entrepreneurial Behaviour and Market Environment," *Review of Economic Studies,* February 1958, p. 131.

490

THE MANAGEMENT
PROCESSES AND
ORGANIZATION THEORY:
A MACRO PERSPECTIVE OF
ORGANIZATIONAL BEHAVIOR

dysfunctional conflict caused by specialization may impede maximizing decisions. The formal structure is separate from the decision behavior of individual participants. Cyert and March point out that "even if individuals maximize pleasure or expected utility, it does not necessarily follow that organizations maximize profits. Likewise, even if individuals do not maximize, it does not necessarily follow that organizations do not."[26]

Simon claims that his model is based on common sense, introspective knowledge, and research of judgmental processes from the behavioral sciences. Many scholars besides Simon have utilized the concept of satisficing in their analyses. Among them are Cyert and March's substitution of acceptable level of profit norm for profit maximization,[27] Chamberlin's use of the concept of ordinary rather than maximum profit,[28] Dean's criteria that are used to determine a reasonable profit,[29] and Gordon's explicit use of satisfactory profits.[30] Simon, however, was the first to put these ideas together into a descriptive model of management decision making. It seems to be most descriptive of realistic management decision-making behavior.

BEHAVIORALLY ORIENTED DECISION TECHNIQUES

The discussion of the quantitative approach to management in the last chapter briefly covered some important mathematically based decision techniques. These quantitative techniques have contributed to a science of decision making. Not as developed, but potentially as important or even more so, are the behavioral decision techniques. Most of these behavioral techniques, at least traditionally, have revolved around the concept of participation.

Participation as a technique means that individuals or groups are involved in the decision-making process. It can be formal or informal, and it entails intellectual and emotional as well as physical involvement. The actual amount of participation in making decisions ranges from one extreme of no participation, wherein the superior makes the decision and asks for no help or ideas from anyone, to the other extreme of full participation, where everyone connected with or affected by the decision is completely involved. In practice, the degree of participation will be determined by several factors. One management book suggests three: "(1) who initiates ideas; (2) how completely a subordinate carries out each phase of decision making—diagnosing, finding alternatives, estimating consequences, and making the

[26]R. M. Cyert and James G. March, "Organization Factors in the Theory of Oligopoly," *Quarterly Journal of Economics,* February 1956, p. 47.

[27]Ibid.

[28]Edward H. Chamberlin, *The Theory of Monopolistic Competition,* Harvard, Cambridge, 1942, p. 105.

[29]Joel Dean, *Managerial Economics,* Prentice-Hall, New York, 1951, pp. 33–39.

[30]R. A. Gordon, "Short-Period Price Determination in Theory and Practice," *American Economic Review,* June 1948, p. 271.

choice; and (3) how much weight an executive attaches to the ideas he receives."[31] The more there is of each of these factors, the higher will be the amount of participation.

In today's organizations there is much pseudoparticipation. Because of participation's popularity in the early human relations movement, many managers have attempted to incorporate it into their decision-making processes. However, like many other organizational behavior concepts and techniques, participatory techniques often end up being more fiction than fact. As one writer notes: "Some managers speak of developing a 'sense' of participation in their employees. They exhort them to get their 'shoulders to the wheel and all push together.' They try to persuade their people to work more enthusiastically to perform jobs and activities designed and regulated exclusively by management."[32] These are examples of pseudoparticipation. The managers are trying to get their subordinates involved in the task but not in the decision-making process.

Individual, group, and program participation techniques

Participatory techniques can be applied informally on an individual or group basis or on a formal program basis.[33] Individual participation techniques are those in which a subordinate somehow affects the decision making of a superior. Group participation utilizes consultative and democratic techniques. Under consultative participation, the superiors ask for and receive involvement from subordinates, but they maintain the right to make the decision. In the democratic form, there is total participation and the group, not the individual head, makes the final decision by consensus or majority vote.

Examples of formal programs of participation include the autonomous work groups in the sociotechnical projects described in Chapter 8 and also junior boards of executives, collective bargaining between union and management, union-management cooperation committees, Scanlon Plan committees, and suggestion plans. The junior board, first used at McCormick & Company, enables junior executives to participate in top management decision making. Normally, the junior executives are limited to an advisory role. Collective bargaining, defined as the negotiation and administration of an agreement between labor and management over wages, hours, and employment conditions, is generally not associated with participatory techniques of decision making. Yet technically, if the union is a legally elected bargaining agent for the employees, the union participates through collective bargaining in the decisions affecting them. Union-management cooperation committees are formally established to encourage participation of union members in practically all areas of management decision making. Such a committee is usually set up as a last resort to save an organization from closing down.

---

[31]Newman et al., op. cit., 2d ed., 1967, p. 534.

[32]Dale S. Beach, *Personnel*, 2d ed., Macmillan, New York 1970, p. 55.

[33]See: ibid., pp. 567–578, for an expanded discussion of the various types of participation.

492

THE MANAGEMENT
PROCESSES AND
ORGANIZATION THEORY:
A MACRO PERSPECTIVE OF
ORGANIZATIONAL BEHAVIOR

The Scanlon Plan is a special form of labor-management cooperation. The plan, originated by Joseph Scanlon (who was at first with the steel workers union and later MIT) over forty years ago, consists of a system of committees which encourages labor to participate in management decisions. The unique feature of the Scanlon Plan is that the rewards for an individual's successful suggestion are equally divided among all members of the group. A recent comprehensive analysis of the Scanlon Plan tested several hypotheses that were derived out of the extensive literature on the plan over the past thirty years. By examining twenty-three firms that have or had the Scanlon Plan in operation it was concluded that success was positively related to: (1) the average level of participation in decision making reported by employees; (2) the number of years the company had been using the plan; and (3) management's, especially the chief executive officer's, attitudes and expectations of the plan.[34]

Commonly used suggestion plans or boxes are also a formal type of participation program. If employee responses are properly handled and adequately rewarded, the suggestion box can be a very effective method of obtaining participation in the decision-making process from anyone in the organization.

There are many positive and negative attributes of the participatory techniques of decision making. One problem, already mentioned, is the tendency toward pseudoparticipation. This can lead to a boomerang effect regarding employee satisfaction. If the superior claims to want participation from subordinates but never lets them become intellectually and emotionally involved and never utilizes their suggestions, the results may be disastrous. Also, participation can be very time-consuming, and it has the same general disadvantages that are attributed to committees in Chapter 11. From a behavioral standpoint, however, the advantages far outweigh the disadvantages. Most of the benefits are touched upon throughout this book. Perhaps the biggest advantage is that the participation techniques recognize that each person can make a meaningful contribution to the attainment of organizational objectives.

Group decision techniques

Practically all the advances that have been made in decision-making techniques over the past several years have been quantitative in nature and are applied to the routine and sometimes risk types of decisions. To date, only the participative behavioral techniques discussed so far have been available to managers, and there have been only scattered attempts to develop new techniques for helping make the basic and risk-uncertainty types of decisions. Yet it is the latter decisions which provide the major challenge facing modern management. Recently, Delphi and nominal grouping have emerged to offer some help in making basic and risk-uncertainty decisions.

---

[34]J. Kenneth White, "The Scanlon Plan: Causes and Correlates of Success," *Academy of Management Journal*, June 1979, pp. 292–312.

The Delphi technique Although Delphi was first developed by N. C. Dalkey and his associates in 1950 at the Rand Corporation's Think Tank, it has only recently become popularized as a technique to assist in making risk-uncertainty decisions, e.g., doing long-range forecasting. Today, numerous organizations in business, education, government, health, and the military are using Delphi. No decision technique will ever be able to predict the future completely but the Delphi technique seems to be as good a crystal ball as is currently available.

The technique, named after the oracle at Delphi in ancient Greece, has many variations, but generally it works as follows:

1. A panel of experts on the particular problem at hand is drawn from both inside and outside the organization. Usually these panel members are never in face-to-face interaction with one another.
2. Each expert is asked to make *anonymous* predictions. For example, the panelists in one Rand session were asked to estimate the year when 20 percent of the world's food supply would come from ocean farming. Half thought it would occur before the year 2000, the other half thought it would be later.
3. Each panelist then gets a composite feedback of the way the other experts answered the questions.
4. Based upon the feedback, new estimates are made and the process is repeated several times.[35]

A major key to the success of the technique lies in its anonymity. Keeping the responses of panel members anonymous eliminates the problem of "saving face" and encourages the panel experts to be more flexible and thus to benefit from the estimates of others. In the traditional interacting group decision technique, the experts may be more concerned with defending their vested positions than they are with making a good decision. The major objectives of the Delphi process have been summarized by Delbecq, Van deVen, and Gustafson as follows:

1. To determine or develop a range of possible program alternatives
2. To explore or expose underlying assumptions or information leading to different judgments
3. To seek out information which may generate a consensus on the part of the respondent group
4. To correlate informed judgments on a topic spanning a wide range of disciplines
5. To educate the respondent group as to the diverse and interrelated aspects of the topic[36]

Many organizations testify to the success they have had so far with the Delphi technique. McDonnell Douglas Aircraft uses the technique to forecast the future uncertainties of commercial air transportation. Weyerhaeuser, a building supply company, uses it to predict what will happen in the construction business, and Smith, Kline, and French, a drug manufacturer, uses it to study the uncertainties of medicine. TRW, a highly diversified,

---

[35]"Forecasters Turn to Group Guesswork," *Business Week*, Mar. 14, 1970, p. 130.

[36]André L. Delbecq, Andrew H. Van deVen, and David H. Gustafson, *Group Techniques for Program Planning*, Scott, Foresman, Glenview, Ill., 1975, pp. 10–11.

494

THE MANAGEMENT
PROCESSES AND
ORGANIZATION THEORY:
A MACRO PERSPECTIVE OF
ORGANIZATIONAL BEHAVIOR

technically oriented company, has fourteen Delphi panels averaging seventeen members each. The panels suggest products and services which have future marketing potential and predict technological developments and significant political, economic, social, and cultural events. Besides business applications, the technique has been used successfully on various problems in government, education, health, and the military. For example, Delphi was used to obtain predictions concerning the impact of a new land-use policy upon population growth, pollution, agriculture, taxes, etc.,[37] and to help set priorities and objectives for a large professional association.[38] In other words, Delphi can be applied to a wide variety of program planning and decision problems in any type of organization.

The major criticisms of the Delphi technique center on its time consumption, cost, and Ouija-board effect. The third criticism implies that, similar to the parlor game of that name, Delphi can claim no scientific basis or support. To counter this criticism, Rand has attempted to validate Delphi through controlled experimentation. The corporation set up panels of nonexperts who use the Delphi technique to answer questions such as "How many popular votes were cast for Lincoln when he first ran for President?" and "What was the average price a farmer received for a bushel of apples in 1940?" These particular questions were used because the average person does not know the exact answers but knows something about the subjects. The result of these studies showed that the original estimates by the panel of nonexperts were reasonably close to being correct, but with the Delphi technique of anonymous feedback, the estimates greatly improved. Rand Corporation's N. C. Dalkey offers the following conclusion: "We have proved Delphi works, but we must convince the scientific and technical experts that they are doing something significant."[39]

Nominal group technique Closely related to Delphi is the nominal grouping approach of group decision making. Nominal grouping has been used by social psychologists for a couple of decades. A nominal group is simply a "paper group." It is a group in name only because no verbal exchange is allowed between members. In group dynamics research, social psychologists would pit a fully interacting group against a nominal group (a group of individuals added together on paper but not verbally interacting). In terms of number of ideas, uniqueness of ideas, and quality of ideas, research has found nominal groups to be superior to real groups.[40] The general conclusion is that interacting groups inhibit creativity. This, of course,

---

[37]Jerome Kaufman and David H. Gustafson, *Multi-County Land Use Policy Formation: A Delphi Analysis*, Technical Report of the Department of Industrial Engineering, University of Wisconsin, Madison, 1973.

[38]Fred Luthans and Thomas E. Balke, "Delphi Technique Helps Set ASFSA Goals," *School Foodservice Journal*, June 1974, pp. 40–41.

[39]"Forecasters Turn to Group Guesswork," op. cit., p. 134.

[40]The classic study is Donald W. Taylor, P. L. Berry, and C. H. Block, "Does Group Participation When Using Brainstorming Facilitate or Inhibit Creative Thinking," *Administrative Science Quarterly*, vol. 3, June 1958, pp. 23–47. Follow-up studies support their findings.

applies only to idea generation because the interactive effects of group members is known to have a significant effect on other variables. The latter effects were given attention in Chapter 11, on group dynamics.

When the nominal grouping approach is used as a specific technique for decision making in organizations, it has been labeled NGT (nominal group technique) by Delbecq and Van deVen. NGT consists of the following specific steps:

1. Silent generation of ideas in writing
2. Round robin feedback from group members to record each idea in a terse phrase on a flip chart
3. Discussion of each recorded idea for clarification and evaluation
4. Individual voting on priority ideas with the group decision being mathematically derived through rank ordering or rating[41]

The difference between this approach and Delphi is that the NGT members are usually acquainted with one another, have face-to-face contact, and communicate directly with each other. Although more research is needed, there is some evidence that NGT leads to many more ideas than traditional interacting groups and may do as well as or slightly better than groups using Delphi.[42] However, one study did find that NGT groups did not perform as well as interacting groups whose participants were pervasively aware of the problem given the group and where there were no dominant persons who inhibited others from communicating ideas.[43] Thus, as in most of the techniques discussed in the book, there are moderating effects. A review of the existing research literature on Delphi and NGT concluded:

In general, the research on both Delphi and nominal group techniques suggests that they can help improve the quality of group decisions because they mitigate the problems of interacting groups—individual dominance and groupthink. A skillful chairperson, therefore, may adapt these techniques to particular decision-making situations.[44]

Artificial intelligence techniques

Computers, of course, have revolutionized management approaches to certainty-routine types of decisions. In the future, computers may also have a significant impact on the more basic, risk-uncertainty decisions. This possibility lies in the development of artificial intelligence.

The newest generation of computers emphasizes the software (programming), rather than the hardware, aspects. Through new software techniques

[41]Delbecq et al., op. cit., p. 8.

[42]A. H. Van de Ven, *Group Decision-Making Effectiveness*, Kent State University Center for Business and Economic Research Press, Kent, Ohio, 1974.

[43]Thad B. Green, "An Empirical Analysis of Nominal and Interacting Groups," *Academy of Management Journal*, March 1975, pp. 63–73.

[44]David R. Hampton, Charles E. Summer, and Ross A. Webber, *Organizational Behavior and the Practice of Management*, 3rd ed., Scott, Foresman, Glenview, Ill., 1978, p. 258.

496

THE MANAGEMENT
PROCESSES AND
ORGANIZATION THEORY:
A MACRO PERSPECTIVE OF
ORGANIZATIONAL BEHAVIOR

such as heuristic programming, the electronic computer is starting to take over activities formerly reserved for the human brain. Hall observes that "whereas up to now technology has extended or even taken over what men do with their physical equipment—their hands and eyes and legs—with our generation for the first time the computer is providing brain power."[45]

There are many pro and con arguments about the computer's capability to think. Albers, after reviewing both sides, concluded:

Present-day computers can "think" in the sense that they have the capacity to make such logical choices. The programmer provides the instructions as to when and how a choice is to be made; the computer then automatically makes these choices as information is processed. . . . There would appear to be no absolute barrier to the development of computers that simulate the human thinking apparatus.[46]

Although many people fear that a "thinking" computer may take over the world, this idea seems more science fiction than reality. Computers like HAL 9000 in Stanley Kubrick's movie *2001—A Space Odyssey* are possible but not probable. The catch is that computers will never be able to make a value decision (to determine what is ethically right or wrong) unless humans choose to live in a computer culture. But, with heuristic programming capabilities, the computer may be a definite aid in the basic, risk-uncertainty realm of management decision making.

The classic definition of *heuristic* was given by Polya as follows:

Heuristic, or heuretic, or "ars inveniendi" was the name of a certain branch of study, not very clearly circumscribed, belonging to logic, or to philosophy, or to psychology, often outlined, seldom presented in detail, and as good as forgotten today. The aim of heuristic is to study the methods and rules of discovery and inventing. . . . Heuristic, as an adjective, means "serving to discover."[47]

In short, heuristics can be considered a sophisticated technique of controlled trial and error.

When applied to decision making, heuristics combines the systems and behavioral approaches because it considers both major variables and the reactions and feelings of people in the system. "In other words, heuristics allows the decision maker to consider less-than-rational paths and thus preclude frustration when more preferable alternatives are somehow available."[48] The real key for decision making is its adaptability to computer programming.

The traditional algorithmic method of computer programming consists of tracing through each step to a guaranteed solution. The solution is based on input variables. At the other extreme is stochastic programming, which uses trial and error. The stochastic solution is based on intuitive conjecture

---

[45]Douglas T. Hall, "Potential for Career Growth," *Personnel Administration*, May–June 1971, p. 27.

[46]Albers, op. cit., pp. 283–284 and 286.

[47]G. Polya, *How to Solve It*, Princeton, Princeton, N.J., 1945, p. 102.

[48]John G. Hutchinson, *Management Strategy and Tactics*, Holt, New York, 1971, p. 126.

or speculation and is tested against known evidence or measurements. Such an approach has potential for solving long-range, strategy decisions for management. The heuristic approach is in between the algorithmic and stochastic approaches. Heuristic programming uses an exploratory method of solving a problem. It continually evaluates progress and through analysis of results permits determination of the next step leading to solution. This is similar to the way a human thinks and makes a judgment. For example, a person playing chess does not attempt to calculate all future moves every time a piece is moved. This would be virtually impossible. Instead, the human chess player uses judgment, memory, and trial and error to plan the next move.[49] This is how heuristic programming works.

Heuristic programming closely resembles what is known about human thinking processes. It is this almost human capacity that gives heuristic programming nearly unlimited potential applicability and has led Simon to state: "I think you can say that the computer is now showing intuition and the ability to think for itself. Some of us don't see any principles or reason that would prevent machines from becoming more intelligent than man."[50] At present, artificial intelligence is still in its formative stages of development. It has been successfully applied to the development of strategies and countermoves in games like checkers and chess. The fact that it is theoretically possible to develop decision strategies and learn from experience opens up new vistas for application to the basic and risk-uncertainty decisions. Simon has predicted, "There is now good reason to believe that the processes of nonprogrammed decision making will soon undergo as fundamental a revolution as the one which is currently transforming programmed decision making in business organizations."[51] A major factor in this decision-making revolution will undoubtedly be heuristic programming of the computer. Much of the future handling of all types of decisions promises to be largely dependent upon the computer.

THE CONTROL PROCESS

Besides decision making, the other most important and widely recognized function in the management process is control. Like decision making, control has important implications for the study of organizational behavior. For example, Lawler and Rhode note:

The issue of how information and control systems affect behavior is a critical one for anyone interested in the determinants of organizational effectiveness. . . . Information and control systems are such an important part of complex organizations it is impossible to explain much of the behavior that takes place in organizations without examining information and control systems.[52]

---

[49]See *Wall Street Journal*, June 18, 1973, p. 1.

[50]Ibid.

[51]Simon, *The New Science of Management Decision*, op. cit., p. 21.

[52]Edward E. Lawler, III, and John Grant Rhode, *Information and Control in Organizations*, Goodyear, Pacific Palisades, Calif., 1976, p. xiii.

498

THE MANAGEMENT
PROCESSES AND
ORGANIZATION THEORY:
A MACRO PERSPECTIVE OF
ORGANIZATIONAL BEHAVIOR

The first step in the analysis of the control process is to clear up some of the common misconceptions about it. Some of the misconceptions stem from the negativism attached to the common usage of the term. The American cultural value of individual freedom is supposedly threatened by any form of control. Highly simplified, the argument goes that freedom is good and control is bad. Despite this widely held value, the daily life of every American is highly controlled from waking to the ringing of the alarm clock in the morning to watching the 10 or 11 o'clock news at night. Inside as well as outside the organization, today's employees have many rules to follow—where to park, when to punch the time clock or report to the office, how to comply with safety regulations, and what to wear are just a few examples. In addition, there is the controlling atmosphere inherent in the superior-subordinate authority relationship which exists in every formal organization.

More specific behavioral implications of control are given later, but for now it can be said that control per se is not categorically "bad" for the individual. Although they do not readily admit it, most people probably prefer some degree of control over their lives because it gives them some stability and contributes to their general welfare and safety. Nevertheless, the negative connotation of control still exists and is amplified by the ways in which controls have been traditionally set, implemented, and used in formal organizations.

Meaning of control

Despite the many misconceptions about the nature of control, there is, surprisingly, general agreement about its formal definition. Fayol's definition, which he gave in 1916, set a precedent that has been followed through the years and is commonly accepted today. In the very last section of his book, he states: "In an undertaking, control consists in verifying whether everything occurs in conformity with the plan adopted, the instructions issued and principles established. It has for its object to point out weaknesses and errors in order to rectify them and prevent recurrence. It operates on everything, things, people, actions."[53] Most management experts follow the Fayol definition, but more recently, definitions of control have taken on more of a systems orientation. For example, systems writers have the following to say about control: "We shall define control as that function of the system which provides adjustments in conformance to the plan; the maintenance of variations from system objectives within allowable limits."[54] The cybernetic system concept in particular is an important conceptual basis for the organizational control process. Automatic feedback control mechanisms play a significant role in steering the modern organization. The general systems approach emphasizes feedback, which is an inherent part of any

---

[53]Henri Fayol, *General and Industrial Management*, translated by Constance Storrs, Pitman, London, 1949, p. 107.

[54]Richard A. Johnson, Fremont E. Kast, and James E. Rosenzweig, *The Theory and Management of Systems*, 3d ed., McGraw-Hill, New York, 1973, p. 74.

control process. Control decisions are traditionally based upon the feedback that is obtained from accounting information in the upward system of an organization.

The new emphasis is also on the feedforward aspects of control. This feedforward approach recognizes that the feedback process alone is not enough for effective control. The input variables of a system are controlled in a feedforward system. It has been pointed out that "a shift must be made away from emphasis on quickly available data on final results to quickly available data on those input variables that lead to final results. It is a means of seeing problems as they develop and not looking back—always too late—to see why a planning target was missed."[55]

The very existence of the control process implies that the other management processes are not perfect. The tremendous complexity of the modern organization, combined with certain psychological dependencies of personnel on order and stability, makes the control process a necessity. For example, because of an organization's size and complexity, planning decisions do not always work out in practice. Moreover, the organizational communication process can easily break down. A control process is required to anticipate and point out these types of difficulties and to try to get them corrected. In addition, many of the problems at which the control process is aimed are human in nature. An example: "In the absence of control, an individual tends to allow results to stray from plans or orders. Anarchy is more than he can stand, for it permits him to work so poorly that it may trouble his conscience."[56] The behavioral impact of control is much more far-reaching than is implied by this statement. Yet the key to interpreting this statement is the word *absence*. The absence of any organizational controls would probably lead to anarchy and psychological problems because people have learned to depend on various controls in their daily lives. The argument in the behavioral approach to management is not whether controls are to exist but rather how they are to be set and used in the modern organization. The control process per se is necessary for the attainment of objectives and ultimately for the very survival of the organization.

Basic elements of control

Inherent in the definition of control are three basic elements. First, control sets the standards and objectives which serve as the guideline for performance. Second, control measures and evaluates inputs and performance according to the standards and objectives. Third, control takes corrective action in the form of a control decision. Sometimes control is mistakenly equated with only one of the three elements. The control process includes all three elements and is very broad in scope.

Objectives and standards The objectives-and-standards phase of the control process is closely related to the management function of planning.

---

[55]Harold Koontz and Robert W. Bradspies, "Managing through Feedforward Control," *Business Horizons*, June 1972, pp. 25–36.

[56]McFarland, op. cit., p. 393.

500

THE MANAGEMENT
PROCESSES AND
ORGANIZATION THEORY:
A MACRO PERSPECTIVE OF
ORGANIZATIONAL BEHAVIOR

"Every objective, every goal of the many planning programs, every activity of these programs, every policy, every procedure, and every budget become standards against which actual or expected performance might be measured."[57] Control standards and objectives are set for each organizational unit and range from a small work group at the bottom to the governing board at the top.

Traditionally, control units were structurally defined and assigned as a budget area. Recently, because of behavioral influence, the trend has been toward identifying control units by area of responsibility. The responsibility units are often expressed as profit centers. This type of "responsibility accounting" can be traced back to Sloan's profit-centered concept of decentralization, which he installed in General Motors in the 1920s. The philosophy and practice of responsibility-centered control are now beginning to be implemented in most modern organizations. The controllable variables are distinguished from the uncontrollable ones when standards are being set for performance. For example, overhead items (heat, light, water, and depreciation) or union wage rates cannot generally be controlled by middle- or lower-level unit managers. Therefore, these uncontrollable variables would be excluded from their standards for performance.

Measurement and evaluation   Once standards have been set, the next phase of the control process is to measure and evaluate inputs and performance. Measurement for inputs and outcomes may take the form of either personal observation or sophisticated managerial accounting procedures. Personal observation is the most widely used method of measuring in the control process. It is relied upon especially when controlling human performance. For example, a skilled supervisor is "able to judge output by observing the pace of his workers; quality can be evaluated by personally inspecting the work in progress; and an estimate of morale and attitudes results from seeing employees, listening to their spontaneous remarks, and obtaining responses to questions."[58]

Not everyone is capable of obtaining and using observation to measure performance effectively. What the visual sense picks up, the perceptual interpretation, and the reality may be three completely different things, as was discussed in detail in Chapter 4. The complex psychological process of perception greatly influences the use of personal observation as a measuring technique. In addition, the other psychological processes of learning and motivation strongly affect observation. Besides having a complicating psychological impact, personal observation is very time-consuming. Despite these real and potential problems, most management experts maintain that personal observation is one of the best ways to control people.[59]

Traditionally, accounting theory and practice concentrated on providing

---

[57]Harold Koontz and Cyril O'Donnell, *Principles of Management,* 6th ed., McGraw-Hill, New York, 1976, p. 657.

[58]Henry L. Sisk, *Principles of Management,* 2d ed., South-Western Publishing Company, Cincinnati, 1973, p. 649.

[59]Koontz and O'Donnell, op. cit., p. 671.

information for external users. In recent years, the emphasis in accounting has shifted to internal or management usage. Managerial accounting generates much objective information, and it has become a major method of measurement in the control process. Lawler and Rhode note, "In most organizations financial control systems are the most prominent and play a central role in influencing the behavior of individuals both inside and outside organizations."[60]

Corrective control decisions   The third and final element of the control process is corrective action taken in the form of a control decision. Merely setting standards and measuring and evaluating inputs and performance do not achieve control. A control decision must be made in order for the control process to be complete. The third phase occurs in the same place as the first phase—the decision-making center of the dynamic management process. For example, suppose that a deviation from standards is detected by the measuring devices. An evaluation may lead to one of the following conclusions: the standards were set wrong; there is a need to "tighten up" and obtain conformance between standards and inputs or performance; new motivational techniques are needed to gain compliance with standards; or maintenance of the current deviation should be attempted. Each of these possible conclusions requires a corresponding control decision. If the first conclusion is adopted, the decision will be to reexamine present standards and/or make new ones. With the second conclusion, the decision may be to reprimand or fire the personnel involved and put on more pressure. The third conclusion may lead to a decision that installs a new wage-incentive plan or supervisory style. For the fourth conclusion, the decision would be to maintain the status quo and continue to do things as they have been done in the past.

In effect, the manager who is trying to control is like the captain of a ship.[61] The captain receives information on the location and bearing of his ship and then adjusts his course in order to arrive at the planned destination. In a similar manner, the manager receives feedforward or feedback information about the inputs or performance of his unit and then makes a control decision that will accomplish the unit's objectives.

BEHAVIORAL IMPLICATIONS OF CONTROL

The behavioral approach to management has probably caused more concern about control than about any of the other management processes. Much of this concern is a carry-over from the assumption that any form of control restricts individual freedom. The introductory discussion attempted to modify this totally negative attitude toward control. Some forms and degrees of control are essential and are even desired by most people. On the other hand, organizational controls, when put into practice, often create a

---

[60]Lawler and Rhode, op. cit., p. 4.

[61]This analogy is made in Newman et al., op. cit., p. 597.

502

THE MANAGEMENT
PROCESSES AND
ORGANIZATION THEORY:
A MACRO PERSPECTIVE OF
ORGANIZATIONAL BEHAVIOR

situation where personnel attempt to work against, rather than with, the control system. In a typical control process, personnel frequently try to reap the rewards of good results for themselves but shift the blame for poor results to someone else. The N.I.H. factor (not invented here) seems to go into effect whenever anything goes wrong. Some of the specific behavioral opposition to control includes "disagreement with standards, reporting procedures (including the amount, nature, and frequency of reports), cost allocations pertaining to the control systems, and, in some cases, the need for control itself."[62]

Although there is undoubtedly justifiable criticism of the design, implementation, and use of control, there seems to be no legitimate argument against the need for control itself. After all, "An individual's perception of freedom is not necessarily maximized by an absence of control."[63] Controls can create more predictability in a person's own behavior and in the behavior of other relevant persons in the situation. The individual tends to equate predictability with freedom.

In summary, there is nothing behaviorally wrong with the control process per se. The key to organizational effectiveness is to obtain an optimum mix composed of freedom *and* control. Both are necessary, and too much of either may have a detrimental effect on organizational performance. What the exact mix turns out to be depends upon many variables. Retracing the three elements of the control process in terms of their direct impact on behavior should help clarify this analysis.

The impact of standards and objectives on behavior

A fundamental assumption in the behavioral approach to management is that humans generally react negatively to standards imposed from above. Beginning with the findings of the bank wiring room phase of the Hawthorne studies, there has been much evidence supporting this assumption. For example, basing his conclusions upon extensive research findings on the effects of control standards used in industry, William F. Whyte stated that full effort is received from "probably less than 10 percent of the work force. In the sorts of situations we have been describing, the other nine-tenths of the force will refuse, more or less, to respond in full measure."[64] While there are many possible reasons for this situation, part of the problem lies in the negative reaction that employees have to imposed standards.

Why do standards bother organizational personnel? The first chapter suggested that the bank wirers at Hawthorne restricted output because of their fear of unemployment, because they believed management would raise the standard, because they felt they were protecting slower coworkers, and

---

[62]Dan Voich, Jr., and Daniel A. Wren, *Principles of Management*, Ronald, New York, 1968, p. 263.

[63]Theo Haimann and William G. Scott, *Management in the Modern Organization*, Houghton Mifflin, Boston, 1970, p. 445.

[64]William F. Whyte, *Money and Motivation*, Harper & Row, New York, 1955, p. 49.

because tacit approval was given by management. In most respects, these same reasons still hold true today. Some other possibilities for the negative reaction are the following:

1. There may be a lack of understanding of standards because they are imposed without any accompanying explanation of their need and value.
2. Regardless of how carefully standards have been set and flexibility built in, unexpected conditions may make accomplishing the standard difficult or impossible but the person or persons involved get blamed for the poor performance.[65]

Furthermore, often the control standard has become a symbol for all the dysfunctional characteristics of modern bureaucratic organizations. Standards may represent impersonality, abstract rules, and even oppression to organizational personnel.

Nevertheless, standards, objectives, or goals are a necessary part of an effective control process and may be very important to human performance as Chapter 8 pointed out. The following are three suggested ways to make control standards more compatible with human behavior:

1. Standards must be established in such a way that they are recognized as legitimate. This requires that the method of deriving standards must be understood by those affected, and that standards must reflect the actual capabilities of the organizational process for which they are established.
2. The individual organization member should feel that he has some voice of influence in the establishment of his own performance goals. Participants of those affected in the establishment of performance objectives helps establish legitimacy of these standards.
3. Standards must be set in such a way that they convey "freedom to fail." The individual needs assurance that he will not be unfairly censured for an occasional mistake or for variations in performance which are outside his control.[66]

These points indicate that the key to overcoming difficulties and obtaining a positive response to control standards depends on human inputs. The person or persons who are going to be affected by and evaluated according to the standard or objective should have an input into how it is formulated, implemented, and utilized. If the people concerned have this opportunity, they will tend to respond more positively; if they do not, they may react negatively.

The impact of measurement and evaluation on behavior

Organization members may also be dissatisfied with the way they are measured and evaluated under traditional control procedures. The following are some possible reasons for dissatisfaction:

1. Control measures may not be timely enough.

---

[65]Sisk, op. cit., pp. 690–691.

[66]Raymond E. Miles and Roger C. Vergin, "Behavioral Properties of Variance Controls," *California Management Review*, Spring 1966, p. 59.

504

THE MANAGEMENT
PROCESSES AND
ORGANIZATION THEORY:
A MACRO PERSPECTIVE OF
ORGANIZATIONAL BEHAVIOR

2. Control measures only get at the surface; they don't begin to measure all that is being done.

3. Control measures only concentrate on deviations; they don't account for effort.[67]

Typical of the reactions from personnel that express displeasure with traditional control measures and evaluation is the manager of a repair-parts department who stated, "We've no kick about the goals you set. The trouble with the controls is, we don't get credit for the work we do." Another example is the member of a maintenance department who commented, "You can't measure the breakdown that didn't happen."[68]

The key to obtaining a positive reaction to measurement and evaluation is closely tied to the way the standards were set in the first phase of the control process. If the affected person has helped set the standards and if performance is accurately measured against those standards, the reaction will tend to be more positive. Obviously, there are a lot of if's in measurement and evaluation, but a positive impact can be, and is being, accomplished in some modern control systems.

The impact of corrective control decisions on behavior

Whether a small child in the home or an adult employee in a modern organization, people in general dislike being corrected. When the measurement and evaluation reveal that there is a deviation between standards and performance, the people affected sense a threatening and ego-damaging implication that they personally are at fault, so they often react by blaming the control system. Some persons "find it difficult to accept the facts of life, and so develop a sense of frustration. Because a frustrated person needs some relief, it is only natural for him to put part of the blame on the mechanism that tells him he is not as good as he thinks he ought to be."[69] In other words, the control mechanism is blamed for any real or imagined personal failures. Besides their threatening nature and the danger of ego deflation, corrective control decisions openly expose an individual's failures to peers, superiors, and subordinates. This exposure may badly undermine the person's need for social support.

Corrective decisions are a necessary part of the control process. The clue to obtaining a positive reaction lies in the sensitivity and empathy that are required when correcting a person. Chapters 9 and 10 on learning and organizational behavior modification emphasized that if a change in behavior is deemed necessary, reinforcement is more effective than punishment. Positive control of behavior is more effective than negative control. When the control process indicates that inputs or performance are not in accordance with standards, the corrective decision should not only show that something is going wrong; it should also point out why this happened and what is necessary to correct the situation. Furthermore, not all control

[67]Sisk, op. cit., pp. 691–692.

[68]Newman et al., op. cit., p. 626.

[69]Ibid., p. 627.

decisions are corrective in purpose. As noted earlier, decisions may be made to anticipate or to motivate or maintain the status quo.

The impact of budgets on behavior

Budgets are an important special case for the analysis of the behavioral impact of control because they are the target of much criticism from behaviorally oriented management writers. The budget is often pictured as a straitjacket for human behavior and is said to allow no room for initiative, flexibility, or freedom. Most of the research support for this view comes from a classic study on the effect of budgets on supervisory personnel, conducted by Chris Argyris. The study consisted of field research on three small plants, supplemented by other research findings. Major attention was given to the impact that manufacturing budgets have on first-line supervisors. The exploratory approach led Argyris to conclude that at least four human problems can result from budgets:

1. Budget pressure tends to unite the employees against management, and tends to place the factory supervisor under tension. This tension may lead to inefficiency, aggression, and perhaps a complete breakdown on the part of the supervisor.
2. The finance staff can obtain feelings of success only by finding fault with factory people. These feelings of failure among factory supervisors lead to many human relations problems.
3. The use of budgets as "needlers" by top management tends to make each factory supervisor see only the problems of his own department.
4. Supervisors use budgets as a way of expressing their own patterns of leadership. When this results in people getting hurt, the budget, in itself a neutral thing, often gets blamed.[70]

Argyris believes that the reason why budgets have such a negative impact on behavior stems from their pressuring effect on humans. Budgets become devices which pressure individuals into joining groups. A group formed in this way often has objectives which are contrary to the organizational objectives. Argyris described the pattern as follows:

1. First, the individuals sense an increase in pressure.
2. Then they begin to see definite evidences of the pressure. They not only feel it; they can point to it.
3. Since they feel this pressure is on them personally, they begin to experience tension and general uneasiness.
4. Next, they usually "feel out" their fellow workers to see if they too sense the pressure.
5. Finding out that others have noted the pressure, they begin to feel more at ease. It helps to be able to say, "I'm not the only one."
6. Finally, they realize that they can acquire emotional support from each other by becoming a group. Furthermore, they can "blow their top" about this pressure in front of their group.[71]

---

[70]Chris Argyris, "Human Problems with Budgets," *Harvard Business Review*, January–February 1953, p. 108.

[71]Ibid., p. 100.

506

THE MANAGEMENT
PROCESSES AND
ORGANIZATION THEORY:
A MACRO PERSPECTIVE OF
ORGANIZATIONAL BEHAVIOR

In summary, individuals being pressured by a budget can join a group and thereby reduce the pressure, relieve the tension, and make themselves more secure.

Standards and objectives, measurement and evaluation, corrective control decisions, and budgets do not have to have a negative effect on behavior. The next section explores some approaches that may lead to a positive behavioral impact from the organizational control process.

Behavioral approaches to control

Behavioral approaches are only beginning to have an influence on the organizational control process. Up to the last few years, the approach to controlling the organization seemed to follow what Roethlisberger called "the vicious-cycle syndrome." By this he meant that "the breakdown of rules begot more rules to take care of their breakdown or the breakdown of close supervision encouraged the use of still closer methods of supervision and as a result, the continuous search and invention of new control systems to correct for the limitations of previous ones."[72]

Behaviorally oriented management theorists have urged that controls break out of this vicious cycle. Several important behavioral trends in control are emerging. Some of the more important are movements toward:

1. Participative budgeting
2. Diagnostic rather than punitive responses during evaluation
3. Goals set on an individual basis
4. A coaching, rather than a directive, role for superiors
5. Supplying control information to people on the firing line
6. Measurement of employee attitudes[73]

In addition there is, of course, the goal-setting approach described in Chapter 8. Setting goals and providing feedback (which is closely tied into the control process) can lead to improved human performance and MBO (management-by-objectives) systems may be able to lead to more effective overall planning and control.

Other new, specifically behavioral approaches to control, such as human resource or human asset accounting, are also slowly beginning to have an affect. Human resource accounting formally recognizes the monetary value of human resources in an organization. For example, if a good employee leaves the organization, its assets are reduced by a certain dollar amount. There are also definite replacement costs associated with employee turnover. Although most accounting systems have detailed cost data on the use of paper cups for dispensing drinking water, they generally do not generate or

---

[72]Fritz J. Roethlisberger, "Contributions of the Behavioral Sciences to a General Theory of Management," in Harold Koontz (ed.), *Toward a Unified Theory of Management,* McGraw-Hill, New York, 1964, p. 54.

[73]Edmund P. Learned and Audrey T. Sproat, *Organization Theory and Policy,* Irwin, Homewood, Ill., 1966, p. 85.

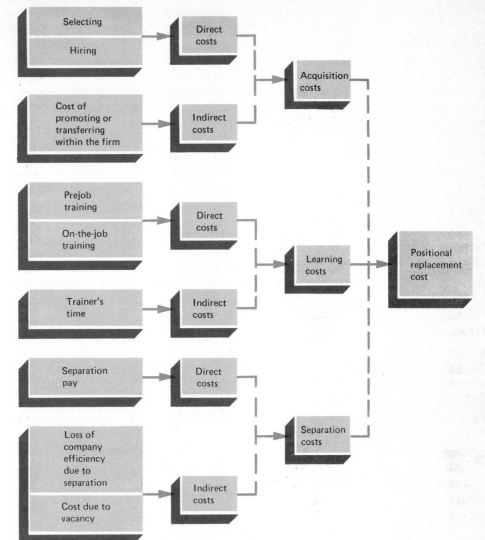

**Figure 17-3
Employee
replacement
costs. (*Source:*
Eric G. Flamholtz,
"Human Resource
Accounting:
Measuring
Positional
Replacement
Costs," *Human
Resource
Management,*
Spring 1973, p.
11.)**

analyze employee replacement costs. Figure 17-3 shows some of the indirect and direct costs that should be recognized in employee replacement analysis and control.

Analogous to replacement, when a good employee joins the organization, the assets will increase by the value of the new employee. Rensis Likert suggests that the following types of variables be considered when calculating the value of new or existing human resources: level of intelligence and aptitudes; level of training; quality of leadership; and quality of decision making, communication, and control.[74] Conflict can be of both positive and

---

[74]Rensis Likert, *The Human Organization,* McGraw-Hill, New York, 1967, p. 148.

508

THE MANAGEMENT
PROCESSES AND
ORGANIZATION THEORY:
A MACRO PERSPECTIVE OF
ORGANIZATIONAL BEHAVIOR

negative value in calculating the worth of human assets. "If bickering, distrust and irreconcilable conflict become greater, the human enterprise is worth less; if the capacity to use differences constructively and engage in cooperative teamwork improves, the human organization is a more valuable asset."[75]

Human resource accounting gives unprecedented recognition to the value of humans in organizations. Traditionally, this human value has been badly neglected. The new emphasis has led to the entire accounting function's becoming more behaviorally oriented. In the past, accounting controls, in terms of both design and use, were greatly influenced by the public function of the auditor.[76] In other words, balance sheets and operating statements were geared to the stockholders and the government, not to the internal organizational control process. In the last few years, this situation has been changing. As explained in an article in a professional accounting magazine:

A school of behavioral accountants has sprung up in the last decade that believes their responsibility extends beyond the classification and transmission of information to include the effect of this information on the users' behavior. These accountants are attempting to improve the effectiveness of accounting reports by applying the findings of behavioral science. They are interested not only in the behavior of report users, but also that of the persons who prepare reports and others who may be directly affected, such as those being reported on.[77]

Although the techniques of control are becoming more behaviorally oriented and although there is a movement toward techniques such as participative budgeting and human resource accounting, if the control process is to be fully compatible with the human being, a sense of self-control must ultimately be developed. The background and specific strategies of self-control are covered in the last chapter of the book.

SUMMARY

This chapter has been devoted to two of the most important functions in the management process: decision making and control. Decision making is defined as choosing between two or more alternatives. However, viewed as a process, the actual choice activity is preceded by gathering information and developing alternatives. Types of management decisions include personal decisions and basic and routine organizational decisions. The relevant behavioral models for analyzing decision-making rationality include the completely rational classical economic models on one extreme; Herbert

---

[75]Ibid., p. 149.

[76]Eliot D. Chapple and Leonard R. Sayles, *The Measures of Management*, Macmillan, New York, 1961, p. 70.

[77]Robert K. Elliott, "Aspects of Behavioral Accounting," *World*, Fall 1970, p. 17.

Simon's intentionally rational, satisficing *administrative man* in the middle range; and the irrationally based social models of psychology on the other extreme. Each of these models gives insights into decision-making rationality, but Simon's administrative man is probably most descriptive of its actual practice. The techniques for decision making have been dominated mainly by quantitative models. New, effective techniques applicable to the more basic decisions have not kept pace with management science techniques. The participative techniques do not begin to approach the sophistication of the quantitative models. Yet it is the basic, uncertain management decisions which are crucial for organizational success. Group techniques such as Delphi and NGT and artificial intelligence from the computer offer some hope for the future.

The management control process consists of three basic elements: (1) standards and objectives, (2) measurement and evaluation, and (3) corrective action. The first phase is closely associated with the planning function. The standards and objectives that are set reflect the performance levels and criteria for management plans. Management can measure and evaluate inputs and performance against standards and objectives in several ways. Measurement largely depends on personal observation and managerial accounting. The last phase of the control process occurs when a corrective control decision is made.

All three elements of control have a significant impact on human behavior in organizations. The behavioral theorists have aimed a great deal of criticism at the ways in which management has traditionally controlled. The problem is not with control per se but rather with how controls have been set and used in practice. Recently, there has been a definite trend toward making controls more behaviorally compatible, through such techniques as participative budgeting and human resource accounting. The ultimate goal is to create self-control among organizational participants.

QUESTIONS FOR DISCUSSION AND REVIEW

1. What are the three steps in Simon's decision-making process? Relate these steps to an actual decision.
2. Describe the essential differences between personal and organizational decisions and between basic and routine decisions.
3. Compare and contrast the economic model and the social model.
4. Describe the major characteristics of Simon's "administrative man." Do you think this model is descriptive of practicing executives? Defend your answer.
5. Explain a hypothetical situation where Delphi and/or NGT could be used.
6. What role do you feel artificial intelligence will play in the future of managerial decision making?
7. Explain the statement, "The existence of the control process implies that the decision-making and communication processes are not perfect."
8. What is the difference between feedforward and feedback control? Give an example of feedforward control.

510

THE MANAGEMENT
PROCESSES AND
ORGANIZATION THEORY:
A MACRO PERSPECTIVE OF
ORGANIZATIONAL BEHAVIOR

9. What are the three basic elements of the control process? Briefly describe the major facets of each element. What are the behavioral implications of each?

CASE:

HARRY SMART—OR IS HE?

Harry Smart, a very bright and ambitious young executive, was born and raised in Boston and graduated from a small New England college. He met his future wife, who was also from Boston, in college. They were married the day after they both graduated cum laude. Harry then went on to Harvard, where he received an MBA. He was now in his seventh year with Brand Corporation, which was located in Boston.

As part of an expansion program, the board of directors of Brand decided to build a new branch plant. The president personally selected Harry to be the manager at the new plant and informed him that a job well done would guarantee him a vice presidency in the corporation. Harry was appointed chairman, with final decision-making privileges, of an ad hoc committee to determine the location of the new plant. In the initial meeting, Harry explained the ideal requirements for the new plant. The members of the committee were experts in transportation, marketing, distribution, labor economics, and public relations. He gave them one month to come up with three choice locations for the new plant.

A month passed and the committee reconvened. After weighing all the variables, the experts recommended the following cities in order of preference: Kansas City, Los Angeles, and New York. Harry could easily see that the committee members had put a great deal of time and effort into their report and recommendations. A spokesperson for the group emphasized that there was a definite consensus that Kansas City was the best location for the new plant. Harry thanked them for their fine job and told them he would like to study the report in more depth before he made his final decision.

After dinner that evening he asked his wife, "Honey, how would you like to move to Kansas City?" Her answer was quick and sharp. "Heavens, no!" she said. "I've lived in the East all my life, and I'm not about to move out into the hinterlands. I've heard the biggest attraction in Kansas City is the stockyards. That kind of life is not for me." Harry weakly protested, "But, honey, my committee strongly recommends Kansas City as the best location for my plant. Their second choice was Los Angeles and the third was New York. What am I going to do?" His wife thought a moment, then replied, "Well, I would consider moving to New York, but if you insist on Kansas City, you'll have to go by yourself!"

The next day Harry called his committee together and said, "Gentlemen, you should all be commended for doing an excellent job on this report. However, after detailed study, I am convinced that New York will meet the needs of our new plant better than Kansas City or Los Angeles. Therefore, the decision will be to locate the new plant in New York. Thank you all once again for a job well done."

1. Did Harry make a rational decision?
2. What model of decision rationality does this incident support?

3. What decision techniques that were discussed in the chapter could be used by the committee to select the new plant site?

CASE: LAKE INDUSTRIES

Lake Industries is a small textile mill in northern Wisconsin that manufactures woolen clothing. For many years Lake has had a reputation for high-quality, long-lasting sportswear. Most of their employees were hired right after World War II. Most had fought in the war, returned home, and gone to work for Lake, the biggest employer in the small town. In recent years, these employees have begun to retire and are being replaced by young men and women from Milwaukee, the largest city in the state, which is 100 miles south. The labor pool in town dried up many years ago and Milwaukee people who cannot find jobs at home migrate north to fill the openings at Lake Industries.

In recent years the quality of the clothing has badly deteriorated. The materials are still the best that money can buy, but the workmanship on the clothes is very sloppy and getting worse. Customers in the immediate region are beginning to cut back on their purchases of Lake Industries apparel, and the hard-earned reputation is beginning to crumble. The chief operating executive has held several meetings with his staff, and the problem seems to be that the production controls are breaking down. The older production supervisors complain that the new, younger workers refuse to be controlled, and spot checks with rank-and-file employees (old and young) indicate that the existing quality control has seemed to become an end in itself. Many of the old-timers mention that self-controls have been replaced by tight, bureaucratic controls in recent years. The chief executive is determined to turn the situation around. He feels that the company will have to start from scratch and reexamine the whole concept of control and institute some new control techniques to improve the quality of their clothes.

1. What do you think are some of the problems contributing to the quality deterioration of this company's products?

2. Analyze the finding that the "older production supervisors complain that the new, younger workers refuse to be controlled." What does this have to say about the control process at Lake? What about the statement that "self-controls have been replaced by tight, bureaucratic controls"?

3. What would be involved in the reexamination of the whole concept of control at Lake? What would be involved in each of the three phases of control?

CLASSICAL ORGANIZATION THEORY AND DESIGN

BUREAUCRATIC RED TAPE*

W. F. Numrich is president of the Deever Construction Company in Marietta, Ohio. A few years ago he bid on his first construction project under the Housing and Urban Development (HUD) program 236. This HUD program subsidizes mortgage interest for middle income families. The project that Deever bid upon was a 125-unit apartment complex in Parkersburg, West Virginia, called Pinewood Village. Deever was the successful bidder on the project and a proposal was submitted to HUD. This proposal specified that construction could commence in the early fall and be completed within eighteen months. HUD responded that the project starting date was too optimistic because of the necessary approval forms and other paper work that HUD had to complete before construction could get underway. HUD finally agreed to a November starting date. The agency, in fact, did not finish the processing of the proposal until November of the following year—twelve months after they had agreed to. In the interim, the Davis-Bacon section of the Department of Labor increased the minimum wage rate that would apply to the construction project. This new rate increased the labor costs to Deever Construction by $80,000. When Mr. Numrich attempted to pass the cost along to HUD by increasing the proposal costs, HUD responded by indicating the entire proposal had to be denied if he insisted on an additional $80,000. HUD insisted that the cost increase should be included in a change order later on in the project. Once Pinewood Village was half completed, Mr. Numrich issued a change proposal to cover the $80,000 additional labor cost. This was denied by HUD. However, HUD did indicate that Numrich could resubmit the proposed change later. After the project was completed, the change order was again submitted and was again turned down. The end result was a project that was completed two years later than originally proposed and at a cost of at least $80,000 (there were obviously inflationary increases in the costs of materials over the two years delay)

---

*Adapted from "The Frustration of Building for HUD," *Business Week,* Aug. 27, 1979, pp. 18–22.

512

more than originally proposed. The bureaucratic machinery at HUD moved very slowly. Mr. Numrich's problems with the Pinewood Village project could be attributed to bureaucratic red tape. As a result of this type of experience many firms are beginning to shy away from doing business with bureaucratically structured government agencies like HUD.

The first two chapters in this macro part of the book have given attention to the management processes. This chapter and the next are concerned with organization theory and design. Organization structure represents the skeletal framework for organizational behavior. As the discussion of the conceptual model in Chapter 3 pointed out, the organization structure is the dominant environmental factor that interacts with the person and the behavior. This chapter presents the organization from the viewpoint of classical theory and design. The bureaucratic model of organization dominates the classical approach. After presenting and discussing this model, the chapter gives an overview and analysis of some of the extensions and modifications represented by the concepts of centralization-decentralization, flat-tall, departmentation, and line-staff. Behavioral implications are given attention throughout the chapter.

THE BUREAUCRATIC MODEL

A logical starting point in the analysis of any theory is the ideal. Max Weber, who was presented in Chapter 2 as one of the pioneers of modern sociology, was concerned with an ideal organization structure called a *bureaucracy*. His concern was a natural extension of his interest in the development and change of Western society. He believed that rationalization was the most persistent cultural value of Western society. On an organizational level, the bureaucracy represented a completely rational form.

The characteristics of bureaucracy

Weber specified several characteristics of an ideal organization structure. The four major ones are the following:

1. *Specialization and division of labor.* Weber's bureaucracy contained: "A specified sphere of competence. This involves (a) a sphere of obligations to perform functions which has been marked off as part of a systematic division of labour (b) The provision of the incumbent with the necessary authority. . . . (c) That the necessary means of compulsion are clearly defined and their use is subject to definite conditions."[1] This statement implies that Weber recognized the importance of having the authority and power to carry out assigned duties. In addition,

---

[1]A. M. Henderson and Talcott Parsons (trans. and ed.), *Max Weber: The Theory of Social and Economic Organization*, Free Press, New York, © 1947 by Oxford, New York, p. 330.

514

THE MANAGEMENT
PROCESSES AND
ORGANIZATION THEORY:
A MACRO PERSPECTIVE OF
ORGANIZATIONAL BEHAVIOR

the bureaucrats must know the precise limits of their sphere of competence so as not to infringe upon that of others.

2. *Positions arranged in a hierarchy.* Weber stated, "The organization of offices follows the principle of hierarchy; that is, each lower office is under the control and supervision of a higher one."[2] This bureaucratic characteristic forces control over every member in the structure. Some organization theorists, such as Herbert Simon, have pointed out that hierarchy is in the natural order of things. An example lies in the biological subsystems, such as the digestive and circulatory, which are composed of organs, the organs composed of tissues, and the tissues composed of cells. Each cell is in turn hierarchically organized into a nucleus, cell wall, and cytoplasm. The same is true of physical phenomena such as molecules, which are composed of electrons, neutrons, and protons.[3] In a manner analogous to the biological and physical structures, hierarchy is a basic characteristic of complex organizational structures.

3. *A system of abstract rules.* Weber felt a need for "a continuous organization of official functions bound by rules."[4] A rational approach to organization requires a set of formal rules to ensure uniformity and coordination of effort. A well-understood system of regulations also provides the continuity and stability that Weber thought were so important. Rules persist, whereas personnel may frequently change. They may range from no smoking in certain areas to the need for board approval for multithousand-dollar capital expenditures.

4. *Impersonal relationships.* It was Weber's belief that the ideal official should be dominated by "a spirit of formalistic impersonality, without hatred or passion, and hence without affection or enthusiasm."[5] Once again, Weber was speaking from the viewpoint of ideal rationality and not of realistic implementation. He felt that in order for bureaucrats to make completely rational decisions, they must avoid emotional attachment to subordinates and clients/customers.

The four characteristics just described are not the only ones recognized and discussed by Weber. Another important aspect of ideal bureaucracy is that employment is based on technical qualifications. The bureaucrat is protected against arbitrary dismissal, and promotions are made according to seniority and/or achievement. In total, it must be remembered that Weber's bureaucracy was intended to be an ideal construct: no real-world organization exactly follows the Weber model. The widely recognized modern organization theorist Peter M. Blau summarizes Weber's thinking as follows:

Weber dealt with bureaucracy as what he termed an ideal type. This methodological concept does not represent an average of the attributes of all existing bureaucracies (or other social structures), but a pure type, derived by abstracting the most characteristic bureaucratic aspects of all known organizations.[6]

The ideal is only the starting point, not the end, of organizational analysis.

----

[2]Ibid., p. 331.

[3]Herbert A. Simon, *The New Science of Management Decision*, Harper & Row, New York, 1960, pp. 40–41.

[4]Henderson and Parsons, op. cit., p. 330.

[5]Ibid., p. 340.

[6]Peter M. Blau, *Bureaucracy in Modern Society*, Random House, New York, 1956, p. 34.

Conditions for bureaucratization

Blau outlined four historical conditions which help promote the development of a bureaucratic form of organization.[7] They are:

1. Money economy
2. Capitalistic system
3. Protestant ethic
4. Large size

Blau carefully points out that all four conditions are *not* necessary in order for bureaucracy to exist. For example, the bureaucratic organizations of ancient civilizations, plus the widespread existence of bureaucratic organizations in contemporary noncapitalistic and non-Protestant countries such as Russia, give ample evidence that especially points 2 and 3 above are not prerequisites. Nevertheless, each of Blau's conditions, including capitalism and Protestantism, may help create an atmosphere that is conducive to a bureaucratic form of organization structure. But it is size that is unquestionably the single most important condition that leads to bureaucratization, and that can overcome the absence of a money economy, capitalism, or Protestantism.

All characteristics of a bureaucracy are built around the framework of large-scale administrative tasks. Bureaucratic adaptability to large size is well documented in history. The administration of the large system of waterways in ancient Egypt; the maintenance of a far-reaching system of roads in the Roman Empire; and the control over millions of people's religious lives by the Roman Catholic Church could probably not have been accomplished without the bureaucratic form of organization. To varying degrees all large organizations of modern society, regardless of economic or religious orientation, are also bureaucracies. Large business, industrial, governmental, church, military, hospital, union, and educational organizations throughout the contemporary world are bureaucratic in nature. In order to survive and maintain some degree of efficiency in accomplishing their goals, most of these large organizations have greatly depended upon hierarchy, specialization, rules, and impersonality.

The relevant question is not whether today's organizations are using the bureaucratic principles because, to a large degree, they all are. Rather, the critical question for contemporary analysis of classical organization theory is whether the functions of bureaucracy outweigh some of the very serious dysfunctions. Weber can be legitimately accused of ignoring this question. He almost completely disregarded, or at least deemphasized, the dysfunctional consequences of the bureaucratic model. A very close reading of Weber's work does indicate that he recognized certain conflicts or dilemmas inherent in bureaucracy. However, he so greatly stressed the functional attributes, either explicitly or implicitly, that the significant dysfunctions were never properly considered in his classic organizational analysis.

---

[7]Ibid., pp. 36–40.

516

THE MANAGEMENT
PROCESSES AND
ORGANIZATION THEORY:
A MACRO PERSPECTIVE OF
ORGANIZATIONAL BEHAVIOR

BUREAUCRATIC DYSFUNCTIONS

With the exception of Weber, other sociologists and philosophers have been very critical of bureaucracies. For example, Karl Marx believed that bureaucracies were used by the dominant capitalist class to control the other, lower social classes. According to Marx, bureaucracies are characterized by strict hierarchy and discipline, veneration of authority, incompetent officials, lack of initiative or imagination, fear of responsibility, and a process of self-aggrandizement.[8] This interpretation of bureaucracy is basically a list of functions opposite to what Weber proposed.

The Weber model can serve equally well in analyzing either the functional or the dysfunctional ramifications of classical organization structure. The characteristic of specialization is a good illustration. The Weber bureaucratic model emphasizes that specialization serves efficiency. The model ignores, but can be used to point out, the dysfunctional qualities of specialization. Empirical investigation has uncovered both functional and dysfunctional consequences. In other words, specialization has been shown to lead to increased productivity and efficiency but also to create conflict between specialized units to the detriment of the overall goal of the organization. For example, specialization may impede communication between units. The management team of a highly specialized unit has its own terminology, similar interests, attitudes, and personal goals. Because "outsiders are different," the specialized unit tends to withdraw into itself and not fully communicate with units above, below, or horizontal to it.

What was said of specialization also holds true for the other characteristics of bureaucracy. The functional attributes of hierarchy are that it maintains unity of command, coordinates activities and personnel, reinforces authority, and serves as the formal system of communication. In theory, the hierarchy has both a downward and an upward orientation, but in practice it has often turned out to have only a downward emphasis. Thus, individual initiative and participation are often blocked, upward communication is impeded, and there is no formal recognition of horizontal communication. Personnel who only follow the formal hierarchy may waste a great deal of time and energy.

Bureaucratic rules probably have the most obvious dysfunctional qualities. Contributing to the bureaucratic image of red tape, rules often become the ends for more effective goal attainment. The famous management consultant Peter Drucker cites the following common misuses of rules that require reports and procedures:

1. First is the mistaken belief that procedural rules are instruments of morality. They should only be used to indicate how something can be done expeditiously, not determine what is right or wrong conduct.
2. Secondly, procedural rules are sometimes mistakenly substituted for judgment. Bureaucrats should not be mesmerized by printed forms; they should only be used in cases where judgment is not required.

---

[8]Rolf E. Rogers, *Organizational Theory*, Allyn and Bacon, Boston, 1975, p. 4.

3. The third and most common misuse of procedural rules is as a punitive control device from above. A bureaucrat is often required to comply to rules that have nothing to do with his job. An example would be the plant manager who has to accurately fill out numerous forms for staff personnel and corporate management which he cannot use in obtaining his own objectives.[9]

Drucker would like to see every procedural rule put on trial for its life at least every five years. He cites one case where all the reports and forms of an organization were totally done away with for two months. At the end of the suspension, three fourths of the reports and forms were deemed unnecessary and were eliminated.[10]

The impersonal quality of the bureaucracy has even more dysfunctional consequences than specialization, hierarchy, and rules. Behaviorally oriented organization theorists and researchers, including Robert K. Merton and Philip Selznick, two widely known scholars, have given a great deal of attention to the behavioral dysfunctions of bureaucratic structures. Merton concluded that one major behavioral consequence of bureaucratic structuring is the disruption of overall goal attainment. He felt that exaggerated adherence to bureaucratic rules and discipline affects participants' personalities to the point where the rules and discipline become ends in themselves.[11] Selznick made specific recommendations for overcoming some of the behavioral dysfunctions of bureaucracy. Most of his insights were gained from his noted study of the Tennessee Valley Authority. He was convinced that more enlightened organizational concepts, such as delegation of authority, must be incorporated into bureaucratic structures for them to become workable, cooperative systems.[12]

CLASSIC RESEARCH ON BUREAUCRACIES

Besides the work by Merton and Selznick, the classic research on bureaucratic structuring conducted by Alvin Gouldner has particularly important insights for the study of organizational behavior and marks the beginning of some modern organization theory concerns such as the importance of environmental variables, for example technology.[13] An intensive, three-year case analysis was made of the bureaucratization of a gypsum plant. This organization employed 225 workers, 75 in the mining operation and 150 in the various departments in the surface plant. The critical variables studied were the change of leadership and the mining-surface environmental distinction.

---

[9]Peter Drucker, *The Practice of Management*, Harper & Row, New York, 1954, pp. 133–134.

[10]Ibid., p. 135.

[11]Robert K. Merton, *Social Theory and Social Structure*, Free Press, Glencoe, Ill., 1949, pp. 153–157.

[12]Philip Selznick, *TVA and the Grass Roots*, University of California Press, Berkeley, Calif., 1949, especially part three, pp. 217–266.

[13]Alvin W. Gouldner, *Patterns of Industrial Bureaucracy*, Free Press, Glencoe, Ill., 1954.

518

THE MANAGEMENT
PROCESSES AND
ORGANIZATION THEORY:
A MACRO PERSPECTIVE OF
ORGANIZATIONAL BEHAVIOR

Change in leadership

The old management in the plant studied was classified by Gouldner as an indulgency pattern. This leadership pattern operated in a very informal and lenient manner under "Old Doug," the plant manager. He ran a pretty loose ship, as is evident in the following comment of a surface worker. "I really like to work in this place. . . . There is nobody coming around pushing you all the time. The boys at the top are certainly lax in their treatment. There is none of this constant checking up on the job. . . . Your free time is your own."[14]

When Old Doug died, a new manager, given the pseudonym of Vincent Peele, took over the plant. The indulgency pattern died along with Old Doug. Mr. Peele was anxious to integrate himself into the existing organization but found he was unable to cope with the informal methods and relationships that were part of the indulgency pattern. One worker noted that Peele was the opposite of Old Doug and that he failed to adapt to Doug's style of management. The worker observed that Peele "always came around checking on the men and standing over them. As long as production was going out Doug didn't stand over them. Peele is always around as though he doesn't have faith in the men like Doug."[15]

Soon after Peele assumed command, he replaced the indulgency pattern with a very formal bureaucratic style, including strict rules and discipline. The method of handling absenteeism typified the contrast between the old and the new. "Among other things, Vincent is cracking down on absenteeism. . . . Doug used to go right out and get the men. . . . He would hop into his car, drive down to their house and tell the men that he needed them. . . . Vincent doesn't stand for it, and he has let it be known that any flagrant violations will mean that the man gets his notice."[16]

One of Peele's strategies was to fire subordinates who were not able to give him complete loyalty and adapt to his new bureaucratic methods. The replacements were loyal outsiders who were sympathetic to his cause. The disciplinary moves perpetuated the bureaucracy, but the firing of Old Doug's management team and their replacement by outsiders further alienated the workers from Peele. Their reaction only caused Peele to institute more and stricter rules and discipline.

The impact of the environment on bureaucratization

The second important aspect of the study was the effect that differing environments had on Peele's bureaucratization. The study has some interesting implications for contingency management and organization design. Two clearly separate environments existed in the surface plant and in the mine. In the surface environment, bureaucratization worked out quite well and was even reluctantly accepted by the workers. In the mine, workers literally refused to adapt to the bureaucratic form of organization. The miners'

---

[14]Ibid., p. 46.

[15]Ibid., p. 81.

[16]Ibid., p. 80.

informal group norms and differing belief system were strong enough to resist the formal bureaucratic methods. The very inherent dangers of mining resulted in a completely different set of attitudes toward work and authority. Often, the miner's life itself depended on the procedures and rules that existed. Therefore, a miner felt justified in refusing orders from the top because "down here we are our own bosses." Furthermore, to escape the pressures of the dangerous work, an occasional drinking spree that resulted in not showing up for work the next morning was acceptable to the miners. The head of the mine, "Old Bull," scoffed at Peele's no-absenteeism rule as "red tape." He complained that "if we laid off a man for absenteeism, we'd have to lay off four or five all the time."[17] Peele forced his form of bureaucracy on the mine unsuccessfully. If he had used a contingency approach, this could have been avoided.

Implications of Gouldner's research

Gouldner's study clearly pointed out that certain physical and psychological conditions must exist in order for bureaucracy to be functional. However, before broad generalizations are made, it must be remembered that this was a case study. Gouldner himself stated, "As a case history of only one factory, this study can offer no conclusions about the 'state' of American industry at large, or about the forces that make for bureaucratization in general."[18] Nevertheless, the study pointed up the importance of environmental variables in organizational structure. It represents a landmark case for contingency management and organization design. The study also docu-

[17]Ibid., p. 151.
[18]Ibid., p. 231.

Table 18-1

SUMMARY OF CHARACTERISTICS OF GOULDNER'S THREE PATTERNS OF BUREAUCRACY

Mock	Representative	Punishment-centered
1. Rules are neither enforced by management nor obeyed by workers.	1. Rules are both enforced by management and obeyed by workers.	1. Rules are enforced by either workers or management and evaded by the other group.
2. Usually, little conflict occurs between the two groups.	2. A few tensions but little overt conflict is generated.	2. Relatively great tension and conflict are entailed.
3. Joint violation and evasion of rules are buttressed by the informal sentiments of the participants.	3. Joint support for rules is buttressed by informal sentiments, mutual participation, initiation, and education of workers and management.	3. Rules are enforced by punishment and supported by the informal sentiments of *either* workers or management.

Source: Adapted from Alvin W. Gouldner's *Patterns of Industrial Bureaucracy*, Free Press, Glencoe, Ill., 1954, p. 217. Used with permission.

520

THE MANAGEMENT
PROCESSES AND
ORGANIZATION THEORY:
A MACRO PERSPECTIVE OF
ORGANIZATIONAL BEHAVIOR

mented the importance and power of the informal structure in an organization.

Gouldner definitely refined and extended Weber's classic model. Through his research, he was able to determine the aspects of bureaucracy that created tensions. He identified three bureaucratic patterns: *mock*, *representative*, and *punishment-centered*. The characteristics of these three types of bureaucracy are summarized in Table 18-1. Both the representative and the punishment-centered forms have certain parallels with the Weber model. The key difference between Gouldner's three types is the extent to which rules are enforced. Evidence from his research indicated that a punishment-centered bureaucracy creates the most tension and generates the most complaints about dysfunctions such as red tape and impersonality.

THE FATE OF BUREAUCRACY

Many modern organization theorists are predicting the complete disappearance, or at least a drastic modification, of the classical bureaucratic structure. Warren Bennis has probably been the most vocal prophet of its death. He contends that "the bureaucratic form of organization is becoming less and less effective; that it is hopelessly out of joint with contemporary realities; that new shapes, patterns, and models are emerging which promise drastic changes in the conduct of the corporation and of managerial practices in general."[19] Most people can testify to the following types of experiences from their own observations of a bureaucracy:

1. Bosses without (and underlings with) technical competence
2. Arbitrary and zany rules
3. An underworld (or informal) organization which subverts or even replaces the formal apparatus
4. Confusion and conflict among roles
5. Cruel treatment of subordinates based not on rational or legal grounds but upon inhumanity.[20]

The above observations support the red tape, bureaupathic image of the bureaucratic form of organization. Victor Thompson describes the often existing "bureaupathology" thus:

Everyone has met the pompous, self-important official at some time in his life, and many have served under autocratic, authoritarian superiors. Employees who seem to be interested in nothing but a minimal performance of their own little office routines are numerous enough, and impersonal treatment of clients and associates that approaches the coldness of absolute zero is not, sadly, uncommon.[21]

Observations such as the above have led most people to readily accept popular Parkinson's "Laws" (for example, bureaucratic staffs increase in

---

[19]Warren Bennis, "Beyond Bureaucracy," *Trans-Action*, July–August 1965, p. 31.
[20]Ibid., p. 32.
[21]Victor A. Thompson, *Modern Organization*, Knopf, New York, 1961, p. 23.

inverse proportion to the amount of work done[22]) and the more recent "Peter Principle" (managers rise to their level of incompetence in bureaucracies[23]). These "laws" and "principles" have received wide public acceptance because everyone has observed and experienced what Parkinson and Peter wrote about. But as one organizational scholar has noted:

These two writers have primarily capitalized on the frustrations toward government and business administration felt by the general public, which is not familiar with the processes necessitated by large-scale organization. Parkinson and Peter made a profit on their best sellers; they added little to the scientific study of organizations.[24]

In addition to the popularized criticisms of bureaucracy, a more academic analysis also uncovers many deficiencies. Bennis summarized some of them as follows:

1. Bureaucracy does not adequately allow for personal growth and the development of mature personalities.
2. It develops conformity and "group-think."
3. It does not take into account the "informal organization" and the emergent and unanticipated problems.
4. Its systems of control and authority are hopelessly outdated.
5. It has no juridical process.
6. It does not possess adequate means for resolving differences and conflicts between ranks, and most particularly, between functional groups.
7. Communication (and innovative ideas) are thwarted or distorted due to hierarchical divisions.
8. The full human resources of bureaucracy are not being utilized due to mistrust, fear of reprisals, etc.
9. It cannot assimilate the influx of new technology or scientists entering the organization.
10. It modifies personality structure, so that people become and reflect the dull, gray, conditioned "organization man."[25]

Also from an academic viewpoint, Thompson states that bureaupathology occurs because "the growing imbalance between the rights of authority positions, on the one hand, and the abilities and skills needed in a technological age, on the other, generates tensions and insecurities in the system of authority."[26] Thompson regards this growing imbalance between ability and authority as the most symptomatic characteristic of modern bureaucracy.

Parkinson, Peter, Bennis, and Thompson represent the extreme critics of bureaucratic organization. Nevertheless, during the past few years popular writers, scholars, practitioners, and the general public have felt increasing dissatisfaction and frustration with classical bureaucratic structures. In the

---

[22]Northcote Parkinson, *Parkinson's Law and Other Studies in Administration*, Houghton Mifflin, Boston, 1957.

[23]Laurence J. Peter, *The Peter Principle*, Morrow, New York, 1969.

[24]Rogers, op. cit., p. 4.

[25]Bennis, op. cit., p. 33.

[26]Thompson, op. cit., p. 23.

522

THE MANAGEMENT
PROCESSES AND
ORGANIZATION THEORY:
A MACRO PERSPECTIVE OF
ORGANIZATIONAL BEHAVIOR

case of the public, the consumerism movement is largely a result of dissatisfaction with bureaucracies. The argument is not that the classical bureaucratic theorists were necessarily wrong but, rather, that the times have rendered their concepts and principles no longer relevant. Bureaucratic organization is thought to be too inflexible to adapt readily to the dynamic nature and purpose of many of today's organizations and public needs. Flexibility and adaptability are necessary requirements for modern organization structures. The increasing size of organizations, in terms of both mergers and internal growth, the advent of the computer, and the tremendous strides made in all types of technology are but a few of the things which have contributed to a new organizational environment. Sociologist Charles Perrow probably best summarizes the current situation facing many bureaucracies thus: "The rate of change is so rapid, the new techniques so unproven and so uncertain, the number of contingencies so enormous, that the bureaucratic model is only partly applicable . . . Something else is needed."[27] The rest of this chapter and the next discuss this "something else" besides bureaucratic principles that can be used to structure today's organizations.

EXTENSIONS OF CLASSICAL CONCEPTS OF ORGANIZATIONS

Besides the bureaucratic and classical aspects of organization, a concern with vertical and horizontal structural arrangements has emerged over the years. Vertical analysis concentrates on centralization versus decentralization and flat-versus-tall structuring. These concerns are modifications of the classical principles of delegation and span of control. Decentralization expands the principle of delegation to the point of an overall philosophy of organization and management. A *tall* organization structure means a series of narrow spans of control, and a *flat* structure incorporates wide spans. The bureaucratic principle of hierarchy is also closely related to the vertical concept.

Horizontal structural analysis is concerned with organizing one level of the hierarchy. The concepts of departmentation and line-staff represent this approach. They are derived chiefly from the bureaucratic doctrine of specialization. Departmentation concentrates on organizing each level to attain optimal benefit from high degrees of specialization. The staff concept attempts to resolve the vertical and horizontal conflicts that appeared in the classical scheme. In general, the concepts discussed in the rest of this chapter carry the classical concepts one step further. They give greater weight to the human element and recognize that simple, mechanistic structural arrangements are not satisfactory for complex organizations.

Centralization and decentralization

The terms *centralization* and *decentralization* are freely tossed about in management and organization theory literature and theoretical practice of

---

[27]Charles Perrow, *Organizational Analysis: A Sociological View*, Wadsworth, Belmont, Calif., 1970, p. 60.

management and organization design. Most often, both the scholar and the practitioner neglect to define what they mean by the concept. There are three basic types of centralization-decentralization.

One is the geographical or territorial concentration (centralization) or dispersion (decentralization) of operations. For example, the term *centralized* can be used to refer to an organization that has all its operations under one roof or in one geographical region. On the other hand, the dispersion of an organization's operations throughout the country or the world is a form of decentralization. The word *geographical* is often not stated, thereby adding to the confusion.

A second type is *functional* centralization and decentralization. A good example is the personnel function of an organization. A separate personnel department that performs personnel functions for the other departments is said to be centralized. However, if the various functional departments, e.g., marketing, production, and finance, handle their own personnel functions, then personnel is considered to be decentralized. Figure 18-1 shows how functional centralization-decentralization would appear on a simplified organization chart. Both geographical and functional centralization and decentralization are descriptive terms rather than analytical.

**Figure 18-1
Functional
centralization-
decentralization.**

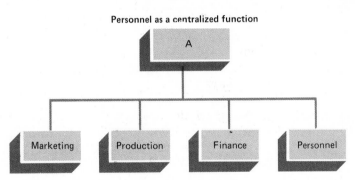

Personnel as a centralized function

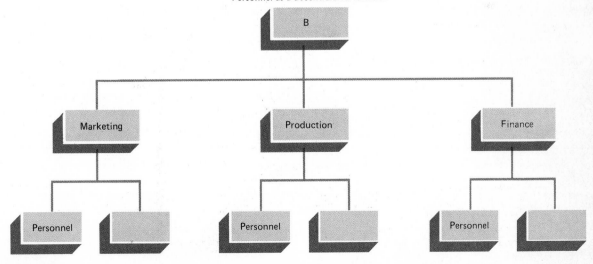

Personnel as a decentralized function

524

THE MANAGEMENT
PROCESSES AND
ORGANIZATION THEORY:
A MACRO PERSPECTIVE OF
ORGANIZATIONAL BEHAVIOR

The third type is the only analytical use of the concept. This is where the terms *centralization* and *decentralization* refer to the retention or delegation of decision-making prerogatives or command. From an organization theory and analysis standpoint, this third type is the most relevant use of the concepts centralization and decentralization. They are relative concepts because every organization structure contains both features, and the concepts differ only in degree.

Contrary to common belief, it is not possible to determine whether an organization is centralized or decentralized by merely looking at the organization chart. The determining factor is how much of the decision making is retained at the top and how much is delegated to the lower levels. This amount of retention or delegation is not reflected on the organization chart.

Determining decentralization Both management writers and practitioners generally favor decentralization. It represents one of the "in" concepts and identifies the advocate as a modern-thinking theorist or practitioner. Centralization has taken on the connotation of being traditional and even authoritarian. Albers observed:

In recent years, decentralization has become the golden calf of management philosophy. It has been lauded by such terms as "more democratic," "a step toward world peace," "greater freedom of spirit," and "less authoritarian." The implicit assumption is that centralization reflects the opposite of these worthy qualities.[28]

Although most contemporary managers say they advocate the values of decentralization, in reality their use of the concept turns out to be more fiction than fact. A typical case is the executive who gives a speech at the Rotary Club luncheon praising the values of decentralization. More often than not, these individuals are likely to be practicing a high degree of centralization although they may truly think they are running a thoroughly decentralized operation. Obviously, the mere verbalization of decentralization by top management is not sufficient to determine the extent of decentralization. Ernest Dale has formulated some objective criteria that can be very helpful in measuring the extent of decentralization. He states that as decentralization increases:

1. The greater the number of decisions made lower down the management hierarchy.
2. The more important the decisions made lower down the management hierarchy. For example, the greater the sum of capital expenditure that can be approved by the plant manager without consulting anyone else, the greater the degree of decentralization in this field.
3. The more functions affected by decisions made at lower levels. Thus, companies which permit only operational decisions to be made at separate branch plants are less decentralized than those which also permit financial and personnel decisions at branch plants.
4. The less checking required on the decision. Decentralization is greatest when no

---

[28]Henry H. Albers, *Principles of Management*, 3d ed., Wiley, New York, 1969, p. 186.

check at all must be made; less when superiors have to be informed of the decision after it has been made; still less if superiors have to be consulted before the decision is made. The fewer people to be consulted, and the lower they are on the management hierarchy, the greater the degree of decentralization.[29]

Optimum degree of decentralization   So far, the discussion has probably implied that decentralization is somehow better than centralization. In truth, neither concept is an ideal or intrinsically good or bad. Generally speaking, decentralization is much more compatible with the behavioral aspects of management. This relevancy is due in part to the lower-level participation in decision making that results from decentralization. Increased motivation is an extremely important by-product. Besides the behavioral benefits, more effective decisions are possible because of the speed and first-hand knowledge that decentralization provides. Decentralization also affords invaluable experience in decision making for lower-level executives. Finally, it allows more time for top management to concentrate on policy making and creative innovation. Centralization "produces uniformity of policy and action, lessens risks of error by subordinates who lack either information or skill, utilizes the skills of central and specialized experts, and enables closer control of operations."[30] The findings of Robert Duncan, a modern organization theorist, on the advantages and disadvantages of decentralized structures are summarized in Table 18-2.

---

[29]Ernest Dale, *Planning and Developing the Company Organization Structure*, Research Report 20, American Management Association, New York, 1952, p. 118.

[30]Edwin B. Flippo and Gary Hunsinger, *Management*, 3d ed., Allyn and Bacon, Boston, 1975, p. 183.

Table 18-2

SUMMARY CHARACTERISTICS OF DECENTRALIZED STRUCTURES

Strengths	Weaknesses
1. Suited to fast change and dynamic growth	1. Innovation and growth tend to be restricted to existing project or functional areas
2. High product, project, or program visibility and awareness	2. Difficult to allocate pooled resources (e.g., computer, lab)
3. Full-time, objective task orientation (i.e., dollars, schedules, profits)	3. Shared functions hard to coordinate/integrate (e.g., purchasing)
4. Task responsibility pinpointed and is clearly communicated to customers or clients	4. Deterioration of in-depth competence and expertise—hard to attract technical specialists
5. Multiple tasks processed in parallel, easy-to-cross functional lines	5. Possible internal task conflicts, jurisdictional and priority conflicts
	6. May cause neglect of high level of coordinational integration required in effective organization

Source: Adapted from Robert Duncan, "What Is the Right Organization Structure," *Organizational Dynamics*, Winter 1979, p. 66.

526

THE MANAGEMENT
PROCESSES AND
ORGANIZATION THEORY:
A MACRO PERSPECTIVE OF
ORGANIZATIONAL BEHAVIOR

A model of decentralization Traditionally, the most widely cited model of decentralization has been the General Motors Corporation. Alfred P. Sloan, the "Great Organizer," was primarily responsible for the formulation of the original model. Many people don't realize that centralization, as well as decentralization, played a vital role in his scheme. His model was based on two important premises:

1. The responsibility attached to the chief executive of each operation shall in no way be limited. Each such organization headed by its chief executive shall be complete in every necessary function and enabled to exercise its full initiative and logical development. (Decentralization of operations.)
2. Certain central organization functions are absolutely essential to the logical development and proper coordination of the Corporation's activities. (Centralized staff services to advise the line on specialized phases of the work, and central measurement of results to check the exercise of delegated responsibility).[31]

Simply stated, Sloan's General Motors model suggests *centralized control of decentralized operations.*

Many large industrial organizations have patterned themselves after the Sloan model. This is undoubtedly a major reason why American industry has been able to overcome the economic concept of decreasing returns to scale. This concept states that when a firm gets very large, further growth will result in a proportionately lower amount of output. The chief reasons given for decreasing returns to scale are that a breakdown in communication occurs, there is a loss of control, and a general decline in organization and management efficiency develops. To date in American industry, this point of decreasing returns has not really occurred. The industrial corporations keep growing larger and larger. For example, there are about twenty United States corporations with over $7.5 billion worth of assets each. There are tremendously large organizations with worldwide operations that have hundreds of thousands of employees. One important way they have overcome breakdowns in communication, control, and managerial effectiveness is through centralized control of decentralized operations.

Besides the overall planning, organizing, and controlling advantages of the Sloan type of decentralization, there are also some very practical day-to-day benefits. These advantages were summarized as follows by Peter Drucker, on the basis of interviews with several GM executives who had worked under the Sloan type of structure:

1. The speed and lack of confusion with which a decision can be made.
2. The absence of conflict of interest between corporate management and the divisions.
3. The sense of fairness, appreciation, confidence, and security that comes when organizational "politics" are kept under control.
4. The democracy and informality in management where everyone is free to criticize but no one tries to sabotage.
5. The absence of a gap between the "privileged few" top managers and the "great many" subordinate managers in the organization.

---

[31]Ernest Dale, "Contributions to Administration by Alfred P. Sloan, Jr., and GM," *Administrative Science Quarterly,* June 1956, p. 41.

6. The availability of a large supply of good, experienced leaders capable of taking top responsibility.
7. The inability of weak divisions and managers to ride on the coat tails of successful divisions or trade on past performance.
8. The absence of "edict management" and the presence of public policies which are a product of the experiences of all the people concerned.[32]

Strategy and structure   The Sloan model is the most widely recognized, but not the only, influence on decentralized organization. Alfred D. Chandler, Jr., a professor of history, made a significant contribution to understanding the reasons why organization structure evolves. He proposed a thesis that structure follows managerial strategy.[33] To test this thesis, he made in-depth case studies of the structural changes that occurred in four major companies. Data were obtained from internal company records, correspondence, reports, minutes, and interviews with company executives who had participated in the changes. He discovered that each company eventually evolved into a decentralized structure, but for different reasons. The decentralization of the four companies, very briefly, developed as follows:

1. *Du Pont* went from a centralized to a decentralized structure. Decentralization was needed to accommodate a management strategy of product diversification.
2. *General Motors* was a different situation. As was pointed out in Chapter 1, in the early years of GM there was a lack of centralized control over diverse products and functions. This precarious situation can be attributed to the one-man, authoritative management style practiced by the founder, William C. Durant. In 1920, GM switched to Sloan's model of decentralization. Sloan's strategy of centralized control over decentralized operations put GM back on its feet and was a major contributing factor to its tremendous success.
3. *Standard Oil (New Jersey)* had a different experience. The company had many of the same problems as Du Pont and GM but moved toward decentralization on a piecemeal, unsystematic basis. It differed from the other companies studied by Chandler in that its eventual decentralized structure was not the result of a one-shot, overall policy change. Nevertheless, once more management strategy played a crucial role in instituting the changes to decentralization.
4. *Sears, Roebuck* experienced still another pattern. The company started off with a decentralized organization which proved to be successful because of unclear channels of authority and communication and lack of overall planning. Next the company moved to a highly centralized structure which also proved to be unworkable, but it gradually evolved into a very successful decentralized structure. Once again, managerial strategy preceded the eventual decentralized structure.

After completing these comprehensive case studies, Chandler concluded that decentralized structure was a result of management strategy. This was not necessarily a strategy of decentralization per se but, rather, was a strategy designed to accommodate growth. At least in the companies he studied, the

---

[32]Peter F. Drucker, *Concept of the Corporation*, John Day, New York, 1946, pp. 47–48.

[33]Alfred D. Chandler, Jr., *Strategy and Structure*, Doubleday, Anchor Books, Garden City, N.Y., 1966. The book was originally published by the MIT Press in 1962.

528

THE MANAGEMENT
PROCESSES AND
ORGANIZATION THEORY:
A MACRO PERSPECTIVE OF
ORGANIZATIONAL BEHAVIOR

strategies developed for different reasons. Wide territorial expansion, combinations, and, to a greater extent, product diversification, all played a role. However, overall growth seemed to be the most common denominator of the histories of the decentralized companies Chandler studied.[34]

The recentralization issue Although decentralization has been the "golden calf" for the past couple of decades, many scholars and practitioners are now forecasting a recentralization of organization structure. Even General Motors, the classic textbook example of decentralization, is moving away from the Sloan model toward a more centralized operating structure. One news report noted:

Carried through, the centralization will find GM operating with a single engine division, for example, supplying engines for all car lines, a single assembly division building the cars and supplying the finished product to the sales divisions. Consolidation of other operations, now spread among various divisions, could result in single divisions for forgings, chassis, transmissions, suspension and so on.[35]

Although this development at GM is primarily concerned with the functional, as opposed to decision-making, aspects of centralization-decentralization, it is still of great significance to organizational analysis. Of even greater interest is the reason for the movement toward centralization. Besides taking advantage of some of the managerial-efficiency benefits of centralization, GM may have adopted this strategy in order to avoid antitrust action.[36] Under the Sloan plan, the comparatively autonomous product divisions could be easily separated by the government from the parent corporation, but not under a centralized plan. This, of course, is only speculation, but it is interesting from the standpoint that environmental factors (antitrust suits) can affect organization structure and vice versa. In addition to antitrust, most organizations today are also responding to external environmental pressures such as equal opportunity, environmental protection, and OSHA (Occupational Safety and Health Act) by centralizing. These very real examples point out the open-systems nature of modern organizations. The next chapter will explore these open-systems implications further.

Behavioral implications of decentralization Although delegation was probably the most behaviorally oriented classical principle, decentralization represents an even more concerted attempt to incorporate behavioral ideas into organization structure. Decentralization recognizes and actually capitalizes on the importance of the human element. Most important, decentralization gives an opportunity for individual responsibility and initiative at the lower levels. Because of the popularity of decentralization, many organizations have been stimulated to incorporate the accompanying behavioral ideas. Yet, as has been pointed out, decentralization may be more fiction than

---

[34]Ibid., pp. 50–60.

[35]*Automotive News*, Sept. 20, 1971, p. 1.

[36]Ibid.

fact in actual practice. Moreover, as mentioned earlier, there is a distinct possibility that recentralization may be occurring. Such a turn of events may wipe out the behaviorally oriented advances in organization that have been stimulated by decentralization.

From another viewpoint, there is a convincing argument that decentralization, as practiced, never did have a behavioral impact. Simon gives two reasons for this view:

First, we should observe that the principle of decentralized profit-and-loss accounting has never been carried much below the level of product-group departments and cannot, in fact, be applied successfully to fragmented segments of highly interdependent activities. *Second,* we may question whether the conditions under which middle management has in the past exercised its decision-making prerogatives were actually good conditions from a motivational standpoint.[37]

It is fair to say that, overall, decentralization has supported, and in some cases has stimulated, the behavioral approach to management. At the same time, there is little doubt that a wide discrepancy exists between the theory of decentralization and its practice. Yet, because of its wide acceptance, decentralization has had a definite impact on developing a managerial attitude toward acceptance and implementation of behavioral concepts in organization. However, in the future this may all change because of the movement to recentralize.

Flat and tall structures

In organizational analysis, the terms *flat* and *tall* are used to describe the total pattern of spans of control and levels of management. Whereas the classical principle of span is concerned with the number of subordinates one superior can effectively manage, the concept of flat and tall is more concerned with the vertical structural arrangements for the entire organization. The nature and scope are analogous to the relationship between delegation and decentralization. In other words, span of control is to flat-tall structures as delegation is to decentralization.

The difference between flat and tall structures may be easily seen in the two simplified organization charts in Figure 18-2. The tall structure has very small or narrow spans of control, whereas the flat structure has large or wide spans. In tall structures, the small number of subordinates assigned to each superior allows for tight controls and strict discipline. Classical bureaucratic structures are typically very tall.

The most noteworthy departure from the tall structural concept of organization is attributed to the pioneering work of James C. Worthy, a former vice president of Sears, Roebuck and Company. A number of years ago he was involved with a comprehensive organizational study of Sears.[38] The results obtained from surveys of several hundred company units

---

[37]Herbert A. Simon, *The New Science of Management Decision,* op. cit., pp. 46–47.

[38]James C. Worthy, "Organization Structure and Employee Morale," *American Sociological Review,* April 1950, pp. 169–179; and "Factors Influencing Employee Morale," *Harvard Business Review,* January 1950, pp. 61–73.

530

THE MANAGEMENT
PROCESSES AND
ORGANIZATION THEORY:
A MACRO PERSPECTIVE OF
ORGANIZATIONAL BEHAVIOR

contradicted the classical assumptions about span of control. He found that stores that were organized into flat structures had better sales, profit, morale, and management competence than stores that were formed into tall structures. These results gave empirical evidence to challenge the classical tall structures. Worthy summarized his reasoning as follows: "The emphasis is constantly on *shortening* the span, without giving much more than lip service to the fact that circumstances often differ and that under certain conditions there may be positive advantages in *lengthening* the span."[39]

Advantages and disadvantages   Tall structures assume a role in assessing the value of flat structures similar to that of centralization in assessing the relative merits of decentralization. Tall structures are often negatively viewed in modern organizational analysis. More accurately, there are advantages and disadvantages to both flat and tall structures. Furthermore, flat and tall are only relative concepts; there are no ideal absolutes.

---

[39]James C. Worthy, *Big Business and Free Men*, Harper, New York, 1959, pp. 101–102.

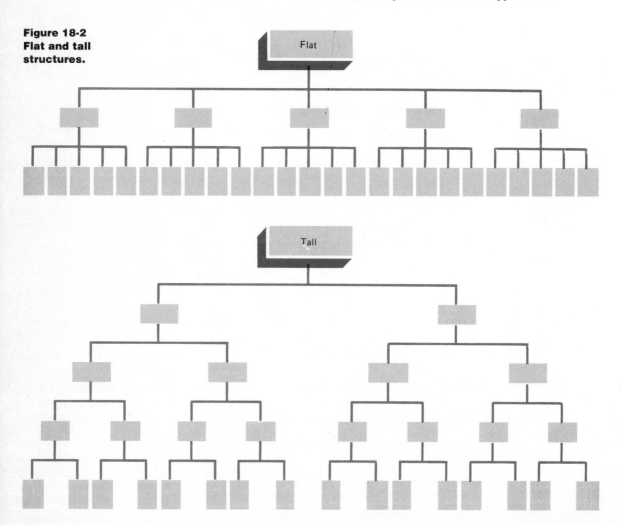

**Figure 18-2
Flat and tall
structures.**

Both charts shown in Figure 18-2 have the same number of personnel. However, the tall structure has four levels of management and the flat one has only two levels. The tall structure has the definite advantage of facilitating closer control over subordinates. Notice that the term *closer* and not *better* control was used. The classicists, of course, equated "closer" with "better"; the more behaviorally oriented theorists do not. The very nature of flat structures implies that superiors cannot possibly keep close control over many subordinates. Therefore, they are almost forced to delegate a certain amount of the work. Thus, wide spans structurally encourage decentralization. The behavioral theorists would say that this opens up the opportunities for individual initiative and self-control.

From a behavioral viewpoint, self-control is much more effective than control imposed from above. This behavioral advantage of flat organizations hinges on the assumption that there are capable people who can produce under conditions of relative independence. In other words, the analysis of flat and tall structures depends a great deal on what hypotheses are made about the basic nature of people. For discussion purposes, Douglas McGregor's Theories X and Y assumptions may be used to assess the merits of flat versus tall structures.

Relationship to Theories X and Y   McGregor's widely recognized traditional Theory X sees humans as innately lazy and in need of close control. In this view, the individual prefers to be told what to do and shuns responsibility. If this is correct, tall structures which encourage close controls would be the most appropriate form of structure. Theory Y takes an essentially opposite view of people, holding that they are not inherently lazy or inherently productive. People's behavior depends on how they have been treated. If they have been held under close controls and given no responsibilities, they will react by being stubborn, uncooperative, or just plain lazy. On the other side of the coin, if they are not given close controls but are assigned responsibility, according to Theory Y they will react by being highly motivated and self-controlled, and they will seek more responsibility. If in fact Theory Y depicts the nature of humans, the flat structure which has built-in loose controls or, more appropriately, ends-oriented controls, and in which a great deal of responsibility is given to subordinates, will be more effective than a tall structure.

As to which view is correct, there are no ready answers. There is no doubt, however, that a simple X or Y interpretation of human behavior is much too abstract and limiting. The chapters in this book give a more comprehensive and meaningful analysis of human behavior than the X and Y theories. In general, however, the assumptions of Theory Y are probably more compatible with what is now known about human behavior than are those of Theory X. But it should be remembered that the nature of organizational behavior is much more complex and varied than is implied by McGregor's theories.

Behavioral implications of flat versus tall   One behavioral implication that is often overlooked in analyzing flat versus tall structures is the opportunity that tall structures offer for more personal contact between

532

THE MANAGEMENT
PROCESSES AND
ORGANIZATION THEORY:
A MACRO PERSPECTIVE OF
ORGANIZATIONAL BEHAVIOR

superior and subordinate. This contact is generally assumed to be negative and conflicting, but it need not be. In a tall structure, the superior may create a positive rapport with his or her subordinate that may not be possible in a flat structure.

Another consideration besides personal contact is the levels of communication in the two structures. In the flat structure there are fewer levels, which means that both downward and upward communication is simplified. There should be less distortion and inaccuracy. The red tape endless communication channels associated with bureaucratic tall structures are not present in a flat structure. On the other hand, the increased equality that exists between subordinates in a flat structure may lead to communication problems. If no status or authority differentials are structurally created, a heavy burden is placed upon horizontal communications. As Chapter 12 brought out, the horizontal communication system is notably deficient in most organizations. The problem may be compounded in flat organizations, where more dependence is placed on this type of communication, but it is not structurally facilitated. Also, coordination may be seriously impaired by a flat structure for the same reason.

Overall, the flat structure, at least from a behavioral standpoint, is generally preferable to the tall. It can take advantage of the positive attributes of decentralization and personal satisfaction and growth. Although managers who have wide spans will have to give a great deal of attention to selecting and training subordinates, a flat structure has the advantage of providing a wealth of experience in decision making. Perhaps Worthy best summarizes the behavioral advantages of flat structures in these words: "Flatter, less complex structures, with a maximum of administrative decentralization, tend to create a potential for improved attitudes, more effective supervision, and greater individual responsibility and initiative among employees."[40]

Together with these advantages, however, it must be remembered that flat structures only *encourage* decentralization and individual responsibility and initiative. The supervisor of a small span does not always keep close control and never decentralize, nor does the supervisor of a large span always create an atmosphere of self-control and decentralization. The degree of centralization or its reverse depends on the overall management and organization philosophy and policies and on individual leadership style and personality. All a flat or tall arrangement does is structurally promote, not determine, centralization or decentralization and the approach taken toward the behavioral aspects of managing.

Departmentation

Departmentation is concerned with horizontal organization on any one level of the hierarchy, and it is closely related to the classical bureaucratic principle of specialization. There are several types of departmentation. Traditionally, purpose, process, persons or things, and place were the

---

[40]Worthy, "Organization Structure and Employee Morale," op. cit., p. 179.

recognized bases for departmentation.[41] In more recent terminology, *product* is substituted for *purpose*, *functional* has replaced *process*, and *territorial* or *geographical* is used instead of *place*. In addition, time, service, customer, equipment, and alpha-numerical have also become recognized types of departmentation. Each of these latter types of departmentation is fairly self-explanatory. Examples of each follow.

1. *Time* may be divided into first shift, second shift, and third shift.
2. *Service* may reflect first class, second class, and tourist class on a passenger ship.
3. *Customer* organization may exist in a large commercial loan department that lends to farmers, small businesses, and large industries.
4. *Equipment* may be broken down in a production unit into drill-press, punch-press, and polishing departments.
5. *Alpha-numerical* may be utilized in telephone servicing where numbers 0000–5000 are placed in one department and 5001–9999 in another.

Because organizations of any size will contain more than one hierarchical level, there will always be different types of departmentation represented. A typical large industrial corporation may be territorially organized on the first major horizontal level, and each succeeding level may be organized by product, function, time, and equipment. Confusion is often created when a given organization is identified as one type of departmentation, e.g., General Motors has traditionally been known as a product-departmentalized structure. The confusion can be cleared up if it is remembered that an organization is identified as one particular type of departmentation because at the primary level, i.e., the first major organizational breakdown, it is organized and identified in this way. General Motors has been known as a product-departmentalized company because the primary level was organized into automotive and nonautomotive product divisions. However, it must be noted that many other types of departmentation are found in the lower levels of GM or any other organization that is designated by only one particular type of departmentation.

Functional departmentation　By far the most widely used and recognized type of departmentation is functional in nature. Koontz and O'Donnell explain the importance that functions play in all organized endeavor:

Since all undertakings involve the creation of utility and since this occurs in an exchange economy, the basic enterprise functions consist of production (creating utility or adding utility to a good or service), selling (finding customers, patients, clients, students, or communicants who will agree to accept the good or service at a price), and financing (raising and collecting, safe-guarding, and expending the funds of the enterprise).[42]

[41]Luther Gulick, "Notes on the Theory of Organization," in Luther Gulick and Lyndall Urwick (eds.), *Papers on the Science of Administration*, Institute of Public Administration, New York, 1937, p. 15.

[42]Harold Koontz and Cyril O'Donnell, *Principles of Management*, 5th ed., McGraw-Hill, New York, 1972, p. 265.

534

THE MANAGEMENT
PROCESSES AND
ORGANIZATION THEORY:
A MACRO PERSPECTIVE OF
ORGANIZATIONAL BEHAVIOR

It logically follows that functional departmentation may be found in all types of organizations. For example, in a manufacturing organization the major functions usually are production, marketing, and finance, the vital functions that enable a manufacturing concern to operate and survive. On the other hand, in a railroad organization the major functions are called *operations*, *traffic*, and *finance*, and in a general hospital they are *medical service*, *housekeeping*, *dietetics*, and *business*. Although the titles are different, the railroad and hospital functions are nevertheless analogous to the manufacturing functions in terms of importance and purpose. The titles of various functional departments may differ among industries and even between organizations within the same industry. All businesses, hospitals, universities, governmental agencies, religious organizations, and the military contain vital functions and can be functionally departmentalized.

The greatest single advantage of functional departmentation is that it incorporates the positive aspects of specialization. Theoretically, functionalism should lead to the greatest efficiency and the most economical utilization of employees. In practice, however, certain dysfunctions that were discussed with regard to specialization may also negate the advantages of functional departmentation. For example, functional empires may be created that conflict to the point of detracting from overall goal attainment. A typical case is the salesperson who is guided by the sales department goal of maximizing the number of units sold. In order to sell 2000 units to a customer, this salesperson may have to promise delivery by the end of the week and to require no money down. The production department, on the other hand, has a goal of keeping costs as low as possible and therefore does not carry a very large inventory. It cannot possibly supply the customer with 2000 units by the end of the week. Finance has still another goal. It must keep bad debt expense at a minimum and therefore must require substantial down payments and thorough credit checks on every customer. In this situation, the sales department is in conflict with production and finance. If the salesperson goes ahead and makes the sale under the conditions in the example, the customer will not receive the order on time and if and when it is received may not be able to pay the bill. In either or both outcomes, the company goals of customer goodwill and bad debt expense minimization will suffer because of the salesperson's action.

It is easy to place the blame in the above example on the individual salesperson or on the lack of management coordination and communication. They are both definitely contributing factors. However, an equal, if not overriding, difficulty is the subgoal loyalties that are fostered by functionalization. A true story told by Peter Drucker provides an example of this mentality.

A railroad company reported a $20,000 per year cost item for broken glass doors in their passenger stations. Upon investigation it was found that a young accountant had "saved" the company $200 by limiting each station to one key for the rest room. Naturally, the key was always lost and the replacement cost only 20 cents. The catch, however, was that the key cost was set up by financial control to be a capital expenditure which required approval from the home office. This home office approval accompanied by the appropriate paperwork took months to accomplish. On the other hand, emergency repairs could be paid immediately out of the station's cash account. What bigger emergency than not being able to get into the bathroom? Each station had an axe and the result was $20,000 for broken bathroom glass doors.[43]

The presentation of such examples does not imply that conflict is always bad for the organization. In fact, as Chapter 13 pointed out, many modern organization theorists think that conflict has a good effect on the organization that, in fact, outweighs the bad. Yet, as in the cases cited above, where functionalization creates conflict that hinders overall goal attainment, conflict is detrimental.

Product departmentation　At the primary level, many organizations have chosen to organize along product or unit rather than along functional lines. The product form of departmentation is particularly adaptable to the tremendously large and complex modern organizations. It goes hand in hand with profit-centered decentralization. It allows the giant corporations, such as General Motors, General Electric, and Du Pont, to be broken down into groups of self-contained, smaller product organizations. Thus, the advantages of both large and small size can occur in one large organization.

The classical principle of specialization was earlier said to be the greatest benefit derived from functional departmentation. Although often ignored, specialization can also be applied to product departmentation. This was brought out as follows: "The executive who heads a battery manufacturing department generally knows more about production than other functional executives, but he also knows more about batteries than other production executives."[44] However, a greater advantage of organizing on a product basis is the matter of control. Because of their self-contained nature, product departments are very adaptable to accounting-control techniques and management appraisal. Product department performance, measured according to several different criteria, can usually be objectively determined. Another advantage is that product departments can be readily added or dropped with minimum disruption to the rest of the organization.

As a structural form, product departmentation is very compatible with the behavioral approach. Many of the conflicts that exist in the upper level under functional departmentation are generally resolved by product departmentation. Under product organization, however, the functional conflicts may disappear at the upper levels but reappear in the lower levels that are functionalized. Yet, from the standpoint of overall organization goals, functional conflict at lower levels may be preferable. Besides reducing the potential for conflict, product division lends itself to many of the same behavioral advantages found in decentralization and flat structures. They include more opportunity for personal development, growth, and self-control. Once again, this is not a universal truth, because the advantages still depend on many other personal and organizational variables. All in all, however, product or unit organization, through its self-contained character-

---

[43]Peter Drucker, *The Practice of Management*, Harper, New York, 1954, p. 125.

[44]Albers, op. cit., 4th ed., 1974, p. 95.

536

THE MANAGEMENT
PROCESSES AND
ORGANIZATION THEORY:
A MACRO PERSPECTIVE OF
ORGANIZATIONAL BEHAVIOR

istics, is potentially more structurally adaptable to the behavioral aspects of organization than is functional departmentation.

The staff concept of organization

Staff organization goes way back in history. The military is given credit for its development. As early as the seventeenth century, Gustavus Adolphus of Sweden used a military general staff. The Prussians, with some influence from the French, refined the theory and practice of this concept. At the beginning of the twentieth century, the European version of military staff was installed in the United States armed forces. However, it was not until after the Great Depression that the staff concept was widely adapted to American business and industry.

Staff is not a clear-cut organizational concept. It often creates confusion and problems for the organization. In assessing the staff concept, Koontz and O'Donnell state that "there is probably no area of management which causes more difficulties, more friction, and more loss of time and effectiveness."[45] Many of the problems stem from conflicting definitions regarding line and staff and the hybrid forms of staff used by many organizations. The military has escaped some of these problems because they have precisely defined and successfully implemented a pure staff system. The difference between the pure forms of line and staff is that line carries command or decision-making responsibilities whereas staff gives advice.

The military staff concept   Table 18-3 summarizes the function, authority, and responsibility for the line and for the three types of military staff: personal, special, and general. The key to the success of military staff is that unity of command is maintained while simultaneously advantage is taken of high degrees of specialization. The line commander has several "heads" but gives orders from only one mouth. Traditionally, the specialized back-up provides the line commander with what is termed "completed staff action." All the commander must do is approve or disapprove a decision and issue the covering order under his or her name.

In reality, military staff officers have a great deal of implied authority even though, technically, their role is limited to advising. The informal organization knows that staff officers are close to the "old man" and can

---

[45]Koontz and O'Donnell, op. cit., p. 302.

Table 18-3

SUMMARY OF THE CHARACTERISTICS OF MILITARY STAFFS

Position	Function	Authority	Responsibility
Line	Executive	Direct	General
Personal staff	Personal aid	None	Personal
Special staff	Specialized	Indirect	Functional
General staff	Functional aid	Representative	Coordinative

Source: Ernest Dale and Lyndall F. Urwick, *Staff in Organization,* McGraw-Hill, New York, 1960, p. 102. Used with permission.

always revert to formal channels in the name of the commander. The actual amount of implied authority of staff officers depends on the leadership style and personality of the line commander. Some line commanders insist on approving all staff reports and activities and on issuing the orders themselves; others do not want to be bothered with details and allow their staff officers to exercise authority in implementing as well as designing plans and activities. However, even in the latter case commanders must still maintain some degree of control, but they will usually manage by exception. On the whole, the military staff has proved to be one of the most effective concepts applied to large-scale organization structure.

The modified staff concept   Almost every type of modern organization has attempted to adopt to some degree the military staff concept. In contrast to the military, however, business, hospital, educational, and government organizations have not given proper attention to defining operationally the difference between line and staff. In the military, there definitely exists an informal, implied staff authority, but everyone understands the system and realizes that conflicts can be resolved by reverting to pure line-staff relationships. Unfortunately, this is generally not the case in other types of organizations. What usually develops is a lack of understanding of the line-staff roles and relationships, which often results in a breakdown of communication and in open conflict. A typical example is the business corporation which has a myriad of line-staff roles and relationships. It is not unusual to find many lower and middle managers who do not really know if and when they are line or staff. One reason is that they generally wear more than one hat. Normally, managers are line within their own departments and become line or staff when dealing with outside departments. The manager's functional authority is often not spelled out in the policies of the organization. As a result, personal conflicts and dual-authority situations are rampant. Chapter 13 gave specific attention to the problems of role ambiguity and conflict that can result from such line-staff relationships.

Although these weaknesses exist in a hybrid staff concept, benefits have also been derived. The larger, more technologically complex organizations have been almost forced to depend greatly on an executive staff organization. In general, these staff organizations have accomplished their purpose. Yet, from a behavioral viewpoint, one of the dominant themes associated with the staff concept is the great amount of conflict that is generated.

Line-staff conflicts   Line-staff conflicts have been one of the most commonly identifiable problem areas associated with the behavioral approach to management. The classic research of Melville Dalton is a good example of this analysis.[46] Also covered in Chapter 11 on informal organization, his case study of Milo (a pseudonym), a factory of 8000 employees, has become a classic analysis of line-staff conflict. Through detailed observations, he was able to record actual conflict that occurred between line and

---

[46]Melville Dalton, *Men Who Manage*, Wiley, New York, 1959; "Conflicts between Staff and Line Managerial Officers," *American Sociological Review,* June 1950, pp. 342–350; and "Changing Staff-Line Relationships," *Personnel Administration*, March–April 1966, pp. 3–5 and 40–48.

538

THE MANAGEMENT
PROCESSES AND
ORGANIZATION THEORY:
A MACRO PERSPECTIVE OF
ORGANIZATIONAL BEHAVIOR

staff personnel at this plant. One of his major conclusions was that line managers often view staff advice as a threat. An example was the case of R. Jefferson, a staff engineer who devised a new plan for tool room operations. At least two line supervisors admitted privately to Dalton that the plan had merit, but they nevertheless rejected it. One of them, H. Clause, explained why.

Jefferson's idea was pretty good. But his damned overbearing manner queered him with me. He came out here and tried to ram the scheme down our throats. He made me so damn mad I couldn't see. The thing about him and the whole white-collar bunch that burns me up is the way they expect you to jump when they come around. Jesus Christ! I been in this plant twenty-two years. I've worked in tool rooms, too. I've forgot more than most of these college punks'll ever know. I've worked with all kinds of schemes and all kinds of people. You see what I mean—I've been around, and I don't need a punk like Jefferson telling me where to head in. I wouldn't take that kind of stuff from my own kid—and he's an engineer too. No, his [Jefferson's] scheme may have some good points, but not good enough to have an ass like him lording it over you. He acted like we *had* to use his scheme. Damn that noise! Him and the whole white-collar bunch—I don't mean any offense to you—can go to hell. We've got too damn many bosses already.[47]

In support of the classic conflict situation, Dalton documented that at Milo the staff personnel were substantially younger and had more formal education than the line supervisors. Combined with social factors, these personal characteristics were given as the major factors explaining the conflicts which existed at Milo. However, in a later study, Dalton found some indication that the traditional line-staff conflict model may be changing, at least in some industries. His study of Transode Corporation, a fictitious name given to an electronics firm that employed a highly technical engineering staff that had no official hierarchy and a group of line officers who were formed into a strict hierarchy, provided insights into how conflict can be reduced. In this situation, friction was decreased by "assigning each individual a specific authority, by obscuring status symbols and by stressing symbols of science, quality, and service that allowed all officers to share the luster of association with a vital product."[48]

A very simple solution to help alleviate line-staff conflict and improve communications would be for all staff personnel to use the approach of "sell before tell" when dealing with line personnel. Taken philosophically and literally, this approach has great merit for improving line-staff relationships in any organization.

SUMMARY

Bureaucracy dominates classical organization theory and structure. Weber's bureaucratic model consists of specialization, hierarchy, rules, and impersonal relationships. Weber believed that this model was an ideal organiza-

---

[47]Dalton, *Men Who Manage,* op. cit., p. 75.

[48]Dalton, "Changing Staff-Line Relationships," op. cit., p. 45.

tion structure that would lead to maximum efficiency. Unfortunately, it does not always turn out this way in practice. In fact, there are probably as many dysfunctions as there are functions of a bureaucracy. Specialization or hierarchy can lead to organizational efficiencies, but either can also provoke detrimental conflict and impede the communication process. Rules often become ends in themselves rather than means to assist goal attainment, and everyone can attest to the dysfunctional consequences of the impersonal characteristic. Because of these and a number of other dysfunctions, many of today's theorists are predicting the decline and fall of the classical bureaucratic form of organization. Decentralization, flat structures, departmentation, and staff organization have developed to extend and modify the pure bureaucratic and classical principles of organization. In general, the behavioral approach is more compatible with the modified concepts.

QUESTIONS FOR DISCUSSION AND REVIEW

1. What are the major characteristics of the Weber bureaucratic model? Discuss the functions and dysfunctions of each.
2. Do you agree or disagree with those who are predicting the fall of bureaucracy? Defend your answer.
3. What are the various kinds of centralization and decentralization? Which one is most relevant to organizational analysis? Why?
4. Defend centralization as an important organizational concept. Do the same for decentralization.
5. Critically analyze functional versus product (unit) departmentation.
6. How does the military line-staff concept differ from most other organizations' line-staff structure?
7. Why does conflict develop between line and staff? How can it be resolved?

CASE:

THE GRASS IS GREENER—OR IS IT?

Alice Jenkins had been a supervisor of caseworkers in the county welfare department for nine years. The bureaucratic procedures and regulations were becoming so frustrating that she finally decided to look for a job in private industry. She had an excellent education and employment record and soon landed a supervisory position in the production end of a large insurance firm. After a few weeks on her new job she was having coffee with one of the supervisors of another department. She said, "I just can't win for losing. I quit my job at county welfare because I was being strangled by red tape. I thought I could escape that by coming to work in private industry. Now I find out that it is even worse. I was under the illusion that private industry did not have the bureaucratic problems that we had in welfare. Where can I go to escape these insane rules and impersonal treatment?"

1. Is Alice just a chronic complainer, or do you think it was as intolerable at her former and present job as she indicates? Do you think Alice is typical of most employees in similar types of positions?
2. How would you answer Alice's last question? Can you give an example of a large organization that you are familiar with that is *not* highly bureaucratized? Does the county welfare department or the insurance company have to be bureaucratized?

540

THE MANAGEMENT
PROCESSES AND
ORGANIZATION THEORY:
A MACRO PERSPECTIVE OF
ORGANIZATIONAL BEHAVIOR

3. Can the concepts of decentralization, flat structures, departmentation, and staff be used in a welfare department or in the clerical area of a large insurance company? Give some examples if possible.

CASE:

GETTING RID OF THE BUREAUCRATS AND RED TAPE

Rodney Palmer was appointed the director of a volunteer agency in a large city. He thought he was a good organizer; his style was to give people "space", let them be free to "do their own thing." He personally felt that bureaucratic systems were stifling and distasteful. He strongly felt that bureaucracies were at the root of most of the problems that government agencies had in effectively serving the people. Now that he was in charge of a community agency he had a chance to prove himself right. The first thing he did was to abolish the organization chart. From now on the person who thought up a new program would have to come to Rodney for approval. In addition, the various people in and outside the agency would come to him if they had problems and he would work with them directly on the budgeting process. He would personally appropriate and monitor funds for all programs. In this form of organization, Rodney reasoned, there would be less wasting of time and better community service. Long committee meetings and never-ending bureaucratic approval processes and red tape could be cut. "Doggone it," Rodney said to himself, "this approach to organization will get this agency rolling."

Very soon Rodney began to see evidence that he was right. The agency did start rolling. Programs were expanding and people got very excited because now somebody finally took action on their ideas. A new vitality and optimism entered the agency. Many of the oldtimers (Rodney called them "bureaucrats") in the agency were initially miffed and some quit, but Rodney felt the agency was better off without them because they just wanted power and now he kept them from obtaining it. Besides, he reasoned that most of the people who left were on the approval committees anyway and since he was now making all approvals himself they wouldn't be missed.

About two years after Rodney assumed command of the agency he was admitted to the hospital with what was diagnosed as "mental exhaustion." He had been working an average of seventy-two hours a week trying to manage the expanding number of programs by himself. While contribution sources had increased the budget for the agency by several thousand dollars, the number of programs had doubled and required a couple of hundred thousand additional dollars. Obviously, the agency was under severe strain to fund all the programs. People in and outside the agency had become very upset and frustrated over the funding restrictions. The agency couldn't beg or borrow any more funds and an investigative reporter for the local newspaper had charged misappropriation and embezzlement in more than one of the agency's programs.

1. How do you explain the short- and long-range impact of Rodney's organization structure for this agency? Did he do the right thing?
2. If you were now called in to replace Rodney, how would you organize the agency? How would you incorporate decentralization, unit departmentation, wide spans, and staff structuring into this agency? Would this structure serve the community more effectively?

MODERN ORGANIZATION THEORY AND DESIGN

MERGERS PRESSURE MODERN ORGANIZATION DESIGNS*

Besides causing economic, technological, and social pressures, the increasing amount of merger activity has greatly contributed to the restructuring of modern organizations. In the last couple of years alone there have been an estimated 4000 mergers affecting U.S. corporations. These mergers can lead to tremendous human and/or organizational difficulties. Managers and operations need to be coordinated between sometimes very diverse organizations. One of the notorious failures of merged organizations was that of the New York Central and the Pennsylvania Railroads. The severe personality problems among top management personnel and the failure to properly integrate the structures of the two companies led to a multibillion-dollar failure only 867 days after the merger was completed. Many other mergers have led to similar problems in the coordination of operations and the integration of key management personnel. For example, President David M. DeMotte of Sea World, Inc., has had some difficulty in adapting after his company was acquired by Harcourt Brace Jovanovich. Suddenly, instead of being the chief executive officer of the organization, he has a boss to please and this has proved difficult to live with at times. Rudolph Eberstadt, Jr., former president of Microdot, Inc., had the same problems when his company was merged with Northwest Industries. This merger led to Eberstadt's resignation within a year of the takeover. Obviously, the coordination of operations and the integration of the key managerial staff is an important consideration for modern organization theory and design.

---

*Adapted from "After the Merger: Keeping Key Managers on the Team," *Business Week,* Oct. 30, 1978, pp. 136–145; and Joseph R. Daughen and Peter Binzen *The Wreck of the Penn Central,* Little, Brown, Boston, 1971.

542

THE MANAGEMENT
PROCESSES AND
ORGANIZATION THEORY:
A MACRO PERSPECTIVE OF
ORGANIZATIONAL BEHAVIOR

The last chapter was concerned with the traditional theories and practices of structuring organizations. As indicated, these classical approaches are still very much in evidence today, but all areas of modern society are undergoing a process of dramatic change. This is especially true of formal organizations. Traditional ways of structuring are no longer always relevant to the modern organization. New theories and structural designs are emerging to meet the demands of growth, complexity, and change. In general, the modern approach to organization assumes more complexity and is more comprehensive in nature. For example, Robert Duncan has recently noted that, "organization structure is more than boxes on a chart; it is a pattern of interactions and coordination that links the technology, tasks, and human components of the organization to ensure that the organization accomplishes its purpose."[1] The present chapter reflects this more comprehensive theoretical understanding of organizations and presents some specific, newer structural designs. The introductory section discusses the behavioral, systems, information processing, and contingency theories of organization. This is followed by a description and an analysis of project, matrix, and free-form organization designs.

MODERN ORGANIZATION THEORY

Chester Barnard had an early influence on the break with classical thinking on organizing. In his significant book, *The Functions of the Executive*, he defined a formal organization as a system of consciously coordinated activities of two or more persons.[2] It is interesting to note that in this often cited definition, the words *system* and *persons* are given major emphasis. People, not boxes on an organization chart, make up a formal organization. Barnard was critical of the existing classical organization theory because it was too descriptive and superficial.[3] He was especially dissatisfied with the classical bureaucratic view that authority came from the top down. Barnard, utilizing a more analytical approach, took an opposite viewpoint. As Chapter 14 pointed out, he maintained that authority came from the bottom up. Furthermore, he cited four conditions that must be met before a person will decide to accept a communication as being authoritative:

1. He can and does understand the communication.
2. At the time of his decision he believes that it is not inconsistent with the purpose of the organization.
3. At the time of his decision he believes it to be compatible with his personal interest as a whole.
4. He is able mentally and physically to comply with it.[4]

---

[1]Robert Duncan, "What's the Right Organization Structure?" *Organizational Dynamics*, Winter 1979, p. 59.

[2]Chester I. Barnard, *The Functions of the Executive*, Harvard, Cambridge, 1938, p. 73.

[3]Ibid., p. vii.

[4]Ibid., p. 165.

This analysis has become known as the *acceptance* theory of authority. Barnard recognized that not every executive order can be consciously analyzed, judged, and either accepted or rejected. Rather, most types of orders fall within a person's "zone of indifference." If an order falls within the zone, the person will respond without question, but if it falls outside the zone, he or she will question and accept or reject it. The width of the zone depends upon the degree to which the inducements exceed the burdens and sacrifices.[5]

Besides authority, Barnard stressed the cooperative aspects of organization. This concern reflects the importance which he believed the human element has in organization structure and analysis. It was Barnard's contention that the existence of a cooperative system was contingent upon the human participants' ability to communicate and their willingness to serve and strive toward a common purpose.[6] Under such a premise, the human being plays the most important role in the creation and perpetuation of formal organization.

From this auspicious beginning, modern organization theory has evolved in four major directions. First are the behaviorally oriented theories. These theories take up where Barnard left off; they stress the important role that individuals and groups play in organizations. The next major development in organization theory was to view the organization as a system made up of interacting parts. Especially the open-systems concept, which stresses the input of the external environment, has had a tremendous impact on modern organization theory. This was followed by an analysis of organizations in terms of their ability to process information in order to reduce the uncertainty in managerial decision making. Finally, the most recent development in organization theory has been the contingency approach. The premise of the contingency approach is that there is no single best way to organize. The organizational design must be fitted to the existing environmental conditions. Obviously, all of these approaches are very closely related, and the contingency approach in particular tries to integrate them all. The following sections discuss these four modern theoretical approaches to organization in more detail. They serve as the foundation for the actual design of practicing organizations, which is covered in the last half of the chapter.

Behavioral organization theories

There are many behaviorally oriented organization theories which, of course, are very relevant and closely related to organizational behavior. The major behavioral organization theories deal with balance, roles, and groups.

The balance theory of organizations Barnard originally stressed and Herbert Simon later refined the theory of organizational equilibrium or

---

[5]Ibid., pp. 168–169.
[6]Ibid., p. 82.

544

THE MANAGEMENT
PROCESSES AND
ORGANIZATION THEORY:
A MACRO PERSPECTIVE OF
ORGANIZATIONAL BEHAVIOR

balance. Both Barnard and Simon brought out the importance of the human decision to participate in an organization. This concern takes two areas into consideration: the behavior of participants in joining, remaining in, or withdrawing from organizations; and the balance of inducements and contributions for all participants, measured in terms of their individual "utilities."[7] Essentially, this analysis becomes almost a theory of motivation. March and Simon conclude:

Decisions to participate in the organization—either to enter or to withdraw— . . . focus attention on the motivational problems involved in using human beings to perform organizational tasks. . . . Participation decisions are both more complex and more important to the organization than their position in classical theory would suggest.[8]

In structural terms, Simon depicts the organization as a three-layered cake. On the bottom layer are the basic work processes. The middle layer consists of the routine, programmed decisions, and the top layer is made up of unprogrammed decisions of a policy and control nature.[9] Despite the three-layered concept, he emphasizes the importance and inevitability of the hierarchical nature of organizations. But he admits that the basis for drawing departmental lines may change. "Product divisions may become even more important than they are today, while the sharp lines of demarcation among purchasing, manufacturing, engineering, and sales are likely to fade."[10]

Role theories of organizations   The role concept provides a theoretical construct for organization. A role was defined in Chapter 13 as the expectations one has of a position; the role is one of the smallest but most widely used units of analysis in sociology. Applied to organizations, each participant who occupies a position would have certain expectations from others and him- or herself as to what would be involved in this role. The organization could be thought of as a system of roles, and when these roles interact with one another, the organization could more realistically be pictured as a system of overlapping role sets.

Robert L. Kahn is most closely associated with the role set theory of organization. In Kahn's view the organization is made up of overlapping and interlocking role sets. These role sets would normally transcend the boundaries of the classical conception of organizations. Figure 19-1 gives an example of the role concept of organization. The figure shows only three possible role sets from a large manufacturing organization. The purchasing agent, executive vice president, and design engineer are called the focal persons of the sets shown. The supplier's and consultant's roles are vital in their respective sets but would not be included within traditional organiza-

---

[7]James G. March and Herbert A. Simon, *Organizations*, Wiley, New York, 1958, p. 84.

[8]Ibid., p. 110.

[9]Herbert A. Simon, *The New Science of Management Decision*, Harper & Row, New York, 1960, p. 40.

[10]Ibid., p. 50.

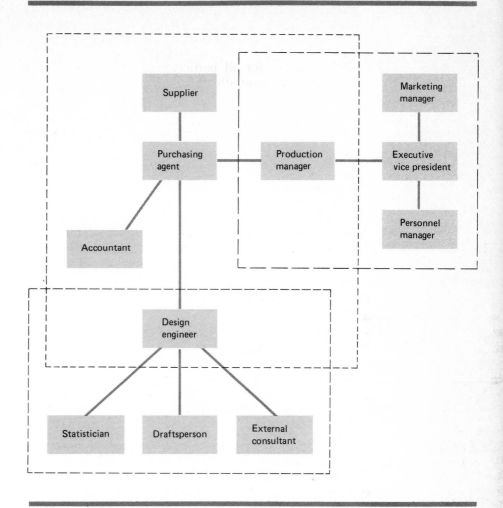

**Figure 19-1
Organization as
overlapping role
sets.**

tional boundaries. They are external to the classical organization. The design engineer is a member of the purchasing agent's role set but is also a focal person for another role set. The production manager is shown as a member of two role sets.

The overlaps can result in role conflicts and ambiguities such as were discussed in Chapter 13. Such dynamics become important in organizational analysis. For example, Kahn and his colleagues found that role conflict will be greater if the role set includes insiders as well as those outside the organizational boundaries. They also found that role conflict and ambiguity tend to be greater the higher the rank of the focal person in the role set.[11] In any case, the overlapping role set conception differs greatly from the

[11]R. L. Kahn, D. M. Wolfe, R. P. Quinn, J. D. Snowe, and R. A. Rosenthal, *Organizational Stress: Studies in Role Conflict and Ambiguity*, Wiley, New York, 1964.

546

THE MANAGEMENT
PROCESSES AND
ORGANIZATION THEORY:
A MACRO PERSPECTIVE OF
ORGANIZATIONAL BEHAVIOR

classical bureaucratic approach. However, it must be remembered that the role sets mainly describe for theoretical purposes what really goes on in an organization. The role theory approach is not necessarily suggesting that this is how organizations should (normatively) be structured in actual practice. On the other hand, similar to the group approach which follows, the role set idea has definite implications for practice and organization design.

Group theory of organization   After the role, the group is the next largest unit of sociological analysis. Rensis Likert has the most widely recognized group theory of organization. He felt that instead of the traditional individual-to-individual relationships in organizations, a more accurate depiction is a group-to-group relationship, with each individual serving as a linking pin. This linking pin idea, although conceptually very simple, represents an actual model for organization structure. Figure 19-2 depicts the model. It is based on the concept of every individual functioning as a linking pin for the organization units above and below one's own unit. Under this arrangement, every individual is a vital member of two groups. Each participant is the group leader of the lower unit and a group member of the upper unit. Thus, in the linking-pin structure, there is a group-to-group conceptualization of organization.

The linking-pin structure gives the organization an upward orientation. Communication, supervisory influence, and goal attainment are all focused upward. This is in contrast to the classical hierarchical structure, which fosters a downward orientation. In later work, Likert added horizontal (lateral) linkages to the model. Figure 19-3 recognizes the need for formalizing lateral linkages for communication, influence, motivation, and coordination purposes. He states his reason for the horizontal dimension as follows:

Lateral communication and interaction may occur through an informal organization. Since such activity is in violation of the formal system, it is less effective, however, than when done as a legitimate part of the formal system. This is equally true with

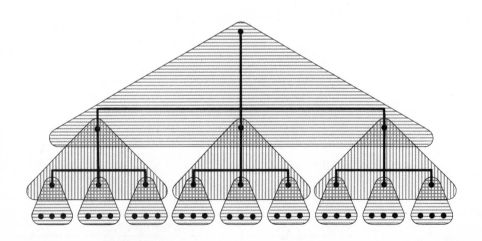

**Figure 19-2
Likert's linking-pin
model. (*Source:
Rensis Likert, New
Patterns of
Management,
McGraw-Hill, New
York, 1961, p. 105.
Used by
permission.*)**

**Figure 19-3
Vertical and
horizontal linking
pins. (*Source:*
Adapted from
Rensis Likert, *The
Human
Organization*,
McGraw-Hill, New
York, 1967, pp.
168–169. Used by
permission.)**

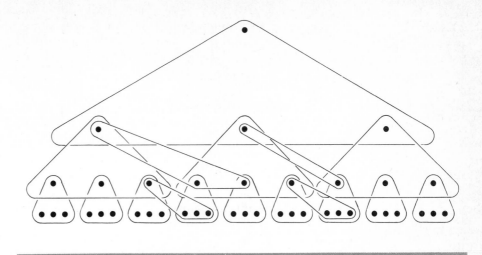

regard to the exercise of influence and the creation of the motivational forces required for cooperative coordination.[12]

Likert is very careful to point out the important role that group processes play in the linking-pin structure. All groups must be equally effective because the failure of any one group will have adverse consequences for the entire organization. In other words, the linking-pin chain is only as strong as its weakest link. To protect the group chain from breaking, Likert recommends additional staff groups and ad hoc committees. These adjuncts provide multiple overlapping groups through which linking functions are performed and the organization is bound together.[13]

Advantages and disadvantages of the linking-pin model   Proponents of the linking-pin idea are often accused of doing nothing more than drawing triangles around the traditional hierarchical arrangements. Other criticisms are that the linking-pin organization encumbers and slows down the decision-making process and generally has the same disadvantages as committees. These criticisms, for the most part, seem legitimate. The overlapping-group form of organization structure has definite limitations and disadvantages. However, the key question for organizational analysis is whether the advantages outweigh the admitted disadvantages. It has been noted that groups, as found in the linking-pin structure, provide opportunities for participation, contributions to planning, open communication, and commitments that produce binding decisions.[14] It is only logical that if people feel they are a vital part of two groups (the one in which they are a subordinate member and the one in which they are the head), they will be

---

[12]Rensis Likert, *The Human Organization*, McGraw-Hill, New York, 1967, p. 170.

[13]Rensis Likert, *New Patterns of Management*, McGraw-Hill, New York, 1961, p. 115.

[14]Bernard M. Bass and Edward C. Ryterband, *Organizational Psychology*, Allyn and Bacon, Boston, 1979, p. 317.

548

THE MANAGEMENT
PROCESSES AND
ORGANIZATION THEORY:
A MACRO PERSPECTIVE OF
ORGANIZATIONAL BEHAVIOR

more loyal to both groups and will exchange information freely and accept decisions more readily in both groups. Individuals will also exert more real upward influence under this arrangement. The latter point is stressed by Likert. Research findings support his conclusion that the ability to exert an upward influence affects not only morale and motivation, but also productivity and performance.[15]

In summary, it is probably true that the linking-pin idea only emphasizes and facilitates what is theoretically supposed to occur under the classical hierarchical structure. In reality, however, the hierarchy too often ends up having only a downward orientation, while upward and lateral communications are inhibited by the individual-to-individual authority structure. The general disadvantages of group action—the slowness in particular—must be weighed against the advantages. From a behavioral standpoint, the linking-pin arrangement, with the positive additions that are derived from lateral linkages, may be preferable to the traditional hierarchy.

Systems theory applied to organizations

The systems approach recognizes and, in most cases, fills modern organizational requirements which were either ignored or only partially solved by the classical approach. In particular, the following questions, which focus on necessary requirements for the survival of modern organizations, are compatible with a systems approach.

1. What are the strategic parts of the system?
2. What is the nature of their mutual dependency?
3. What are the main processes in the system which link the parts together and facilitate their adjustment to each other?
4. What are the goals sought by systems?[16]

The systems approach to management, which was covered in Chapter 16, stresses the interrelatedness and interdependency among the elements of a specified whole. With regard to organization theory, the whole is the formal organization, and the interrelated/interdependent parts include structure, management processes, and technology. As with any systems approach, each of the major parts of the organization may be broken down into interrelated/interdependent subparts. For example, in this book structure is divided into classical and modern structural elements; management processes include decision making and control; and technology is viewed as the mechanical techniques and total human knowledge used to obtain organization objectives. Each major subsystem in turn can be broken down further and further. Such a view of the formal organization represents only one conceptualization. Modern organization theory is far from unified. Each writer and researcher in organization and management give a different emphasis and breakdown of the elements. For example, Jay Lorsch identifies the following elements in his view of an organization: (1) structure, (2)

---

[15]Likert, *New Patterns of Management*, op. cit., p. 114.

[16]William G. Scott, "Organization Theory: An Overview and an Appraisal," *Academy of Management Journal*, April 1961, p. 16.

planning, measurement, and evaluation schemes, (3) rewards, (4) selection criteria, and (5) training.[17] Despite divergent viewpoints, the systems approach, more than any other conceptual approach, has unified organization theorists to view the organization as a whole made up of interrelated and interdependent parts. This view of organizations reflects the concept of synergism. The *synergistic effect* means that the whole organization is greater than the sum of its parts. This is an outgrowth of and closely related to the gestalt school of psychological thought covered in Chapter 2. It encourages theorists and practitioners to view the organization as a whole rather than as a series of unrelated parts.

The organization as an open system

Both the closed- and open-systems approaches discussed in Chapter 16 are utilized in modern organization theory and practice. However, in today's dramatically changing environment an open-systems approach is becoming much more relevant and meaningful. Last chapter's discussion of how General Motors is moving toward a more centralized structure for antitrust reasons clearly illustrates the point. "The open system is in continual interaction with its environment and achieves a 'steady state' or dynamic equilibrium while still retaining the capacity for work or energy transformation."[18]

The simplest open system consists of an input, a transformation process, and an output. This is graphically depicted thus:

Inputs $\longrightarrow$ **Transformation processes** $\longrightarrow$ **Outputs**

A system cannot survive without continuous input, the transformation, and output.

There are many types of inputs, transformation processes, and outputs.[19] For example, one kind of input actually enters the open system in the "closed" sense. In other words, this type of input has a direct effect on the internal system rather than an outside effect—in systems jargon, it loads the system. Another type of input affects the system in an "open" sense. Generally, this input would consist of the entire environmental influence on the system, as shown in the GM example discussed in the previous chapter. Still another kind of input takes the form of replacement or recycling. When a component of the system is ejected or leaves, the replacement becomes an input. This recycling process perpetuates the system. Specific examples of inputs into a business organization include monetary, material, and human resources.

At the heart of the open system are the processes, operations, or channels which transform the inputs into outputs. Here is where the internal

---

[17]Jay W. Lorsch, "Organization Design: A Situational Perspective," *Organizational Dynamics*, Autumn 1977, p. 3.

[18]Fremont E. Kast and James E. Rosenzweig, *Organization and Management*, 2d ed., McGraw-Hill, New York, 1974, p. 110.

[19]Stanley D. Young, *Management: A Systems Analysis*, Scott, Foresman, Glenview, Ill., 1966, pp. 16–18; and John B. Miner, *Management Theory*, Macmillan, New York, 1971, pp. 26–38.

550

THE MANAGEMENT
PROCESSES AND
ORGANIZATION THEORY:
A MACRO PERSPECTIVE OF
ORGANIZATIONAL BEHAVIOR

organizational design plays an important role. The transformation process consists of a logical network of subsystems which lead to the output. The subsystems are translated into a complex systems network that transforms the inputs into the desired outputs.

The third and final major component of any simple open system is the output. This is represented by the product, result, outcome, or accomplishment of the system. Stability and reliability are two major criteria that can be used to judge the output performance of the system. *Stability* refers to the continuity of the output of the system, and *reliability*, as in the testing sense, refers to the consistency and the error rate of the output.[20] Specific examples of the outputs of a business organization system that correspond to the inputs of monetary, material, and human resources are profit or loss, product sales, and role behaviors.

The simple open-systems concept has universal applicability. Any biological, human, social, economic, or technical phenomenon can be conceptualized in open-systems terms. As has been shown, an economic institution receives inputs of people, raw materials, money, laws, and values. The system then transforms these inputs via complex organizational subsystems into outputs, such as products, services, taxes, dividends, and pollution. From an organization structure standpoint, the critical factor is the design of the transformation process. Oddly, this transformation design involves a closed-systems analysis. In other words, the closed system is a subsystem of the open system. The closed-systems aspects of the transformation process are concerned with the interrelated and interdependent organizational subsystems of structure, processes, and technology. These subsystems must be organized in such a way that they will lead to maximum goal attainment or output.

Information processing view of organizations

The recent view of organizations as information processing systems facing uncertainty serves as a transition between systems theory, which has just been discussed, and contingency theory, which is discussed next. The information processing view makes three major assumptions about organizations.[21] First, organizations are open systems that face external, environmental uncertainty (e.g., technology or the economy) and internal, work-related task uncertainty. Jay Galbraith defines task uncertainty as "the difference between the amount of information required to perform the task and the amount of information already possessed by the organization."[22] The organization must have mechanisms and be structured in order to diagnose and cope with this environmental and task uncertainty. In particular, the organization must be able to gather, interpret, and use the appropriate

---

[20]Young, *Management: A Systems Analysis*, op. cit., pp. 17–18.

[21]These assumptions are identified in Michael L. Tushman and David A. Nadler, "Information Processing as an Integrating Concept in Organization Design," *Academy of Management Review*, July 1978, pp. 614–615.

[22]Jay Galbraith, *Designing Complex Organizations*, Addison-Wesley, Reading, Mass., 1973, p. 5.

information to reduce the uncertainty. Thus, the second assumption is as follows: "Given the various sources of uncertainty, a basic function of the organization's structure is to create the most appropriate configuration of work units (as well as the linkages between these units) to facilitate the effective collection, processing, and distribution of information."[23] In other words, organizations are information processing systems. The final major assumption of this view deals with the importance of the subunits or various departments of an organization. Because the subunits have different degrees of differentiation (i.e., they have different time perspectives, goals, technology, etc.), the important question is not what the overall organization design should be, but rather, "(a) What are the optimal structures for the different subunits within the organization (e.g., R&D, sales, manufacturing); (b) What structural mechanisms will facilitate effective coordination among differentiated yet interdependent subunits?"[24]

Taking the answers to these questions as a point of departure, Tushman and Nadler draw on the extensive relevant research to formulate the following propositions about an information processing theory of organizations:

1. The tasks of organization subunits vary in their degree of uncertainty.
2. As work-related uncertainty increases, so does the need for increased amounts of information, and thus the need for increased information processing capacity.
3. Different organizational structures have different capacities for effective information processing.
4. Organizations will be more effective when there is a match between information processing requirements facing the organization and information processing capacity of the organization's structure.
5. If organizations (or subunits) face different conditions over time, more effective units will adapt their structures to meet the changed information processing requirements.[25]

The above propositions summarize the current state of knowledge concerning the information processing view of organizations. Although the focal point of this approach is the interface between environmental uncertainty (both external and internal) and information processing, it is very closely related to and, some organization theorists would argue, could even be subsumed under the contingency approach.

Contingency organization theory

Analogous to the development of management as a whole has been the recent emphasis given to contingency views of organization theory and design. Open-system theory and information processing recognize environmental input, but the contingency approach goes one step further and relates this environment to specific organization structures. The starting point for

---

[23]Tushman and Nadler, op. cit., p. 614.

[24]Ibid., p. 615.

[25]Ibid.

552

THE MANAGEMENT
PROCESSES AND
ORGANIZATION THEORY:
A MACRO PERSPECTIVE OF
ORGANIZATIONAL BEHAVIOR

contingency organization theory is generally recognized to be some significant research conducted at England's Tavistock Institute,[26] by Joan Woodward,[27] and Burns and Stalker.[28] These pioneering efforts have since been refined by James Thompson[29] and Lawrence and Lorsch,[30] and most recently, the Aston group[31] (a group of researchers from the University of Aston in England) and Charles Perrow.[32] While it is not within the scope of this chapter to review in detail all of this research, the pioneering work of Woodward and Lawrence and Lorsch is still the most significant and is representative of contingency organization research. Each of the others have somewhat different emphases, but the key is that all contingency theorists relate the environment to organizational structure.

The Woodward study   Before the Woodward studies, most theorists had viewed the organization as rather narrow and had given little if any attention to environmental variables such as technology. Woodward openly challenged this narrow perspective. She felt that technology plays a role equal to, if not more important than, the roles of structure and processes. Her research findings tended to support a contingency view of organizations.

The major study encompassed about a hundred British (South Essex) firms. They were classified under one of the three following distinct types of productive technological environments:

1. *Unit and small batch.* This type of technology depends upon self-contained units that make products according to customer specifications; prototypes; and large equipment in stages.
2. *Large batch and mass.* This technology is characterized by mass production of large batches of goods. A moving assembly line is typically thus employed.
3. *Process.* This type of technology facilitates the intermittent production of chemicals or continuous-flow production of such substances as liquids, gases, or crystals.

After classifying the firms according to the type of technology they employed, Woodward examined the internal organizational variables of structure, human relations, and status. The results of this analysis are summarized in Table 19-1. In Woodward's own words:

---

[26]The most famous Tavistock study is E. L. Trist and K. W. Bamforth, "Some Social and Psychological Consequences of the Longwall Method of Coal-Getting," *Human Relations*, February, 1951, pp. 3–38.

[27]Joan Woodward, *Industrial Organization*, Oxford, London, 1965.

[28]Tom Burns and G. M. Stalker, *The Management of Innovation*, Tavistock Publications, London, 1961.

[29]James Thompson, *Organizations in Action*, McGraw-Hill, New York, 1967.

[30]Paul R. Lawrence and Jay W. Lorsch, *Organization and Environment*, Harvard Business School, Division of Research, Boston, 1967.

[31]Examples of the Aston group's research would be: D. S. Pugh, D. J. Hickson, S. Hinings, and C. Turner, "The Context of Organization Structure," *Administrative Science Quarterly*, March 1969, pp. 91–114; and D. J. Hickson, D. S. Pugh, and D. C. Pheysey, "Operations Technology and Organizational Structure," *Administrative Science Quarterly*, September 1969, pp. 378–397.

[32]Charles Perrow, *Organizational Analysis*, Wadsworth, Belmont, Calif., 1970.

Among the organizational characteristics showing a direct relationship with technical advance were: the length of the line of command; the span of control of the chief executive; the percentage of total turnover allocated to the payment of wages and salaries; and the ratios of managers to total personnel, of clerical and administrative staff to manual workers, of direct to indirect labour, and of graduate to non-graduate supervisory in production departments.[33]

As Leonard Sayles notes, "The structural differences could hardly have been accounted for by difference in management philosophy, the advice of consultants, or trial and error. . . . Not only the form but the substance follows from technology."[34] Yet Woodward herself backs off from an extreme position on the role of technology in formal organization structure by concluding:

It is not suggested that the research proved technology to be the only important variable in determining organizational structure. . . . Technology, although not the only variable affecting organization, was one that could be isolated for study without too much difficulty. The patterns which emerged in the analysis of the data indicated that there are prescribed and functional relationships between structure and technical demands.[35]

---

[33]Woodward, op. cit., p. 51.

[34]Leonard R. Sayles, "Managing Organizations: Old Textbooks Do Die!" *Columbia Journal of World Business*, Fall 1966, p. 84.

[35]Woodward, op. cit., pp. 50–51.

Table 19-1

SUMMARY OF WOODWARD'S FINDINGS

Type of technology	Organization structure	Human relationships	High status functions
Unit	Avg. span of control for 1st-line super., 21–30; median number reporting to top exec., 4; median levels of management, 3; and top management committees instead of single head, 12%	Small intimate groups, much participation, permissiveness, and flexibility in job inter-relationships	Development personnel Skilled workers Draughtsmen Experienced managers
Mass or batch	Span for 1st-line super., 41–50; reporting to top exec., 7; levels of mgt., 4; and mgt. committees, 32%	Clear-cut duties, line-staff conflict, and generally bad industrial relations	Production personnel (line and staff)
Process	Span for 1st-line super., 11–20; reporting to top exec., 10; levels of mgt., 6; and mgt. committees, 80%	Good interpersonal relations like the unit technology and little conflict or stress	Maintenance personnel Young, technically competent managers

Source: Adapted from Joan Woodward, *Industrial Organization,* Oxford, London, 1965, pp. 50–67.

554

THE MANAGEMENT
PROCESSES AND
ORGANIZATION THEORY:
A MACRO PERSPECTIVE OF
ORGANIZATIONAL BEHAVIOR

It is these "functional relationships" between environment variables (technology in this case) and organization structure which have contingency implications. Follow-up studies have substantiated the Woodward findings,[36] and the more recent work by Perrow has expanded Woodward's rather narrow production-oriented technological classifications to broader knowledge-based technology.[37] Figure 19-4 shows the Perrow classification of technology. Like Woodward, he then relates each technological environment to a particular organization structure as indicated in the figure.

Lawrence and Lorsch contingency study   Another landmark study that supports the contingency organization theory was done by Lawrence and Lorsch. For their study, they selected ten firms from three industries (plastics, foods, and containers) on the basis of differing rates of technological change and impacts from different sectors of the environment.[38] They analyzed the internal environment of these organizations according to the dimensions of *differentiation* (differences among managers in various functional departments according to goals, time, interpersonal orientation, and formality of structure) and *integration* (the status of interdepartmental relations, coordination, or collaboration). Then taking a contingency approach, they examined how differences in external environments were related to differences in internal environments and these, in turn, to the integrating mechanisms of the organization.

The results of the Lawrence and Lorsch study indicated that the internal organization variables have a complex relationship with each other and with external environment variables. It was found that the more turbulent, diverse, and complex the external environment was for an organization, the more differentiated the subunits/departments were and the greater the need

---

[36] William L. Zwerman, *New Perspectives on Organization Theory*, Greenwood, Westport, Conn., 1970.

[37] Perrow, op. cit.

[38] Lawrence and Lorsch, op. cit.

	Few exceptions	Many exceptions
Analyzable problems	ROUTINE TECHNOLOGY (Bureaucratic structure)	ENGINEERING TECHNOLOGY (Decentralized structure)
Unanalyzable problems	CRAFT TECHNOLOGY (Projectlike structures with problem solvers who have experience and craft knowledge)	NONROUTINE TECHNOLOGY (Open, organic structure adaptable to complexity and change)

**Figure 19-4
The Perrow
contingency model
of organization
structure.**

for elaborate organizational integrating mechanisms. For example, the plastics firms had the most turbulent, complex environments, and it followed that they were highly differentiated in the various subunits and had to have elaborate integrating mechanisms in order to be successful. The opposite was found in the container firms, who face a relatively stable, routine environment: they had low differentiation in the subunits and the fewest integrating mechanisms. The firms in the food industry face an environment in between these two extremes, and the amount of differentiation and integration also fell in between.

Put into the "if-then" contingency framework suggested in Chapter 16, the Lawrence and Lorsch's findings can be summarized as follows:

1. *If* the environment is uncertain and heterogeneous, *then* the organization should be relatively unstructured and have widely shared influence among the management staff.
2. *If* the environment is stable and homogeneous, *then* a rigid organization structure is appropriate.
3. *If* the external environment is very diverse and the internal environment is highly differentiated, *then* there must be very elaborate integrating mechanisms in the organization structure.

Other contingency studies and theories The Lawrence and Lorsch study is not the final word on the contingency approach to organization. Their sample was too small and no independent variables were manipulated, so that both the internal and external (generalizability) validity could be questioned. In addition, there is some evidence that the measures used in the study were invalid.[39] However, in combination with other contingency studies, the contingency approach has enough empirical evidence to lend support to its continued development. Particularly to be noted in this context is the earlier Burns and Stalker study of twenty British firms, which found that *mechanistic* organizations (highly specialized and centralized firms which encourage loyalty and obedience) were effective in stable environments, while *organic* organizations (firms that were vertically coordinated, had unstructured job definitions, and utilized communication based on advice rather than commands) were effective in dynamic environments.[40] The recent work of Jay Galbraith and Robert Duncan is also significant.

Galbraith's analysis of organizations Jay Galbraith ties the Lawrence and Lorsch work on differentiation and integration to an information processing perspective.[41] He stresses the need to balance differentiation and integration. As an organization grows and attempts to cope with environ-

---

[39]Henry Tosi, Ramon Aldag, and Ronald Storey, "On Measurement of the Environment: An Assessment of the Lawrence and Lorsch Environmental Uncertainty Scale," *Administrative Science Quarterly*, March 1973, pp. 27–36.

[40]Burns and Stalker, op. cit.

[41]See: Jay Galbraith, *Designing Complex Organizations*, Addison-Wesley, Reading, Mass.. 1973; and Jay Galbraith, *Organization Design*, Addison-Wesley, Reading, Mass., 1977.

556

THE MANAGEMENT
PROCESSES AND
ORGANIZATION THEORY:
A MACRO PERSPECTIVE OF
ORGANIZATIONAL BEHAVIOR

mental complexity and uncertainty, it tends to become more differentiated by adding diverse subunits. This increased differentiation will then cause an imbalance with the existing integrating mechanisms and a breakdown in the necessary information processing that is required for successful performance. For example, a fast-growing firm may lose a major contract with a customer because the salesperson can't get adequate information from production and finance in order to close the deal. In other words, the integrating mechanisms from the differentiated subunits fail to provide the necessary information for effective performance.

To restore the balance between differentiation and integration, Galbraith suggests the organization must either reduce its need to process information (e.g., by adding more resources, creating self-contained tasks, or having more effective management of the external environment) or increase its capacity to process information (e.g., by expanding vertical information systems or creating lateral relations that cut across lines of authority).[42] The suggested strategies for decreasing or increasing information processing to restore the balance of differentiation and integration are related to organization designs. For example, in Figure 19-5 Galbraith suggests seven alternatives for organizationally creating lateral relations and information flows across lines of authority. He makes the type of organization design that is appropriate (bureaucratic at one extreme and matrix at the other) contingent upon environmental (specifically, task) uncertainty. He states that "in order to be effective, organizations will utilize these forms in proportion to the amount of task uncertainty. Thus, as task uncertainty increases, the organization will sequentially adopt these mechanisms up through the matrix organization."[43]

Galbraith certainly makes a contribution to contingency organization theory. The problem is the lack of research support for his ideas and the contingency relationships he suggests. However, he does offer specific guidelines to the practicing manager. Such practical guidelines are the strength of the contingency approach.

---

[42]Galbraith, op. cit., 1977, p. 49.

[43]Ibid., p. 112.

Figure 19-5 Galbraith's contingencies for improving information processing by lateral relations cutting across traditional lines of authority. (Source: Adapted from Jay Galbraith, *Organization Design*, Addison-Wesley, Reading, Mass., 1977, p. 112.)

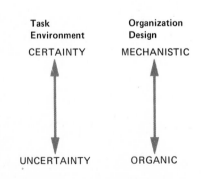

Task Environment	Organization Design	Specific Strategies
CERTAINTY UNCERTAINTY	MECHANISTIC ORGANIC	1. Direct contact among managers 2. Creation of liaison role for two interdependent departments 3. Creation of temporary task forces for several interdependent departments 4. Use of permanent teams 5. Creation of integrating role 6. Change to managerial linking role 7. Establishment of the matrix form of organization

Duncan's decision tree analysis of organizations   Robert Duncan has recently suggested a specific decision-making process that the practicing manager can use in selecting the appropriate structure to "fit" environmental demands. A contingency theorist, Duncan, like Galbraith, uses an information processing view of the organization and concludes from his research that "when organizational structure is formalized and centralized, information flows are restricted and, as a consequence, the organization is not able to gather and process the information it needs when faced with uncertainty."[44] Thus, he suggests the need to contingently relate various organization designs to the environment.

Although Duncan recognizes that there are a number of potential organization designs available to managers, he feels that they can be lumped together into two general types: functional (the highly specialized, bureaucratic structures discussed in the last chapter) and decentralized (the more modern, self-contained decision units discussed in the last chapter and the project structures discussed next in this chapter). He relates these two designs to the nature of the goals and environment as shown in Figure 19-6.

[44]Duncan, op. cit., pp. 60–61.

**Figure 19-6
Duncan's decision tree for contingent application of organization design.
[*Source:* Reprinted with permission from Robert Duncan, "What's the Right Organization Structure?" *Organizational Dynamics,* Winter 1979, (New York: *AMACOM,* a division of American Management Associations), p. 72.]**

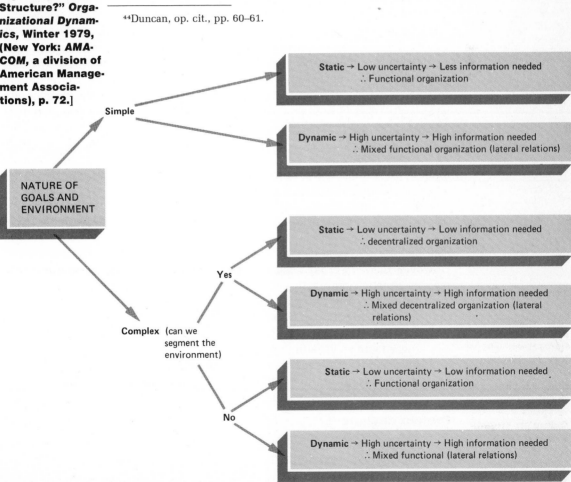

Static → Low uncertainty → Less information needed
∴ Functional organization

Dynamic → High uncertainty → High information needed
∴ Mixed functional organization (lateral relations)

Static → Low uncertainty → Low information needed
∴ decentralized organization

Dynamic → High uncertainty → High information needed
∴ Mixed decentralized organization (lateral relations)

Static → Low uncertainty → Low information needed
∴ Functional organization

Dynamic → High uncertainty → High information needed
∴ Mixed functional (lateral relations)

NATURE OF GOALS AND ENVIRONMENT

Simple

Complex (can we segment the environment)

Yes

No

558

THE MANAGEMENT
PROCESSES AND
ORGANIZATION THEORY:
A MACRO PERSPECTIVE OF
ORGANIZATIONAL BEHAVIOR

Notice that he also indicates when the functional or decentralized designs should be supplemented with some form of lateral relations such as a task force, team, or matrix.

This decision tree approach gives practicing managers even more specific guidelines for appropriate organization design than does Galbraith's approach. Duncan emphasizes that with the tremendous change that most organizations have been experiencing in recent years, there is a need for such contingency guidelines to switch back and forth. For example, he notes that the motor home–recreational vehicle industry faced a relatively simple, static environment until the oil embargo hit several years ago. Then, all of a sudden, this industry was faced with a very complex, dynamic environment. The firms in this industry could have used the guidelines suggested in the decision tree to restructure themselves.

Specifically, there are four major advantages to the practice of management by the decision tree approach:

1. It provides a *broad framework* for identifying the key factors a manager should think about in considering an organization design.
2. It forces the manager to *diagnose* the decision environment.
3. It causes managers to think about *how much interdependence* there is among segments of the organization.
4. Once the organization is in either a functional or decentralized structure, the decision tree points out what can be done to meet the *increased needs for information* through the use of lateral relations.[45]

This practical approach to organization structure provided by Duncan serves as a good point of departure for describing and analyzing the modern organization designs.

MODERN ORGANIZATION DESIGNS

Along with organization theorists, many practicing managers are becoming disenchanted with traditional ways of designing their organizations. Up to the last few years, most managers attempted only timid modifications of classical structures and balked at daring experimentation and innovation. However, many of today's managers have finally overcome this resistance to making drastic organizational changes. They realize that the simple solutions offered by the classical theories are no longer adequate for many of their complex problems. In particular, the needs for flexibility, adaptability to change, and overcoming environmental uncertainty are among the biggest challenges facing a growing number of modern organizations. The following sections describe and analyze some of the newer structural models that have been designed and implemented to meet these challenges.

Project designs

From a rather restricted beginning in the aerospace industry and in those firms having contracts with the Department of Defense, the use of project

---

[45]Ibid., p. 79.

designs has increased in all organizations that require a great deal of planning, research, and coordination. In addition to the aerospace industry, it is becoming widely used in other industrial corporations and also in financial institutions, health care facilities, governmental agencies, and educational institutions. For example, the project design has been credited with successfully downsizing General Motors autos in response to the gasoline shortage crisis. Normally, such a major undertaking would be very cumbersome and complex and would take a very long time. But by creating project teams for the various divisions, GM was able to successfully accomplish this major effort in less than two years.[46]

The most salient characteristic of project organization, and the most radical departure from classical organization structures, is the existence of horizontal and diagonal relationships. It has been noted that these horizontal and diagonal arrangements have sufficient strength and permanency to become in reality the modus operandi of the project organization.[47]

Projects of various degrees of importance and magnitude are always under way in an organization. The project structure is created when management decides to focus a great amount of talent and resources for a given period on a specific project goal. There are several criteria that should be explored before an organization moves to a project structure. One writer feels that the character of a project should be

1. Definable in terms of a specific end result;
2. A unique or infrequent effort to the existing management group;
3. Complex with respect to the degree of interdependence among tasks; and
4. [Such that its] stake in the outcome is extremely critical to the organization.[48]

These criteria are effective guidelines for assessing the desirability of project structures.

Types of project structures

There are several types of project structures.[49] One is the *individual* project organization. This consists of only the project manager. Figure 19-7 shows that the project managers under this design have no activities or personnel reporting directly to them. The project manager, along with the heads of quality control, research and development, contract administration, and scheduling, acts in a staff capacity to the general manager. The project manager must rely on influence and persuasion in performing a monitoring role with direct line authority exercised only by the general manager. Richard Hodgetts discovered four leadership techniques that were success-

[46]Charles G. Burck, "How GM Turned Itself Around," *Fortune*, Jan. 16, 1978, pp. 92–96.

[47]David I. Cleland and William R. King, *Systems Analysis and Project Management*, McGraw-Hill, New York, 1968, p. 151.

[48]John M. Stewart, "Making Project Management Work," *Business Horizons*, Fall 1965, pp. 57–59.

[49]C.J. Middleton, "How to Set Up a Project Organization," *Harvard Business Review*, March–April 1967, p. 78.

560

THE MANAGEMENT
PROCESSES AND
ORGANIZATION THEORY:
A MACRO PERSPECTIVE OF
ORGANIZATIONAL BEHAVIOR

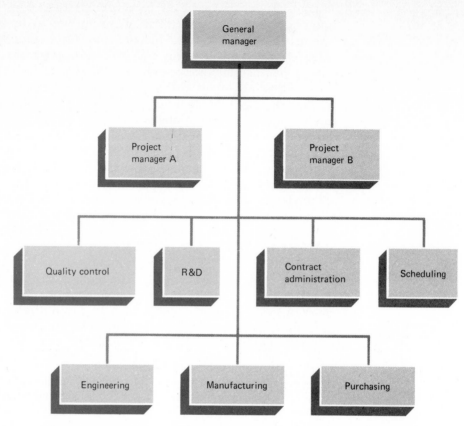

**Figure 19-7
Individual project
organization.**

fully used by project managers who suffered from such an "authority gap":
negotiation, personality and/or persuasive ability, competence, and reciprocal favors.[50]

A second variation is the *staff* project design. Under this arrangement,
the project manager is provided staff backup for project activities, but the
primary functional tasks of the organization are performed by the traditional
line departments. The project managers only have authority and control over
the staff backup for their project. However, as with the individual project
design, the project managers under a staff design must rely on leadership
techniques rather than on line authority over the primary functional areas.
The same is true only to a lesser degree in the *intermix* form of project
organization. In the intermix design the project managers have staff personnel and selected primary functional heads reporting directly to them. A
fourth type is termed *aggregate* project organization. Here, project managers
have all the personnel necessary for the project. They have staff and
functional line personnel reporting directly to them. Figure 19-8 shows that
the project managers under the aggregate design have full authority over the
entire project. In reality, the aggregate project organization is very similar to

---

[50]Richard M. Hodgetts, "Leadership Techniques in the Project Organization," *Academy of
Management Journal*, June 1968, p. 219.

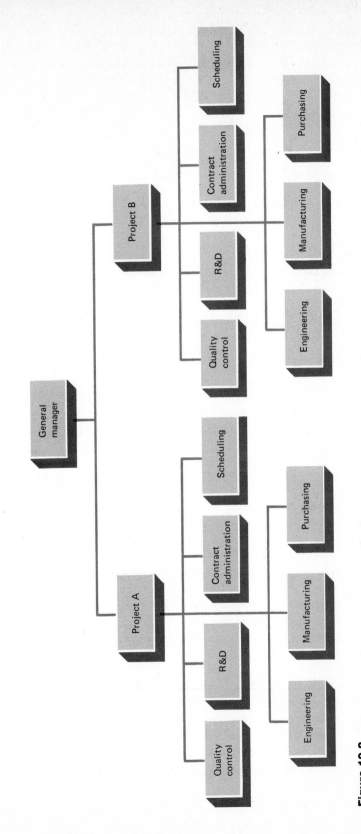

Figure 19-8
Aggregate project organization.

562

THE MANAGEMENT
PROCESSES AND
ORGANIZATION THEORY:
A MACRO PERSPECTIVE OF
ORGANIZATIONAL BEHAVIOR

the traditional product or unit form of departmentation that was presented in the last chapter.

There are other possible variations besides the individual, staff, inter-mix, and aggregate designs, and the project organization almost always coexists with the more traditional functional structure. But project experts stress that even though there are many similarities between project and functional organizations, project managers must take a new approach to their job.

1. He must become reoriented away from the purely functional approach to the management of human and nonhuman resources.
2. He must understand that purposeful conflict may very well be a necessary way of life as he manages his project across many vertical, organizational lines.
3. He must recognize that project management is a dynamic activity where major changes are almost the order of the day.[51]

These three statements make it clear that the project concept is a philosophy of management as well as a form of structural organization. The project viewpoint is quite different from the functional one. Table 19-2 summarizes some of the major differences.

Matrix designs

When a project structure is superimposed on a functional structure, the result is a matrix. Sometimes the matrix organization is considered to be a form of project organization, and the terms are used interchangeably. However, a more accurate portrayal would show that the matrix organization is a project organization *plus* a functional organization, rather than a variation of a project organization. The project overlay provides a horizontal, lateral dimension to the traditional vertical orientation of the functional organization. Figure 19-9 represents a very simplified matrix organization. Here, the functional department heads have line authority over the special-ists in their departments (vertical structure). The functional specialists are then assigned to given projects (horizontal structure). These assignments are usually made at the beginning of each project by a collaboration between the appropriate functional and project managers.

It has recently been argued that the matrix structure evolves as shown in Table 19-3. Also the matrix structure was mentioned earlier in this chapter in relation to both Galbraith's and Duncan's contingency models. They suggested that matrix designs are a way to obtain lateral relations that cut across lines of authority.

Direct violation of classical principles Matrix designs violate the traditional organizational principles. The hierarchy principle and unity of command are flagrantly violated. Furthermore, the matrix concept does not coincide with the usual line-staff arrangements discussed in the last chapter. Obviously, a great deal of conflict is generated in matrix organization. An

---

[51]Cleland and King, op. cit., p. 152.

Table 19-2

A COMPARISON OF THE PROJECT VERSUS THE FUNCTIONAL ORGANIZATION

Phenomenon	Project viewpoint	Functional viewpoint
Line-staff organizational dichotomy	Vestiges of the hierarchal model remain, but line functions are placed in a support position. A web of authority and responsibility relationships exists.	Line functions have direct responsibility for accomplishing the objectives; the line commands, staff advises.
Scalar principle	Elements of the vertical chain exist, but prime emphasis is placed on horizontal and diagonal work flow. Important business is conducted as the legitimacy of the task requires.	The chain of authority relationships is from superior to subordinate throughout the organization. Central, crucial, and important business is conducted up and down the vertical hierarchy.
Superior-subordinate relationship	Peer-to-peer, manager-to-technical expert, associate-to-associate relationships are used to conduct much of the salient business.	This is the most important relationship; if kept healthy, success will follow. All important business is conducted through a pyramiding structure of superiors-subordinates.
Organizational objectives	Management of a project becomes a joint venture of many relatively independent organizations. Thus, the objective becomes multilateral.	Organizational objectives are sought by the parent unit (an assembly of sub-organizations) working within its environment. The objective is unilateral.
Unity of direction	The project manager manages across functional and organizational lines to accomplish a common inter-organizational objective.	The general manager acts as the head for a group of activities having the same plan.
Parity of authority and responsibility	Considerable opportunity exists for the project manager's responsibility to exceed his or her authority. Support people are often responsible to other managers (functional) for pay, performance reports, promotions, and so forth.	Consistent with functional management; the integrity of the superior-subordinate relationship is maintained through functional authority and advisory staff services.
Time duration	The project (and hence the organization) is finite in duration.	Tends to perpetuate itself to provide continuing facilitative support.

Source: David I. Cleland, "Understanding Project Authority," *Business Horizons,* Spring 1967, p. 66. Used with permission.

564

THE MANAGEMENT
PROCESSES AND
ORGANIZATION THEORY:
A MACRO PERSPECTIVE OF
ORGANIZATIONAL BEHAVIOR

organizational specialist with IBM has observed that, besides fostering conflict, the matrix structure discourages informal groups and the nurturing of supervisor-subordinate relations. After ten years experience with the transition from traditional hierarchical to matrix organizations, he concluded that the matrix structure "has seemingly reduced participant motivation for all but the most aggressive personalities and has reduced corporate loyalty and identification with the organization."[52] These disadvantages are balanced by many positive aspects of matrix organization.

Advantages of matrix designs The matrix organization attempts to combine the best of both worlds. In an eclectic manner, it includes the positive aspects of both the functional and project designs. These advantages can be summarized as follows:

1. The project is emphasized by designating one individual as the focal point for all matters pertaining to it.
2. Utilization of manpower can be flexible because a reservoir of specialists is maintained in functional organizations.

---

[52]Michael V. Fiore, "Out of the Frying-Pan into the Matrix," *Personnel Administration,* July–August 1970, p. 6.

**Figure 19-9
An example of a
matrix design.**

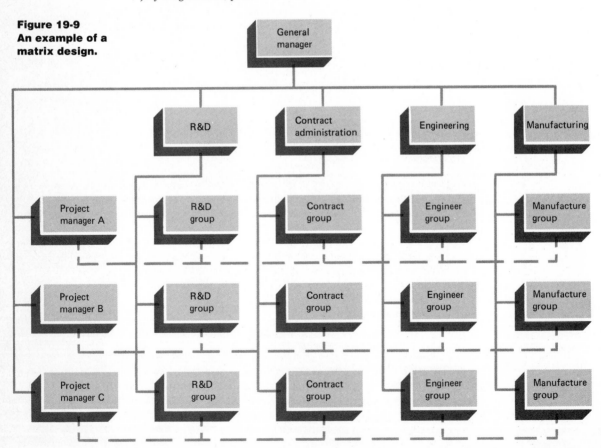

Table 19-3

DETERMINANTS OF THE EVOLUTIONARY STAGES OF MATRIX DESIGN

Organization design	Determinants
Functional ⟶	1. Efficiency is the major objective. 2. Competitive advantage is along a parameter such as technology, price, performance, or delivery. 3. Markets are relatively stable and predictable. 4. There is a narrow range of products with long-term perspectives.
Project ⟶	1. There are several simultaneous objectives (e.g., performance, cost, price, schedule, technology, and efficiency). 2. There is moderate market change. 3. There are differentiated clients/customers and markets. 4. There is a moderate number of products or projects. 5. There are specified time horizons for each client/customer or project. 6. There is interconnectedness between outside and local organization.
Product/matrix ⟶	1. Innovation is the major objective. 2. There are differentiated products, markets, and customers/clients. 3. High variability and uncertainty characterize the product-market mix. 4. The time perspective for products varies from medium to long.
Matrix ⟶	1. There are the same determinants as for product/matrix.

Source: Adapted from Harvey F. Kolodny, "Evolution to a Matrix Organization," *Academy of Management Review,* October 1979, p. 551.

3. Specialized knowledge is available to all programs on an equal basis; knowledge and experience can be transferred from one project to another.
4. Project people have a functional home when they are no longer needed on a given project.
5. Responsiveness to project needs and customer desires is generally faster because lines of communication are established and decision points are centralized.
6. Management consistency between projects can be maintained through the deliberate conflict operating in the project-functional environment.
7. A better balance between time, cost and performance can be obtained through the built-in checks and balances (the deliberate conflict) and the continuous negotiations carried on between the project and the functional organizations.[53]

   Theorists who advocate a matrix structure maintain that these advantages outweigh the inherent disadvantages. Many contemporary organizations which are facing tremendous structural and technical complexity have no choice but to move to such an arrangement. The critical need for coordina-

[53]Cleland and King, op. cit., p. 172.

tion and functional interrelationships can be met by adding a horizontal dimension to the functional structure.

Making the matrix effective As Galbraith and Duncan pointed out, in many modern organizations a lateral *interface* has developed. It occurs when people, departments, or systems must meet to support one another, integrate the existing differentiation, and reduce the environmental uncertainty. Interface, more precisely, is "the contact point between relatively autonomous organizations which are nevertheless interdependent and interacting as they seek to cooperate to achieve some larger system objective."[54] Such an interface can result in either conflict or cooperation. Like the project design, the matrix organization depends on effective leadership to overcome the obstacles and attain the positive attributes of coordination and communication. In this regard, the following conclusion has been drawn: "The scalar indeterminacy which exists between project managers and department managers gives rise to a number of transactions that can be only described as political."[55] Some matrix experts maintain that only significant conflicts should be presented to a common superior for resolution. In other words, they recommend that management by exception become the rule in a matrix organization. The right of appeal should not be exercised unless the following two criteria are met:

1. The issue is clearly drawn, with alternatives and costs described.
2. It is a salient project-functional issue.[56]

This type of systematic approach helps to overcome some of the potential difficulties of matrix organizations. This type of organization design will undoubtedly become more widely used in the future to meet the demands of increased differentiation and the ever increasing complexity and uncertainty of the external environment. Like project structure, the application so far has been in the aerospace industry. But many other large, complex organizations are turning to this structure. *Business Week* recently reported that corporations such as General Electric, TRW Systems, Citicorp, Dow Corning, and Shell Oil are currently using a matrix design.[57] The matrix should be measured against the same high standards that are applied to other types of structures.

Free-form organizations

Closely related to the project and matrix models are the free form, sometimes called the *naturalistic* or *organic*, structures of modern organization. The

---

[54]Daniel A. Wren, "Interface and Interorganizational Coordination," *Academy of Management Journal*, March 1967, p. 71.

[55]William G. Scott and Terence R. Mitchell, *Organization Theory*, Irwin, Homewood, Ill., 1972, p. 64.

[56]Cleland and King, op. cit., p. 178.

[57]"How to Stop the Buck Short of the Top," *Business Week*, Jan. 16, 1978, p. 82.

free-form model is based on the premise that the purpose of an organization is to facilitate the management of change. To accomplish this objective, the structural arrangements are highly adaptable and flexible. There are no prescribed or rigid roles and the internal structure is now allowed to solidify.[58]

Under the free-form concept, there is no one way of organizing. Organizations that operate under the free-form concept tailor-make the structure to fit their particular needs at a particular time. Usually, the traditional, departmentalized functional structure is replaced by self-contained profit centers. These organizational units are results-oriented and their members are managed as a team. Individual action within a team attempts to incorporate the behavioral approach to management. Participation, self-control, individual initiative, independent judgment, open communication, and sensitivity are some of the human factors that are encouraged and facilitated by free-form organization.

In a sense, the free-form organization is merely an extension of the "Great Organizer" Alfred Sloan's model of decentralization. An executive group at the top of the organization maintains centralized control over highly decentralized profit centers. Keeping the profit centers autonomous facilitates the management of change because whole units can be dropped or added with little disruption to the rest of the organization.

Besides the decentralized pattern, there are two major characteristics common to all free-form organizations. First, they make extensive use of computerized information systems, especially to evaluate the performance of various organizational units. Second, they are populated by young, dynamic managers who are willing to accept calculated risks. These executives usually have had previous experience in one of the firms which pioneered the free-form concept. The firms include Litton Industries, Xerox Corporation, and Textron, Inc.[59]

Companies that have come to depend on a free-form structure are those which must be highly adaptive to products or services that are on the frontiers of public consumption (for example, pollution control devices) or high-demand industrial, consumer, or military products (for example, electronic devices, lenses and frames, and space-age hardware).[60] The free-form structure provides the opportunity for technological and operational leverage. Technologically, it can take advantage of external changes and the transfer of new knowledge. Operationally, it can easily spread, reduce, or prune to meet economic, technological, or social contingencies, even in the short run.[61] Many types of organizations, including

---

[58]For discussions of free-form organizations, see Dalton E. McFarland, *Management: Principles and Practices*, 4th ed., Macmillan, New York, 1974, pp. 161–163; and John J. Pascucci, "The Emergence of Free-Form Management," *Personnel Administration*, September–October, 1968, pp. 33–41.

[59]Pascucci, op. cit., p. 38.

[60]Ibid., pp. 37–38.

[61]Ibid., p. 38.

568

THE MANAGEMENT
PROCESSES AND
ORGANIZATION THEORY:
A MACRO PERSPECTIVE OF
ORGANIZATIONAL BEHAVIOR

conglomerates[62] and highly technical firms, have found the free-form structure to fit their needs.

SUMMARY

Modern organization theory was presented from the perspective of the behavioral, systems, information processing, and contingency approaches. The behaviorally oriented approaches include the balance theory of inducements and contributions, the overlapping role set description of organizations from role theory, and the group theory represented by linking pins on a group-to-group basis. Systems theory emphasizes the synergistic effect of organizations (the whole is greater than the sum of the parts) and the impact of the external environment, which is expressed through open-systems analysis. The information processing approach views the importance of information flows in an organization to cope with internal differentiation and external environmental uncertainty. Contingency theory gives specific attention to the environment by relating it to organization structure and design. The Woodward and Lawrence and Lorsch studies gave initial empirical support to the contingency approach and the more recent work of Galbraith and Duncan shows a great deal of promise.

The new organizational models that have recently come on the scene have been designed by practitioners primarily to meet their dramatically changing needs. The project, matrix, and free-form structures represent a significant departure from the classical, bureaucratic model. The new structures flagrantly violate classical principles such as unity of command and equal authority and responsibility. Nevertheless, organizations with technologies that require flexibility and adaptability to change are willing to sacrifice the classical concepts. Only time will tell whether the new structural forms are suitable replacements for classical structure. On the other hand, there seems little doubt that the new designs in general and the systems, information processing, and contingency concepts in particular have already proved themselves valuable enough to become a significant part of organization theory and practice.

QUESTIONS FOR DISCUSSION AND REVIEW

1. What was Chester Barnard's contribution to organization theory?
2. How does Likert's linking-pin model differ from the traditional hierarchical structure?
3. What are two ways that the systems concept can be applied to organizations? Discuss each.

---

[62]In a *Fortune* list of forty-six conglomerates (companies with eight or more categories of business), twelve are considered to use free-form structures. See Thomas O'Hanlon, "The Odd News about Conglomerates," *Fortune*, June 15, 1967, pp. 175–177, for a discussion of conglomerates.

4. How does the open-system theory differ from the information processing and contingency approaches? How does the open-system concept apply to organizations? How does the information processing concept apply to organizations? How does the contingency concept apply to organizations?

5. What are some different types of project structures? How does the project manager differ from the traditional functional manager?

6. The matrix design of organization is variously said to rest on classical, behavioral, systems, information processing, and contingency bases. Explain how each of these approaches could serve as the basis for the matrix design.

CASE: THE OUTDATED STRUCTURE

Jake Harvey had a position on the corporate planning staff of a large company in a high technology industry. Although he had spent most of his time on long-range, strategic planning for the company, he was appointed to a task force to reorganize the company. The president and board of directors were concerned that they were losing their competitive position in the industry because of an outdated organization structure. Being a planning expert, Jake convinced the task force that they should proceed by first determining exactly what type of structure they have now, then determine what type of environment the company faces now and in the future, and then design the organization structure accordingly. In the first phase they discovered that the organization was currently structured along classical bureaucratic lines. In the second phase they felt that they were competing in a highly dynamic, rapidly growing, and uncertain environment that required a great deal of flexibility and response to change.

1. What type(s) of organization design do you feel this task force should recommend in the third and final phase of the approach to their assignment?

2. Explain how the behavioral, systems, information processing, and contingency theories of organization can each contribute to the analysis of this case.

3. Do you think Jake was correct in his suggestion of how the task force should proceed? What types of problems might develop as by-products of the recommendation you made in question 1?

CASE: AFRAID TO ASK

Ralph Worth had been a project manager for a high technology transportation equipment company for the past three years. He had worked in various line and staff jobs in the production area for several years before his present job. When he took the project management job he was very uncertain whether the company was doing the right thing by moving to this project design. He felt that the old method of each functional department having full say over its own particular phase of the task was working well. In his role as project manager, Ralph was completely responsible for every facet of the project (quality specifications, supplies, finish dates, etc.). He was never told, and he was afraid to ask, how much authority he had over the project. He just went ahead and gave orders to everyone in the functional departments that he had to work with.

570

THE MANAGEMENT
PROCESSES AND
ORGANIZATION THEORY:
A MACRO PERSPECTIVE OF
ORGANIZATIONAL BEHAVIOR

He did sense a lot of backlash from the functional managers who resented their apparent loss of power and the intrusion of the new project managers. Ralph was not sure how he could handle these problems. The functional managers were his friends; he had worked for some of them before. Ralph felt that he was caught in the middle. He did not want to start really bucking the functional managers, but he knew that he and he alone was responsible for the project, especially if something went wrong. So far Ralph was keeping things on schedule and meeting all the specifications on the project. However, he was not sure how long he or the project design would last.

1. What type of project design is Ralph apparently working in? Should his role be clarified by top management?
2. Do you think this company is better off under this project structure? Do you agree with Ralph's concern that both he and the project design may not last?

CASE STUDY AND EXPERIENTIAL EXERCISES FOR PART 5

CASE:
A TEAM APPROACH[1]

The Inland Division of the General Motors Corporation supplies the firm with equipment such as steering wheels, foam seats, ball joints, and padded dashboards. While this is but a small portion of all the hardware found on today's automobile, the division currently accounts for around $300 million in annual sales.

For the past decade Inland's general manager, Thomas O. Mathues, has been operating the firm under a very open, participatory organization structure, which is designed to stop the division's 600 line managers from getting lost in the shuffle. His brand of team organization design includes the following kinds of characteristics:

1. Teams of twenty-five to seventy-five members operate internally as individual companies and are responsible for one or more of the division's product lines.
2. Rotating team chiefs, who are specialists in manufacturing, product engineering, or production engineering, serve as boss for four months each year when the product cycle is especially relevant to their talents.
3. A nine-member division staff acts as a board of directors for each of the teams, reviewing progress at quarterly board meetings at which up to a dozen members of a single team may discuss problems such as quality control and manufacturing performance.

Mr. Mathues began deemphasizing the traditional bureaucratic structure soon after taking over the helm about a decade ago. The major reason he cites for going to the new structural design is the improvement it permits in decision response time. As was reported in *Business Week,* "In forming the teams, the first step was to bring together managers involved in engineering and manufacturing. Later the teams became more autonomous as salaried employees were added for such functions as purchasing, finance, and sales. Recently, the teams have been trying, with mixed results, to bring hourly workers into the team effort as well."

The primary objective of this team approach was to deemphasize the little functional empires that were developing under the traditional organization structure. These empires often worked at cross purposes with each other and the overall organization because individual managers associated themselves with departments rather than with the organization. For example, it was not

[1]The data in this case can be found in: "GM's Test of Participation, "*Business Week,* Feb. 23, 1976, pp. 88, 90.

571

572

THE MANAGEMENT
PROCESSES AND
ORGANIZATION THEORY:
A MACRO PERSPECTIVE OF
ORGANIZATIONAL BEHAVIOR

atypical to find someone saying "I'm a quality control guy and I'm not really very interested in your production problems." Now all of that has changed because people currently think of themselves as all being on the same team. And in getting the job done, these teams have wide operating latitude, often acting like semiautonomous units. As reported in *Business Week:*

All team members have access to information necessary for general management of the team, such as selling price, competitive position in the marketplace, and materials costs for their product. Based on the data, each team makes up its own annual operating budget, giving up—on paper—50% of its profits for taxes and 70% of its after-tax earnings to GM as "dividends." Whatever is left, plus depreciation, the teams may use for capital investment. Any remaining profit is "loaned" to the division at 9% interest. But, if the team's capital needs are unusually high, it can "borrow" from the division at the same rate of interest. Last year, for example, a bumper rub-strip team had to take out a substantial loan to buy a new $500,000 rubber mixing machine to replace one carried on the books at only $250,000.

The managers at Inland say that the design is working smoothly because everyone has a chance to participate in the decision-making process. In addition, they claim that this new form of organization allows materials to be altered and engineering innovations to be made much more quickly than before, thereby reducing costs. In the case of material alterations and cost reduction, for example, a production engineer made a recommendation about product design that wound up reducing the amount of vinyl in steering wheels, thereby saving the division 10 percent of its vinyl costs. In another case, the bumper rub-strip team persuaded the division's rubber compounders to change their formulas, thereby reducing the number of carbon blacks in inventory from thirteen to six and saving the division $30,000 annually.

Of course, no one is saying that this team approach is favored by all. Some people dislike having to think in terms of "we" rather than "I." And then there is the problem associated with controlling and providing needed information to all of these people. This takes a great amount of time but is absolutely essential for coordinated team action. Finally, company managers admit that they are still having little success involving hourly workers in this team approach. At present, only a handful of the 5500 hourly personnel have joined these teams. As Mr. Mathues has pointed out, "The question is how to make it intelligible that our well-being and theirs is tied together. We have yet to find an entirely appropriate way."

Still, it is hard to argue with the overall success that the division has had with this new organizational concept. Although Inland will not release either sales or earning figures, Mr. Mathues says that there is clear evidence that the new design is working well. Since phasing in the team approach, he reports, sales in constant dollars (eliminating the effect of inflation) have increased by 45 percent per employee, 35 percent per salaried employee, and 20 percent per square foot of plant space. As a result, it appears that the new team design at Inland will continue to be the organizational philosophy of the future.

1. Is the organization structure used by Inland classical or modern? Explain. What organization theory(s) is it based upon?
2. In what way do you think the participatory feature helps account for Inland Division's apparent success?
3. In addition to participation, what other kinds of benefits does Inland's structure seem

to have compared to the traditional bureaucratic structure? What are the implications for management processes such as decision making and control?

4. If this new structure is superior to a traditional one, why do the hourly employees not join in? How would you propose to get them more involved?

EXERCISE:
ORGANIZA-TIONS

Goals:

1. To identify some of the important organizations in your life
2. To determine relevant, specific characteristics of organizations
3. To describe some of the important functions of management in organizations

Implementation:

Read the "Overview" and "Procedure" sections. Complete the "Profile of Organizations" form which follows those sections.

Overview:

Undoubtedly, you have had recent experiences with numerous organizations. Ten to fifteen minutes of reflective thinking should result in a fairly large list of organizations. Don't be misled by thinking that only large organizations, such as your college or General Motors, are relevant for consideration. How about the clinic with the doctor(s), nurse(s), and secretary/bookkeeper? Or the corner garage or service station? The local tavern, McDonald's Golden Arches, and the neighborhood theater are all organizations. You should have no difficulty listing several organizations with which you have had recent contact.

The second part of the exercise, however, gets tougher. You are asked to describe several of the key characteristics of the organizations that you have listed. One of the major issues in studying and describing organizations is deciding *what* characteristics or factors are important. Some of the more common characteristics considered in the analysis of organizations are:

1. Size (small to very large)
2. Degree of formality (informal to highly structured)
3. Degree of complexity (simple to complex)
4. Nature of goals (what the organization is trying to accomplish)
5. Major activities (what tasks are performed)
6. Types of people involved (age, skills, educational background, etc.)
7. Location of activities (number of units and their geographic location)

You should be able to develop a list of characteristics that you think are relevant for each of your organizations.

Now to the third, final, and most difficult task. Think about what is involved in the *management* of these organizations. For example, what kinds of functions do their managers perform? How does one learn the skills necessary to be an effective manager? Would you want to be a manager in any of these organizations?

In effect, in this exercise we are asking you to think specifically about organizations you have been associated with recently, develop your own conceptual model for looking at their characteristics, and think more specifically about the managerial functions in each of these organizations. You probably

574

THE MANAGEMENT
PROCESSES AND
ORGANIZATION THEORY:
A MACRO PERSPECTIVE OF
ORGANIZATIONAL BEHAVIOR

already know a great deal more about organizations and their management than you think. This exercise should be useful in getting your thoughts together.

Procedure:

Step 1 Prior to class, list up to 10 organizations (e.g., work, living group, club) in which you have been involved or with which you have had recent contact.

Step 2 Enter five organizations from your list on the following form.

1. List the organization.
2. Briefly outline the characteristics that you consider most significant.
3. Describe the managerial functions in each of these organizations.

Step 3 During the class period, meet in groups of five or six to discuss your list of organizations, the characteristics you consider important, and your descriptions of their management. Look for significant similarities and differences across organizations.

Step 4 Basing your selections on this group discussion, develop a list entitled "What we would like to know about organizations and their management." Be prepared to write this list on the blackboard or on newsprint and to share your list with other groups in the class.

PROFILE OF ORGANIZATIONS

Organization	Key characteristics	Managerial functions
1. _____	_____	_____
	_____	_____
	_____	_____
	_____	_____
2. _____	_____	_____
	_____	_____
	_____	_____
	_____	_____
	_____	_____
3. _____	_____	_____
	_____	_____
	_____	_____
	_____	_____
	_____	_____
4. _____	_____	_____
	_____	_____
	_____	_____
	_____	_____
	_____	_____
5. _____	_____	_____
	_____	_____
	_____	_____
	_____	_____

EXERCISE:

PAPER PLANE CORPORA- TION

Goals:

1. To work on an actual organizational task
2. To experience the managerial functions of organizing, decision making, and control

Implementation:

Unlimited groups of six participants each are used in this exercise. These groups may be directed simultaneously in the same room. Approximately a full class period is needed to complete the exercise. Each person should have assembly instructions and a summary sheet, which are shown on the following pages, and ample stacks of paper (8-1/2 by 11 inches). The physical setting should be a room large enough so that the individual groups of six can work without interference from the other groups. A working space should be provided for each group.

1. The participants are doing an exercise in production methodology.
2. Each group must work independent of the other groups.
3. Each group will choose a manager and an inspector, and the remaining participants will be employees.
4. The objective is to make paper airplanes in the most profitable manner possible.
5. The facilitator will give the signal to start. This is a ten-minute, timed event utilizing competition among the groups.
6. After the first round, everyone should report their production and profits to the entire group. They also should note the effect, if any, of the manager in terms of the performance of the group.
7. This same procedure is followed for as many rounds as there is time.

PAPER PLANE CORPORATION: DATA SHEET

Your group is the complete work force for Paper Plane Corporation. Established in 1943, Paper Plane has led the market in paper plane production. Presently under new management, the company is contracting to make aircraft for the U. S. Air Force. You must establish an efficient production plant to produce these aircraft. You must make your contract with the Air Force under the following conditions:

1. The Air Force will pay $20,000 per airplane.
2. The aircraft must pass a strict inspection made by the facilitator.
3. A penalty of $25,000 per airplane will be subtracted for failure to meet the production requirements.
4. Labor and other overhead will be computed at $300,000.
5. Cost of materials will be $3000 per bid plane. If you bid for ten but only make eight, you must pay the cost of materials for those you failed to make or which did not pass inspection.

576

THE MANAGEMENT
PROCESSES AND
ORGANIZATION THEORY:
A MACRO PERSPECTIVE OF
ORGANIZATIONAL BEHAVIOR

INSTRUCTIONS FOR AIRCRAFT ASSEMBLY

 STEP 1: Take a sheet of paper and fold it in half, then open it back up.

 STEP 2: Fold upper corners to the middle.

 STEP 3: Fold the corners to the middle again.

 STEP 4: Fold in half.

 STEP 5: Fold both wings down.

STEP 6: Fold tail fins up.

 COMPLETED AIRCRAFT

SUMMARY SHEET

Round 1:

Bid: _____ Aircraft @ $20,000.00 per aircraft = _____

Results: _____ Aircraft @ $20,000.00 per aircraft = _____

Less: $300,000.00 overhead

_____ × $3000 cost of raw materials

_____ × $25,000 penalty

Profit: _____

Round 2:

Bid: _____ Aircraft @ $20,000.00 per aircraft = _____

Results: _____ Aircraft @ $20,000.00 per aircraft = _____

Less: $300,000.00 overhead

_____ × $3000 cost of raw materials

_____ × $25,000 penalty

Profit: _____

Round 3:

Bid: _____ Aircraft @ $20,000.00 per aircraft = _____

Results: _____ Aircraft @ $20,000.00 per aircraft = _____

Less: $300,000.00 overhead

_____ × $3000 cost of raw materials

_____ × $25,000 penalty

Profit: _____

HUMAN RESOURCE MANAGEMENT APPLICATIONS, ORGANIZATION DEVELOPMENT, AND PERSONAL DEVELOPMENT

SELECTION AND APPRAISAL

PARTICIPATORY SELECTION AND APPRAISAL*

Cobe Laboratories, Inc., a Lakewood, Colorado, manufacturer of medical therapeutic systems, has embarked on an unusual approach to selection and appraisal. The philosophy of this company is expressed by Enno Fritz, the production superintendent, as follows: "Any time you have more than one person dealing with a subject, you're going to get better-quality input. The process may be a bit slower and you have to work at keeping things moving, but the more input, the better the decision." The company's selection and appraisal process for new personnel follows this philosophy. For example, when a prospect is being considered for a job, instead of the usual interview with the personnel manager, he or she may have up to as many as fourteen interviews with people throughout the firm. After the relevant manager is sold on the prospect in the initial interview, then the other interviews are scheduled. Fritz explains how he handles the selection process. "Each interviewer receives a copy of the resume and application, and speaks to the person for about half an hour. Then an interview form is filled out and returned to me. If I am sold on the applicant and one interviewer isn't, I ask why. Usually, through additional communication, the problem can be solved. I have the final say, but I always consider input." Appraisals are also based on group input. Evaluations are made every six months by a committee two levels above the employee.

*Adapted from "How One Company Gives Its Employees a Say," *Management Review,* November 1979, p. 48.

582

HUMAN RESOURCE
MANAGEMENT
APPLICATIONS,
ORGANIZATION
DEVELOPMENT, AND
PERSONAL DEVELOPMENT

Although all of the chapters so far have been at least indirectly concerned with applications and many are directly aimed at human resource management, this chapter is concerned with two remaining areas of application that organizational behavior can make to human resource management. The first half of the chapter is devoted to selection. Tests and interviews have traditionally been the major selection tools. However, because of legal ramifications of tests, alternative selection techniques such as assessment centers are being developed and increasingly used. All three selection techniques (tests, interviews, and assessment centers) are presented here and analyzed. The last half of the chapter gives attention to performance appraisal. Like those of selection, the purposes and techniques of appraising human performance are undergoing major changes. The significant issues and some of the traditional and emerging techniques are presented and analyzed.

SELECTION

Until recently, most organizations depended heavily upon tests and interviews to select personnel for either entry-level jobs or, internally, to select someone for transfer or promotion. Now many organizations have turned away from tests completely, and a growing number are foregoing interviews as well. What is the reason for this drastic turn of events? The answer mainly lies in the changing social and legal climate. After examining the legal climate for testing, the nature and use of tests, interviews, and assessment centers will be presented and analyzed.

The legal climate for testing

The passage of the Civil Rights Act in 1964 did not spell doom for testing. In fact, immediately after the passage of the act, testing experienced a boom period. According to Title VII of the Act, employers could not discriminate on the basis of race, creed, sex, or national origin, but they could exclude anyone on the basis of how they scored on "an objective test that doesn't discriminate." Of course, all organizations that used tests in the selection process claimed that their tests met this criterion. Then, in 1971, the U. S. Supreme Court ruled in *Griggs v. Duke Power Company* that in order to use a test as the basis of selection, the test had to be proved valid. In other words, the test had to measure what it was supposed to measure; it had to be able to predict successful job performance. In this case, Duke Power hired blacks as long as they could pass the selection tests. But when challenged in court, the company could not prove that the tests related to job performance (shoveling coal). The Court in an 8-to-0 vote decided that the test was discriminatory. The reaction across the country was dramatic. Instead of validating their tests, which they should have been doing all along if in fact the test was going to be an effective selection tool, a great number of organizations simply dropped testing.

The reasoning in dropping testing from the selection process seemed to be, "If we drop testing, it will prove we don't discriminate." The industrial psychologists, many of whose jobs were at stake, countered that it was not tests that discriminated but rather the people who used the test results. The latter reasoning has also come under attack in the academic community in relation to intelligence testing and racial differences.

In addition to *Griggs v. Duke Power*, there have been some other landmark cases that also have been interpreted by practitioners as making it tough to use tests. For example, in *Albemarle Paper Company v. Moody*, the Supreme Court held that minimal evidence of job-relatedness was insufficient. The court ruled that an employer must be able to show a significant amount of evidence that their selection procedures follow EEOC (Equal Employment Opportunity Commission) guidelines and are job related. As indicated in this case, the EEOC is becoming increasingly vigorous in enforcing the Civil Rights Act. The EEOC went from a budget of $2.25 million and a handful of staff members immediately after passage of the Act in 1964 to a budget of $43 million and a staff of about 2000. Many organizations have simply chosen to drop testing rather than take on the powerful EEOC.

It is important to note that neither the Civil Rights Act nor the subsequent court cases have banned testing as a selection device—only those tests have been banned that are designed, intended, or used to discriminate. Yet because of the fear of not being able to prove validity of employment tests, there is little question that testing is not used as much as it was several years ago as a selection device. Nevertheless, understanding the concept and types of tests available is still useful for the study of organizational behavior.

Testing has played a very important role in the past and, if a test is validated, there is no reason why testing cannot be a useful selection technique. The same goes for interviews. Every organization still uses interviews in one form or another, but they may go the way of tests unless they have proven validity. In part, the assessment center approach has become important in the last few years because so far it has been judged to be compatible with EEOC requirements.

Types of tests

A *test* can be defined as a systematic procedure for comparing the responses of two or more persons. The test supposedly represents a sampling of the test takers' behavior. With the qualifications discussed above (i.e., they have been proved valid), tests can be used for selection but can also be used for evaluation, placement, promotion, transfer, and research. Besides the many uses of tests, there are also many ways to classify tests.

One way to categorize tests is an individual versus group. *Individual tests* consist of one examiner and one person taking the test and have two major advantages. First, misinterpretations of directions and test items are kept to a minimum, and second, the examiner's observation can supplement the information given on the test and contribute additional information for the final evaluation. The Wechsler Adult Intelligence Scale (WAIS) is a good

584

HUMAN RESOURCE
MANAGEMENT
APPLICATIONS,
ORGANIZATION
DEVELOPMENT, AND
PERSONAL DEVELOPMENT

example of an individual test. In *group tests*, one examiner or psychometrist administers a test to two or more persons. The group tests have traditionally been used more frequently because they are more economical and less time consuming.

Another way to classify tests is by speed versus power. A *speed test* has items of equal difficulty that are to be answered in a specified period of time. The object is to answer as many questions as possible in the allotted time. A *power test* has items of increasing difficulty and time is not a factor. Its purpose is to measure certain kinds of capabilities.

Perhaps the most familiar differentiation is seen in tests for aptitude versus achievement. An *aptitude test* is designed to measure potential ability, and it attempts to predict success. Experience or past achievement is not supposed to influence the outcome of the test. An *achievement test* also measures ability, but actual ability—not potential ability, like the aptitude test. Achievement tests measure past learning and experience. In reality, of course, there is a fine line between aptitude and achievement tests. Often the only real difference between the two is how the test is interpreted and used. If the test is used to measure potential, it is an aptitude test. However, if the same test is used to judge how much has been learned, it may be considered an achievement test.

Intelligence tests   A major factor in measuring individual differences is intelligence. It is an oddity that intelligence-test results provide the only operational definition of intellectual capacity. In other words, about the only operational definition of intelligence is that it is what an intelligence test measures. This brings to mind a dog chasing its tail but does point out the complexity of operationally defining and measuring this elusive individual capacity.

The general intelligence test is normally scored according to the well-known intelligence quotient or IQ. Intelligence tests such as the Stanford-Binet Intelligence Scale determine the mental age of the person taking the test. The IQ is obtained by dividing the mental age (M. A.) by the person's actual or chronological age (C. A.) and multiplying the result by 100(M. A./C. A. $\times$ 100). An IQ of 100 is considered average. Widely used tests of mental abilities besides the Stanford-Binet are the Wechsler Adult Intelligence Scale, Otis Self-Administering Test of Mental Ability, Wonderlic Personnel Test, Miller Analogies Test, and the Concept Mastery Test.

Personality tests   The complexity associated with intelligence testing is compounded by trying to measure personality. Most of the problem can be traced to the difficulty of defining personality. As Chapter 5 pointed out, there is little agreement on a practical or analytical definition and almost no agreement on an operational definition of personality. This glaring problem has, of course, contributed to the controversy surrounding testing and to its declining use as a selection tool.

There are two major ways of measuring and describing personality—the self-report personality inventories and the projective techniques. The self-report approach relies on paper-and-pencil tests that can usually be answered by "true" or "false." They are based on the assumption that the personality consists of a group of traits. The purpose of the tests is to measure traits such as masculinity-femininity, introversion-extroversion, dominance-submissiveness, and independence-dependence. The results are usually shown on an overall personality profile. The biggest problem with self-report personality tests is that they are designed and interpreted on the basis of a priori rather than empirical data and can be easily faked. An important exception is the highly regarded Minnesota Multiphasic Personality Inventory (MMPI), which has empirically validated dimensions and scales that identify faking.

The other approach to testing personality is by projective means. In contrast to the self-report tests, projective tests attempt to assess the whole personality rather than a set of traits. The best-known projective tests are the word association and Rorschach inkblot tests and the Thematic Apperception Test (TAT). Word association tests are one of the oldest kinds of tests used in the behavioral sciences. Even Wilhelm Wundt, the founder of modern psychology, utilized the technique in his study of thought processes. Word associations are still widely used in assessing personality for clinical purposes.

The Rorschach and the TAT present a series of stimuli to the test taker. In the Rorschach, the stimuli consist of unstructured inkblots, whereas in the TAT a series of realistic pictures is presented. Subjects respond to the stimulus by telling a story about what they see. In doing this the test takers project their personalities. Using some predetermined guides, a qualified psychologist or psychometrist will then interpret these projections and make conclusions about the individual's personality.

Interest tests A third major category of tests traditionally used for selection is the interest test. Besides selection, however, these tests can be used in vocational counseling and career planning and are also adaptable to problems relating to job satisfaction. The two most commonly used interest tests are the Strong Vocational Interest Blank (VIB) and the Kuder Preference Record. These two tests were originally designed to measure professional and semiprofessional occupational interests. The newer Minnesota Vocational Interest Inventory tests the interests for lower-level jobs in an organization.

Since interests are closely linked with personality, interest tests are plagued with some of the same problems as personality tests. For instance, responses can be easily faked. Furthermore, before maturity, most people's interests are not stabilized, and therefore results are often meaningless. Although the Strong VIB attempts to determine how successful people in various occupations answer the questions, most interest tests start off with preconceived notions of how a member of a given occupation *should* respond to the questions. In other words, except for a few tests like the Strong, interest tests are not empirically validated.

586

HUMAN RESOURCE
MANAGEMENT
APPLICATIONS,
ORGANIZATION
DEVELOPMENT, AND
PERSONAL DEVELOPMENT

The validity concept

Validity has been mentioned throughout the discussion so far. It is *the* key concept for discussing the value of testing as a selection tool or for any other uses. Managers' ignoring validity is the major reason testing is in the precarious situation it is today as a selection technique. It is not only the social and legal climate or the EEOC that has "done testing in." Rather, the real root of the problem is the long-standing refusal of organizations to validate their selection process. Miles suggests there are two reasons for this state of affairs: ignorance and lack of incentive to do so. "The costs of poor selection processes are, in the main, either hidden or borne by persons outside the organization, whereas the costs of carrying out the careful analysis and evaluation which experts argue should underlie a good selection program appear high and the returns uncertain."[1] Now, with legislation and EEOC enforcement, tests that are used *must* be validated. Regardless of the legislative implications, the simple fact is that if a test is not valid, it is useless, can be dangerous and misleading, and *should not* be used.

Exactly what is meant by this important concept? First of all, it should be pointed out that validity is a fairly elusive concept and; as Robert Guion, a recognized expert on validity, has pointed out, it has never enjoyed much precision of definition, and there is currently a lot of "loose talk" about it. This is especially true when "a bewildering number of adjectives have been attached to it, each delimiting some aspect of a broader meaning."[2] He feels that both practitioners and scholars need to be reminded of three important properties or characteristics of validity in general:[3]

1. Validity is an evaluation, not a fact. Validity can be expressed in broad terms (e.g., high or good, moderate or satisfactory, weak or poor) instead of precise quantities or numbers. "To confuse an interpretation of validity with an obtained validity coefficient is probably our most mortal, or at least most mortifying, linguistic sin."[4]
2. Validity is an evaluation of the inferences about the test drawn from scores and is not an evaluation of the test per se. Other things (e.g., motivation of the person taking the test) enter into the test *score* besides the test itself.
3. Validity is both derived from and refers to variance in a set of scores. This means that the score of an individual "may be evaluated as more or less valid only if it has been previously determined that a set of scores from a substantial number of other individuals similarly tested is a valid set."[5]

The above points put validity into its proper perspective but still do not really define the term. Very simply, validity means that the test measures what it is supposed to measure. As Guion noted, much of the confusion about validity results from the adjectives that are used with the term. For

---

[1]Raymond E. Miles, *Theories of Management*, McGraw-Hill, New York, 1975, p. 169.

[2]Robert M. Guion, "Content Validity: Three Years of Talk—What's the Action?" *Public Personnel Management*, November–December, 1977, p. 407.

[3]Ibid., p. 408.

[4]Ibid.

[5]Ibid.

example, *face* validity, which most tests depend upon, is a pseudo type of validity and refers only to the surface appearance of the test. In someone's subjective judgment, the test *should* measure what it is supposed to measure. This is a normative, as opposed to empirical, judgment. It is now recognized that face validity is virtually useless and can be very misleading. Now, attention is being focused on the different types of empirically derived validity. An examination of these different types of validity is vital to the understanding of selection procedures, of appraisal (discussed in the last half of this chapter), and of research and understanding of organizational behavior in general.

Types of validity

Traditionally it was assumed that there was one type of validity, which could be determined by a single study. Now it is recognized that there are several different types of validity, and a number of investigations are needed to assess it. Although there are variations of each, the three major categories of validity are generally recognized to be content, predictive, and construct.

Content validity   This type of validity is concerned with the extent to which the items on the test are representative of the behavior or dimensions they are trying to measure. In other words, is the test an adequate sample of the universe of situations it is supposedly representing? Since content validity largely reflects a sampling process, it must for the most part depend on rational, judgmental analysis rather than on empirical analysis.

In employment applications, the test must be judged to represent the job performance domain in order to have content validity. On relatively simple job proficiency (e.g., a typing test) or job knowledge tests, content validity can be accurately judged (by the jobholder, supervisor, or outside expert), and if the test is systematically analyzed it will probably hold up to EEOC guidelines for validation.[6] However, on more abstract jobs such content validity would be inadequate. More criterion-based predictive or construct validity would be required.

Predictive validity   In content validity the criterion is the representativeness of the test. Obviously, this is quite subjective and can slip into being mere face validity. Predictive validity, on the other hand, calculates an objective, statistical relationship between the test predictors and an outside criterion. Figure 20-1 shows how this approach to predictive validity can be used.

In the bivariate scatterplot, a strong positive correlation is shown between the test scores and the performance criterion. Each dot represents an employee's score on the test and his or her resulting level of performance. If management wanted to use this test to predict who would be successful performers if they set the score as indicated, the hits far outnumber the

---

[6]"Questions and Answers on the Federal Executive Agency Guidelines on Employee Selection Procedures," *Federal Register*, vol. 42, 1977, pp. 3820–3825.

588

HUMAN RESOURCE
MANAGEMENT
APPLICATIONS,
ORGANIZATION
DEVELOPMENT, AND
PERSONAL DEVELOPMENT

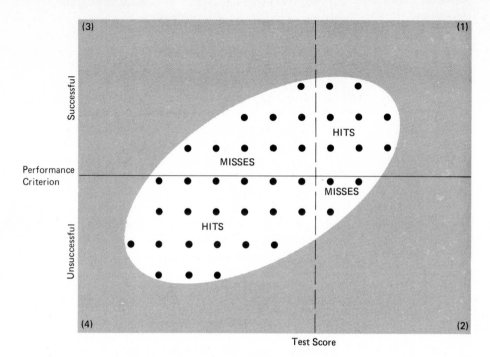

**Figure 20-1
A predictive
validity
scatterplot.**

misses. In other words, their test would have predictive validity in this case. The "hits" (in quadrant 1 those who would have been selected and turned out successful and in #4 those who would not have been selected and would have turned out unsuccessful) show the value of such predictive tests. On the other hand, the "misses," even though in the minority, are sacrificed. Especially of concern would be those in quadrant 3—they would not have been selected but would have turned out successful. Can the organization or the society as a whole afford these "misses"? Obviously, the answer depends on the type of job (e.g., in selecting astronauts, the selection score would be set so high that there would be no misses in the second quadrant and a lot of misses in the third quadrant) and the social consciousness/responsibility of the organization (e.g., is the organization eliminating minorities and/or women in quadrant 3 who could have turned out to be successful?).

Korman suggests the following steps for a comprehensive predictive validity approach to employee selection:[7]

1. Do a thorough job analysis to determine the characteristics and required job behaviors that will lead to successful performance.
2. Derive hypotheses about the types of people who would most likely fit the demands of the job.

---

[7]Abraham K. Korman, *Organizational Behavior*, Prentice-Hall, Englewood Cliffs, N.J., 1977, pp. 238–249.

3. Decide what test(s) would most likely measure individual differences in job applicants on the relevant variables of the job.
4. Administer the test(s) to an applicant sample (selections are not made at this time).
5. After the applicants have been hired and have been at work for a sufficient amount of time, calculate the correlation between their test scores and their actual job performance.
6. Cross-validate or replicate the last two steps.
7. Determine the scores that will be needed to predict success and set up the necessary guidelines for administering this selection procedure.

Such a systematic predictive validity approach to selection can effectively meet EEOC requirements. A major problem, of course, is finding an outside "success criterion." Except for "widget-making" types of jobs this is difficult.

Construct validity Both content and predictive (i.e., criterion-related) validity have proved to be useful for determining the value of tests used in selection for relatively straightforward, routine jobs. But for more complex, abstract jobs, tests that try to measure concepts or constructs such as personality dimensions (aggressiveness, confidence, self-esteem, etc.) or leadership have been commonly used. Construct validity is concerned with whether such tests really do measure the psychological concept in question.

In the final analysis, the other forms of validity become subsumed by construct validity; it is the crux of the whole selection process and has significant implications for how research is done in the whole field of organizational behavior. Guion supports this view when he states: "All validity is at its base some form of construct validity. . . . The most salient of the traditionally identified aspects of validity—the only one that is salient— is construct validity. It *is* the basic meaning of validity."[8] In addition to the comprehensive nature of construct validity, it may also be the overlooked key to research progress in organizational behavior as a whole. As Chapters 2 and 15 pointed out, the widely used questionnaires used to gather data on constructs such as job satisfaction and leadership[9] may not be valid. So construct validity considerations are important not only to selection, but to widely used questionnaire methods in organizational behavior research as well.

Unlike content or predictive validity, construct validity draws on a number of studies and sources in order to make an evaluation. Thus, it is both a logical and an empirical process.[10] The construct validation approach

---

[8] Guion, op. cit. p. 410.

[9] For a review that is critical of the construct validity of commonly used leadership tests see: Chester A. Schriesheim and Steven Kerr, "Theories and Measures of Leadership: A Critical Appraisal of Current and Future Directions," in James G. Hunt and Lars L. Larson (eds.) *Leadership: The Cutting Edge*, Southern Illinois University Press, Carbondale, Illinois, 1977, pp. 9–45.

[10] Wayne Cascio, *Applied Psychology in Personnel Management*, Reston Publishing Company, Reston Va., 1978, p. 95.

590

HUMAN RESOURCE
MANAGEMENT
APPLICATIONS.
ORGANIZATION
DEVELOPMENT, AND
PERSONAL DEVELOPMENT

would involve what measurement experts call a nomological network (i.e., a system of interrelated concepts, propositions, and laws), where observable characteristics are related to other observables, observables to theoretical constructs, or one theoretical construct to another theoretical construct.[11] In order to have construct validity, there must be some convergence of the scores from different measurement techniques (e.g., a standardized test and an observational system) that purportedly measure the same dimension of a construct. This is called *convergent validity*. In addition, there must be *discriminant validity* (i.e., the test that supposedly measures the construct should be *unrelated* to the scores of instruments that are not supposed to measure the construct in question). Thus, construct validity involves both convergent and discriminant validity and can be determined by innovative experimental and statistical procedures such as the multi trait-multi method (MTMM) matrix.[12]

The reliability concept

The other major concept of testing, though not nearly as important as validity, is reliability. In order for a test to be valid it must also be reliable. *Test reliability* refers to the *accuracy* of measurement and the *consistency* of results. Test reliability is not nearly as difficult to achieve as is validity. Normally, all that is required for a high degree of reliability is control over the testing conditions. As long as directions are clear, the environment is comfortable, the test is long enough, and ample time is given, there is no problem with test reliability. About the only aspect of test reliability that is difficult to control is the attitude and motivation of the person taking the test. If test takers do not try to do their best, the test will not be reliable.

Even though tests are usually very reliable, it does not automatically follow that they will be valid. The test may be accurately and consistently measuring the wrong variables. The major challenge facing the use of tests comes not from reliability but from validity. It will be necessary to concentrate more on content, predictive, and, especially, construct validity in the future.

Interviewing techniques for selection

Interviews are often called the most used but least useful selection technique. Interviews can also be used for counseling employees and for gathering data for research. An *interview* can be defined as a conversation with a purpose. Analysis of the word itself (literally, "to see between") implies a process of interaction. The interaction between the interviewer and the interviewee is a very complex phenomenon. In fact, it is so complex and imprecise that interviewing can probably better be considered an art rather than a science.

---

[11]L. J. Cronbach and P. E. Meehl, "Construct Validity in Psychological Tests," *Psychological Bulletin*, vol. 52, 1955, pp. 281–302.

[12]D. T. Campbell and D. W. Fiske, "Convergent and Discriminant Validation by the Multitrait-Multimethod Matrix," *Psychological Bulletin*, vol. 56, 1959, pp. 81–105.

There is considerable evidence to suggest that interviews may be even less valid for use in selection than tests.[13] There are many reasons for this. A summary of the existing studies on interviewing finds the following problems:

1. In an unstructured interview, material is not consistently covered.
2. When interviewers obtain the same information, they are likely to weigh it differently. What is positive information to one interviewer may turn out to be negative to another.
3. Interviewers have great difficulty in reliably and validly assessing traits other than intelligence or mental ability.
4. Interviewers in unstructured interviews tend to make their decisions early in an interview, that is, before all the information is in.
5. Interviewers give more weight to negative information than to positive information.[14]

Research is beginning to accumulate on the various aspects of interviewing. Table 20-1 summarizes this research. These findings should be used in trying to make the interview more effective as a selection technique.

---

[13]Eugene C. Mayfield, "The Selection Interview: A Re-evaluation of Published Research," *Personnel Psychology*, Autumn 1964, pp. 239–260; Donald P. Schwab, "Why Interview? A Critique," *Personnel Journal*, February 1969, pp. 126–129; and Enzo Valenzi and I. R. Andrews, "Individual Differences in the Decision Process of Employment Interviewers," *Journal of Applied Psychology*, August 1973, pp. 49–53.

[14]Lyman W. Porter, Edward E. Lawler, and J. Richard Hackman, *Behavior in Organizations*, McGraw-Hill, New York, 1975, p. 145.

Table 20-1

SUMMARY OF RESEARCH FINDINGS ON INTERVIEWING

1. Interviewers tend to develop a stereotype of a good candidate and then seem to match applicants with stereotypes.
2. Biases are established early in the interview.
3. During an interview in which the applicant is accepted, the interviewer talks more and in a more favorable tone than in an interview in which the applicant is rejected.
4. Interviewers are influenced more by unfavorable than by favorable information.
5. Seeing negative candidates before positive candidates will result in a greater number of favorable acceptances than the other way around.
6. There are reliable and consistent individual differences between people in the total number of people seen as being acceptable.
7. Factual written data seem to be more important than physical appearance in reaching judgments, and this increases with interviewing experience.
8. Situational measures of behavior designed to simulate job conditions are weighted more heavily than ability tests, which are, in turn, weighted more heavily than personality tests.
9. Although the immediately previous job applicant has an influence on ratings of the current applicant, the effect seems to be relatively small.
10. An interviewee is awarded a more extreme evaluation when proceeded by an interviewee of opposing value.

Source: Adapted from Abraham Korman, *Organizational Behavior*, Prentice-Hall, Englewood Cliffs, N.J., 1977, pp. 260–261.

592

HUMAN RESOURCE
MANAGEMENT
APPLICATIONS,
ORGANIZATION
DEVELOPMENT, AND
PERSONAL DEVELOPMENT

Interviews should always be used in conjunction with other selection tools. A selection decision should not be made on the basis of an interview alone. In addition, there are certain techniques and procedures that can be used to improve the art' of interviewing. Although interviews can be directive or nondirective and structured or unstructured, the interview should always be planned in advance. In the directive/structured interview, a detailed guide should be prepared and the items asked should be validated in the same way that test items are validated. For the nondirective/unstructured interview the overall atmosphere is important to its success. "The ideal usually sought is a permissive situation in which the respondent is encouraged to voice his frank opinions without fearing that his attitudes will be revealed to others and without the expression of any surprise or value judgment by the interviewer."[15] In the conduct of the interview, the interviewer must consciously play the role of a reporter, not that of an antagonist, debater, or evangelist. The closing of the interview is critical. At the end of the interview, an open-ended question is useful to "clear the air" between interviewer and interviewee. It is important to the long-range objective of the organization that a good rapport exist when the interview is terminated.

If correctly handled, interviews as a selection tool can avoid the problems associated with testing. At present, interviews are still widely used; but if selection decisions are going to be based on them, they are going to have to have proved validity. Most employers would be justifiably reluctant to hire people without interviewing them. But unless the interview can be shown to have validity, interviews may be eliminated in the future.

Assessment centers

In response to the problems associated with using tests in the selection process, especially in selection for supervisory/managerial positions and in the promotion process, an increasing number of organizations in both the private and public sectors are turning to the use of assessment centers. The exact meaning and methods of assessment centers have been somewhat unclear. Recently a professional assessment center group did establish a set of specific guidelines of exactly what is meant by an assessment center. Briefly summarized, these dimensions are:[16]

1. Multiple assessment techniques, including at least one simulation exercise, must be used.
2. Multiple assessors with prior training must be used.
3. Selection or development judgments/decisions must be based on pooled information from assessors and techniques.
4. Overall evaluations must be made by assessors at a time separate from that of actual observation.
5. Simulation exercises must be tested prior to use to ensure that they provide reliable, objective, and relevant information for the organization in question.

---

[15]Claire Selltiz et al., *Research Methods in Social Relations*, rev. ed., Holt, New York, 1959, p. 575.

[16]J. L. Moses, et al., "Standards and Ethical Considerations for Assessment Center Operations," *Task Force on Development of Assessment Center Standards*, Third International Congress on the Assessment Center Method, Quebec, May 1975.

6. The various dimensions, attributes, characteristics, or qualities that are evaluated must be derived from an analysis of relevant job behaviors.
7. The purpose of the techniques used is to provide information in evaluating the dimensions, attributes, or qualities previously determined.

Such specifically defined standards as the above should help rule out techniques that use only panel interviews or only one specific simulation exercise or only a test battery from being called an assessment center.

The dimensions derived from a detailed job analysis for a managerial position that would be evaluated in an assessment center might include: organizing and planning, perception and analysis, decision making, decisiveness, leadership, sensitivity to people, oral communications, written communications, and adaptability.[17] Table 20-2 outlines the content and conduct of a typical two-day assessment center. At the end of the two days the assessors would meet to pool and thoroughly discuss their observations and the results of the exercises for each participant. A summary evaluation would then be used to select the individual for the job in question. Their rapid growth in popularity (from about a dozen large firms in 1970, most notably AT&T, to an estimated 4000 organizations today[18]) and research backup for validation of the process, make assessment centers one of the biggest success stories in the applied aspects of organizational behavior.

In addition to their use in the selection process, assessment centers are also being touted as an important tool in the overall development process of modern organizations. For example, assessment centers can help identify training needs for the organization; identify and develop employees, especially minorities and women, who have managerial potential; improve employees' performance in their present job; and help in employees' developmental and career planning. However, like any fast-rising technique, assessment centers have had some growing pains (i.e., there have been misunderstandings), and overzealous statements regarding their value have been made.

It is true that the activities of assessment centers have had considerable research backup in support of their predictive validity[19], and the approach has held up very well in some recent court tests. The original eight-year longitudinal predictive validity study conducted at AT&T in the 1960s by Douglas Bray and his colleagues still serves as the foundation for the approach.[20] Despite this relatively impressive research support, recently there have been some concerns about assessment centers.

---

[17]Stephen L. Cohen and Larry Sands, "The Effects of Order of Exercise Presentation on Assessment Center Performance: One Standardization Concern," *Personnel Psychology*, Spring 1978, p. 40.

[18]Joyce D. Ross, "A Current Review of Public Sector Assessment Centers: Cause for Concern," *Public Personnel Management*, January–February 1979, p. 41.

[19]For reviews of the validity of assessment centers see: J. R. Huck, "Assessment Centers: A Review of the External and Internal Validation," *Personnel Psychology*, Summer, 1973, pp. 191–212; A. Howard, "An Assessment of Assessment Centers," *Academy of Management Journal*, March 1974, pp. 115–134; and R. J. Klimoski and W. J. Strickland, "Assessment Centers—Valid or Merely Prescient," *Personnel Psychology*, Autumn 1977, pp. 353–360.

[20]D. W. Bray and D. L. Grant, "The Assessment Center in Measurement of Potential for Business Management," *Psychological Monographs*, vol. 80, no. 17, no. 625, 1966.

594

HUMAN RESOURCE
MANAGEMENT
APPLICATIONS,
ORGANIZATION
DEVELOPMENT, AND
PERSONAL DEVELOPMENT

Table 20-2

A TYPICAL TWO DAY ASSESSMENT CENTER

Day 1   Orientation meeting

Management game—"Conglomerate."
Forming different types of
conglomerates is the goal, with
four-person teams of participants
bartering companies to achieve their
planned result. Teams set their own
acquisition objectives and must plan
and organize to meet them.

Background interview—A one-
and-a-half-hour interview conducted by
an assessor.

Group discussion—"Management
Problems." Four short cases calling for
various forms of management judgment
are presented to groups of four
participants. In one hour the group,
acting as consultants, must resolve the
cases and submit its recommendation in
writing.

*Individual fact-finding and
decision-making exercise*—"The
Research Budget." Participants are told
that they have just taken over as division
manager. Each is given a brief
description of an incident in which the
predecessor has recently turned down a
request for funds to continue a research
project. The research director is
appealing for a reversal of the decision.
The participant is given fifteen minutes
to ask questions to dig out the facts in
the case. Following this fact-finding
period, he or she must present a
decision orally with supporting
reasoning and defend it under
challenge.

Day 2

In-basket exercise—"Section Manager's
In-Basket." The contents of a section
manager's in-basket are simulated.
Participants are instructed to go through
the contents, solving problems, answering
questions, delegating, organizing,
scheduling and planning, just as they
might do if they were promoted suddenly
to the position. An assessor reviews the
contents of the completed in-basket and
conducts a one-hour interview with each
participant to gain further information.

*Assigned role leaderless group
discussion*—"Compensation Committee."
The Compensation Committee is meeting
to allocate $8000 in discretionary salary
increases among six supervisory and
managerial employees. Members of the
committee (participants) represent
departments of the company and are
instructed to "do the best you can" for
the employee from their department.

*Analysis, presentation, and group
discussion*—"The Pretzel Factory." This
financial analysis problem has the
participant role-play a consultant called in
to advise Carl Flowers of the C. F. Pretzel
Company on two problems: what to do
about a division of the company that has
continually lost money, and whether the
corporation should expand. Participants
are given data on the company and are
asked to recommend appropriate courses
of action. They make their
recommendation in a seven-minute
presentation, after which they are formed
into a group to come up with a single set
of recommendations.

Source: William C. Byham, "The Assessment Center as an Aid in Management Development," *Training
and Development Journal,* December 1971.

One concern centers around the fact that most of the validation studies
have been restricted to large business organizations (AT&T, General Electric,
IBM, Sears, and Standard Oil). But with increasing use of assessment centers
in a wide variety of contexts, especially in the public sector, requirements
may differ, and thus there may be a need for different kinds of evaluation
research.[21] One public personnel administration expert noted:

---

[21]Howard, op. cit., p. 131.

There is a concern that public personnel administrators may now have some knowledge of *how* to conduct an assessment center, but close observation has shown that many do not have an understanding of why they're doing what they're doing. . . . A number of in-house as well as externally contracted assessment centers are being conducted in the public service which, to all outward appearances, are very marginal in terms of meeting the criteria for a reliable and valid center.[22]

In addition to these general observations, the courts are also becoming sensitive to *how* the assessment center is being conducted. For example, in a case where the city of Omaha, Nebraska, used the assessment center to select the deputy police chief, the validity was upheld, but the judge questioned some of the methods used.

In addition to the concerns about the conduct of assessment centers, there is also concern about generalizing the positive results obtained for selection to training, development, and career planning. One study found that this extended use of assessment centers may be more talk than reality. Only a few of the sixty-five organizations surveyed (all of whom have used assessment centers for a number of years) indicated that they follow administrative practices which deal with the long-term utilization of assessment center results. For example, only about half reported that the assessee's immediate supervisor gets feedback of the evaluation or discusses training and development needs, and only about a third of the organizations reported that developmental plans were initiated as a result of participation in the assessment center or that assessment center staffs monitored subsequent development of assessees. In addition, only two uses (identifying strengths and weaknesses and making promotional decisions) of the ten suggested for assessment centers are moderately utilized at present by the surveyed organizations. Training, development, and career planning uses do not seem common in these organizations with assessment centers.[23]

There is little question that the assessment center is a much more comprehensive and valid approach to selection than are tests and interviews. By use of the simulated exercises, the approach is much more directly related to job performance than is a question on a personality test asking whether the employee likes to sleep with a light on or not. The big companies have given a great deal of effort and financial support for relating actual job dimensions to the exercises used in their assessment centers. At this stage of the development of assessment centers, the procedures and actual conduct of the sessions in medium-sized and smaller business firms and the potential of the approach for use outside the selection process must be given further attention. Overall, the future looks very bright for the use of assessment centers in the selection, training and development, and career planning processes of organizations.

---

[22]Ross, op. cit., p. 42.

[23]Larry D. Alexander, "An Exploratory Study of the Utilization of Assessment Center Results," *Academy of Management Journal*, March 1979, pp. 154–155.

596

HUMAN RESOURCE
MANAGEMENT
APPLICATIONS,
ORGANIZATION
DEVELOPMENT, AND
PERSONAL DEVELOPMENT

PERFORMANCE APPRAISAL

Performance appraisal represents an important applications area for organizational behavior. Traditional techniques for performance appraisal have been handled fairly ineffectively and are coming under the scrutiny of equal opportunity advocates regarding their validity. In this section, after the purposes and trends in performance appraisal have been discussed, three major approaches to performance appraisal will be examined: judgment-based rating procedures, observable-job-behavior–based procedures, and overall control and objective end-results-oriented procedures.

Purposes and trends in performance appraisal

In recent years the purposes of performance appraisal have greatly expanded. It used to be solely a means of differentiating among hourly employees for wage increases, transfers, promotions, and layoffs. Today, performance appraisals are used not only for the above but also as a means of communication, motivation, and development of all employees in the organization. In addition, because of the extremely important value of employees (both pragmatically in cost terms and in the contribution they make to the success of the organization), the appraisal process is a major method of controlling the human assets. Such human controls are necessary if organizations are to survive and grow in the coming years.

Table 20-3 summarizes the specific trends that have taken place in appraisal. Formerly, the emphasis was on narrowly based subjective ratings of personal traits. Table 20-4 is meant as a jest but it is not too far from the truth of how appraisals used to be, and in many cases still are, made. The new emphasis is on objective appraisal of performance. A review of the available research findings concluded that the following characteristics would make up an ideal performance appraisal system:

1. Measures are used that are inclusive of all the behaviors and results that should be performed.
2. The measures used are tied to behavior and as far as possible are objective in nature.
3. Moderately difficult goals and standards for future performance are set.
4. Measures are used that can be influenced by an individual's behavior.
5. Appraisals are done on a time cycle that approximates the time it takes the measures to reflect the behavior of the persons being evaluated.
6. The persons being evaluated have an opportunity to participate in the appraisal process.
7. The appraisal system interacts effectively with the reward system.[24]

The above obviously represents the ideal, but the various judgmental, behavioral, and end-results techniques should strive to incorporate as many as these characteristics as possible.

---

[24]Porter, Lawler, and Hackman, op. cit., p. 339.

Table 20-3

CHART SUMMARIZING CHANGING EMPHASIS IN PERFORMANCE APPRAISAL OVER THE YEARS

Item	Former emphasis	Present emphasis
Terminology	Merit rating	Employee appraisal, Performance appraisal
Purpose	Determine qualification for wage increase, transfer, promotion, layoff	Development of the individual; improved performance on the job
Application	For hourly paid workers	For technical, professional, and managerial employees
Factors rated	Heavy emphasis upon personal traits	Results, accomplishments, performance
Techniques	Rating scales with emphasis upon scores. Statistical manipulation of data for comparison purposes	Management by objectives, mutual goal setting, critical incidents, group appraisal, performance standards, less quantitative
Post-appraisal interview	Supervisors communicate ratings to employees and try to sell their evaluations, seek to have employees conform to supervisor's views	Supervisor stimulates employees to analyze themselves and set own objectives in line with job requirements; supervisor is helper and counselor

Source: Dale S. Beach, *Personnel,* 3d ed., Macmillan, New York, 1975, p. 336. Used with permission.

Judgmental techniques for performance appraisal

The traditional and still most commonly used appraisal technique is for supervisors to rate their subordinates' personal traits (e.g., neatness, dependability, initiative, or drive) or categories of traits (e.g., cooperation, quantity of work, quality of work, overall attitude, or job knowledge). These traits may evolve out of a systematic job analysis but are usually subjectively determined and have only face validity for job performance.

The ratings are usually recorded on a form that forces the rater to mark items on a 1-to-5 or 1-to-7 scale. Such ratings are vulnerable to common rater errors such as the following:

1. *Distribution.* These errors are the result of overrating (leniency) underrating (strictness), rating everyone about average (central tendency), or simply failing to discriminate among ratees. A forced distribution (i.e., only 15 percent can be rated high, 15 percent must be rated low, only 20 percent can be rated good, 20 percent must be rated poor, and 30 percent must be rated average) can help overcome this problem. However, this assumes that such a distribution does exist in the group being rated. Such an assumption may not always be true.
2. *Halo or stereotyping.* Here the error is to make the overall rating on the basis of one or a few traits. For example, the ability to get along well with others or the length of a guy's hair may generalize to all the traits being rated. Raters must be careful to avoid such generalizations.

598

HUMAN RESOURCE
MANAGEMENT
APPLICATIONS, ORGANIZATION
DEVELOPMENT, AND
PERSONAL DEVELOPMENT

3. *Recency and primacy.* Recency errors occur when the person is rated on the basis of very recent performance and primacy errors occur when the rating is based on the previous rating. By keeping and using detailed performance records over time, these errors can be minimized.

Besides recognition of the above rating errors, there is also accumulating research evidence to support the following conclusions about raters and ratees in performance appraisals:[25]

1. Rating ability may be positively related to intelligence.
2. There is a positive relationship between the effectiveness of the supervisor and the ability to discriminate between good and poor employees.
3. Special training (e.g., in clinical psychology) may not help in rating other people accurately.
4. The closer the propinquity (physical proximity) between the rater and the ratee, the higher the ratings.
5. The more the rater engages in analytical rather than global thinking, the more likely he or she will differentiate among others.
6. Those who exhibit good behaviors are more likely to be rated accurately than those who exhibit poor behaviors.

Although academicians are highly critical of the trait-rating approach to performance appraisal, it remains the most widely used technique. More acceptable judgmental techniques are various ranking schemes, multirater procedures, and critical incident methods. In *simple ranking*, the rater

[25]Korman, op. cit., p. 359.

Table 20-4

APPRAISAL FORM USING PERSONAL TRAITS

Personal traits	Far exceeds job requirements	Exceeds job requirements	Meets job requirements	Needs some improvement	Does not meet minimum requirements
Quality	Leaps tall buildings with a single bound	Must take running start to leap over tall buildings	Can only leap over a short building or medium one with no spires	Crashes into buildings when attempting to jump over them	Cannot recognize buildings at all, much less jump over one
Timeliness	Is faster than a speeding bullet	Is as fast as a speeding bullet	Not quite as fast as a speeding bullet	Would you believe a slow bullet?	Wounds self with bullets when attempting to shoot the gun
Initiative	Is stronger than than a locomotive	Is stronger than a bull elephant	Is stronger than a bull	Shoots the bull	Smells like a bull
Adaptability	Walks on water consistently	Walks on water in emergencies	Washes with water	Drinks water	Passes water in emergencies
Communication	Talks with God	Talks with the angels	Talks to self	Argues with self	Loses those arguments

rank-orders all the ratees from highest to lowest. In *alternation ranking*, the rater first chooses the best ratee, then the worst, next the second best and second worst are chosen, and so forth until all the ratees have been ranked. A third type of ranking is called the *paired comparision* method. In this method, for every trait every ratee is compared to every other ratee in pairs. Each of these ranking techniques is usually considered to be more effective than traditional forced-choice ratings.

Recently, a *multiple-rater* technique (where a number of relevant raters pool their judgments on each ratee) is offered as being the most promising judgmental procedure. "Proposed advantages of multi-rater techniques include their potential for capturing a wide range of performance data and reduced bias resulting from aggregation of a variety of expert perspectives."[26]

The *critical incident method* has also received recent attention as a desirable alternative to traditional forced-choice rating techniques. Under this procedure, the supervisor and/or other knowledgeable observers record especially effective and ineffective anecdotes or incidents involving the ratee throughout the rating period. Supposedly these incidents are related to job performance. When review time rolls around records of these incidents kept over the period are assembled and serve as the basis for the appraisal. At least these incidents are based on observable behaviors instead of the traditionally unobservable, highly subjectively perceived personal traits of the ratees. The critical incident method allows for more objective judgments and serves as the point of departure for the behaviorally oriented appraisal methods.

Behaviorally anchored rating scales (BARS)

Assessment centers resulted from dissatisfaction with traditional testing techniques used for selection, and a parallel development has occurred in appraisal: dissatisfaction with traditional judgmental procedures used in appraising employee performance has led an increasing number of organizations to move toward behaviorally based techniques. Behavioral expectancy scales (BES) go back a couple of decades, but only in recent years have these techniques made a significant impact on appraisal practices. Today, this approach, now commonly called behavioral anchored rating scales or BARS, is picking up support because it is, at least potentially, more compatible with the validity requirements dictated by the current legal climate surrounding appraisal practices.

The BARS approach gets away from measuring subjective personal traits and instead measures observable, critical behaviors that are related to specific job dimensions. BARS takes advantage of many of the modern, effective approaches to the evaluation of personnel. First of all, behaviors, and not unobservable traits of employees, are measured. Second, BARS is aimed at specific dimensions of job performance. This makes the technique

---

[26]Michael Keely, "A Contingency Framework for Performance Evaluation," *Academy of Management Review*, July 1978, p. 432.

600

HUMAN RESOURCE
MANAGEMENT
APPLICATIONS.
ORGANIZATION
DEVELOPMENT, AND
PERSONAL DEVELOPMENT

much more compatible with EEOC requirements, which were discussed at the beginning of the chapter. Third, the people who are actually involved with the job participate in determining the job dimensions and the development of the scales. Such participation greatly enhances acceptance of the technique. Fourth, because the evaluation is in terms of specific behaviors, the rater can give objective feedback on how the ratee performed and what specific behavior the ratee must exhibit to improve. Such feedback is much more effective than the vague, subjective feedback given in traditional rating methods. Finally, the technique is highly adaptable to evaluating "nonwidget" types of jobs. Most white-collar jobs and practically all jobs in nonprofit organizations, both of which are becoming increasingly important all the time, do not have number of widgets sold or produced as a measure of performance. BARS provides an effective way of measuring the performance on these types of jobs because critical behaviors, and not the number of widgets, are evaluated.

One of the most important aspects of BARS is that the job dimensions and scales are developed from scratch for each job. Although the recommended steps vary slightly from author to author, the original procedure described by Smith and Kendall is usually followed.[27] The steps in developing BARS include the following:

1. *Identify performance measures.* Knowledgeable, relevant people, usually supervisors, staff personnel, and the jobholder, are asked to identify the important dimensions of the job in question. These dimensions may be the same or different from what traditional job analysis would turn up.
2. *Identify critical behaviors.* Through the use of critical incidents, the participants in step 1 are asked to identify the critical behaviors (both effective and ineffective) for the job dimensions identified in step 1. These are usually stated in a few short sentences or phrases and use the terminology of the job in question.
3. *Retranslation.* The critical behaviors identified in step 2 are next retranslated, usually by another group of participants. Each member of the group is asked to assign the various critical behaviors identified in step 2 to the job dimension that it best describes. Those critical behaviors that the majority assign to the job dimension that was intended are kept for further development. This retranslation process assures the reliability of the critical behaviors (consistent, accurate behaviors for the job dimensions).
4. *Scale development.* Those critical behaviors that survive the retranslation are next numerically scaled (usually from 1 to 7 or 1 to 9) to a level of performance that each is perceived to represent. The final value for each critical behavior is the average (to the nearest whole number) of values of those making the estimates.
5. *The BARS instrument.* The product of the preceding steps is a vertical scale (1 to 7 or 1 to 9) for each job dimension. Figure 20-2 shows an example for the job dimension "absorb and interpret policies" for interviewers and claims deputies in a state labor department. The nine behaviors on the scale are the critical behaviors that were retranslated, i.e., there was high rater agreement on these. They were assigned the values 1 through 9 according to the scaling procedure of step 4.

The research on BARS indicates mixed findings. Some studies find that

---

[27]Patricia C. Smith and L. M. Kendall, "The Retranslation of Expectations: An Approach to the Construction of Unambiguous Anchors for Rating Scales," *Journal of Applied Psychology*, April 1963, pp. 149–155.

the BARS technique is more effective than traditional rating techniques in reducing rating errors such as leniency, central tendency, and halo,[28] but another study found that BARS resulted in significantly higher ratings than a numerically anchored scale.[29] As for whether BARS does in fact get at independent performance dimensions and whether the critical behaviors are

[28]J. P. Campbell, M. D. Dunnette, R. D. Arvey, and L. W. Hellervik, "The Development and Evaluation of Behaviorally Based Rating Scales," *Journal of Applied Psychology*, vol. 57, 1973, pp. 15–22; Cheedle W. Millard, Fred Luthans, and Robert L. Ottemann, "BARS: A New Breakthrough for Performance Appraisal," *Business Horizons*, August 1976, pp. 70–72.

[29]W. C. Borman and W. R. Vallon, "A View of What Can Happen When Behavioral Expectation Scales Are Developed in One Setting and Used in Another," *Journal of Applied Psychology*, vol. 59, 1975, pp. 197–201.

Absorb and Interpret Policies—learns new policies and procedures with a minimum of instruction.

Interviewers and claims deputies must keep abreast of current changes and interpret and apply new information. Some can absorb and interpret new policy guides and procedures quickly with a minimum of explanation. Others seem unable to learn even after repeated explanations and practice. They have difficulty learning and following new policies. When making this rating, disregard job knowledge and experience and evaluate ability to learn on the job.

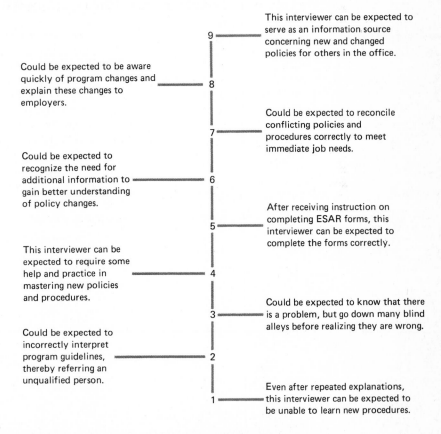

Figure 20-2 An example of BARS. (*Source: Cheedle W. Millard, Fred Luthans, and Robert L. Ottemann, "BARS: A New Breakthrough for Performance Appraisal," Business Horizons, August 1976, p.69.)*

602

HUMAN RESOURCE
MANAGEMENT
APPLICATIONS,
ORGANIZATION
DEVELOPMENT, AND
PERSONAL DEVELOPMENT

reliable, a review article concludes, "It is clear that research on BARS to date does not support the high promise regarding scale independence. . . . In short, while BARS may outperform conventional rating techniques, it is clear that they are not a panacea for obtaining high interrater reliability."[30] Despite the legitimate warnings that BARS is not a panacea, because those with knowledge of the job make a direct input into the development of the BARS technique in each application, a strong case can be made for content validity.[31] But as the earlier discussion on test validity pointed out, predictive and, especially, construct validation of instruments such as BARS is needed. One recent analysis pointed out, "A number of theoretical problems exist which underline the development and implementation of behaviorally anchored rating scales in particular and all performance evaluation procedures in general."[32] This observation, of course, implies that without theoretical clarification, BARS may not have construct validity. But at least by concentrating on observable behaviors and having content validity, BARS seems to be a significant improvement over traditional rating techniques in appraising employee performance. By the same token, more theoretical development and research on its predictive and construct validity is certainly needed in the future.

The role of control in performance appraisals

So far, the discussion of appraisal has been concerned with judgment and behaviorally based techniques. A third widely recognized category of performance appraisal evolves out of the established control system of an organization and concentrates on end results. Chapter 17 discussed the control process in detail, and so it will not be discussed further here, except to say that the information generated by this system can be important to the performance appraisal process. For instance, accounting data generated by the financial system can be very helpful in making appraisals (e.g., what is the return on investment of the individual's profit center?) and the standards or objectives set in the control process can be used to evaluate employee performance. This latter aspect of control is, of course, where management-by-objective (MBO) systems can and do play a vital role in performance appraisal. MBO was defined in Chapter 8 as a systematic approach to the setting of objectives (goal setting) and *appraising by results*. Since Chapter 8 was concerned with goal setting, this aspect of MBO was emphasized. Now, in this discussion, appraisal by results is given separate attention.

Appraisal by results

Appraisal by results is most closely associated with the control aspect of MBO. As a performance appraisal technique, it differs from judgment rating

---

[30]Donald P. Schwab, Herbert Heneman, III, and Thomas A. Decotiis, "Behaviorally Anchored Rating Scales: A Review of the Literature," *Academy of Management Proceedings,* 1975, p. 223.

[31]Campbell et al., op. cit.

[32]Robert S. Atkin and Eward J. Conlon, "Behaviorally Anchored Rating Scales: Some Theoretical Issues," *Academy of Management Review,* January 1978, p. 119.

techniques and behaviorally based techniques in that the focus is on ends rather than means. It is an objective way to appraise some fairly subjective, abstract managerial jobs. The person is evaluated according to the end results obtained as compared to the mutually (between the supervisor and the subordinate) set objectives. In addition, the evaluation is concerned with the reasons why the person did or did not meet the standards or accomplish the objectives that were mutually determined.

Many organizations combine their planning process with appraisal by results. For example, General Electric pinpointed key-results areas, using the question, "Will continued failure in this area prevent the attainment of management's responsibility for advancing General Electric as leader in a strong, competitive economy, even though results in all other key result areas are good?" The eight key-results areas determined in this way were: profitability, market position, productivity, product leadership, personnel development, employee attitudes, public responsibility, and balance between short-range and long-range goals.[33] Concentrating on these key-results areas allows managers considerable freedom to operate but gives some fairly objective data with which to appraise them.

Emphasizing end results recognizes the role of the external (open-systems) environment. Drucker makes the point that results in business organizations exist *only* on the outside, and it is much more difficult for managers to control these outside variables than inside variables. He notes that even the most internally efficient buggy whip companies are not in business today.

It is of little value to have the most efficient engineering department if it designs the wrong product. The Cuban subsidiaries of U. S. companies were by far the best run and, apparently, the most profitable—let alone the least "troublesome"— of all U. S. operations in Latin America. This was, however, irrelevant to their expropriation. And it mattered little, I daresay, during the period of IBM's great expansion in the fifties and sixties how "efficient" its operations were; its basic entrepreneurial idea was the right, the effective one.[34]

In the long run, how managers handle the outside environmental variables, such as technological developments, economic conditions, social values, and the political and legal climate, will affect the very survival of their respective organizations. Only in an appraisal-by-results approach can managers be evaluated along these dimensions.

Being diagnostic, appraisal by results does not automatically reward conformance with standards or punish deviation from standards. This diagnostic characteristic, plus the fact that appraisal by results can be environmentally oriented, does not mean that it is an easy or, to use Douglas McGregor's term, a "soft" approach to appraisal. On the contrary, appraisal

---

[33]Robert W. Lewis, "Measuring, Reporting and Appraising Results of Operations with Reference to Goals, Plans and Budgets," in *Planning, Managing and Measuring the Business: A Case Study of Management Planning and Control at General Electric Company*, Controllership Foundation, Inc., New York, 1955, pp. 30–31.

[34]Peter F. Drucker, *Management*, Harper & Row, New York, 1974, p. 497.

604

HUMAN RESOURCE
MANAGEMENT
APPLICATIONS.
ORGANIZATION
DEVELOPMENT, AND
PERSONAL DEVELOPMENT

by results is a very demanding and stringent approach. If the appropriate philosophical base exists and is carefully implemented, appraisal by results can be an effective evaluation approach. However, as the discussion of MBO in Chapter 8 pointed out, whereas there is considerable research on the value of goal setting, the overall MBO process (which includes appraisal by results) has little research backup. One exception relevant to appraisal by results has been the relatively extensive research conducted by the General Electric Company on the impact that the appraisal by results interview has on the subordinate's subsequent job performance. These findings can be summarized as follows:

1. Comprehensive annual performance appraisals are of questionable value.
2. Coaching should be a day-to-day, not a once-a-year, activity.
3. Criticism has a negative effect on the achievement of goals.
4. Defensiveness resulting from critical appraisal produces inferior performance.
5. Praise has little effect one way or the other.
6. Performance improves most when mutually agreeable, specific goals are established.
7. Participation by the employee in the goal-setting procedure produces favorable results when the employee is accustomed to working under high participation levels. When employees are accustomed to working under low participation levels, they work best on goals set by the manager.
8. Interviews designed primarily to improve a subordinate's performance (with the supervisor in the role of counselor) should not at the same time be used to determine his or her salary or promotion (with the supervisor in the role of judge).[35]

Not all of these findings from the General Electric studies have been verified by subsequent research, but they can serve as tentative guidelines to make the appraisal by results technique more effective. However, as with all the other selection and appraisal techniques discussed in this chapter, in the final analysis, appraisal by results needs to be validated to be of long-term value to the organization and to meet the demands of public policy with regard to a discrimination-free appraisal process.

SUMMARY

This chapter has examined two important areas of application from organizational behavior for more effective human resource management: selection and appraisal. Traditionally, the selection process has been heavily dependent on test results. Today, because of legal interpretations and enforcement, organizations are required to validate their selection tests. Although they should have been validating their tests all along, many organizations have now simply chosen to drop their testing programs. It is important to realize that civil rights legislation and the EEOC do not ban all tests, only those that are used to discriminate on the basis of race, creed, sex, religion, or national origin. By understanding the concept of validity and

---

[35]Cascio, op. cit., p. 342.

doing content and predictive validity studies on the selection instruments and ultimately striving to attain construct validity, the selection process of organizations can not only meet the requirements of the social and legal climate but also become more effective in managing human resources. Interviews are the other widely used traditional way of selecting people. Although interviewing is commonly referred to as the most used but least useful selection technique, the art of interviewing can be improved by better planning and by employing certain skills. The newest, most comprehensive technique of selection which is more directly related to job performance and has generally proved to have content and predictive validity is the assessment center. This selection technique has been a success story so far, but some concerns now emerging will need attention in the future.

Like selection, performance appraisal has been undergoing change in recent years. The pressures from the legal climate that selection has experienced over the past decade are now starting to be felt in the appraisal process as well. Organizations are going to have to face the same validity requirements for appraisal as they have for selection. The three general categories of appraisal are judgmental (the traditional trait-rating and the more recent ranking and critical incident methods), behavioral (BARS), and end-result (appraisal by results). In general, the more objective behavioral and end-results techniques seem more effective than the judgmental techniques and have more potential for reaching validation goals. Both selection and appraisal will receive increasing attention in the coming years because they make a significant contribution to the practice of human resource management.

QUESTIONS FOR DISCUSSION AND REVIEW

1. What is the current legal status of the use of tests for selection? Do you think this is fair? Why or why not?
2. What is validity? How do content, predictive, and construct validities differ from one another?
3. In your own words, what is an assessment center? Do you feel this is a good way to select people? Why or why not?
4. What is involved in BARS? Would you rather be rated by a BARS approach or a traditional judgmental technique which measures personal traits. Why?
5. How does the organizational control process fit into performance appraisal?
6. How does appraisal by results differ from BARS and a trait-rating approach? What kinds of jobs would appraisal by results be most compatible with?

CASE:
HOSPITAL
CONSULTANT

You have been hired as a consultant for setting up a comprehensive human resource management program for General Hospital. After interviewing the personnel manager, you decide that major attention must be given to selection and appraisal. You find out that at present the hospital uses the following approaches:

606

HUMAN RESOURCE
MANAGEMENT
APPLICATIONS,
ORGANIZATION
DEVELOPMENT, AND
PERSONAL DEVELOPMENT

Selection. A battery of personality, intelligence, and aptitude tests is used to hire hourly paid employees. There is no evidence that these tests have been validated. In addition, the personnel manager's assistant gives a short interview and the interviewee fills out a standard application blank. On the basis of the test scores, interview, and application blank, selection decisions are made. Managerial personnel are selected on the basis of an interview with the administrator.

Appraisal. The hourly people have an annual appraisal made by their immediate supervisor. This amounts to the supervisor filling out a checklist of the employee's personal traits such as initiative and dependability. No formal evaluations are made of managerial employees. The latter are felt to be professionals and not in need of formal performance appraisals.

1. Based on the present selection and appraisal processes that are used by this hospital, what recommendations would you make and why? Be specific in your recommendations and your reasoning.

2. Comment on the last statement under *Appraisal.* Do professionals need to be evaluated? Why or why not?

3. Would your answer to the first question change if this was a business organization rather than a hospital? How and why?

CASE:
BUCKING TRADITION

Esther Khone was hired as a personnel staff specialist for the Yukon Company. Yukon produces fiberglass shells for use in camping and recreational vehicles. The company had experienced a tremendous growth rate over the past decade. Esther was hired because the top management of Yukon was becoming very concerned with the problems of selecting needed new employees and appraising currently employed ones. The existing policy was for each supervisor to make his or her own policy with respect to selection and appraisal. For example, supervisors did all the interviewing for new positions in their respective departments and made a year-end subjective evaluation of each subordinate. This had worked okay when the company was very small, but it wasn't working well in the expansion situation of recent years. In addition, the top management is now concerned because several complaints have been filed with the EEOC compliance office. So far nothing has happened, but the personnel manager has painted a pretty bleak picture unless things change drastically. Viewing the situation realistically, management knows that each supervisor cannot really be expected to know the current state of the art of personnel selection, keep up with antidiscrimination laws and EEOC guidelines, and utilize the latest appraisal techniques. By the same token, top management has been reluctant to have the personnel department assume all responsibilities for selection and appraisal because of the tradition of letting supervisors hire and evaluate their own people. This was felt necessary so that there would be supervisory acceptance of new employees, and the best way to control and motivate employees was for supervisors to be in charge of evaluating them. Furthermore, the supervisor's acceptance of any changes in the current practices would be crucial to the success of those changes. When she was hired, Esther was charged with deciding whether the current selection and appraisal system should be maintained or whether entirely new policies and procedures should be set up.

1. What would you do if you were Esther? What specific programs would you set up for selection? For appraisal?
2. How would you answer the management concerns about their "traditions" and about supervisory acceptance?

ORGANIZATION DEVELOPMENT

AN OPEN CLIMATE FOR GROWTH AND DEVELOPMENT AT TCA*

About a decade ago Tax Corporation of America (TCA) was in trouble. The president recently related how a new approach to organization development (OD) turned things around. In addition, now that things are straightened out and the firm has begun to grow rapidly, their OD approach has greatly contributed to successful planned change. The approach has been simply to create a climate of openness and trust. This has largely been accomplished through the example of the top management team. For instance, to encourage people to speak out and open up at meetings, the top executives openly admit mistakes in front of employees and admit that their ideas do not always work. The president, Robert Dulsky, noted, "We can also show we value free speech by grabbing the first good employee suggestion, implementing it, and providing recognition to the employe." To reduce hierarchical conflicts, meetings are often organized for people only at the same level, and to discourage interdepartmental conflict, employees from the same department are not allowed to cluster when seated at a meeting. To get a fresh outlook and to stimulate new ideas, key meetings are sometimes held away from the office. To ensure openness, an outside consultant sits in on meetings that cover touchy subjects. The president describes the consultant's role as follows: "He defuses emotional situations by encouraging participants to get feelings out. If personality flare-ups overshadow objectives, he takes over the meeting. As a respected neutral figure, he has greater distance and perspective than emotionally involved executives. Likewise, employees with problems can open up to him as an intermediary, and he keeps these discussions completely confidential." TCA feels that this open climate gives employees a chance to realize their potential and boosts their morale, and, perhaps most important, the company's sales have tripled since the program began.

---

*Adapted from Robert J. Dulsky, "How To Gain from Give-and-Take Sessions with Employees," *Management Review,* August 1979, pp. 32–33.

608

Whereas the last chapter presented and analyzed some specialized human resource management applications, in this chapter a more macro, overall application approach is presented. The term *organization development*, or simply OD, represents this approach. OD has become recognized as the applied arm of the field of organizational behavior and is mainly concerned with the planned change of complex organizations. The development of an organization's human resources and its improved performance are the major aims of OD efforts. Many of the concepts and techniques (e.g., assessment centers, job enrichment, MBO, and O.B. Mod.) discussed in previous chapters could be considered part of OD. However, this chapter is directly concerned with the general issue of the management of change and with widely recognized OD techniques.

After a general discussion of the impact of change, the overall characteristics of OD are explored. Then the three traditional OD techniques of sensitivity training, grid training, and survey feedback are presented and analyzed. Next, attention is given to other modern OD interventions, particularly the interpersonal/intergroup OD interventions of process consultation, third-party peacemaking, and team building. Next, the increasingly popular approach to interpersonal relations and development called transactional analysis is discussed. Finally, the overall track record of OD is examined and some new techniques are explored.

THE IMPACT OF CHANGE

Everyone today is keenly aware of and concerned about change. The following observation summarizes the fact of the inevitability of change:

We may not recognize it or otherwise be cognizant of it; we may oppose it or we may even try to accelerate it. No matter what our position may be, change makes its course in the evolution of human effort. Change may take place so slowly that it is not perceptible in one generation or even two, or it may occur with such rapidity that we are left somewhat breathless in the wake of the waves.[1]

There is little doubt of the dominant role that change has played in contemporary society, and this is nowhere more evident than in organizations. All of today's organizations are vibrating from the forces of change.

A wide variety of forces bombarding the modern organization make change inevitable. These forces can be categorized into three broad areas:

1. The highly competitive marketplace in the private, and also in many respects the public, sector of the economy
2. The tremendously accelerating rate of technological advance
3. The highly volatile changes that are occurring in both the physical and social environment[2]

---

[1] Blair J. Kolasa, *Introduction to Behavioral Science*, Wiley, New York, 1969, p. 348.

[2] James J. Donnelly, Jr., James L. Gibson, and John M. Ivancevich, *Fundamentals of Management*, rev. ed., Business Publications, Austin, Tex., 1975, pp. 269-270.

HUMAN RESOURCE
MANAGEMENT
APPLICATIONS,
ORGANIZATION
DEVELOPMENT, AND
PERSONAL DEVELOPMENT

In order to remain competitive, organizations must forge ahead on all three fronts. Neither private nor public organizations can compete in today's marketplace by standing still or going backward. If they do, they go the way of the buggy whip factory. They die in the long run. Change as a technological force is probably most visible. There have been technological advances through the ages, but not at this *rate* of change.

The *total* accumulation of scientific knowledge is presently doubling about every ten years. One expert on the subject compares the rapidly developing technology with an automobile "whose driver is steadily pressing down on the accelerator of an increasingly powerful engine. The view behind recedes more quickly, the surrounding scenery becomes more quickly unfamiliar, and the speed of the movement gives one a feeling of strangeness and insecurity."[3] Others have noted that today's managers are in a situation analogous to one described by Lewis Carroll in *Alice in Wonderland*: "You have to run as fast as you can to stay where you are."[4]

An example of the impact that changing technology can have on an organization is what happened at National Cash Register (NCR) a couple of years ago. A tiny silicone chip was invented that replaced most of the mechanical parts used in making cash registers. Formerly a cash register had several thousand parts, and now the technologically advanced register has only a few hundred parts. This technological change had a tremendous impact on all aspects of this organization. For example, in its Dayton, Ohio facility the workforce was reduced from 20,000 to 5000, and worldwide the workforce went from 103,000 to 65,000. Not only the number but the nature of the jobs was also drastically changed. Although not all changes are quite as dramatic as those facing NCR, all modern organizations have been facing technological change in recent years.

Besides competition and technology, the physical/ecological and social environments are also rapidly changing. The energy crisis and the concern over environmental protection dominates the everyday life of contemporary society. Suddenly, it has been realized that limited physical resources accompanied by a deteriorating ecological balance present a tremendous challenge.[5]

The same is true of the social environment. Like technological or physical/ecological change, social change has occurred throughout human history, but not at its current rate. People growing up in the 1920s (who are in their sixties and seventies today) had a vastly different sociocultural environment contributing to value development from that of people growing up in the 1960s (who are in their twenties and thirties today) or today. An interesting contrast between these two sociocultural environments would be the young man growing up in the 1920s who got his thrills by getting into an

---

[3]Cameron P. Hall, *Technology and People*, Judson Press, Valley Forge, Pa., 1969, p. 35.

[4]Keith Davis and Robert L. Blomstrom, *Business and Society*, 3d ed., McGraw-Hill, New York, 1975, p. 115.

[5]For an expanded analysis of these challenges see: Fred Luthans, Richard M. Hodgetts, and Kenneth R. Thompson, *Social Issues in Business*, 3d ed., Macmillan, New York, 1980.

older friend's "tin lizzie" (Model T Ford), filled it up with 10 cents per gallon gas, and went racing down a cow path at 18 mph guzzling "bootleg" gin. This contrasts with the young man in the 1960s or 1970s who got his thrills by getting into his older friend's "vet" (Chevrolet Corvette), filled it up with $1.10 a gallon gas, and went racing down an interstate highway at 118 mph smoking a "joint" (marijuana cigarette).[6] The contrasts of the 1920s versus the 1960s and 1970s are "tin lizzies" versus "vets," 10 cents per gallon versus $1.10 per gallon gas, cow paths versus interstate highways, 18 mph versus 118 mph, and alcohol versus drugs. The 1920s situations were probably just as thrilling and daring as the 1960s and 1970s situations, but the speed was different. Recent times represent a fast-paced, 118 mph type of technical, economic, and sociocultural environment.

One result of this contrast between "then" and "now" sociocultural environments is a differing set of values for the people growing up during these times. In other words, people in their sixties or seventies will tend to have a different set of values from people in their twenties or thirties. One contemporary theorist labels this a *value gap* and pinpoints six value areas that are especially relevant to managing people in modern organizations.

1. There is now more concern about values per se, not just different values.
2. Action is more important. Merely talking about values is not enough. One's values must be backed by action.
3. Values such as integrity, honesty, openness, and realness are more important.
4. In general, values are more humanistic. There are different motivating factors.
5. There is increased concern for the ultimate social value of one's work.
6. Authority based on expertise, personal style, and convictions or accomplishments is more legitimate than authority based on age or position.[7]

Like the technological changes, these new social values have a tremendous impact on contemporary organizations. Only through a systematic, planned change effort can these challenges be met. Organization development (OD) has emerged to help in this effort of planned change for organizational effectiveness.

CHARACTERISTICS OF ORGANIZATION DEVELOPMENT

Traditionally, the management of change and the development of human resources were handled in a variety of ways. Bennis identified eight types of traditional change programs which management relied upon: (1) exposition and propagation, (2) elite corps, (3) human relations training, (4) staff, (5) scholarly consultation, (6) circulation of ideas, (7) developmental research, and (8) action research. Although recognizing that each of these change

---

[6]This example is adapted from one used by Professor Morris Massey, University of Colorado, in a lecture heard by the author.

[7]Douglas T. Hall, "Potential for Career Growth," *Personnel Administration*, May-June 1971, pp. 18–19.

612

HUMAN RESOURCE
MANAGEMENT
APPLICATIONS,
ORGANIZATION
DEVELOPMENT, AND
PERSONAL DEVELOPMENT

programs has some positive attributes, Bennis believes that inherent in each is some bias or flaw which weakens its effectiveness. As examples, he notes that graduates of human relations training programs often act like nonalumni shortly after returning to their organizational base; that the staff programs may be limited by the unresolved conflicts between line and staff; and that the elite strategy may focus on the individual and not the organization.[8]

Paul Lawrence is also critical of the highly simplistic nature of traditional approaches to change. In a classic paper he recommended techniques like putting people's needs into the design of technological systems or making special efforts to help newly formed work groups to develop meaningful team relations quickly. However, in a retrospective analysis made fifteen years later, he was not so confident about these relatively simple solutions. He stated that "they do not always enable management to prevent situations from developing in which some individuals win while others lose."[9]

OD: The modern approach to the management of change

The modern approach to the management of change and the development of human resources is called *organization development*. Although there is still not a universally agreed upon definition, Bennis suggests that OD is

a response to change, a complex educational strategy intended to change the beliefs, attitudes, values, and structure of organizations so that they can better adapt to new technologies, markets, and challenges, and the dizzying rate of change itself.[10]

More recently, French and Bell have offered this comprehensive definition:

Organization development is a long-range effort to improve an organization's problem-solving and renewal processes, particularly through a more effective and collaborative management of organization culture—with special emphasis on the culture of formal work teams—with the assistance of a change agent, or catalyst, and the use of the theory and technology of applied behavior science, including action research.[11]

Using the above types of definitions as a point of departure and summarizing what the leaders in the OD movement emphasize, Filley, House, and Kerr suggest that several elements make up the modern OD

[8]Warren G. Bennis, "Theory and Method in Applying Behavioral Science to Planned Organizational Change," *Journal of Applied Behavioral Science*, October–November–December 1965, p. 346.

[9]Paul R. Lawrence, "How to Deal with Resistance to Change," *Harvard Business Review*, May–June 1954, reprinted with retrospective commentary in Gene Dalton and Paul Lawrence (eds.), *Organizational Change and Development*, Dorsey-Irwin, Homewood, Ill., 1970, p. 196.

[10]Warren G. Bennis, *Organization Development: Its Nature, Origins, and Prospects*, Addison-Wesley, Reading, Mass., 1969, p. 2.

[11]Wendell L. French and Cecil H. Bell, Jr., *Organization Development*, 2d ed., Prentice-Hall, Englewood Cliffs, N.J., 1978. p. 14.

approach to the management of change.[12] The following summarizes the major characteristics of OD.

1. *Planned change.* Bennis was one of the first to emphasize the need for systematic, planned change. This "planned" emphasis separates OD efforts from other kinds of more haphazard changes that frequently occur in modern organizations.
2. *Comprehensive change.* Most OD experts emphasize that OD efforts generally involve a "total system." The entire organization or an identifiable unit within it is the unit of analysis.
3. *Emphasis upon work groups.* Although some OD efforts are aimed at individual and organizational change, most are oriented toward groups. There is a sociological flavor to much of OD.
4. *Long-range change.* OD experts emphasize that the process takes months or, in some cases, years, to implement. Although there is pressure for quick results, the OD process is not intended to be a stopgap measure.
5. *Participation of a change agent.* Most OD experts stress the need for an outside, third-party "change agent" or catalyst. "Do-it-yourself" programs are discouraged.
6. *Emphasis upon intervention and action research.* The OD approach results in an active intervention in the ongoing activities of the organization. Action research attacks practical problems but differs from applied research in that the researcher (change agent) is involved in the actual change process in OD.

The desired organizational outcomes of OD efforts include increased effectiveness, problem solving, and adaptability. For human resource development, OD attempts to provide opportunities to be "human" and to increase awareness, participation, and influence. An overriding goal is to integrate individual and organizational objectives.[13]

Historical development of OD

As with other behavioral approaches, it is difficult to pinpoint the precise beginning of OD. French and Bell, who have done the most work on the historical development of OD, feel that "organization development has emerged from applied behavioral science and social psychology and from subsequent efforts to apply laboratory training and survey-feedback insights into total systems."[14] Thus, the two major historical stems for OD are laboratory training and survey feedback. The work of the pioneering social psychologist Kurt Lewin was instrumental in both approaches. Today, almost every organization of any size is pursuing some form of organization development.

TRADITIONAL APPROACHES TO OD

Laboratory training applications to OD have two major techniques. One is the historically significant T-group or sensitivity training approach, and the

---

[12]Alan C. Filley, Robert J. House, and Steven Kerr, *Managerial Process and Organizational Behavior,* 2d ed., Scott, Foresman, Glenview, Ill., 1976, p. 488.

[13]Ibid., pp. 489–490.

[14]French and Bell, op. cit., p. 27.

614

HUMAN RESOURCE
MANAGEMENT
APPLICATIONS,
ORGANIZATION
DEVELOPMENT, AND
PERSONAL DEVELOPMENT

other is. the widely used grid training. After a discussion of these two techniques, the survey-feedback stem of OD is presented and analyzed. These three techniques represent the traditional, but still widely used, approaches to OD.

Sensitivity training

The sensitivity or T(training)-group approach evolved from the group dynamics concepts of Kurt Lewin. The first specific sensitivity training session was held in 1946 on the campus of the State Teachers College in New Britain, Connecticut. The more widely recognized beginning was in 1947 at the National Training Laboratory in Bethel, Maine. Besides Lewin, Kenneth Benne, Leland Bradford, and Ronald Lippitt played important roles in the early sensitivity training effort.

Since the beginning at Bethel, sensitivity training has become a technique widely used by a variety of professionals (psychotherapists, counselors, educators, nurses, social workers, religious workers, and organizational trainers and consultants).[15] There are at least six major target populations at which laboratory training is aimed:

1. Professional helpers with educational and consultative responsibilities (workers in religion, wives of corporation presidents, school superintendents, classroom teachers, juvenile court judges, and youth workers)
2. Middle and top management
3. Total membership of a given organization (Red Cross executives, a family, or a business organization)
4. Laymen and/or professionals in a heterogeneous occupational group
5. Children, youth, and college students
6. Persons with different cultural and/or national backgrounds[16]

This list points out that sensitivity training has very diverse applications. However, for present discussion purposes, it is viewed in terms of its use as a technique of organizational development.

Goals of sensitivity training Sensitivity training attempts to accomplish many different goals. Some training sessions stress the personal development aspects, others stress the ways to become a more effective group member, and still others stress both. Overall, traditional sensitivity training is *process*- instead of task-oriented, and it focuses on the following:[17]

1. To make participants increasingly aware of, and sensitive to, the emotional reactions and expressions in themselves and others
2. To increase the ability of participants to perceive, and to learn from, the consequences of their actions through attention to their own and others' feelings

---

[15]Leland Bradford, Jack R. Gibb, and Kenneth Benne (eds.), *T-Group Theory and Laboratory Method*, Wiley, New York, 1964, p. ix.

[16]Kenneth Benne, Leland Bradford, and Ronald Lippitt, "The Laboratory Method," in Bradford et al., op. cit., pp. 19–22.

[17]Ibid., pp. 16–17.

3. To stimulate the clarification and development of personal values and goals consonant with a democratic and scientific approach to problems of social and personal decision and action

4. To develop concepts and theoretical insights which will serve as tools in linking personal values, goals, and intentions to actions consistent with these inner factors and with the requirements of the situation

5. To foster the achievement of behavioral effectiveness in transactions with the participants' environments

Figure 21-1 relates and summarizes these major process variables. In a systems sense, these variables interact and are interdependent with one another.

Because of the rapid growth in popularity of sensitivity training and the tremendous emotional impact, both pro and con, that it has on people, many misconceptions exist. To clear up these misconceptions and at the same time to gain a better understanding of what sensitivity training is all about, Argyris lists the things which sensitivity training is *not:*[18]

1. Sensitivity training is not a set of hidden, manipulative processes by means of which individuals can be brainwashed into thinking, believing, and feeling the way someone might want them to without realizing what is happening to them.

2. Sensitivity training is not an educational process guided by a staff leader who is covertly in control and who by some magic hides this fact from the participants.

3. The objective of sensitivity training is not to suppress conflict or to get everyone to like one another.

4. Sensitivity training does not attempt to teach people to be callous and disrespectful of society and to dislike those who live a less open life.

5. Sensitivity training is neither psychoanalysis nor intensive group therapy.

6. Sensitivity training is not necessarily dangerous, but it must focus on feelings.

7. Sensitivity training is not education for authoritarian leadership. Its objective is to

---

[18]Chris Argyris, "T-Groups for Organizational Effectiveness," *Harvard Business Review,* March–April 1964, pp. 68–70.

**Figure 21-1
Interacting
process variables
in sensitivity
training.** *Source:*
**Leland P. Bradford,
"Membership and
the Learning
Process," in
Leland P. Bradford
et al., eds.,
*T-Group Theory
and Laboratory
Method,* Wiley,
New York, 1964, p.
215. Used with
permission.)**

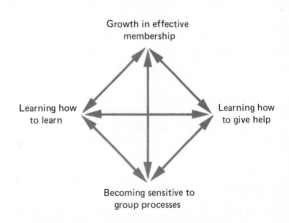

616

HUMAN RESOURCE
MANAGEMENT
APPLICATIONS,
ORGANIZATION
DEVELOPMENT, AND
PERSONAL DEVELOPMENT

develop effective, reality-centered leaders. The most sensitivity training can do is help individuals to see certain unintended consequences and costs of their leadership and to develop other leadership styles if they wish.

8. Sensitivity training does not guarantee change as a result of attendance at the training sessions.

Design and conduct of sensitivity laboratories Sensitivity training may be designed as either a "stranger-lab" or a "cousin-" or "family-lab." In the stranger-labs, the participants are from different organizations and therefore do not know one another. The sequence of events runs something like this:[19]

1. In the beginning, there is an intentional lack of directive leadership, formal agenda, and recognized power and status. This creates a behavioral vacuum which the participants fill with enormously rich projections of traditional behavior.
2. In the second phase, the trainer becomes open, nondefensive, and empathetic, and expresses his or her own feelings in a minimally evaluative way. However, the major impact on each participant comes from the feedback received from the here-and-now behavior of the other group members.
3. In the third phase, interpersonal relationships develop. The members serve as resources to one another and facilitate experimentation with new personal, interpersonal, and collaborative behavior.
4. The last phase attempts to explore the relevance of the experience in terms of "back-home" situations and problems.

In the cousin-labs, the participants are from the same organization but not the same subunit, while in the family-labs they are all from the same subunit. These cousin- and family-labs are used more frequently in organizational development than the stranger-labs are. The conduct of these two labs may be the same as that described for the stranger-lab, but, more often, greater attention is given to intergroup linkages. Typically, in the cousin- and family-labs there is an interfacing of diagnostic surveys, interviews, and confrontation sessions dealing with a variety of policy, problem-solving, and interpersonal issues.[20]

Evaluation of sensitivity training Both the critics and the advocates of sensitivity training defend their position emotionally. George Odiorne, one of the leading critics, reported that he had incurred personal attacks from the other side. Personalized rebuttals to Odiorne's position typically take the following line of reasoning: "The very fact that you attack sensitivity training indicates that you are in favor of autocratic management and therefore *need* sensitivity training to straighten out your personal inadequacies."[21] Odiorne hints that this type of argument, which sets itself above and immune to attacks, is a sure sign of weakness. This type of heated debate still continues, but finally research evidence is starting to accumulate.

A recent comprehensive review of OD techniques by Porras and Berg found that process-oriented laboratory training (as opposed to task-oriented

---

[19]Andre Delbecq, "Sensitivity Training," *Training and Development Journal*, January 1970, p. 33.

[20]Ibid.

[21]George S. Odiorne, *Training by Objectives*, Macmillan, New York, 1970, p. 51.

laboratory training, which is now known as team building and will be covered later in the chapter) is the second most researched OD intervention (after team building), but had the lowest rate of positive change in both process and outcome variables.[22] In the eight scientific studies contained in this analysis of sensitivity training, it was concluded that there was a 44 percent substantial positive change on process variables (i.e., the types of interactive variables shown in Figure 21-1) and an equal 44 percent positive impact on outcome variables (e.g., profits, costs, absenteeism, turnover, or employee satisfaction).

The findings of the Porras and Berg review are somewhat surprising on two counts. First, although sensitivity training was relatively not as effective as other OD techniques, it still had some positive impact. Second, although sensitivity training is aimed mainly at improving the process variables it had an equal effect on outcome variables. But despite this somewhat favorable report on the effect of sensitivity training, there is some evidence that practitioners are not too enthusiastic about using sensitivity training. For example, a survey of personnel directors of large firms found that about twice as many respondents indicated that they would *not* recommend the use of sensitivity training as said they would recommend it.[23] Therefore, even though there is some evidence that sensitivity training can have a positive impact, practitioners' apparent reluctance to use it is probably justified. There is little question that sensitivity training has been subjected to many unwarranted generalizations and abuses. These problems must be corrected if it is to be a truly effective organization development technique for the future. Its spin-off of task-oriented team building has and probably will continue to be a more viable and effective OD technique.

Grid training

Grid training is an outgrowth of the managerial grid approach to leadership discussed in Chapter 15 and is an instrumented approach to laboratory training. Benne explains the nature of the instrumented approach as follows:

In the instrumented T-group, the trainer is removed from direct participation in the group. In his place, a series of self-administered instruments are introduced. The feedback provided by the compilation and analysis of the data provided by all members in responding to these instruments serves as a principal steering mechanism in the group's development and in the learnings which members achieve.[24]

A 9,9 position on Blake and Mouton's leadership grid shown in Chapter 15, indicating a maximum concern for both people and production, is an implied goal of grid training. A more comprehensive step-by-step approach

---

[22]Jerry I. Porras and P. O. Berg, "The Impact of Organization Development," *Academy of Management Review*, April 1978, pp. 259–260.

[23]William J. Kearney and Desmond D. Martin, "Sensitivity Training: An Established Management Development Tool?" *Academy of Management Journal,* December 1974, pp. 755–760.

[24]Kenneth D. Benne, "History of the T-Group in the Laboratory Setting," in Bradford et al., op. cit., p. 129.

618

HUMAN RESOURCE
MANAGEMENT
APPLICATIONS.
ORGANIZATION
DEVELOPMENT, AND
PERSONAL DEVELOPMENT

is taken when grid training is used in OD. Whereas sensitivity training is more of a tool for OD, the grid training approach offers a complete plan for organization development. Blake and his colleagues explain:

The Grid helps to give businessmen a language system for describing their current managerial preferences. It also involves classroom materials and an educational program for designing more productive problem-solving relationships. Even more important, the program is meant to be taught and applied by line managers over a time span involving six overlapping phases.[25]

Summarized, the six phases of grid training for OD are the following:[26]

1. *Laboratory-seminar training.* The purpose of this first phase is to introduce the participants to the overall concepts and materials used in grid training. The seminars that are held are not like therapeutic sensitivity training. There is more structure and concentration on leadership styles than on developing self-insights and group insights.
2. *Team development.* This is an extension of the first phase. Members of the same department are brought together to chart how they are going to attain a 9,9 position on the grid. In this stage, what was learned in the orientation stage is applied to the actual organizational situation.
3. *Intergroup development.* Whereas the first two phases are aimed at managerial development, this phase marks the beginning of overall organization development. There is a shift from the micro level of individual and group development to a macro level of group-to-group organization development. Conflict situations between groups are identified and analyzed.
4. *Organizational goal setting.* In the manner of management by objectives, in this phase the participants contribute to and agree upon the important goals for the organization. A sense of commitment and self-control is instilled in participants.
5. *Goal attainment.* In this phase the participants attempt to accomplish the goals which they set in the fourth phase. As in the first phase, the participants get together, but this time they discuss major organizational issues and the stakes are real.
6. *Stabilization.* In this final phase, support is marshaled for changes suggested earlier and an evaluation of the overall program is conducted.

These six phases of grid training may take from three to five years to implement, but in some cases they may be compressed into a shorter period of time.

Most of the support for grid training has come from its founders, Robert R. Blake and Jane S. Mouton. They and their colleagues have maintained over the years that "managerial and team effectiveness *can* be taught by managers with outside assistance. Furthermore, it appears that this type of educational strategy can help to make significant contributions to organizational effectiveness."[27] In one report where the grid program was carried to the lowest level of the firm, they noted:

---

[25]Robert R. Blake, Jane S. Mouton, Louis B. Barnes, and Larry E. Greiner, "Breakthrough in Organization Development," *Harvard Business Review*, November–December 1964, p. 134.

[26]Ibid., pp. 137–138.

[27]Ibid., p. 155.

Specific advantages have been shown in the gain in dollar savings. Plant-wide practical application of cooperative effort toward greater effectiveness is shown by: decreased time of plant units' tasks, such as unit shutdowns; increased use of capacities and energies of plant personnel through union-management agreed-upon arrangements; . . . and a greater personal interest and involvement in the work.[28]

In their latest work, *The New Managerial Grid,* they continue to suggest that research indicates that grid training is very effective.[29] The recent Porras and Berg review of OD gives some support to their claims. Although Porras and Berg found it to have the least rigorous research (along with survey feedback), of the four studies they reviewed, grid training was found to have a 43 percent substantial positive impact on process variables, and of the three studies examining the impact on outcome variables, there was a 68 percent positive impact.[30] The impact of grid training on outcome variables was higher than any of the other OD techniques but, again, this finding was based on only three studies. Conclusions are still tentative at this point, because more and better research is needed in the future before any firm conclusions can be drawn; nevertheless, the use of grid training does seem to be justified. One thing is certain: it is very widely used. One estimate was that at least 20,000 persons have participated in public grids, while an additional 200,000 have attended in-company grid learning sessions. The conclusion is that the managerial grid is the single most popular approach to organization development.[31]

Survey feedback

Besides laboratory training (sensitivity or grid) the other major thrust in the development of OD has come from survey research and feedback of the data. Once again Kurt Lewin had the original influence in survey feedback, but for the last thirty-five years the approach has been most closely associated with the University of Michigan's Institute for Social Research (ISR).

As the terminology indicates, this approach to OD surveys the unit of analysis (e.g., a work group, department, or whole organization) by means of questionnaires and feeds back the data to those who generated them. The data are used in the action research sense of diagnosing problems and developing specific action plans to solve the problems. The questionnaire can be either tailor-made for each situation or, as has been more common in recent years, a standardized version is researched and developed by the ISR. A number of revisions have been made through the years, but the typical ISR questionnaire provides data on the following areas.[32]

---

[28]Robert R. Blake, Jane S. Mouton, Richard L. Sloma, and Barbara P. Loftin, "A Second Breakthrough in Organization Development," *California Management Review,* Winter 1968, p. 78.

[29]Robert R. Blake and Jane S. Mouton, *The New Managerial Grid,* Gulf, Houston, Texas, 1978.

[30]Porras and Berg, op. cit.

[31]"Using the Managerial Grid to Ensure MBO," *Organizational Dynamics,* Spring 1974, p. 55.

[32]See James C. Taylor and David G. Bowers, *Survey of Organizations: A Machine-Scored Standardized Questionnaire Instrument,* Institute for Social Research, University of Michigan, Ann Arbor, 1972, pp. 3–4.

620

HUMAN RESOURCE
MANAGEMENT
APPLICATIONS,
ORGANIZATION
DEVELOPMENT, AND
PERSONAL DEVELOPMENT

Leadership

1. Managerial support
2. Managerial goal emphasis
3. Managerial work facilitation
4. Managerial interaction facilitation
5. Peer support
6. Peer goal emphasis
7. Peer work facilitation
8. Peer interaction facilitation

Organizational climate

9. Communication with company
10. Motivation
11. Decision making
12. Control within company
13. Coordination between departments
14. General management

Satisfaction

15. Satisfaction with company
16. Satisfaction with supervisor
17. Satisfaction with job
18. Satisfaction with pay
19. Satisfaction with work group

Normally an external consultant will accumulate, present, and interpret the data for the group. The consultant will then, usually in a process consultation or team-building approach (covered in the next section) help the group diagnose and solve its problems.

ISR has conducted a relatively great amount of research over the years on their questionnaire instrument and on survey feedback as an OD intervention. For example, in one comprehensive study by ISR's David Bowers, various OD interventions (survey feedback, interpersonal process consultation, task process consultation, sensitivity training, simple data handback to appropriate superiors/control, and no treatment/control) were analyzed.[33] Thousands of subjects from twenty-five organizational systems in ten companies were asked to fill out questionnaires that provided data similar to the nineteen dimensions outlined above under leadership, organizational climate, and satisfaction. This data were gathered before and after the OD interventions. The results showed that the survey feedback intervention had the most favorable impact on the respondents. Groups whose average respondent reported positive rather than negative change from the survey feedback were 72 percent for organizational climate, 85 percent for managerial leadership, 100 percent for peer leadership, and 85 percent for satisfaction. Even the control condition of merely handing back survey data

[33]David G. Bowers, *Development Techniques and Organizational Change: An Overview of Results from the Michigan Inter-Company Longitudinal Study*, Technical Report, Office of Naval Research, Arlington, Va., September 1971.

to appropriate supervisors (with no group processing in the sense of diagnosing problems and developing action plans as in the survey-feedback approach) had a much more positive impact on managerial leadership, peer leadership, and satisfaction than did the other OD techniques.

This impressive study does lend credibility to the survey-feedback approach to OD. But it must be interpreted with some caution. First of all, the survey-feedback technique is the only one that "fanned out" throughout the entire organizations studied and concerned itself with the combinations of structural, technical, and interpersonal issues of consequence to the whole organization. The other techniques were more limited in their applications (e.g., the consultants spent most of their time with top management) and therefore there were no spillover effects.[34] Second, one could question the sole use of questionnaire responses as dependent measures to evaluate the impact.[35] Multiple measures would have been much more effective, and at least from a human resource management perspective, some hard perform-ance measures to assess the impact on outcome variables would have been more meaningful.[36] The Porras and Berg review did analyze three rigorous studies on survey feedback that indicated it had a 53 percent substantial positive change on such outcome variables.[37] So, even though there are some possible reservations, the research is fairly supportive of the effectiveness of a survey-feedback approach to OD.

OTHER MODERN OD TECHNIQUES

As indicated, the two major historical stems in OD are laboratory training (sensitivity and grid) and survey feedback. Both of these are still important OD intervention strategies. However, today there are many other important techniques used in OD. Table 21-1 gives a typology of the most widely recognized OD interventions according to the unit of analysis.

As shown, sensitivity training can be used as a major OD intervention at both the intraindividual and interpersonal levels; survey feedback is applied at both the interpersonal/intergroup and total organization level; and grid training in its various phases or as a whole is applied to all three levels. Although there are other OD interventions that are sometimes used at the intraindividual (e.g., life and career planning, which helps individuals

---

[34]Bernard M. Bass and Edward C. Ryterband, *Organizational Psychology*, 2d ed., Allyn and Bacon, 1979, p. 481.

[35]For a critical analysis of the use of questionnaire measures such as those used by the Michigan group see: Fred Luthans and Tim Davis, "Operationalizing a Behavioral Approach to Leader-ship," *Proceedings of the Midwest Academy of Management*, 1979, pp. 144–155; and Chester A. Schriesheim and Steven Kerr, "Theories and Measures of Leadership: A Critical Appraisal of Current and Future Directions," in J. G. Hunt and L. L. Larson (eds.), *Leadership: The Cutting Edge*, Southern Illinois University Press, Carbondale, Ill., 1977, pp. 9–45.

[36]For a comprehensive review of multiple measures to assess the impact of organizational development techniques see: Diane L. Lockwood and Fred Luthans, "Multiple Measures to Assess the Impact of Organizational Development," *The 1980 Annual Handbook for Group Facilitators*, University Associates, San Diego, Calif. pp. 233–245.

[37]Porras and Berg, op. cit.

622

HUMAN RESOURCE
MANAGEMENT
APPLICATIONS,
ORGANIZATION
DEVELOPMENT, AND
PERSONAL DEVELOPMENT

Table 21-1

TYPES OF MAJOR OD INTERVENTIONS

Unit of analysis	Major OD interventions
Intraindividual	Sensitivity training (therapeutic)
	Grid training (Phase 1)
Interpersonal (group) and intergroup (different groups are substituted for different individuals in intergroup applications)	Sensitivity training (family and cousin)
	Grid training (Phases 1, 2, and 3)
	Survey feedback
	Process consultation
	Third-party peacemaking
	Team building
Total (system) organization	Grid training (all phases)
	Survey feedback

identify strengths and weaknesses in order to focus on their life and career objectives and how they can achieve them) and total organization (e.g., technostructural interventions that strategically improve the technical or structural inputs) levels, most of the modern, widely used OD efforts are aimed at the interpersonal/intergroup level. Besides the sensitivity training, grid training, and survey-feedback techniques, which have already been discussed, three of the most important interventions at the interpersonal/intergroup level are process consultation, third-party peacemaking, and team building.

Process consultation

Process variables were introduced in the discussion of sensitivity training, and as the terminology suggests, the process consultation, or P-C, approach to OD is concerned with the processes that take place within a group or between groups and the consultant. Edgar Schein, the leading writer and consultant on P-C, depicts the role of the outside consultant as helping "the client to perceive, understand, and act upon process events which occur in the client's environment."[38] The underlying assumption of P-C is that the process consultant can effectively help diagnose and solve important problems facing modern organizations. Schein points out that the consultant is mainly concerned with processes such as "the various human actions which occur in the normal flow of work, in the conduct of meetings, and in formal and informal encounters between members of the organization. Of particular relevance are the client's own actions and their impact on other people."[39] Specific areas at which P-C is aimed include communication, functional roles of group members, group problem solving and decision making, group norms and growth, leadership and authority, and intergroup processes.

---

[38]Edgar H. Schein, *Process Consultation: Its Role in Organization Development*, Addison-Wesley, Reading, Mass., 1969, p. 9.

[39]Ibid.

Schein lists the following specific steps which the consultant would follow in a P-C program of OD:[40]

1. *Initiate contact.* This is where the client contacts the consultant with a problem that cannot be solved by normal organization procedures or resources.
2. *Define the relationship.* In this step the consultant and the client enter into both a formal contract spelling out services, time, and fees and a psychological contract. The latter spells out the expectations and hoped-for results of both the client and the consultant.
3. *Select a setting and method.* This step involves an understanding of where and how the consultant will do the job that needs to be done.
4. *Gather data and make a diagnosis.* Through a survey using questionnaires, observation, and interviews, the consultant makes a preliminary diagnosis. This data gathering occurs simultaneously with the entire consultative process.
5. *Intervene.* Agenda-setting, feedback, coaching, and/or structural interventions can be made in the P-C approach.
6. *Reduce involvement and terminate.* The consultant disengages from the client organization by mutual agreement but leaves the door open for future involvement.

There are two major advantages of a P-C approach to OD. First of all, P-C is aimed at important interpersonal and intergroup problems facing today's organizations. Second, although an outside consultant is used, with the accompanying advantages, the P-C approach is aimed at helping organizations help themselves. The disadvantages of P-C are that the participants are not as intensively involved in the process as in some of the other OD techniques and it generally takes two or three years of sustained involvement, which requires a great deal of commitment and cost. To date, although Chris Argyris has developed some innovative approaches to evaluating P-C[41] and there are some cases citing its effectiveness,[42] rigorous research evaluating this approach has not been conducted. The Bower's study cited earlier found both interpersonal P-C and task P-C to have less affect on the questionnaire respondents' reactions than survey feedback.[43] But obviously, more research than this is needed before any conclusions can be drawn.

Third-party peacemaking

A special case of process consultation is third-party peacemaking, which is specifically aimed at resolving interpersonal/intergroup conflict. Like P-C, it examines the processes involved, makes a diagnosis of the reasons for the conflict, and through the third-party consultant facilitates a constructive confrontation and a resolution of the conflict. The approach is based on the modern assumptions of conflict that were examined in detail in Chapter 13. Richard Walton is most closely associated with third-party peacemaking.

---

[40]Ibid., pp. 79–131.

[41]See: Chris Argyris, *Organization and Innovation*, Homewood, Ill., 1965.

[42]For example, see: Schein, op. cit., pp. 126–129; and Gordon Lippitt, *Organization Renewal*, Appleton-Century-Crofts, New York, 1969.

[43]Bowers, op. cit.

624

HUMAN RESOURCE
MANAGEMENT
APPLICATIONS,
ORGANIZATION
DEVELOPMENT, AND
PERSONAL DEVELOPMENT

He feels that this approach may lead to constructive outcomes of conflict by ensuring mutual motivation on the part of the principals; creating parity in their situational power; synchronizing their negative and positive moves; providing social support and process expertise that enhances openness; performing a translation function; and adjusting the tension to optimum levels.[44] The intervention made by the consultant can be either passive, with the consultant simply being present and available in the confrontation, or active, with the consultant taking the following types of steps:

1. Gather relevant data by interviewing the principles in the conflict.
2. Select the place and structure the context of the confrontation meeting.
3. Make a direct intervention in the process by doing actions such as the following:
   a. Refereeing the interaction process
   b. Initiating agenda
   c. Encouraging and participating in feedback
   d. Giving a diagnosis and prescription
   e. Assisting the principals to plan and prepare for further dialogue after the confrontation[45]

The advantage of third-party peacemaking is that it is a systematic approach to dysfunctional conflict resolution. The disadvantage is that the conflict can become worse if not handled properly. To avoid compounding the problem, there must be a highly skilled consultant. Walton suggests that the profile for the ideal third-party peacemaker is one who has (1) high professional expertise regarding social processes; (2) low power over the fate of the principals; (3) high control over the confrontation setting and processes; (4) moderate knowledge about the principals, issues, and background factors; (5) neutrality or balance with respect to substantive outcomes, personal relationships, and conflict resolution methodology.[46] As with process consultation, there are testimonial cases that try to evaluate third-party consultation,[47] but as yet there is no rigorous research available.

Team building

Both process consultation and third-party peacemaking are specialized OD interventions that are closely associated with a very few leading advocates and practicing consultants. Of wider appeal and application is team building. Whereas sensitivity training "scares off" many managers because of the controversy surrounding it and the potentially harmful psychological implications inherent in it, team building is seen as accomplishing some of the same process goals as sensitivity training but tends to be much more task-oriented. Table 21-2 shows that team building activities can be applied to either "family" groups or special groups (e.g., task forces, committees, or

[44]Richard E. Walton, *Interpersonal Peacemaking: Confrontations and Third-Party Consultation,* Addison-Wesley Publishing Company, Inc., Reading, Mass., 1969, p. v.

[45]Ibid., pp. 148–150.

[46]Ibid., pp. 15–69.

[47]Ibid.

Table 21-2

VARIOUS APPROACHES TO TEAM BUILDING

Family groups (members from the same organizational unit)	Special groups (start-up teams, task forces, committees, interdepartmental groups)
1. Task accomplishment (e.g., problem solving, decision making, role clarification, goal setting, etc.)	1. Task accomplishment (e.g., special problems, role and goal clarification, resource utilization, etc.)
2. Building and maintaining effective interpersonal relationships (e.g., boss-subordinate relationships and peer relationships)	2. Relationships (e.g., interpersonal or interunit conflict, and underutilization of each other as resources)
3. Understanding and managing group processes and culture	3. Processes (e.g., communications, decision making, and task allocations)
4. Role analysis technique for role clarification and definition	4. Role analysis technique for role clarification and definition
5. Role negotiation techniques	5. Role negotiation

Source: Adapted from Wendell L. French and Cecil H. Bell, *Organization Development*, 2d ed., Prentice-Hall, Englewood Cliffs, N.J., 1978, p. 119.

interdepartmental groups) within the organization. Ignoring for the time being some specialized problems dealing with process variables, in general it can be said that team building has replaced sensitivity training in organization development efforts aimed at improving overall performance. Perhaps with the exception of widely marketed, commercially based grid training, there is little question that team building has become the most popular OD technique in recent years. French and Bell go as far as to say that "probably the most important single group of interventions in OD are the team-building activities the goals of which are the improvement and increased effectiveness of various teams within the organization."[48]

As an OD process, team building generally follows the classic change procedure originally formulated by Kurt Lewin:

1. *Unfreezing.* The first task is to make the team aware of the need for change. A climate of openness and trust is developed so that the group is ready for change.
2. *Moving.* Basically using a survey-feedback technique, the team makes a diagnosis of where they are and develops action plans to get to where they want to go.
3. *Refreezing.* Once the plans have been carried out and an evaluation has been made, the team starts to stabilize into more effective performance.

The above, of course, represents only a very general idea of what team building is all about and can also apply to the other OD techniques.

A more specific team-building program actually used in a large industrial plant is described as follows:[49]

---

[48]French and Bell, op. cit., p. 119.

[49]Warren R. Nielsen and John R. Kimberly, "The Impact of Organizational Development on the Quality of Organizational Output," *Academy of Management Proceedings*, 1973, pp. 528–529.

626

HUMAN RESOURCE
MANAGEMENT
APPLICATIONS,
ORGANIZATION
DEVELOPMENT, AND
PERSONAL DEVELOPMENT

1. *Team skills workshop.* The production teams in this plant first went through a two-and-a-half-day workshop that mainly consisted of a series of experience-based exercises. The purpose of this first phase was essentially to unfreeze the various teams and get them ready to accept change.

2. *Data collection.* In a questionnaire survey, data were collected on organizational climate, supervisory behavior, and job content from all first-line supervisors in the program.

3. *Data confrontation.* The consultants presented the teams with the data gathered in step 2. The teams, with the consultant present, openly discussed problem areas, established priorities, and made some preliminary recommendations for change.

4. *Action planning.* Based on what went on in step 3, the teams then developed specific plans for the changes to be actually carried out on the job.

5. *Team building.* The first four phases were preliminary to the actual team building. In this phase, each team met as a whole to identify barriers to effectiveness, developed ways of eliminating the barriers, and agreed upon plans to accomplish the desired changes.

6. *Intergroup building.* In this final phase there were two-day meetings held between various teams that were interdependent in accomplishing goals. The purpose of this phase was to establish collaboration on shared goals and problems and to generalize the OD effort to the total organization.

This program took over a year to complete. The outside consultant in a team-building OD approach such as the above plays an important facilitative role but is not as central to the approach as in process consultation or third-party peacemaking.

The advantages of team building are all those that are attributed to old-fashioned teamwork. The process can create a team effort in an open, participatory climate. There can be improved communication and problem solving, and individual team members can experience psychological growth and improve their interpersonal skills. For example, one research study found that four trained teams reported significantly higher levels of group effectiveness, mutual influence, and personal involvement and participation than did the eight control groups.[50] Evaluation of the six-step program described above also found that the program produced a positive impact on organizational performance (quality of output and profit but not quantity of output) and favorably affected the attitudes and perceptions of the members of the teams studied.[51]

As the above studies indicate, there is relatively more and better research on team building than on any of the other OD techniques. Porras and Berg found by far more acceptable research studies (40 percent of the thirty-five studies which met their minimum criteria) on team building than on any other OD technique. Of the fourteen team-building studies that examined process variables, 45 percent had a substantial positive change, and of the three studies that analyzed the impact on outcome variables, 53 percent were

[50]Frank Friedlander, "The Impact of Organizational Training Laboratories upon Effectiveness and Intervention of Ongoing Work Groups," *Personnel Psychology,* Autumn 1967, pp. 289–308.

[51]John R. Kimberly and Warren R. Nielsen, "Organizational Development and Change in Organizational Performance," *Administrative Science Quarterly,* June 1975, pp. 191–206.

deemed to have a substantial positive change.[52] Thus, even though there is more research on team building than on other OD techniques, the balance is still greatly in favor of examining process variables over performance variables. In other words, as with the other OD techniques discussed in this chapter and the other human resource applications discussed in the other chapters, more research is needed on team building, but its potential for the future seems great.

TRANSACTIONAL ANALYSIS

Transactional analysis, or TA, is given separate attention in this chapter because it is not part of the mainstream of OD. Most OD experts do not feel that TA is a full-fledged intervention strategy; rather, they treat it as a useful tool to help people better understand themselves and their affect on others. The application of TA is not limited to OD efforts. Similar to sensitivity training, TA has diverse applications in counseling and is widely used to analyze group dynamics and interpersonal communication. As an OD tool, it has been pointed out that the purpose of TA is to "help the people involved better understand their own ego states and those of others, to understand the principles behind transactions and games, and to interact in more meaningful ways with one another."[53]

Eric Berne is usually credited with starting the TA movement with his best-selling book *Games People Play*, and Thomas Harris's book *I'm OK—You're OK* further popularized TA. More recent books by James and Jongeward are more relevant to OD applications.[54] TA is very popular today and has a wide appeal. In many respects it is a fad and is sometimes confused with the equally popular transcendental meditation (TM) movement. However, TA has been able to transcend the fad stage because it is based on a well-developed psychoanalytic theoretical base. A major reason for its popularity, and where Freud and other pioneering psychoanalytic theorists failed, is that it uses very understandable, everyday, relevant terminology. Everyone can readily relate to the concepts and practice of TA. The following sections give attention to the three major areas of transactional analysis: ego states, transactions, and strokes and games. The last section will comment on its application and value as an OD technique.

Ego states

Chapter 3 contained a discussion of the Freudian psychoanalytic model and Chapter 5 was devoted to the structure of personality. The ego plays a central

---

[52]Porras and Berg, op. cit.

[53]Huse, op. cit., p. 290.

[54]Muriel James and Dorothy Jongeward, *Born to Win*, Addison-Wesley, Reading, Mass., 1971; Dorothy Jongeward and contributors, *Everybody Wins: Transactional Analysis Applied to Organizations*, Addison-Wesley, Reading, Mass., 1973; and Dorothy Jongeward and Philip Seyen, *Choosing Success*, Wiley, New York, 1978.

628

HUMAN RESOURCE
MANAGEMENT
APPLICATIONS,
ORGANIZATION
DEVELOPMENT, AND
PERSONAL DEVELOPMENT

role in the Freudian model. In the structure of the human personality, the ego represents reality, and it rationally attempts to keep the impulsive id and the conscience of the superego in check. The ego is a hypothetical construct because it is not observable; it is used to help explain the complex dynamics of the human personality. TA uses this psychoanalytic theory as background for identifying three important ego states: child, adult, and parent. These three ego states are roughly equivalent to the Freudian concepts of id (child), ego (adult), and superego (parent). A more detailed look at the three ego states is necessary to understand TA and how it can be used in OD.

Child (C) ego state　This is the state where the person acts as an impulsive child. This "child" state could be characterized by being either submissive and conforming (the dutiful child) or insubordinate, emotional, joyful, or rebellious (the "little brat"). In either case the child state is characterized by very immature behavior. An example would be the employee who, when reprimanded by the boss for doing something known to be correct, responds by saying, "You know best. Whatever you say, sir." Another example would be the secretary who tells a coworker, "My boss makes me so mad sometimes I could scream" and then proceeds to break into tears. Both examples illustrate immature, childlike behaviors.

Adult (A) ego state　In this state the person acts like a mature adult. In the adult state people attack problems in a "cool-headed," rational manner. They gather relevant information, carefully analyze it, generate alternatives, and make logical choices. In the adult state people do not act impulsively or in a domineering way. In dealings with other people, the adult state is characterized by fairness and objectivity. An example would be the sales manager who, when presented with a relatively high expense account by a subordinate, replies, "Well, this appears high, but we will have to look at the reasons for it. It may be that our other salespersons' expenses are too low to do the kind of job that needs to be done."

Parent (P) ego state　In this state people act like domineering parents. Individuals can be either overly protective and loving or stern and critical. The parent state is also illustrated by those who give standards and rules for others. They tend to talk down to people and to treat others like children. An example would be the supervisor who comes up to a group of workers and says, "Okay, you guys, stop fooling around and get to work. You have to earn your keep around here."

Transactions between ego states

It should be pointed out that people generally exhibit all three ego states, but one state may dominate the other two. The strong implication is, of course, that the adult state is far superior to the child or parent state, at least for effective interpersonal relations. However, the TA authors generally stress that all three ego states are necessary to a healthy personality. More important than the ego state per se is how one ego state matches or conflicts with another ego state in interpersonal relations. As James and Jongeward note, "Anything that happens between people will involve a transaction between their ego states. When one person sends a message to another, he expects a response. All transactions can be classified as (1) complementary, (2) crossed, or (3) ulterior."[55] Analysis of these transactions is at the very heart of TA.

Complementary transactions   Figure 21-2 shows three possible complementary transactions. As shown, transactions are complementary if the message sent or the behavior exhibited by one person's ego state receives the appropriate and expected response from the other person's ego state. For example, suppose that the two people interacting in Figure 21-2, are a boss and an immediate subordinate. In (a), the boss says, "Joe, I want you to be more careful in filling out a report on even the smallest accident. OSHA requirements are getting really tough, and we have to do better." The subordinate in case (a) replies, "Gee, boss, I really don't have time to fill out those dumb reports, but if you think I should, I will." In (b), the superior and subordinate both interact in an adult manner. For example, the boss says, "Joe, I would like your input on a report I am writing on how to improve the efficiency of the department." Joe responds by saying, "You bet, Jack. I have been gathering a lot of cost data over the past couple of months, and as soon as I analyze it, I would like to sit down with you and discuss it." In (c) the subordinate possesses the parent state and the boss represents the child state. Although rarer than the other two cases, an example might be the following dialogue:

Joe: Jack, I wish you would give more attention to maintenance around here. I can't do my job well unless you give me the proper support.

---

[55]James and Jongeward, op. cit., p. 24.

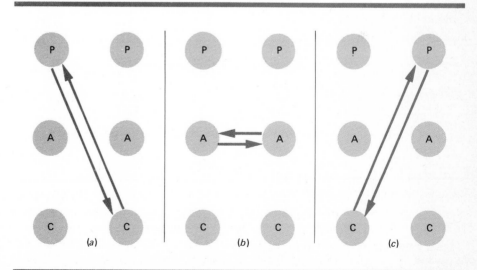

**Figure 21-2
Complementary
transactions.**

630

HUMAN RESOURCE
MANAGEMENT
APPLICATIONS,
ORGANIZATIONAL
DEVELOPMENT, AND
PERSONAL DEVELOPMENT

The boss: Heaven's sake! What do you want from me? You guys drive me up a wall. I can't take it anymore.

Once again it should be pointed out that although the adult-to-adult complementary transactions are probably most effective for organizational interpersonal relations, communication and understanding can also occur in the parent-child complementary transactions.

Crossed transactions A crossed transaction occurs when the message sent or the behavior exhibited by one person's ego state is reacted to by an incompatible, unexpected ego state on the part of the other person. There are many more possible crossed transactions than there are complementary transactions. Figure 21-3 shows one crossed transaction that would typically occur in an organizational setting. As shown, the boss treats his subordinate as a child but the subordinate attempts to respond on an adult basis. The dialogue in this example might be as follows:

Boss: I have told you over and over that I want those reports in on time. You are either going to have to meet my deadlines or look for another job.

Subordinate: I did not realize that the timing of the reports was so critical. I will have to reorder my priorities.

Crossed transactions are the source of much interpersonal conflict in an organization. The result can be hurt feelings and frustrations on the part of the parties involved and possible dysfunctional consequences for the organization.

Ulterior transactions The most complex are the ulterior transactions. These can be very subtle, but, like the crossed transactions, they are generally very damaging to interpersonal relations. As shown in Figure 21-4 the ulterior transactions always involve at least two ego states on the part of one person. The individual may say one thing (e.g., project an adult state, as

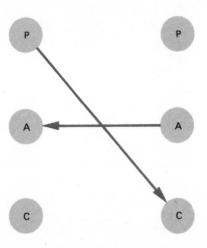

**Figure 21-3
Crossed
transactions.**

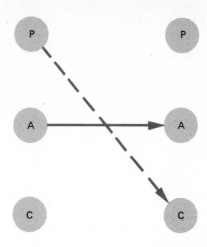

**Figure 21-4
Ulterior
transactions.**

indicated in Figure 21-4) but mean quite another (e.g., the parent state, as shown by the dashed line in Figure 21-4). Although there are many other possibilities besides the one shown in Figure 21-4, an example is this typical one in organizations, where the boss says, "My door is always open, come in so we can air your problems and together reach a rational solution" (adult state), when what he really means is: "Don't come whining to me with your troubles. Find an answer yourself. That is what you're getting paid for" (parent state). Obviously, these ulterior transactions are the most difficult to identify and deal with in transactional analysis.

Strokes and games in TA

The three ego states and the three types of transactions are the basic elements of TA. In addition, however, there are other concepts and dynamics inherent in the TA approach. Two of the more important are strokes and games.

The concept of strokes TA experts feel that everyone has to have strokes. Using the common meaning of the word, this simply means that starting out as an infant and throughout one's life, a person needs cuddling, affection, recognition, and praise. Not everyone is turned on by the same strokes. (In the vernacular of TA this is stated as "different strokes for different folks.") But everyone needs them. It may be a simple "Good morning" or a pat on the back every once in a while. If people do not get such positive strokes, they will seek out negative strokes. The latter case may be the outgrowth of childhood experiences. People in this case tend to discount any attempts to give them positive strokes. Obviously, this TA concept of strokes is very closely related to the learning concept of reinforcement. For example, positive strokes could be thought of as social reinforcers.

632

HUMAN RESOURCE
MANAGEMENT
APPLICATIONS.
ORGANIZATIONAL
DEVELOPMENT, AND
PERSONAL DEVELOPMENT

The games people play TA is also concerned with the ways that people structure their time. James and Jongeward suggest that people learn withdrawal, rituals or pastimes, games, activities, and intimacy to occupy their time.[56] The meanings of each of these are self-explanatory, and going into depth on each of them is beyond the scope of this discussion. However, a brief look at the games people play is especially relevant to some of the things that go on in modern organizations.

Eric Berne, who is most closely associated with the games aspect of TA and, of course, wrote the best-selling book *Games People Play*, which was pointed out as starting the TA movement, defines a game as "a recurring set of transactions, often repetitious, superficially plausible, with a concealed motivation; or, more colloquially, a series of moves with a snare, or 'gimmick.' "[57] Those involved in a game are usually not aware of it until the "snare" is drawing tight. The outcome of games is almost always a win-lose proposition. Straightforward as well as devious people commonly play games. Games that are frequently played in organizations are summarized in Table 21-3.

The games summarized in the table are only representative examples of the games people play in organizations. Anyone who has spent some time working can readily identify with many of these and other games that people play in organizational life.

Evaluation of TA as an OD technique

As noted in the introductory comments on TA, most OD experts consider TA a tool rather than an intervention strategy for OD. Yet it is becoming increasingly popular with management practitioners. Many companies in a wide variety of industries have sponsored TA programs for their managerial personnel and certain key positions such as customer service representatives. Questionnaire instruments which identify dominant ego states of people and exercises that help people understand and analyze their transactions with others have been developed.

When used as an OD approach, TA has attempted to develop more adult states in people and complementary transactions with others. TA is also used in certain phases of the interpersonal OD techniques of process consultation, third-party peacemaking, and team building. There is some recent evidence that its use as an OD technique is having increased acceptance. After a comprehensive analysis of TA as an OD technique, Bowen and Nath offer the following guidelines for successful application:

1. If TA is to be employed in OD, it will be more effective if introduced early in the diagnostic phase.
2. The planning, action, and stabilization phases should be designed to encourage continued application of the TA framework.

---

[56]Ibid., pp. 56–63.

[57]Eric Berne, *Games People Play*, Grove Press, New York, 1964, p. 48.

Table 21-3

GAMES PEOPLE PLAY IN ORGANIZATIONS

Name of game	Brief description of game
1. Now I've Got You, You S.O.B. (N.I.G.Y.S.O.B.)	One employee gets back at another by luring her into what appears to be a natural work relationship. Actually the situation is rigged so that the other will fail. When the inevitable mistake is made, the game player pounces on the associate and publicly embarrasses her.
2. Poor Me	The person depicts himself to the boss as helpless. Criticisms for inadequate performance are avoided because the boss truly feels sorry for the individual, who may actually begin to feel sorry for himself.
3. Blemish	The boss appears to be objectively evaluating an employee's total performance. In reality, the boss is looking for some minor error. When the error is found, the employee is berated for the poor performance, the inference being that the whole project/task/report is inadequate.
4. Hero	The boss consistently sets up situations where employees fail. At some point, the boss steps in to save the day miraculously.
5. King of the Hill	The boss sets up situations where employees end up in direct competition with her. At the end, she steps in and demonstrates her competence and superiority while publicly embarrassing her employees.
6. Cops and Robbers	An employee continuously walks a fine line between acceptable and unacceptable behavior. The boss wastes unnecessary time desperately trying to catch the employee, while the employee stays one step ahead and laughs to himself through the day.
7. Prosecutor	The employee carefully carries around a copy of the union contract or organization regulations and investigates management practices. This employee dares the boss to act in an arbitrary manner. Once he does, the employee files a grievance and attempts to embarrass the boss.
8. If It Weren't for You . . .	The employee discusses her problems openly but carefully works the conversation around so that she can rationalize her failure by blaming the boss for everything that goes wrong.
9. Yes, but . . .	In this game the boss responds with "Yes, but . . ." to every good answer or idea that the subordinate may have. By doing this the boss can maintain a superior position and keep subordinates in their place. It represents a form of pseudoparticipation, i.e., the boss asks for participation but answers every suggestion with "Yes, but . . ."

Source: Adapted from Fred Luthans and Mark J. Martinko, *The Practice of Supervision and Management,* McGraw-Hill, New York, 1979, pp. 386–387, which in turn is adapted from the literature on transactional analysis.

634

HUMAN RESOURCE
MANAGEMENT
APPLICATIONS,
ORGANIZATION
DEVELOPMENT, AND
PERSONAL DEVELOPMENT

3. The application of TA in OD should only be undertaken within a broader framework of a systems model of OD.
4. Where TA is employed as an unfreezing mechanism, it is probably most effective to employ the general pattern of experiential activity followed by cognitive input and analysis of the activity, rather than beginning with the cognitive element.
5. TA will tend to be of greatest value in OD designs emphasizing interpersonal relationships and process consultation.
6. Employing a TA approach to change does not reduce the demands for interpersonal competence on the part of the consultant.[58]

Such guidelines are certainly helpful but the actual effectiveness of TA approaches to OD are largely unknown.

To date, only a few studies have attempted to evaluate the impact that a TA intervention has had on attitudes or behaviors of employees in work organizations and these have had mixed results. For example, one study in the customer service department of a large utility did find that those employees trained in TA reacted very favorably, learned the concepts, and found evidence of significant improvements in employees' perceptions of customer satisfaction at the beginning and end of transactions. However, even though customers' ratings of employee behavior were significantly more favorable during and after the TA intervention as compared to pre-intervention levels, and selected areas of departmental performance improved, when compared to a control group who did not receive the TA intervention there were no significant differences.[59]

Besides this very sparse research, about the only evidence of the value of TA as an OD technique is the testimony of TA consultants and the results of a few questionnaire studies that asked participants how well they liked the TA program and whether they thought it did them any good back on the job. All the TA consultants, of course, give glowing testimony to the effectiveness of TA.[60] The same is true of the questionnaire studies. The participants are generally very positive about the TA program and feel that it has done some good back on the job.[61] However, as Huse notes, "Since the results of most of these programs are given in anecdotal or questionnaire-response form, the true value of TA and its long-term influence on employees, groups, or the larger social system have yet to be determined."[62] In other words,—and the

---

[58]Donald D. Bowen and Raghu Nath, "Transactional Analysis in OD: Applications Within the NTL Model," *Academy of Management Review*, January 1978, pp. 86–87.

[59]Mark J. Martinko and Fred Luthans, "An Experimental Analysis of the Effectiveness of a Transactional Analysis Program in Industry," *Proceedings of the Midwest Academy of Management*, 1978, pp. 279–290. For a couple of other systematic evaluations of TA in a work setting see: D. D. Ely and J. T. Morse, "TA and Reinforcement Theory," *Personnel*, March–April 1974, pp. 38–41; and N. Nykodym, "Transactional Analysis: A Strategy for the Improvement of Supervisory Behavior," *Proceedings of the Midwest Academy of Management*, 1977, pp. 346–357.

[60]For example, see: Jongeward and contributors, op. cit.

[61]Ibid. In particular, see pp. 99–101; and Lynn Randall, "Red, White and Blue TA at 600 MPH"; Susan Sinclair, "TA Improves Customer Contacts"; and Kathy O'Brien Tiano, "Transactional Analysis Applied to Mountain Bell," which are all found in Jongeward, op. cit.

[62]Huse, op. cit., p. 291.

reader is probably getting tired of seeing this at the end of each section, but it is nevertheless true—more research is needed on the relatively new and exciting applications of TA to the field of organizational behavior.

OD IN PERSPECTIVE

OD is beginning to mature. On the one hand it is now clear that OD is not going to be a panacea for all of management's problems. On the other hand, it is also clear that OD can definitely help to meet the challenges that change and complexity present to modern human resource management and organizational effectiveness. The recent Porras and Berg comprehensive review of research in OD, which was cited in the discussion of the various OD techniques, sheds some important new light on the impact of OD. Although overall they found relatively little systematic research evidence on OD, their conclusions do counter some of the traditional assumptions about OD. For example, the data did not support the assumption that OD makes people happier/more satisfied, and, also contrary to common belief, they found that OD had at least an equal impact on outcome variables (e.g., profits, costs, productivity, absenteeism, turnover, and employee satisfaction) as it did on process variables (e.g., openness, self-awareness, goal emphasis, decision making, motivation, and influence).[63]

For those interested in "bottom-line" impacts of intervention strategies, OD may possess a heretofore overlooked advantage. However, before becoming too optimistic about the value of OD and overturning all the negative assumptions about it, Porras and Berg do point out that "the data support the belief that OD does not have an important impact on overall organizational processes but instead impacts primarily on the individual."[64]

Thus, the value of OD as a group and/or organization-wide approach to change is not supported by the data reviewed by Porras and Berg. This conclusion is also consistent with others who observed and argued that OD rarely diffuses throughout the entire organization and is too limited.[65] Like any other technique or approach that has been discussed in other chapters of the book (e.g., job enrichment, goal setting, or O.B. Mod.), the successes rather than the failures of OD tend to be reported in the literature. Yet, to the credit of the OD experts they are beginning publicly to air some of their failures in books and articles, in the spirit of learning from their mistakes.[66]

---

[63]Porras and Berg, op. cit., pp. 263–264.

[64]Ibid., p. 264.

[65]Richard Walton, "The Diffusion of New Work Structures: Explaining Why Success Didn't Take," *Organization Dynamics,* Winter 1975, pp. 3–22; and George Strauss, "Organizational Development—Credits and Debits," *Organizational Dynamics,* Winter 1973, pp. 2–19.

[66]For example, see the book by Philip H. Mirvis and David N. Berg, *Failures in Organization Development and Change,* Wiley, New York, 1977, for cases of failures by the leading OD consultants/writers, or an article by Charles E. Kozoll, "Success and Failure with Organization Development," *Training HRD,* May 1978, pp. 26–28.

HUMAN RESOURCE
MANAGEMENT
APPLICATIONS,
ORGANIZATION
DEVELOPMENT, AND
PERSONAL DEVELOPMENT

NEW OD TECHNIQUES FOR THE FUTURE

Overall, the future of OD looks fairly promising. The OD techniques are becoming more systematized and there are more and better trained internal and external change agents. There are also a few new approaches that deserve mentioning. For example, based on the findings of Porras and Berg, Ouchi and Price suggest that there may be an error in the direction of causality between cohesive work groups/teams and organizational success. They maintain that cohesive teams are a result rather than the cause of organizational success.[67] If this is true, then they reason that structuring the organizational environment/climate to yield the productive teams is the key to successful OD.

The approach that Ouchi and Price are recommending has traditionally been called the sociotechnical approach to OD, which is similar to the sociotechnical approaches to job design discussed in Chapter 8. Ouchi and Price recommend a Japanese-style type Z organization environment. In contrast to the traditional American bureaucratic organization, the characteristics of type Z organizations are: (1) long- rather than short-term employment; (2) slow rather than rapid evaluation and promotion; (3) moderate rather than specialized careers; (4) consensual rather than individual decision making; (5) implicit, informal control with explicit measures rather than explicit, formal control; and (6) holistic rather than sequential concern.[68] In essence, they are suggesting the need for a *cultural* rather than just a sociotechnical approach to OD. This, of course, would require a very comprehensive, all-encompassing approach to OD.

At the other extreme from cultural OD is a suggestion by Thomas Peters of the need to look at very simplistic, but very pragmatic, approaches to managing change.[69] He tries to counter the pessimism of many modern theorists who claim that organizations are so complex that they can never be managed effectively (e.g., James March calls today's organizations "garbage cans" in which problems, participants, and choices circle aimlessly around, connecting—with resultant decisions—only occasionally) and counter the unrealistic normative prescriptions of traditional OD. His proposal is for a set of mundane, informal tools that are embedded in management's daily activities. In other words, instead of a sophisticated, massive reorganization or OD effort, he suggests that managers should follow simple rules such as the following:

1. *Spend time.* Spending time exerts, in itself, a "claim" on the decision-making system.
2. *Persist.* Having more patience than other people often results in adoption of a chosen course of action.
3. *Exchange status for substance.* One of the most effective ways to gather support for programs is to reward allies with visible tokens of recognition.

---

[67]William G. Ouchi and Raymond L. Price, "Hierarchies, Clans, and Theory Z: A New Perspective on Organization Development," *Organizational Dynamics*, Autumn 1978, p. 27.

[68]Ibid., p. 39.

[69]Thomas J. Peters, "Symbols, Patterns, and Settings: An Optimistic Case for Getting Things Done," *Organizational Dynamics*, August 1978, pp. 3–23.

4. *Facilitate opposition participation*. Often those outside the formal decision centers overestimate the feasibility of change; encouraged to participate, they will often become more realistic.

5. *Overload the system*. Bureaucracies chew up most projects, but on the other hand, some sneak through; merely launching more projects is likely to result in more successes.

6. *Provide garbage cans*. Organizations endlessly argue issues; to induce desired outcomes, put "throw-away" issues at the top of agendas (to absorb debate) saving substantive issues for later.

7. *Manage unobtrusively*. Certain actions can influence the organization pervasively but almost imperceptibly; moreover, the resulting changes will persist with little further attention.

8. *Interpret history*. By articulating a particular version of events, the leader can alter people's perception of what has been happening; whoever writes the minutes influences the outcome.[70]

Peters gives a very complete analysis of these and other similar change tools and cites specific examples in practice that back up their usefulness. Such pragmatic, but potentially powerful, change tools are readily available to managers in today's organizational garbage cans. By following this latest suggested approach, OD may have come the full circle. But like the other techniques discussed in this book, contingent and combined application of both the traditional and these newer approaches is the key for the future course of successful OD.

SUMMARY

Organizations today are faced with tremendous forces for change. A systematic, planned way of managing this change is through the process of organization development. The two major traditional paths of OD come from laboratory training (both sensitivity and grid) and survey feedback. The more recent approach to OD is to utilize more specialized techniques such as process consultation, third-party peacemaking, and team building. Finally, the increasingly popular transactional analysis is beginning to be used in organization development. However, like the other techniques and approaches, more rigorous research and contingency applications need to be forthcoming. Yet there is little question that OD has a fairly bright future in helping solve some of the tremendous challenges facing management.

QUESTIONS FOR DISCUSSION AND REVIEW

1. What are some of the major forces for change that are confronting today's organizations?
2. What are some of the major characteristics of organization development?
3. In your own words, briefly describe the three traditional approaches to OD. Discuss some of their major advantages and limitations.

---

[70]Ibid., p. 6.

638

HUMAN RESOURCE
MANAGEMENT
APPLICATIONS,
ORGANIZATION
DEVELOPMENT, AND
PERSONAL DEVELOPMENT

4. In your own words, briefly describe the other major OD techniques. What would be the major steps in a team-building approach to OD?
5. What are the three ego states in TA? Give an example of each of the three major transactions. What are strokes in TA? Give examples of some you have received in the last day or two. Can you describe any TA games you have been involved in lately?
6. Do you think the mundane tools for change suggested by Peters can have a significant impact? How would this approach compare to say a team-building approach to OD?

CASE:
CHANGE AT MIDSOUTH GAS AND ELECTRIC

Midsouth Gas and Electric is being challenged by almost unbelievable forces for change. For example, up to a few years ago the marketing department was charged with the responsibility of increasing the customers' use of gas and electricity; the power generation branch of the company had the "green light" on unlimited expansion with no worries about the effects of pollution from the power plant; and the personnel department used tests to hire the kind of people that "fit into the Midsouth family." Now all this has drastically changed. The company has launched into a public relations effort to have customers decrease their consumption of gas and electricity; the power generation arm of the company is faced with extremely limited resources and is facing some very costly lawsuits from the government and conservationists unless it does something very quickly about its pollution problems; and under EEOC pressures the personnel department has eliminated its testing program and feels it must give preferential treatment to minorities and women.

Faced with this type of change, the chief executive of Midsouth feels that it is time that the company launched into a full-scale organization development program. The personnel of Midsouth are experiencing uncertainties, frustrations, and just plain confusion. Interdepartmental and interpersonal conflicts are occurring throughout the company. All areas of organizational performance are beginning to decline. The future looks very bleak for Midsouth Gas and Electric.

1. You have been hired as a consultant to develop an organization development program for Midsouth. Weighing the pros and cons of the traditional and more specialized OD techniques, what kind of program would you propose? Why?
2. Could transactional analysis be used in the OD program for Midsouth? How? Could the mundane tools suggested by Peters be used?
3. Do you think that this company can turn itself around by the OD program you propose? What do you think the major problems will be? What do you think the major benefits will be?

CASE:
THE HIGH-PRICED OD CONSULTANT

The middle managers of a large firm were told by corporate personnel that a group of consultants would be calling on them later in the week. The purpose of the consultants' visit would be to analyze intergroup relations throughout the firm. The consultants had been very effective in using an OD intervention called team building. Their particular approach used six steps. When their approach was explained to the managers, a great deal of tension was relieved. They had initially thought that team building was a lot of hocus-pocus, like sensitivity training, where people attack each other and let out their aggressions by heaping abuse on those they dislike. By the same token, these managers generally felt that perhaps the consultants were not needed. One of them put it this way, "Now that we understand what is involved in team building, we can go ahead and conduct the sessions ourselves. All we have to do is to choose a manager who is liked by everyone and put him in the role of the change agent/consultant. After all, you really don't need a high-priced consultant to do this team-building stuff. You just have to have a good feel for human nature." The other managers generally agreed. However, the corporate personnel director turned their suggestion down. He hired the OD consultants to do the team building.

1. What is a team-building approach to organization development? Do you think the managers had an accurate view of the technique? How does it differ from sensitivity training?
2. Do you think the managers had an accurate view of the role of the external consultant? Do you agree or disagree with the corporate personnel director for turning down their suggestions? Why?

SELF-MANAGEMENT, CAREER DEVELOPMENT, AND THE FUTURE

AN INNOVATIVE PERSONAL AND CAREER DEVELOPMENT PROGRAM

The Bendix Corporation has a strong commitment to their employees, and the South Bend plant of the Energy Controls Division is translating that commitment into action. They have chosen to use the assessment center approach as one means to select their managerial personnel. Their assessment center acts as a screening device in the selection procedure. However, in addition, the company has implemented a voluntary program whereby current employees can use the assessment center in order to assess their own strengths and weaknesses for personal and career development. Company counselors will help individual employees improve themselves and chart out their own career plans aimed at enhancing their promotability within the Bendix Corporation. This program is open to all employees, including clerical workers and staff specialists. Company officials feel the program has improved the morale of employees and has aided in building a stronger commitment and loyalty to Bendix. Employees feel that the company is more concerned about them as individuals and is actively attempting to help them and develop their potential. Since the adoption of the program, there has been a greater reliance on promotion from within at Bendix, with resulting savings in personnel costs. According to outside observers, the program should also receive high marks along the lines of affirmative action. This type of innovative program can be an indication of things to come.

In this last chapter, self-management and career planning and development are examined. Traditionally, management in general and organizational behavior in particular have focused on how to more effectively manage organizations, groups, and individual subordinates. How to more effectively manage oneself has been almost completely ignored, except for some accolades concerning positive thinking and the recently popular time management guidelines. But, in the final analysis, self-management may be the basic prerequisite for effective management of organizations, groups, and individual subordinates; in fact, it has recently been suggested that behavioral self-management may be the important missing link, or at least the overlooked first step in the inductive chain, for managerial effectiveness.[1] The first part of the chapter gives the meaning, theoretical and research background, specific strategies for application, and the experience to date on this self approach to management.

The second part of the chapter is concerned with career planning and development. A natural follow-up to self-management, career planning and development is receiving increasing attention and a new emphasis in organizational behavior and human resource management. Traditionally, there was only passing interest in careers, e.g., in how young people make career choices and in the use of interest tests in the selection process. Now, with values toward work and quality of life changing rapidly, the development and planning of careers has become a major focus for both individual employees and the organizations that employ them. Employees have suddenly realized that their careers make a significant contribution to the quality of their work life and thus life in general, and organizations are beginning to recognize the importance of this for the satisfaction of their employees and, most importantly, for their performance. The career planning and development process is described and analyzed, and some specific techniques and strategies are presented.

The chapter—and the book—ends with a brief look into the crystal ball at the future course of the field of organizational behavior and its various applications for more effective human resource management.

BEHAVIORAL SELF-MANAGEMENT

In the past, whenever discussions of self-management were brought up, the importance of positive thinking, will power, or perhaps self-motivation were brought out. This approach to self-management certainly didn't do any harm, and may have done some people some good. However, as a systematic approach to more effective management, a *behavioral* approach to self-management is required. Some representative definitions of behavioral self-control are the following: "A person displays self-control when in the relative absence of immediate external constraints, he engages in behavior whose previous probability has been less than that of alternatively available

---

[1]Fred Luthans and Tim R. V. Davis, "Behavioral Self-Management: The Missing Link in Managerial Effectiveness," *Organizational Dynamics*, Summer 1979, pp. 42–60.

642

HUMAN RESOURCE
MANAGEMENT
APPLICATIONS,
ORGANIZATION
DEVELOPMENT, AND
PERSONAL DEVELOPMENT

behaviors;"[2] "self-control refers to those behaviors that an individual deliberately undertakes to achieve self-selected outcomes. The individual employee selects the goals and implements the procedures to achieve these goals."[3] When applied more to a management context, a relevant definition of self-control and the one that will be the basis of this discussion is "The manager's deliberate regulation of stimulus cues, covert processes, and response consequences to achieve personally identified behavioral outcomes."[4] In addition to this definition, there are three conditions that need to be met before the approach is called behavioral self-management or simply BSM:

1. The individual manager is the proactive agent of change.
2. Relevant stimulus cues, cognitive processes, and response consequences must be brought under control by the manager.
3. The manager must be consciously aware of how a personally identified target outcome is being achieved.[5]

The above definitions and criteria make a clear distinction between BSM and traditional positive thinking approaches to self-management, or even time management approaches. In the case of time management, prescriptive guidelines are offered (e.g., delegate more, reduce paper work, establish goals, etc.), but exactly *how* to accomplish these guidelines or how to deal with other-imposed or self-imposed environmental antecedents and consequences is not offered. There is considerable theoretical and research backup for behavioral self-management. After briefly examining this backup for BSM, some of the specific strategies that tell the manager how to change behaviors are presented, and the applications to date and the implications for the future are analyzed.

Theoretical and research background for BSM

Chapter 9 indicated that behavioral self-control is a vital part of social learning theory, along with modeling and cognitive mediating processes. As pointed out in that chapter, it is important to recognize that the social learning approach is a behavioral theory and depends heavily upon classical and operant principles. Thus, behavioral self-management also draws upon these principles.

To B. F. Skinner, the notion of self-control is no different from other forms of operant behavioral control. In the strict (i.e., Skinnerian) operant interpretation, behavior is deemed to be under the control of the stimulus environment (i.e., the antecedent, discriminant stimulus) and the contingent consequences, irrespective of whether these are manipulated by individuals themselves or by others in the environment. In other words, under the

[2]Carl E. Thoresen and Michael J. Mahoney, *Behavioral Self-Control*, Holt, New York, 1974, p. 12.

[3]Henry P. Sims, Jr., "Managing Behavior Through Learning and Reinforcement," in Don Hellriegel and John W. Slocum, Jr., *Organizational Behavior*, 2d ed., West, St. Paul, 1979, p. 205.

[4]Luthans and Davis, op. cit., p. 43.

[5]Ibid.

operant view, behavioral self-control depends on the individual's ability to manage the stimulus environment and the contingent consequences. However, just as social learning theory accepts the operant principles but goes beyond them, so does the approach to BSM suggested here.

A social learning theoretical base for BSM encompasses the operant premise of the importance of the antecedent and consequent environment; in addition, however, it recognizes and gives attention to the role of cognitive mediating processes (i.e., thoughts, feelings and self-evaluative behavior), and it recognizes that the antecedents and consequences can be covert (i.e., inner and unobservable) as well as overt (i.e., external and observable). This extension from the operant to the social learning view is also represented by a move from the three-term Antecedent-Behavior-Consequence functional analysis used in the operant behavior modification approach (see Chapter 10) to the four-term Stimulus-Organism-Behavior-Consequence functional analysis used in the social learning approach to BSM. This S-O-B-C model was fully discussed in Chapter 3 and can be used as a framework for managers using BSM to identify the relevant variables in their application of the technique.

To date, most of the research on and applications for self-control have been in clinical and educational psychology. A number of studies in these areas have demonstrated that systematic self-management can have desirable results. For example, in one educational application students' study habits were greatly improved by managing the environmental contingencies so that their desk was made strictly a place for studying and nothing else,[6] and in another study the use of self-recording alone led to an increase in appropriate study behavior and a decrease in inappropriate behavior.[7] In the clinical/behavioral therapy area there are numerous studies that have demonstrated the effectiveness of self-control programs to deal with problem behavior such as obesity, smoking, alcoholism, drug addiction, sexual abnormalities, psychiatric disorders, and marital difficulties.[8]

Most of this research on self-management in educational and clinical psychology is quite limited and narrow (e.g., the study on the effect of self-recording on study habits had only two subjects); these studies' handling of methodological issues such as the use of multiple measures, the employment of adequate controls, and meeting criteria for internal and external validity and reliability is not always adequate. Thus, the application of self-management in educational and clinical psychology is not automatically generalizable to management settings. Unlike O.B. Mod., which has a growing body of research support in its application to work

---

[6]W. M. Beneke and M. B. Harris, "Teaching Self-Control of Study Behavior," *Behavior Research and Therapy*, vol. 10, 1972, pp. 35–41.

[7]M. Broden, R. V. Hall, and B. Mitts, "The Effects of Self-Recording on the Classroom Behavior of Two Eighth-Grade Students," *Journal of Applied Behavior Analysis*, vol. 4, 1971, pp. 191–199.

[8]Representative studies on self-control in clinical psychology can be found in many journals such as *Behavior Therapy*, *Behavior Research and Therapy*, and *Journal of Applied Behavior Analysis*.

644

HUMAN RESOURCE
MANAGEMENT
APPLICATIONS,
ORGANIZATION
DEVELOPMENT, AND
PERSONAL DEVELOPMENT

settings, BSM is just getting started as a technique to improve managerial effectiveness. But so far, some specific strategies for BSM application for those in work settings have been identified, and the experience, although limited to date, is very promising for improving managerial effectiveness.

Strategies for BSM

Besides the use of the S-O-B-C functional analysis to help identify and more effectively manage the environmental contingencies and the cognitive mediating processes, there are two major strategies for BSM—stimulus and consequence management—and a number of other possible strategies that can be incorporated into these two, or in some cases stand on their own.

Stimulus management   This strategy is concerned with the antecedent or stimulus side of BSM. Called *stimulus control* in behavior modification, in BSM the stimuli can be either covert or overt. Stimulus management involves the gradual removal of or only selective exposure to stimuli that evoke behaviors whose frequency the manager is trying to decrease or which he or she wants to eliminate altogether. At the same time, or alternatively, the manager would deliberately introduce new cuing stimuli, or rearrange existing stimuli in order to evoke behavior that he or she wants to create or whose frequency is to be increased.

For example, managers who want to decrease the time spent in idle chitchat with subordinates could have their secretaries screen all visits and apply certain criteria before a subordinate is allowed into the office. This method of stimulus management—the removal or selective exposure of the stimulus (visiting subordinates)—will decrease the amount of unproductive time spent chatting with subordinates. This same strategy could also be applied to the manager who wants to increase informal interactions with subordinates. She could arrange weekly appointments with each subordinate or have her and her subordinates' coffee breaks scheduled together. The introduction of the new stimulus (have the subordinate come up to the office) or arranging the existing stimuli (scheduling their coffee breaks to coincide) would evoke more informal interactions with subordinates.

Consequence management   This second major strategy for BSM concentrates on the consequence side of the behavior. It involves the contingent application of new reinforcers or the rearrangement of existing ones to increase the behavior in subsequent frequency, or punishers to decrease it. This strategy is basically the same as the intervention strategies for O.B. Mod. discussed in Chapter 10, except that the self-reinforcers and punishers can be covert as well as overt.

An example of a self-reinforcement strategy would be the manager who wants to limit her weekly staff meetings to an hour. When she is able to do this she could reinforce herself by having a cup of coffee (overt) or by simply congratulating herself and feeling good about it (covert). If she does not keep the meeting time to an hour she could punish herself by staying after work the amount of time over the hour (overt) or simply admonish herself and feel bad about it (covert).

Analogous to the findings in research on behavior modification that rewards tend to be more effective than punishers, it is also generally found, in at least clinical applications, that self-reinforcement is a more effective strategy for BSM than is self-punishment. The problem with self-punishment, besides people's tendency only to suppress rather than change the behavior, is that if a punishment is too aversive the person just won't use it. Thus, the dilemma for self-punishment as a strategy for BSM is to find a punisher that will in fact decrease the behavior but, at the same time, not be so aversive that the person will avoid using it.

Other strategies Besides the two main strategies for BSM, there are slight variations of each in addition to several other possibilities. A variation of stimulus management—more accurately, a part of stimulus management—is the goal-setting procedure discussed in Chapter 8. Self–goal setting can serve as both a cuing stimulus and feedback, and accomplishment of progress and attainment of self-goals can be the reinforcers. The same is true of a self-recording strategy. In a feed forward-feedback sense, self-recording can both serve as a reminder and a cue for the behavior ("I have to record every hour," or every day, or every occurrence), and also reinforce it ("I can see the progress I am making from the records I am keeping"). Thoresen and Mahoney suggest that self-observation is the first step in any program of self-change ("the person must first know what is happening *before* any self-change program is initiated"—and that self-recording is the very "life blood" of effective self-control methods.)[9] Finally, the rehearsal and modeling techniques that were discussed in Chapter 9 could be used in self-control. Manz and Sims give the following example: "A salesman could rehearse his sales approach both covertly and overtly. By rehearsing a sales presentation he might, in fact, refine his approach. Furthermore, by imagining the desirable consequence of a successful sale, he might positively affect his feelings of confidence and enhance the effectiveness of the rehearsal."[10]

Examples of the application of BSM

As indicated earlier, research on and application of BSM are just getting underway. However, a few applications have been systematically analyzed.[11] A number of line and staff managers in a wide variety of positions such as advertising, retailing, manufacturing, and public service have applied BSM in the hope of increasing their effectiveness. For example, one assistant manager in a retail store determined that one of her major problems detracting from her effectiveness was her overdependence on her boss. With the help of the researchers she used BSM to try to reduce this behavior.

She first used the S-O-B-C model to functionally analyze and identify the

[9]Thoresen and Mahoney, op. cit., p. 41.

[10]Charles C. Manz and Henry P. Sims, "Self-Management: A Substitute for Leadership," *Midwest Academy of Management Proceedings*, 1979, p. 380.

[11]The examples and discussion in this section are drawn from Luthans and Davis, op. cit., pp. 51–59.

646

HUMAN RESOURCE
MANAGEMENT
APPLICATIONS,
ORGANIZATION
DEVELOPMENT, AND
PERSONAL DEVELOPMENT

relevant environmental and cognitive variables. She then set up a combination stimulus and consequence management strategy to decrease her visits (i.e., her dependence) with the boss. This strategy mainly consisted of self-recording. She maintained a record of the number of times she resisted going to see the boss when she normally would have and she also kept track of the number of times she did visit with the boss and what was discussed. The index card she carried and the notebook record she kept served to cue the appropriate behavior (i.e., resist visiting boss and take her own action), and the feedback served to reinforce the appropriate and punish the inappropriate behavior.

Using a reversal design (see Chapter 2 for discussion of this design) to evaluate the intervention, it was concluded that the BSM technique did indeed have its intended effect on the targeted behavior. Figure 22-1 shows the results. Both the boss and this manager were pleased with the results that BSM was able to bring about. Once the study was over, the assistant manager reported that she would go back to using BSM to control this behavior and would try to use the approach on other dysfunctional behaviors as well.

Another example is an advertising manager who applied BSM to three critical behaviors that were targeted for analysis and change: processing paperwork, leaving the office without telling anyone, and failure to fill out a daily expense form. Such dysfunctional behaviors are in line with what Mintzberg found to be the realistic problems facing the modern manager.[12] In

---

[12]Henry Mintzberg, *The Nature of Managerial Work*, Harper & Row, New York, 1973.

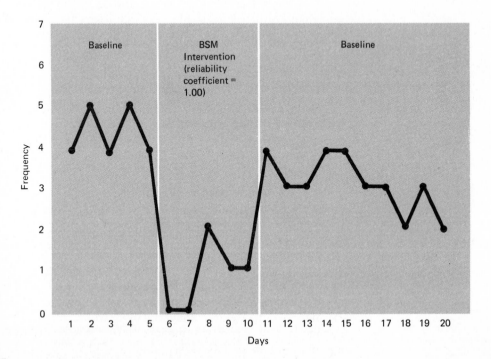

**Figure 22-1
A reversal design to analyze the effects of BSM on a manager's dependence behaviors. (*Source:* Fred Luthans and Tim R. V. Davis, "Behavioral Self-Management: The Missing Link in Managerial Effectiveness," *Organizational Dynamics*, Summer 1979, p. 53.)**

other words, the more important-sounding, but highly unrealistic and in some cases nonexistent, management activities such as strategic planning or matrix management were not the problems facing this manager. He had problems with too much paper work, keeping his staff informed of his whereabouts, and meeting bureaucratic requirements such as filling out his expense vouchers. A BSM approach is especially adaptable to these mundane, yet cumulatively very important, activities that contribute to managerial effectiveness.

After carefully analyzing the paperwork process in S-O-B-C terms, the manager, in conjunction with the researcher, set up a combination stimulus and consequence strategy to reduce the number of unprocessed paper items at the end of each day. In particular, the inflows of paperwork items were categorized and the behaviors to be performed by both the manager and his secretary were cognitively clarified. For example, the secretary now screened out some of the items according to certain criteria and presented other items in consolidated form. The manager, instead of vacillating over each item and then putting it on even higher piles on his desk, now either acted immediately, noted an action step, or put it in his out box. He also employed a self-monitoring strategy whereby he recorded each item by category and noted what action was taken and transferred this data in summary form to a wall chart display. This self-monitoring provided both feed forward (cuing stimulus) and feedback (reinforcement from progress). Figure 22-2 shows the significant results. The numbers along the upper graph represent the total number of incoming paperwork items. Obviously, the number of unprocessed items on the desk during the baseline period (average 9.4) was greatly reduced when the manager applied the BSM approach (average of only .22).

The same type of approach (i.e., S-O-B-C functional analysis, and stimulus and consequence management strategies to change the targeted behavior in the desired direction) were applied to leaving the office without informing the staff, and filling out the expense vouchers. Figure 22-2 shows that these dysfunctional behaviors also dramatically improved after the manager used a BSM approach. The use of the multiple-baseline design (see Chapter 2 for a discussion of this design) lends considerable support to the conclusion that the BSM intervention was responsible for the improvement in this manager's dysfunctional behaviors. The manager was able to exercise self-control over dysfunctional behaviors and the result was that he was a more effective manager.

A final word about BSM

Behavioral self-management is certainly not the final word on managerial effectiveness. Table 22-1 shows that there are some con as well as pro arguments for BSM, but the pro arguments outweigh the con. It may be an important missing link and, taken in combination with the other techniques and approaches discussed in this book, can have significant implications and make an input into managerial effectiveness. One thing is certain: Before managers can expect to manage individual subordinates, groups, and organizations more effectively, they will have to manage themselves more effectively. BSM provides a systematic approach to such self-management.

648

HUMAN RESOURCE
MANAGEMENT
APPLICATIONS,
ORGANIZATION
DEVELOPMENT, AND
PERSONAL DEVELOPMENT

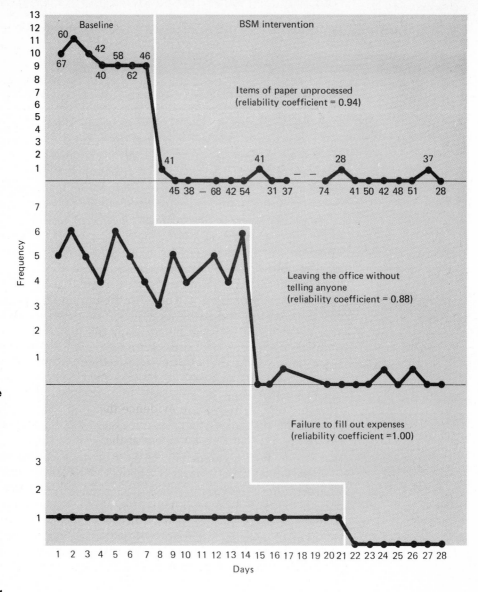

**Figure 22-2
A multiple-baseline
design to analyze
the effects of BSM
on a manager's
dysfunctional
behaviors.
(Source: Fred
Luthans and Tim
R. V. Davis,
"Behavioral
Self-Management:
The Missing Link
in Managerial
Effectiveness,"
Organizational
Dynamics, Summer
1979, p. 56.)**

CAREER PLANNING AND DEVELOPMENT

A discussion of career planning and development is a good follow-up to and
logical extension of self-management, and is a fitting conclusion to the book.
The topic of careers, both from an individual and an organizational
perspective, has just emerged as an important area of study in organizational
behavior, and it is now recognized to have important implications for the

Table 22-1

ARGUMENTS FOR AND AGAINST A BEHAVIORAL SELF-MANAGEMENT (BSM) APPROACH

Pro arguments for BSM	Con arguments for BSM
1. There is a need for self-management skills as well as organizational management skills.	1. Some managers neither want to nor can control their behavior.
2. Attention is given to measurable changes in the situation-cognition-behavior dynamics rather than measurable changes in attitudes.	2. BSM deals with the minutiae of behaviors and is slow and tedious.
3. An interactional rather than goal-oriented approach to managerial behavior is taken.	3. BSM involves a strong personal commitment to change.
4. An individual—rather than group—centered approach to organizational change and development is taken.	4. BSM requires behavioral self-recording and careful display of the data.
5. There is a closer relationship between theory and practice.	5. Self-control techniques are as yet untested as a "general" strategy of increasing managerial effectiveness.
6. There is a more ethically defensible approach to behavior change.	

Source: Adapted from Fred Luthans and Tim R. V. Davis, "Behavioral Self-Management: The Missing Link in Managerial Effectiveness," *Organizational Dynamics*, Summer 1979, pp. 47–51.

practice of human resource management. The recent academic and professional literature reflects this attention (e.g., a recent review lists some ninety citations on career planning and development) and there are a growing number of books on the subject.[13] However, as in other areas of organizational behavior, there is some evidence that despite the "press" given to new approaches to career planning and development, they are not really being implemented to any great extent at the present time.

A recent survey of large organizations found very little being done on formal career planning and development.[14] Yet both the practitioners surveyed and certainly the academicians in the field of organizational behavior and management realize that with the dramatically changing social climate, the time for emphasis on career planning and development has arrived, and it will be even more important in the near future. With changing values toward life in general and work in particular and the legal climate demanding equal opportunity for minorities and women, careers take on central importance.

After first exploring some of the meanings and perspectives, attention

---

[13]For example, see: Douglas T. Hall, *Careers in Organizations*, Goodyear, Santa Monica, California, 1976; Edgar H. Schein, *Career Dynamics: Matching Individual and Organizational Needs*, Addison-Wesley, Reading, Mass., 1978; John Van Maanen, *Organizational Careers: Some New Perspectives*, Wiley, New York, 1977; and Mariann Jelinek (ed.), *Career Management*, St. Clair Press, Chicago, 1979.

[14]John W. Seybolt, "Career Development: The State of the Art among the Grass Roots," *Training and Development Journal*, April 1979, pp. 16–20.

650

HUMAN RESOURCE
MANAGEMENT
APPLICATIONS,
ORGANIZATION
DEVELOPMENT, AND
PERSONAL DEVELOPMENT

will turn to an organizational and then an individual approach to career planning and development.

The meaning and dynamics of career planning and development

Once again, there is considerable confusion concerning definitions of career planning and development. Hall has identified at least four distinct ways in which the term *career* is used in the popular and behavioral science literature: (1) as *career advancement*, i.e., upward mobility in an organization; (2) as a *profession*, i.e., in some occupations there is a clear pattern or ladder of advancement representing a career (lawyers, professors, military officers, business executives, etc.), while other jobs that do not meet this criterion are not considered to be careers; (3) as a *lifelong sequence of jobs*, i.e., the individual's job history; and (4) as a *lifelong sequence of role-related experiences*, i.e., individuals' subjective perceptions of their jobs—their changing aspirations, satisfactions, self-conceptions or attitudes.[15] Hall draws on these definitions of *career* to make the following formal definition: "The career is the individually perceived sequence of attitudes and behaviors associated with work-related experiences and activities over the span of the person's life."[16] His assumptions are that *career* per se does not imply success or failure; a career can best be judged by the person being considered; it is made up of both behaviors and attitudes; and it is a process or sequence of work-related experiences.

Viewing this definition of careers in the context of the study of organizational behavior and human resource management also needs clarification, for there has been considerable misunderstanding regarding the meaning and use of career planning and development. Some managers mistakenly think that career planning is a replacement for workforce planning, and others equate it with affirmative action programs. It is now generally recognized that career planning is not a replacement for workforce planning (i.e., it is not concerned only with forecasting or developing workforce information systems), and although it can and should incorporate the goals of equal opportunity employment and affirmative action, it involves much more. Most of the confusion surrounding the place of career planning in organizational behavior and human resource management can be clarified if it is broken down into its organizational and individual components. Table 22-2 points out some of the similar and different characteristics of these two perspectives. A closer look at each will lead to the best understanding and use of career planning and development.

Organization career planning and development

Traditionally, organizations have shown only passing interest in the career planning and development of their employees. This process has been pretty much left up to the individual employee and, at most, supervisors have felt a paternalistic responsibility to give advice and guidance to their subordi-

---

[15]Hall, op. cit., pp. 2-3.
[16]Ibid., p. 4.

Table 22-2

ORGANIZATIONAL AND INDIVIDUAL CAREER PLANNING AND DEVELOPMENT

Characteristics of organizational career planning and development	Characteristics of individual career planning and development
Contribution to organizational goals	Contribution to individual goals
Ensure affirmative action	Career mobility for minorities and women
Provide materials for career planning and development	Identification of the life stages
Provide workshops for career planning and development	Self-assessment
Provide professional counseling on careers	Career goal setting
Train management in career counseling	Career path development
Organization development and job redesign	Assessment of progress
Innovative programs for special career needs (e.g., job sharing and parental leaves)	
Modified work schedules	

nates. As the survey cited earlier indicated, this still seems to be the case in most organizations. However, a growing number are beginning to realize that such an informal, haphazard approach to this important process may be very costly in terms of employee satisfaction and performance. In particular, organizations are beginning to recognize the following:[17]

1. Employees' career experiences and outcomes directly affect their performance, level of absenteeism, work quality, and turnover, all of which have a significant impact on the organization's overall goals.
2. Careers are a target for implementing affirmative action policies and programs to ensure equal opportunity in employment.
3. Since careers are such a central part of most people's overall quality of life, and since the quality of life is of growing importance to most people, then it behoves organizations to help employees plan and develop so that they can attain satisfying career opportunities.
4. Given that the sluggish growth of the economy is making career opportunities more limited than in the recent past, organizations must give more systematic and careful attention to the career process if employees are to meet their personal goals.

In short, organizations should realize that career planning and development can make them more effective and is a way of promoting the compatibility between personal and organizational objectives.

Specific organizational approaches The specific way that career planning and development is handled varies considerably from organization to organization, ranging all the way from a total, comprehensive

---

[17]Douglas T. Hall and Marilyn A. Morgan, "Career Development and Planning," in W. Clay Hamner and Frank L. Schmidt (eds.), *Contemporary Problems in Personnel*, rev. ed., St. Clair Press, Chicago, p. 205.

652

HUMAN RESOURCE
MANAGEMENT
APPLICATIONS,
ORGANIZATION
DEVELOPMENT, AND
PERSONAL DEVELOPMENT

organizational entry-to-exit approach on the one extreme to a self-guided workbook or one-shot annual workshop on the other extreme. The following are some examples of programs and techniques, all or some of which could be used by any one organization:

1. Devices designed to aid the individual in self-assessment and increased self-understanding. These are normally workbooks, workshops, and one-on-one career counseling sessions.
2. Devices designed to communicate opportunities. These range from the dictionary of occupational titles to listings or postings of job openings to descriptions of careers and jobs transmitted through individuals.
3. Career counseling through interviews. Counseling sessions may be conducted by managers, counseling professionals, personnel and educational specialists, and people outside the organization.
4. Workshops or educational activities designed to assist the individual in goal setting and establishing action plans for change.
5. Educational and experimental programs that prepare the individual with skills and knowledge for new activities and new careers, or that enhance capability for the current job.
6. Organizational development and job design and development programs that aim at restructuring work for improved personal growth and enhanced job satisfaction.
7. Programs that enhance the individual's opportunities to make job and career changes. These may be rotational programs, employee-transfer request systems, opportunity search systems external to the organization, and general how-to books on job and career change.[18]

Representative of some actual career programs in industry would be:[19]

1. *General Electric.* GE has developed a set of four workbooks/manuals that cover (a) the employee's initial exploration of life issues that affect career decisions; (b) a career planning guide for the employee; (c) a guide to facilitate effective career interviews with employees; (d) suggestions on how to design and conduct career planning workshops and seminars. These materials are available throughout the company to assist in career planning and development efforts.
2. *Minnesota Mining and Manufacturing.* The 3M program consists of the following dimensions: (a) a concerted effort (e.g., meetings and referrals) to communicate an awareness and use of program services for careers; (b) a career information center which contains information on career paths (not openings) in the company, aids for career planning, self-development programs, and a career counseling staff; (c) management training on career counseling; (d) career growth workshops (four sessions over four weeks that aid individuals assess themselves and their current job, make action plans, and hold discussions with the boss); and (e) transition workshops that provide intensive help to those identified as available for transfer.
3. *IBM.* IBM has a general, corporation-wide program that involves primarily managerial training in career counseling and provides printed and cassette materials to support career planning and development. The key element is a voluntary annual supervisor-subordinate career counseling session. A one-page action plan results from this session. In addition, many IBM facilities give more extensive support in terms of workbooks and workshops.

[18]Donald B. Miller, "Career Planning and Management in Organizations," *S.A.M. Advanced Management Journal,* Spring 1978, reprinted in Jelinek, op. cit., pp. 357–358.

[19]Ibid., pp. 355–356.

Innovative programs for special career needs In addition to the commonly used workbook and workshop techniques, a more comprehensive and more expensive commitment to career planning and development would include innovative approaches to special needs. An example would be an affirmative action approach to ensure the career progress of minorities and women. Especially with more women entering the labor market and dual-career families becoming more common, innovative approaches such as *job sharing* (two people, usually husband and wife, share one full-time job), *in-house day care centers, parental leave time* (not just for maternity reasons, and for both sexes), and *modified work schedules* (flexitime and four-day work week) are being advocated. Except for modified work schedules, these approaches to date are not being widely implemented.[20]

Flexitime and four-forty workweeks Flexitime has been widely used in Europe for years and is gaining popularity in this country. There is some research evidence that it has a favorable impact on employee satisfaction and performance.[21] Flexitime allows more employee control over starting and quitting times and thus is an aid to the careers of young parents and dual-career families. The four-forty scheduling (four days a week, ten hours a day) allows for more liesure time (i.e., three-day weekends) that may help parents and may also be more compatible with contemporary life-styles and energy shortages. There is some evidence, although it is still not definitive, that this four-forty scheduling has a favorable impact on employees.[22]

Although more research on the impact of these innovative programs as well as on the whole area of organizational career planning and development is needed, there seems little doubt that with the way things are going (in terms of changing social and work values, the declining economy, the energy crisis, changing sex roles, and decreasing productivity), all organizations are going to have to pay more attention to the career process of their employees.

Individual career planning and development

As Table 22-2 indicated, there is considerable overlap between organizational career planning and development and the individual approach. Obviously, the career techniques used by the organization are aimed at the individual employee, but the objectives have a different perspective. This section first explores the various adult life stages that correlate with the

---

[20]Seybolt, op. cit.

[21]For example, see: Robert T. Golembieski, Samuel Yeager, and Rich Hilles, "Factor Analysis of Some Flexitime Effects: Attitudinal and Behavioral Consequences of a Structural Intervention," *Academy of Management Journal,* September 1975, pp. 500–509; and Barron H. Harvey and Fred Luthans, "Flexitime: An Empirical Analysis of Its Real Meaning and Impact," *MSU Business Topics,* Summer 1979, pp. 31–36.

[22]For example, see: John Ivancevich and Herbert Lyon, "The Shortened Work-Week: A Field Experiment," *Journal of Applied Psychology,* vol. 62, 1977, pp. 34–37, and Cheedle W. Millard, Diane L. Lockwood, and Fred Luthans, "The Impact of a Four-Day Workweek on Employees," *MSU Business Topics,* Spring 1980, pp. 31–37.

654

HUMAN RESOURCE
MANAGEMENT
APPLICATIONS,
ORGANIZATION
DEVELOPMENT, AND
PERSONAL DEVELOPMENT

person's career and then gives a specific career planning and development model that could actually be used by the reader.

Adult life stages Just as Chapter 5 indicated that an individual's personality can be analyzed in terms of certain identifiable states of development, it has also become popular in recent years to do the same for adult life stages. The work of Daniel Levinson in particular has received considerable recent attention in both the academic[23] and popular literature.[24] He believes that "the life structure evolves through a relatively orderly sequence throughout the adult years"[25] and, unlike other stage theories that are event-oriented (e.g., marriage, parenthood, or retirement), his is age-based. In particular, he believes there is little variability (a maximum of two or three years) in four identifiable stable periods:

1. Entering the adult world (ages 22–28)
2. Settling down (33–40)
3. Entering middle adulthood (45–50)
4. Culmination of middle adulthood (55–60)

He identifies four transitional periods:

1. Age thirty transition (28–33)
2. Mid-life transition (40–45)
3. Age fifty transition (50–55)
4. Late adult transition (60–65)

Like their counterparts in personality theory and development, the adult life stage theories such as Levinson's have a lot of intuitive and popular appeal, but, also like the personality stage theories, they may not hold up under systematic research. For example, a recent study utilizing longitudinal data found no support for Levinson's hypotheses that there should be greater variability in work attitudes during transitional compared to stable developmental periods or that the greatest variability occurs during the mid-life transition.[26] In other words, there may be such individual differences among people that the stage theories don't really hold up. Nevertheless, as a general guideline, and always recognizing there will be individual differences, these stage theories can be useful for individual career planning and development.

Hall has synthesized the Levinson and other adult stage theories (in particular the work of Erikson and Super) into an overall model for career

---

[23]For example, see: Daniel J. Levinson, "Periods in the Adult Development of Men: Ages 18 to 45," *The Counseling Psychologist,* vol. 6, 1976, pp. 47–59; and Daniel J. Levinson, "The Mid-Life Transition: A Period in Adult Psychosocial Development," *Psychiatry,* Vol. 40, 1977, pp. 99–112.

[24]For example, see: Daniel J. Levinson, "Growing up with the Dream," *Psychology Today,* vol. 20, 1978, pp. 20–31 and 89; and his latest book, Daniel J. Levinson, *The Seasons of a Man's Life,* Knopf, New York, 1978.

[25]Levinson, *The Seasons of a Man's Life,* op. cit., p. 49.

[26]Richard E. Kopelman and Michael Glass, "Test of Daniel Levinson's Theory of Adult Male Life Stages," *National Academy of Management Proceedings,* 1979, pp. 79–83.

stages. Figure 22-3 shows that there are four major career stages. During the first stage there is considerable *exploration*. The young employee is searching for an identity and undergoes considerable self-examination and role tryouts. This stage usually results in taking a number of different jobs and is, in general, a very unstable and relatively unproductive period in the person's career. In the second stage, *establishment*, the employee begins to settle down and indicate a need for intimacy. This is usually a growing, productive period in the employee's career. The third stage of *maintenance* is where the person levels off into a highly productive plateau and has a need for generativity (the concern to leave something to the next generation). This need often leads the person to a paternalistic or perhaps a mentor role for younger subordinates. As shown in Figure 22-3 the person may either have a growth spurt or become stagnant and decline during this third career stage. The final stage, *decline*, is self-explanatory. The person indicates a need for integrity (i.e., the person needs to feel satisfied with his or her life choices and overall career). With the recent changes in mandatory retirement laws, better medical treatment, and the expectations of society concerning "gray power," this last stage may be undergoing drastic change in the years ahead. Older employees may overcome the heretofore assumed decline in this stage of their careers.

The career stage model can help individuals gain a better understanding of their future and assist in their career planning and development process.

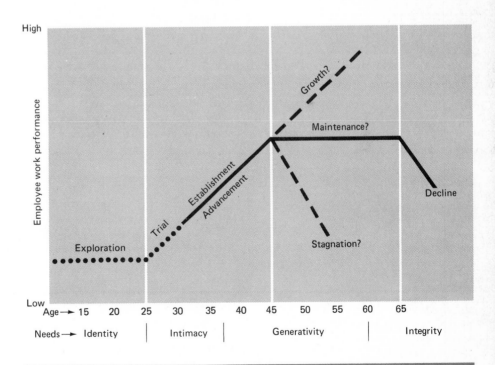

**Figure 22-3
A career stage
model. (*Source:*
Adapted from
Douglas T. Hall,
*Careers in
Organizations,*
Goodyear, Santa
Monica, Calif.,
1976, p. 57.)**

656

HUMAN RESOURCE
MANAGEMENT
APPLICATIONS,
ORGANIZATION
DEVELOPMENT, AND
PERSONAL DEVELOPMENT

A specific model for individual career planning and development Just as the first part of this chapter pointed out that behavioral self-management may be an important dimension of overall managerial effectiveness, in the final analysis, individuals themselves must also come to grips with their own career planning and development. The organizational approach can provide the needed resources and assistance, and knowledge of the various career stages can be helpful, but a specific model for individual career planning and development is needed to effectively guide individuals in their career choices and paths to reach their personal goals.

Figure 22-4 provides a simple but useful model for individual career planning and development. Briefly summarized, the steps in this model are as follows:

1. *Self-assessment.* The aim of this initial step is to get to know oneself as well as possible. There are a number of ways and techniques that can help in self-assessment. Some of these include performance appraisals, self-evaluation guidelines or checklists, subordinate/peer assessments, professional assessments from counselors using tests and interviews, assessment centers as discussed in Chapter 20, and informal feedback on a lifelong basis.[27] These should be used in combination to gain as much insight as possible. As one expert on career

---

[27]Fred Luthans and Mark J. Martinko, *The Practice of Supervision and Management,* McGraw-Hill, New York, 1979, pp. 462–467.

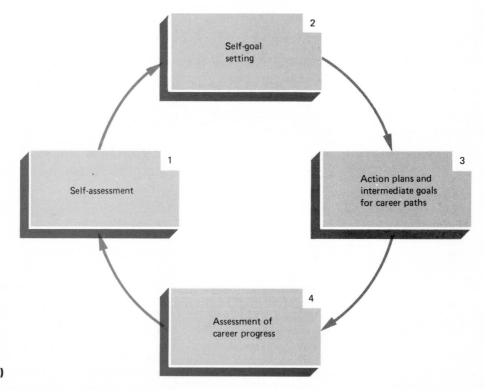

**Figure 22-4
An individual self-management model for career planning and development.** (*Source:* Adapted from Fred Luthans and Mark J. Martinko, *The Practice of Supervision and Management,* McGraw-Hill, New York, 1979, p. 462.)

development states, "To know one's self, then, is considered to be a sine qua non of mature career development."[28]

2. *Identifying major career goals.* As Chapter 8 pointed out, goal setting can lead to improved performance. The same is true for self–goal setting for effective career planning and development. For example, an experimental study concludes that there is "convincing evidence that conscious goal-setting plays an important role in the process of self-directed behavior change."[29] One needs to set goals in order to know in what direction one is headed and to experience psychological success. Some experiential exercises are available[30] to help in this self–goal setting process, and a few suggested techniques, such as the somewhat gruesome obituary approach (the person writes his or her own obituary covering areas such as career accomplishments, educational credentials, hobbies and pastimes, and major disappointments and unfulfilled dreams) or the flash-forward approach (the person attempts to create visual images of the future) may help set career goals. The following simple guidelines may prove the most useful: (a) be realistic; (b) set priorities; (c) deal with strengths and weaknesses; and (d) maintain flexibility.[31]

3. *Planning paths and intermediate steps.* This is the action planning step to make sure that the self-goals that were set in the previous step are actually accomplished. In making the action plans to accomplish ultimate goals, it is important to identify relevant intermediate or subgoals that will assist and keep the person on the right path. Some examples of formal intermediate steps might include changing jobs, getting more or different formal education, getting additional training/development within or outside the organization, gaining relevant experience outside the job, becoming active in professional organizations, and self-development from reading or taking correspondence courses.[32] Some more informal, pragmatic guidelines to follow in terms of facilitating the path to career goals would be:

   a. Maintain the widest set of options.
   b. Don't be blocked by immobile superiors.
   c. Become a crucial subordinate to a mobile superior.
   d. Always favor increased exposure and visibility.
   e. Be prepared to practice self-nomination.
   f. Leave an organization at your own convenience.
   g. Rehearse before quitting.
   h. Plan for a multicareer.[33]

   The above are very similar to the political strategies for power discussed in Chapter 14. To be realistic, effective career planning must consider these political dynamics of the process.

4. *Assessing career progress.* Like any good model for planning and development,

---

[28]John O. Crites, *Theory and Research Handbook, Career Maturity Inventory,* McGraw-Hill, New York, 1973, p. 23.

[29]David A. Kolb and Richard E. Boyatzis, "Goal Setting and Self-Directed Behavior Changes," in Jelinek, op. cit., p. 30.

[30]For example, see exercises such as "Life Planning" or "Career Problems" in Douglas T. Hall, Donald D. Bowen, Roy J. Lewicki, and Francine S. Hall, *Experiences in Management and Organizational Behavior,* St. Clair Press, Chicago, 1975.

[31]Luthans and Martinko, op. cit., pp. 468-471.

[32]Ibid., pp. 472–476.

[33]Eugene E. Jennings, *Routes to the Executive Suite,* McGraw-Hill, New York, 1971.

658

HUMAN RESOURCE
MANAGEMENT
APPLICATIONS,
ORGANIZATION
DEVELOPMENT, AND
PERSONAL DEVELOPMENT

the individual career model stresses the need for a built-in assessment of progress. Feedback of actual progress toward intermediate and ultimate career goals must be periodically checked. A discrepancy between planned and actual progress (favorable or unfavorable) may result in adjustments in action plans and intermediate goals and/or changing ultimate career goals. Once the ultimate goals are attained, the individual may want to repeat the steps of the model.

The individual career planning and development model is only a guide, but it can actually be used by the reader to more effectively manage his or her career and ultimately have a more fulfilling life. Studying the topics covered in this book should lead to a better understanding of human behavior in organizations. Combined with the various techniques presented throughout, this knowledge plus practical experience can be molded into a satisfying career in management. As the introductory chapter pointed out, the challenge for managers today and in the future lies on the human, not the technical, side of organizations. Thus, the study of organizational behavior can make a significant contribution to a successful management career.

THE FUTURE

Some trends for the future of the field of organizational behavior are beginning to emerge. Some of these trends are evident in the way that this book has changed in structure and in the topics that have been included, comparing the first edition with the second and now with the third edition. First of all, it can be said that organizational behavior has truly arrived as an identifiable field of academic study and has definite implications for the effective management of human resources in modern, complex organizations. This recognition of organizational behavior as a legitimate academic and applied field should become even greater in the future.

Second, there is now a clear distinction between organizational behavior and other areas such as general management or personnel administration. For example, organizational behavior is concerned with human behavior in organizations while personnel management is recognized as a function of the organization and mainly is concerned with topics such as wage and salary administration or labor relations. In addition, the micro-macro split in organizational behavior that has recently emerged should become even more pronounced in the future. As in this third edition of the present book, organizational behavior is headed more toward micro topics of analysis (e.g., perception, personality, motivation, learning, power, and leadership) rather than more macro-oriented analysis of the management processes and organization theory and design.

Third, the topical coverage of the field of organizational behavior will be moving more away from the traditional general topics in behavioral science (e.g., perception, personality, and group dynamics) toward topics more specifically identified with organizational behavior per se (goal setting, job design, organizational behavior modification, job conflict and stress, organizational power and politics, informal organization, managerial roles, organizational communication, managerial leadership, selection, appraisal, organization development, behavioral self management, and career development). The exceptions here are the two mainstays of experimental psychology—motivation and learning. These two should continue to be important areas in organizational behavior. But whereas motivation has in the past had a much greater role in the study of organizational behavior, in the future, learning may have an equal, if not even more important, role to play in terms of both theory and practice. This is true not only of operant learning theory but also of the newly emerging social learning theory.

Finally, and this of course most students and practitioners will be happy to hear, the trend of making organizational behavior more applications-oriented should continue. The successive editions of this text have evidenced this trend toward applications. The field of organizational behavior is clearly aimed at the more effective management of human resources. With emphasis on areas such as goal setting, job design, organizational behavior modification, political strategies, leadership styles, selection, appraisal, organization development, behavioral self-management, and career planning and development, this aim at application should become clearer and is more likely to hit the target of more effective human resource management in the years to come.

SUMMARY

In this concluding chapter three areas have been covered—behavioral self-management, career planning and development, and the future of organizational behavior. It is logical for these to come last because in a sense these topics bring the study of organizational behavior full circle. In behavioral self-management (BSM) it is recognized that in the final analysis—or perhaps it is the first step—managers must be able to effectively manage themselves before they can expect to manage subordinates, groups, or organizations. Based on social learning theory, BSM utilizes S-O-B-C functional analysis and entails both stimulus and consequence management strategies. Some preliminary studies of the application of BSM indicate that this approach may have considerable promise for changing managers' dysfunctional behavior and making them more effective.

Like behavioral self-management, career planning and development helps close the circle of the study of organizational behavior. The best way to present this increasingly important topic is in terms of an organizational and an individual perspective. The organizational perspective is concerned with the contribution that individuals, in their careers, can make to organizational goals. Most organizational career planning and development approaches also are tied into affirmative action goals for minorities and women. The typical approach for organizational career planning and development would be to provide materials (e.g., workbooks or cassettes), workshops, counseling services, training for managers and, possibly, organization development and job redesign efforts. Needed for the future are innovative programs for special career needs. In particular, there is growing evidence to support the positive impact of modified work schedules (flexitime and four-forty work

660

HUMAN RESOURCE
MANAGEMENT
APPLICATIONS,
ORGANIZATION
DEVELOPMENT, AND
PERSONAL DEVELOPMENT

weeks) on employee satisfaction and performance, and such schedules are very compatible with certain career needs. The individual approach to career planning and development is geared more toward personal goals and self-management of one's career. Recognition that people go through certain adult stages (e.g., exploration, establishment, maintenance, and decline) and following a specific model (self-asessment, self–goal setting, action planning and intermediate goals, and assessing progress) can be helpful to all individuals in managing their careers and, in turn, improving the overall quality of their lives.

The future of the field of organizational behavior looks very bright and exciting. Although there will be some shifting emphases in conceptual framework and topical coverage, the "bottom line" is that the study and application of the areas covered in this book will help make better, more effective, managers of the most important and underutilized resource in any organization—PEOPLE. The effective management of people (both others and self) is really what organizational behavior is all about.

QUESTIONS FOR DISCUSSION AND REVIEW

1. What is the definition and criterion of behavioral self-management (BSM)? How does this differ from traditional positive thinking approaches to self-control? How does it differ from time management?
2. What is the theoretical base for BSM? What role do operant principles play? How can the S-O-B-C framework apply to BSM?
3. Identify and give an example of stimulus and consequence management in BSM.
4. What are some ways that the term *career* is used? What is the best definition and use of the term as used in the context of career planning and development?
5. In your own words summarize some of the dimensions and applications of an organizational approach to career planning and development.
6. Do you agree with the adult stage theories? Can you give personal examples of relatives or friends to support your answer? Do you think your life will follow these stages?
7. Using the model for individual career planning and development, apply, in a rough, general way at least, steps 1, 2, and 3 to yourself.
8. Do you agree with the view in the crystal ball of the future of organizational behavior? Do you have anything to add or subtract?

CASE:
THE PLUMP MODEL

You are concerned with your weight. You have a good part-time job while going to college with the local department store modeling clothes for their ads for TV and newspapers. Your weight has increased markedly since you started the job. You think that the problem may be related to the dorm food that you have been eating, but you have little chance to change that. Each dorm has its own kitchenette and that includes a refrigerator. There is a "fast-food–chain row" within walking distance of the dorm. You are making good money from your modeling job but your budget is still very tight. You must eat at the dorm, yet occasionally you splurge and eat at Hamburger Heaven. You are having difficulty finding something that is rewarding enough to help you lose weight. It is also difficult to lose weight because it is such a slow process. It is also difficult when most of your friends in the dorm want you to go out for a "quick bite" and "liquid refreshments" on a nightly basis. You hate to say no to them because you do value their friendship and enjoy yourself whenever you go out with them. Yet you really feel that you need to lose some weight in order to look good and maybe keep your job.

1. Analyze your behavior in S-O-B-C terms.
2. What would be a stimulus management strategy to lose weight? What would be a consequence strategy?

CASE:
"IS THAT ALL THERE IS?"

Ed Jobobs had worked for Fairway, Inc., since graduating from college twenty-five years ago. His goal had always been to have a good, high-paying job and live a comfortable life in the suburbs with a nice family. He had accomplished that goal. He was the head of the sales department, made $45,000 (including fringe benefits), had a lovely two-story home and a model family (a good wife and two now grown-up children who had never given them any problems). Now all of a sudden the lyric of a Peggy Lee song of a few years back began to haunt him. Over and over he could hear her singing "Is that all there is?" It was clear to Ed that he would never progress any further in the company. The challenge the job used to offer was now gone. His two kids had graduated from college and one had moved to the West Coast and the other had moved to the East Coast. Last week his wife announced that she was going back to college to take some accounting courses, get a CPA, and go to work full-time for a public accounting firm. Ed felt depressed, lonely, and unsure of himself. He didn't know where or whom to turn to. He had at least twenty years of work left in him but he had no idea where he was going to go from here.

1. What stage is Ed going through?
2. If Ed came to you, what advice would you give him? How, if at all, could Ed's company give him any help? Should they? Why?
3. How about Ed's wife, could she use career planning and development? How?

CASE STUDY AND EXPERIENTIAL EXERCISES FOR PART 6

CASE:
A CHALLENGE OF SURVIVAL FOR HUMAN RESOURCE PROGRAMS

Many modern organizations have a lot of nice things to say about the need for management selection, appraisal, and development programs. However, when there are downturns in the economy, it seems as if these particular programs are some of the first to be cut. For example, during the recession of the mid-1970s, Chrysler, Corning Glass, National Bank of Chicago, and the New York Telephone Company all began to prune their long-established human resources programs. In Chrysler's case, 20,000 white-collar workers were laid off, and these programs were all but eliminated. One Chrysler manager explained that things were so bad that in order to hang on to some of their good people, high-potential employees either had to be transferred to other jobs or dropped to a lower grade job just to keep them. Why are human resource programs given the ax so quickly? An article in *Business Week* explains why management development programs have problems:[1]

Management development is vulnerable because it is expensive, time-consuming, and complex to administer. It means, almost by definition, having a managerial surplus. IBM, for example, has three or four potential replacements for each of several hundred top jobs. It also means moving managers in and out of jobs, sometimes just when they are beginning to make a contribution, to give them breadth of experience. That kind of talent transfer can be expensive not just because it temporarily drags down efficiency, but because the physical moves that accompany many such job changes are today more costly than ever.

Of course, not everyone cuts back all their human resource programs during an economic slump. Firms like Xerox, Exxon, AT&T, and Citicorp see no real alternative to selection and appraisal programs. After all, who wants to go out and fill a slot from the outside every time there is an opening? Some managers, however, point out that a new chief executive tends to bring his own team with him or her. And these people, in turn, bring their personnel. As a result, regulars within the firm never get to move up because there are too many people brought in ahead of them. To maintain managerial mobility and potential, some firms simply refuse to cut back on selection, appraisal, and career development programs.

---

[1] The data on this case can be found in: "How Companies Raise a New Crop of Managers," *Business Week,* Mar. 10, 1975, pp. 45–46, 48.

Companies committed to human resource programs use all different types of approaches, but there seem to be three common threads: (a) they are built deep into the system and involve every level of the hierarchy; (b) these programs are seen as part of every manager's job; (c) top management support and long-term commitment must be unwavering.

How well have the firms following this philosophy succeeded? Results indicate that they have done very well. Take the case of Thomas Theobald, who heads Citibank's World Corporation Group, which lends money to major multinational corporations. His job is to oversee the progress of some 300 officers scattered all over the globe. In staffing these positions, Mr. Theobald likes to take people right out of school, give them basic training in such fundamentals as cash flow accounting, and then put them to work under close supervision. Here they are monitored and appraised every few months. During this process, those who can make sensible judgments are separated from those who cannot. The good people are moved into positions of greater responsibility and opportunity. Other firms use different approaches to hasten the development and career process of their people. As the report in *Business Week* notes:

Some attempt to compress work experience by giving developing managers short-term special assignments on high-level task forces or making them assistants to division or corporate executives. For example, Stanley Rosenthal, now a 34-year-old partner at Peat, Marwick, Mitchell & Co. in Chicago spent two years in the company's department of professional practices in New York. The department's 12 partners and 30 managers have no direct client responsibility but work on quality control and advise the operating officers on knotty accounting problems. "You get two years of intensive problem solving and when you return to your office you are recognized as being current in SEC matters and accounting practices," Rosenthal says. "Often you get more difficult assignments." Rosenthal's service on the practices department probably hastened his being made a partner last summer, a year after he returned from New York, not only because he was abreast of developments in the profession, but also because it increased his visibility in the Chicago office.

Other firms like to combine a study program with one of work experience for career development. For example, the First National Bank of Chicago has newly hired managers who attend graduate business school at night for two-and-one-half years and work in various jobs in the bank from one to six months. This group feel it is a "fast track" because the firm slots them right into the management mode and gives them wide experience almost immediately. They apparently like this approach because the bank's retention rate is 82 percent.

Peat, Marwick & Mitchell, the accounting firm, places even stronger emphasis on formal course work. The firm offers courses at its 105 domestic operating offices and runs its own education center in New York City, making dozens of courses available for staff, managers, and partners. The firm has been very pleased with the results so far.

One of the biggest arguments against human resources programs is that no one knows for sure whether the payoff justifies the expenditures. Peat, Marwick & Mitchell estimate that they spend at least $10 million annually for employee development including time spent on coursework. Others, like First National Bank of Chicago, put the expenditures at about $31,000 for each employee in its "night graduate school, job rotation program." Meanwhile, in the case of a

664

HUMAN RESOURCE
MANAGEMENT
APPLICATIONS,
ORGANIZATION
DEVELOPMENT, AND
PERSONAL DEVELOPMENT

firm like Exxon, the company feels that these programs are so much a part of the management structure that it cannot be singled out and calculated.

In the last analysis, the question comes down to one of cost benefit. Are these programs worth the cost, regardless of whether the company can put a dollar figure on it? If the answer is yes, then even during economic slumps, companies will attempt to bolster their programs and, at worst, not let them be cut back too drastically. And this is exactly what has happened among some firms in recent years. The *Business Week* article states:

Many companies with traditionally strong development programs are preserving what they can even in the face of deep sales slumps. GM is moving managers infrequently and has curtailed recruiting. But some of the management development survives. "Results of the program have changed," says William B. Chew, director of GM's human resources management activity, "but that doesn't change the need for the program."

1. Besides the programs that are discussed in very general terms by these big companies, what specific techniques for the selection process should these companies implement? What are some current selection issues that they should be aware of? How will your suggested techniques deal with these issues?
2. What appraisal techniques would you recommend? Why?
3. What organization development techniques would you recommend? Why?
4. Should these firms be concerned with specific career development programs and techniques? Why or why not?
5. Given how you have answered the questions above, why is it that the very survival of these programs is often at stake when anything goes wrong? What arguments would you make for the continuance or even expansion of human resource programs?

EXERCISE:

SELECTION AND APPRAISAL: THE CASE OF NAYLOR PRODUCT CORPORATION

Goals:

1. To study the difficult choices a manager faces in using performance-related information in making selection and appraisal decisions
2. To consider the performance criteria used within one organization

Implementation:

Set up groups of four to eight students for the forty-five to sixty minute exercise. The groups should be separated from each other and asked to converse only with their group members.

Before forming the groups, each person should complete the exercise alone and then join the group and reach a decision within the time allotted. Each person should read the following:

The Naylor Product Corporation is a medium-sized manufacturing company located in the suburbs of Tampa, Florida. The company is nonunionized and has attempted during the past two years to incorporate an objective performance review system designed purposefully to provide feedback to employees. The system is designed to be objective, time-oriented, and representative.

The loss of a contract bid to a competitor has forced the Naylor management to consider laying off one, two, or three of the poorest performers next week in the generator-contracting unit. This unit produces generators that are sold to electronics firms. The layoff may only be temporary, but management wants to be sure that they have been fair in presenting an objectively based decision to the employees.

The eight people in the unit that is to be cut back to five are the following:

1. Max Rogers: white; age forty-two; married; three children; two years of high school; fourteen years with the company.
2. Tom Banks: black; age thirty-seven; widower; two children; high-school graduate; eight years with the company.
3. Marsha Beloit: white; age twenty-four; single; high-school graduate; two years with the company.
4. Ray Lasifer: white; age fifty; single; finished junior college while working; fifteen years with the company.
5. Nina Palmond: white; age thirty-six; married; four children; high-school graduate; three years with the company.
6. Steve Castro: hispanic; age forty; married; one child; high-school graduate; four years with the company.
7. John Sailers: white; age thirty-nine; divorced; two children; two years of college; seven years with the company.
8. Bob Wilks: white; age forty-two; married; no children; one year of college; nine years with the company.

The company has evaluated these generator unit employees on a number of factors, listed in the following exhibit. The ratings shown in the exhibit have been averaged over the past eighteen months of performance appraisals.

NAYLOR MANAGEMENT MOST RECENT PERFORMANCE APPRAISAL OF GENERATOR EMPLOYEES

Employee	Average weekly output*	% of defective generators†	% absent‡	Cooperative attitude¶	Loyalty to company	Potential for advancement	Initiates personal development attitudes
Max Rogers	19.8	4.9	7.3	good	good	fair	no
Tom Banks	21.7	5.3	8.9	poor	fair	fair	no
Marsha Beloit	17.6	0.9	1.4	excellent	good	good	yes
Ray Lasifier	20.2	4.7	14.2	excellent	excellent	fair	no
Nina Palmond	20.1	9.6	10.3	poor	fair	poor	no
Steve Castro	19.8	3.4	7.1	good	fair	poor	no
John Sailers	18.1	4.8	6.0	good	good	fair	no
Bob Wilks	22.6	7.0	4.6	fair	fair	good	yes

*Higher score designates more quantity of output.

†Lower score designates fewer defective generators.

‡Lower score designates less absenteeism.

¶The ratings possible are poor, fair, good, excellent.

666

HUMAN RESOURCE
MANAGEMENT
APPLICATIONS,
ORGANIZATION
DEVELOPMENT, AND
PERSONAL DEVELOPMENT

Instructions for the exercise:

1. Each person is to rank the employees from 1 (the first to be laid off) to 8 (the last to be laid off). The individual rankings should be given to the instructor on a sheet of paper before the person joins the assigned group.

2. Each group of four to eight people is to reach a ranking consensus. These rankings are to be placed on a sheet of paper with a brief explanation for the rationale used to arrive at the final order.

EXERCISE:

ORGANIZA-
TION DEVEL-
OPMENT
AT J.P. HUNT

Goals:

To experience an OD technique—in this case the use of survey feedback—to diagnose strengths and weaknesses and develop an action plan

Implementation:

Set up groups of four to eight members for the one-hour exercise. The groups should be separated from each other and asked to converse only with members of their own group. Each person should read the following:

J. P. Hunt department stores is a large retail merchandising outlet located in Boston. The company sells an entire range of retail goods (e.g., appliances, fashions, furniture, and so on) and has a large downtown store plus six branch stores in various suburban areas.

Similar to most retail stores in the area, employee turnover is high (i.e., 40 to 45 percent annually). In the credit and accounts receivable department, located in the downtown store, turnover is particularly high at both the supervisor and subordinate levels, approaching 75 percent annually. The department employs approximately 150 people, 70 percent of whom are female.

Due to rising hiring and training costs brought on by the high turnover, top department management began a turnover analysis and reduction program. As a first step, a local management consulting firm was contracted to conduct a survey of department employees. Using primarily questionnaires, the consulting firm collected survey data from over 95 percent of the department's employees. The results are shown in the following exhibit, by organizational level, along with industry norms developed by the consulting firm in comparative retail organizations.

SURVEY RESULTS FOR J. P. HUNT DEPARTMENT STORE: CREDIT AND ACCOUNTS RECEIVABLE DEPARTMENT

Variable	Survey results*			Industry norms*		
	Managers	Supervisors	Non-supervisors	Managers	Supervisors	Non-supervisors
Satisfaction and rewards						
Pay	3.30	1.73	2.48	3.31	2.97	2.89
Supervision	3.70	2.42	3.05	3.64	3.58	3.21
Promotion	3.40	2.28	2.76	3.38	3.25	3.23
Coworkers	3.92	3.90	3.72	3.95	3.76	3.43
Work	3.98	2.81	3.15	3.93	3.68	3.52
Performance-to-intrinsic rewards	4.07	3.15	3.20	4.15	3.85	3.81
Performance-to-extrinsic rewards	3.67	2.71	2.70	3.87	3.81	3.76
Supervisory behavior						
Initiating structure	3.42	3.97	3.90	3.40	3.51	3.48
Consideration	3.63	3.09	3.18	3.77	3.72	3.68
Positive rewards	3.99	2.93	3.02	4.24	3.95	3.91
Punitive rewards	3.01	3.61	3.50	2.81	2.91	3.08
Job characteristics						
Autonomy	4.13	4.22	3.80	4.20	4.00	3.87
Feedback	3.88	3.81	3.68	3.87	3.70	3.70
Variety	3.67	3.35	2.22	3.62	3.21	2.62
Challenge	4.13	4.03	3.03	4.10	3.64	3.58
Organizational practices						
Role ambiguity	2.70	2.91	3.34	2.60	2.40	2.20
Role conflict	2.87	3.69	2.94	2.83	3.12	3.02
Job pressure	3.14	4.04	3.23	2.66	2.68	2.72
Performance evaluation process	3.77	3.35	3.19	3.92	3.70	3.62
Worker cooperation	3.67	3.94	3.87	3.65	3.62	3.35
Work-flow planning	3.88	2.62	2.95	4.20	3.80	3.76

*The values are scored from 1, very low, to 5, very high.

Instructions for the exercise

1. Individually, each group member should analyze the data in the exhibit and attempt to identify and diagnose departmental strengths and problem areas.
2. As a group, the members should repeat step 1 above. In addition, suggestions for resolving the problems and an action plan for feedback to the department should be developed.

NAME INDEX

SUBJECT INDEX